ROUTLEDGE HA DERADICALISATION AND DISENGAGEMENT

The *Routledge Handbook of Deradicalisation and Disengagement* offers an overview of the historical settings, theoretical debates, national approaches and practical strategies to deradicalisation and disengagement.

Radicalisation and violent extremism are major global challenges, and as new violent extremist groups and environments emerge, there is an increasing need for knowledge about how individuals physically exit these movements and how to change their mindset. Historically, much of the focus on these topics has been highly securitised and militarised; by contrast, this volume explores the need for more community-based and 'soft' approaches. The handbook includes discussions from both right-wing/left-wing political and religiously inspired deradicalisation processes.

The handbook is organised into three parts:

1. definitions, backgrounds and theories;
2. actors;
3. regional case studies.

This handbook will be of much interest to students, researchers, scholars and professionals of deradicalisation, counterterrorism, political violence, political extremism, security studies and international relations in general.

Stig Jarle Hansen is a professor and leader of the international relations programme at the Norwegian University of Life Science.

Stian Lid is a researcher at the Norwegian Institute for Urban and Regional Research at Oslo Metropolitan University.

ROUTLEDGE HANDBOOK OF DERADICALISATION AND DISENGAGEMENT

Edited by Stig Jarle Hansen and Stian Lid

LONDON AND NEW YORK

First published 2020
by Routledge
2 Park Square, Milton Park, Abingdon, Oxon OX14 4RN

and by Routledge
605 Third Avenue, New York, NY 10017

First issued in paperback 2022

Routledge is an imprint of the Taylor & Francis Group, an informa business

Publisher's Note
The publisher has gone to great lengths to ensure the quality of this reprint but points out that some imperfections in the original copies may be apparent.

British Library Cataloguing-in-Publication Data
A catalogue record for this book is available from the British Library

Library of Congress Cataloging-in-Publication Data
Names: Hansen, Stig Jarle, editor. | Lid, Stian, editor.
Title: Routledge handbook of deradicalisation and disengagement / edited by Stig Jarle Hansen and Stian Lid.
Description: Abingdon, Oxon ; New York, NY : Routledge, 2020. | Includes bibliographical references and index.
Identifiers: LCCN 2019036250 (print) | LCCN 2019036251 (ebook) | ISBN 9781138229969 (hbk) | ISBN 9781315387420 (ebk)
Subjects: LCSH: Terrorism–Prevention. | Terrorism–Rehabilitation. | Radicalism–Rehabilitation.
Classification: LCC HV6431 .R6825 2020 (print) | LCC HV6431 (ebook) | DDC 363.325/16–dc23
LC record available at https://lccn.loc.gov/2019036250
LC ebook record available at https://lccn.loc.gov/2019036251

ISBN: 978-1-03-240057-0 (pbk)
ISBN: 978-1-138-22996-9 (hbk)
ISBN: 978-1-315-38742-0 (ebk)

DOI: 10.4324/9781315387420

Typeset in Bembo
by Swales & Willis, Exeter, Devon, UK

CONTENTS

ILLUSTRATIONS

Figures

Tables

EDITORS

Stig Jarle Hansen works primarily within the fields of organised crime, religion and politics, as well as deradicalisation and disengagement within a Norwegian and African context. His latest book *Horn, Sahel and Rift: Fault-lines of the African Jihad* is a comparative study of African Jihadist organisations. Hansen is a world-leading expert on Islamism in the Horn of Africa, and has commented for CNN, BBC, Al Jazeera, Reuters, CCTV 4 and many other international media outlets. He is currently leading Norway's only master's programme in international relations.

Stian Lid is researcher at the Norwegian Institute for Urban and Regional Research at Oslo Metropolitan University, Norway. He works primarily within the field of countering violent extremism and crime prevention in Norway and East Africa, and has been a key researcher in the research component of the Norwegian action plan against radicalisation and violent extremism. He is also one of the editors of the Norwegian book *Forebygging av radikalisering og voldelig ekstremisme* (translation: prevention of violent extremism) which was published in 2019. Several of his projects have focused on various actors' engagement and cooperation in countering violent extremism and promoting disengagement, deradicalisation and reintegration processes.

CONTRIBUTORS

Amarnath Amarasingam is an Assistant Professor in the School of Religion at Queen's University in Ontario, Canada. He is also a Senior Research Fellow at the Institute for Strategic Dialogue, and an Associate Fellow at the International Centre for the Study of Radicalisation. He is the author of *Pain, Pride, and Politics: Sri Lankan Tamil Activism in Canada* (2015). His research interests are in radicalisation, terrorism, diaspora politics, post-war reconstruction and the sociology of religion. He is the editor of *Sri Lanka: The Struggle for Peace in the Aftermath of War* (2016), the author of several peer-reviewed articles and book chapters, has presented papers at over 100 national and international conferences and has written for *The New York Times*, *The Washington Post*, *Politico*, *The Atlantic*, *Vice News*, *Foreign Affairs* and *War on the Rocks*.

Anneli Botha is a Senior Lecturer at the Department of Political Studies and Governance at the University of the Free State in Bloemfontein, South Africa. She also serves as an independent consultant on radicalisation, deradicalisation, reintegration and counterterrorism in Africa. During the period 2003 till 2016 she worked as a senior researcher on terrorism at the Institute for Security Studies (ISS) in Pretoria, South Africa. Anneli has travelled extensively throughout Africa.

Marina Chernikova completed her PhD in Social Psychology at the University of Maryland, USA, in 2018. In her dissertation, she aimed to identify personality traits that can predict unethical behaviour. Her PhD research also included various other projects on motivation, personality and the psychology of terrorism.

Irina A. Chindea is an Associate Political Scientist with the Washington DC office of the RAND Corporation. For her doctoral dissertation, Irina has conducted extensive field research in Mexico, Colombia and El Salvador. She holds a PhD in International Relations and an MA in Law and Diplomacy from the Fletcher School at Tufts University. Prior to joining RAND, she was a post-doctoral research fellow in the International Security Program at the Belfer Center at Harvard's Kennedy School, and a Visiting Assistant Professor with University at Albany (State University of New York, USA).

Tina Wilchen Christensen is currently working as Mentorship Advisor for RUSI, the Royal United Services Institute for Defence and Security Studies' programme, focusing on preventing recruitment to violent extremist organisations in Kenya. She is also an assistant professor at the Danish School of Education, Aarhus University, Denmark. Christensen's research examines ways into and especially out of violent militant groups with a particular focus on exit and the processes of developing an alternative identity to that of a violent extremist. Dr Christensen has an MPhil in Social Anthropology from the University of Oslo, Norway and a PhD from Roskilde University, Denmark.

Anja Dalgaard-Nielsen is Director of the Institute for Strategy at the Royal Danish Defence College and Professor (part-time) at the Centre for Risk Management and Societal Safety, University of Stavanger. Previously she directed the Danish Security and Intelligence Service's Preventive Security Department. Dr Dalgaard-Nielsen holds a PhD from Johns Hopkins University School of Advanced International Studies, an MA in Political Science from the University of Aarhus, and an MA in Public Governance from Copenhagen Business School.

Bertjan Doosje is a researcher at the Social Psychology Department at the University of Amsterdam. His work focuses on intergroup/intercultural relations, with a focus on group-based emotions and radicalisation. He is currently supervising PhDs and post-docs in projects examining: (1) repatriation of children of ISIS-returnees to the Netherlands and Belgium for 6 years; (2) the impact of local programmes aimed at preventing radicalisation; (3) how social trust is related to intergroup contact; (4) how recognition of emotional expressions can improve relations between newcomers from Syria and Dutch people; and (5) how experiences of misrecognition as a fully accepted group member can be associated with low trust in authorities. His research has been financed by the EU, Dutch Research Council, Volkswagen Foundation and several Ministries in the Netherlands. He has published numerous articles and several books and reports about (de-)radicalisation as well as emotions.

Jennifer Philippa Eggert is a researcher and practitioner working on gender, political violence, preventing and countering violent extremism (PVE/CVE), Islam(ism), migration and development. She is currently Head of Research at the Humanitarian Academy for Development, Research Advisor for the Women Muslim Advisory Project and Non-executive Director for We Rise UK. Previous positions have taken her to the universities of Warwick, Oxford Brookes, Princeton and Colorado. She has also worked in the non-governmental organisation sector and with an international organisation. Jennifer holds a PhD in Politics (with a focus on female fighters), an MSc in Conflict Studies and a BA in Social and Cultural Sciences. She has worked in research, civic education, counterextremism, intercultural exchange and international development in the UK, Germany, France, Austria, Bosnia, Bulgaria, Palestine, Lebanon, Jordan, Yemen and Pakistan.

Mohammed Samir Elshimi is a Preventing and Countering Violent Extremism (P/CVE) Advisor to the UN Office of Counter-Terrorism (UNOCT) and is responsible for helping national governments develop their P/CVE Strategies and National Action Plans. He is the author of *De-radicalisation in the UK Prevent Strategy: Security, Identity and Religion.*

Allard R. Feddes is an Assistant Professor at the Social Psychology Department of the University of Amsterdam, the Netherlands. He is generally interested in how group membership influences how we think (cognition), feel (emotion) and behave. He has studied processes of (de-)radicalisation since 2011.

Rached Ghannouchi is perhaps one of the most prominent Islamic philosophers of the 20th century. He was named one of *Time*'s 100 most influential people in the world in 2012 and *Foreign Policy*'s top 100 global thinkers. In 2016 he received the Jamnalal Bajaj Award for promoting Gandhian values outside India, and was crucial in the process that led to Tunis' peaceful transition into democracy in the Arab spring. He received his certificate of attainment degree, equivalent to the Baccalauréat, in 1962 from the University of Zaytouna. He studied philosophy at the University of Damascus, graduating in 1968.

Amy-Jane Gielen is a PhD candidate at the University of Amsterdam, the Netherlands. Her dissertation is on the evaluation of countering violent extremism (CVE). She also works as an independent researcher and consultant on (the effectiveness of) CVE for Dutch ministries and municipalities. She has previously worked as an intervention provider for families of foreign fighters and females who travelled to Syria.

Phil Gurski is the President and CEO of Borealis Threat and Risk Consulting. He worked as a Senior Strategic Analyst at the Canadian Security Intelligence Service, specialising in violent Islamist-inspired home-grown extremism and radicalisation as well as a Senior Multilingual Analyst at Communications Security Establishment. Mr Gurski has presented on violent Islamist-inspired home-grown extremism and radicalisation across Canada and around the world and is a frequent commentator on Canadian and international media. He is the author of five books on terrorism, including the forthcoming *When Religion Kills: How Extremists Justify Violence Through Faith* (Lynne Rienner).

Jakob Ilum is former Head of Countering Violent Extremism programmes in the Danish Security and Intelligence Service, where he initiated a close collaboration with police districts, municipalities and civic society. He is currently working with the City of Copenhagen on Creative City programmes. Jakob Ilum holds an MA in Political Science from the University of Aarhus and an MA in Media and Communication Studies from Goldsmiths College, University of London.

Christian Kaunert is Chair of Policing and Security, as well as Director of the International Centre for Policing and Security at the University of South Wales. He is also the Leader of the Cognate Research Group on Policing and Security at the University of South Wales. Previously, he served as Academic Director and Professor at the Institute for European Studies, Vrije Universiteit Brussel; Professor of International Politics; Head of Discipline in Politics; and the Director of the European Institute for Security and Justice, a Jean Monnet Centre for Excellence, at the University of Dundee. Prior to that, he was Marie Curie Senior Research Fellow at the European University Institute Florence, Senior Lecturer in EU Politics and International Relations at the University of Salford and Lecturer in European Politics at the University of Wales, Aberystwyth. Professor Kaunert holds a PhD and MSc(Econ) in International Politics from the University of Wales, Aberystwyth, as well as a BA(Hons) in European Business from Dublin City University (Ireland).

Bahadar Nawab is Chairman of the Department of Development Studies at COMSATS University Islamabad (CUI) Abbottabad Campus. Nawab has an interdisciplinary academic and research background in Environment and Development Studies. His core area of specialisation is Post Crises Development, Conflict, Peace and Development. Nawab has completed and is currently pursuing several national and international research and capacity-building grants and programmes. Bahadar Nawab Khattak is currently working on research grants of regional conflict, peace and development; community policing; Afghan refugees and the impact of conflict on the business community in Pakistan.

Daniel Koehler is the Founding Director of the German Institute on Radicalization and De-radicalization Studies (GIRDS – www.girds.org), the Editor in Chief of the *Journal for Deradicalization* (www.journal-derad.com) and editorial board member of the International Centre of Counter-Terrorism (ICCT) in The Hague. His work can be followed via Twitter (@GIRD_S).

Arie W. Kruglanski is Distinguished University Professor of Psychology at the University of Maryland, USA. He is the recipient of the National Institute of Mental Health Research Scientist Award, the Distinguished Scientific Contribution Award from the Society of Experimental Social Psychology and the Donald Campbell Award for Outstanding Contributions to Social Psychology from the Society for Personality and Social Psychology. He presently serves as co-founder and senior investigator at the National Center for the Study of Terrorism and the Response to Terrorism. His research interests are in the domains of human judgement and decision making, the motivation–cognition interface, group and intergroup processes, the psychology of human goals and the social psychological aspects of terrorism.

Sarah Léonard is Professor of Social Sciences at the University of the West of England (UWE) Bristol, UK. Prior to taking up her post at UWE Bristol, she was Associate Professor in International Affairs, Associate Dean Research and Head of Department of International Affairs, at Vesalius College, Vrije Universiteit Brussel (Belgium). Previously, she served as Senior Lecturer in Politics at the University of Dundee, Marie Curie Research Fellow at Sciences Po Paris and Lecturer in International Security at the University of Salford. Professor Léonard holds a PhD in International Politics from the University of Wales, Aberystwyth, a Master of Arts in Russian and Eurasian Studies from the University of Leeds, as well as an MA in European Studies and a BA in Politics (International Relations) from the Université Catholique de Louvain, Belgium.

Liesbeth Mann studied social psychology and Holocaust and genocide studies at the University of Amsterdam, the Netherlands. In 2017 she obtained her PhD at the same university. Her PhD project dealt with the experience of humiliation in interpersonal, intragroup and intergroup contexts. As part of this project she also studied the role of humiliation in radicalisation and terrorism. Related to this she was involved in a large-scale EU project on processes of violent radicalisation and terrorism, called SAFIRE, and she worked on a project on the resilience of the Dutch population against radicalisation and extremism, commissioned by the Dutch Ministry of Justice and Security.

Fathali M. Moghaddam's most recent books are *Threat to Democracy: The Appeal of Authoritarianism in an Age of Uncertainty* (2019, APA Books) and *Mutual Radicalization: How Groups and Nations Drive Each Other to Extremes* (2018, APA Books). Since 2014 he has served as the editor of *Peace and Conflict: Journal of Peace Psychology* (an American Psychological Association journal). Moghaddam serves as the Director of the Interdisciplinary Program in Cognitive Science and is Professor of Psychology, Georgetown University.

Erica Molinario is a Post-doctoral Research Associate at the University of Maryland, College Park. Her research focuses on motivation, social norms, social identity and intergroup processes. In her work, she focuses on understanding the psychological and social circumstances that lead to violent and non-violent forms of extremism. She is currently working on projects aimed at studying the psychology of refugees, the attitudes of the host communities in Europe and the Middle East and the risk factors for radicalisation.

Lars Nickolson graduated *cum laude* as a Master in Philosophy in 2008. He was involved with counter-radicalisation policy as a researcher and advisor working within and outside of the Dutch government. He is currently a PhD candidate at the Department of Political Science of the University of Amsterdam.

Paige Pascarelli received her MA in International Relations and Religion from the Frederick S. Pardee School of Global Studies at Boston University, and her BA from Connecticut College. She was the recipient of the Pardee School's Ambassador Hermann Frederick Eilts Thesis Award. She has presented her work at the Society for Terrorism Research conference, and is published in the *Behavioral Sciences of Terrorism and Political Aggression* journal and *Lawfare*. She previously was a research assistant for Dr Jessica Stern and at George Washington University's Program on Extremism.

Arie Perliger is director of the graduate programme in Security Studies, at the School of Criminology and Justice Studies, University of Massachusetts Lowell (UML). In the past 20 years, Dr Perliger has studied extensively issues related to terrorism and political violence, security policy and politics, politics of the Far Right in Israel, Europe, and the United States, Middle Eastern politics and the applicability of social network analysis to the study of social phenomena. His studies have appeared in eight books and monographs, and in more than 40 articles and book chapters by publishers such as Columbia University Press, Routledge, Security Studies, Political Studies, Social Forces and others. Dr Perliger is the Editor-in -Chief of the journal *Democracy and Security*, member of the editorial board of *Studies in Conflict and Terrorism* and a regular reviewer for various publishers and journals such as Columbia University Press, Chicago University Press, *American Political Science Review*, *Journal of Politics*, *Journal of Peace Research* and *Political Psychology*.

Hans-Jakob Schindler currently works as the Senior Director at the Counter Extremism Project (CEP) in New York and is a member of the Advisory Board of the Global Diplomatic Initiative in London and a member of the Board of Directors of Compliance and Capacity Skills International (CCSI) in New York.

Mubin Shaikh is a deradicalised ex-extremist, and ex-undercover operative for the Canadian Security Intelligence Service and Royal Canadian Mounted Police (RCMP) Integrated National Security Enforcement Team (INSET). He worked multiple classified infiltration operations and his final assignment became public in the 'Toronto 18' terrorism case of 2006, when 11 violent extremists were convicted after five hearings over four years. Shaikh has a Master of Policing, Intelligence and Counter Terrorism (Macquarie), is an external subject matter expert to the United Nations Security Council, US Special Operations Command and trains police, intelligence and special operations forces. He was extensively involved with the ISIS social media boom, countering their views using Islamic sources, and has since dealt with the Foreign Terrorist Fighter file, including returnees and rehabilitation.

Lihi Ben Shitrit is an Assistant Professor at the School of Public and International Affairs, University of Georgia, Athens. She is the author of the book *Righteous Transgressions:*

Women's Activism on the Israeli and Palestinian Religious Right (2015, Princeton University Press), alongside many other articles and book chapters.

Bhavna Singh is Associate Fellow at the Centre for Air Power Studies, New Delhi, and is currently pursuing her PhD from the Centre for East Asian Studies, Jawaharlal Nehru University. She was a Senior Research Officer with the Institute of Peace and Conflict Studies (IPCS), New Delhi (2010–2013) and was later associated with the V-Dem project based at Gothenburg University, Sweden (2013–2017). Her work focuses on Chinese nationalism, subregionalism and China's foreign policy. She is particularly interested in separatist and sub-national tendencies in the regions of Xinjiang, Tibet, Taiwan and Inner Mongolia. She is the author of the book *China's Discursive Nationalism: Contending in Softer Realms* (Pentagon Press, New Delhi, 2012) and co-editor of *India, China and Sub-regional Connectivities in South Asia* (Sage, 2015) and has written for several esteemed journals, such as *Economic and Political Weekly, Mainstream Weekly, Nam-today, World Focus, Epilogue* and the *China Daily*, and several web portals like the ISN-ETH Zurich. She was part of the youth exchange delegation between China and India in the year 2008, was nominated to the Taiwan Study Camp for Future Leaders of South Asia in 2010 and participated in the One Belt One Road Summit, organised by Shaanxi University in 2016.

Jessica Stern is a Research Professor at Boston University's Pardee School of Global Studies. She has taught courses on counterterrorism for 20 years – at Boston University, Harvard and CIA University. She is the coauthor with J.M. Berger of *ISIS: The State of Terror*; and the author of *My War Criminal: Encounters with an Architect of Genocide* (forthcoming), *Denial: A Memoir of Terror, Terror in the Name of God* and *The Ultimate Terrorists*. Stern served on President Clinton's National Security Council Staff, and was included among seven 'thinkers' in *Time* magazine's 2001 series profiling 100 innovators.

Hicham Tiflati has a PhD in Religious Studies, a master's in Education, and a bachelor's in Islamic Law. He is a humanities professor at John Abbot College and a fellow at the German Institute for Radicalization and Deradicalization (GIRDS). Hicham has worked closely with families and individuals affected by terrorism and done fieldwork in Germany, Turkey, Morocco and Canada. His research focuses on radicalisation, disengagement from violent extremism, Muslim identity construction and Islamic schooling. He has academic and research interests in topics such as deradicalisation, countering violent extremism, Muslim identities, citizenship and the role of religious education in (re)shaping identities.

David Webber is Assistant Professor at the L. Douglas Wilder School of Government and Public Affairs at Virginia Commonwealth University. His research examines the social psychological factors involved in violent extremism.

Ikrom Yakubov is a Lecturer in Intelligence and Security Studies at the University of South Wales. His research interests overlap between intelligence, international relations, intelligence–policy relations, terrorism and counterterrorism, security studies and policing. In his PhD dissertation, Ikrom researched the role of intelligence (CIA and SIS-MI6) in securitisation processes.

Martine Zeuthen is a Senior Research Fellow in the National Security Studies programme at the Royal United Services Institute (RUSI). She is a Danish anthropologist (MSc) and currently studying a PhD in Crime and Security Studies at University College London. She is based in Nairobi and set up RUSI's operation in East Africa. She focuses on extremism and radicalisation, countering violent extremism, programme management and research methodology. Martine is leading the CVE work in East Africa and she led the Strengthening Resilience to Violent Extremism in the Horn of Africa (STRIVE) programme and the follow-on, STRIVE II, as well as many other research-based CVE projects.

ACKNOWLEDGEMENTS

We would like to thank all the contributors to this book, who took it upon themselves to go through quite a rigorous and extensive peer review process, including comments from both practitioners and theoreticians. The book strove to reflect diversity amongst its contributors, with high-quality experts from institutions in Africa and Asia participating together with a mix of leading experts and up-and-coming new talents from Europe and North America, as well as experienced practitioners in the field of deradicalisation and disengagement. In the process of gathering the various contributions and ensuring their quality, we have been given extensive assistance. We received highly valuable comments on drafts from Uzair Ahmed, Atle Mesøy, Tom Pettinger, Robin Malmros Andersson, Clarke Jones, Arild Schou, David Hansen, Salma Abdalla, Lars Gule, Upali Pannilage, Gina Lende, Linda Noor, Petter Nesser, Laila Bokhari, Thomas Hegghammer, Clifford Collins Omondi Okwany, John McNeish, Shai Divon, Geir Orderud, Laila Bokhari, and Christopher Anzalone, as well as others. Ida Berry at Birmingham University has been outstanding in helping us transcend language barriers.

We would also like to thank Routledge, and their editor Andrew Humphrys for his advice, help and patience, and the Norwegian Research Council for funding through our Jihadi War Economy project.

Stig Jarle Hansen
Stian Lid

1

WHY DO WE NEED A HANDBOOK ON DISENGAGEMENT AND DERADICALISATION?

Stig Jarle Hansen and Stian Lid

Radicalisation and violent extremism are global challenges. Although the allure of the Islamic State weakened when the latter faced battlefield defeats in Syria and Iraq, the Islamic State has gained recruits in other places, and racist and hate groups have increased their activities in the West (Kennedy, 2014; Koehler, 2016; Pestano, 2016). There are no signs of these challenges diminishing in the future; rather the contrary. The rise of the Islamic State saw between 27,000 and 31,000 fighters travelling to Syria and Iraq, many of whom returned to their home countries after the battlefield defeats suffered by the Islamic State after 2014. The Islamic State has also mobilised sympathisers around the world (Khalil and Shanahan, 2016). There are also numerous reports on increasing right-wing violence in many larger countries, such as the United States (Jones, 2018).

As new and violent extremist groups and environments emerge, there is an increasing need for knowledge of not only how individuals physically exit these movements, but also how to change their mindset and how to stimulate the deradicalisation and disengagement processes. As of today, a veritable marketplace for new deradicalisation and disengagement efforts has been established. Not all of the new actors are serious. Moreover, the knowledge foundation was, at times, lacking (for examples, see Hansen, Lid, and Okwani, 2019; Schulze, 2008). A plethora of methods has been used, and a large number of different types of deradicalisation and disengagement programmes have been developed for different arenas (Speckhard, 2011). Yet, the expansion was based upon uncertain foundations, difficult dilemmas and imperfect understandings (Altier, Thoroughgood, and Horgan, 2014; Dechesne, 2011; Feddes, 2015; Schuurman and Bakker, 2016). The literature focusing on the disengagement and deradicalisation programmes has primarily been more isolated descriptions of specific programmes or countries, and many studies have focused on prison-based offender rehabilitation programmes. The regional focus in the studies or edited volumes has mainly been on the Middle East or South Asia or on the Western perspective (Koehler, 2017, pp. 28–30).

The aim of this book is to start to fill some of these gaps in the literature on disengagement and deradicalisation. This volume has the ambition of contributing with new knowledge on the approaches, strategies and initiatives taken by various implementing actors globally to support disengagement and deradicalisation processes. The book includes new perspectives on the softer approaches to counterterrorism applied by transnational organisations, local governments, civil society, religious actors, prisons and others. In addition to its global perspectives, it will include specific regional chapters, and contain both the perspectives of practitioners and researchers, and regional and global organisations. The book will shed light on the various debates around different approaches to and thinking around disengagement and deradicalisation processes in addition to bringing forward new and less known perspectives not only from a theoretical angle, but also from a more practical perspective in relation to experiences and lessons learned from specific groups and areas.

Concept and problems

One of the major problems is the definition of radicalisation, as well as disengagement and deradicalisation (Altier, Thoroughgood, and Horgan, 2014; Bjørgo and Horgan, 2009; Koehler, 2017). The lack of conceptual and theoretical clarity has "led to political and practical action executed with largely absent theoretical frameworks or clear-cut concepts" (Koehler, 2017, p. 2). A rough point of departure would be to look at a process in which a person's commitment to ideological violence is reduced, differentiating deradicalisation and disengagement from prevention. Prevention is actually to be implemented before a person has the ideological commitment to violence. However, there are grey areas between prevention, disengagement and deradicalisation. Following Koehler in this book, prevention is a part of deradicalisation work partly to prevent recidivism into violent or extremist behaviour and thought patterns after an intervention has taken place, reducing existing commitment to the group and cause. Prevention also comes into play with cases in early stages of radicalisation, where one can try to prevent further radicalisation, which is where intervention and preventative methods mix. The key to deradicalisation, however, is to intervene with an existing commitment to a violent extremist group and ideology and to reduce that commitment.

It is possible to group definitions of deradicalisation into a "narrow" type that only includes rejection of ideological violence, and a "broad" version that includes rejection of an ideological worldview that could legitimise violence; the former type is often referred to as disengagement. During the first phase of the British Prevent programme, it may be that violent action is to be avoided, sometimes defined as disengagement – a mere physical and behavioural role change. However, the target could also be more comprehensive, such as changing the radical worldview itself. The target could also be a combination of the two. The first version becomes close to "disengagement" – behaviour changes – while the ideological or psychological aspects are left aside (Bjørgo and Horgan, 2009; Horgan, 2009; Koehler, 2017). Some researchers will maintain that disengagement is the more feasible option; others would say that without addressing the ideology's attraction points there is a much higher risk of re-radicalisation and failure to exit. Successful programmes based on both views exist.

A focus-changing worldview could quickly develop into "thought policing" and even alienate potential allies by attempting to police opinions rather than actions (Edwards, 2016). Indeed, the end state you should "deradicalise" from is in itself contested. "Radical" is perceived as a relative concept (Schmid, 2013; Sedgwick, 2010). Some even see radicalisation as in some cases reflecting something positive, such as an inclination to act to improve society, that needs to be harnessed. Reidy (2019), for example, sees altruism as an important feature in such processes that can be harnessed, also for humanitarian purposes, avoiding violence in the process. There have been several efforts to define and make distinctions between "problematic" radicals and acceptable and unproblematic radicals; for instance, making the distinction between "(open-minded) radical" and "(close-minded) extremist" or between "violent extremist" and "non-violent extremist" (Schmid, 2013, p. 10). One has to keep in mind that deradicalisation programmes run in totalitarian, or semi-totalitarian, regimes, and a focus on deradicalisation as changing a mindset can be misused (Aggarwal, 2013; Joseba and Douglass, 1996; Smyth, Gunning, Jackson, Kassimeris, and Robinson, 2008; Winkler, 2006). Deradicalisation could easily become an excuse to prevent political activism for promoting democracy, political dialogue or the promotion of minority rights. Indeed, it could serve as a justification for avoiding deeper societal changes, as expressed by Al Jazeera's Margot Kiser with regard to deradicalisation programmes in East Africa: "It [deradicalisation] seems a concept 100% politicised even before out the gate."[1] Even in Western countries, the attempted change of a person's religious or political opinions is morally questionable, as these are usually protected by democratic freedoms and not subjected to criminalisation. Some of these problems are also encountered in disengagement; after all, disengagement from groups striving for non-violent change in authoritarian regimes is another form of enhancing those regimes.

However, while deradicalisation and disengagement have an oppressive potential, they are also potential alternatives to the use of force. As shown by Hansen (2017), deradicalisation and disengagement can in some cases empower minorities, as they become seen as key allies in such processes. Deradicalisation can also be a soft alternative to security services and police. We should emphasise *can* here, as deradicalisation often is implemented by the police and/or other security services and can be used for intelligence or evidence gathering (Koehler, 2017). A separation between security services and the deradicalisation programme might present deradicalisation as a clearer alternative to the use of the police, and avoid reduction of trust in and legitimacy of the social services that provide deradicalisation programmes. However, a separation might lead to cooperation and coordination problems between various pertinent agencies. Access to relevant information from, for example, school and health services, depending also on the interpretation of the local legal framework, and police intentions of pursuing prosecution might hinder the use of deradicalisation programmes, or hamper the flow of information from the police to institutions doing deradicalisation (Lid, Winsvold, Søholt, Hansen, Heierstad, and Klausen, 2016).

There are other problems when trying to implement radicalisation programmes as well. Problems with implementing disengagement and deradicalisation programmes include the tendency to neglect the wider environment, under-prioritising the intersection between deradicalisation and reintegration, and how contextual factors mediate the success of these two (Marsden, 2017, p. 3; Clubb and Tapley, 2018). Instead, the problem is positioned in the mind of the individual (Marsden, 2017, p. 3). Successful disengagement and deradicalisation involve both leaving the extremist environment and re-engaging with the non-extremist milieu (Barelle, 2015).

To measure success is also hard. Comparative studies are rare (El-Said, 2015; Horgan and Braddock, 2010); wider comparative studies of strategies have often not been done, a fact that we will attempt to remedy in this book. Second, in some cases, programmes have been so secretive that it becomes hard to assess their success or failure (El-Said, 2015; Hansen, Lid, and Okwani, 2019). Third, the process of leaving extremism, avoiding recidivism and fully reintegrating into mainstream society is a process that goes far beyond programmes, and is influenced by the reintegrating communities and contextual factors which shape the capacity to facilitate or resist reintegration. The complexity of factors that influence the reintegration process significantly complicate measuring the success of programmes (Clubb and Tapley, 2018). Moreover, some deradicalisation programmes depend on the participants themselves taking active steps to participate, leading to self-selection that might in turn enhance the success rate. Re-activism amongst imprisoned terrorists is also lower than for the common prison population, thus re-activism on its own might not be such a good indicator of success (Koehler, 2017).

Different types of goals also give different rates of success. A programme focusing on removing problematic ideology and behaviour is more complex than a programme that only focuses on behaviour, and success becomes harder to operationalise, making it harder to compare the programmes. This in turn opens up a wider discussion over cost efficiency. For example, in the United States, deradicalisation programmes have been limited compared to Europe, and very often implemented by private actors. Nevertheless, the United States has had relatively few radical jihadist groups and foreign fighters joining the Islamic State compared to European countries (Bakker and Singleton, 2016; Soufan Group, 2015).

There has been a lack of a thorough discussion of the type of territorial presence of groups from which individuals are to be removed. Radical groups may range from what resemble insurgency outfits to small clandestine networks, and such groups can actually control territories in a civil war-like scenario, or have a semi-territorial presence enabling them to punish participants in deradicalisation programmes, where working in radical groups actually pays better than other jobs (Hansen, 2019). Situations arise where radical groups actually have links to parts of the authorities (ibid). Targeting also needs to be discussed, as research increasingly shows that some of these networks, clustered in areas with relatively similarly socioeconomic characteristics, are for example more vulnerable to foreign recruitment than others (Perliger and Milton, 2016). Targeting can also lead to stigmatisation of wider groups if not carefully implemented (O'Toole, Meer, DeHanas, Jones, and Modood, 2016). Gender is also seldom discussed in the deradicalisation literature, although both the Islamic State and right-wing groups have placed the issue on the agenda (Braunthal, 2009).

This book hopes to highlight some of these problems, sometimes giving solutions, but at other times at least presenting the dilemmas and theoretical consequences. Indeed, the problems are many. Yet, deradicalisation and disengagement are important themes, because of the scope of the activities implemented in their name, as well as because of the number of genuine idealists involved. They do provide a tool to use against radical groups. The above problems should be seen as problems to be solved or dilemmas to be handled. Deradicalisation has great potential, which is as yet untapped. There are definitively both ethical problems and problems with regard to the lack of knowledge, as well as when it comes to the interaction between researchers, practitioners and even former participants, to make these projects more efficient. This book is also a way to promote such interaction, and bring conceptual differences to the forefront, thus contributors are allowed some conceptual freedom, yet categories of types of disengagement and deradicalisation are still needed.

Categorising disengagement and deradicalisation

Disengagement and deradicalisation is a field that is in need of being systematised, and categorisation may help us when studying the wider subject field; for example, different mechanisms of leaving, the different actors involved in the disengagement/deradicalisation process and variations in their roles.

The process of disengagement and deradicalisation can, for example, be voluntary or involuntary/forced. However, some programmes in prisons can be understood as a hybrid between voluntary and involuntary, taking into account the circumstances in detention facilities (El-Said, 2015). Second, the efforts are either individual or collective, and these processes may be distinctive. The latter refer to programmes or efforts addressing entire groups or organisations. Third, as discussed above, the process of leaving radical or extremist groups can be physical and/or psychological (disengagement or deradicalisation). Finally, the processes are permanent or temporary (Ferguson, 2010). In addition to these critical distinctions, we can draw a line between those who leave extremism on their own, without any support from formal institutions (governmental and non-governmental), which it is argued are the majority of former high-ranking terrorists and low-level extremists (Barelle, 2015; Horgan, 2009), and those who receive any kind of support. The latter group is the group primarily discussed in the chapters in this volume.

Another significant distinction when understanding the processes of leaving is between push and pull factors. Push factors are experiences related to an individual's involvement in a particular social movement that drive him or her away and include disillusionment with the group's strategy or actions, loss of faith in the ideology, disagreements with group leaders or members, and burnout. Pull factors are influences outside the group that attract the person to a more rewarding alternative than continuing in the movement or group, such as the promise of amnesty or material rewards, desire to marry and have a family, and the demands of a conventional career. Hence, many of the relevant factors are personal factors that are difficult for others to influence, but a range of factors, both push and pull factors, are relevant in the effort to persuade individuals to leave extremism (Altier, Boyle, Shortland, and Horgan, 2017; Bjørgo, 2016). If a more holistic approach to disengagement and deradicalisation is taken, the perspective of sustained disengagement is distinct between various levels of integration (Barelle, 2015). Minimal levels of engagement are those that do not wish to engage with mainstream society, even if they have stopped using violence or other radical methods. The cautious level of engagement with society after exiting extremism is undertaken by those persons engaged in a limited or hesitant manner. They are not reaching their full potential for happiness or wellbeing. A positive level of engagement represents full integration, and this occurs when individuals enjoy healthy and functional relationships with people around them, irrespective of their group categorisations (ibid).

There are also some critical distinctions between actors who implement initiatives, activities or programmes for promoting disengagement and deradicalisation processes. There is an important distinction between government and non-government actors (Bjørgo and Horgan, 2009). Yet this handbook also shows the relevance of often neglected transnational actors such as the United Nations and the European Union. Operators in the wider field of disengagement and deradicalisation include the police, the intelligence service and other security forces, prison, state social services, public health institutions, religious institutions (both government-controlled and non-government-controlled), civil society actors, aid organisations and political parties.

There are variations in the roles of these different actors. An actor involved in disengagement and deradicalisation can serve as the *main implementer* who designs the programmes and handles the financial aspects. Many such actors can also serve as *agents*, acting on behalf of another institution. Some might serve as *contributors*, taking responsibility for parts of the programmes. Last, and perhaps of least importance, are the *external advisors*, the actors who host awareness programmes and facilitate the training of trainers. Most of the actors mentioned above can serve in all of these roles. Different countries might prefer different configurations of agents, main implementers, external advisors and contributors. In the United States, municipality administrations have traditionally had fewer services to implement than Scandinavian municipalities, which very often are the major agents in implementing the welfare state services. This may be why municipalities enjoy a prominent role in the Scandinavian disengagement and deradicalisation arena, although the same implementers are notably absent from the American arena. Similarly, organisations doing development activities, such as the Department for International Development, will be involved in disengagement and deradicalisation in Asia and Africa.

The practical partnership arrangements will influence implementation. As mentioned earlier, the involvement of justice sector actors may create fear of misuse of the programmes for intelligence purposes. On the other hand, a correct mix of actors may create expertise, enhance information flows and introduce mechanisms of checks and balances.

Outline of the book

The handbook is divided into three parts. The first is a general part focusing on overreaching issues; the second explores the involvement of various actors in promoting disengagement and deradicalisation; the third is a set of case studies from around the world to introduce the reader to the interaction between the local context, overreaching issues and variations in organisations. The first part starts with Daniel Koehler, who will set the stage for the rest of the book by discussing the key concepts of disengagement and deradicalisation, before Stig Jarle Hansen gives a brief historical overview of these concepts and shows how these concepts are developed from wider relevant fields. The book proceeds with a chapter on the viability of phase-based models to deradicalisation, written by Liesbeth Mann, Lars Nickolson, Allard R. Feddes, Bertjan Doosje, and Fathali M. Moghaddam, and continues with David Webber, Marina Chernikova, Erica Molinario and Arie W. Kruglanski's discussion of the most common psychological approaches to deradicalisation and disengagement, showing direct and indirect mechanisms of deradicalisation. An under-analysed field is the role of gender in deradicalisation and disengagement work, which will be explored by Jennifer Philippa Eggert. Stig Jarle Hansen then contextualises deradicalisation and disengagement in the light of disarmament, demobilisation, and reintegration and the territorial presence of the radical group involved. Arie Perliger analyses important aspects of deradicalisation, disengagement, and reintegration of foreign fighters.

The second part, focusing on various actors, starts with Jessica Stern and Paige Pascarelli's description of challenges faced by deradicalisation programmes in prison. It continues with the analyses of the role of municipalities and local governments written by Stian Lid, Tina Wilchen Christensen's analysis of the role of civil society, and Rached Ghannouchi's description of the potential of religion in deradicalisation work. The next three chapters analyse the role of transnational organisations. First, Hans-Jakob Schindler presents United Nations work on the field, second, Sarah Léonard, Christian Kaunert, and Ikrom Yakubov analyse the involvement of the European Union. Anneli Botha then proceeds to discuss the engagement of the African Union (AU).

The last part of the book focuses on regional case studies. This part starts in Europe with the chapters about disengagement and deradicalisation strategies and initiatives in Benelux written by Amy-Jane Gielen; the chapter about the UK is written by Mohammed Samir Elshimi and, finally, Anja Dalgaard-Nielsen and Jakob Ilum analyse the situation in Scandinavia. Thereafter, we move to the East and start with a chapter written by Bhavna Singh exploring the Chinese context, before Bahadar Nawab analyses South Asia. Next, Lihi Ben Shitrit explores deradicalisation in the Israeli–Palestinian context.

The book's focus then moves on to Africa, where Martine Zeuthen explores disengagement and deradicalisation work in the shadow of the Harakat al Shabaab and the Islamic State. The last regional area includes the chapter on disengagement and deradicalisation in North America by Mubin Shaikh, Hicham Tiflati, Phil Gurski, and Amarnath Amarasingam, and Irina Chineda ends with a study of Latin American work against right- and left-wing radical groups. In the conclusion the editors, Stig Jarle Hansen and Stian Lid, bring together the main findings and ideas of this handbook.

Note

1 Correspondence with the writer.

References

Aggarwal, Neil Krishan (2013). "Mental discipline, punishment and recidivism: Reading Foucault against deradicalisation programmes in the War on Terror." *Critical Studies of Terrorism*, 6(2), 262–278.

Altier, Mary Beth, Christian N. Thoroughgood, and John G. Horgan (2014). "Turning away from terrorism: Lessons from psychology, sociology, and criminology." *Journal of Peace Research*, 51(5), 647–661.

Altier, Mary Beth, E.L. Boyle, Neil, D. Shortland and John G. Horgan (2017). "Why they leave: An analysis of terrorist disengagement events from eighty-seven autobiographical accounts." *Security Studies*, 26(2), 305–332.

Bakker, Edwin, and Mark Singleton (2016). "Foreign fighters in the Syria and Iraq conflict: Statistics and characteristics of a rapidly growing phenomenon." In A. de Guttry, F. Capone and C. Paulussen (Eds.), *Foreign fighters under international law and beyond* (pp. 9–25). Berlin: TMC Asser Press.

Barelle, Kate (2015). "Pro-integration. Disengagement from and life after extremism." *Behavioral Sciences of Terrorism and Political Aggression*, 7(2), 129–142.

Bjørgo, Tore (2016). *Preventing crime: A holistic approach*. Basingtoke and New York: Palgrave Macmillan.

Bjørgo, Tore, and John Horgan (2009). "Introduction." In T. Bjørgo and J. Horgan (Eds.), *Leaving terrorism behind. Individual and collective disengagement*. London: Routledge.

Braunthal, Gerhard (2009). *Right-wing extremism in contemporary Germany*. New York: Palgrave Macmillan.

Clubb, Gordan, and Marina Tapley (2018). "Conceptualising de-radicalisation and former combatant re-integration in Nigeria." *Third World Quarterly*, 39(11), 2053–2068.

Dechesne, Mark (2011). "Deradicalization: Not soft, but strategic." *Crime Law and Social Change*, 55(4), 287–292. doi: 10.1007/s10611-011-9283-8

Edwards, Phil (2016). "Closure through resilience: The case of prevent." *Studies in Conflict & Terrorism*, 39(4), Political Resilience to Terrorism in Europe, 292–307.

El-Said, Hamed (2015). *New approaches to countering terrorism. Designing and evaluating counter radicalization and de-radicalization programs*. Basingtoke: Palgrave Macmillan.

Feddes, Allard R. (2015). *Socio-psychological factors involved in measures of disengagement and deradicalization and evaluation challenges in Western Europe*. Washington, DC: Middle East Institute.

Ferguson, Neil (2010). "Disengaging from terrorism." In A. Silke (Ed.), *The psychology of counter-terrorism* (pp. 111–123). London: Routledge.

Hansen, Stig Jarle (2017). "Empowerment, militarization, CVE and deradicalization (The Case of Kenya and Somalia)." *Paper presented at African security workshop 22–23 November.*

Hansen, Stig Jarle (2019). *Horn, Sahel and rift, fault-lines of the African jihad*. London: Hurst.

Hansen, Stig Jarle, Stian Lid, and Clifford Collin Omondi Okwani (2019). "Countering violent extremism in Somalia and Kenya: Actors and approaches." *NIBR Working Paper 2019:106.*

Horgan, John (2009). *Walking away from terrorism: Accounts of disengagement from radical and extremist movements*. New York: Routledge.

Horgan, John, and Kurt Braddock (2010). "Rehabilitating the terrorists? Challenges in assessing the effectiveness of de-radicalization programs." *Terrorism and Political Violence*, 22(2), 267–291. doi: 10.1080/09546551003594748

Jones, Seth G. (2018). "The rise of far-right extremism in the United States." *CSIS brief*, November 7.

Zulaika, Joseba, and William Douglass (1996). *Terror and taboo: The follies, fables, and faces of terrorism*. London: Routledge.

Kennedy, Michael (2014). *Far right-wing extremism and xenophobia in contemporary Russia*. Berlin: GRIN Verlag GMBH.

Khalil, Lydia, and Rodger Shanahan (2016). "Iraq and Syria: How many foreign fighters are fighting for ISIL?" *The Telegraph*, March 24.

Koehler, Daniel (2016). "Right-wing extremism and terrorism in Europe current developments and issues for the future." *PRISM*, 6(2), 84–105.

Koehler, Daniel (2017). *Understanding deradicalization: Methods, tools and programs for countering violent extremism*. New York: Routledge.

Lid, Stian, Marte Winsvold, Susanne Søholt, Stig Jarle Hansen, Geir Heierstad, and Jan Erling Klausen (2016). "Forebygging av radikalisering og voldelig ekstremisme – Hva er kommunenes rolle?" *NIBR Rapport* 2016:12.

Marsden, Sarah (2017). *Reintegrating extremists. Deradicalisation and desistance*. London: Palgrave Macmillan.

O'Toole, Therese, Nasar Meer, Daniel Nilsson DeHanas, Stephen H. Jones, and Tariq Modood (2016). "Governing through Prevent? Regulation and contested practice in State–Muslim engagement." *Sociology*, 50(1), 160–177.

Perliger, Ariel, and Daniel Milton (2016). *From cradle to grave: The lifecycle of foreign fighters in Iraq and Syria*. West Point: Combating Terrorism Centre.

Pestano, Andrew V. (2016) "Islamic State can't afford to recruit foreign fighters anymore." *UPI news*, April 27, www.upi.com/Top_News/World-News/2016/04/27/Islamic-State-cant-afford-to-recruit-foreign-fighters-anymore/4571461751913/

Reidy, Ken (2019). "Benevolent radicalization: An antidote to terrorism." *Perspectives on Terrorism*, 13(4), 1–13.

Schmid, Alex P. (2013). *Radicalisation, de-radicalisation, counter-radicalisation: A conceptual discussion and literature review*. The Hague: ICCT.

Schulze, Kirsten E. (2008). "Indonesia's approach to Jihadist deradicalization." *CTC Sentinel*, 1(8).

Schuurman, Bart, and Edwin Bakker (2016). "Reintegrating jihadist extremists: Evaluating a Dutch initiative, 2013–2014." *Behavioral Sciences of Terrorism and Political Aggression*, 8(1), 66–85.

Sedgwick, Mark (2010). "The concept of radicalization as a source of confusion." *Terrorism and Political Violence*, 22(4), 479–494.

Smyth, Marie Breen, Jeroen Gunning, Richard Jackson, George Kassimeris, and Piers Robinson (2008). "Critical terrorism studies – an introduction." *Critical Studies on Terrorism*, 1(1), 1–4.

Soufan Group (2015) "Foreign Fighters in Syria and Iraq." *Soufan group report*, December.

Speckhard, Anne (2011). "Deradicalization/disengagement strategies: Challenging terrorist ideologies and militant Jihadis." In Laurie Fenstermacher, Special Rapporteur, and Anne Speckhard (Eds.), *Social sciences support to military personnel engaged in counter-insurgency and counter-terrorism operations*: Report of the NATO Research and Technology Group 172 on Social Sciences Support to Military Personnel Engaged in Counter-Insurgency and Counter-Terrorism Operations Symposium held in St. Petersburg, Russia June 18–20.

Winkler, Carol (2006). *In the name of terrorism: Presidents on political violence in the post-World War II era*. Albany, NY: State University of New York Press.

PART I

Definitions, backgrounds and theories

2
TERMINOLOGY AND DEFINITIONS

Daniel Koehler

'Deradicalization' has increasingly become a buzzword in counter-terrorism circles around the world in recent years. Even though research into individual exit processes from violent extremist groups dates back at least to the late 1980s (Aho, 1988), rehabilitation programs for civil war combatants (disarmament, demobilization, reintegration – DDR) have been conducted since 1989 (Muggah, 2005, p. 244) and whole terror groups have disavowed violent means on many occasions in the past (e.g. Ashour, 2009; El-Said, 2012; Ferguson, 2010), the relatively young term 'deradicalization' began to emerge and enter the international discourse mainly through Middle Eastern countries' attempts to use theological debates on terrorist prisoners, aiming to convince them to abandon militant jihadist ideology as a part of the 'Global War on Terror' initiated by the United States of America after the September 11 attacks. While state-run programs like those in Yemen (Johnsen, 2006) and Saudia Arabia (Boucek, 2007; El-Said & Barrett, 2012) starting just a few years after 9/11 were pivotal to spread the deradicalization concept into the general public (e.g. *Time* magazine: Ripley, 2008) and to spark further academic interest (e.g. Bjørgo & Horgan, 2009; Horgan, 2009b; Mullins, 2010; Noricks, 2009), some programs (governmental and non-governmental) in Europe had already been working extensively on diverting right-wing extremists away from violence and terrorism since the mid-1990s (Bjørgo, 1997; Bjørgo & Carlsson, 2005). Very early, though, leading experts have found the 'lack of conceptual clarity in the emerging discourse on deradicalization striking' (Bjørgo & Horgan, 2009, p. 3). It seemed that the term was being applied to a wide array of policies and tools with 'virtually no conceptual development in the area' (Horgan, 2009b, p. 17). With the outbreak of the Syrian civil war in 2011 and the emergence of terrorist semi-states like the so-called 'caliphate' of the terror organization Islamic State in Iraq and Syria (ISIS) (Honig & Yahel, 2017) and the global increase in 'foreign fighter' travel movements to unprecedented levels (Hegghammer, 2013), governments around the world have been under pressure to develop and implement various different responses to the perceived threat of returned and radicalized combatants (e.g. Vidino, 2014). In 2014, the United Nations Security Council released Resolution 2178, urging all member states to establish effective rehabilitation measures for returning fighters from Syria and Iraq (UNSC, 2014). Similarly, the revised European Union Counter Terrorism Strategy places strong importance on 'disengagement and exit strategies' (EU, 2014, p. 11). Hence, it is fair to say that programs and strategies that could roughly be described as 'deradicalization' measures have gained global significance in the fight against terrorism, recruitment into violent extremism and violent radicalization. However, terminology remains unclear and potentially inhibits development in the field, as Altier, Thoroughgood, and Horgan (2014, p. 647) found 'that existing research remains devoid of conceptual clarity' with synonymous and inconsistent use of different terms.

Of course, deradicalization as a concept is by etymology tied to its opposite: 'radicalization', an equally contested and controversial term. However, research into radicalization processes and pathways leading to violent extremism, terrorism and violence has received much more academic and public attention than deradicalization, with an extensive and almost unmanageably large body of publications and studies from various different disciplines. Nevertheless, conceptual clarity and a more or less shared understanding of basic terms are absolutely indispensable for any academic or practical development and advancement in a field with so many expectations placed upon it, especially since 'much of our understanding of the causal processes of disengagement from terrorism remains theoretical or speculative and under-researched' (Gill, Bouhana, & Morrison, 2015, p. 245).

This chapter aims to give an overview of the most important terms, concepts and frictions within the different argumentations and schools of thought. It points out where the radicalization and deradicalization discourse might have disconnected from the necessities of so called 'front-line practitioners' who are tasked with achieving success in working with individuals with different violent extremist and terrorist backgrounds, as well as with those vulnerable and under high risk of entering extremist movements. Funding and establishment of such programs in the field have gained exponential traction regardless of the conceptual unclarity among academics and policy makers. This holds the danger of uninformed or conceptually weak programs being implemented in practice, working with high-risk individuals. Hence, this chapter will also suggest ways to reconsolidate the current academic discourse with the practical field regarding key terms and concepts.

Radicalization

Before turning to a discussion of the term deradicalization, it is necessary to shed some light on the process it claims to counter or reverse: 'radicalization'. Having entered the mainstream political, media and academic discourse after the London terror attacks of July 7, 2005 (Sedgwick, 2010), the term is widely understood to describe a 'process by which an individual adopts an extremist ideology' (Braddock, 2014, p. 62). Before the term entered the discourse, academics and policy makers usually referred to 'root causes' of terrorism (Neumann, 2008, p. 4). The European Commission sees 'radicalization' as a process of 'embracing opinions, views and ideas which could lead to acts of terrorism' (Reinares et al., 2008, p. 5). Similarly focusing on the aspect of violence, Bosi, Demetriou and Malthaner (2014a, p. 2) understand this individual change as 'a process forming through strategy, structure, and conjuncture, and involving the adoption and sustained use of violent means to achieve articulated political goals'. Whether or not the use of violence is actually a key aspect of radicalization remains contested and led to the distinction between violent and non-violent radicalization (Bartlett & Miller, 2012). Non-violent radicalization is seen as 'the social and psychological process of incrementally experienced commitment to extremist political or religious ideology' by Horgan and Braddock (2010, p. 152). This means that: 'radicalization may not necessarily lead to violence, but is one of several risk factors required for this' (ibid.). Violent radicalization on the other hand is defined by the same scholars as:

> the social and psychological process of increased and focused radicalization through involvement with a violent non-state movement. Violent radicalization encompasses the phases of a) becoming involved with a terrorist group and b) remaining involved and engaging in terrorist activity; it involves a process of pre-involvement searching for the opportunity to engage in violence and the exploration of competing alternatives; the individual must have both the opportunity for engagement as well as the capacity to make a decision about that engagement
>
> (*ibid.*)

or, in the words of Bartlett and Miller, violent radicalization means simply the 'radicalization that leads to violence' and non-violent radicalization 'the process by which individuals come to hold radical views in relation to the *status quo* but do not undertake, aid, or abet terrorist activity' (Bartlett & Miller, 2012, p. 2 [italics in original]).

Alternatively, some scholars have argued to speak of 'cognitive' (focusing on extremist beliefs) and 'behavioral' radicalization (focusing on extremist actions) (Neumann, 2013). This dichotomy between psychological and physical sides of the process will be mirrored in the concept of deradicalization as well. However, violent and non-violent radicalization have both received considerably more academic attention in recent decades compared with deradicalization, and the abundant body of literature focusing on radicalization from various different fields has resulted in numerous metastudies attempting to summarize the state of the art (e.g. Borum, 2011a, 2011b; Christmann, 2012; Dalgaard-Nielsen, 2008a, 2008b, 2010; Horgan, 2008; Reinares et al., 2008). Nevertheless, the term 'radicalization' itself remains a source of confusion and no widespread consensus exists about what it actually means and which components are necessary to define it (Pisoiu, 2011, p. 10; Sedgwick, 2010). Mainly due to the use of the term in at least three different contexts with three different agendas (the 'security', 'integration' and 'foreign policy' contexts; see Sedgwick, 2010, p. 479), clear-cut definitions are scarce and vary greatly in content and scope. While the 'security' agenda focuses on radicalization as a security threat, the integration agenda, according to Sedgwick, is mainly concerned with political polarization about immigration politics. Lastly, the 'foreign policy' agenda uses the concepts of 'radical' and 'radicalization' as labels to justify certain policies by state actors, for example supressing national opposition, aligned to international discourses, e.g. the 'war on terror'. In consequence, Sedgwick suggests abandoning the idea of being 'radical' and 'radicalization' as absolute concepts and recognizing their relative and dynamic nature.

One way to define the core of radicalization beyond the use of violence is, for example, the individual's motive to fundamentally alter the surrounding environment. In this regard, Moskalenko and McCauley (2009) have suggested introducing the concept of 'activism' as the legal counterpart to illegal 'radicalism'. Echoing this notion, Dalgaard-Nielsen (2010, p. 798) defines 'radicalization' as 'a growing readiness to pursue and support far-reaching changes in society that conflict with, or pose a direct threat to, the existing order'. Pointing to the fact that 'radicalization' is, in fact, a label used to interpret a certain behavior by outsiders, De Vito (2014, p. 72) sees 'radicalization' as 'a shift in the contents and/or forms of contention that, in relation to previous contents and/or forms of contention, is perceived as an escalation by (some) historical agents and/or by external observers'. As noted by Pisoiu (2011, p. 12), most definitions actually describe a result, rather than the process or mechanism of radicalization as such. Suggesting that one should understand 'radicalism' as a 'political ideology with the objective of inducing sweeping change based on fundamental or "root" principles' (Pisoiu, 2011, p. 23) means that 'radicalization' implies a twofold process: on the one hand a growing desire for (fundamental) change, and on the other an increasing importance of 'root' (referring to the Latin word *radix* for 'root' or 'base') principles.

Furthermore, one can identify roughly four schools within research looking at processes of 'radicalization': the sociological, social movement, empirical (for the first three, see Dalgaard-Nielsen, 2010) and psychological schools. The 'sociological' school (e.g. Kepel, 2004; Kepel & Milelli, 2008; Khosrokhavar, 2005, 2006; Roy, 2004) sees the main reason for radicalization lying with the individual, who reclaims a lost identity in an environment perceived as hostile (Dalgaard-Nielsen, 2010). The 'social movement' (and 'framing') theorists claim, however, that radicalization occurs due to networks, group dynamics, peer pressure and a constructed reality (e.g. Sageman, 2004, 2007a, 2007b; Wiktorowicz, 2004). Within the literature on social movements, another group of scholars have developed an approach labelled 'contentious politics' (Bosi, Demetriou, & Malthaner, 2014b; Della Porta, 2013; McAdam, Tarrow, & Tilly, 2001; Tarrow, 1998), looking at the relational aspects of violence and between social movements in conflict with each other. Research within this framework has shown that radicalization leading to violence is the result of mutual processes involving 'competition between movement activists and opponents, especially in the form of escalating policing but also of competitive escalation within the social movement sector, as well as within social movement families' (Della Porta, 2013, p. 94). Indeed, once thoroughly scrutinized, it becomes clear that radicalism (including radicalization) does not '"come upon" the regular political institutions, but emerges within and around them' (Pisoiu, 2011, p. 24) and therefore the exchange between the different groups, movements, individuals and societies becomes essential to understand the phenomenon. One approach to theoretically conceptualize that exchange was suggested by Koehler (2015), which essentially sees a radical social movement connected to its surrounding mainstream ideology through infrastructure (e.g. events, rituals, clothing, subcultural products) and its own ideology. Radical social movements need to negotiate a middle ground between attacking and destroying a negative, as well as winning over a positive, target society. Caught in this competition over ideological efficacy, the social space between these movements with their own goals and collective identities and the target societies provides the fertile ground for individual and collective radicalization in Koehler's model.

The 'empiricists', in contrast, try to find individual-level motivations and socio-economic profiles and draw the theories inductively (Nesser, 2004; Slootman & Tillie, 2006). One outcome of this school is the classification of different types of members within extremist groups with different radicalization processes, motives and backgrounds – e.g. the 'leader', the 'protégé', the 'misfit' and the 'drifter' (Nesser, 2004).

The fourth school can be called 'psychological', with one main author being John Horgan (Horgan, 2005, 2008, 2017). Horgan points to the fact that no 'terrorist' profile has been found and most studies do not look into the socio-psychological dynamics between 'push' and 'pull' factors. Horgan (2008, pp. 6–7) states that emotional vulnerability, dissatisfaction with current political activity, identification with victims, belief that the use of violence is not immoral, a sense of reward and social ties in the radical group, among others, are very important factors for understanding how these dynamics lead to the use of violence.

In addition to these studies focusing on individual pathways into extremism and terrorism, other scholars have attempted to identify radicalization models and the necessary steps or phases an individual has to go through on the path to violent extremism. To name only a few and most widely cited, the first major radicalization model theory was published in 2007 by the New York Police Department Intelligence Division (Silber & Bhatt, 2007) using 11 case studies of jihadist-motivated radicalization in Western countries and describing a four-step model ('pre-radicalization', 'self-identification', 'indoctrination', 'jihadization').

Another widely recognized model was designed by Marc Sageman (2004, 2007a, 2007b), who also identified a four-step process. His phases, however, do not need to follow each other in one sequence, but rather constantly appear during an individual radicalization process: moral outrage; specific interpretation or worldview; contextualization with personal experiences; and mobilization through interactive networks.

Inspired by Sageman's studies, Michael Taarnby (2005) developed his own radicalization model based on an in-depth analysis of the 9/11 cell from Hamburg incorporating eight stages: individual alienation and marginalization; a spiritual quest; a process of radicalization; meeting and associating with like-minded people; gradual seclusion and cell formation; acceptance of violence as legitimate political means; connection with a gatekeeper in the know; and going operational.

As a last example of the many different process models looking at violent radicalization, Moghaddam's (2005) famous 'staircase' model includes three individual levels (dispositional factors), one organizational level (situation) and one environmental level (socio-economic). Moghaddam uses the metaphor of a staircase in a house where everyone lives on the ground floor. However, a small group of people are driven by a psychological process to gradually move up the stairs, during which the group is constantly reduced. If a person reaches the top, terrorist attacks become almost inevitable, as together with the upward movement the number of individual decisions are constantly narrowed down.

All these process models point to the fact that individual radicalization pathways are gradual processes spanning over a certain time span and involving different cognitive and behavioral steps. One benefit of identifying these steps and pathways would be to eventually identify persons at risk of or already engaged in radicalization, in order to initiate an adequate intervention. This aim implies that radicalization processes are visible or noticeable in the first place, an aspect increasingly seen in doubt as part of the 'lone wolf' radicalization theory (e.g. Bakker & de Graaf, 2010; Feldman, 2013; Spaaij, 2010, 2011). There is, however, strong indication that even 'lone wolf' radicalization processes rarely, if ever, happen completely unnoticed by the affective environment or associate gatekeepers (Gill, Horgan, & Deckert, 2014). This opens the possibility to provide specialized support for communities and families to recognize potential radicalization processes and intervene.

Those definitions and process models presented above have so far described what a violent radicalization process is and what it may look like in terms of individual steps towards violence. Most theories and especially the process models identifying phases and steps within the radicalization processes remain more or less deterministic in their attempts to identify biographical factors or root causes of radicalization. Empirically, the search for a terrorist profile has thoroughly failed:

> Neither psychological nor other research has revealed qualities unique to those who become involved in terrorism, or the existence of singular pathways into (and out of) terrorism. Though terrorist profiles exist in a broad sense, no meaningful (i.e., having predictive validity) psychological profile has been found either within or across groups. If anything, the composition of terrorist groups is remarkable for its diversity.
>
> *(Horgan, 2017, p. 200)*

Hence, there is a need for concepts of radicalization that focus more on the psychological mechanisms behind the process as such, rather than individual factors and root causes.

It was suggested by Koehler (2016, pp. 65–94) to understand radicalization as a process of individual depluralization of political concepts and values (e.g. justice, freedom, honour, violence, democracy) on the one hand and an increase in ideological urgency to act against a framed problem on the other. With a higher degree of individual internalization of the notion that no other alternative interpretations of the (individually prioritized) political concepts and values exist (or are relevant), one can show (e.g. in syntax, language and behavior) the progression of the radicalization process. This in turn creates a value conflict with the surrounding mainstream value system, which was seen by Schwartz (2017) to be one of the main driving factors of political alienation, or more precisely, the process of disconnection from the mainstream value system with the potential for ending in violent behavior. This internalization of ideologically framed political concepts and problems can be emotional and/or intellectual, which in itself is not dangerous to any society. The important link here is the fusion (and combination) with a certain type of ideology that inherently denies individual freedom (or equal rights) to anyone who is not part of the radical person's in-group and thus the degree of ideological incompatibility with the mainstream political culture.

It is clear that the term 'ideology' plays a major role in understanding radicalization. A major function of every ideology is to 'cement the word–concept relationship' and to 'attach a single meaning to a political term' (Freeden, 1994, p. 156). Thus, every ideology strives to 'decontest' the range of meanings that can possibly be attached to central political concepts. 'Decontestation' or 'depluralization' is, in fact, the core dynamic of radicalization, which at the beginning postulates and defines specific religious or political problems (e.g. the suffering of Muslims in Syria, unemployment of members of the 'Aryan' race) and contextualizes these with the recruit's individual biographical experiences and background in order to connect global or abstract issues with micro-social events (e.g. conflicts in the family, discrimination). Through this mechanism, other individual or social problems and issues are gradually pushed aside or integrated into the main problem set defined by the ideology. Typically fostered and driven through the tactical use of propaganda material, connection with charismatic leaders and mentors and the assignment of group-specific tasks, the individual is integrated into a 'contrast society' connecting the radical social movement with the mainstream environment (Koehler, 2015), in which the basic ideological tenets are intertwined with individual values, political concepts and beliefs.

During the process of depluralization, these values and concepts are gradually rewritten, restructured and redefined. This alone is nothing extraordinary, as every ideology typically functions in that way. Violent radical ideologies, however, constantly erase and negate alternative or competing definitions of the ideology's core values and concepts and try to establish a monopoly in this regard. At the same time, the propaganda and group dynamics constantly increase the urgency and importance of the core problems stated through the movement and ideology. On the one hand, this is an automatic result of any depluralization process by simply erasing or devaluating other problems. On the other hand, radical social movements deliberately overstate the importance of their core issues in order to trigger activism and commitment more effectively. Consequently, a psychological tension is built up within the recruit for which the movement offers a solution: the praised future vision. At the end of the process, the recruit only recognizes one problem subsuming every other or simply being much more important than all other issues, only one viable solution and one perfect vision for the future. Simultaneously, the individual's understanding of core political concepts and values has dramatically changed according to this new problem–solution–vision triad.

A maximally radicalized person in this sense does not recognize an alternative concept, for example, of 'justice', 'freedom' or 'honour', and even reacts aggressively towards different viewpoints. As the problematic aspect of 'violent radical ideologies' lies within the inherent inequality between human beings, the *decreasing* number of alternative concepts, values, problems and solutions in combination with an *increasing* urgency of the main problem forces each person inevitably (in case the process is not interrupted) to eventually cross the individual point at which the use of violence is the only option to resolve the tension. Non-violent solutions have been declared ineffective or useless and are not adequate to the perceived importance of the problem anymore. Slowly (or sometimes rather quickly) reaching that critical point is the 'time bomb effect' – a mechanism underlying every form of radicalization. If these processes do not lead to violence, the individual's (or group's) ideology is not in direct, or only modest, contrast with the mainstream political culture and surrounding ideology. It is therefore of great importance to what degree the surrounding environment perceives the individual or group as a direct threat or political competitor and reacts accordingly, whether repressive or not – a course of action which fosters depluralization processes and the use of violence, as has been reflected in the social movement literature and especially the contentious politics approach to radicalization, which includes the relational field and contextualization of violence to explain the individual or collective move towards violence (Bosi, Demetriou, & Malthaner, 2014b).

Deradicalization

As noted above, the term 'deradicalization' has been widely used with conceptual unclarity and been used synonymously and inconsistently with other terms (Altier et al., 2014). Horgan and Taylor (2011, p. 175), for example, listed 'rehabilitation', 'reform', 'counseling', 'reconciliation', 'amnesty', 'demobilization', 'disbandment', 'dialogue' and 'deprogramming' as concepts competing and sometimes exchangeable with deradicalization. In addition, Koehler (2016) named 'reintegration', 're-education', 'desistance' (primary, secondary and tertiary), 'disaffiliation' and 'debiasing'. All these terms roughly describe a similar process of turning from a position of perceived deviance or conflict with the surrounding environment towards moderation and equilibrium. This process can take numerous different forms, for example, voluntary or involuntary; permanent or temporary; individual or collective; and psychological or physical (Koehler, 2016, p. 14).

It is obvious that all these concepts and terms describe a psychological and physical process essentially measured by individuals' or groups' degree of accordance, respectively conflict, with the legal, ideological or moral views of the surrounding majority (or mainstream) environment. Hence, deradicalization and its competing concepts have to be understood as terms marking a specific kind of societal negotiation between a community and perceived deviants aiming at conflict reduction. Most of these concepts and terms (including deradicalization) imply that the source for the conflict lies with the 'deviant' other, who must be somehow aligned with the position of the mainstream majority, assuming that an increased alignment automatically reduces conflict. Deradicalization, and most of these competing concepts, therefore have to navigate a precarious borderline between reducing plurality of opinions and convictions on the one hand, sometimes even crossing the threshold to infringe upon central core freedoms guaranteed in all Western democratic countries, and reducing sources of violent conflict based on extremist thought patterns, ideologies or group dynamics on the other. This inherent struggle with moral legitimacy of the deradicalization concept (i.e. the attempted change of a person's or group's political or religious opinion, which are oftentimes not illegal), at least in Western countries, was described in detail by Koehler (2016, pp. 201–210) and has to be the background for the following conceptual and definitional remarks.

The inherent moral legitimacy conflict is one of the reasons that deradicalization's most important competing concept is 'disengagement' and both are usually used in combination with each other. Looking at some definitions by leading academic experts, the main difference between deradicalization and disengagement is the focus on ideology, or more precisely the psychological side of exiting a violent extremist milieu. Horgan and Braddock (2010, p. 152), for example, define disengagement as:

> the process whereby an individual experiences a change in role or function that is usually associated with a reduction of violent participation. It may not necessarily involve leaving the movement, but is most frequently associated with significant temporary or permanent role change. Additionally, while disengagement may stem from role change, that role change may be influenced by psychological factors such as disillusionment, burnout or the failure to reach the expectations that influenced initial involvement. This can lead to a member seeking out a different role within the movement

and deradicalization as:

> the social and psychological process whereby an individual's commitment to, and involvement in, violent radicalization is reduced to the extent that they are no longer at risk of involvement and engagement in violent activity. Deradicalization may also refer to any initiative that tries to achieve a reduction of risk of re-offending through addressing the specific and relevant disengagement issues.
>
> *(Horgan & Braddock, 2010, p. 153)*

More specifically, Braddock (2014, p. 60) points out that deradicalization is a 'psychological process through which an individual abandons his extremist ideology and is theoretically rendered a decreased threat for re-engaging in terrorism'.

Hence, at a first glance, the main difference between disengagement and deradicalization is if reduction of the ideological commitment (deradicalization) or physical role change and desistance from illegal behavior (disengagement) is the main focus of the process. However, it is more complex than that. Horgan (2009a, p. 19), for example, notes that, even if psychologically reducing commitment to a violent extremist group is the goal, deradicalization (i.e. reduction in ideological commitment) does not have to be part of the process and might not even be a likely outcome. Using the term 'psychological disengagement' as synonymous with 'deradicalization' (Horgan, Altier, Shortland, & Taylor, 2016, p. 11), he found that, in his large sample of interviews with former terrorists he collected between 2006 and 2008, 'almost all could be described as disengaged, the vast majority of them could not be said to be "deradicalized"' (2009a, p. 27). In this differentiation between disengagement and deradicalization, another term, 'ideology', again plays a significant role.

To complicate this even further, ideology and its role in entering, as well as leaving, extremist milieus has essentially divided the discourse specifically on deradicalization into a 'broad' and 'narrow' school (Clubb, 2015), with the first aiming to achieve rejection of ideological-based violence and the latter including various other ideological aspects as well. Furthermore, while it has been argued that disengagement, i.e. the mere physical role change and desistance from crime, would be more feasible and realistic (e.g. Noricks, 2009), other scholars have pointed out that in order to reduce recidivism of extremist offenders, it is necessary to address 'beliefs and attitudes that drive violent behavior' (Braddock, 2014, p. 60). Not addressing these underlying beliefs and attitudes, as well as the individual psychological factors of attraction, might increase the chance of a failed exit process and the risk of re-radicalization (Koehler, 2016; Rabasa, Pettyjohn, Ghez, & Boucek, 2010). However, beliefs, attitudes and factors of attraction might overlap with the milieu's ideology, but they don't have to be entirely equal. Other parts of the collective identity or oppositional culture within the extremist environment can also provide a pull factor. In that sense, 'ideology', as explained above in the section on 'radicalization', is better understood as a dynamic set of political values and ideals, which is constantly renegotiated between the individual and the collective, albeit to a differing degree of involvement from both sides.

It is important to note here that the term deradicalization has been used to describe both the process of exiting an extremist environment on the one side and the wider practical activity by programs or mentors on the other. Practitioners in the field tend not to distinguish between the role of ideology in the exit process when describing their activities, but rather see every form of assisted departure from an extremist milieu and reintegration into a non-extremist life as 'deradicalization'. Bringing together the terminology of the wider deradicalization field at this point, the different forms of exiting can be defined according to the degree of ideological removal (from the weakest to the strongest): physical disengagement, psychological disengagement or deradicalization (narrow) and deradicalization (broad). These processes can overlap and an individual might go through all or only one of them in different order. For example, physical disengagement might lead to a narrow deradicalization, which might lead to a broad one in the long run (Clubb, 2017). It must also be recognized that these developments are not a one-way process but also include setbacks and reversals. Some aspects of the ideology or group might regain attractiveness, for example, in the form of another extremist ideology or group. This essentially means that 'deradicalisation should not be considered a psychological return to some pre-radicalised state' (Braddock, 2014, p. 62) but as a new development in itself.

Shifting the focus to deradicalization as a practical activity, another set of terms and concepts have entered the discourse. One common classification used in connection to deradicalization is the trifold prevention matrix from Caplan (1964), being rooted in clinical psychiatry and dubbed 'Public Health Model'. 'Primary' prevention in this matrix aims to prevent a deviant behavior from occurring in a non-infected system. 'Secondary' prevention aims to avert its solidification, when it is already present and 'tertiary' prevention in consequence aims to prevent this element from recurring in the future. As intended by Caplan, every intervention in tertiary prevention essentially aims to prevent recidivism. This mechanism was echoed when deradicalization as practical activity was seen as programs reducing risk of terrorist recidivism (Horgan & Altier, 2012). In this context, academics and practitioners have seen deradicalization activities as tertiary prevention (e.g. Harris-Hogan, Barrelle, & Zammit, 2015).

Another classification concept from using a prevention-based terminology applied to deradicalization was introduced by Gordon Jr (1983), who, in contrast to Caplan, only looked at a state of non-infection. 'Universal' prevention in this concept aims to introduce wide, easy and cheap measures of preventative care, e.g. a healthier nutrition. 'Selective' prevention aims to introduce more differential methods targeting a group with a higher risk of infection, while 'indexed' prevention aims at those with a high risk. Objection to that framework was, for example, raised by Koehler (2016), who argued that preventing recidivism is just one necessary (and later) part of deradicalization, which must reduce individual physical and psychological commitment to the extremist group and ideology in the first place. In addition, using a classification scheme from clinical psychiatry might imply a pathological nature of radicalization and deradicalization, which can have a significant negative impact on practitioners' self-understanding and the cognitive opening of the program participants.

Next to these classifications from mental health and disease control, attempts to counter violent radicalization processes have been commonly referred to as 'countering violent extremism' (CVE) programs (e.g. Cherney et al., 2017; Harris-Hogan et al., 2015). These are usually understood to be preventative in nature and to be 'an approach intended to preclude individuals from engaging in, or materially supporting, ideologically motivated violence' (Williams, 2017, p. 153). It would be more accurate, however, to see CVE as the umbrella category under which prevention-oriented initiatives (i.e. before a person radicalizes to a point of using violence) and intervention-oriented initiatives (i.e. deradicalization and disengagement of persons who are already radicalized to the point of using violence) are subsumed. The first is commonly referred to as 'counter-radicalization' or 'preventing violent extremism' (PVE) programs and the latter as deradicalization, rehabilitation or reintegration program.

Naturally, there is no clear distinction between prevention- or intervention-oriented methods and programs in practice as radicalization processes are not linear and dynamic as well. Hence, whether or not a person is not yet 'radical enough' for deradicalization is mostly impossible and even futile to answer, which is why most practitioners do not differentiate as clearly the different terms and concepts as the academic discourse might suggest. Case managers or mentors who are in touch with the client, participant or beneficiary have to decide on an individual case-by-case basis which tools and methods to choose. In reality, prevention- and intervention-oriented tools form a methods-blend aiming to achieve effects on all levels: preventing further radicalization; decreasing physical and psychological commitment to the radical milieu and thought pattern or ideology; preventing return to violence and extremism; increasing resilience to extremist ideologies or groups; and assisting to build a new self-sustained life and identity. Usually, reference points for mentors and case managers are the time spent in the extremist environment, position or rank in the group and quantity and severity of crimes committed in the name of the extremist ideology. The question of individual conviction or the degree of internalization of that extremist ideology is in many cases never fully answered but rather addressed through a methods mix, including a variety of different approaches (for an overview see: Koehler, 2016). Even though it is seen as a major necessity of high-quality deradicalization work to base the methods mix for individual counselling on a detailed account of the client's risk factors and needs (Koehler, 2017b), tools for adequate risk assessment are contested (Sarma, 2017) and so are attempts to identify root causes or driving factors of a violent radicalization. Practitioners mostly assume some connection between identified biographical friction points or traumatic experiences, as well as somehow expressed factors of attraction (e.g. action and adventure seeking, quest for significance, search for loyalty, camaraderie and honour), which is embodied in the extremist group or ideology. As outlined by Koehler (2015), violent radical milieus are not monolithic, static and clearly separated groups but rather in constant exchange with their positive and negative target societies through infrastructure and ideology. As there are multiple ways in and out of these contrast societies (i.e. the mechanism of interaction between the radical group and mainstream environment), it is also possible to move within these milieus. Motivations for joining can, but do not have to, be connected to reasons for leaving. In consequence, as radicalization is a context bound phenomenon 'par excellence' (Reinares et al., 2008, p. 7), so is deradicalization. Practitioners constantly have to adapt their methods and tools to the individual context of the client combined with the goal to achieve a maximum of disengagement or deradicalization possible.

Conclusion

The aim of this chapter is to provide an overview of the most important terms and definitions used by academics and practitioners in the deradicalization landscape, which not only includes various key concepts around leaving a violent extremist or terrorist milieu, but also how to understand the process of entering that environment. It is clear that both key terms (radicalization and deradicalization) are connected to a third key term: ideology. Experts from both academia and the practitioner field see a psychological and physical side of radicalization and deradicalization, which led to the introduction of additional terms (e.g. disengagement). In addition to the question of the importance of ideology during enter and exit processes, the role of violence is key to understanding the various rifts within the terminological discourse. As a natural marker of legal and illegal activism, the use of violence provides an easy way to assess if a person has crossed the line into the criminal space or left it in case of abstaining from violence. Without a doubt, however, individuals undergo a psychological process of change before they reach that threshold and after moving back. Arguably, that process of change is key for prevention- or rehabilitation-oriented external support. As entering and exiting violent extremism and terrorism follow highly individual and context-specific pathways, in which political concepts and ideas (ideology) intertwine with biographical and situational factors, these change processes hardly follow a linear development and can be impacted (positively or negatively) by significant others in the affective environment.

While academics have stressed the necessity for clear-cut definitions and concepts (e.g. to differentiate between deradicalization and disengagement), practitioners have pointed out the need for flexibility in choosing approaches and methods for each individual case, which also means being able to shift between deradicalization and disengagement goals and tools for an individual client. One of the biggest challenges, therefore, is to reconnect the academic discourse around terms and concepts of deradicalization to practitioners' needs and understanding of the day-to-day work with their clients.

One possible way to achieve this might be to focus on quality standards in deradicalization work, which is essential to improve evaluability, as well as identification and transfer of good practices by academics on the one hand and more flexibility on the practitioners' side on the other. Because one part of quality standards in deradicalization is conceptual clarity (Koehler, 2017a, 2017b), in order to choose adequate methods and tools but also to understand and recognize when to alter the approach, there is also the requirement for practitioners to be sufficiently equipped for the complex and individual nature of radicalization and deradicalization. Hence, quality standards could be the connecting bridge between the academic and practitioner discourse on terms and definitions.

References

Aho, J. A. (1988). Out of hate: A sociology of defection from neo-nazism. *Current Research on Peace and Violence, 11*(4), 159–168.

Altier, M. B., Thoroughgood, C. N., & Horgan, J. G. (2014). Turning away from terrorism: Lessons from psychology, sociology, and criminology. *Journal of Peace Research, 51*(5), 647–661. doi:10.1177/0022343314535946

Ashour, O. (2009). *The deradicalization of jihadists: Transforming armed Islamist movements*. New York and London: Routledge.

Bakker, E., & de Graaf, B. (2010). Lone wolves. The Hague: ICCT. Retrieved from www.icct.nl/download/file/ICCT-Bakker-deGraaf-EM-Paper-Lone-Wolves.pdf

Bartlett, J., & Miller, C. (2012). The edge of violence: Towards telling the difference between violent and non-violent radicalization. *Terrorism and Political Violence, 24*(1), 1–21. doi:10.1080/09546553.2011.594923

Bjørgo, T. (1997). *Racist and right-wing violence in Scandinavia: Patterns, perpetrators, and responses*. Oslo: Aschehoug.

Bjørgo, T., & Carlsson, Y. (2005). Early intervention with violent and racist youth groups. Norsk Utenrikspolitisk Institutt (NUPI), Oslo, Paper No. 677. Retrieved from www.files.ethz.ch/isn/27305/677.pdf

Bjørgo, T., & Horgan, J. (2009). *Leaving terrorism behind: Individual and collective disengagement*. London and New York: Routledge.

Borum, R. (2011a). Radicalization into violent extremism I: A review of social science theories. *Journal of Strategic Security, 4*(4), 7.

Borum, R. (2011b). Radicalization into violent extremism II: A review of conceptual models and empirical research. *Journal of Strategic Security, 4*(4), 37.

Bosi, L., Demetriou, C., & Malthaner, S. (2014a). A contentious politics approach to the explanation of radicalization. In L. Bosi, C. Demetriou, & S. Malthaner (Eds.), *Dynamics of political violence. A process-oriented perspective on radicalization and the escalation of political conflict* (pp. 1–23). Farnham, UK: Ashgate.

Bosi, L., Demetriou, C., & Malthaner, S. (2014b). *Dynamics of political violence: A process-oriented perspective on radicalization and the escalation of political conflict*. Farnham, UK: Ashgate.

Boucek, C. (2007). Extremist reeducation and rehabilitation in Saudi Arabia. *Terrorism Monitor, 5*(16), 1–4.

Braddock, K. (2014). The talking cure? Communication and psychological impact in prison de-radicalisation programmes. In A. Silke (Ed.), *Prisons, terrorism and extremism: Critical issues in management, radicalisation and reform* (pp. 60–74). London: Routledge.

Caplan, G. (1964). *Principles of preventive psychiatry*. New York: Basic Books.

Cherney, A., Sweid, R., Grossman, M., Derbas, A., Dunn, K., Jones, C., ... Barton, G. (2017). Local service provision to counter violent extremism: Perspectives, capabilities and challenges arising from an Australian service mapping project. *Behavioral Sciences of Terrorism and Political Aggression*, 1–20. doi:10.1080/19434472.2017.1350735

Christmann, K. (2012). Preventing religious radicalisation and violent extremism. A systematic review of the research evidence. Retrieved from www.gov.uk/government/uploads/system/uploads/attachment_data/file/396030/preventing-violent-extremism-systematic-review.pdf

Clubb, G. (2015). Deradicalisation, disengagement and the attitudes-behavior debate. In C. Kennedy-Pipe, G. Clubb, & S. Mabon (Eds.), *Terrorism and political violence* (pp. 258–266). London: Sage.

Clubb, G. (2017). *Social movement de-radicalisation and the decline of terrorism: The morphogenesis of the Irish republicanism movement*. New York; London: Routledge.

Dalgaard-Nielsen, A. (2008a). Studying violent radicalization in Europe I: The potential contribution of social movement theory: DIIS Working Paper.

Dalgaard-Nielsen, A. (2008b). Studying violent radicalization in Europe II: The potential contribution of socio-psychological and psychological approaches: DIIS Working Paper.

Dalgaard-Nielsen, A. (2010). Violent radicalization in Europe: What we know and what we do not know. *Studies in Conflict & Terrorism, 33*, 797–814.

De Vito, C. G. (2014). Processes of radicalization and deradicalization in Western European prisons (1965-1986). In L. Bosi, C. Demetriou, & S. Malthaner (Eds.), *Dynamics of political violence. A process-oriented perspective on radicalization and the escalation of political conflict* (pp. 71–90). Surrey, UK: Ashgate.

Della Porta, D. (2013). *Clandestine political violence*. Cambridge, UK: Cambridge University Press.

El-Said, H. (2012). Clemency, civil accord and reconciliation: The evolution of Algeria's deradicalization process. In H. El-Said & J. Harrigan (Eds.), *Deradicalising violent extremists: Counter-radicalisation and deradicalisation programmes and their impact in Muslim majority states* (pp. 14–49). London: Routledge.

El-Said, H., & Barrett, R. (2012). Saudi Arabia: The master of deradicalization. In H. El-Said & J. Harrigan (Eds.), *Deradicalising violent extremists: Counter-radicalisation and deradicalisation programmes and their impact in Muslim majority states* (pp. 194–226). London: Routledge.

EU. (2014). Revised EU strategy for combating radicalisation and recruitment to terrorism. (5643/5/14). Brussels. Retrieved from http://register.consilium.europa.eu/doc/srv?l=EN&f=ST%209956%202014%20INIT

Feldman, M. (2013). Comparative lone wolf terrorism: Toward a heuristic definition. *Democracy and Security*, *9*(3), 270–286. doi:10.1080/17419166.2013.792252

Ferguson, N. (2010). Disengaging from terrorism. In A. Silke (Ed.), *The psychology of counter-terrorism* (pp. 111–123). London: Routledge.

Freeden, M. (1994). Political concepts and ideological morphology. *Journal of Political Philosophy*, *2*(2), 140–164. doi:10.1111/j.1467-9760.1994.tb00019.x

Gill, P., Bouhana, N., & Morrison, J. (2015). Individual disengagement from terrorist groups. In C. Kennedy-Pipe, G. Clubb, & S. Mabon (Eds.), *Terrorism and political violence* (pp. 243–257). London: Sage.

Gill, P., Horgan, J., & Deckert, P. (2014). Bombing alone: Tracing the motivations and antecedent behaviors of lone-actor terrorists. *Journal of Forensic Sciences*, *59*(2), 425–435. doi:10.1111/1556-4029.12312

Gordon, J. R. (1983). An operational classification of disease prevention. *Public Health Reports*, *98*(2), 107–109.

Harris-Hogan, S., Barrelle, K., & Zammit, A. (2015). What is countering violent extremism? Exploring CVE policy and practice in Australia. *Behavioral Sciences of Terrorism and Political Aggression*, *8*(1), 6–24. doi:10.1080/19434472.2015.1104710

Hegghammer, T. (2013). Number of foreign fighters from Europe in Syria is historically unprecedented. Who should be worried? *The Washington Post–The Monkey Cage*, 27.

Honig, O., & Yahel, I. (2017). A fifth wave of terrorism? The emergence of terrorist semi-states. *Terrorism and Political Violence*, 1–19. doi:10.1080/09546553.2017.1330201

Horgan, J. (2005). *The psychology of terrorism*. London; New York: Routledge.

Horgan, J. (2008). From profiles to pathways and roots to routes: Perspectives from psychology on radicalization into terrorism. *Annals of the American Academy of Political and Social Science*, *618*, 80–94.

Horgan, J. (2009a). Individual disengagement: A psychological analysis. In T. Bjørgo & J. Horgan (Eds.), *Leaving terrorism behind: Individual and collective disengagement* (pp. 17–29). London and New York: Routledge.

Horgan, J. (2009b). *Walking away from terrorism: Accounts of disengagement from radical and extremist movements*. London and New York: Routledge.

Horgan, J. (2017). Psychology of terrorism: Introduction to the special issue. *The American Psychologist*, *72*(3), 199–204.

Horgan, J., & Altier, M. B. (2012). The future of terrorist deradicalisation programs. *Georgetown Journal of International Affairs, Summer/Fall* (2012), 83–90.

Horgan, J., Altier, M. B., Shortland, N., & Taylor, M. (2016). Walking away: The disengagement and deradicalisation of a violent right-wing extremist. *Behavioral Sciences of Terrorism and Political Aggression*, *9*(2), 63–77. doi:10.1080/19434472.2016.1156722

Horgan, J., & Braddock, K. (2010). Rehabilitating the terrorists? Challenges in assessing the effectiveness of deradicalisation programs. *Terrorism and Political Violence*, *22*(2), 267–291. doi:10.1080/09546551003594748

Horgan, J., & Taylor, M. (2011). Disengagement, deradicalisation, and the arc of terrorism: Future directions for research. In R. Coolsaet (Ed.), *Jihadi terrorism and the radicalisation challenge: European and American experiences* (pp. 173–186). Farnham: Ashgate.

Johnsen, G. (2006). Yemen's passive role in the war on terrorism. *Terrorism Monitor*, *4*(4), 7–9.

Kepel, G. (2004). *The war for Muslim minds. Islam and the West*. Cambridge, MA: Belknap Press.

Kepel, G., & Milelli, J.-P. (2008). *Al Qaeda in its own words*. Cambridge, MA: Belknap Press.

Khosrokhavar, F. (2005). *Suicide bombers. Allah's new martyrs*. London: Pluto Press.

Khosrokhavar, F. (2006). Terrorism in Europe. In D. Hamilton (Ed.), *Terrorism and international relations* (pp. 23–38). Washington DC: Center for Transatlantic Relations.

Koehler, D. (2015). Contrast societies. Radical social movements and their relationships with their target societies. A theoretical model. *Behavioral Sciences of Terrorism and Political Aggression*, 7(1), 18–34. doi:10.1080/19434472.2014.977325

Koehler, D. (2016). *Understanding deradicalization. Methods, tools and programs for countering violent extremism*. Oxon/New York: Routledge.

Koehler, D. (2017a). How and why we should take deradicalization seriously. *Nature Human Behaviour, 1*, 0095. doi:10.1038/s41562-017-0095

Koehler, D. (2017b). Structural quality standards for work to intervene with and counter violent extremism. Retrieved from www.kpebw.de/wp-content/uploads/Handbuch-KPEBW-engl.pdf

McAdam, D., Tarrow, S. G., & Tilly, C. (2001). *Dynamics of contention*. Cambridge, UK and New York: Cambridge University Press.

Moghaddam, F. M. (2005). The staircase to terrorism: A psychological exploration. *American Psychologist, 60*(2), 161–169.

Moskalenko, S., & McCauley, C. (2009). Measuring political mobilization: The distinction between activism and radicalism. *Terrorism and Political Violence, 21*(2), 239–260. doi:10.1080/09546550902765508

Muggah, R. (2005). No magic bullet: A critical perspective on disarmament, demobilization and reintegration (DDR) and weapons reduction in post-conflict contexts. *The Round Table, 94*(379), 239–252.

Mullins, S. (2010). Rehabilitation of Islamist terrorists: Lessons from criminology. *Dynamics of Asymmetric Conflict, 3*(3), 162–193. doi:10.1080/17467586.2010.528438

Nesser, P. (2004). *Jihad in Europe. Exploring the motivations for Salafi-Jihadi terrorism in Europe post-millennium*. Oslo: Department of Political Science, University of Oslo.

Neumann, P. (2008). Introduction. *Perspectives on Radicalisation and Political Violence. Papers from the First International Conference on Radicalisation and Political Violence*. (pp. 3–7). London: International Centre for the Study of Radicalisation.

Neumann, P. (2013). The trouble with radicalization. *International Affairs, 89*(4), 873–893. doi:10.1111/1468-2346.12049

Noricks, D. M. E. (2009). Disengagement and deradicalization: Processes and programs. In P. K. Davis & K. Cragin (Eds.), *Social science for counterterrorism. Putting the pieces together* (pp. 299–320). Santa Monica: Rand Corporation.

Pisoiu, D. (2011). *Islamist radicalisation in Europe. An occupational change process*. New York: Routledge.

Rabasa, A., Pettyjohn, S. L., Ghez, J. J., & Boucek, C. (2010). Deradicalizing Islamist extremists. Retrieved from Santa Monica www.rand.org/content/dam/rand/pubs/monographs/2010/RAND_MG1053.pdf

Reinares, F., Alonso, R., Bjørgo, T., Della Porta, D., Coolsaet, R., Khosrokhavar, F., … De Vries, G. (2008). Radicalisation processes leading to acts of terrorism. Retrieved from www.rikcoolsaet.be/files/art_ip_wz/Expert%20Group%20Report%20Violent%20Radicalisation%20FINAL.pdf

Ripley, A. (2008, Mar. 13). Future revolutions. 4. Reverse radicalism. *Time Magazine*.

Roy, O. (2004). *Den globaliserede islam*. Copenhagen: Vandkunsten.

Sageman, M. (2004). *Understanding terror networks*. Philadelphia: University of Pennsylvania Press.

Sageman, M. (2007a). *Leaderless Jihad. Terror networks in the twenty-first century*. Philadelphia: University of Pennsylvania Press.

Sageman, M. (2007b). Radicalization of global Islamist terrorists. Retrieved from www.hsgac.senate.gov/download/062707sageman

Sarma, K. M. (2017). Risk assessment and the prevention of radicalization from nonviolence into terrorism. *American Psychologist, 72*(3), 278–288.

Schwartz, D. C. (2017). *Political alienation and political behavior*. New York: Routledge.

Sedgwick, M. (2010). The concept of radicalization as a source of confusion. *Terrorism and Political Violence, 22*(4), 479–494. doi:10.1080/09546553.2010.491009

Silber, M. D., & Bhatt, A. (2007). *Radicalization in the West – The homegrown threat*. New York: New York City Police Department Intelligence Divison.

Slootman, M., & Tillie, J. (2006). *Processes of radicalization. Why some Amsterdam Muslims become radicals*. Amsterdam: Institute for Migrations and Ethnic Studies. University of Amsterdam.

Spaaij, R. (2010). The enigma of lone wolf terrorism: An assessment. *Studies in Conflict & Terrorism, 33*(9), 854–870. doi:10.1080/1057610x.2010.501426

Spaaij, R. (2011). *Understanding lone wolf terrorism: Global patterns, motivations and prevention*. London: Springer Science & Business Media.

Taarnby, M. (2005). Recruitment of Islamist terrorists in Europe. Trends and perspectives. Retrieved from www.investigativeproject.org/documents/testimony/58.pdf

Tarrow, S. (1998). *Power in movement: Social movements and contentious politics*. Cambridge, UK: Cambridge University Press.

UNSC. (2014). *Resolution 2178 (2014)*. S/RES/2178 (2014). New York: United Nations Security Council.

Vidino, L. (2014). *Foreign fighters: An overview of responses in eleven countries.* Retrieved from Zurich www.css.ethz.ch/content/dam/ethz/special-interest/gess/cis/center-for-securities-studies/pdfs/Foreign_Fighters_2014.pdf

Wiktorowicz, Q. (Ed.). (2004). *Islamic activism. A social movement theory approach.* Bloomington, IN: Indiana Universtiy Press.

Williams, M. J. (2017). Prosocial behavior following immortality priming: Experimental tests of factors with implications for CVE interventions. *Behavioral Sciences of Terrorism and Political Aggression, 9*(3), 153–190. doi:10.1080/19434472.2016.1186718

3

CONCEPTS AND PRACTICES

A brief history of disengagement and deradicalisation

Stig Jarle Hansen

The history of disengagement and deradicalisation is complex. The concept of deradicalisation is rather new, while the concept of disengagement is older, yet its use exploded after 11 September 2001, and the growth of the Islamic State in the Levant. Yet, to start an exploration of disengagement and deradicalisation practices and theory with 11 September 2001 is misleading and loses much of the conceptual and practical heritage of the field as it stands today. Yet, this historical analysis also has to be limited due to the number of pages available for this chapter in this volume, and this chapter will mainly focus on individual and meso-level disengagement, rather than collective disengagement at group level. Attempts to get individuals to end criminal behaviour, and/or to stop believing in specific ideologies or religious systems deemed to be dangerous for society, have been ongoing for more than a century, and some of the concepts and techniques used today can be traced back to programmes established between World War I and the turn of the millennium.

The belief that criminals and perpetrators of violence can be rehabilitated (vs. the idea that only containment or deterrence worked) was crucial for these activities, and indeed the deradicalisation and disengagement programmes of today. Yet, there are some notable differences between penal rehabilitation and today's deradicalisation programmes. It should be remembered that the aim of a deradicalisation/disengagement programme is not necessarily to focus on a criminal or illegal context. The group from which the individual is to disengage might not have been criminalised; some deradicalisation/disengagement programmes may focus on the post-criminal space, while many others explicitly work in the pre-criminal space.

Often, but not always, a focus on pre-criminal space entails a different logic than a focus on the post criminal space. The pre-criminal space consists of actors that have yet to commit a crime, they are not in the care of law enforcement, and cannot, in general, be detained against their will. The early works on rehabilitation subsequently also influenced work on rehabilitation from criminal gangs, and the general field of criminology, and through these fields influenced today's deradicalisation and disengagement programmes.

The idea of criminal rehabilitation gained credibility from the late 19th century (McLennan 2008, 177; Brockway 1883, 44). Education and re-education was seen as an important tool in the early phase. Rehabilitation (of which one of the main tools was education, both to gain a future economic income but also to gain empathy and understanding of, and sympathy with, both democracy and society) was in some cases seen as a way of breaking a "cage" that was created by previous habits, social learning from criminal family members and criminals, towards creating the "normal person", a "citizen" with values supporting society (Brockway 1910; Winslow 1912), yet researchers also understood the weakness of the way success rates were measured (Kavanagh 1921; Tibbitts 1933).

The trend reached its high-water mark in the 1950s (Garland 2001).[1] The larger field of rehabilitation and encouraging desistance (the cessation of offending or other antisocial behaviour) is a field with long traditions, although there was a period when related programmes were seen as inefficient by criminologists in the late 1970s and early 1980s (Cullen 2013; Halleck and Witte Ann 1977; Serrill 1975). Notable relevant experiences and indeed research were also gathered from the re-education programmes targeting National Socialists (Nazis), both as prisoners of war during World War II as well as in post-war Europe. Anti-cult programmes, programmes targeting criminal offenders and gang members, as well as the anti-right-wing programmes of the 1980s and 1990s clearly have influenced today's deradicalisation and disengagement programmes. Although not applying the term "deradicalisation" and limiting the use of the term "disengagement", "exit" programmes targeting right-wing groups were prevalent in the late 1990s, and lessons and concepts from these programmes were directly incorporated into the deradicalisation and disengagement programmes of today; indeed, some of the practitioners are the same. Indeed, all of the genres that deradicalisation and disengagement draw upon share some of the characteristics of the discussion of disengagement and deradicalisation, including disagreements about conceptualisations, discussions of the use and abuse of power and force, and discussions (in the fields of re-education, anti-cult work and programmes targeting right-wing organisations only) of the importance of change of ideology vs. change of behaviour.

Yet there are also noticeable problems with these genres that mirror gaps in today's discussions, such as the western and Middle Eastern, and limited South East Asian focus of the research, and lack of focus on the paradoxes of the situations where groups that are to be deradicalised actually are drawn into power-sharing agreements to create peace, such as, for example, Latin American cases (see Chapter 24), and in cases where radicals actually control territories (see Chapter 7).

The interaction between politics and disengagement/deradicalisation has also often been avoided in discussions, yet this was a vital factor in ending re-education of Nazis after World War II, and today deradicalisation and disengagement face the challenges of being implemented for political purposes by totalitarian countries. The practices and discussions of these previous attempts at "re-education", "deprogramming", "rehabilitation", creating "desistance" and facilitating "exit" all hold important practical lessons for today, with practical techniques as well as theoretical discussions of use for present-day practitioners.

This chapter will start with the "re-education" programmes targeting Nazis, and subsequently present "deprogramming" from cults, the history behind changes in thinking around desistance and rehabilitation of criminals and facilitating exit in right-wing groups, following the chronological order of when these fields were established, and the most important discussions within them.

Re-educating Nazis

During World War II and after, various allied countries and new regimes in the old axis countries engaged in re-educating Nazis. The target here was to both change an ideological world view (which was seen as dangerous in itself, also leading to racist behaviour that was not necessarily illegal) and a tendency to political violence. At first these programmes targeted prisoners of war. The army psychological warfare units were initially ascribed a great deal of the responsibility for what was to be defined as *re-education* (Hartenian 1987). Yet, there was scepticism towards re-education programmes, with the sceptics often assuming that the Nazi defeat in World War II and the punishment of Nazi leaders would be all that was needed to destabilise the ideology.

How did these efforts work? The American "idea factory" at Fort Kearney, for example, conducted "training of trainers" targeting oppositional German prisoners, already sceptical about the Nazi ideology, into producing a wider prisoner-of-war newspaper called *Der Ruf* (*The Call*), to be distributed to the wider prisoner-of-war population (Kandarian 2016). Yet the US had problems with identifying Nazi hard-line entrepreneurs in their prisoner camps, and at the start of the war some of these elements thwarted de-ideologisation, and were able to use cohesion to maintain the Nazis worldwide even in the camps (Bernard, O'Connell, Thurston, Villamizar, Loredo, Sulivan and Goulka 2011). In one sense, the US touched upon one of the neglected elements in present-day deradicalisation and disengagement studies, namely how counter-measures and organisational disciplinary mechanisms on behalf of extremists influence deradicalisation and disengagement work, as discussed by Hansen in this volume. The Americans learned to dismantle disciplinary structures by removing individuals deemed to be essential for maintaining them, a lesson that interestingly had to be relearned during the American deradicalisation and disengagement efforts in Camp Bucca in Iraq 70 years later. They discovered that such individuals should be separated from the prisoners.

The Soviets, on the other hand, attempted to use the German command hierarchy identifying older officers with anti-Nazi sympathies who held authority but at the same time were willing to counter the Nazi intelligence. The latter also set up ideologically focused Antifa (anti-fascist) classes. The Soviet approach was different in the sense that their programmes also educated cadres intended to be future leaders in a post-war Germany; this elite was intended to become a bulwark against fascist ideology, but also a future governing elite of Soviet-led Eastern Europe, as a cadre replacing Nazism with communism. Indeed, parts of the American re-education programme were impossible for the Soviets to adapt, as it would undermine their own ideology, such as the American emphasis on democracy training (ibid. 12).[2]

The UK differed from the two other allies, in the sense that a lot of the responsibility for re-education was put on a civilian institution, the Political Intelligence department of the Foreign Office (Staff writer 1946). The British methods consisted of lectures, discussions, instructional films, books and newspapers. It is important to note that the British, as well as the Americans, attempted to stress collective guilt on behalf of Nazi Germany; a vital element was to highlight German violations of human rights. Indeed, later all three allies were to attempt this approach, to develop a German sense of collective responsibility through guilt, even at a collective national level (Janowitz 1946).

Peace led to change, and re-education had to be combined with the day-to-day workings of occupation. The new institutions thus emphasised cold and orderly governance, and stressed that propaganda should be based on the truth, yet a collective guilt was attempted to be induced (Hartenian 1987). The US emphasised a holistic approach: it was the whole of their sector of Germany that was to be re-educated, yet in one sense the "collective guilt" approach contradicted a "cadre" approach focusing on individual allies amongst the German population, and the latter, in the interest of the ease of governing the occupied zone, was prioritised. Pragmatism, and the new world setting, the onslaught of the cold war, sabotaged US, Soviet and UK efforts at re-education; several former Nazis were incorporated in intelligence services, in governance and inside research; punishment become more lenient; the re-education programmes faltered, the US and Soviet zones gained more self-determination; and less importance was put on re-education. There are many signs that re-education had problems, as relatively extreme attitudes were maintained by many in the war generation, and the real change occurred when a new generation started to probe into what happened during World War II.

Re-education illustrates how political pragmatism might influence deradicalisation and disengagement today, because it shows how politics and opportunism play into such programmes in situations where former enemies are to be incorporated into new political arrangements (such as, for example, right-wing groups in Latin America, or indeed the Taliban in Afghanistan), and how a totalitarian regime has limited its repertoire in deradicalisation and disengagement work. Yet the lessons from "re-education" have tended to be lost in disengagement and deradicalisation programmes today, while there is a direct intellectual link to the criminal rehabilitation discussions going back more than a century.

Deprogramming cult members

From the late 1960s, 1970s and 1980s, there was a growth of alternative religious groups in the west. Smaller religious societies emerged, and in some cases non-western religions established themselves in the west (Robbins 1988; Thomas 2005). Some of these new religious groups were in many cases seen as isolating new group members from the outside world. In some cases the new groups were taking economic advantage of recruits and behaved in an authoritarian way – activities that spurred both private groups and various governments to develop anti-cult programmes. "Deprogramming" was put on the agenda (see, for example, Bainbridge 1978; Balch 1980; Damrell 1977; Festinger, Riecken and Schachter 1956; Keiser and Keiser 1987; Lewis 2012). Cult membership was defined as a problem to the extent that the American Psychiatric Association (2000) defined the "disorder" as a phenomenon "that may occur in individuals who have been subjected to periods of prolonged and intense persuasion (e.g., brainwashing, thought reform, or indoctrination)". Yet, while psychiatrists viewed the problem as therapeutic and individual, sociologists tended to view the problem as a product of small-group dynamics (Lewis 2012: 163–164), and that the loyalties created through personal bonding were an obstacle to deprogramming.

Some of the deprogramming efforts drew on the works of Berger and Luckman (1966), seeing "deprogramming" as a social (re-)construction of subjective reality, questioning the plausibility structure of cult programming. Another popular model was Scheins' (1961) deepening of Lewin's (1951) concepts of *unfreezing*, *changing* and *freezing* concepts. *Unfreezing* meant the induction of a need or a motive to change; changing meant:

> influence of information, arguments, models to be imitated or identified with, etc., which provide a direction of change toward a new equilibrium, usually by allowing

> the person to learn something new, redefine something old, re-evaluate or reintegrate other parts of his personality or belief system.

Changing meant integration of the new framework into the person's beliefs and practices, and *freezing* meant entrenching these. The idea was to contest the plausibility structure of the cult's ideology. The ideology's credible views of reality were to be challenged with "conversation fabric" and moral community through which a legitimating apparatus for the whole sequence of transformation is provided (Berger and Luckman 1966). Authors such as Wright (Wright 1988; Kim 1979, 201) suggested that this could be done through:

> (1) a breakdown in members' insulation from the outside world; (2) unregulated development of dyadic relationships within the communal context; (3) highlighting the lack of success in achieving world transformation by the cult; and (4) highlighting inconsistencies between the actions of leaders and the ideals they symbolically represent.

In practical deprogramming this meant that programmes attempted to cause: (1) a breakdown in insulation from the outside world (by physically removing the member from her or his cult group); (2) a highlighting of the inconsistencies between group ideals and the actions of leaders; (3) the increased pull of family ties; (4) the presentation of an alternative belief system; (5) pointing out internal inconsistencies within the group's belief system (as differentiated from inconsistencies between ideals and practices); and (6) offering an alternative explanation for the individual's recruitment and membership – the exploitation/mind control ideology. Techniques mirrored the World War II era re-education, focusing on truth and rational argumentation, but also included isolation and sleep deprivation; physical discomfort and insults were a crucial part of most of these efforts; as were to a certain extent "brainwashing" techniques, although the latter were contested and alternative deprogramming techniques were developed. It should be noted that some of these theories, including the theories of Wright, who actually was one of the first to conceptualise disengagement, and sketched out theories of sequential withdrawal from cults, were to have a direct influence on both exit programmes for neo-Nazis and future deradicalisation and disengagement programmes for jihadists, for example through the works of Tore Bjørgo (Bjørgo and Horgan 2008, 6).

Deprogramming quickly became a lucrative business. Perhaps it was the profitability of the "business" that drove actors within the "business" to increase their scope, and define the churches and faith society to be targeted under the wider deprogramming agendas, including socialists and the Episcopal Church, as the scope expanded. The underlying problem was the definition of what was "normal", what was the type of mind-set expected to be held, and the definitions of "normality" increasingly varied. In one sense "deprogramming" also held many important lessons for disengagement and deradicalisation; firstly, the perennial question of what a "radical" mind-set is, and how there is a thin line between deradicalisation and brainwashing for political purposes, and secondly, what commercial pressure and commercial interests can potentially do to deradicalisation and disengagement programmes and their scope.[3]

Evaluations also found other faults with deprogramming programmes. Richardson and Kilbourne (1983) criticised the simplified assumption that deception by necessity was a vital strategy for cult leaders and the assumption that cult members lacked free will, as well as the inherent sampling bias created by an over-reliance upon the accounts of former, possibly disgruntled cult members. Systemic evaluations also illuminated problems that today are mirrored in deradicalisation and disengagement programmes. Byong-suh Kim (1979) suggested that anger was felt by the participants even when they left deprogramming, partly after the use of force. Several evaluations also suggested that deprogramming seems to be much more effective at desocialisation (disrupting the old plausibility structure) than it is at resocialisation (providing a new system of meaning and attachments).

As the programmes expanded, several anti-cult "parent power" groups were established, beginning in local communities and spreading nationally and internationally. Mental health professionals became increasingly involved, as did lawyers; the toolbox was also enlarged, expanding from only focusing on traditional coercive deprogramming through "kidnapping" to rehabilitation (in "half-way house" settings where individuals had to come of their own free will) and overt and/or covert non-coercive "exit counselling" (Lewis 1986). The term "exit counselling" gained popularity and was later to emerge as an important concept in deradicalisation and disengagement (Crawford 1984, 1–7; Hassan 1990). In this sense there is a direct historical connection and continuity between the deprogramming efforts and current-day deradicalisation and disengagement programmes. Yet the kidnapping technique (which many deprogramming programmes did not practise) and the problems of establishing the success criteria for programmes encouraging voluntary defection all contributed to harsh critiques being raised against deprogramming in the 1970s and early 1980s.

Rehabilitation, desistance and anti-gang work

The criticism against deprogramming was mirrored by a general criticism of rehabilitation as a toolkit to prevent criminals from reoffending in the 1970s and 1980s, after several studies found such programmes to be inefficient (Lipton, Martinson and Wilks 1975; Martinson 1974). Several studies found no or little effect of these programmes (Martinson 1974). The research was in hindsight criticised for being based on meta-studies, that often were based poor quality non-random-sampled research, equalling them with random-sampled research drawing upon more rigorous research designs (Davis, Steele, Bozick, Williams, Turner, Miles, Saunders and Steinberg 2014). The new trend coincided with a political trend that focused on deterrence rather than rehabilitation, and with sociological theories pointing to the role of society over individuals in causing crime (Mullins 2010, 176). Yet, there were rehabilitation programmes that survived, and gang-related programmes continued.

Rehabilitation studies again gained in popularity by the 1990s. Many researchers saw changes in age cohorts as the most efficient way of preventing re-entrance into crime, a variable beyond rehabilitation programmes (Matza 1967). Others discouraged the view that the choice between crime and not offending was a binary choice, viewing desistance (the cessation of offending or other antisocial behaviour, although the precise definition is contested) as a long and complex non-linear process, similar to deradicalisation, but with former offenders at times reoffending while involved in the process (Farrall and Bowling 1999; Maruna 2001; Shadd and Farrall 2004; Sampson and Laub 1993; Warr 1998). Criminologists also discovered some of these effects, as the life cycle effect varied between types of criminals defined according to their type of criminal activity (Farrington 1986; Hirschi and Gottfredson 1983). Matza (1967) introduced the concept of *drift* to stipulate how individuals could *drift* in and out of crime, rather than leave crime forever. A general finding was that, while factors such as marriage (although the influence of marriage was seen as depending on the strength of the emotional bond created by marriage), education and even military training were related to reducing crime, these factors varied according to individual psychological traits, as well as the category of crime committed. Sampson and Laub (1993), suggested that strong social bonds in the form of employment, marriage, and so on, created bonds that prevented individuals from reoffending. Maruna (2001) focused on creating an enhanced reflective thought process amongst offenders, in addition to realistic opportunities; later McNeill, Farrall, Lightowler and Maruna (2012) expanded on this argument, stressing the difference between *primary desistance*, meaning a lull or crime-free gap in a criminal career, and *secondary desistance,* meaning a change in the way that an ex-offender sees him- or herself. Essentially, secondary desistance is about ceasing to see oneself as an offender and finding a more positive identity; it is about successfully changing identity and deconstructing the criminal label; in this sense the emphasis was put on self-reflection.

Later Don, Bonta and Wormith (2006) developed the principles of "risk", "need" and "responsivity", where service provision increases as estimates of the individual risk of reoffending increase, indeed suggesting that the targeting of high-risk reoffenders actually led to larger reductions in recidivism. The need principle states that interventions must target "criminogenic needs", focusing on variables such as offence history, antisocial personality traits (such as impulsivity and aggressiveness), pro-criminal attitudes, social environment, substance abuse, school or work life. Social learning was encouraged, tailored to suit individual offender characteristics. In this sense it was suggested that there was no such thing as "one size fits all". Yet, there was a general confirmation that one of the tools that had been employed over a long period of time (Hazard 1940; Nolan 1955; Seeman 1963), education (both academic and vocational), was of major importance, with studies finding up to 43% lower odds of recidivism (Davis, Steele, Bozick, Williams, Turner, Miles, Saunders and Steinberg 2014, 14).

Some of the findings from the study of rehabilitation and desistance from crime have also been found and led to implementation techniques for programmes designed to get gang members to leave criminal gangs.[4] Gang membership usually had a shorter duration than the average time a person was doing crime (Thornberry 1998). Research also suggested that the reasons for leaving youth gangs were positively influenced by social bonds, such as emotional ties with outsider peers, family or friends (Bartolomé-Gutiérrez and Rechea-Alberola 2006; Vigil 1988). Work on youth gangs also illustrated that violence could lead to defections, but that social stigmatisation of a gang actually served to keep the group together (Hastings, Dunbar and Bania 2011).

S. Tonks and Z. Stephenson's meta-study (Tonks and Stephenson 2018), studying the wider field of gang studies, suggested that *victimisation* (friends who were injured, personal injuries, fear of future violence from the gang), *disillusionment* (often arising from the lack of loyalty to an individual demonstrated by a gang), *maturation* (life cycle-focused), *physical removal* and *self-reflection* were the most important factors creating defections. Yet, other writers such as Klein (1995) suggested that many failures in anti-gang programmes often were caused by lack of attention and understanding of the group dynamics within the gang, indicating that strategies causing defection needed to take this into account.

Anti-gang projects to encourage defections from gangs were developed, and focused on physical forms of support, such as finding a safe place to go, and providing education, training, job opportunities and peer mentoring or addressing social determinants of health. Psychological counselling, cognitive-behavioural development and suppressive methods (e.g. arrest, incarceration) are widely used by such gang-focused programmes today (Hastings, Dunbar and Bania 2011, 9). Several of these anti-crime and anti-gang procedures are directly incorporated in today's deradicalisation programmes.[5] Importantly, some of these models, such as the Danish Aarhus model, building upon cooperation between schools, social services and police, date back to the 1980s (Koehler 2016, 150), with their roots in crime prevention, today the Aarhus model, or important elements of it, form the foundation of many deradicalisation and disengagement efforts in Scandinavia (see Chapter 18). Notably, crime prevention efforts did not include ideological components, since crime often was seen as driven by the desire for profit rather than ideology; several of the programmes did however encourage self-reflection over individual identity and the individual's position in life.

Dissociati, "the third wave" and "social reinsertion"

By the mid-1970s and 1980s several researchers also began to focus more explicitly on terrorism, in many cases studying how the organisations that had made up what Rapoport (2002) had branded the third wave of terrorism had met their end. In Ireland, the Glencree Centre for Peace and Reconciliation was founded in 1974, supporting dialogue between victims and former perpetrators in Ireland for peace and reconciliation purposes, but also becoming an element in a wider focus of restorative and retributive justice. Some claimed that it had a deradicalising effect, whereas others saw it as a vessel to promote Irish Republican Army (IRA) influence, through its use of IRA members (Alonso and Bada 2016, 984).

Italy launched *pentiti* (penitent) laws, reducing punishment for prisoners who turned state witnesses, and created a new category of *dissociati* (disassociated) prisoners, who cooperated with criminal investigations and showed regret, but were not expected to testify; this created defections from the Brigata Rosso (Red Brigade) (Geipel 2007, 448). Donatella Della Porta (1992) studied the Italian Government's strategies of *dissociati* scheme, interestingly initiated by prisoners, and formalised in 1987.

In Spain "social reinsertion" policy was first introduced from 1982, when the ETA Político-Militar (ETA-PM) split into two factions, with one advocating non-violence while the other promoted a continuation of the terrorist campaign. Prisoners who identified with the non-violent faction could apply through the courts for early release if violence was publicly renounced, links with ETA were severed, a declaration of respect for the law was signed and there was a recognition of the misery caused. The conditions were met by signing a legal document (Silke 2011). The Spanish social reinsertion programme was relatively successful, with Geipel (2007, 451) assessing that more than 300 individuals were released and reinserted into society – none rejoined ETA. Inside prisons Spain developed their own tactics. Spanish authorities split up the prisoners from ETA so that they avoided the build-up of ETA's organisational hierarchies within prison that could pressurise individual ETA prisoners not to disassociate themselves from the organisation (Alonso 2011, 701). Interestingly, the active use of organisational cells to counter disengagement efforts within prison, even to run units outside prison, had been attempted by the German Rote Arme Faction (Red Army Faction) in the 1970s (Geipel 2007, 457), and Spain actively hindered such attempts. Yet, outside events, such as internal discord over the killings of civilians, and organisational discussions over the use of violence, also contributed to a more general organisational transformation (Ibid). Notably ETA also tried to take hostages to influence Spanish state prison politics, without success, and also, more successfully, attempted to put social pressure on the families of ETA prisoners, illustrating how an actor actually attempts to influence and interact with the deradicalisation policies targeting it (Alonso 2011, 701–702).[6]

A common theme for many of the attempts to counter the "third wave" of terrorist organisations was a mix of stick and carrot, an emphasis on programmes to create disengagement in combination with deterrence and punishment, and the more lenient policies of the early 1970s hardened as time passed. Importantly, the social reintegration programmes of the third wave live on, for example in Sri Lanka's attempt to reintegrate the Liberation Tigers of Tamil Eelam (Kruglanski, Gelfand, Bélanger, Gunaratna and Hettiarachchi 2014), and there is direct continuity to today's deradicalisation and disengagement programmes, as some of the institutions and individuals involved in the third-wave efforts are involved in deradicalisation and disengagement programmes today.

Yet the word deradicalisation was not used for projects dealing with the third-wave terrorist groups, and many of the European programmes dealt with groups in decline. Nor was the focus mainly on strategies to get individuals to leave these groups; academic work studying the end of third-wave terror groups mirrored this tendency (see, for example, Crenshaw 1991; Ross and Gurr 1989). This type of research seldom drew upon the wider fields of rehabilitation and desistance studies.

Exit and disengagement from neo-Nazi and right-wing groups

However, the increased studies of defections from neo-Nazi groups did draw upon ideas from rehabilitation and desistance research. Central to these developments was the emergence of exit counselling for neo-Nazis, to reduce recruitment and facilitate disengagement. Initially, cooperation between researchers and practitioners was close, and the anti-cult literature and anti-cult disengagement practices had influence, for example in the Swedish organisation Fri (Free) (Bjørgo 1997, 238). Some of the models from anti-cult work, mostly not focusing directly on deprogramming and the use of force, but rather on exit and exit counselling, were developed further by researchers such as Tore Bjørgo, based on the work of anti-cult experts suggesting that many members of right-wing organisations did not join because of ideology, but from provocation and anger, the need for protection, drifting (changing groups at random) and pure thrill seeking, as a substitute father figure, because of friends, as a type of youth rebellion and for status (ibid.). Reasons for exiting included losing faith in the ideology, losing status, becoming dissatisfied with the activities of the group (often because of partying), burn-out, getting older and limited career prospects.

However, the most important contribution of Bjørgo was perhaps his work inspired by Helmut Willems' classic division of perpetrators of xenophobic violence into four categories: ideologically motivated right-wing extremists; xenophobic ethnocentrists; criminalised and marginalised youth; and followers (ibid. 48–50; Willems 1993, 1995). Bjørgo suggests that in these types the ideologically motivated right-wing extremist and the xenophobic ethnocentrist are less categorised by weak socioeconomic variables and family relations, and the first category is more ideologically motivated than the others.

Interestingly, Petter Nesser follows similar ideas (2015), launching his categories as *entrepreneurs*, *protégés*, *misfits* and *drifters*, illustrating the potential similarities between right-wing and jihadist structures. This categorisation had potentially great therapeutic consequences for potential deradicalisation attempts. Different elements of typical programmes simply fit different types of perpetrators differently, for example, with ideology being less important to *followers*. Importantly, Bjørgo advocated that the ideal types are distributed unevenly between various right-wing groups, and that they need different treatment.

The Norwegian exit programme highlighted the importance of parental networks, reinforcing parental efforts to create exit and to set borders. The strongest aspects of the Norwegian approach were probably that exit activities became integrated into the normal activities of established public agencies, such as municipalities; to some extent it drew on previous crime prevention experiences (Bjørgo, Halhjem and Knudstad 2001). The Swedish programme, started in 1998 by former neo-Nazi Kent Lindhal, was mostly staffed by former participants in the neo-Nazi or White Power movement. In some cases, as with the youth house Fryshuset in Stockholm, the exit programme drew on older youth organisations as well (Christensen 2015, 101). The Swedish programme was reactive in the sense that former neo-Nazis who wanted out needed to make contact with the programme to be included. In all of these programmes the focus was on disengagement, focusing on individuals already in an extremist organisation, and on behavioural change rather than ideological change. It was often assumed that neo-Nazis had joined because of reasons other than ideology and that ideology was acquired after joining the group, and in some cases because of the habitual implementation of rehabilitation and desistance techniques adopted from criminology and crime prevention programmes. There is also a direct link to present-day deradicalisation and disengagement programmes, from exit programmes, with Germany's Hayat programme being based on experiences gained from EXIT-Deutschland, a deradicalisation programme focusing on deradicalising neo-Nazis (Koehler 2016, 185).

Enter "deradicalisation"

While present-day practitioners in deradicalisation and disengagement would nod in recognition to terms such as "exit", "exit counselling" and "disengagement", the word "deradicalisation" was not used. The term "radicalisation" has only relatively (Sedgwick 2010) recently, post-11 September 2001, entered the mainstream political and scientific debate. Early attempts to do what we today call "deradicalisation" of jihadists were attempted in Yemen, which initiated religious dialogue with its returning foreign fighters through the Committee for Religious Dialogue in September 2002 (Willems 2004). In August 2003 Singapore acted, through their government Religious Rehabilitation Group from 2002, focusing on religious dialogue and counselling (Hassan 2007). In Saudi Arabia, their rehabilitation and demobilisation campaign started in 2004 after the 2003 domestic terrorist attacks (Boucek 2008), while Indonesia started their religious dialogue programmes from 2005, one of which was based on former jihadist instructors (Schulze 2008). Yet, none of these early programmes were branded "deradicalisation" or "disengagement". In 2006 the Americans launched their Detainee Rehabilitation Program in their Iraqi prisons, designed by several experts (one of whom has written a chapter in this book), containing, amongst other elements, psychological counselling.

"Deradicalisation" was also used by the EU. The EU's countering violent extremism framework was initially concerned with "radicalisation and recruitment", developed by the EU Council's Working Group on Terrorism in September 2005. However, the EU framework illustrates a wider problem with deradicalisation: the lack of proper conceptualisation. "Radicalisation" was not explicitly defined; it is described as the "practical steps an individual must take to become involved in terrorism" (European Union strategy for combating radicalisation and recruitment, 2005). In 2009 Germany launched their AG Deradikalisierung that also included subgroups working on countering violent extremism (focused on counter-narratives) (Endres 2014, 4).[7] As more deradicalisation programmes started to emerge, on a relatively larger scale around 2011–2015, these programmes often contained elements from earlier crime prevention programmes and exit programmes, as well as often bringing elements from deprogramming. Several explicit attempts were introduced to strengthen the family as an alternative social bond. Germany pioneered family support as part of their counter-radicalisation strategy when they launched their family hotline in 2012 (Gielen 2015, 21–48), set up by the Federal Office for Migration and Refugees (BAMF).

In the footsteps of the expansion, discussions over how to measure success followed (Feddes and Gallucci 2015). Yet, as illustrated by Elshimi in this book (Chapter 17), the exact meaning of "deradicalisation" was not fully resolved, and even within various programmes the meaning changed over time, and was filled with new context. The discussion over the difference between "deradicalisation" and "disengagement", with some researchers arguing for the merits of the latter and that the former should no longer be used (Bjørgo and Horgan 2008), also stirred up debate, although often not directly influencing practitioners. Some researchers, like Borum (2012), wanted to abandon the concept of radicalisation entirely, removing the usefulness of deradicalisation as an antonym.

Lessons forgotten and topics neglected?

There are lessons neglected, links neglected and gaps in knowledge identified by a study of the historic past of deradicalisation and disengagement programmes. Yet, the history of the wider fields relevant for disengagement and deradicalisation can give us clues as to the relevant dynamics, and the lessons that researchers and practitioners drew from these in the past. Ongoing discussions over conceptual clarity mirror similar discussions in the past. As was the case with many of the discussions in the past, these discussions will often not be settled fully, but contribute to increased understanding of the field. Operationalisation and the measurement of success, with classical criminology preferring to follow individuals for long periods of time (resource demanding), and changes in the estimates of how successful rehabilitation was, for example, suggest that caution is needed when trying to establish success rates of deradicalisation and disengagement programmes, and how studies over longer periods of time perhaps are needed to correctly assess such rates. Indeed, many of these debates have actually been ongoing within relevant subfields for more than 100 years. The paradox is perhaps that the wish for rapid progress and the sense of urgency hinder such studies; one wishes for success, and in some cases for support for new programmes.

The history of the wider field also illustrates how deradicalisation and disengagement could be politicised. There is a balance between a focus on ideology and faith in contrast to just changing behaviour, but perhaps also how this can and should vary according to the group dynamics and composition of the group from which individuals are to be deradicalised/disengaged. The de-nazification experience also suggests that deradicalisation and disengagement have to take into account the opposing command hierarchy and structures that can be used to sabotage such efforts, themes dealt with by Hansen in this book, also suggested by Spanish experiences in the 1980s, and lessons learned from other more recent efforts.

It could be argued that there are differences between present-day deradicalisation/disengagement and several of these fields, for example between criminal rehabilitation and disengagement from jihadist groups, where participation in criminal activities does not need ideological conviction. It should be remembered that programmes that contained self-reflection and reflection on identity were an important part of rehabilitation and desistance work, and that not all jihadists or neo-Nazis are driven by ideological conviction. Moreover, as argued by Mullins (2010), many of the jihadists of today are increasingly becoming similar in profile to many of the criminal profiles targeted for rehabilitation in the past, with a general tendency towards developing from cadre-based entities to a broader recruitment pattern.

It could be argued that perhaps the major lesson from the field is that internal group dynamics and personal traits vary, and that techniques to bring about disengagement and deradicalisation have to vary. There simply is no "one size fits all". Yet, the history of the wider field illustrates some gaps in the discussions and some tendencies towards "one size fits all" discussions. One such weakness is the sole focus on western states and the lack of incorporation of lessons learned and understanding of local dynamics. Outside South East Asia, the Middle East, Europe and North America, this book attempts to address this by including the chapters of Zeuthen, Botha, Chindea, Diallo, Nawab and Singh on various regions and states around the world. A second weakness is perhaps the lack of focus on the role to be played by regional and global organisations, as addressed by Léonard, Kaunert and Yakubov, Botha and Schindler in this volume.

Notes

1 The watershed for the introduction of the rehabilitation principle was the so-called "Declaration of Principles" promulgated by the 1870 Congress of the National Prison Association.
2 In the end the Americans also emphasised cadre training, but only from 1945 onwards.
3 The reluctance towards "deprogramming" seemingly was greater in the United States than in Europe, highlighting a larger continental European will to define religious groups as inciting problematic behaviour (Robbins 2001).
4 The definition of "gangs" did however create controversy (see Ball and Curry 1995; Brown 2000; Gordon 2000; Hallsworth and Young 2004).
5 Indeed, some theorists (such as Tore Bjørgo) have been active within both fields.
6 In 2007 Spain launched another scheme, the "Nanclares scheme", encouraging ETA prisoners to disengage themselves from the organisation in return for prison privileges, including early and temporary release (Alonso and Bada 2016, 987).
7 Ag Deradikaliserung was a part of the "Joint Counter-Terrorism Center" (GTAZ) in Berlin. The GTAZ itself had been set up in 2004 as a coordination and cooperation body for the German agencies and institutions involved in counterterrorism efforts. See Said and Fouad (2018).

References

Alonso, Rogelio. (2011) "Why Do Terrorists Stop? Analyzing Why ETA Members Abandon or Continue with Terrorism", *Studies in Conflict & Terrorism* 34(9), 696–716.

Alonso, Rogelio and Javier Díaz Bada. (2016) "What Role Have Former ETA Terrorists Played in Counterterrorism and Counterradicalization Initiatives in Spain?", *Studies in Conflict & Terrorism* 39(11), 982–1006.

American Psychiatric Association. (2000) *The Diagnostic and Statistical Manual of Mental Disorders (DSM 4)*, Washington: APA Publishing, 532.

Bainbridge, William S. (1978) *Satan's Power: A Deviant Psychotherapy Cult*, San Francisco: University of California Press.

Balch, Robert W. (1980) "Looking behind the Scenes in a Religious Cult: Implications for the Study of Conversion", *Sociological Analysis* 41(2), 137–143.

Ball, Richard A. and David Curry. (1995) "The Logic of Definition in Criminology: Purposes and Methods for Defining 'Gangs'", *Criminology* 33(2), 225–245.

Bartolomé-Gutiérrez, Raquel and Cristina Rechea-Alberola. (2006) "Violent Youth Groups in Spain", *Young* 14(4), 323–342.

Berger, Peter L. and Thomas Luckman. (1966) *The Social Construction of Reality*, New York: Penguin.

Bernard, Cheryl, Edward O'Connell, Catherin Thurston, Andres Villamizar, Elvira Loredo, and Jeremiah Goulka. (2011) *The Battle behind the Wire, U.S. Prisoner and Detainee Operations from World War II to Iraq*, Washington: RAND Corporation.

Bjørgo, Tore. (1997) *Racist and Right-wing Violence in Scandinavia, Patterns, Perpetrators and Responses*, Oslo: Tano Aschehough.

Bjørgo, Tore and John Horgan. (2008) "Introduction", in Tore Bjørgo and John Horgan (eds), *Leaving Terrorism Behind: Individual and Collective Disengagement* (pp. 3–21), New York: Routledge.

Bjørgo, Tore, Odd Arild Halhjem, and Taran Knudstad. (2001) *EXIT – Ut av voldelige ungdomsgrupper: Kunnskap, erfaringer og metoder i lokalt tverrfaglig og tverretatlig arbeid*, Oslo: Voksene for barn. http://www.vfb.no/xp/pub/topp/prosjekter/exit/50403.

Borum, Randy. (2012) "Radicalization into Violent Extremism I: A Review of Social Science Theories", *Journal of Strategic Security* 4(4), 7–36.

Boucek, Christopher. (2008) "Saudi Arabia's 'Soft' Counterterrorism Strategy: Prevention, Rehabilitation, and Aftercare", *Carnegie Papers* 97.

Brockway, Zebulon R. (1883) "Needed Reforms in Prison Management", *The North American Review* 137(320), 40–48.

Brockway, Zebulon R. (1910) "The American Reformatory Prison System", *American Journal of Sociology* 15(4), 454–477.

Brown, Rupert. (2000) *Group Processes Dynamics within and between Groups*, Oxford: Blackwell.

Christensen, Tina W. (2015) "How Extremist Experiences Become Valuable Knowledge in EXIT Programmes", *Journal for Deradicalisation* 2(3), 92–134.

Crawford, Lynn. (1984) "Snap Out of It: Steven Hassan's New Deprogramming Method", *City Paper (Washington, D.C.)* 4(26), 1–7.

Crenshaw, Martha. (1991) "How Terrorism Declines", *Terrorism and Political Violence* 3(1), 69–87.

Cullen, Francis T. (2013) "Rehabilitation, beyond Nothing Works", *Crime and Justice* 42(1), 299–376.

Damrell, Joseph. (1977) *Seeking Spiritual Meaning*, Beverly Hills: Sage.

Davis, Lois M., Jennifer L. Steele, Robert Bozick, Malcolm V. Williams, Susan Turner, Jeremy N. V. Miles, Jessica Saunders, and Paul S. Steinberg. (2014) "How Effective Is Correctional Education for Incarcerated Adults?", in Steele Davis, Williams Bozick, Miles Turner, Jessica Saunders and Paul S. Steinberg (eds), *How Effective Is Correctional Education, and Where Do We Go from Here? The Results of a Comprehensive Evaluation* (pp. 7–18), Washington: Rand Corporation.

Della Porta, Donatella. (1992) "Institutional Responses to Terrorism: The Italian Case", *Terrorism and Political Violence* 4(4), 151–170.

Don, Andrews, James Bonta, and Stephen Wormith. (2006) "The Recent Past and Near Future of Risk and/or Need Assessment", *Crime and Delinquency* 52, 7–27.

Endres, Frank. (2014) "The Advice Centre on Radicalisation of the Federal Office for Migration and Refugees", *Journal EXIT-Deutschland* 4(2).

Farrall, Stephen and Benjamin Bowling. (1999) "Structuration, Human Development and Desistance from Crime", *British Journal of Criminology* 39(2), 253–268.

Farrington, David P. (1986) "Age and Crime", *Crime and Justice* 7(1), 189–250.

Feddes, Alard and Marcello Gallucci. (2015) "A Literature Review on Methodology Used in Evaluating Effects of Preventive and De-radicalisation Interventions", *Journal for Deradicalisation* 2(5).

Festinger, Leon, Henry Riecken, and Stanley Schachter. (1956) *When Prophecy Fails: A Social and Psychological Study of a Modern Group that Predicted the Destruction of the World*, Minneapolis: University of Minnesota Press.

Garland, David. (2001) *The Culture of Control Crime and Social Order in Contemporary Society*, Chicago: University of Chicago Press.

Geipel, Gary L. (2007) "Urban Terrorists in Continental Europe after 1970: Implications for Deterrence and Defeat of Violent Nonstate Actors", *Comparative Strategy* 26(5), 439–467.

Gielen, Amy-Jane. (2015) "Supporting Families of Foreign Fighters. A Realistic Approach for Measuring the Supporting Families of Foreign Fighters", *Journal for Deradicalization* 2(2), 1–28.

Gordon, Robert M. (2000) "Criminal Business Organizations, Street Gangs and 'Wanna-be' Groups: A Vancouver Perspective", in Schneider (ed), *Gangs* (pp. 49–71), New York: Routledge.

Halleck, Seymour J. and D. Witte Ann. (1977) "Is Rehabilitation Dead?", *Crime and Delinquency* 23(3), 372–382.

Hallsworth, Simon and Tara Young. (2004) "Getting Real About Gangs", *Criminal Justice Matters* 55, 1–13.

Hartenian, Larry. (1987) "The Role of Media in Democratizing Germany: United States Occupation Policy 1945-1949", *Central European History* 20(2), 145–190.

Hassan, Muhammad H. (2007) "Counter-Ideological Work, Singapore Experience", in Anne Aldis and P. Herd Graeme (eds), *The Ideological War on Terror, World-wide Strategies for Counter-Terrorism* (pp. 18-38), New York: Routledge.

Hassan, Steven. (1990) *Combatting Cult Mind Control: The #1 Best-selling Guide to Protection, Rescue, and Recovery from Destructive Cults*, Rochester: Park Street Press.

Hastings, Ross, Laura Dunbar, and Melania Bania. (2011) *Leaving Criminal Youth Gangs: Exit Strategies and Programs*, Ottawa: University of Ottawa.

Hazard, John N. (1940) "Trends in the Soviet Treatment of Crime", *American Sociological Review* 5(4), 566–576.

Hirschi, Travis and Michael Gottfredson. (1983) "Age and the Explanation of Crime", *The American Journal of Sociology* 89(3), 552–584.

Janowitz, Morris. (1946) "German Reactions to Nazi Atrocities", *American Journal of Sociology* 52(2), 141–146.

Kandarian, Paul E. (2016) "The Secret Pow Camp that Fought Nazi Ideology", *The University of Rhode Island blog* 1 September, https://web.uri.edu/quadangles/the-secret-pow-camp-that-fought-nazi-ideology/ (accessed 13 March 2019).

Kavanagh, Marcus A. (1921) "The Adjustment of Penalties", *American Bar Association Journal* 7(9), 461–466.

Keiser, Thomas W. and Jaqueline Keiser. (1987) *The Anatomy of Illusion: Religious Cults and Destructive Persuasion*, Springfield: Charles C Thomas Pub Ltd.

Kim, Byong-suh. (1979) "Religious Deprogramming and Subjective Reality", *Sociological Analysis* 40(3), 197–207.

Klein, Malcom W. (1995) *The American Street Gang*, Oxford: Oxford University Press.

Koehler, Daniel. (2016) *Understanding Deradicalization: Methods, Tools and Programs for Countering*, New York: Routledge.

Kruglanski, Arie, Michele J. Gelfand, Jocelyn Bélanger, Rohan Gunaratna, and Malkanthi Hettiarachchi. (2014) "De-radicalising the Liberation Tigers of Tamil Eelam (LTTE): Some Preliminary Findings", in Andrew Silke (ed), *Prisons, Terrorism and Extremism: Critical Issues in Management, Radicalisation and Reform* (pp. 183–196), New York: Routledge.

Kurt, Lewin. (1951) *Field Theory in Social Science: Selected Theoretical Papers*, New York: Harper & Row.

Lewis, James R. (1986) "Reconstructing the "Cult" Experience: Post-Involvement Attitudes as a Function of Mode of Exit and Post-Involvement Socialization", *Sociological Analysis* 47(2), 151–159.

Lewis, James R. (2012) *Cults: A Reference and Guide*, New York: Routledge.

Lipton, Douglas, Robert Martinson, and Judith Wilks. (1975) *The Effectiveness of Correctional Treatment: A Survey of Treatment Evaluation Studies*, New York: Praeger.

Martinson, Robert. (1974) "What Works? – Questions and Answers about Prison Reform", *The Public Interest*, New York 35.

Maruna, Shadd. (2001) *Making Good: How Ex-Convicts Reform and Rebuild Their Lives*, Washington DC: American Psychological Association Books.

Matza, David. (1967) *Delinquency and Drift*, Piscataway: Transaction Publishers.

McLennan, Rebecca. (2008) *The Crisis of Imprisonment: Protest, Politics, and the Making of the American Penal State 1776-1941*, Cambridge, UK: Cambridge University Press.

McNeill, Fergus, Farrall Stephen, Claire Lightowler, and Shadd Maruna. (2012) "Re-Examining Evidence-based Practice in Community Corrections: Beyond 'a Confined View' of What Works", *Justice Research and Policy* 14(1), 35–60.

Mullins, Sam. (2010) "Rehabilitation of Islamist Terrorists: Lessons from Criminology", *Dynamics of Asymmetric Conflict* 3(3), 162–193.

Nesser, Petter. (2015) *Islamist Terrorism in Europe, a History*, London: Hurst Publishers.

Nolan, James B. (1955) "Athletics and Juvenile Delinquency", *The Journal of Educational Sociology* 28(6), 263–265.

Rapoport, David. C. (2002) "The Four Waves of Rebel Terror and September 11", *Anthropoetics* 8(1), 1–16.

Richardson, James T. and B. Kilbourne. (1983) "Classical and Contemporary Applications of Brainwashing Models: A Comparison and Critique", in Bromley (eds), *The Brainwashing Deprogramming Controversy*, New York: Edward Mellen Press.

Robbins, Thomas. (1988) *Cults, Converts and Charisma, the Sociology of New Religious Movements*, London: Sage.

Robbins, Thomas. (2001) "Combating 'Cults' and 'Brainwashing' in the United States and Western Europe: A Comment on Richardson and Introvigne's Report", *Journal for the Scientific Study of Religion* 40(2), 29–45.

Ross, Jeffery I. and Ted R. Gurr. (1989) "Why Terrorism Subsides: A Comparative Study of Canada and the United States", *Comparative Politics* 21(4), 405–426.

Said, Behnam and Hazim Fouad. (2018) "Countering Islamist Radicalisation in Germany: A Guide to Germany's Growing Prevention Infrastructure", *ICCT Policy Brief* 9.

Sampson, Robert J. and John H. Laub. (1993) *Crime in the Making: Pathways and Timing Points through Life*, Cambridge, MA: Harvard University Press.

Schein, Edgar. (1961) *Coercive Persuasion: A Socio-psychological Analysis of the "Brainwashing" of American Civilian Prisoners by the Chinese Communists*, New York: W.W. Norton.

Schulze, Kirsten E. (2008) "Indonesia's Approach to Jihadist Deradicalization", *CTC Sentinel* 1(8).

Sedgwick, Mark. (2010) "The Concept of Radicalization as a Source of Confusion", *Terrorism and Political Violence* 22(4), 479–494.

Seeman, Melvin. (1963) "Alienation and Social Learning in a Reformatory", *American Journal of Sociology* 69(3), 270–284.

Serrill, Michael S. (1975) "Is Rehabilitation Dead?", *Corrections Magazine* 1(May–June), 21–32.

Shadd, Maruna and Stephen Farrall. (2004) "Desistance from Crime: A Theoretical Reformulation", *Kolner Zeitschrift Fur Soziologie Und Sozialpsychologie* 43, 171–194.

Silke, Andrew. (2011) "Disengagement or Deradicalization: A Look at Prison Programs for Jailed Terrorists", *CTC Sentinel* 4(1).

Staff writer (1946). "Denazification at Wilton" *Evening Standard*, 18 March 1946.

Thomas, Scott. (2005) *The Global Resurgence of Religion*, London: Palgrave.

Thornberry, Terence P. (1998) "Membership in Youth Gangs and Involvement in Serious and Violent Offending", in Rolf Loeber and David P. Farrington (eds), *Serious & Violent Juvenile Offenders: Risk Factors and Successful Interventions* (pp. 147–166), Thousand Oaks: Sage Publications, Inc.

The European Union. (2005) "European Union strategy for combating radicalisation and recruitment", Brussels: Justice and Home Affairs Council meeting, 1 December.

Tibbitts, Clark. (1933) "Penology and Crime", *American Journal of Sociology* 38(6), 896–904.

Tonks, Sarah and Zoe Stephenson. (2018) "Disengagement from Street Gangs: A Systematic Review of the Literature", *Psychiatry, Psychology and Law* 25, 21–49.

Vigil, James D. (1988) "Group Processes and Street Identity: Adolescent Chicano Gang Members", *Ethos* 16(4), 421–445.

Warr, Mark. (1998) "Life-course Transitions and Desistance from Crime", *Criminology* 36(2), 162–181.

Willems, Helmut. (1993) *Fremdenfeindliche Gewalt: Einstellungen Täter Konflikteskalation*, Berlin: Leske+Budrich.

Willems, Helmut. (1995) "Development, Patterns and Causes of Violence against Foreigners in Germany: Social and Biographical Characteristics of Perpetrators and the Process of Escalation", *Terrorism and Political Violence* 7(1).

Willems, Peter. (2004) "Unusual Tactics", *The Middle East No.* 349.

Winslow, John B. (1912) "The President's Address", *Journal of the American Institute of Criminal Law and Criminology* 3(4), 327–340.

Wright, Stuart A. (1988) "Leaving New Religious Movements: Issues, Theory and Research", in Bromley (ed), *Falling from the Faith* (pp. 143–165), Newbury Park: Sage.

4

EXPLORING THE VIABILITY OF PHASE-BASED MODELS IN (DE)RADICALIZATION

Liesbeth Mann, Lars Nickolson, Allard R. Feddes, Bertjan Doosje, and Fathali M. Moghaddam

Particularly since the tragedy of 9/11, there has been increased research attention on radicalization and terrorism, defined as "politically motivated violence, perpetrated by individuals, groups, or state-sponsored agents, intended to instill feelings of terror and helplessness in a population in order to influence decision making and to change behavior" (Moghaddam, 2005, p. 161). In line with Kurt Lewin's (1951) dictum that "there is nothing so practical as a good theory" (p. 169), much of this research has involved theory development. Theoretical models of radicalization must explain how and why people radicalize in such a way that they are motivated to kill others, and sometimes themselves, apparently for their purported ideals. An important assumption of such models is that radicalization towards terrorism tends to take place through a gradual *process*, which is often divided into distinctive phases describing how individuals (and/or groups) become increasingly engaged with extreme ideologies and groups. An influential metaphor that is used to describe these successive phases is that of the staircase. In *The Staircase to Terrorism* (Moghaddam, 2005, 2009), radicalization is envisioned as a narrowing staircase connecting five floors that are each characterized by specific psychological processes. Other such "phase models" differ in regard to the emphasis they place on specific (psychological) aspects or processes, but they are similar in their view of radicalization as a process involving different successive phases leading to increased commitment to extremist ideologies and the use of violence. In each of these phases certain psychological processes play a role in shaping this commitment.

To date, much less attention has been paid to similar processes in the opposite direction —that is, different phases and corresponding factors that could explain deradicalization and disengagement from extremist groups (e.g., Feddes, 2015; Horgan, 2008a). The field is expanding, however (e.g., Koehler, 2017). For example, Moghaddam (2009) used his own staircase model to terrorism to discuss options for deradicalization.

One could argue that any phase model that describes the path *towards* radicalization or engagement can also be used to explain the path *leading away* from radicalization or engagement. However, one should be careful not to simply regard the processes of disengagement and deradicalization as mirror images of engagement and radicalization (e.g., Bjørgo, 2011; Moghaddam, 2009). Still, it may be worthwhile considering which specific psychological factors that have been identified to contribute to radicalization in each different phase could also in some way be involved and coopted to reverse this process.

The primary goal of this chapter is to explore the extent to which phase-based models can be used to accurately describe the process of deradicalization. In addition, we will examine how this provides clues about which psychological processes could be targeted through specific interventions in different phases of the deradicalization process. To recognize the necessity for such knowledge, one can point to the phenomenon of foreign fighters participating in the war in Syria, and more specifically their (imminent) return to their Western countries of origin (e.g., Byman, 2015). It is valid to assume that these returnees remain in some key respects radicalized. Therefore, it is imperative that we make more rapid progress in understanding deradicalization processes. Phase-based models, however, may not only prove their worth in these cases of "advanced radicalization," but are also helpful in determining which psychological factors are at play at earlier stages of radicalization. In other words, they enable a preventative approach that aims to halt the emergence of new home-grown terrorists and foreign fighters (see also Horgan, 2008b, on phase-specific counter-terrorism initiatives).

This chapter is structured as follows. First, we briefly describe some of the existing phase models that focus on movement to terrorism and discuss the main points of criticism levied against this type of model. Second, we present an overarching phase model of (de)radicalization which covers the most important aspects of the abovementioned existing theories, and aims to overcome some of the limitations. Within this model, we distinguish between different (kinds of) concrete external trigger factors that could explain why individuals move from one phase to the next, different underlying psychological needs, and specific psychological aspects of resilience which play a role in various phases of the process. In the concluding paragraphs, we briefly explore some of the main implications of our phase model for theory and practice as well as some ideas for future scientific research.

Phase models to and from terrorism

Most existing social psychological models of radicalization distinguish between several phases (see King & Taylor, 2011, for a review). For example, Moghaddam (2005, 2009) uses the metaphor of a staircase in a building to explain how a very small number of people (relative to the total size of a population) radicalize from the ground floor to the top (fifth) floor of the building where they commit a terrorist act. On each floor of this staircase certain psychological processes can influence the decision to either climb up or remain at the same level. This decision depends on people's perceptions of the doors and spaces that are open to them on each of the floors. Importantly, the staircase is narrowing: the higher up one climbs, the smaller the number of individuals on each floor. Thus, only very few people actually reach the top floor of the building. From the nine different specializations engaged in terrorism (Moghaddam, 2007), only one type reaches the "top" floor. These individuals are radicalized to such an extent that they are willing and able to commit terrorist attacks, sometimes killing themselves as well as others.

Similar phase models have, for example, been by outlined by Borum (2003), Wiktorowicz (2004), McCauley and Moskalenko (2008), Sageman (2008) and Horgan (2008a, 2008b). These models all envisage radicalization as a gradual process involving discrete successive phases, but they differ in their distinctions between phases and their emphasis on specific psychological processes that characterize these phases. Moreover, although Horgan

(2008a) does include disengagement from terrorism as a distinct phase in his model, most phase models ignore processes of disengagement and deradicalization.

Such phase models can be criticized on several aspects. First, as King and Taylor (2011) point out, many phase models assume that relative deprivation plays an important role at the initial stages of radicalization. However, one could also envision phase-based models that place identity-related issues, needs related to meaning seeking, or a need for adventure more centrally (see Feddes, Nickolson, & Doosje, 2015, for a review). Furthermore, it may be that the process of radicalization is more dynamic in that different needs are important at different phases for different people. For example, one person may join an extremist group because of identity-related needs (safety, friendship), while in later phases the need to counter injustice may play a more important role for this individual. For another person, the need for justice may be particularly important at an earlier stage, while identity-related needs become stronger over time when he or she forms stronger bonds in the group membership phase or before committing violent acts.

A second criticism on phase models is that they assume that radicalization is a linear process, while it may also just emerge as a combination of different factors (see also Lygre, Eid, Larsson, & Ranstorp, 2011; Veldhuis & Staun, 2009). However, not all phase models presume linearity. For example, Sageman (2008) describes radicalization among Muslims as an emergent non-linear process consisting of a sense of moral outrage about perceived injustices (e.g., the war in Iraq), a specific interpretation of the world (the "Western war against Islam"), resonance with personal experiences (e.g., unemployment, discrimination), and mobilization through networks (via face-to-face peer groups and online forums). These factors should, according to him, not be regarded as part of different consecutive stages, but they are simply important elements in the process towards radicalization. Similarly, viewing radicalization as a non-linear process, radicalization and deradicalization can repeatedly alternate and merge or flow into one another in different phases of the process(es) (i.e., Sageman, 2008). An example of this is the phenomenon that some extremists switch sides by starting initiatives to counter radicalization themselves, for example by working with governments they previously opposed (Schmid, 2014).

A third point of criticism on phase models is that these models do not explain why or under what circumstances a person moves from one phase to the next. The models somehow assume that individuals move up the radicalization phases without going into what causes an individual to become vulnerable to radicalization, to join a group, or to become prepared to commit a violent act. This is connected to a fourth weakness of traditional phase-based models, namely that they are overly broad. That is, each phase is characterized by very broad and unspecific indicative factors (e.g., a "changed appearance") that in themselves may not signal violent radicalization or even radicalism at all (Veldhuis & Staun, 2009). When such broad factors are used to identify people who are radicalizing, mistakes are easily made and this may result in the stigmatization of people from certain (vulnerable) groups, potentially even creating a self-fulfilling prophecy.

A final point of critique on existing phase models of radicalization is that they use vulnerability of individuals to radicalize as a starting point. However, in order to understand deradicalization it is critical to also focus on what determines whether a person is resilient to radicalization, or resilient to outside attempts to deradicalize (see also Mann, Doosje, & Kruglanski, 2018).

Phase models, we argue, provide a valuable starting point to understand deradicalization. However, the limitations of these models should be acknowledged and addressed. In this chapter, we take these limitations into account by providing a more nuanced approach towards phase-based models and integrate this with recent insights on trigger factors, underlying psychological needs, and aspects of resilience against (de)radicalization. In an attempt to extend existing phase models to the process of deradicalization, we take a general phase model that summarizes previous work (Doosje et al., 2016) as a starting point and will discuss this in terms of deradicalization.

A general phase model of deradicalization

Building on previous models, Doosje et al. (2016) distinguish three subsequent phases in the process of radicalization, which also apply to the process of deradicalization when reversed. The basic elements of this model (Figure 4.1) are: (1) a vulnerability phase, in which a person is more or less sensitive to a radical ideology; (2) a group membership phase, in which the individual is a member of a radical group; and (3) an action phase, in which the individual is ready to act in line with the group's ideals and ideology, even by means of violence. We will first broadly describe these three phases, and then discuss the trigger factors, psychological needs, and individual resilience which are involved in the movement of an individual from one phase to the other—in either direction—in more detail.

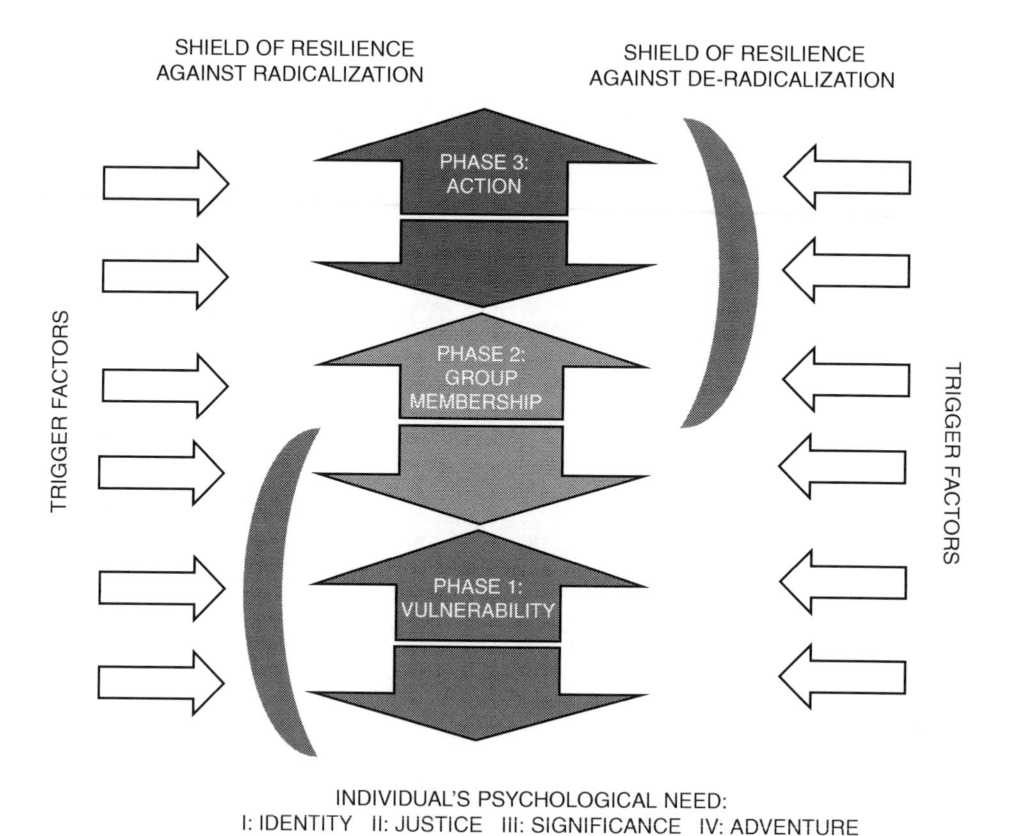

Figure 4.1 The (de)radicalization process and its determinants.
Source: Adapted from Doosje, de Wolf, Mann, and Feddes (2017).

Phase 1: the vulnerability phase

There are many people who might be relatively (or potentially) sensitive to radicalization because they are confronted with certain structural conditions, which are often also called *root factors*. Such root factors range from one's socio-economic position (and corresponding feelings of relative deprivation), uncertainty about one's place (or "integration") in society, or frustrations about world affairs—such as the wars in the Middle East (i.e., Kruglanski & Fishman, 2009). For example, Moghaddam's (2005) staircase model emphasizes the millions of people in this phase who experience frustration and shame or humiliation as a result of perceived unfair treatment and personal or fraternal relative deprivation.

Such factors may constitute the "background music" to radicalization, but we cannot argue that all those people affected are actually involved in a radicalization process. In other words, by themselves these structural root causes are not sufficient when explaining or predicting terrorism, but have to be complemented with other factors, on the individual and group level (Forest, 2005; Newman, 2006; Schuurman, Bakker, & Eijkman, 2018). It is often only when a specific context or event renders their situation increasingly precarious or hopeless that they might experience a "cognitive opening" (Wiktorowicz, 2004), be propelled on a "quest for significance" (Kruglanski et al., 2013), or embark on a search for somewhere to belong (Buijs, Demant, & Hamdy, 2006; Winter, 2015). In other words, in those cases individuals are not only (potentially) sensitive but also vulnerable, and actively looking for solace or a remedy to their situation.

Phase 2: the group membership phase

A radical group might very well be a remedy to one's situation, and provide solace and belonging. In this phase an individual becomes a member of such a group, be it directly physical or first virtual and later physical. Central to this phase is increasing mutual commitment between the group and the new member. Increased commitment to the morality of the terrorist organization can grow through the development of a parallel life that is secret and isolated, and in which strong and absolute affiliation with other members and the group leader is the norm. In line with Social Identity Theory (Tajfel & Turner, 1979) people are generally motivated to view the *ingroup* as superior to *outgroups*, thus showing ingroup favoritism. In particular under conditions of perceived group threat, they also regard outgroups as inferior to the ingroup, engaging in outgroup derogation. This mechanism plays an important role in radical groups. The individual adheres to the norms and values of the group more and more strongly, starts to devalue outgroups, and burn bridges with original social circles. This leads to the development of a strong "us-versus-them" categorization of the world and the terrorist group gains in perceived legitimacy; it is considered a justified means to an idealized end. Thus, in this context, terrorism increasingly becomes a justified strategy. The so-called "slippery slope" mechanism (McCauley & Moskalenko, 2008) is also important in this context. This refers to a mechanism of increasing self-radicalization via justification of past behavior by the adoption of new (radical) beliefs and values. This is comparable to what happened to participants who administered increasingly intense shocks to their (alleged) victims in Milgram's famous experiments (Milgram, 1974; and see; McCauley & Moskalenko, 2008).

Phase 3: the action phase

In this phase the individual is ready to act in accordance with the group's ideals, for example, by planning or executing an attack (Doosje et al., 2016). Moghaddam (2005) argues that, at this stage, individuals are selected and trained to side-step the inhibitory mechanisms that could hold them back from wounding or killing others and themselves. This happens through categorization of civilians as the enemy outgroup and dehumanizing them, and through a process of social distancing by (over)emphasizing differences between ingroup and outgroup. Those who are selected to commit terrorist acts are being prepared and equipped.

These three phases in principle are broad enough to describe deradicalization as well, since this process is often described as comprised of intermediate (or partial) steps away from violent extremism-inspired action. The distinction between disengagement (i.e., the cessation of terrorist behavior) and deradicalization (i.e., the elimination of one's belief in a violent, extremist ideology) is especially relevant here (Altier, Thoroughgood, & Horgan, 2014). In our current model, the former constitutes only a partial step towards full deradicalization, and—depending on the definition of terrorist behavior—could entail a move towards either the group membership or vulnerability phase. Deradicalization in its common sense, however, is also not unambiguous here, since leaving an ideology behind could still mean that the individual in question is vulnerable ór potentially sensitive to renewed radicalization. By making these specific distinctions between those phases, the model thus provides clarity in discussions about such concepts. From now on, we will speak of deradicalization as a term denoting a process that encompasses all these phases.

Moving between phases: triggers, needs, and resilience

The phase model described above is an overarching model in the sense that it does not describe a radicalization process by distinguishing specific substantive factors that apply to each (de)radicalizing individual. Rather, corresponding with recent insights in such processes, it allows for a multitude of different routes including various (and varying) factors (e.g., Sieckelinck, Sikkens, Van San, Kotnis, & De Winter, 2019). In this section, we will elaborate on these (interrelated) factors, being (external) trigger factors, psychological needs, and aspects of resilience. Together, these factors drive processes of radicalization as well as deradicalization, and through this elaboration the added value of radicalization in conjunction with deradicalization in a phase-based model will become clear. Below we discuss how factors involved in radicalization can also play a role in deradicalization.

Trigger factors in the (de)radicalization process

Triggers are concrete external events that can play a decisive role in both radicalization and deradicalization (Feddes et al., 2015). In terms of phase models of (de)radicalization, trigger factors could help understand why a person moves from one phase to another (Figure 4.1). There are two broad categories of trigger factors that are identified in such movements: "catalysts" and "turning points." An event is termed a catalyst when it slows down or speeds up the (de)radicalization process. This would mean that a person experiences an incident that makes him or her move up or down on the staircase of radicalization. An event is considered a turning point if a person who is radicalizing and moves from one phase to the next experiences an event that leads him or her to "turn around" and move to a lower phase and deradicalize. Trigger factors can be found at the level of the individual (micro-level), the level of the group (meso-level), and the global or societal level (macro-level).

At the start of a process of radicalization, certain life experiences (generally seen as pertaining to the micro-level) often function as triggers. The loss of a family member, for example, is such a trigger factor (Pyszczynski et al., 2006; Sieckelinck & De Winter, 2015). It can lead to an existential (or identity) crisis which may leave the individual more vulnerable to the influence of radical worldviews which provide solace and meaning. On the other hand, *gaining* a family (member) can set in motion a process of deradicalization. Becoming a parent, for example, can be such a turning point, by instilling (new) meaning to one's life—and adding the fear of potentially losing touch with your child as a result of your radical path (Sieckelinck & De Winter, 2015). Altier et al. (2014) point to marriage (which is often accompanied by the desire to start a family) as such a turning point, similarly emphasizing the heightened costs of involvement in terrorism and providing alternatives outside of the (radical) group. With these opposite triggers, we see a kind of mirror relation: The loss of a family member may propel the individual into the vulnerability phase and thus starts the radicalization process, while gaining a family (member) could signal the start of the deradicalization process, and lead to a retreat from the group phase towards (or even beyond) that same vulnerability phase.

The experience of violence is a similar event, which is often traumatic but also involves a sense of injustice (why me/that person?). Van der Valk and Wagenaar (2010) indicate that experiencing violence could be a trigger factor for both radicalization and deradicalization. Based on interviews with former right-wing extremists in the Netherlands, they note that experiences with violence can trigger a person to join an extremist group or can lead to further radicalization. However, for some individuals, the use of violence by group members influenced their decision to leave the group and thereby set in motion a process of deradicalization (see also Demant, Slootman, Buijs, & Tillie, 2008).

While the trigger factors described above are mainly associated with the move towards (and perhaps beyond) the vulnerability phase—from two directions—there are also important triggers that surround the phase of group membership. One of the most influential events leading to such group membership is the encounter or connection with (a) radical individual(s). Recruitment into radical groups often happens via people's networks, their personal connections (e.g., McCauley & Moskalenko, 2008). Mutual connectedness can even lead a whole group of friends to join a terrorist organization at once, via so-called "block recruitment" (McCauley & Moskalenko, 2008, p. 421; see also Kruglanski et al., 2014). These connections are often made or exploited as a result of chance encounters (Schuurman, 2017; Weggemans, Bakker, & Grol, 2014). However random, these encounters do play an important role in the process, by linking one's vulnerability and the associated emotions with a solution. This is aptly illustrated by the following quote by former radical Maajid Nawaz:

> It was not until a recruiter of Hizb ut-Tahrir approached me and confronted me with my anger that I became enthusiastic about the Caliphate which offered me an explanation and a dream. I connected my anger to radical Islam, a disgusting ideology. That step made me radical.
>
> *(De Wever, 2015)*

Chance encounters can also have the opposite effect, however, and lure a radical or extremist individual away from his or her group. This could mean getting to know a person belonging to the "enemy," such as a right-wing extremist's brother's girlfriend with a migrant background (Sieckelinck et al., 2019, p. 16), or it could take the shape of positive interactions with moderate individuals with more mainstream beliefs, causing individuals to question their involvement in the group (Altier et al., 2014). Another factor that may play an important role in deradicalization at the group membership level or the action level is disappointment in fellow group members (Bjørgo, 2011; Van der Valk & Wagenaar, 2010).

There are also trigger factors which do not have such a mirror-like relation: they do not occur in the beginning of the radicalization and deradicalization process. Rather, they play a role at the *start* of the radicalization process and the *end* of deradicalization. This is the case with triggers that concern family relations, such as divorce. Such events are often cited as being very influential in starting the radicalization process (Corner & Gill, 2014; Geelhoed, 2012; Lankford, 2012; Sieckelinck & De Winter, 2015). The role of family relations in deradicalization, however, is confined to the ending of that process, as family members often do not seem to spark that process, but mainly prove their worth in facilitating it, and providing a "safe landing" for those who have already decided to turn their backs on the radical group (Sieckelinck & De Winter, 2015). Similarly, losing a job is often cited as an important event pushing an individual towards radicalization (Corner & Gill, 2014; Kleinmann, 2012), while finding a job can provide perspective and thereby the decisive push for individuals to lead a more conventional life (Altier et al., 2014).

It is not only the case that the same *kind* of trigger factor plays a role—be it mirrored or not—in both radicalization and deradicalization, however. It can also be the very same event itself which leads to different results, depending on the situation and the individual in question. For instance, an often-cited event is incarceration and detention (e.g., Doosje et al., 2016), which has influenced some (radicalizing) individuals to persist in their path but left others reflecting on their choices and veering away from radical groups and ideals. But also, the earlier-mentioned events of marriage and becoming a parent could have both a radicalizing and a deradicalizing effect (Sieckelinck & De Winter, 2015).

Finally, events on a macro-level—that is, the level of society, politics, and culture—are even more prone to fulfill the various functions in the (de)radicalization process described above, and are perhaps less bound to the various phases of which these processes consist. Sometimes, they can fulfill a mirrored function, one example being the establishment of the Caliphate by extremist group Islamic State in 2014 as a trigger for (further) radicalization—by joining a group ("the winners") or even to proceed to the final action phase—and the fall of that same Caliphate as a trigger for deradicalization.

Not much is known about the conditions or psychological processes that determine whether an event results in further radicalization or deradicalization. However, based on social strain theory (Agnew, 1992), it can be predicted that the stronger the impact of the trigger, the more recent it is, and the longer its duration, the more likely it is that this results in a shift from one phase to the next. A clustering of multiple triggers may also add to the likelihood of shifting between phases. One might hypothesize the same to be true for the role of triggers in deradicalization. One promising avenue of future research in this respect could be identifying the underlying motivation of individuals, as outlined in the next section.

Underlying psychological needs

Whether an individual is susceptible to a trigger factor or not also depends on that person's underlying motivations or psychological needs. In the literature a distinction is made between different *types* of (potential) radical individuals (Bjørgo, 2011; Buijs et al., 2006; Feddes et al., 2015; Macdougall, Van Der Veen, Feddes, Nickolson, & Doosje, 2018; Venhaus, 2010). Four categories can be distinguished: identity seekers, justice seekers, significance seekers, and sensation seekers. *Identity seekers* are mainly driven by a quest for social status and a need to belong to a social group. From a deradicalization perspective these individuals would be particularly susceptible to trigger factors such as the disintegration of their extremist group or being disappointed by their fellow members or leaders (e.g., Altier et al.,

2014). *Justice seekers* are those individuals who believe their social group is being treated unfairly and generally is less well off than it deserves. Events that counter these perceptions would possibly be important triggers to deradicalize for these individuals. Furthermore, justice seekers may be susceptible to trigger factors showing the inability of an extremist group to obtain their goal. *Significance seekers* are primarily driven by a quest for significance. Individuals who experience a traumatic event, such as the death of close friends or family, may feel particularly attracted to ideologies which can provide more substantial meaning to their existence. Finding an alternative goal in life may trigger individuals to focus their attention away from the extremist group. Finally, *sensation seekers* are those individuals who actively seek excitement and adventure. These individuals may be triggered to deradicalize by, for example, being excluded from the action by their group or the disintegration of their group, and may be lured into satisfying this need for sensation in other ways. Furthermore, unmet expectations can also stir a process of deradicalization among these individuals. For example, one's daily life in an extremist group can be much less exciting and adventurous than one had expected or hoped for (Altier et al., 2014).

The two shields of resilience

Resilience against extreme ideas can be conceptualized as "the potential to resist, oppose and/or ignore extremist influences". In Figure 4.1, we display two shields of resilience. First, as illustrated on the left side of Figure 4.1, most people have a "natural" shield of resilience against extreme ideas. However, certain micro- (individual), meso- (group, organizational), or macro- (societal) level factors may weaken this shield and may make a person sensitive to extreme ideas and thus enter a vulnerability phase. In the group membership and action phase, this shield of resilience against extreme ideas has been further damaged or even completely destroyed.

As illustrated by the right side of Figure 4.1, members of radical groups in the group membership and action phase also create a shield of resilience, but in this case against those views that challenge the radical ideology. This is the second, "inverted" shield of resilience. For example, members of radical groups are encouraged to end contact with people outside the radical group (Bjørgo & Carlsson, 2005). This increases the importance of the radical group and the ability to build a shield of resilience against moderate views. This shield becomes stronger the more people become committed to the terrorist group. Thus, resilience as a personal characteristic may protect an individual from radicalizing, but once radicalized, a similar type of resilience may "protect" someone from deradicalization.

This also implies that, whereas in the vulnerability phase it makes sense to strengthen resilience to radicalization, in the group membership phase it would be more effective to try to deconstruct certain elements of people's resilience to deradicalization. Sometimes, building resilience against radicalization may entail the same strategies as building resilience against deradicalization. An example is: offering a counter-narrative to extremist propaganda; this could work mainly in a preventive way, but in some cases, it might stimulate people who are already radicalized to a certain extent to question the message of extremist groups (Van Eerten, Doosje, Konijn, De Graaf, & De Goede, 2017). At other times, specific factors should be targeted.

Conclusions

In this chapter we critically examined phase models of radicalization and extended them to the process of deradicalization. We explained how trigger factors, underlying psychological needs, and individual resilience against (de)radicalization can cause people to move between different phases in the process of (de)radicalization. Although in this chapter we focused more on the process of deradicalization, in general we think it is important to employ a phase-based model which considers radicalization in conjunction with deradicalization. As we saw in this review, some factors that play a role in the radicalization process may also play an important role in the process of deradicalization (e.g., losing a loved one may result in radicalization but engaging in a love relationship may result in deradicalization). In line with this idea, some recent empirical research (Sieckelinck et al., 2019) uses a biographical approach to describe the radicalization and deradicalization of specific persons; an idiographic approach without fixed cross-individual factors but rather a unique sequence of events and combination of factors for each case. Decoupling radicalization and deradicalization would not be fruitful within such an idiographic approach, because it is the same person radicalizing and deradicalizing in different circumstances.

Phase models are a valuable approach to (de)radicalization as they may help researchers and practitioners determine what level of radicalization or deradicalization an individual is at and which specific social psychological factors are relevant in each phase.

The use of phase-based models to conceptualize processes of deradicalization and the use of such models as a starting point to design interventions imply a consideration of the different psychological factors and potential triggers that are at work in each phase. This also results in a need for different types of interventions, aimed at people in different phases of the process and in different roles in terrorist organizations (see also Moghaddam, 2009). It is also important to consider the specific objective of the intervention; disengagement is usually easier to accomplish than complete deradicalization. Importantly, when designing interventions, the individual situation of potential radicals should always be kept in mind, as well as the specific context, to prevent overgeneralizations and assumptions about the phase someone is in. In line with this, Veldhuis and Staun (2009) suggest that it is "essential to examine the causes rather than the courses of radicalization, and in doing so to perceive radicalization as an 'embedded individual process' that occurs in the individual within a specific social and environmental context" (p. 3).

We would like to emphasize that previous criticism on (the use of) phase-based models should be taken seriously. Some criticisms on phase models were already outlined, such as the fact that radicalization and deradicalization are not always linear processes but dynamic. For example, individuals moving up or down the staircase (or whichever phase metaphor is used) of terrorism may skip steps as a result of certain trigger factors. This, we argue, makes it even more important for professionals to be able to determine in which specific phase the individual currently is and to be aware of potential trigger factors speeding up or slowing down the process. As indicated before, conceptualizing both radicalization as well as deradicalization as two parts of a similar process can help to emphasize the non-linear character of the process.

The concepts of trigger factors and psychological resilience point to important new research avenues. In particular, more research is needed that takes into account multiple factors in explaining radicalization and deradicalization. For example, more research into the specific interplay between psychological processes and people's shield of resilience (at what stage does it change and how?), external trigger factors, and underlying psychological needs (i.e., needs related to identity, justice, significance, or sensation) in each phase of deradicalization may prove worthwhile. Such research can inform the development of more effective interventions that specifically target individuals or groups in a certain phase of radicalization.

References

Agnew, R. (1992). "Foundation for a general strain theory of crime and delinquency", *Criminology, 30*, 47–87.

Altier, M. B., Thoroughgood, C. N., & Horgan, J. G. (2014). "Turning away from terrorism: Lessons from psychology, sociology, and criminology", *Journal of Peace Research, 51*, 647–661.

Bjørgo, T. (2011). "Dreams and disillusionment: Engagement in and disengagement from militant extremist groups", *Crime, Law, and Social Change, 55*, 277–285.

Bjørgo, T., & Carlsson, Y. (2005). *Early intervention with violent and racist youth groups.* (NUPI Working Papers, issue 667). Oslo: Norwegian Institute of International Affairs. Retrieved from www.css.ethz.ch/en/services.html

Borum, R. (2003). "Understanding the terrorist mind-set", *FBI Law Enforcement Bulletin, 72*, 7–10.

Buijs, F. J., Demant, F., & Hamdy, A. (2006). *Strijders van eigen bodem. Radicale en democratische moslims in Nederland [Homegrown Warriors: Radical and democratic Muslims in the Netherlands].* Amsterdam: Amsterdam University Press.

Byman, D. (2015). "The homecomings: What happens when Arab foreign fighters in Iraq and Syria return?", *Studies in Conflict & Terrorism, 38*, 581–602.

Corner, E., & Gill, P. (2014). "A false dichotomy? Mental illness and lone-actor terrorism", *Law and Human Behavior, 39*, 23–34.

De Wever, R. (2015, April 6). "De strijd tegen extremisme begint met die voor mensenrechten, stelt deze ex-jihadist [The battle against extremism starts with the one for human rights, poses this former jihadist]", *De Correspondent.* Retrieved from www.decorrespondent.nl

Demant, F., Slootman, M., Buijs, F., & Tillie, J. (2008). *Decline and disengagement: An analysis of processes of de-radicalization.* Amsterdam: Institute for Migration & Ethnic Studies [IMES].

Doosje, B., Moghaddam, F. M., Kruglanski, A. W., de Wolf, A., Mann, L., & Feddes, A. R. (2016). "Terrorism, radicalization and deradicalization", *Current Opinion in Psychology, 11*, 79–84.

Doosje, B., de Wolf, A. B., Mann, L., & Feddes, A. R. (2017). "Radicalisering en de-radicalisering", in P. J. van Koppen, J. W. de Keijser, R. Horselenberg, & M. Jelicic, eds., *Routes van het Recht. Over de rechtspsychologie* (pp. 131–146). Den Haag, Nederland: Boom Juridisch.

Feddes, A. R. (2015). "Socio-psychological factors involved in measures of disengagement and deradicalization and evaluation challenges in Western Europe", in *Understanding deradicalization: Pathways to enhance transatlantic common perceptions and practices.* Middle East Institute/Fondation pour la Recherche Stratégique, 1-17. Retrieved from http://www.mei.edu

Feddes, A. R., Nickolson, L., & Doosje, E. J. (2015). *Triggerfactoren in het radicaliseringsproces [Trigger factors in the radicalization process].* The Hague/Amsterdam: Expertise-unit Sociale Stabiliteit/University of Amsterdam.

Forest, J. J. F. (2005). "Exploring root causes of terrorism: An introduction", in J. J. F. Forest, ed., *The making of a terrorist, Volume III: Root causes* (pp. 1–16). Westport/London: Praeger Security International.

Geelhoed, F. (2012). "Purification and resistance: Glocal meanings of Islamic fundamentalism in the Netherlands", *Doctoral dissertation*, Erasmus School of Law (ESL).

Horgan, J. (2008a). "Deradicalization or disengagement: A process in need of clarity and a counterterrorism initiative in need of evaluation", *Perspectives on Terrorism, 2, 5.* Retrieved from www.terrorismanalysts.com/pt/index.php/pot/article/view/32/html

Horgan, J. (2008b). "From profiles to pathways and roots to routes: Perspectives from psychology on radicalization into terrorism", *Annals of the American Academy of Political and Social Science, 618*, 80–94.

King, M., & Taylor, D. M. (2011). "The radicalization of home-grown Jihadists. A review of theoretical models and social psychological evidence", *Terrorism and Political Violence, 23*, 602–622.

Kleinmann, S. M. (2012). "Radicalization of homegrown Sunni militants in the United States: Comparing converts and non-converts", *Studies in Conflict and Terrorism, 35*, 278–297.

Koehler, D. (2017). *Understanding deradicalization: Methods, tools and programs for countering violent extremism.* New York, NY: Routledge.

Kruglanski, A. W., Bélanger, J. J., Gelfand, M., Gunaratna, R., Hettiarachchi, M., Reinares, F., Orehek, E., Sasota, J., & Sharvit, K. (2013). "Terrorism—A (self) love story: Redirecting the significance quest can end violence", *American Psychologist, 68*, 559–575.

Kruglanski, A. W., & Fishman, S. (2009). "Psychological factors in terrorism and counterterrorism: Individual, group, and organizational levels of analysis", *Social Issues and Policy Review, 3*, 1–44.

Kruglanski, A. W., Gelfand, M. J., Bélanger, J. J., Sheveland, A., Hetiarachchi, M., & Gunaratna, R. (2014). "The psychology of radicalization and deradicalization: How significance quest impacts violent extremism", *Political Psychology, 35*, 69–93.

Lankford, A. (2012). "A comparative analysis of suicide terrorists and rampage, workplace, and school shooters in the United States from 1990 to 2010", *Homicide Studies, 17*, 255–274.

Lewin, K. (1951). *Field theory in social science; selected theoretical papers*. D. Cartwright, ed. New York, NY: Harper & Row.

Lygre, R. B., Eid, J., Larsson, G., & Ranstorp, M. (2011). "Terrorism as a process: A critical review of Moghaddam's 'staircase to terrorism'", *Scandinavian Journal of Psychology, 52*, 609–616.

Macdougall, A. I., Van Der Veen, J., Feddes, A. R., Nickolson, L., & Doosje, B. (2018). "Different strokes for different folkes: The role of psychological needs and other risk factors in early radicalization", *International Journal of Developmental Science, 12*, 37–50. Doi:10.3233/DEV-170232.

McCauley, C., & Moskalenko, S. (2008). "Mechanisms of political radicalization: Pathways toward terrorism", *Terrorism and Political Violence, 20*, 415–433.

Milgram, S. (1974). *Obedience to authority: An experimental view*. New York, NY: Harper and Row.

Moghaddam, F. M. (2005). "The staircase to terrorism: A psychological exploration", *American Psychologist, 60*(2), 161–169.

Moghaddam, F. M. (2007). *From the terrorists' point of view*. Westport, CT: Praeger.

Moghaddam, F. M. (2009). "Deradicalisation and the staircase from terrorism", in D. Canter, ed., *The faces of terrorism: Multidisciplinary perspectives* (pp. 277–292). Malden, MA, USA: John Wiley.

Newman, E. (2006). "Exploring the 'root causes' of terrorism", *Studies in Conflict & Terrorism, 29*, 749–772.

Pyszczynski, T., Abdollahi, A., Solomon, S., Greenberg, J., Cohen, F., & Weise, D. (2006). "Mortality salience, martyrdom, and military might: The great Satan versus the axis of evil", *Personality and Social Psychology Bulletin, 32*, 525–537.

Sageman, M. (2008). "A strategy for fighting international Islamist terrorists", *The Annals of the American Academy of Political and Social Science, 618*, 223–231.

Schmid, A. P. (2014). "Violent and non-violent extremism: Two sides of the same coin", *ICCT Research Paper*.

Schuurman, B. W. (2017). *Becoming a European homegrown jihadist: A multilevel analysis of involvement in the Dutch Hofstadgroup, 2002-2005*. (PhD Thesis). Institute of Security and Global Affairs, Faculty of Governance and Global Affairs, University of Leiden.

Schuurman, B., Bakker, E., & Eijkman, Q. (2018). "Structural influences on involvement in European homegrown jihadism: A case study", *Terrorism and Political Violence, 30*(1), 97–115.

Sieckelinck, S. M. A., & De Winter, M. (2015). "Formers & families: Transitional journeys in and out extremisms in the UK, Denmark and The Netherlands", The Hague: NCTV.

Sieckelinck, S., Sikkens, E., Van San, M., Kotnis, S., & De Winter, M. (2019). "Transitional journeys into and out of extremism. A biographical approach", *Studies in Conflict & Terrorism, 42*(7), 662–682.

Tajfel, H., & Turner, J. C. (1979). "An integrative theory of intergroup conflict", in W. G. Austin & S. Worchel, eds., *The social psychology of intergroup relations* (pp. 33–47). Monterey, CA: Brooks-Cole.

Van der Valk, I., & Wagenaar, W. (2010). *Monitor racism & extremism: Entry and exit from extreme right*. Amsterdam, The Netherlands: Amsterdam University Press.

Van Eerten, J. J., Doosje, B., Konijn, E., De Graaf, B., & De Goede, M. (2017). *How to prevent radicalization or stimulate deradicalization? An evaluation of counter-narrative programs using social media*. Amsterdam/Utrecht/The Hague: University of Amsterdam, Free University Amsterdam, Utrecht University, Ministry of Security & Justice.

Veldhuis, T., & Staun, J. (2009). "Islamist radicalisation: A root cause model", Danish Centre for International Studies and Human Rights. Retrieved from www.diis.dk/files/media/publications/import/islamist_radicalisation.veldhuis_and_staun.pdf

Venhaus, J. (2010). "Why youth join Al-Qaeda", *United States Institute of Peace*. May 2010. Retrieved from www.usip.org/publications/why-youth-join-al-qaeda

Weggemans, D., Bakker, E., & Grol, P. (2014). "Who are they and why do they go? The radicalisation and preparatory processes of Dutch jihadist foreign fighters", *Perspectives on Terrorism, 8*, 100–110.

Wiktorowicz, Q. (2004). "Joining the cause: Al-Muhajiroun and radical Islam", *Paper presented at the Roots of Islamic Radicalism conference*, Yale University, Cambridge, MA, 8 – 9 May 2004.

Winter, C. (2015). *The virtual 'caliphate': Understanding Islamic State's propaganda strategy*. London, UK: The Quilliam Foundation.

5

PSYCHOLOGICAL APPROACHES TO TERRORIST REHABILITATION

Direct and indirect mechanisms of deradicalization

David Webber, Marina Chernikova, Erica Molinario, and Arie W. Kruglanski

In this chapter, we discuss the psychology underlying various approaches toward terrorist rehabilitation. These programs operate worldwide and vary considerably. They operate in vastly different regions. They target different varieties of extremism (e.g., of the white supremacy, nationalist, or religious variety) and different clientele (e.g., former terrorists imprisoned for their crimes, or extremists voluntarily seeking help to leave a radical movement). And they utilize different methods of rehabilitation. The purpose of the present chapter is not to focus on these differences, but to take stock of the similarities—to examine the common underpinnings of these approaches, and discuss the underlying mechanisms through which these seemingly disparate methods can facilitate rehabilitation.

"Rehabilitation" is a loaded term that holds different meanings for different people. When it comes to the rehabilitation of terrorists, there is disagreement as to what can be realistically achieved. The debate typically centers on two possible outcomes. The first potential outcome is *deradicalization*. That is, rehabilitation can aim to disabuse clients of a violence-promoting narrative used by terrorist organizations to justify, inspire, and reward violence for the cause. It follows that, after renouncing the ideology, the client no longer has a reason to engage in violence, and terrorist behavior should subside. The second potential outcome is *disengagement*. Disengagement is merely behavioral change. It involves abandoning one's personal involvement in violence, while still remaining committed to the ideology and maintaining the toxic beliefs that motivate violence (Horgan 2008). Indeed, the reasons that terrorists give for abandoning their violent ways often have little to do with changes in ideological beliefs (Altier, Boyle, Shortland, and Horgan 2017). Moreover, Horgan (2008, Horgan and Altier 2012) noted that many rehabilitation methods—e.g., vocational training, education, community building, or connecting terrorists with individuals who have been successfully rehabilitated—do not directly work toward changing a client's endorsement of terrorist ideology, and therefore seem more akin to disengagement than deradicalization.

The present chapter sees less distinction between these outcomes when it comes to rehabilitation programs. Specific methods employed by rehabilitation programs can be easily categorized by their surface features into those that should deradicalize (e.g., ideological argumentation/counseling with a religious scholar) and those that should disengage (e.g., vocational training and community building). However, that does not mean that addressing ideological belief is the only route toward deradicalization, or that increasing one's education or imparting life skills cannot facilitate deradicalization. Instead, we propose that the two types of methods should be categorized as those that *directly* lead to deradicalization, and those that *indirectly* facilitate it. Toward this aim, the present chapter integrates the two models of disengagement and deradicalization to provide insight into the mechanisms through which rehabilitation programs can achieve deradicalization.

Theories of disengagement and deradicalization

Push and pull factors

An oft-cited disengagement perspective identifies the "push and pull" factors that increase the likelihood of disengagement (e.g., Altier, Thoroughgood, and Horgan 2014; Bjørgo 2009; Horgan 2009; Reinares 2011). *Push factors* represent various forms of disillusionment with the internal workings of a terrorist organization. They include disappointment with the organization's ability to achieve political goals, frustration with the (lack of) camaraderie, hypocritical behavior of fellow members, or changes in belief about the veracity of the organization's ideology. In essence, push factors are circumstances within the organization that push one away. *Pull factors*, on the other hand, represent external influences that may attract an extremist individual, and pull him or her away from the organization. Included in this category are employment or family desires, financial incentives for leaving the organization, amnesty for crimes committed, or positive interactions with either "enemy" forces (e.g., a white supremacist having positive interactions with a foreigner) or members of the mainstream. Recent evidence culled from autobiographies of former terrorists suggests that disengagement is more likely to be driven by push (vs. pull) factors, with the most prevalent push factors being disillusionment with either the strategy or membership of the organization (Altier et al. 2017).

3N theory

The 3N perspective identifies a nexus of three factors, referred to as the 3Ns—psychological *needs*, ideological *narratives*, and social *networks*—that facilitate radicalization (Dugas et al. 2016; Jasko, LaFree, and Kruglanski 2017; Kruglanski, Jasko, Chernikova, Dugas, and Webber 2017; Webber and Kruglanski 2016; Webber et al. 2018b). The model starts with the notion that extremism involves a motivational imbalance, wherein a violent extremist is willing to forgo other important concerns of the human condition (i.e., family obligations, career aspirations, safety, or normative proscriptions of violence) to achieve a highly valued goal (the *need*). On the surface, that goal may appear to be ideological and conjoined with the goals of the terrorist organization, such as establishing the Caliphate within the Middle East or expelling an occupying force from one's homeland. Psychologically speaking, however, these ideological goals are attained in the service of fundamental concerns for personal significance; through their attainment one can feel important, earn respect, and believe that he or she matters to others (e.g., Kruglanski, Xiaoyan, Mark, Shira, and Edward 2009; Kruglanski et al. 2014, 2017).

A common way in which radicalization occurs is that an individual experiences some form of personal humiliation, stigma, discrimination, or oppression that occasions a loss of personal significance. These negative circumstances then motivate one to remedy these feelings of insignificance, leading individuals to turn to violent extremism (e.g., Jasko et al. 2017; Kruglanski et al. 2009, 2013, 2014, 2017; Victoroff, Adelman, and Matthews 2012; Webber, Klein, Kruglanski, Brizi, and Merari 2017). Through exposure to ideologies crafted by terrorist organizations that promise honor to those who fight for the cause, and that legitimize violence perpetrated against an enemy (the *narrative*), insignificant individuals find a potent route toward significance restoration. And lastly, the presence of allies in the cause, or like-minded individuals within one's social group (the *network*), serves to validate the terrorist ideology, and increase one's willingness to transgress normative proscriptions and enlist within the organization.

According to 3N theory, deradicalization (or disengagement) should operate through the same three factors. In other words, deradicalization is the process of restoring motivational balance. If feelings of significance are restored through culturally appropriate mechanisms, the impetus for engaging in violence should be effectively removed (Kruglanski et al. 2017). Likewise, if a terrorist no longer endorses the violence-justifying tenets of a terrorist organization, or has been cut off from the influence of radical others, he or she should be less compelled to remain an extremist.

Integrating perspectives

Together, the push/pull and 3N frameworks provide important insight into terrorist rehabilitation programs. The 3N framework highlights the three major mechanisms by which rehabilitation methods should operate: (1) restoring motivational balance; (2) changing one's endorsement of terrorist ideology; and (3) weakening ties to other extremists. The addition of the push/pull framework highlights the two routes through which each of these mechanisms can be addressed: (1) changing one's positive perspective of the internal workings of terrorist organizations; and (2) luring one away from the grasp of terrorist organizations via external avenues. We therefore organize the remainder of this chapter according to these three mechanisms, and the two routes through which they can be achieved.

(Direct) deradicalization via the narrative

Given that deradicalization is defined as rejection by violent extremists of a terrorism justifying ideology, the most straightforward way to effect that kind of change is to counter the ideological narrative by articulating arguments against it. A key point to remember, however, is that successful deradicalization does not require one to abandon the entire ideology of the extremist organization, but merely those aspects of the ideology that permit and reward the use of violence. Terrorist ideologies, particularly those of a religious nature, cover a vast array of topics that include the goals of the organization and warrants for violence, but also moral prescriptions and general guidelines for everyday behavior. The problem does not lie in those latter beliefs and goals as such, but in the justification of violence as a means toward achieving the goals in question. For instance, we do not perceive the leaders of the Black Lives Matter movement as violent extremists, because they aim to achieve their goals through non-violent and socially mandated routes. Likewise, Tamils or Palestinians fighting for self-determination or equal treatment only become extremists when they come to accept violence as a means toward the attainment of their goals.

Indeed, research has consistently shown that terrorists often choose to end their extremist lifestyles because they no longer believe that violence is the appropriate way to redress their grievances. Former members of Euskadi Ta Askatasuna (ETA) in Spain, for instance, came to perceive violence as counterproductive, given the political gains made across the years (Reinares 2011). Likewise, defectors from ISIS often struggled with the organization's extreme brutality, and questioned the moral warrants advanced by ISIS concerning violence against other Muslims (Neumann 2015). This dynamic is represented in analyses of autobiographies whereby almost 60% of extremists became disillusioned with the strategy or actions of their organization (which often likely centered around issues of violence), but under 30% lost faith in the entire ideology (Altier et al. 2017).

The major difficulty for rehabilitation programs is identifying successful ways to facilitate this disillusionment. Rehabilitation efforts of Islamic extremists have often included religious counseling or religious re-education programs. This has been a major component of the programs in Yemen (Rabasa, Stacie, Jeremy, and Christopher 2010), Singapore (Gunaratna and Hassan 2015), Saudi Arabia (al-Hadlaq 2011), Indonesia (Idris and Taufiqurrohman 2015), Iraq (Rabasa et al. 2010), and China (Zhou 2017), to name a few. Consider the Religious Rehabilitation Group in Singapore: religious clerics and teachers counsel former members of Jemaah Islamiyah to "extricate their negatively imbibed ideology," for instance, by clarifying the meaning of jihad and discussing the non-violent ways in which (spiritual) jihad could be achieved (Gunaratna and Hassan 2015). In Saudi Arabia, detained terrorism suspects complete ten courses on topics such as relations with non-Muslims, excommunication, and jihad (al-Hadlaq 2011). The Indonesian program utilizes former radicals to counsel detainees to renounce violence, but does not challenge the core of their fundamentalist ideals (Idris and Taufiqurrohman 2015).

Unfortunately, the popularity of these programs should not be equated with success. The now defunct Yemeni program presents an interesting case study, as it is one of the only programs to focus solely on explicating terrorist ideology. The program was focused on a dialogue, and operated under the premise that terrorists' actions were based on "faulty intellectual foundations" that could be disputed to effect disengagement (e.g., Horgan and Braddock 2010). Although there is a question as to whether the tactics used in these dialogues were intended to deradicalize or merely secure acquiescence, the program is generally viewed as a failure (Rabasa et al. 2010). Moreover, rehabilitation programs that merely utilize religious counseling have acknowledged its inadequacy. In Indonesia, for instance, officials have acknowledged that economic aid and building of personal connections have been more important to deradicalization than has been ideological argumentation (Idris and Taufiqurrohman 2015). In Iraq, the religious re-education system backfired and may have contributed to the widespread riots in the detention center (Rabasa et al. 2010). Likewise, organizers of the Saudi program learned through experience with early participants that religious argumentation alone may be less effective, and came to emphasize other methods focused on the acquisition of skills to help individuals reintegrate into society upon release (al-Hadlaq 2011). It also seems noteworthy that rehabilitation efforts like those in Sri Lanka (Hettiarachchi 2015) and Eastern Europe (Bjørgo, Van Donselaar, and Grunenberg 2009) do not address ideological beliefs. This decision could simply reflect the fact that the extremists in these programs do not subscribe to religious doctrine to justify their actions, or that the EXIT programs in Europe are geared toward participants who have already chosen to abandon a violent organization. Successes of these programs—the EXIT programs boast very low recidivism rates (Bjørgo et al. 2009), and the Sri Lankan program has been empirically found to reduce the endorsement of violence (Webber et al. 2018b)—suggest that deradicalization can be achieved without confronting the violent narrative head on.

Instead of viewing the purported failure of ideological argumentation as clear evidence that deradicalization cannot be achieved, we propose that deradicalization may be better sought through indirect routes. Disillusionment with terrorist ideology is likely a conclusion that extremists need to come to on their own. Indeed, interviews and analyses of biographies show that extremists often come to this illation (e.g., Kruglanski et al. 2019; Neumann 2015; Reinares 2011). Forcing this conclusion on them through counseling and debate is complicated, likely to be met with resistance, and has the potential to backfire. These debates could spur the targeted individuals to think of arguments of their own to support their belief system, and in so doing, only harden their resolve. In applying the tenets of reactance theory (Brehm 1966) and cognitive dissonance theory (Festinger 1957), Dalgaard-Nielsen (2013) reached a similar conclusion, and proposed that ideological change could be better fostered by spurring behavioral change. Dalgaard-Nielsen further advised abstaining from direct attempts at ideological argumentation "unless it is established by an initial screening, that [the targeted individual] is already experiencing doubt with regard to for example the glorification of violence, the demonization of the presumed enemy, or the absolutist claims of the extremist narrative" (Dalgaard-Nielsen 2013, p. 109). As we elaborate in the following sections, rehabilitation methods that operate on the remaining two Ns—networks and needs—should not only facilitate disengagement, but should indirectly weaken the appeal of the ideology so that it can be more easily cast aside.

(Indirect) deradicalization via the network

Research has consistently found that individuals are often pushed away from extremism when they become disillusioned by actions of their brothers-in-arms. This was found when analyses examined terrorists of multiple nationalities and across ideological spectrums (e.g., Altier et al. 2017; Barrelle 2015), and specifically when examining individuals who had defected from ISIS (e.g., Neumann 2015; Speckhard and Yayla 2016) and the right-wing movement in Germany (Kruglanski et al. 2019). Also, interviews revealed that a common reason for defecting from ISIS was the realization that ISIS soldiers and leaders engaged in "un-Islamic" behaviors forbidden by Shariah law, like smoking and rape (Speckhard and Yayla 2016).

Use of this information in the deradicalization process may be difficult, however, in that enthusiastic ISIS supporters may dismiss it as biased propaganda.

Reducing the impact of the radical network may be accomplished by limiting individuals' contact with their erstwhile comrades and leaders. In residential facilities (like prisons or detention centers) that house many extremists, this is accomplished through housing arrangements that separate the committed ideologues or influencers from the underlings within the organization. One example of this is Major General Stone's method of identifying the hard-core insurgents—the irreconcilables—in Iraqi rehabilitation centers, and separating them from the rest of the prisoners believed to be potentially malleable in their attitudes and beliefs (Rabasa et al. 2010). Although this is likely an insufficient method when used alone, lower-level members should become more receptive to other forms of rehabilitation when freed from the influence of their leaders. This approach also requires a bit of calculation on the part of the rehabilitators. Isolating the influencers poses the risk of further radicalizing them, as experiences of social isolation, restriction of freedom, and what is likely to be viewed as discrimination may serve to only increase feelings of insignificance and worsen the motivational imbalance. The decision therefore becomes: should a program focus on rehabilitating a greater number of low-risk detainees (who are likely to be released into society sooner), or expend most of their efforts on attempting to rehabilitate fewer high-risk militants?

Rather than selecting either of the paths described above, rehabilitation efforts may be geared toward strengthening former extremists' social connections to non-radical networks. For instance, the Sri Lankan program, that focused on rehabilitating former members of the Liberation Tigers of Tamil Eelam (LTTE), brought in successful Tamils (i.e., business owners, film stars, athletes) from within local communities, and sent former militants on field trips in order to build their ties to those communities (Hettiarachchi 2015). Similarly, a mainstay of disengagement programs for right-wing extremists in Europe is connecting the detainees to former comrades who have been successfully deradicalized, and explicitly working to build up the detainees' non-extreme social networks (Bjørgo et al. 2009). These programs, such as the EXIT programs in Germany and Sweden, work outside of the prison context, and aid individuals who have voluntarily made the decision to leave extremist organizations. These persons often find themselves isolated, having previously abandoned all social relationships outside the extreme movement. The EXIT programs help them develop their social skills and introduce them to contacts who can provide much-needed support as former extremists navigate their return to the mainstream.

Rehabilitation efforts that work with detainees and prisoners can expand the non-radical social network, but are often limited in the extent to which they can foster new, meaningful relationships. Thus, many programs work to help them reconnect with existing family members and friends. Assuming the extremists had non-radical friends and family outside the movement (before they fully radicalized), rehabilitation programs attempt to reconnect these individuals by providing family visitations, facilitating communication (letters, emails, phone calls), or offering leave to allow the detainees to attend important family events (funerals, weddings, etc.). These tactics were implemented in the Sri Lankan program (Webber et al. 2018b), the Iraqi program (Rabasa et al. 2010), the Indonesian program (Horgan and Braddock 2010), and others. Any effort that seeks to build new relational ties to non-radical entities will serve to weaken ties to radical entities (cf. Klein and Kruglanski 2013; Zhang, Fishbach, and Kruglanski 2007), and should thus facilitate the exit from violent extremism.

Psychologically speaking, these tactics should facilitate movement away from the terrorist ideology. As Festinger (1954) proposed, other people form the very basis by which we evaluate the appropriateness of our own actions, and maintaining faith in any form of ideology generally requires that those beliefs are shared and consensually validated by others (e.g., Berger and Luckmann 1966). It has been further proposed that individuals are likely to search for consensus, or what is referred to as a shared reality (Hardin and Higgins 1996), to fulfill their epistemic motives for knowledge and certainty. The more ambiguous or difficult the informational environment, the greater the individuals' need to rely on others to validate one's beliefs (e.g., Echterhoff, Higgins, and Levine 2009; Festinger 1954). Endorsing the ideology of a terrorist organization, and especially its warrants for violent behavior, is a particularly difficult task, because it requires ignoring society's general prescriptions against brutality and violence (cf. Kruglanski et al. 2017). That is why the network support for violent extremism is of particular importance and why re-connecting former militants to mainstream networks that oppose extremism is essential.

In this vein, Sageman (2008) argued that terrorist groups often turn into "echo chambers" that promote a spiral of mutual encouragement and the escalation of commitment. In those contexts, individuals are disproportionately exposed to one-sided arguments, and tend to adopt positions which they believe will make them acceptable to their peers. Most importantly, the increased solidarity found within echo chambers leads individuals to hold their own extreme beliefs with greater confidence (Sunstein 2007). Indeed, there is evidence that echo chambers can promote radicalization, particularly in online contexts (Saddiq 2010; Stevens and Neumann 2009; Von Behr, Reding, Edwards, and Gribbon 2013; Warner 2010; Wojcieszak 2009, 2010). In short, if rehabilitation programs can successfully weaken individuals' social ties to radical influences, they would remove a main source of justification for their radical beliefs, thus advancing deradicalization.

(Indirect) deradicalization via the need component

Deradicalization efforts can focus on individuals' psychological need to feel significant in their own and in others' eyes. Individuals join terrorist organizations because they view the organizations as potent means through which significance can be earned (Kruglanski et al. 2009, 2013, 2014, 2017). As with all of the 3N factors of radicalization, disengagement is likely to occur when disillusionment *pushes* an extremist away from the organization—that is, when he or she begins to question whether continued involvement in the movement sufficiently provides him or her with feelings of self-worth. Indeed, this appears to have been true for many ISIS defectors. For instance, one such individual found that his life with ISIS did not meet the standards he was promised, and doubted that his time with the terrorists would help him gain the heroism he so desperately sought (Neumann 2015; see also Tomlinson 2014). Horgan (2009) reported similar sentiments. More broadly speaking, all forms of disillusionment with the organization likely lead individuals to question not only their role in the organization, but their purpose and meaning in life; feelings that contribute to the sense of "burnout" often referenced as a cause of disengagement (e.g., Bjørgo 2011; Della Porta 2009). Disengagement may also occur when one is *pulled* away from the organization because he or she finds other alluring avenues for earning significance. Interviews conducted with former members of the Basque ETA provide a compelling account of this process, as many extremists wanted to make a life for themselves outside of the movement, and attain significance by getting married and starting a family (Reinares 2011).

The latter of these routes—providing alternative forms of significance—is a task that rehabilitation programs can tackle, assuming they have the necessary resources. When participants of these programs are released, their likelihood of returning to the extremist organization is higher if they have no alternative ways to earn a living and provide for their families. In other words, individuals may return to extreme groups because these offer them a means to earn respect and a sense of mattering.

To be sure, the quest for significance is a universal striving that motivates much of human behavior: it has driven some of the greatest innovators, motivated business leaders to secure their next contract, led students to endure the rigors of medical school, and pushed academics to publish. Although the significance motive can be satisfied via extremism, most people attain it in socially acceptable ways. Rehabilitation programs can therefore offer educational and vocational courses that provide their clients with the necessary skills that would increase their likelihood of landing a job after release. Indeed, vocational education constituted a focus of the deradicalization program operating in Sri Lanka (Hettiarachchi 2015; Webber et al. 2018b), Indonesia (Idris and Taufiqurrohman 2015; Horgan and Braddock 2010), Colombia (Horgan and Braddock 2010), Saudi Arabia (al-Hadlaq 2011), and Iraq under Major General Douglas Stone (Rabasa et al. 2010), and others.

For instance, the Sri Lankan program offered LTTE detainees more than 40 vocational training courses based on detainees' traditional family vocations and regional job opportunities, including carpentry, masonry, garment making, mechanics, and cosmetology (Hettiarachchi 2015). Some of the companies involved in these training programs even pledged to hire or provide on-the-job training in their factories after the detainees were released. Colombia offered former guerrillas health care, shelter, clothing, and vocational support (Horgan and Braddock 2010). In the same vein, the Saudi program has helped graduates of their center find suitable jobs, and even offered them assistance in getting married (al-Hadlaq 2011; Lankford and Gillespie 2011). As former members of ETA (and many parents) can attest, marriage and children may provide a sense of significance with which little can compete.

In addition to providing alternative routes to significance, rehabilitation programs should address former militants' current deficits in significance. Vocational and educational courses described above can address this aim. For captured and incarcerated extremists who likely feel hopeless and have been stripped of personal freedom, learning new skills, getting an education, and proving to themselves that they are capable and competent can be highly empowering. Psychological counseling is also important. Based on this logic, the Saudi program offered detained "beneficiaries" courses on social skills, self-management, positive thinking, and art therapy (al-Hadlaq 2011). The Colombian program similarly adopted a person-centered therapeutic approach, including individualized workshops and therapy sessions (Horgan and Braddock 2010). Likewise, psychosocial courses in Sri Lanka tackled topics like interpersonal relations, managing emotions, mindfulness training, and art/creativity therapy (Hettiarachchi 2015). The same is true for treatment of right-wing extremists who are referred to therapists and professional counselors to deal with issues like depression, anxiety, anger management, or changing their damaging ways of thinking (Bjørgo et al. 2009).

Throughout this section, we have referenced often the Sri Lankan deradicalization program. Notwithstanding its alleged flaws (e.g., claims of human rights abuses; Keenan 2007) and the historical context within which the program was launched (i.e., after the defeat of the terrorist group by the government), the Sri Lankan program utilized multiple methods that addressed the former militants' significance motive. It is thus a good case study for investigating whether this approach represents an effective deradicalization tool. Our research team (Webber et al. 2018b) gained access to the population of detainees within the Sri Lankan program, and assessed the effectiveness of rehabilitation using self-report surveys. A longitudinal assessment measured endorsement of terrorist ideology among detainees exposed to the full battery of significance-relevant rehabilitation programs (educational, vocational, and psycho-social), and compared them to detainees who did not have access to these specific programs (see Webber et al. 2018b for more details). After a year of rehabilitation, detainees who participated in the full battery of programs expressed significantly lower ideological extremism than those without access to these programs. Follow-up surveys conducted after the detainees had been reintegrated into society further revealed significantly lower endorsement of violent extremism among the former detainees, as compared to community members who never belonged to the terrorist group in the first place. A final set of analyses revealed that decreased feelings of insignificance were driving this reduction in extremism. For instance, research on reintegrated extremists revealed that those who participated in a greater number of rehabilitation programs reported lower feelings of insignificance, which were subsequently related to lower levels of extremism (Webber et al. 2018b).

These findings suggest that restoring motivational balance can be used as an effective deradicalization tool. Indeed, the main dependent variable in these studies was ideological. Although the Sri Lankan rehabilitation curriculum did not include ideological counter-argumentation (Hettiarachchi 2015), extremists who went through the program expressed less endorsement of terrorist ideology, an effect that persisted for years after their release. Moreover, self-reported feelings of significance were directly implicated as the mechanism underlying this reduction in ideological extremism. It thus appears that when the motivation driving extremism is gratified, the belief in extremist ideology is correspondingly weakened.

Additional research sheds light on one reason why this may occur (Webber et al. 2018a). Consistent with observations made by Barrett (2014), this work examined the degree to which epistemic motivation for certainty and closure (e.g., Kruglanski 2004; Kruglanski and Webster 1996; Webster and Kruglanski 1994) is involved in the endorsement of extremism. We found a positive relation between self-reported insignificance and the need for closure among detained terrorists in Sri Lanka and the Philippines. Arguably, this occurred because significance loss creates an inconsistency between the positive manner in which individuals wish to perceive themselves and the humiliating experience they are having (cf. McGregor, Zanna, Holmes, and Spencer 2001). This induces feelings of uncertainty and anxiety that motivate behavior aimed at restoring certainty (Festinger 1957). More importantly, the increased need for closure was subsequently related to terrorists' endorsement of violent extremism (Webber et al. 2018a). We suggest that this occurred because terrorist ideology provides the closure and certainty that some individuals crave (Hogg, Kruglanski, and Van den Bos 2013). Terrorist ideologies tend to portray the world in clear-cut, black-and-white terms: there is typically a "good" group (the terrorists) and a "bad" group (the enemy to be defeated), with no gray area in between. For instance, the Islamic State identifies clear "us versus them" categories (i.e., true believers vs. infidels), and unequivocally applies the tenets of *takfir* (i.e., excommunication) to determine which is which, enabling the killing of the infidels and thus purifying the world.

In an additional study, we manipulated feelings of insignificance experienced by American participants; some individuals were induced to feel humiliated and insignificant, whereas others were not. Just as occurred in the terrorist samples, participants made to feel insignificant reported a higher need for closure, which was related in turn to the endorsement of an extreme political ideology (Webber et al. 2018a). For instance, liberals became more willing to endorse extreme liberal perspectives like supporting a ban on all firearms, whereas conservatives were more willing to support the notion that firearm sale and use should be completely unrestricted. Importantly, the need for closure was also negatively related to the endorsement of moderate perspectives. So, while participants moved toward the extremes of their ideological beliefs, they likewise became less receptive to moderate policies that allow for some ambiguity (i.e., only restricting the sale of automatic firearms or extended ammunition clips).

Taken together, these studies demonstrate that feelings of insignificance increase one's endorsement of violent extremism by way of inducing a desire for certainty and closure. When individuals experience the motivational imbalance we have discussed, they want to see the world in a clearly delineated manner—and the black-and-white, polarized narratives advanced by terrorist organizations serve this purpose particularly well. Applying these findings to processes of rehabilitation, it becomes apparent that a successful restoration of one's feelings of significance will decrease the appeal of terrorist ideology. With one's motivational balance restored, the self-inconsistency would be removed, and the appeal of extremist ideology would decrease. Likewise, evidence suggests that under those conditions moderate perspectives, such as the moderate versions of Islam being promoted by clerics through religious counseling programs (e.g., Rabasa et al. 2010; Gunaratna and Hassan 2015; al-Hadlaq 2011; Idris and Taufiqurrohman 2015; Zhou 2017), would increase in appeal.

Thus, while tactics that address the significance motive may appear to only address an individual's impetus for becoming a terrorist, in reality, they also reduce the appeal of any closure-affording ideology. This can create a potent cocktail that leads one to cast off his belief in terrorist ideology. Specifically, if one (1) no longer needs the glory promised by the ideology, and (2) no longer finds an unambiguous outlook on the world appealing, one has little reason to retain extremist beliefs. When this approach is combined with tactics that weaken individuals' ties to the radical social network discussed previously, radical ideologies would (3) lose the much-needed validity provided by consensual validation. None of these tactics directly confronts individuals' violence-justifying beliefs, yet they indirectly reduce the pull of the corresponding ideologies and lessen the psychological pressure that may keep one committed to a life of terrorism.

A promising application of the present analysis is that the foregoing tactics should be relatively easy to implement within existing prison systems. Many penitentiaries already offer their inmates some form of educational, vocational, or counseling services. They also often include family visitation programs that help connect inmates to their families. Simply extending these existing programs to terrorist inmates should facilitate indirect deradicalization, and increase the former terrorists' receptivity to ideological change.

Conclusion

In this chapter, we reviewed several deradicalization programs that, for the most part, did not directly work toward changing their participants' endorsement of terrorist ideology. Nonetheless, we argue that these programs can be as effective—if not more effective—in promoting deradicalization as programs that focus directly on challenging terrorists' ideological beliefs. This is because the indirect programs can address the psychological mechanisms that lead to radicalization, thus indirectly reducing the appeal of terrorist ideology and spurring effective deradicalization (and not just mere disengagement).

References

al-Hadlaq, Abdulrahman (2011) "Terrorist rehabilitation: The Saudi experience." In Rubin, Lawrence, Rohan Gunaratna, and Jolene Anne R. Jerard (eds) *Terrorist Rehabilitation and Counter-Radicalisation: New Approaches to Counter-Terrorism*. New York: Routledge, 64–65.

Altier, Mary Beth, Emma Leonard Boyle, Neil Shortland and John Horgan (2017) "Why they leave: An analysis of terrorist disengagement events from eighty-seven autobiographical accounts." *Security Studies* 26, no. 2: 305–332. www.tandfonline.com/doi/full/10.1080/09636412.2017.1280307.

Altier, Mary Beth, Christian Thoroughgood, and John Horgan (2014) "Turning away from terrorism: Lessons from psychology, sociology, and criminology." *Journal of Peace Research* 51, no. 5: 647–661. http://journals.sagepub.com/doi/full/10.1177/0022343314535946.

Barrelle, Kate (2015) "Pro-integration: Disengagement from and life after extremism." *Behavioral Sciences of Terrorism and Political Aggression* 7, no. 2: 129–142.

Barrett, Richard. (2014) *Foreign Fighters in Syria*. New York: The Soufan Group.

Berger, Peter, and Thomas Luckmann (1966) *The Social Construction of Reality: A Treatise in the Sociology of Knowledge*. London: Penguin Books.

Bjørgo, Tore (2009) "Processes of disengagement from violent groups of the extreme right." In Bjørgo, Tore and John G. Horgan (eds) *Leaving Terrorism Behind: Individual and Collective Disengagement*. London: Routledge, 30–48.

Bjørgo, Tore (2011) "Dreams and disillusionment: Engagement in and disengagement from militant extremist groups." *Crime, Law and Social Change* 55, no. 4: 277–285.

Bjørgo, Tore, Jaap Van Donselaar, and Sara Grunenberg (2009) "Exit from right-wing extremist groups: Lessons from disengagement programmes in Norway, Sweden and Germany." In Bjørgo, Tore and John G. Horgan (eds) *Leaving Terrorism Behind: Individual and Collective Disengagement*. London: Routledge, 135–151.

Brehm, Jack (1966) *A Theory of Psychological Reactance*. Oxford: Academic Press.

Dalgaard-Nielsen, Anja (2013) "Promoting exit from violent extremism: Themes and approaches." *Studies in Conflict & Terrorism* 36, no. 2: 99–115.

Della Porta, Donatella (2009) *Leaving Underground Organizations: A Sociological Analysis of the Italian Case*. London: Routledge.

Dugas, Michelle, Jocelyn Bélanger, Manuel Moyano, Birga Schumpe, Arie Kruglanski, Michele Gelfand, Kate Touchton-Leonard, and Noëmie Nociti (2016) "The quest for significance motivates self-sacrifice." *Motivation Science* 2, no. 1: 15–32.

Echterhoff, Gerald, Tory Higgins, and John Levine (2009) "Shared reality: Experiencing commonality with others' inner states about the world." *Perspectives on Psychological Science* 4, no. 5: 496–521.

Festinger, Leon (1954) "A theory of social comparison processes." *Human Relations* 7, no. 2: 117–140.

Festinger, Leon (1957) *A Theory of Cognitive Dissonance*. Stanford, CA: Stanford University Press.

Gunaratna, Rohan, and Mohamed Feisal Bin Mohamed Hassan (2015) "Terrorist rehabilitation: The Singapore experience." In Gunaratna, Rohan and Bin Ali (eds) *Terrorist Rehabilitation: A New Frontier in Counter-Terrorism*. London: Imperial College Press, 41–70.

Hardin, Curtis D. and Tory Higgins (1996) "Shared reality: How social verification makes the subjective objective." In Sorrentino, Richard M. and Edward Tory Higgins (eds) *Handbook of Motivation and Cognition, the Interpersonal Context*. New York: Guilford Press, 28–84.

Hettiarachchi, Malkanthi (2015) "Sri Lanka's rehabilitation programme: The humanitarian mission two." In Gunaratna, Rohan and Bin Ali (eds) *Terrorist Rehabilitation: A New Frontier in Counter-Terrorism*. London: Imperial College Press, 103–131.

Hogg, Michael A., Arie Kruglanski, and Kees Van den Bos (2013) "Uncertainty and the roots of extremism." *Journal of Social Issues* 69, no. 3: 407–418.

Horgan, John (2008) "From profiles to pathways and roots to routes: Perspectives from psychology on radicalization into terrorism." *The ANNALS of the American Academy of Political and Social Science* 618, no. 1: 80–94.

Horgan, John (2009) *Walking Away from Terrorism: Accounts of Disengagement from Radical and Extremist Movements*. New York: Routledge.

Horgan, John and Mary Beth Altier (2012) "The future of terrorist deradicalisation programs." *Georgetown Journal of International Affairs* 13, no. 2: 83–90.

Horgan, John and Kurt Braddock (2010) "Rehabilitating the terrorists?: Challenges in assessing the effectiveness of deradicalisation programs." *Terrorism and Political Violence* 22, no. 2: 267–291.

Idris, Irfan, and Muh Taufiqurrohman (2015) "Current state of Indonesia's deradicalisation and rehabilitation programme." In Gunaratna, Rohan and Bin Ali (eds) *Terrorist Rehabilitation: A New Frontier in Counter-Terrorism*. London: Imperial College Press, 71–101.

Jasko, Katarzyna, Gary LaFree, and Arie W. Kruglanski (2017) "Quest for significance and violent extremism: The case of domestic radicalization." *Political Psychology* 38: 815–831.

Keenan, Alan (2007) "The trouble with evenhandedness: On the politics of human rights and peace advocacy in Sri Lanka." In Fehr, Michael, Gaelle Krikorian, and Yates McKee (eds) *Nongovernmental Politics*. Brooklyn, NY: Zone Books, 88–117.

Klein, Kristen M. and Arie W. Kruglanski (2013) "Commitment and extremism: A goal systemic analysis." *Journal of Social Issues* 69, no. 3: 419–435.

Kruglanski, Arie, and Donna Webster (1996) "Motivated closing of the mind: 'Seizing' and 'freezing.'" *Psychological Review* 103, no. 2: 263–283.

Kruglanski, Arie W. (2004) *The Psychology of Closed Mindedness*. New York: Psychology Press.

Kruglanski, Arie W., Jocelyn J. Bélanger, Michele Gelfand, Rohan Gunaratna, Malkanthi Hettiarachchi, Fernando Reinares, Edward Orehek, Jo Sasota, and Keren Sharvit (2013) "Terrorism: A (self) love story." *American Psychologist* 68, no. 7: 559–575.

Kruglanski, Arie W., Xiaoyan Chen, Mark Dechesne, Shira Fishman, and Edward Orehek (2009) "Fully committed: Suicide bombers' motivation and the quest for personal significance." *Political Psychology* 30, no. 3: 331–357.

Kruglanski, Arie W., Michele J. Gelfand, Jocelyn J. Bélanger, Anna Sheveland, Malkanthi Hetiarachchi, and Rohan Gunaratna (2014) "The psychology of radicalization and deradicalization: How significance quest impacts violent extremism." *Political Psychology* 35, no. S1: 69–93.
Kruglanski, Arie W., Katarzyna Jasko, Marina Chernikova, Michelle Dugas, and David Webber (2017) "To the fringe and back: Violent extremism and the psychology of deviance." *American Psychologist* 72, no. 3: 217–230.
Kruglanski, Arie W., David Webber, and Daniel Koehler (2019) *The Radical's Journey: How German Neo-Nazis Voyaged to the Edge and Back*. New York: Oxford University Press.
Lankford, Adam, and Katherine Gillespie (2011) "Rehabilitating terrorists through counter-indoctrination: Lessons learned from the Saudi Arabian program." *International Criminal Justice Review* 21, no. 2: 118–133.
McGregor, Ian, Mark Zanna, John Holmes, and Steven Spencer (2001) "Compensatory conviction in the face of personal uncertainty: Going to extremes and being oneself." *Journal of Personality and Social Psychology* 80, no. 3: 472–488.
Neumann, Peter (2015) "Victims, perpetrators, assets: The narratives of Islamic State defectors." *The International Centre for the Study of Radicalisation and Political Violence (ICSR)*.
Rabasa, Angel, Stacie Pettyjohn, Jeremy Ghez, and Christopher Boucek (2010) *Deradicalizing Islamist Extremists*. Arlington, TX: National Security Research DIV.
Reinares, Fernando (2011) "Exit from terrorism: A qualitative empirical study on disengagement and deradicalization among members of ETA." *Terrorism and Political Violence* 23, no. 5: 780–803.
Saddiq, Mohamed Abdul (2010) "Whither e-jihad: Evaluating the threat of internet radicalisation." *RSIS Commentaries* 83: 1–4.
Sageman, Marc (2008) "A strategy for fighting international Islamist terrorists." *The ANNALS of the American Academy of Political and Social Science* 618, no. 1: 223–231.
Speckhard, Anne, and Ahmet Yayla (2016) *ISIS Defectors: Inside Stories of the Terrorist Caliphate*. Mclean: Advances Press.
Stevens, Tim, and Peter R. Neumann (2009) "Countering online radicalisation: A strategy for action." *International Centre for the Study of Radicalisation and Political Violence (ICSR)*, 10.
Sunstein, Cass R. (2007) *Republic.com 2.0*. Princeton, NJ: Princeton University Press.
Tomlinson, Simon (2014) "'ISIS made me clean the toilets … and my iPod didn't work': How disenchanted Islamic fanatics are returning home because jihad isn't as glamorous as they hoped." *Daily Mail 2 December*. www.dailymail.co.uk/news/article-2855780/Indian-IS-recruit-goes-home-having-clean-toilets.html.
Victoroff, Jeff, Janice Adelman, and Miriam Matthews (2012) "Psychological factors associated with support for suicide bombing in the Muslim diaspora." *Political Psychology* 33, no. 6: 791–809.
Von Behr, Ines, Anais Reding, Charlie Edwards, and Luke Gribbon (2013) *Radicalisation in the Digital Era: The Use of Internet in 15 Cases of Terrorism and Extremism*. Santa Monica, CA: RAND Corporation. www.rand.org/pubs/research_reports/RR453.html.
Warner, Benjamin R. (2010) "Segmenting the electorate: The effects of exposure to political extremism online." *Communication Studies* 61, no. 4: 430–444.
Webber, David, Maxim Babush, Noa Schori-Eyal, Anna Vazeou-Niewenhuis, Malkanthi Hettiarachchi, Jocelyn Bélanger, Manuel Moyano, Humberto Trujillo, Rohan Gunaratna, Arie Kruglanski, and Michele Gelfand (2018a) "The road to extremism: Field and experimental evidence that significance loss-induced need for closure fosters radicalization." *Journal of Personality and Social Psychology* 114, no. 2: 270–285.
Webber, David, Marina Chernikova, Arie Kruglanski, Michele Gelfand, Malkanthi Hettiarachchi, Rohan Gunaratna, Marc Andre Lafreniere, and Jocelyn Bélanger (2018b) "Deradicalizing detained terrorists." *Political Psychology* 39, no. 3: 539–556.
Webber, David, Kristen Klein, Arie Kruglanski, Ambra Brizi, and Ariel Merari (2017) "Divergent paths to martyrdom and significance among suicide attackers." *Terrorism and Political Violence* 29, no. 5: 852–874.
Webber, David, and Arie Kruglanski (2016) "Psychological factors in radicalization: A '3 N' approach." In Freilich, Joshua D. and Gray LaFree (eds) *The Handbook of the Criminology of Terrorism*. Hoboken, NY: John Wiley & Sons, 33–46.
Webster, Donna, and Arie Kruglanski (1994) "Individual differences in need for cognitive closure." *Journal of Personality and Social Psychology* 67, no. 6: 1049–1062.
Wojcieszak, Magdalena (2009) "'Carrying online participation offline'—mobilization by radical online groups and politically dissimilar offline ties." *Journal of Communication* 59, no. 3: 564–586.

Wojcieszak, Magdalena (2010) "'Don't talk to me': Effects of ideologically homogeneous online groups and politically dissimilar offline ties on extremism." *New Media & Society* 12, no. 4: 637–655.
Zhang, Ying, Ayelet Fishbach, and Arie Kruglanski (2007) "The dilution model: How additional goals undermine the perceived instrumentality of a shared path." *Journal of Personality and Social Psychology* 92, no. 3: 389–401.
Zhou, Zunyou (2017) "Chinese strategy for deradicalisation." *Terrorism and Political Violence*: 1–22.

6

GENDER, DERADICALISATION AND DISENGAGEMENT

Jennifer Philippa Eggert

The ways in which gender and terrorism interrelate and intersect have long been overlooked and underestimated (Cunningham, 2003; Gentry and Sjoberg, 2015; Henshaw, 2016). Whilst in the last 20 years in particular, a substantial body of literature on women and terrorism in various parts of the world has developed, comprehensive studies that focus on gender – rather than women – remain rare (Kimmel, 2018). The topic of gender, terrorism and deradicalisation has gained new interest in large parts of the world since the emergence of the so-called 'Islamic State' (IS) and the subsequent fall of its self-proclaimed 'Caliphate'. The unprecedented numbers of women and girls who joined IS in Syria, Iraq and later Libya (Eggert, 2015) caught the attention of many, who were interested in finding out more about women's motivations to join violent and/or extremist political organisations, the reasons why organisations decide to include women and the wider communal and societal context in which these processes take place. However, the focus often remained on women and terrorism, rather than extending to a wider focus on the role gender plays more generally in terrorism.

To a certain extent, this new interest in the intersection of gender and terrorism was mirrored by an increased interest in the related issue of gender and deradicalisation and disengagement. The question of what role gender plays in deradicalisation and disengagement is of interest to academics – as the topic remains a relatively blind spot in academic literature on (de)radicalisation and (dis)engagement – and to practitioners and policy-makers, who are faced with the challenge of developing and implementing effective deradicalisation and disengagement programmes.

Considering the role of gender in deradicalisation and disengagement is important for two reasons. Firstly, on a practical level, it allows us to develop deradicalisation and disengagement strategies that address the situation of both male and female (former) members of terrorist groups who are willing to exit (or already have exited) the movement. In recent months, much of the attention of academics, practitioners and policy-makers working on deradicalisation and disengagement has been focused on the issue of IS returnees. Indeed, with the relative defeat of IS and the end of the IS 'Caliphate' in Syria and Iraq, the number of returnees is expected to increase (Barrett, 2017) – which poses a considerable challenge to the states and communities in Northern Africa, the Middle

East, Western Europe and beyond, where many former IS members are expected to either return or move to the next.

A significant number of these returnees are women (Brannen, 2017), who often have different practical needs than men. In order to be able to adequately prosecute, rehabilitate and reintegrate these women, gender-sensitive approaches to deradicalisation and disengagement are crucial.

Whilst much of the recent discussion on gender, deradicalisation and disengagement in Europe, the US, the Middle East and parts of Asia has focused on IS, the role of gender in deradicalisation and disengagement strategies necessitates our attention beyond this very mediated organisation. The vast majority of non-state violent political organisations worldwide have female members (Cunningham, 2003; Eager, 2008; Henshaw, 2016). This includes right-wing extremist organisations in Europe and Northern America, the radical Hindutva movement in India, violent left-wing groups in Latin America as well as violent Islamist organisations in various parts of the world – to name just a few of the more prominent examples (Cunningham, 2003; Eager, 2008; Henshaw, 2016). Female participation in violent and/or extremist political organisations is thus truly a global phenomenon that transcends ideological and geographical boundaries (Eggert, 2015).

The second reason why we cannot afford not to integrate gender into deradicalisation and disengagement approaches is that, on an ideological level, gender is at the heart of most terrorist movements. Gender norms constitute an essential factor of the overall ideology of most terrorist organisations (Weilnböck, 2014a, 2014b). Most terrorist groups tend to have very specific expectations of what a man and a woman are supposed to do and be like. There is a very specific link between gender norms and forms of engagement with terrorist organisations. Terrorist groups use gender tactically and strategically, in order to achieve their aims and gain advantages in the struggle for their cause (Bayard de Volo, 2018). It would thus be negligent not to consider gender in strategies aimed at countering radicalisation and engagement in the work with any (former) member of terrorist organisations – male or female (Weilnböck, 2014a, 2014b).

This chapter provides an overview of existing work on gender, deradicalisation and disengagement. In the first section following this introduction, it briefly sketches out existing work on gender and terrorism. Whilst this section is not aimed at providing a detailed discussion of gender and terrorism, it is hoped that it will give the uninitiated reader some context to appreciate why adopting a gender-sensitive approach to deradicalisation and disengagement is crucial. The final section of this chapter identifies common pitfalls in this area and how these might be avoided, overcome or – at the very least – mitigated.

Gender, women and terrorism

In the summer of 2014, the territorial gains of the terrorist group IS in Syria and Iraq highlighted that the group was not simply a terrorist organisation any more but that it was increasingly developing state-like features (Tziarras, 2017). Realising that in order to form a state, the inclusion of women was required, IS leader Abu Bakr Al-Baghdadi started calling on female supporters to join the group's self-proclaimed caliphate in Syria and Iraq (Eggert, 2015). The group started a carefully tailored and professionally executed online campaign targeting both men and women in highly gendered ways (Pearson, 2016, 2017). This targeted campaign proved extremely effective. Unlike other previous hotspots of global terrorism (such as Afghanistan or Chechnya), Syria was much more easily accessible – and the gruesome war affecting millions of Syrian and Iraqi civilians provided plenty of images that

IS effectively incorporated into their propaganda efforts. As a result, thousands of supporters (both male and female) followed Al-Baghdadi's call and joined IS-controlled territory.

The unprecedented numbers of women joining IS (many of whom came from the West) garnered an extraordinary amount of attention by the media, policy-makers and the wider public. As a result, several academic studies of women, gender and IS were published (Eggert, 2015; Hoyle et al., 2015; Jacoby, 2015; Pearson, 2016, 2017; Peresin, 2015; Peresin and Cervone, 2015; Saltman and Smith, 2015). This latest wave of publications on gender and terrorism built upon a (relatively recent) tradition of literature on women, gender and terrorism, which mostly focused on the roles and experiences of women – rather than gender, more broadly speaking. The earliest academic studies of women, gender and terrorism date as far back as the 1980s (Weinberg and Eubank, 1987). However, in terrorism studies, the topic remained relatively neglected until the terrorist attacks in the US on 11 September 2001. In the years following 9/11, a handful of pioneering studies on gender and terrorism were published (Bloom, 2011; Cunningham, 2003, 2007, 2008, 2009, 2010; Dalton and Asal, 2011; Davis, 2013, 2017; Dearing, 2010; Eager, 2008; Ness, 2008; Schweitzer, 2006; Speckhard, 2008, 2009). A separate branch of the literature explores women's participation in right-wing terrorist movements in Northern America and Western Europe, with limited overlap with the broader terrorism literature (see, for example, Blee and Deutsch, 2012). More literature is available by authors who frame women's participation as political violence rather than terrorism. These studies tend to be situated in conflict, war or area studies and often remain relatively separated from the terrorism studies literature – even if both study the same conflicts, movements and organisations.

Most authors working from a terrorism studies perspective who focus on gender tend to examine the roles of women only. Very few authors also take a broader approach to the topic, by including the roles of both men and women as well as dominant gender norms and expectations. Examples include Gentry and Sjoberg (2015), who went beyond analysing why women joined and what their experiences were within the group. Instead, they highlighted how gender was used strategically by the groups and how expectations of what men and women are and should be like are interlinked.

One recurrent theme in much of the literature on gender and terrorism is that gendered stereotypes continue to dominate our perspective on men's and women's roles in terrorist organisations: Whilst women tend to be viewed as victims of terrorism and extremism or actors for peaceful change, men are often presented as perpetrators and supporters of violence. The fact that both men and women are subjected to violence, perpetrate and aim to counter it often remains overlooked.

Similar biases can be found when it comes to analyses of the reasons why individuals decide to join terrorist organisations. Whilst some of the most recent research has found that, overall, men and women join for largely the same reasons (even if their specific experiences are gendered, i.e. affected by their experience of being a man or a woman) (Eggert, 2015), some of the literature continues to describe gender-specific motivations for joining terrorist organisations. One of these debates focuses on the question of coercion vs. free will, or more specifically whether or not men and women decide to join terrorist organisations or whether they are made to do so. Whilst assumptions that women are more frequently coerced into joining persist, some scholars stress that more nuanced perspectives on the topic are required (Henshaw, 2016). In fact, empirical studies point out that most women join out of their free will, which implies that assumptions to the contrary may be based on the women's gender rather than substantial research findings (Henshaw, 2016).

Another dominant assumption is that women join for personal and men for political reasons. This stereotype is reflected in wide parts of the media coverage on terrorism. It also can be found in some of the academic literature on the topic (see, for example, Bloom, 2011). In this context, men's involvement in terrorism is often explained by political grievances or ideological convictions, whereas women's participation tends to be looked at through personal experiences, such as sexual violence, the loss of a loved one, lack of perspective in a male-dominated society and so on. One pertinent example in this case is Mia Bloom's book *Bombshell*, in which all of the four factors for women's participation she identifies are situated on the personal level (Bloom, 2011). Henshaw (2016) has highlighted how problematic such an approach is, as the empirical evidence often points to the importance of both personal and political factors in the decision-making of both men and women. Rather than actual gender-specific differences it is thus often our biases that lead us to assuming there are substantial differences in why men and women engage in terrorism.

Publications that take into account the experiences of men and the role of masculinities remain the exception in their analyses of gender and terrorism. A notable example in this context is the work of Maleeha Aslam (2012) and Michael Kimmel (2018). Aslam and Kimmel argue that men who are unable to live up to the ideals of hegemonic masculinity (and fulfil societal expectations of what a man should be like and achieve) can often be attracted by terrorist organisations, which offer them a way to gain status and redeem their identity as a 'strong man'. Rather than concentrating solely on the individual and the group they join (and perpetuating the stereotype of 'the problematic male'), these approaches advocate instead also taking wider societal norms into account (Ezekilov, 2017; Pearson, 2018). Thus, these studies highlight the link between gender norms upheld by the individual, wider society and the organisation:

> So this is how it works: These young men feel entitled to a sense of belonging and community, of holding unchallenged moral authority over women and children, and of feeling that they count in the world and that their lives matter. Experiencing threats to the lives they feel they deserve leads these young men to feel ashamed and humiliated. And it is this aggrieved entitlement – entitlement thwarted and frustrated – that leads some men to search for a way to redeem themselves as men, to restore and retrieve that sense of manhood that has been lost. Joining up is a form of masculine compensation, an alternate route to proving manhood.
>
> *(Kimmel, 2018)*

Deradicalisation and disengagement approaches that do not consider the link between these gender norms, men's humiliation and their joining of terrorist organisations arguably do not see the full picture.

Gender, deradicalisation and disengagement

If the literature on gender, terrorism and extremism is limited, this is even more so the case when it comes to studies on gender, deradicalisation and disengagement. Most mainstream publications on deradicalisation and disengagement fail to take into account gender altogether (see, for example, Bjorgo and Horgan, 2009; El-Said, 2015; El-Said and Harrigan, 2011; Horgan, 2009; Marsden, 2017). The issue of gender and preventing/countering violent extremism (P/CVE) has received more attention, albeit also at a relatively low level. To date, only a handful of academic studies on gender and P/CVE have been published (including Brown, 2013; Giscard d'Estaing, 2017; Winterbotham and Pearson, 2016). The number of more practice-oriented reports and studies by think tanks, international organisations and non-governmental organisations on gender and P/CVE is slightly higher (see, for example, for more recently published studies and reports: Centre for Human Rights and Global Justice, 2011; Chowdhury Fink et al., 2013, 2016; Cook, 2017; Couture, 2014; Dufour-Genneson and Alam, 2014; Eggert, 2018; GCTF n.d.; Hedayah, 2015; LSE Centre for Women, Peace and Security, 2017; Permanent Mission of the United Arab Emirates to the United Nations and Georgetown University, 2014; Saltman and Smith, 2015; UN Women, 2016). Whilst most of these focus on gender and P/CVE rather than gender and deradicalisation and disengagement, some of these studies can be of use in informing deradicalisation and disengagement work as well, as there often is a certain degree of overlap of issues that emerge in both P/CVE and deradicalisation and disengagement strategies. Similarly, some of the expertise and experience of academics and practitioners with a background in social work, development or women, peace and security can be useful while working on developing strategies and tools on how to incorporate gender into deradicalisation and disengagement approaches. It will hardly ever be possible to adopt these one by one; however, it would be a wasted opportunity to discard existing approaches in neighbouring disciplines and areas of work altogether.

Another issue is the lack of empirical evidence for what works and what does not in gendered approaches to deradicalisation and disengagement. The academic literature on the topic is useful in this context; however, it is extremely limited in scope and breadth. As to the studies published by think tanks, international organisations and non-governmental organisations, many of these are position papers or summaries of meetings rather than empirically grounded analyses. Whilst they can be helpful for practitioners and policy-makers, they only provide anecdotal evidence of lessons learned and best practice. In order to fully understand what role gender plays in deradicalisation and disengagement processes, we need more empirical analyses focusing on this topic.

Adopting gendered approaches to deradicalisation and disengagement is important (1) in order to take into account the needs of women willing to leave violent and/or extremist movements, and (2) in order to effectively counter the ideologies of violent and/or extremist organisations, which are often based on very specific gender norms and ideals.

Firstly, despite the fact that the vast majority of violent and/or extremist political organisations worldwide include female members (Cunningham, 2003; Eager, 2008; Henshaw, 2016), very little support is available for women who want to leave violent and/or extremist organisations – or for women who have already done so. Similar to the lack of academic literature on the topic, there are very few deradicalisation and disengagement programmes that take into account gender. This is problematic because it means that the specific needs of women wanting to leave violent and/or extremist political organisations are overlooked (Radvan and Altmeyer, 2014). This is a problem especially (but by no means exclusively) in organisations that adhere to a gender-conservative ideology. For example, in groups with strict division of labour along gendered lines, women can lack the professional training and experience that would allow them to be independent and make their own living away from the movement. This is of particular relevance if the partner of the woman remains a member of the movement, and thus breaking away from the movement would also mean leaving the breadwinner of the couple and/or family. If children are involved (and in many gender-conservative organisations such as right-wing extremist or Islamist groups, organisational ideology tends to encourage families to have many children), this can be even more challenging (Expert Centre on Gender and Right-Wing Extremism, 2014). Often, the respective movement considers these children as part (even property) of either the husband or the movement the family is a part of. On the other hand, the communities and societies the women (who consider leaving a violent and/or extremist political movement) hail from often regard former members of violent and/or extremist organisations with disdain (Radvan and Altmeyer, 2014). This is particularly the case if the women have been actively involved in perpetrating violence themselves. Evidence from disarmament, demobilisation and reintegration programmes illustrates that reintegration is often particularly challenging for women (UN, 2006). Even in cases where the women joined the organisation against their will (as was the case with the women abducted by Boko Haram in North Western Africa), communities often reject former female members of violent organisations and their children after their return (Ford, 2016). In some cases, this has led the women to return to their former abductors and rejoin the organisation, which would at the very least provide them with the very basics necessary for survival – and the most basic amount of dignity their previous home communities would deny them (Ford, 2016). Considering that perceived marginalisation, isolation and discrimination constitute some of the key factors facilitating and driving radicalisation and involvement in (violent) extremist organisations of both men and women (Eager, 2008; Henshaw, 2016; Saltman and Smith, 2015), it would be negligent to disregard this issue.

However, the specific needs of women wanting to leave violent and/or extremist political organisations are only one reason why it is crucial to incorporate gender into deradicalisation and disengagement approaches. Another factor is the often highly gendered nature of many (violent) extremists' recruitment pathways and strategies, as well as the narratives, ideologies and hierarchies they adhere to once within the group. Gender norms and expectations are often at the heart of violent and/or extremist political organisations, with specific roles pre-defined for both men and women within the movement (Expert Center on Gender and Right-Wing Extremism, 2014; Radvan and Altmeyer, 2014; Weilnböck, 2014a, 2014b; Task Force on Gendered Right-Wing Extremism Prevention, 2016). These gender norms are often used to distinguish the ingroup (which is part of the violent and/or extremist movement) from the outgroup (which is made up of the majority of society and/or community). In many cases, these gender norms are based on harmful concepts of masculinity and femininity, celebrating 'masculine' violence and 'feminine' subordination (Expert Centre on Gender and Right-Wing Extremism, 2014; Radvan and Altmeyer, 2014; Weilnböck, 2014a, 2014b; Task Force on Gendered Right-Wing Extremism Prevention, 2016). It is thus important to take dominant gender norms and expectations into account in deradicalisation and disengagement approaches, in order to gain access to (formerly) radicalised and/or violent individuals, better support them during deradicalisation and disengagement processes and help them in their critical engagement with previously held beliefs. Encouraging a critical engagement with the role harmful masculinities and femininities play both prior to joining and within many violent and/or extremist organisations is particularly important in *deradicalisation* efforts, which are aimed at a disassociation from extremist beliefs. Considering how central gender in general and harmful masculinities and femininities in particular are to many violent and/or extremist movements (and how critical they can be during the radicalisation and engagement process, as outlined in the previous section), it is hard to conceive how extremist ideologies can be countered without also addressing gender.

Common pitfalls and ways to avoid them

Despite the current lack of comprehensive empirical studies on gender, deradicalisation and disengagement, it is possible to identify a number of potential pitfalls and ways to avoid them. Some of these are based on the very limited academic literature on the topic, whilst others rely on anecdotal evidence from practitioners working on gender, deradicalisation and disengagement and/or experts focusing on gender in related fields – such as development, social work or peace and security.

Instead of simplifying matters – adopt comprehensive approaches

One common pitfall in gender, deradicalisation and disengagement strategies is the tendency to not base them on a truly comprehensive approach. This includes several aspects: (1) a tendency towards simplifying gendered victim/perpetrator binaries; (2) the tendency to conflate women with gender and a lack of focus on how masculinities and femininities are constructed; (3) the failure to adopt an intersectional approach; (4) single-level approaches; and (5) an instrumentalisation of gender.

Firstly, in debates on terrorism, extremism and ways of countering them, many often focus on women as victims of terrorism and/or actors for peaceful change (whilst men are seen as perpetrators). However, such binary approaches to the role of gender in terrorism are not rooted in empirical analyses of the topic (Cunningham, 2003; Eager, 2008; Henshaw, 2016). Instead, it is important to acknowledge that both men and women are victims of terrorism, both men and women support and perpetrate terrorism, and both men and women help prevent and counter terrorism. Existing research suggests that men and women largely get involved in terrorism for very similar reasons (Eggert, 2015). However, due to their alleged peaceful and non-violent nature, in many cases, female members of violent extremist movements are less often arrested and convicted than men, which is likely one reason for women's lower numbers in exit programmes in Europe (Alison, 2009; Radvan and Altmeyer, 2014; Weilnböck, 2014a, 2014b). In a similar vein, numerous media reports presented female IS members as 'naïve' or 'brainwashed', unlike their male counterparts (Radvan and Altmeyer, 2014; Eggert, 2015). Deradicalisation and disengagement programmes that aim at effectively reaching and engaging both men and women must thus take into account that victimhood and perpetration are more complex than widespread gender stereotypes may suggest.

Secondly, it is important to bear in mind that the concept of gender goes beyond a focus on or an engagement with women. Whilst much of the academic literature and several programmes implemented in the area focus on women, more recent research and practice tend to look at gender more broadly, and take into account masculinities, femininities, relations between men and women, LGBTIQA issues, homo- and transphobia. When working on deradicalisation and disengagement, it is of particular importance to focus on the construction of masculinities and femininities, as gender ideals are at the very heart of many violent and/or extremist political organisations, as outlined above. Encouraging an active, critical engagement with these gender norms, therefore, is often critical during deradicalisation and disengagement processes.

Thirdly, in order to implement effective deradicalisation and disengagement approaches, it is important to not simply focus on gender but instead adopt an intersectional approach. In other words, it is essential to also take into account other identifiers such as class, race, ethnicity, age, citizenship, faith/religion (or lack thereof), sexuality and the roles these play during processes of deradicalisation and disengagement. For example, whilst it is likely that the needs and experiences of a 25-year-old female right-wing extremist will differ from those of a 25-year-old male right-wing extremist in some ways, they might differ in others from those of a 70-year-old female right-wing extremist – because of the specific ways in which age, gender and ideological orientation intersect in this case.

Fourthly, just as radicalisation and engagement in terrorism and extremism are processes in which individual, organisational, communal and societal factors are at play (Horgan, 2009), the same is true for deradicalisation and disengagement processes. Comprehensive deradicalisation and disengagement processes must thus take into account all of these different levels and address them appropriately.

Finally, the instrumentalisation of gender should be avoided. Several studies of P/CVE identify the instrumentalisation of gender and engagement with women and/or communities as one of the key factors contributing to an alienation of members of already marginalised societal groups (Brown, 2013; Cook, 2017; Giscard d'Estaing, 2017; Winterbotham and Pearson, 2016; Eggert, 2018). This is problematic, because it is unethical, but also because perceived marginalisation, isolation and discrimination are amongst the driving and facilitating factors of radicalisation for both men and women, as outlined above. During processes of deradicalisation and disengagement, such experiences thus have the potential of reinforcing previously held extremist views. Problematic single-issue approaches that should be avoided include strategies focusing on gender only for the purpose of deradicalisation and disengagement, without addressing some of the wider gender-related issues people are facing. For example, people tend to be much less receptive to analyses of harmful masculinities in the violent extremist movements they used to be a part of if the very same gender concepts are perpetuated within wider society (or even within the organisation which works on deradicalising and disengaging this group of people), without being addressed with the same vehemence (Huckerby, 2011). Many communities also tend to be less open to engagement with agencies and organisations that only seem to be interested in gender and/or women's rights when it seems to serve their agenda.

Instead of perpetuating problematic gender stereotypes – avoid them

A second common pitfall in attempts to integrate gender into deradicalisation and disengagement approaches is the tendency to perpetuate problematic gender stereotypes. This problem is often linked to underlying assumptions about women's and men's roles and experiences in violent and/or extremist political movements, as well as in society more broadly.

Women are often perceived to be more prone to non-violent conflict resolution and peaceful change, while men are often presented as perpetrators of violence (Gentry and Sjoberg, 2015). As a result, women's involvement in social and political processes is often seen as 'the' solution to effective peace-building or, indeed, deradicalisation and disengagement. Whilst it is certainly advisable to adopt comprehensive approaches to deradicalisation and disengagement and involve a broad variety of different societal stakeholders (including women), the belief that women are essentially and inherently peace-loving (while men are the opposite) is misleading. Indeed, this belief is contradicted on an empirical level by the many women who play active roles in supporting and perpetrating extremist violence.

Unfortunately, some projects focusing on gender, deradicalisation and disengagement (as well as P/CVE more generally) rely on simplifying, one-sided gender norms and expectations (Task Force on Gendered Right-Wing Extremism Prevention, 2016). As a result, they reinforce and perpetuate these gender stereotypes rather than challenging and deconstructing them. One notorious example in this context are projects focusing on the work with women in their capacity as mothers. When these projects work with mothers only (without also engaging fathers and/or working with women in other capacities), they risk reproducing problematic masculinities and femininities rather than questioning them. Moreover, these projects are often based on the assumption that mothers and/or families can actually prevent and/or counter radicalisation and extremism. Thus, these approaches run the risk of blaming families in general and mothers in particular, if specific counter-extremism and deradicalisation efforts prove to be unsuccessful (Eggert, 2017).

This is not to say that gendered approaches to deradicalisation and disengagement should disregard societal and communal realities altogether and implement the latest developments in gender theory, regardless of the context on the ground. Of course, from a practitioner's view, it will be important to be realistic of what can be achieved in a given context and to take a step-by-step approach that takes into account socio-cultural sensitivities. Nevertheless, it is important to bear in mind potential gender-related risks when planning and implementing gendered strategies to deradicalisation and disengagement, as part of a 'do no harm' approach.

Instead of deepening existing rifts – bridge research, practice, policy-makers and communities

Experience from P/CVE highlights the often considerable divide between researchers, practitioners, policy-makers and communities (Eggert, 2018). Policy-making and practitioners' work are not always informed by research; and the mistrust of communities towards both practitioners and policy-makers (and in some cases even towards researchers) can be deep (Eggert, 2018). From a deradicalisation and disengagement perspective, this is highly problematic. The solution to the divide between researchers on the one hand and practitioners and policy-makers on the other lies in promoting exchange between researchers, policy-makers and practitioners. Existing mistrust from communities is more challenging to tackle. Yet, it is particularly important to do so, for a number of reasons. Firstly, strategic considerations apart, it is unethical to marginalise and alienate communities. Secondly, perceived marginalisation and thinking in black-and-white schemes are an integral part of many radicalisation processes (Alison, 2009; Eager, 2008; Saltman and Smith, 2015) and should thus be addressed (rather than perpetuated) by deradicalisation and disengagement approaches. The alienation of communities is particularly problematic when it comes to communities that already feel marginalised in society, such as many Muslim communities in Western European societies (Brown, 2013; Winterbotham and Pearson, 2016). Finally, engaging in deradicalisation and disengagement is linked to considerable risks for the individual. Trust in the individuals and organisations supporting, facilitating and accompanying deradicalisation and disengagement processes is thus essential. This is why it is in the interest of practitioners involved in deradicalisation and disengagement processes to present themselves as (and indeed, be!) credible and reliable partners, who bridge existing rifts and avoid creating additional ones.

As far as gendered approaches are concerned, avoiding an instrumentalisation of gender is thus crucial. Practitioners working on P/CVE highlight the need to include communities instead, and even more so the need to let communities lead (Eggert, 2018; Expert Centre on Gender and Right-Wing Extremism, 2014; Radvan and Altmeyer, 2014; Task Force on Gendered Right-Wing Extremism Prevention, 2016; Weilnböck, 2014a, 2014b). In the context of gendered approaches to deradicalisation and disengagement, this would, for example, mean that the personal background of practitioners involved in deradicalisation and disengagement processes is to be taken into account, as it could be of relevance in their work. This could include their gender, previous engagement and reputation (or lack thereof) with the respective organisation, movement or community, in addition to other identifiers such as ethnicity, race, age and faith/religion (or lack thereof).

Instead of focusing on short-term – think one step ahead

Lastly, when incorporating gender into deradicalisation and disengagement strategies, it is important to plan for the long term rather than focusing on short-term solutions only. As Weilnböck points out, '(l)eaving attitudes and life styles of violent extremism and group-orientated hatred is a very complicated long-term process of personal change' (Weilnböck, 2014a; see also Bjorgo and Horgan, 2009; Horgan, 2009; Marsden, 2017). As part of a full deradicalisation and disengagement process, change must take place on both an ideological as well as a physical level (Marsden, 2017). (Former) extremists willing to deradicalise and disengage must be supported in distancing themselves both from extremist ideology as well as behaviour – two processes that do not always occur in parallel to each other (Marsden, 2017). It is thus important to develop long-term strategies that provide (former) extremists with viable and sustainable solutions, which take into account the complexity of the process of leaving and distancing oneself from (violent) extremist movements and their ideology. In this context, it is essential to not just see deradicalisation and disengagement as a process that happens on an individual level. Rather, it is important to consider that (former) extremists are also members of groups, communities and a society and that their association with these various societal groups can, and often does, affect the deradicalisation and disengagement process.

As in all deradicalisation and disengagement processes, this must also be borne in mind when adopting gendered approaches to deradicalisation and disengagement. Bearing in mind both the long and short term in gender-sensitive deradicalisation and disengagement processes, could, for example, involve considering how the different stages of deradicalisation and disengagement processes affect men and women. One group that often requires additional support are women with dependent children. If they lack the required opportunities, resources and support networks to cover their and their children's financial (and emotional) needs, they might be able to leave a violent and/or extremist organisation in the short term, but in the long term, maintaining an independent lifestyle away from previous networks that remain part of the movement may prove to be challenging.

Conclusion

Whilst there has been an increased interest in the roles and experiences of women in terrorism in recent years, the role of gender in terrorist movements more broadly often continues to be overlooked. Similarly, in the fight against terrorism, researchers, practitioners and policy-makers are only slowly – but increasingly – becoming aware of the need to take gender into account. Often, this interest manifests inself in a focus on women, which is a first step, but must be followed by more comprehensive approaches that consider gender more broadly. Most of the (very limited) literature which is available on the topic focuses on gender and P/CVE. Much fewer studies have been published on gender and deradicalisation and disengagement. Specifically, very little research and empirical evidence exists on what works and what does not in deradicalisation and disengagement programmes that take gender into account. To a certain extent, insights can be gained from neighbouring areas of work, such as social work, development and – of course – P/CVE. In the mid and long term, however, more (empirical) research on gender and deradicalisation and disengagement is needed.

Gendered approaches to deradicalisation and disengagement are needed for two reasons. Firstly, men and women who are undergoing processes of deradicalisation and disengagement can have gender-specific needs and experiences. Without the required knowledge and experience in this area, it is impossible to provide the gender-specific assistance and support that are often required. Considering the fact that both men and women are active members of the vast majority of terrorist organisations worldwide, the issue is likely to remain of relevance in the foreseeable future. Secondly, harmful gender norms and ideals (often based on 'male violence' and 'female submission') are an essential part of the ideology of many terrorist organisations, and often play a crucial role in the radicalisation and engagement process, especially – but not exclusively – in right-wing extremist and Islamist groups. Challenging these norms is thus an integral part of deradicalisation and disengagement processes.

When integrating gender into deradicalisation and disengagement processes, it is crucial to take a comprehensive approach to the topic (rather than oversimplifying matters), to avoid problematic gender stereotypes (rather than perpetuating them), to focus on bridging research, practice, policy-makers and communities (rather than deepening existing divides) and to see deradicalisation and disengagement as a process (rather than focus on short-term solutions and outcomes only). There are no easy, one-kind-fits-all solutions to including gender in deradicalisation and disengagement processes. Just as radicalisation and involvement in terrorism are complex, complicated and often very long processes, so too are deradicalisation and disengagement. However, it is the well-being and security of our communities and societies that are at stake. Not taking into account all the aspects that play a role in deradicalisation and disengagement – including gender – is thus simply not an option.

References

Alison, Miranda (2009) *Women and Political Violence: Female Combatants in Ethno-National Conflict*. London: Routledge.

Aslam, Maleeha (2012) *Gender-Based Explosions: The Nexus Between Muslim Masculinities, Jihadist Islamism and Terrorism*. Tokyo: United Nations University Press.

Barrett, Richard (2017) *Beyond the Caliphate: Foreign Fighters and the Threat of Returnees*. The Soufan Center. http://thesoufancenter.org/research/beyond-caliphate/.

Bayard de Volo, Lorraine (2018) *Women and the Cuban Insurrection: How Gender Shaped Castro's Victory*. Cambridge, UK: Cambridge University Press.

Bjorgo, Tore, and Horgan, John (2009) *Leaving Terrorism Behind: Individual and Collective Disengagement*. London: Routledge.

Blee, Kathleen, and Deutsch, Sandra (2012) *Women of the Right: Comparisons and Interplay Across Borders*. University Park, PA: Pennsylvania State University Press.

Bloom, Mia (2011) *Bombshell: Women and Terrorism*. Philadelphia, PA: University of Pennsylvania Press.

Brannen, Kate (2017) "How Should We Deal with ISIS Women and Children Foreign Fighters Returning Home?" *Newsweek*. 25 October 2017. www.newsweek.com/how-should-we-deal-isis-women-and-children-foreign-fighters-returning-home–692861.

Brown, Katherine E. (2013) "Gender and Counter-Radicalisation: Women and Emerging Counter-Terror Measures." In Margaret L. Satterthwaite, and Jayne Huckerby (eds) *Gender, National Security, and Counter-Terrorism: Human Rights Perspectives* (pp. 36–59). London: Routledge.

Center for Human Rights and Global Justice (2011) *A Decade Lost: Locating Gender in U.S. Counter-Terrorism*. New York: NYU School of Law. http://chrgj.org/documents/a-decade-lost-locating-gender-in-u-s-counter-terrorism/.

Chowdhury Fink, Naureen, Barakat, Rafia, and Shetret, Liat (2013) "The Roles of Women in Terrorism, Conflict, and Violent Extremism: Lessons for the United Nations and International Actors." *Policy Brief.* Center on Global Counterterrorism Cooperation, April 2013. www.globalcenter.org/wp-content/uploads/2013/04/NCF_RB_LS_policybrief_1320.pdf.

Chowdhury Fink, Naureen, Zeiger, Sara, and Bhulai, Sara (2016) "A Man's World? Exploring the Roles of Women in Countering Terrorism and Violent Extremism." *Special Report.* April. www.globalcenter.org/publications/a-mans-world-exploring-the-roles-of-women-in-countering-terrorism-and-violent-extremism/.

Cook, Joana (2017) "Avoiding the Pitfalls of Prevent." *Occasional Paper.* Washington, DC: Georgetown Institute for Women, Peace and Security.

Couture, Krista London (2014) "A Gendered Approach to Countering Extremism: Lessons Learned from Women in Peacebuilding and Conflict Prevention Applied Successfully in Bangladesh and Morocco." Policy Paper, Brookings. July 2014. www.brookings.edu/research/a-gendered-approach-to-countering-violent-extremism-lessons-learned-from-women-in-peacebuilding-and-conflict-prevention-applied-successfully-in-bangladesh-and-morocco/.

Cunningham, Karla (2003) "Cross-Regional Trends in Female Terrorism." *Studies in Conflict and Terrorism*, 26, pp. 171–195.

Cunningham, Karla (2007) "Countering Female Terrorism." *Studies in Conflict and Terrorism*, 30, pp. 113–129.

Cunningham, Karla (2008) "The Evolving Participation of Muslim Women in Palestine, Chechnya, and the Global Jihadi Movement." In Cindy Ness (ed) *Female Terrorism and Militancy: Agency, Utility, and Organization* (pp. 84–99). London: Routledge.

Cunningham, Karla (2009) "Female Survival Calculations in Politically Violent Settings: How Political Violence and Terrorism Are Viewed as Pathways to Life." *Studies in Conflict and Terrorism*, 32, pp. 561–575.

Cunningham, Karla (2010) "Female Participation in the Iraqi Insurgency: Insights into Nationalist and Religious Warfare." In Robin M. Chandler, Lihua Wang, and Linda K. Fuller (eds) *Women, War, and Violence: Personal Perspectives and Global Activism* (pp. 205–218). Berlin: Springer.

Dalton, Angela, and Asal, Victor (2011) "Is It Ideology or Desperation: Why Do Organizations Deploy Women in Violent Terrorist Attacks?" *Studies in Conflict and Terrorism*, 34, pp. 802–819.

Davis, Jessica (2013) "Evolution of the Global Jihad: Female Suicide Bombers in Iraq." *Studies in Conflict and Terrorism*, 36, pp. 279–291.

Davis, Jessica (2017) *Women in Modern Terrorism: From Liberation Wars to Global Jihad and the Islamic State.* Lanham, MD: Rowman and Littlefield.

Dearing, Matthew (2010) "Like Red Tulips at Springtime: Understanding the Absence of Female Martyrs in Afghanistan." *Studies in Conflict and Terrorism*, 33, pp. 1079–1103.

Dufour-Genneson, Ségolène, and Alam, Mayesha (2014) "Women and Countering Violent Extremism." Georgetown Institute for Women, Peace and Security. *Special Report.* https://giwps.georgetown.edu/sites/giwps/files/I2A%20-%20Women%20and%20Countering%20Violent%20Extremism.pdf.

Eager, Page Whaley (2008) *From Freedom Fighters to Terrorists: Women and Political Violence.* Farnham: Ashgate.

Eggert, Jennifer Philippa (2015) "Women Fighters in the 'Islamic State' and Al-Qaeda in Iraq: A Comparative Analysis." *Journal of International Peace and Organization*, 90, pp. 363–380.

Eggert, Jennifer Philippa (2017) "Mothers, Bombs, and a Whole Lot of Gender Clichés." *Engenderings.* 29 June 2017. http://blogs.lse.ac.uk/gender/2017/06/29/mothers-bombs-and-a-whole-lot-of-gender-cliches/.

Eggert, Jennifer Philippa (2018) "The Roles of Women in Counter-Radicalisation and Disengagement (CRaD) Processes: Best Practices and Lessons Learned from Europe and the Arab World." *Special Report.* Berlin: Berghof Foundation. www.berghof-foundation.org/fileadmin/redaktion/Publications/Other_Resources/Berghof_Input_Paper_Women_Counterradicalisation.pdf.

El-Said, Hamed (2015) *New Approaches in Fighting Terrorism: Designing and Evaluating Counter Radicalisation and Deradicalisation Programs.* Basingstoke: Palgrave Macmillan.

El-Said, Hamed, and Harrigan, Jane (2011) "In Search of a Deradicalisation Strategy." In Jane Harrigan, and Hamed El-Said (eds) *Globalisation, Democratisation and Radicalisation in the Arab World* (pp. 237–271). Basingstoke: Palgrave Macmillan.

Expert Centre on Gender and Right-Wing Extremism (2014) "Overlooked and Underrated: Women in Right-Wing Extremist Groups in Germany: Theoretical Analysis and Practical Recommendations for

State and Civil Society." *Special Report*. www.amadeu-antonio-stiftung.de/w/files/pdfs/fachstelle/140407_overlooked-and-underrated.-german-women-in-right-wing-extremist-groups.pdf.

Ezekilov, Jossif (2017) "Gender 'Men-Streaming' CVE: Countering Violence Extremism by Addressing Masculinities Issues." *Reconsidering Development*, 5(1), pp. 2–7.

Ford, Liz (2016) "Women Freed from Boko Haram Rejected for Bringing 'Bad Blood' Back Home." *Guardian*. 16 February 2016. www.theguardian.com/global-development/2016/feb/16/women-freed-boko-haram-rejected-for-bringing-bad-blood-back-home-nigeria.

GCTC (Global Counterterrorism Forum) (n.d.). "Good Practices on Women and Countering Violent Extremism." *Special Report*. www.thegctf.org/Portals/1/Documents/Framework%20Documents/A/GCTF-Good-Practices-on-Women-and-CVE.pdf.

Gentry, Caron, and Sjoberg, Laura (2015) *Beyond Mothers, Monsters, Whores: Thinking About Women's Violence in Global Politics*. London: Zed Books.

Giscard d'Estaing, Sophie (2017) "Engaging Women in Countering Violent Extremism: Avoiding Instrumentalisation and Furthering Agency." *Gender and Development*, 25(1), pp. 103–118.

Hedayah (2015) "Policy and Program Recommendations: Role of Women in Countering Radicalisation and Violent Extremism." *Special Report*. www.hedayahcenter.org/Admin/Content/File-3032016135138.pdf.

Henshaw, Alex L. (2016) *Why Women Rebel: Understanding Women's Participation in Armed Rebel Groups*. London: Routledge.

Horgan, John (2009) *Walking Away from Terrorism. Accounts of Disengagement from Radical and Extremist Movements*. London: Routledge.

Hoyle, Carolyn, Bradford, Alexandra, and Frenett, Ross (2015) *Becoming Mulan? Female Western Migrants to ISIS*. London: Institute for Strategic Dialogue. www.isdglobal.org/wp-content/uploads/2016/02/ISDJ2969_Becoming_Mulan_01.15_WEB.pdf.

Huckerby, Jayne (2011) *A Decade Lost: Locating Gender in U.S. Counter-Terrorism*. New York: NYU School of Law.

Jacoby, Tami Amanda (2015) "Jihadi Brides at the Intersections of Contemporary Feminism." *New Political Science*, 37(4), pp. 525–542.

Kimmel, Michael (2018) *Healing from Hate: How Young Men Get Into – and out of – Violent Extremism*. Berkeley, CA: University of California Press.

LSE Centre for Women, Peace and Security (2017) "Preventing/Countering Violent Extremism and WPS: Concepts, Practices and Moving Forward." *Key Issues Report*. www.lse.ac.uk/women-peace-security/assets/documents/2017/LSE-WPS-PCVE-Key-Issues-Report.pdf.

Marsden, Sarah (2017) *Reintegrating Extremists: Deradicalisation and Desistance*. London: Palgrave Macmillan.

Ness, Cindy (2008) *Female Terrorism and Militancy: Agency, Utility, and Organization*. London: Routledge.

Pearson, Elizabeth (2016) "The Case of Roshonara Choudhry: Implications for Theory on Online Radicalization, ISIS Women, and the Gendered Jihad." *Policy and Internet*, 8(1), pp. 5–33.

Pearson, Elizabeth (2017) "Online as the New Frontline: Affect, Gender, and ISIS-Take-Down on Social Media." *Studies in Conflict and Terrorism*, 41(11), online first, pp. 1–25.

Pearson, Elizabeth (2018) "Why Men Fight and Women Don't: Masculinity and Extremist Violence." *Special Report*. Tony Blair Institute for Global Change, 13 September 2018. https://institute.global/insight/co-existence/why-men-fight-and-women-dont-masculinity-and-extremist-violence.

Peresin, Anna (2015) "Fatal Attraction: Western Muslimas and ISIS." *Perspectives on Terrorism*, 9(3). www.terrorismanalysts.com/pt/index.php/pot/article/view/427/html.

Peresin, Anna, and Cervone, Alberto (2015) "The Western Muhajirat of ISIS." *Studies in Conflict and Terrorism*, 38(7), pp. 495–509.

Permanent Mission of the United Arab Emirates to the United Nations and Georgetown University (2014) "Women and Countering Violent Extremism." *Summary Document and Analysis*. https://giwps.georgetown.edu/sites/giwps/files/Women%20and%20Countering%20Violent%20Extremism.pdf.

Radvan, Heike, and Altmeyer, Carmen (2014) "Overlooked and Underrated: Women in Right-Wing Extremist Groups in Germany." *Open Democracy*. 2 September 2014. www.opendemocracy.net/can-europe-make-it/heike-radvan-carmen-altmeyer/overlooked-and-underrated-women-in-rightwing-extremi/.

Saltman, Erin Marie, and Smith, Melanie (2015) *'Till Martyrdom Do Us Part'. Gender and the ISIS Phenomenon*. London: ICSR/Institute for Strategic Dialogue.

Schweitzer, Yoram (2006) *Female Suicide Bombers: Dying for Equality? Jaffee Center for Strategic Studies (JCSS) Memorandum* No. 84.

Speckhard, Anne (2008) "The Emergence of Female Suicide Terrorists." *Studies in Conflict and Terrorism*, 31, pp. 995–1023.

Speckhard, Anne (2009)"Female Suicide Bombers in Iraq." *Democracy & Security. Task Force on Gendered Right-Wing Extremism Prevention. 2016. A Critique of "Deradicalization"*. http://gender-und-rechtsextremismus.de/w/files/pdfs/fachstelle/deradicalization.pdf.

Task Force on Gendered Right-Wing Extremism Prevention (2016) "A Critique of 'Deradicalization.'" Berlin: Antonio Amadeu Foundation. https://www.amadeu-antonio-stiftung.de/wp-content/uploads/2019/01/deradicalization.pdf (last accessed 14 October 2019).

Tziarras, Zenonas (2017) "Islamic Caliphate: A Quasi-State, a Global Security Threat." *Journal of Applied Security Research*, 12, pp. 96–116.

UN (2006) "Women, Gender and DDR." http://unddr.org/uploads/documents/IDDRS%205.10%20Women,%20Gender%20and%20DDR.pdf.

UN Women (2016) "Women and Violent Radicalisation in Jordan." www.unwomen.org/en/digital-library/publications/2016/7/women-and-violent-radicalization-in-jordan.

Weilnböck, Harald (2014a) "Rehabilitating Perpetrators of Violent Extremism and Hate Crime: The Importance of Gender-Based Approaches and the Limits of Online Interventions." *Open Democracy*. 2 September. www.opendemocracy.net/can-europe-make-it/harald-weilnb%C3%B6ck/rehabilitating-perpetrators-of-violent-extremism-and-hate-crime.

Weilnböck, Harald (2014b) "Why Should Deradicalisation and Prevention Interventions Be Attentive to Gender Issues?" http://cultures-interactive.de/tl_files/publikationen/Fachartikel/2014_Weilnboeck_Why%20Should%20Deradicalisation%20and%20Prevention%20Intervention%20be%20Attentive%20to%20Gender%20Issues.pdf.

Weinberg, Leonard, and Eubank, William Lee (1987) "Italian Women Terrorists." *Terrorism*, 9, pp. 241–262.

Winterbotham, Emily, and Pearson, Elizabeth (2016) "Different Cities, Shared Stories: A Five-Country Study Challenging Assumptions Around Muslim Women and CVE Interventions." *RUSI Journal*, 161(5), pp. 54–65.

7
DERADICALIZATION OR DDR?

The challenges emerging from variations in forms of territorial control

Stig Jarle Hansen

The deradicalization and disengagement literature has to date tended to focus on disrupting the mechanisms that create loyalty to a small group and how to counter these (Horgan 2005; Sageman 2008; Bjørgo 2009; Noricks 2009; Barrelle 2015; Hwang 2015; Nesser 2015; Horgan, Altier, Shortland and Taylor 2017; Kruglanski, Jasko, Chernikova, Dugas and Webber 2017). In large part, these discussions have focused on situations where adherents were organized in small groups, rather than being a part of a wider and stronger organization. Moreover, these small groups were operating in a state with functioning institutions focusing on identifying, arresting and/or deradicalizing/disengaging those radicalized individuals (Hansen 2017). Al Qaeda's attack on 11 September 2001 had set the focus on militant religiously inspired organizations and loose networks; future religiously inspired radicalism was seen by some as leaderless networks, by others as clandestine networks implementing terror (Sageman 2004, 2008). The territorial expansion of the Islamic State in many ways contributed to a change in the focus on jihadist organizations as clandestine illegal networks, as the wider field re-discovered that jihadist organizations could establish forms of territorial control, extraction and discipline mechanisms that go together with such control (Lia 2015; Hansen 2019).

Yet, this was not a new situation. Territorial control had been pioneered by organizations such as Harakat Al Shabaab (Hansen 2013) and the Taliban (Giustozzi 2009); these developments had to a certain extent been neglected in the deradicalization literature.[1] Within the deradicalization and disengagement literature, right-wing groups are also generally seen as existing as public organizations facing a relatively hostile state in a society where the police in general can maintain law and order (Bjørgo 1995; Kaplan and Bjørgo 1998; Bjørgo and Carlsson 1999; Harris, Gringart and Drake 2018). Tentatively, they were seen as criminal clandestine networks, existing in hiding from state institutions that could prosecute, arrest and indeed deradicalize them (Goldwag 2012; Piazza 2015; Altier, Boyle, Shortland and Horgan 2017). However, as illustrated by Irina A. Chindea in this volume (see Chapter 24), Latin America clearly has right-wing groups de facto controlling territory and implementing violence as a tool of the state they exist in, sometimes supported by the state. Hof (2017) illustrates the possible instrumental use of right-wing groups in Western Europe, and the conflict in Ukraine has put the spotlight on far-right militias, such as the Azov Battalion, which exists as militias, fighting conventional battles, with considerable independence from the Ukrainian state, sometimes protected by elements within the latter.

The cases described above present variations in the fundamental relationship of the organization/network from which an individual is to be deradicalized, and their territorial control, subsequently presenting a fundamental problem for deradicalization and disengagement efforts. A clandestine network of violent right-wingers operating in a hostile state is an entirely different type of challenge than deradicalizing from a right-wing militia, for example, supported by a government, or a right-wing organization controlling territory. In the case of Syria, Iraq, Somalia, Yemen, Afghanistan, Nigeria, Ukraine and others, deradicalization and disengagement had to take place in a conflict, or at best, a post-conflict setting, at worst dealing with large enclaves where a radical organization controls and governs territory. When a radical organization controls territory it has an entirely different repertoire of tools to hinder defections and prevent deradicalization, including the effects of having potentially stronger organization and a new set of income-generating possibilities, and a greater ability to sanction against enemies in the territory they control.

This chapter takes Koehler's definition of radicalization as depluralization, presented in this book as a point of departure, and sees deradicalization as a process of individual repluralization of political concepts and values (e.g. justice, freedom, honour, violence, democracy) on the one hand and a decrease in urgency to act (violently) against a framed problem on the other. In this sense the chapter will focus on both a wider idea of deradicalization that aims to change both perceptions of the world and violent behaviour, as well as a narrower one, that focuses only on disengaging from violent behaviour. The latter focus becomes important for the many recruits who join a radical movement for instrumental reasons, profit and so on, rather than ideological reasons and, as will be argued later in this chapter, these causes become more important as territorial control expands.

The aim of the chapter is to analyse how variations in territorial control influence the strategies that may be applied to deradicalize or disengage individuals. Such strategies have in the past been branded as activities other than deradicalization, as 'reintegration', 're-education', 'desistance' (primary, secondary and tertiary), 'disaffiliation' and 'debiasing'. The process can be voluntary or involuntary; permanent or temporary; individual or collective and might be implemented by different actors (as described in the Introduction), security forces, police forces, non-governmental organizations (NGOs; including religious ones) and even individuals, yet the efficiency of the varying categories of implementers may vary according to variations in territorial control. If an extremist organization controls territory, regular police, for example, will be denied access; if the territories are fought over, NGOs engaged in deradicalization may be vanquished in military campaigns. This means that deradicalization can be quite different in a country that maintains territorial control, such as most Western European countries, compared to war zones such as Syria, Libya and Iraq.

Variations in territorial control have indirectly been explored in contexts related to deradicalization before; for example, cases where armed contestation of territories appears in the form of war or insurgency. For deradicalization and disengagement work in post-conflict and conflict scenarios, it could be argued that one might draw on previous work on demobilizing combatants. Disengagement from insurgents in armed conflict had been a part of the agenda for international actors for years, through so-called disarmament, demobilization and reintegration (DDR) programmes. Traditionally, DDR was seen as attempts to integrate former combatants in civil wars into society in a post-conflict situation. Initially, DDR was implemented after a peace agreement. 'Reinsertion' into the community was one of the major goals, sometimes in connection with United Nations (UN) peacekeeping operations. In order to achieve this, transitional assistance was first offered, including cash payments, in-kind assistance (goods and services) and vocational training (Hanson 2007). The amplified focus on violent Islamists and conflicts such as in northeastern Nigeria, Somalia and Yemen increasingly also meant that there has been pressure to include a disengagement-deradicalization component. Notably writers such as Schmid (2013) and Moghaddam (2009) have defined parts of the DDR agenda as potential components in a deradicalization programme. Cockayne and O'Neil (2015, p. 8) suggested employing the term 'demobilization and disengagement of violent extremists' (DDVE). In many countries, the main effort against extreme groups takes the form of deradicalization components within wider DDR programmes, as illustrated by Botha's and Chindea's chapters in this volume (see Chapters 15 and 24).

Such a hybrid approach to deradicalization does, as the writers suggest, have the same problems as previous DDR programmes. According to Bhandari (2014), security sector reform often hinders DDR. First, DDR can be hampered by the lack of inclusion of oppositional forces in the armed forces, a problem that may increase if the organization from which those individuals to be included come is defined as extremist internationally. The DDR discussion is valuable, highlighting very important issues, such as the need for base-line economic research. Other problems that have been identified include work programmes training combatants for the 'wrong' types of civilian work, i.e. training for work that does not exist in the area. Additionally, economic advantages might create envy or 'fake' combatants who attempt to register for demobilization just to gain advantage. Other problems include lack of stable funding, the lack of a cross-border mechanism to handle militias that transcend borders, as well as a focus on output (demobilized militias) rather than outcome (how the combatants fare after the programme). Daniel Koehler (2016, p. 41) also highlights problems encountered with the cantonment of soldiers to be demobilized, how to measure the success of the programme and a lack of focus on females in these programmes.

Criticism of how DDR actually (mis)functions in a conflict zone was also raised. DDR was originally intended for a post-conflict scenario, and DDR during a conflict entails demobilizing soldiers who are still very much needed for the parties to win a war, and who may be a threat to the opposing side even when demobilized, and thus might face sanctions. The latter type of criticism perhaps illustrates that DDR also becomes strained when the nature of the organization from which individuals are to be demobilized changes. Through the 1990s, the post-conflict focus changed, and DDR was increasingly implemented when armed conflicts were still ongoing. Basically, the organization you were to be deradicalized from changed from an organization that was part of a peace process to an organization engaged in warfare, at times with territorial control, at times hostile to the entity doing DDR (Idris 2016; Richards 2017). Today, UN operations with DDR elements increasingly take place in situations in which one of the belligerents is seen as a spoiler and viewed with hostility by the DDR implementers. The DDR literature is thus valuable for organizations and governments doing deradicalization in conflict zones, as it increasingly has dealt with problems concerning territorial control. DDR has increasingly moved away from an activity you implement after peace, and where the implementer is neutral, to an activity that you do in war time, and where the UN is hostile towards a party involved in a conflict, often against local jihadist groups.

Notably, several of the discussions ongoing in the areas of countering violent extremism and deradicalization, including discussion on the need to change belief vs. the need to change only patterns of violent action, have not yet been touched upon in the DDR literature, which can draw more on the countering violent extremism and deradicalization literature to enhance practical programmes. Some of the findings on disengagement from terrorist groups have not been fully considered (such as the works of Bjørgo and Horgan 2009). Similarly, the DDR literature suggests approaches in settings not normally dealt with in the deradicalization and disengagement literature. DDR focuses on organizations and factions that have stronger command hierarchy, conventional fighting power and strong disciplining mechanisms and not the type of legally accepted organizations, clandestine illegal cells and networks that very often are the focus of deradicalization and disengagement literature.

Yet, the DDR literature suffers from some of the drawbacks also seen in the disengagement and deradicalization literature. *First*, the exact limitation between post-conflict and conflict scenarios can be rather unclear and radical organizations can wield much stronger organizational tools than focused on in the deradicalization literature in situations where they wield stronger forms of control. *Second*, what is interesting in relation to deradicalization is the mechanisms that the organization from which one is to be deradicalized can bring in to counter deradicalization efforts, such as command hierarchy that can punish doubting members, or efficient sanctions against friends and relatives, or economic incentives provided to individuals in order to make them stay. *Third*, the span of organizational toolkits for recruiting increases in areas where radical organizations have control, recruits can be gained through promises of stable jobs, promises of economic rewards to control 'taxing', forced recruitments and through locals attempting to coopt jihadists and right-wing organizations controlling territories to gain support in local conflicts.

The above-mentioned mechanisms of control and recruitment are present in a situation where deradicalization is to take place from a clandestine organization (or cells), operating inside a relatively functioning hostile state. However, the mechanisms grow much stronger in situations where the organization from which one is to be deradicalized is actually controlling territories, or if they are situated in a state that tolerates the organization, or even supports it. In many places, such as Northern Mali or Somalia, territorial control is of another kind where the presence of the organization in question is semi-permanent; they can come and go more or less at will, but not openly establish institutions in a given area, as the opposing forces may be stronger than them and will defeat them in open combat. Thus, even in areas 'cleared' of insurgents and militant actors, their influence might be high. A tense security environment might also force DDR implementers to 'bunker up' (Egeland, Harmer and Stoddard 2011), losing control and monitoring capacity over their projects, including providing security to deradicalize them and their families.

How should one study variations of control mechanisms on behalf of violent extremist organizations, and their consequences for deradicalization and disengagement? Hansen (2019) focused on what territorial control entailed, arguing that in some cases such situations were providing so much stability that insurgency became a misleading term. For months, if not years, there could be no fighting in the core areas controlled by the jihadists. In other phases, territorial control could be limited, but jihadists might nevertheless be able to control the local population, partly because of minimal presence of rival entities amongst the local population. Such a situation is at the time of writing seen in Syria, parts of Afghanistan, Iraq, Somalia, Congo and in Mali, to mention a few examples, and is far from the realities facing deradicalization actors in Europe, North America, Oceania and East Asia. This is perhaps best seen from the fact that the chapters in this book, for example, focusing on East Africa, the African Union and West Africa deal with DDR programmes, while the chapters discussing the Western context deal with more traditional deradicalization settings. Yet these variations and what they mean for the structure of deradicalization efforts have not systematically been explored in the past.

Variations over territorial presence and control

Hansen (2017, 2018) launched a model of variations over territorial presence to understand the dynamics of various jihadist organizations in Africa. These models also tell us something about the capacities of jihadist organizations, and the types of tool needed to deradicalize their members. Rather than presenting a stable 'essence' of the organization, he argues that organizations and organizational dynamics change over time, represented by how much control the organization has in the territories where it has a presence. This will also lead to variations in the types of challenges deradicalization and disengagement programmes face, due to variations in organizational strength and in the original incentives for recruitment, and indeed the incentives for exit.

The model operates with four different ideal types of territorial presence. One type of presence is an accepted presence, meaning that an organization is accepted, in some cases even supported, by state elites. Boko Haram, Al Qaeda in Sudan and Al Qaeda in the Islamic Maghreb (in Mali only) have all at times been tolerated by their host government, even used for governance purposes. In many ways, these organizations were part of a type of governance where non-state armed groups are used by rulers to save money and resources. In some cases, such a configuration would be part of a governance strategy of delegating violence to subgroups in society. Indeed, according to Metz, this has been perhaps one of the most common state strategies in the past (2014, p. 39). Local factions are seen as tools at times by local and central authorities, and their independence and potential/occasional disloyalty may be seen as tolerable (Ibid). This is not too far from the status of several right-wing militias in Ukraine and Russia today, as well as several right-wing militias in the recent past (see Chapter 24). The results of such strategies were often mixed, and the bonds of loyalty between the parties are limited. In the case of jihadists, Al Qaeda, Ansar Dine and Boko Haram have had similar functions for hosting states in periods of their history; in the case of right-wing militias, we have seen similar scenarios in South America, Ukraine and Russia. Importantly, such organizations will have the potential for violence, but need not be violent in the state in which they are based; they can be tools for foreign politics.

The state can also be passive, avoiding supporting or encouraging the organizations. The organizations are so insignificant that they are not noticed by the state, and/or at times their level of violence is not large enough to merit a ban. In both cases, the organizations will most commonly enjoy some legal protection. Organizations are allowed to operate strong organizational hierarchies; they will in general be able to openly gather income locally, again as far as tolerated by the host state. This type of organization might present a considerable challenge for actors striving to do deradicalization and disengagement, as organizational mechanisms and/or economic incentives will be employed, openly and at times supported by the host state, against potential defectors. At times, the host state will even employ violence, or allow the organization in question to use open violence, targeting individuals attempting to leave the organization.

In other cases, the state might be hostile and relatively efficient in attempting to hinder, ban and prosecute the organizations. The most common deradicalization and disengagement programmes are perhaps designed for the last scenario, perhaps the most common scenario concerning illegal radical groups in North America, Europe and Eastern Asia. In this scenario, radical groups are forced underground by state-based law enforcement agencies. The groups operate clandestinely, often based around small clandestine cells, with somewhat limited contacts, as described by Nesser (2015) in his work on European jihadists. Hansen (2019) branded this the clandestine network scenario.

The common denominator for the first two scenarios is that the radical group lives at the mercy of a state, a state that can hinder and curtail them, ultimately holding control, and attempts to surveil and control its own citizens as well. However, in other cases this is not always true. The radical organizations could have extensive mechanisms to surveil and control the local population, and rival the state in even providing governance. Such cases bring us closer to the scenarios described by academic works on DDR, with the existence of organized armed groups that operate more like armies than terrorists or activists. Newer versions of DDR programmes, deployed for a conflict rather than a post-conflict situation, seem more relevant. Yet, these scenarios are not necessarily scenarios of ongoing armed conflicts; rather they are scenarios of ongoing – if necessary, violent – control of the locals by radical movements.

Importantly, one does not necessarily need to control a territory on a permanent basis to control its inhabitants. Due to limited resources, at times because of military doctrine, casualty awareness, geography or a limited will, the enemies of violent extremists could keep themselves in restricted base areas. Odd patrols, time-limited campaigns to reduce numbers of checkpoints or limit enemy expansion, focusing on larger battles rather than controlling the countryside could be all enemy forces actually do. The extremist organizations in question can then have semi-territorial control, where their threats of sanctions are what maintains control rather than possibilities of daily sanctions. As long as the organizations in question manage to show that they can be present at relatively regular intervals, the presence need not be permanent. The groups in question will visit local villages on a regular basis, and have the ability to put up roadblocks, before hostile forces remove them. The ability to enter villages frequently and block transportation for longer periods of time means that villagers remain dependent on them; they need to maintain a good relationship to survive. It also to a certain extent creates a panopticon, where locals have to expect to be watched and to face punishment for disloyalty, even if the organization in question is not constantly present, as the latter can enter into the locals' area on a regular basis and can easily coopt locals to surveil. This is the case in parts of Borno province in Nigeria, and in the Somali countryside.

The organizations in question would have the power to extract resources from locals, partly because of the threat of sanctions against members of the population who do not stay loyal. Yet, loyalty can go beyond the threat of sanctions. Locals need to hedge to avoid violence, and one way to do this is to integrate into the organization in question. By supplying daughters for fighters to marry, or by supplying recruits from a village, one hopes to make the organization in question friendly, even perhaps gain influence on the leadership, or through recruits rising through the ranks. In a semi-territorial scenario, local loyalty, created by integration into an organization, might go beyond a radical worldview, through networks of friends and families, even through forced involuntary recruitment. In some cases, the radical organizations might do governance in some form: traders who sell spoiled food can be stopped, Sharia courts can also implement verdicts in civil cases and thieves can be punished. In some cases, as depicted by Kilkullen's (2013) theory of competitive control, the semi-territorial organization might be better than the alternative corrupt government in their governance. However, at some stages only predictability is needed to create forms of loyalty, with locals preferring a less turbulent and anarchic everyday situation, supporting organizations that provide this (ibid). The fact that the organization in question presents a power that will be there for the future means that the organization might be coopted by locals to settle their own scores (Kalyvas 2003). Recruitment might thus reflect local animosities rather than some radical worldview. To join or integrate into an organization becomes a tool to settle personal and family grudges, with just a weak relationship to ideology. This has potentially great consequences for disengagement and deradicalization efforts. Recruits are not only motivated by the sense of belonging or thrill seeking, or ideological reasons often described by European scholars such as Nesser (2015); they may be inspired by the need for local security and safety, by the wish for better governance, by economic opportunism and indeed by the need to have allies in local conflicts.

The form of territorial control might also be of a more permanent sort. Stable areas are set up, reminding us about what Mapilly calls rebel rulers (2015), and indeed what Brynjar Lia (2015) defines as 'jihadi proto states'. In this case, the group in question holds territorial control, establishing state-like institutions. The long-term target of most of these organizations is not always to be a state in the ordinary sense of the word, presenting a disdain for state borders; it was rather a resurrection of a wider Islamic 'ummah' as a political entity. Indeed the Islamic State announcement of their caliphate was literally called 'breaking/shattering the borders'. While, as claimed by Mapilly (2015, p. 39), juridical statehood gives benefits, these benefits are normally not granted because of the capacity of the entity to govern, but rather because of friends in the international system. Radical right-wing organizations, and especially jihadists, might lack this today.

We are thus not really talking about attempts to capture a state, or indeed to build up a new 'state' in the normal sense of the word, but rather attempts to build institutions to manage territorial control – in the longer run, to create a new type of entity. At times, they can do governance, and sometimes better governance than rivals (Kilkullen 2013) can. Again Kilkullen's theory of competitive control becomes useful, highlighting that 'populations respond to a predictable, ordered, normative system, which tells them exactly what they need to do, and not do, in order to be safe'. At times, organizations will project this image actively in their propaganda (Hansen 2013), Yet, at times, the governance aspect would be less important. Importantly, as claimed by Kilkullen (ibid), 'good governance' is not needed to gain the loyalty of the locals; an entity providing regularity and predictability will often be seen by many as better than chaos and anarchy. And, as claimed by Mancur Olson (1993) in his discussion of stationary vs. rowing bandits, a more permanent type of territorial control does give the incentive to avoid looting and plan more long-term forms of taxing and mechanisms of extraction, since one needs to ensure that the income will be generated by locals also in the longer run. The scenario thus opens up for stronger forms of institution building. Moreover, as claimed by Kilkullen (2013, p. 125), support follows strength, echoing Kalyvas's (2003, p. 12) argument that when conflicts endure locals increasingly cooperate with actors controlling their area. Stable control also means that the organization in question can be seen as a stable income provider. It can be seen as an organization that provides possibilities for a carrier, for personal advance.

The above scenarios might change. It seems clear that a scenario with an ongoing civil war, or where the state traditionally had a weak presence in some of its territories, makes the two last scenarios more likely. The scenarios are not necessarily incremental; they do not reassemble Mao's stages of an insurgency (first controlling a rear area, second using terror and attacking isolated enemy units, then beating the enemy in battle). However, Mao holds valuable insights when claiming that a strategic point would be to lure the enemy into striking back so indiscriminately that the locals are provoked into supporting the insurgents (Rich and Duvesteyn 2014, p. 6). In fact, the four scenarios might be surprisingly stable, and even territorial control and semi-territorial control might involve little fighting. Yet,

Hansen (2018) observes a pattern amongst the African jihadists, where territoriality often transforms into semi-territoriality and semi-territoriality might transform back into territoriality, the two scenarios indicating a serious weakness of the states opposing the extremists in their area of operations. As shown by the defeats of the Islamic State, but also organizations such as the Shabaab and Al Qaeda in the Arab Peninsula before them, more permanent territorial control will often be challenged, especially if, like most jihadist organizations, you exist as a pariah in the international system, with many enemies. The institutions built up can be dismantled; permanent territorial control is lost. This does not mean that control mechanisms are fully lost. Jihadists cannot hope to defeat enemy military forces in large battles. However, their enemies fail to defend the local population against sanctions from the jihadists, often because the former lack a physical presence at a local level.

Semi-territoriality and territoriality have other consequences than an accepted presence, and a clandestine network-based presence. It means more permanent sources of income for locals who want to join an organization. The situation creates openings to join such organizations to gain, for example, administrative positions. Secondly, by joining an organization with more territorial control you can 'hedge' for security, that is protect your community from various types of risks from jihadist organizations, by joining them, or even by marrying into them, support could easily be a strategy for survival. Such cases will have consequences outside the areas of territorial and semi-territorial control. Business persons might need to transport goods through them, and thus at times need to pay tolls when transporting goods, and individuals outside the areas with relatives/friends inside these areas will be influenced by the threat of sanctions, or indeed support of extremists, by these relatives. 'Deradicalizers' might have to face dealing with recruits who may have family and friends living under jihadist-controlled areas, and these relatives might be sanctioned against, as well as having an interest in maintaining a stable relationship with the jihadists. Families, a tool that in Danish deradicalization programmes, for example, is used to facilitate deradicalization, become hard to tap into as a resource if they live in areas controlled by radicals, and might even become a tool that radical organizations use to prevent individuals participating in deradicalization programmes outside the organization's zones of control. Families are a source to be punished and sanctioned if individuals don't fulfil both economic and in other cases personal obligations to the extremist organization in question. In the words of a respondent from the Damboa area of the Borno state of Nigeria, who had experienced Boko Haram:[2]

> when they came to our area for the first time they were not powerful because they have not start the violence but later when they got their arms then they become violent and start to force people to give them money or properties or they may ask you to pay certain amount of money or force you to pay it and you have to or else they will kill you and leave or kill members of your family also.

In one sense, some of the challenges will resemble more 'modern' DDR programmes operating in conflict situations, rather than post-conflict situations. Similar situations have been discussed, such as by Vanda Felbab-Brown (2015). Yet the dynamics would be different from her work; in many ways Felbab-Brown neglects the organizational institutional strength of the jihadists and the possibilities for disciplining recruits (Hansen 2017). A deradicalization or disengagement programme operating in relation to areas where the presence of a group enables territorial control or semi-territorial control should in many ways be different from the deradicalization and disengagement programmes handling cases like the ones in the West where groups to be deradicalized from resemble clandestine networks.

One such difference is related to the strength of the organizational hierarchy of the radical organization, which is more likely to be stronger since it can operate more freely. Several of the factors leading to disengagement in the deradicalization/disengagement literature, such as dissatisfaction with the leadership of a group, personal conflicts, and so on, will face an organizational hierarchy with organizational tools to handle internal conflicts, replace poor sub-commanders and so forth. A stronger organizational hierarchy might also mean more tools for disciplining defectors, for screening communications with out-group members and controlling the information-reaching members.

Hansen (2017) illustrates how the jihadist organizations are easily able to maintain organizational hierarchies in such scenarios, being efficiently able to address potential defectors, still having the organizational ability to address personal conflicts within units and sub-groups, the major factor described by Horgan and Bjørgo (2009), such as bringing about defections from terrorist groups in a Western setting. In addition, loyalty towards the government is hard to maintain as the organizations are perfectly able to inflict serious damage on a hostile local population, by arriving in villages when their enemies are not there, sanctioning defections and opposition. In areas such as Somalia, deradicalization programmes operate in contexts like this. The deradicalization centre in Baidoa exists in a setting where the countryside around the city is plagued by rowing bands of Shabaab fighters. In one sense an MP from the city expressed it like this:

> Not only NGOs working in Deradicalization but also other NGOs or communities at large have problems with AS [Al Shabaab] pressure. And the communities in the rural villages cannot participate in the efforts of AS pressurizing because they are forcefully controlled and threatened by AS. And AS has created that people have no confidence in each other, even among families are suspicious. In this case no one can be mobilized.[3]

In such a situation, the threat of sanctions becomes very real and close:

> For instance, I have seen an escapee in this training and was trained for longer period, as he was in Baidoa, one on motto cycle met him in the streets and asked are you so and so? Then he said yes I am, then suddenly told to ride the motto cycle and after a distance he was slaughtered and his head cut off. Such incidence had happened in Baidoa.[4]

The essences of the two latter scenarios are organizational hierarchy, the need to hedge to protect relatives near radicals, against sanctions, the ability of the jihadists to gather funds, thus encouraging opportunists to join the radicals, and the lack of safety for dissidents to the radicals and their families. These differences will constrain the deradicalization and disengagement programmes going on in the close vicinity of the areas with territorial or semi-territorial control.

Deradicalization/disengagement in accepted presence and clandestine network scenarios

In many ways the standard scenario that deradicalization and disengagement theory focuses on has been the clandestine network scenario and many of the important issues influencing the success rate of deradicalization and disengagement activities in this scenario are discussed in depth in other parts of this book. Arguably, deradicalization and disengagement in an *accepted presence scenario* with state support for radical groups are very different. Active state support for radicals ensures that the resources of the radicals are larger, that legislation and police might be used against actors engaged in deradicalization and disengagement. Yet, there are strategies that can be employed. First, foreign pressure can, as it did in Sudan with Al Qaeda in the 1990s, change the government's attitude towards the radical entities. Second, different elites within the governance structures might have different ideas about the radicals, creating potential allies in deradicalization and disengagement work. This was indeed the case when the Harakat Al Shabaab grew under the protection of the Sharia courts in Somalia in 2006. Parts of the Sharia courts, such as the former warlord Indaadde, were openly hostile to many aspects of the Shabaab ideology. Here the concept of re-pluralization becomes important, as a constraining government might curtail more traditional organized deradicalization programmes, yet similar activities can be organized more informally through discussion fora, broadcasts, and so forth, as happened in Somalia, and indeed Nigeria.

Third, some local institutions might enjoy so much legitimacy that they provide a platform to address ideological issues, or other issues within the radical organizations, such as in the case of Boko Haram. Maiduguri Sheiks managed to address Boko Haram leader Mohamed Yusuf in debates, and defeat him oratorically, despite the latter having ties with regional leaders (Hansen 2019). In Sudan the smaller Muslim Brotherhood, which remained allied to the Egyptian Brotherhood, challenged Turabi's own credentials and could have functioned as a platform for ideological critique, since they had support within the government that protected them. Several NGOs, such as Somalia's El Maan human rights group, also managed to exist and operate in parallel to extremists, although the latter were supported by the government in control (in the case of Somalia, the Sharia Courts (the Islamic Courts Union)).

Yet, the security risks for locals attempting to carry out disengagement/deradicalization attempts are larger than in a clandestine network scenario. At times mounting a direct challenge to radicals might be challenging, hence re-pluralization becomes a key word, as questioning ideological assumptions amongst radicals becomes a safer alternative than opening an outright deradicalization programme for defectors. In a globalized world, internet, and indeed radio and satellite TV, enable deradicalization and disengagement activities from afar, as online counter-narrative programmes also have their effects, as expressed in another chapter in this book. An organization could have an accepted presence even without being supported directly by the state, or in a period after a state ends its support. It could then be in a phase when it enjoys legal protection. In such situations, again the more common deradicalization and disengagement literature becomes more useful, as shown in studies of anti-sect programmes (see, for example, Langone 1993; Bromley and Melton 2002; Henson 2002).

The main actors doing deradicalization in an accepted presence scenario would normally not be a police force, law enforcement or municipalities, as the state remains friendly or neutral to the radicals. NGOs, in combination with external actors, have to be the locus of deradicalization and disengagement.

Territorial/semi-territorial scenarios

The territorial control scenario is also more challenging than a clandestine network scenario. A radical organization with territorial control, such as the Islamic State and Shabaab, will function as a beacon, an example of an 'ideal' state, attracting foreign fighters. It will also often have 'state-like' institutions, including police and intelligence, which can be used to strike down dissidents and NGOs working to counter radical messages, and to identify and neutralize potential defectors. A strong command hierarchy will limit the possibilities for group and personal conflicts to spill over in defections, and will sanction against defectors, as well as limiting the abilities of potential defectors to communicate the need. In cases of full control it is hard to implement any deradicalization and disengagement activities, even when it comes to activities such as criticizing the ideas of the radicals. This was for instance illustrated by the brave example of Al Isha human rights group attempting to stand up to the Shabaab in Baidoa in Somalia when the city was controlled by the latter organization, which resulted in the arrest and severe torture of its leader Alin Hillowle, although the latter managed to escape.

Yet, there are potential advantages for deradicalization and disengagement projects within this scenario as well. Motivations beyond the wish for belonging, the wish for adventure and the belief in an ideology will be present. As illustrated by Kalyvas (2003), locals might, for example, join insurgents to gain advantages in local conflicts, and to improve the security of friends and relatives. Additionally, more permanent organizational structures make it more tempting to join to get a stable income. Third, the radical organization wielding territorial control might simply be better at implementing justice than neighbouring areas (Kilkullen 2013) and present a preferred alternative. Fourth, recruitment might be forced. In this sense, motivations for joining might go beyond motives such as thrill seeking; a wish for belonging and ideology, to seek income, to seek security and to seek stability gains in importance. These motives might present new opportunities to enhance and encourage defections and participation in deradicalization programmes.

While deradicalization and disengagement programmes cannot be established in the zones of control, they can still be established outside these zones, on the borders of territorial control and can attract defectors away from them. In Somalia the deradicalization centres in Baidoa, Mogadishu, Kismayo and Beled Weyne, in addition to NGOs working with deradicalization, operate outside areas controlled by the Shabaab working with defectors or prisoners of war. These centres ran or run deradicalization programmes focusing on challenging several of the advantages offered by Shabaab as an employer in the areas they control, including offering vocational skills training in order to offer alternative careers to Somalis who joined Shabaab to have an income. Yet these programmes, often mimicking the deradicalization programmes in the West mainly dealing with clandestine networks, in general fail to deal properly with potential sanctions facing the relatives of Shabaab defectors coping with local ruptures that create potential for Shabaab recruitment through the mechanisms described by Kalyvas (2003). Potential deradicalization programmes draw closer to DDR programmes, discussed previously in this chapter; indeed, these centres are demobilizing former combatants. Aspects of such deradicalization work will be to provide economic opportunities for defectors who flee, to provide possibilities for safe channels for defectors to flee away from the organization, and possibly strategies to get families out simultaneously with the defectors.

Deradicalization efforts taking place outside the zones of control of the radicals might not be the only applicable strategy. Again, a key word becomes re-pluralization, as described by Koehler in this book (see Chapter 2). Potential strategies become to encourage individuals to defect and escape the zones of control, if possible to establish secure channels to smuggle defectors away from them. This is to create doubt around the ideology, the use of violence, perceptions of the radicals as providers of income and security and perceptions of radicals as useful allies in local conflict. The borders of the territories of a radical group are seldom not porous and messages may penetrate. In Pakistan Sheik Muhamad Tahir ul-Qadri's book on fatwas on terrorism and suicide bombing circulated in the areas of Pakistani Taliban control, criticizing the latter's religious assumptions. Books and publications from religious leaders outside the areas under territorial control by the radicals also served this function in Iraq.

Individuals with ties to the territorial zone might also face sanctions against their family and friends if they defect/disengage, or sanctions against families can at times be used as threats in order to use such individuals as agents for sabotage and assassinations. Inside the zone of control, mechanisms of cohesion in the radical organization can be systematically undermined and the army cohesion literature (Hansen 2017) might provide ideas on how to do this, including weakening organizational hierarchy and command and control systems; yet this is difficult.

Semi-territoriality reassembles the territorial control scenario in the sense that the radical organization wields influence outside the territory where semi-territoriality is wielded, both through the abilities of the radicals to implement sanctions against the friends and families of defectors at will, but also the business communities that need to pay to gain access to the areas. A semi-territorial scenario will also lead to recruits having motivations that differ from clandestine network scenarios. Some of these motives might resemble the territorial control scenario. Recruits might join because they are forcefully recruited; they might join because their families seek to protect themselves from violence by the radicals by having family within the radical organization. Additionally, they might join because of a wish to gain allies for local conflicts. But it becomes less tempting to join for economic reasons, as income generation and taxes become slightly harder than the open taxing in the territorial scenario. Yet, income-generating possibilities are stronger than in the clandestine network scenario.

Semi-territoriality is created by the lack of permanent security for villagers and locals in the countryside: in the words of then President Sharif Hassan of the South West Regional State in Somalia, the 'fly over territories' that few politicians care for, yet that you need to secure and protect to end a conflict.[5] Normally, the police would be responsible, but the police are often focused on crime prevention rather than self-protection, and may have problems in facing rowing insurgents (Hill 2014, p. 101). Sadly, local security becomes very important for deredicalization and disengagement in such a scenario. Relatives, as well as the deradicalized, need to be protected against sanctions, including after leaving the deradicalization disengagement programme in question. Internalization of conflicts on behalf of the radical organizations also means that conflict resolution in regard to local conflicts that might lead to recruitment for radicals needs to be addressed. This means that a deradicalization disengagement programme needs to be more comprehensive, and requires knowledge of the local dynamics of ongoing conflicts, of which some are unrelated to right-wing, left-wing or jihadist extremism. Moreover, these conflicts might, because of the relatively weaker control semi-territoriality gives to the radicals, be more prominent, and more reassembling armed conflict than in the territorial control scenario. Such a scenario becomes more and more important as, for example, the Islamic State increasingly becomes transformed into a semi-territorial organization in the Levant, yet focus on local security is often neglected.

As in the case with territorial control, semi-territoriality means that the radicals have control far outside the areas affected directly. Again, relatives of individuals who live outside the region can face punishment if the individuals in question act against the radicals, and relatives can be used as agents due to pressure against relatives and friends inside territories of semi-territorial control. Again, business community members might choose to pay off radicals to be able to trade in and transport through the areas of semi-territoriality. These issues, as well as the continued presence of radicals in semi-territorial areas, mean that security needs to be a very important priority. Local security is normally a police issue, but police forces are usually too weakly equipped to challenge insurgent-like movements. Moreover, semi-territorial scenarios are often not seen as semi-territorial, as they often emerge after the defeat of a radical group transforming its control away from full territorial control into semi-territorial control, mistakenly being seen as being defeated. Often semi-territoriality is found in the periphery of the state, avoiding the attention that action in larger cities usually attracts to radical organizations. Lack of attention might transform into durability, and radical organizations such as the Shabaab, Lord's Resistance Army and the Allied Democratic Forces have maintained themselves in such scenarios for years.

The DDR literature has much to offer practitioners running deradicalization/disengagement in semi-territorial/territorial scenarios. The importance of local security in the semi-territorial zone, and the necessity to understand internalization of local conflicts, remain some of the major drawbacks. In one sense, one size does not fit all when it comes to deradicalization and disengagement; one also has to take the toolkit of the opponent into account, as well as the causes for joining an organization. These two items vary depending on the type of control of territory, and thus variations from an accepted presence, a clandestine network, semi-territorial control and territorial control should be taken into account.

Notes

1 Notable exceptions were Daniel Koehler (2016), who allocated a whole subsection to the topic. Malet and Hayes (2018) also studied disarmament, demobilization and reintegration (DDR) in relation to deradicalization and disengagement in an otherwise very good article focusing on foreign fighters returning from Syria. However, their exploration of DDR uses few cases to draw examples from. The article also neglects the fact that DDR is intended for war zones, and ignores the fact that many of today's DDR programmes have deradicalization and disengagement components focusing on ideology and worldviews of the former militia soldiers, suggesting that DDR focuses on behavioural changes only.
2 Interview with nickname 'TALL', conducted in Maiduguri, 1 August 2018.
3 Group interviews with MP's Baidoa, 20 April 2017. Conducted by Isha Human rights group for Linnea Gelot and Stig Jarle Hansen.
4 Group interviews with rural elders, 20 April 2017. Conducted by Isha Human rights group for Linnea Gelot and Stig Jarle Hansen.
5 Interviews with Sheik Sharif, Oslo, 20 July 2018.

References

Altier, Mary B., Emma L. Boyle, Neil D. Shortland, and John Horgan (2017). "Why They Leave: An Analysis of Terrorist Disengagement Events from Eighty-seven Autobiographical Accounts." *Security Studies*, 26(2), 305–332.
Barrelle, Kate (2015). "Pro-integration: Disengagement from and Life after Extremism." *Behavioral Sciences of Terrorism and Political Aggression*, 7(2), 129–142.
Bhandari, Pittambar (2014). "Integration Issue of Ex-combatants in Nepal: Provisions and Prospects." *Journal of Conflict and Public Policy*, 1(1), 11–20.
Bjørgo, Tore (1995). *Terror from the Extreme Right*, New York: Routledge.
Bjørgo, Tore (2009). "Process of Disengagement from Violent Groups of the Extreme Right," in Tore Bjørgo and John Horgan (Eds.), *Leaving Terrorism Behind: Individual and Collective Disengagement* (pp. 30–48). Milton Park, London; New York: Routledge.
Bjørgo, Tore, and Yngve Carlsson (1999). *Vold, rasisme og ungdomsgjenger: Forebygging og bekjempelse* [Violence, Racism and Youth: Prevention and Combat], Oslo: Tano.
Bjørgo, Tore, and Horgan, John (2009). *Leaving Terrorism Behind*, New York: Routledge.
Bromley, David G., and J. Gordon Melton (2002). *Cults, Religion, and Violence*, Cambridge, UK: Cambridge University Press.

Cockayne, James, and Siobhan O'Neil (2015). "Introduction," in James Cockayne and Siobhan O'Neil (Eds.), *UN DDR in an Era of Violent Extremism: Is It Fit for Purpose?* (pp. 14–36). United Nations University Centre for Policy Research, technical report.

Egeland, Jan, Adele Harmer, and Abby Stoddard (2011). *To Stay and Deliver, Good Practice for Humanitarians in Complex Security Environments*, New York: Independent study commissioned by the Office for the Coordination of Humanitarian Affairs (OCHA) Policy and Studies Series.

Felbab-Brown, Vanda (2015). "DDR in the Context of Offensive Military Operations, Counterterrorism, CVE and Non-Permissive Environments Key Questions, Challenges, and Considerations," in James Cockayne and Siobhan O'Neil (Eds.), *UN DDR in an Era of Violent Extremism: Is It Fit for Purpose?* (pp. 37–63). United Nations University Centre for Policy Research, technical report.

Giustozzi, Antonio (2009). *Empires of Mud: Wars and Warlords of Afghanistan*, London: Hurst.

Goldwag, Arthur (2012). *The New Hate: A History of Fear and Loathing on the Populist Right*, New York: Pantheon Books.

Hansen, Stig Jarle (2013). *All Shabaab in Somalia, the History and Ideology of a Militant Islamist Group*, London: Hurst.

Hansen, Stig Jarle (2017). "Unity under Allah, Cohesion Mechanisms in Jihadist Organizations in Africa." *Armed Forces and Society*, November (online).

Hansen, Stig Jarle (2019). *Sahel, Rift and the Horn, the Fault Lines of African Jihad*, London: Hurst.

Hanson, Stephanie (2007). "Disarmament, Demobilization, and Reintegration (DDR) in Africa." *Council of Foreign Relations Backgrounder*, 15 February 2007.

Harris, Kira J., Eyal Gringart, and Deirdre Drake (2018). "Leaving Ideological Groups Behind: A Model of Disengagement." *Behavioral Sciences of Terrorism and Political Aggression*, 10(2), 9–108.

Henson, Keith H. (2002). "Sex, Drugs, and Cults. An Evolutionary Psychology Perspective on Why and How Cult Memes Get a Drug-like Hold on People, and What Might Be Done to Mitigate the Effects." *Human Nature Review*, 2, 343–355.

Hill, Alice (2014). "Insurgency, Counterinsurgency and Policing," in Paul B. Rich and Isabelle Duvesteyn (Eds.), *The Routledge Handbook of Insurgency and Counterinsurgency* (pp. 98–108). London: Routledge.

Hof, Tobias (2017). "From Extremism to Terrorism: The Radicalization of the Far Right in Italy and West Germany." *Contemporary European History*, 412–431. 24 May.

Horgan, John (2005). *The Psychology of Terrorism*, London: Routledge.

Horgan, John, Mary B. Altier, Neil D. Shortland, and Max Taylor (2017). "Walking Away: The Disengagement and Deradicalisation of a Violent Right-wing Extremist." *Behavioral Sciences of Terrorism and Political Aggression*, 9(2), 63–77.

Hwang, Julie Chernov (2015). "The Disengagement of Indonesian Jihadists: Understanding the Pathways." *Terrorism and Political Violence*, 277–295. Summer 2015.

Idris, Irfat (2016). "Lessons from DDR Programmes." *Helpdesk Research Report*, 1 June.

Kalyvas, Stathis N. (2003). "The Ontology of 'Political Violence': Action and Identity in Civil Wars." *Perspectives on Politics*, 1(3), 475–494.

Kaplan, Jeffery, and Tore Bjørgo (1998). *Nation and Race: The Developing Euro-American Racist Subculture*, Boston: Northeastern University Press.

Kilkullen, David (2013). *Out of the Mountains, the Coming Age of the Urban Guerilla*, London: Hurst.

Koehler, Daniel (2016). *Understanding Deradicalization: Methods, Tools and Programs for Countering Violent Extremism*, New York: Routledge.

Kruglanski, Arie W., Katarzyna Jasko, Marina Chernikova, Michelle Dugas, and David Webber (2017). "To the Fringe and Back: Violent Extremism and the Psychology of Deviance." *American Psychologist*, 72(3), 217–230.

Langone, Michael (1993). *Recovery from Cults: Help for Victims of Psychological and Spiritual Abuse*, New York: W.W. Norton.

Lia, Brynjar (2015). "Understanding Jihadi Proto-States." *Perspectives on Terrorism*, 9(4).

Malet, David, and Rachel Hayes (2018). "Foreign Fighter Returnees: An Indefinite Threat?" *Terrorism and Political Violence*, 30, 1–17.

Mapilly, Zachariah C. (2015). *Rebel Rulers, Insurgent Governance and Civilian Life during War*, Chapel Hill: Cornell University Press.

Metz, Steven (2014). "Rethinking Insurgency," in Paul B. Rich and Isabelle Duvesteyn (Eds.), *The Routledge Handbook of Insurgency and Counterinsurgency* (pp. 32–45). London: Routledge.

Moghaddam, Fathali M. (2009). "Deradicalisation and the Staircase from Terrorism," in David Canter (Ed.), *The Faces of Terrorism: Multidisciplinary Perspectives* (pp. 275–290). New York: John Wiley & Sons.

Nesser, Petter (2015). *Islamist Terrorism in Europe: A History*, London: Hurst.

Noricks, Darcy (2009). "Disengagement and Deradicalization: Processes and Programs. How Does Terrorism End?" in Paul Davis and Kim Cragin (Eds.), *Social Science for Counterterrorism: Putting the Pieces Together*. Santa Monica, CA: Rand Corp RAND report.

Olson, Mancur (1993). "Dictatorship, Democracy, and Development." *American Political Science Review*, 87(3), 567–576.

Piazza, James A. (2015). "The Determinants of Domestic Right-wing Terrorism in the USA: Economic Grievance, Societal Change and Political Resentment." *Conflict Management and Peace Science*, 52–80. 13 March.

Rich, Paul B., and Isabelle Duvesteyn (2014). "The Study of Insurgency and Counter Insurgency," in Paul B. Rich and Isabelle Duvesteyn (Eds.), *The Routledge Handbook of Insurgency and Counterinsurgency* (pp. 1–21). London: Routledge.

Richards, Joanne (2017). "Demobilizing and Disengaging Violent Extremists: Towards a New UN Framework." *Stability: International Journal of Security and Development*, 6(1), 14. doi:10.5334/sta.543.

Sageman, Marc (2004). *Understanding Terror Networks*, Philadelphia: University of Pennsylvania.

Sageman, Marc (2008). *Leaderless jihad*, Philadelphia: University of Pennsylvania.

Schmid, Alex P. (2013). "Radicalisation, Deradicalisation, Counter-Radicalisation: A Conceptual Discussion and Literature Review." *ICCT Research Paper*, March 2013.

8

"WELCOME" HOME

Deradicalization of Jihadi foreign fighters

Arie Perliger

The growing interest among academics and intelligence security agencies about the phenomenon of Jihadi foreign fighters generated a significant literature which sought to identify the dynamics that lead individuals to abandon their home and travel to countries they have never before visited in order to risk their lives in the name of an ideology that they knew little about before their radicalization (Hegghammer 2010; Holman 2015; Malet, Foreign Fighter Mobilization and Persistence in a Global Context 2015; Mustapha 2013; Nilsson 2015; Stenersen 2011). These efforts indeed helped to decipher some aspects of the radicalization process of foreign fighters, and their socialization into the Jihadi lifestyle. However, they interestingly paid somewhat less attention to the main reason behind the initial interest in foreign fighters, which is the threat they represent upon their decision to leave their organization or areas of conflict, and return to their home country, and how we can facilitate policies that will ensure their rehabilitation and re-integration into society (Gurski 2016).

The current chapter aims to present and analyze important aspects of deradicalization and social re-integration of foreign fighters. After providing a brief conceptualization and historical context of the phenomenon of foreign fighters, the chapter will proceed to discuss current attempts to promote and execute deradicalization programs among foreign fighters and the unique challenges these efforts are facing. The concluding section of the chapter will review policy and theoretical insights which hopefully can help better understand the dynamics and processes which are related to the deradicalization of foreign fighters and how they should be addressed when devising relevant policies.

Who is a foreign fighter?

More than any other event, the Paris attacks in November 2015 heighten the attention of policymakers and security practitioners to the threat of returning foreign fighters. This is not just because of the fact that six out of the ten members of the Brussels cell – which was responsible for the attack as well as the Brussels attack in early 2016 – fought in the ranks of ISIS in Syria/Iraq (Parlapiano et al. 2015), but mainly because it demonstrated how the unique characteristics of foreign fighters could help terrorist organizations to dramatically elevate the level of sophistication and execution of their attacks. Simply put, the combination of significant military experience which was gained by members of the Brussels cell during their "tour" in Syria/Iraq, with their familiarity of the Western/European social and security setting, helped them in plotting and perpetrating simultaneous attacks in multiple locations, against different types of targets, and by using multiple tactics. Such a combination of elements in a terrorist operation is fairly exceptional and previously was witnessed just during the Mumbai attacks in 2008 and very few other cases previously (especially during the 1970s).

As with the case of the concept of terrorism, the growing interest in foreign fighters didn't necessarily lead to a consensus regarding the defining features of the phenomenon, or simply put, who should be considered a foreign fighter. One of the reasons for the conceptual inconsistency may be related to the fact that the phenomenon of violent political parties which mobilize recruits and supporters from foreign countries is not new and changed over time.

Two fairly well-known early cases of conflicts that attracted foreign fighters are the Greek struggle for independence during the 1820s and the Spanish civil war between 1936 and 1939. In both cases, the conflict was restricted to a specific national territory, and focused on the desire to change the socio-political order in a specific country via a civil war which reflected a clash between what can be characterized as universal ideologies (in the case of Greece, the idea of national self-determination and anti-colonialism, and in the case of Spain liberal democracy and opposition to fascism) (Perliger and Milton 2016). Recent cases of political struggles that attract foreign fighters, what Cohen and Barak term "Modern Sherwood Forest" (Cohen and Barak 2013), seem to have different characteristics. Jihadi groups that recruit foreign fighters reject nationalist sentiments and the concept of the nation-state and aspire to engage in a global, violent struggle. Thus, Jihadi foreign fighters naturally can be inclined to act against their home state upon returning. Moreover, Jihadi groups espouse an exclusive religious ideology, which allows just members from specific religious communities (selective recruitment) to join them. Lastly, not as in the past, many of the Jihadi foreign fighters participate in violent campaigns against their home countries (or in opposition to their home countries' declared interests) which complicate the normative and legal/operational aspects of potential counter-policies (Perliger and Milton 2016).

The diversity in the strategies that are being implemented by the groups which recruit foreign fighters also doesn't help to reach consensus about the nature of the phenomenon. For example, there are different views regarding the question of whether individuals who are being paid should be considered foreign fighters (or be considered mercenaries) (Hegghammer 2010), as well as with regard to those who are fighting in a neighboring country or in "border wars." Similarly, it is not clear if someone who received training by a specific group, and then returned to his home country to conduct an operation, but didn't participate in any violent operations in foreign countries, should be considered a foreign fighter. Indeed, in many cases it is extremely challenging to identify the specific role of the foreign fighter in areas of conflict.

Despite the conceptual confusion, several important characteristics seem to be shared by most experts (Bakke 2013; Bryan 2010; Hegghammer 2010; Malet 2013). These include: (1) the lack of affiliation to the country where the fighting is happening; (2) the joining to a non-state entity; and (3) the role of transnational ideology as a motivating factor. Malet further distinguishes between the following classes of fighters (Malet 2013):

(a) Transnational insurgents – members of groups that extend operations across borders into states external to the civil conflict.
(b) Foreign-trained fighters – individuals who have traveled abroad to receive paramilitary training or participate in an insurgency and then return to their home countries to participate in a civil war or commit a terrorist attack.

(c) Foreign terrorists – individuals who travel to another state in order to perpetrate a terrorist attack.
(d) Foreign fighters – individuals who travel to another country (where they are not citizens) to join an insurgency.

Since the current chapter focuses on deradicalization of foreign fighters in the Jihadi context, and the threat that they represent upon their return, it will focus mainly on the second category of foreign fighters.

Deradicalization programs for foreign fighters

Several characteristics of foreign fighters are especially relevant when evaluating the potential security threat that they represent. The first is naturally the military experience and skill set that they acquire during their "tour" in areas of conflicts. Data collected from open sources illustrate that around 90% of the Jihadi foreign fighters attended military training camps and that a similar percentage eventually served as foot soldiers, rather than in support/logistical units, or in any leadership position (Perliger and Milton 2016). The fact that the foreign fighters suffer from a high death rate further reflects their intensive engagement in violent military operations. Hence, it is clear that most foreign fighters do not just receive military training, but have the opportunity to sharpen their military skills in actual military activities.

Additionally, the joining to Jihadi groups and the time spent with other Jihadists, which facilitate the socialization into the Jihadi lifestyle and ideological framework, may further strengthen the foreign fighters' solidarity with other Jihadists, as well as their commitment to the violent Jihadi struggle at large. Such a dynamic may create difficulties for returning foreign fighters who attempt to re-integrate into their original communities. Lastly, foreign fighters' attributes (military experience and ideological commitment) combined with their familiarity with various aspects of their home countries (language, culture, etc.) and their ability to move freely because of their citizenship status make them particularly useful for Jihadi groups that are interested in operating in Western countries.

The growth in the number of Western foreign fighters, and the expectation that some of them will eventually return to their home countries, eventually convinced several countries to adapt their existing counter-radicalization and disengagement programs in order to meet with this new challenge. But before discussing these adaptations, it is important to briefly review the main premise of deradicalization programs which were developed following 9/11 and the spread of Jihadi violence all over the globe.

The post-9/11 programs traditionally focused less on efforts of ideological disengagement (i.e., deradicalization) and more on helping individuals to disengage from the social network/framework which facilitates their radicalization or to support them if they decide to disengage voluntarily. More specifically, they tried to identify individuals which as a result of a specific event/process were more open to consider disengaging from radical groups, such as personal experience/trauma, disillusionment with the group's leaders or goals, exhaustion from living under stress or pressure from others (family, spouse) to leave the group. Once such an individual was identified, he or she received access to a plethora of support mechanisms which were aiming to help him or her rehabilitate and re-integrate back into his or her community (Bjørgo and Horgan 2009; Fink and Hamed 2011; Horgan and Braddock 2010). To illustrate, in Norway and Sweden specific "exit" programs were developed in order to allow members of violent neo-Nazi groups to leave their respective groups and to integrate back into the general, "normative," society. These programs relied heavily on non-profit organizations and the families, in order to provide the radicalized individuals with access to various social services that will facilitate their re-integration into society (Ramalingam 2014; Smith 2015). In other countries, similar programs include the transferring of the individuals (and sometimes their families) to new locations, in addition to access to social services and financial incentives (Colombia is a case in point, as FARC (Revolutionary Armed Forces of Colombia) members were relocated from their home towns to other areas of the country, and then went through orientation programs that were aiming at exposing them to the fallacies of FARC's propaganda, as well as helping them integrate back into mainstream society) (Ribetti 2009).

At the same time, many countries also included counter-propaganda efforts in their programs (or what some term as the ideological dimension of deradicalization) which were based mostly on the dissemination of information which fulfills one of the following objectives (Gregg 2010; Kohler 2014; Ryan 2007; Schori Liang 2015): (1) exposing the hypocrisy/corruption of the organization or its leaders, especially when the latter are not behaving in accordance with the group's ideology; (2) exposing inconsistencies in the group's ideological platform, or disagreements between ideological leaders – for example, many efforts were made by Western law enforcement to publicize Nazir Abbas' (top Jemaah Islamiyah leader) statement that Bin-Laden's 2000 fatwa (religious ruling) about the need to kill Americans and Jews everywhere is a false ruling that should be ignored; (3) exposing when possible the ineffectiveness of the group's operations and use of violence; (4) illustrating the advantages of non-violent means of protest or political activism; and (5) focusing on the life of the terrorist – dispelling the myth that the terrorist's life is glamorous or provides access to material or social benefits. These efforts in many cases emphasize how badly members are being treated by the groups' leaders and their heavy sacrifices. Overall, this information is supposed to foster cognitive dissonance in the radicalized individual and to motivate him to break the emotional attachment to the "collective" and ideological perceptions represented by the militant group.

In many ways, however, foreign fighters represent a more challenging problem in comparison to regular home-grown radicalized individuals, who were the main focus of most deradicalization programs until the last few years. To begin with, it is extremely difficult to track their moves upon their return and to gain valuable information about their experiences and personality characteristics (for example, how much they are still committed to Jihadi ideology). In many cases the states are unware of the returning foreign fighters. This explains why, according to an Interpol report, by 2015 fewer than 20% of European foreign fighters were identified (Stock 2015). In addition, in contrast to home-grown terrorists, foreign fighters are more likely to suffer from an array of psychological pathologies which are reflected in post-traumatic stress disorder (PTSD), emotional instability, and behavioral unpredictability (Briggs and Silverman 2014). Lastly, again, unlike most home-grown Jihadists, many of the foreign fighters can eventually become important assets for law enforcement and the intelligence agencies as a result of their military experience and close familiarity with their organizations. Thus, rehabilitation and re-integration can also facilitate their usage as intelligence sources and active participants in the deradicalization of other foreign fighters.

It seems that two important classifications need to be exercised in order to gain a better context and analytical clarity regarding deradicalization of foreign fighters. First, it is important to note that experts tend to identify two "types" of deradicalization policies (Lister 2015). The "soft" or "liberal" approach is focusing on the mobilization of the family and in some cases also other actors within the foreign fighter's community, as a support mechanism, as well as on a more nuanced approach to the risk he represents (Briggs and Silverman 2014; Lister

2015). In other words, it is based on the premise that the primary social network has the best resources to "pull" the radicalized individual back to a normative lifestyle (they are the most familiar with him, and he has some level of emotional commitment to them) as well as the fact that he can represent a "living counter-narrative." The hard approach, on the other hand, is focusing on detaining and then distancing/deportation of returning foreign fighters (Briggs and Silverman 2014; Lister 2015). The second useful classification differentiates between deradicalization programs in Western democracies and in Muslim countries. The different types of polities are facing different legal and cultural challenges, as well as different characteristics of the foreign fighters they "export" and then absorb. In the next sections, both types of approaches and polities' deradicalization efforts of foreign fighters will be analyzed.

Deradicalization of foreign fighters in Western democracies

Probably the most-known program which adopted a "soft" approach is the German HAYAT ("life" in Arabic) which is run by the Center for Democratic Culture (ZDK) in Berlin. It is an extension of a previous initiative which was active between 2007 and 2010 and provided a consultation service to family members of far-right radicalized youth (Koehler 2013). In order to empower the family members to directly engage in helping with the disengagement or deradicalization of the radicalized family member, HAYAT's counseling services provide the family information about the groups and ideology which facilitate the radicalization of the family member, as well as training in the appropriate methods to interact with a radicalized individual (Koehler 2013; Lister 2015). For example, family members are trained to identify behaviors or communications which may be an indication that the radical individual has started to develop doubts regarding his decision to adopt a Jihadi lifestyle and views, and then to exploit these doubts to further inform him about the related moral and practical costs of his decision to adopt radical views, and to help him to disengage from radical activities. The counseling also aims to identify cases of ideological radicalization which are not likely to lead to violent activities (and then try to help the family to cope with the new ideological views of the relative, without engaging in direct deradicalization efforts), as well as identifying the underlying motivations of the radicalization which is important in order to make informed decisions about the exact methods that family members should employ to help the radicalized relative (Kohler 2014; Lister 2015).

As stated above, in recent years HAYAT was modified so it can provide effective help to families of (would-be or returning) foreign fighters. At the pre-travel phase, the counseling is focused on trying to convince (or if necessary prevent by legal means) the radical family member not to travel to areas of conflict. In the post-travel phase, the focus is on working with experts and law enforcement in order to maintain communication with the family member and to gather information about his activities, while identifying possible mechanisms that can facilitate his return. In addition, family members are provided therapy treatments in order to reduce their anxiety. If the foreign fighter eventually returns, the program focuses on initial risk assessment, and then on providing help to the family so it can become a supportive environment which will be able to prevent further radicalization of the family member or even convince him to abandon his militant behaviors/views. At this stage, if the individual is continuing to practice behaviors which indicate that he is a security threat, the program will focus on helping the family to cope with the situation, and prevent other members from radicalizing, while law enforcement will deal directly with the threat represented by the returning foreign fighter (Koehler 2013; Lister 2015).

Another fairly well-known program which adopted a "soft" approach is the one exercised in Denmark. Denmark's initial counter-radicalization program, "A Common and Safe Future," was launched in 2005, and in its 2009 revision, it recognized for the first time the need to deal with the risk of traveling/returning Danish citizens to/from areas of conflict (Project Denmark: Extremism and Counter Extremism 2015). The emphasis of the Danish program is on promoting policies that will encourage Danish foreign fighters to return to the country, as well as to facilitate effective re-integration. Therefore, it provides several services to the foreign fighters immediately upon their return, including medical and psychological treatments, and counseling regarding future occupational and educational opportunities and housing solutions (Briggs and Silverman 2014; Project Denmark: Extremism and Counter Extremism 2015). Thus, the premise is that providing a solution to the socio-economic needs of the returning foreign fighters, can both facilitate their re-integration as well as motivate those of them who have doubts about their ideological choices, to try and return to Denmark. As in Germany, also in Denmark, the primary social networks of the returning foreign fighters are mobilized to help in their deradicalization. Families of returnees are offered counseling and guidance and are also asked to provide a supportive home to the returning foreign fighter. In addition, initiatives which focus on dialog and cooperation between the relevant communities, social services, educational and religious institutions, and law enforcement are part of these efforts, although more in the preventive stage. To conclude, the Danish program also fosters cooperation and coordination with local initiatives. For example, in the framework of the "Aarhus initiative," government agencies worked with local organizations to deal with the issue of local returnees (the city of Aarhus is a significant "exporter" of foreign fighters) (Briggs and Silverman 2014; Lasse and Sedgwick 2012).

The tendency of some programs to concentrate on the utilization of family members as a "pull" mechanism presents several potential challenges. To begin with, while the family can provide emotional support and a safe space, it is much less effective in dealing with socio-economic challenges. Some of the studies which looked into Western foreign fighters identified that it is not just that they usually come from minority groups which suffer from structural economic discrimination, but also from the lower socio-economic echelons of these communities (Perliger and Milton 2016). Thus, they seem to be motivated at least partially by the lack of upward mobilization opportunities. Therefore, it seems that deradicalization models which combine both emotional and socio-economic support (i.e., the Danish model) may be a better solution. In addition, data collected in recent years specify that foreign fighters are in many cases second- and third-generation immigrants. This may hint that at least some of the reasons for their decision to travel to the Middle East is related to feelings of alienation and miscommunication with other members of their family. Many stories of foreign fighters depict polarized and contentious inter-generational relationships (which in families of immigrants are highly common), which prevented the parents identifying in advance their son's/daughter's intentions, and crippled their ability to deal effectively with their radicalization. Lastly, it is important to remember that the emotional attachment of family members to their radicalized son/daughter/brother/sister can make it difficult for them to acknowledge concerning developments in his or her behavior/attitudes and lead to the failure of the deradicalization effort.

Another challenge which is not necessarily specific to foreign fighters is related to the tendency of more conservative families to avoid the use of counseling services and to embrace more radical and stricter versions of the Islamic faith. Considering that some found that the stronger the level of piety of the family (Davis and Cragin 2009), the greater are the chances that some members will be radicalized, this seems to suggest that utilizing family as a "pull" mechanism can work just when there is already some inherent resistance within the family to radical Islamic narratives.

Some democracies adopted what can be considered a "harder" approach when devising programs to deal with the threat of returning foreign fighters. The UK, for example, utilizes an umbrella program titled CONTEST to manage various counter-radicalization/terrorism efforts (Rabasa et al. 2010). Within CONTEST two sections are most relevant to our discussion. The first is focused on the funding of national and local counter-radicalization initiatives (mainly via the "channel" program which utilizes partners within the community to provide pre-criminal intervention), as well as on integration efforts (this strand of the program was titled "Prevent"). The second focuses on the conviction, arrest, and quick deportation of radicalized individuals (this strand of the program was titled "Pursue") (Griffith-Dickson, Dickson and Ivermee 2014). Thus, in many ways, both represent different attitudes within CONTEST. However, the latter seems more prominent, especially in the context of foreign fighters. This is reflected by the high number of returning foreign fighters detained and arrested (around 80%), as well as by the hardening of specific counter-foreign fighters' policies (Committee, Home Affairs 2009). Moreover, the fact that British foreign fighters are distributed between several correctional facilities to reduce the possibility of in-prison radicalization (that is, foreign fighters radicalizing other inmates) naturally hinders the ability to effectively utilize resources aiming to promote foreign fighters' rehabilitation. Lastly, unlike in Germany or Denmark, CONTEST seems to focus more on empowering communities rather than utilizing the primary social network of the returning foreign fighter. The "concept" of a family is absent from the language of CONTEST, except for a recommendation to help them enroll in formal parenting programs (Committee, Home Affairs 2009).

The focus on communities' empowerment in the UK generated significant criticism for at least two reasons (Githens-Mazer and Lambert 2010). The first is that it fostered public designation of Muslim communities as hubs of radicalization, which facilitated animosity between them and the general public. The second was that it put the responsibility on community leaders rather than on those who are in closer interactions with the radicalized individual. In addition, the focus on conviction and detention, as well as deportation, possibly undermines the willingness of family members to cooperate with the authorities, and may also deter foreign fighters who were interested in returning and disengaging from their group.

Deradicalization of foreign fighters in Muslim countries

While most of the discussion about the security threat from foreign fighters can be described as Western-centric, data show that the number of foreign fighters from Muslim countries is several times higher than that of Western foreign fighters (Dodwell, Milton and Rassler 2016). Consequently, it is not surprising that several countries in the Middle East and North Africa attempted to devise deradicalization programs, which were also utilized to mitigate the threat of returning foreign fighters. Most of these programs included a combination of counter-narrative efforts, counseling, and vocational training.

Saudi Arabia, the number-one "exporter" of Jihadi foreign fighters (Dodwell, Milton and Rassler 2016), established several new rehabilitation centers since 2014 to treat Saudi foreign fighters returning from Syria/Iraq. These centers worked as an extension of the Prevention, Rehabilitation, and After-Care (PRAC) program which has been run in Saudi Arabia since 2004. As with the case of "home-grown" Jihadists, the focus is on ideological training/

counseling which was supposed to expose the inconsistencies and fallacies of the Jihadi narrative (Horgan and Braddock 2010; Rabasa et al. 2010). The program also fosters family involvement in the rehabilitation process, in order to ensure that after his release, the former radicalized individual will have a stable supporting environment. Interestingly, recently the Saudi government also utilized its official TV networks to support the program, by broadcasting testimonies of former foreign fighters refuting the Jihadi narrative (Zelin and Prohov 2014). Overall, it seems that ideological counter-indoctrination is the backbone of the Saudi program, while more marginal elements provide additional support and a constructive environment to the returning foreign fighter (Bakrania 2014; Rabasa et al. 2010; Zelin and Prohov 2014). It is important to note however that Saudi Arabia may have deterred some of its foreign fighters from returning when it released a royal decree in 2014 announcing that any citizen who fought in a conflict abroad would be imprisoned for 3–20 years. The decree also clarified that Saudis who join, endorse, or give moral or material aid to groups it classifies as terrorist or extremist organizations, whether inside or outside the country, would face prison sentences of 5–30 years.

Other Muslim countries which endeavored to implement similar programs or to promote policies which will facilitate re-integration of foreign fighters faced significant challenges in executing and maintaining their programs. In Tunisia, the government adopted in 2016 a plan, which was utilized successfully in some Latin American countries (i.e., see, for example, the case of the M14 and FARC in Colombia), of initiating an amnesty program. More specifically, returning foreign fighters who were not involved in actual killings during their "tour" in Syria, and who publicly expressed their regret and remorse for traveling to Syria/Iraq were supposed to be given amnesty (Zelin and Prohov 2014). While it is unclear to what extent this program was implemented, as shortly after it was announced the government faced mass protest and political backlash (Gall 2017), it seems that at least several hundred were indeed given amnesty and received help in re-integrating into society. Nonetheless, most foreign fighters who returned in 2016 and 2017 were arrested after the government decided to build special prisons to accommodate the returning foreign fighters, and government officials announced that returning foreign fighters would be arrested in accordance with Tunisian counter-terrorism laws (Watanabe 2015). Latest testimonies seem indeed to confirm that the Tunisian government abandoned any intention to adopt "soft" re-integration policies or deradicalization programs. For example, Ridha Raddaui, a Tunisian lawyer and civil rights activist, stated that "families of suspects and fighters who have returned are persecuted rather than supported" (Gall 2017).

Tunisia's neighboring countries seem to have made even less progress in developing effective deradicalization or re-integration programs. In both Morocco and Algeria, the governments established strong control over the religious establishment and the curriculum of religious educational institutions, in order to prevent the penetration of Jihadi elements, and ensure that religious education does not facilitate radicalization (Bakrania 2014). In addition, the governments of both countries initiated vocational programs to help people in their early professional career in finding employment. However, no deradicalization programs were formed to deal with returning foreign fighters, and, as in Tunisia, in both Morocco and Algeria they are usually incarcerated immediately upon their return (Bakrania 2014).

In the rest of the countries in the region, there is even less inclination to utilize "soft" measures. Hence, it seems that most Muslim countries prefer to utilize their criminal justice system and "hard" punishment measures, rather than investing in deradicalization efforts. This policy trend can be explained by addressing more broadly the contextual dynamics which are in play in most Muslim countries with regard to the foreign fighters' problem.

To begin with, in comparison to most Western countries, most Muslim countries face tremendous challenges in tracking and monitoring their citizens who became foreign fighters. This is because they are dealing with much greater numbers, as well as because of the inherent limitations of their intelligence agencies and law enforcement. Most of the literature which covers the counter-terrorism efforts of these countries emphasizes the inability of many Arab countries to gain accurate data about their citizens who travel to areas of conflict (Bakrania 2014).

Another challenge that is usually ignored by experts is the unique linkage between the political and religious establishments in many Middle Eastern countries. The fact that many political leaders provide patronage to specific religious streams/institutions, in return for political support and legitimacy, facilitates a deradicalization program which focuses on ideological transformation, rather than on socio-economic mechanisms as well as the utilization of strong mechanisms of monitoring over religious institutions. However, this dynamic frames the conflict with the Jihadist as a religious-ideological dispute, rather than a battle against illegal and immoral violent practices, and thus, benefits jihadists on several grounds. It allows them to present themselves as a legitimate opposition to oppressive political leaders, as well as more easily to utilize religious rhetoric as a justification for their violent struggle. Lastly, this puts governments under greater pressure to support and nurture alternative religious streams.

Another problem which most Middle-Eastern countries face is related to their non-democratic and non-liberal characteristics. Regimes which for decades based their policies on the premise of aggressive treatment and response to opposition groups, and did not base their rule on the concept of popular legitimacy, will find it naturally difficult to adopt policies which are based on concessions, and re-integration of individuals who represent potential ideological opposition.

Conclusions: theoretical and policy insights

One of the common threads within the deradicalization literature is the consensus regarding the great difficulties in evaluating the effectiveness of deradicalization and re-integration policies (Bakrania 2014). This is no different in the case of deradicalization of foreign fighters. While conventional assessment methods try to identify how many of the participants in these programs were able to re-integrate into society and abandoned their radical views, in the case of foreign fighters the application of such methods is more complicated. It is not always clear if the returning foreign fighters are still devoted to the Jihadi ideological framework, or if they returned because their experience "opened their eyes" and exposed them to the deficiencies of the Jihadi lifestyle and ideological paradigm. Moreover, in many cases it is not also clear if the returnees actually engaged in violent or illegal activities (beyond joining a Jihadi group). As a result, foreign fighters who did not resume their radical activities upon their return cannot necessarily serve as a measure of the effectiveness of deradicalization programs. In addition, as with the case with programs which are focusing on home-grown radicals, it is difficult to identify personal ideological transformations and to distinguish them from behavioral ones. Simply put, it is difficult to ascertain how much the fact that the individual is not involved any more in Jihadi activities really reflects a change of heart.

But the probably more important question is related to the potential of deradicalization of people who in many ways already fulfilled their radical aspiration and became part of the Jihadi struggle (i.e., foreign fighters). Academic literature which is focusing on the psychological and sociological processes related to deviant behaviors usually depict a feedback loop between cognition and behavior, and that in many instances behavioral tendencies are the ones which are responsible for rooting specific cognitive and emotional perceptions. Therefore, it is understandable why so many of the young individuals who travel to join Jihadi groups have limited familiarity with Jihadi ideology, but it is also fair to hypothesize that their actual involvement in ideological and military engagements upon their joining a Jihadi group will intensify their attachment to the Jihadi ideology. If this is indeed the case, it is fair to ask: how effective can deradicalization programs be when dealing with individuals who already manifested their devotion by risking their lives? In other words, some may argue that foreign fighters cannot be the subject of deradicalization efforts since they are the manifestation of the failure of such efforts.

Identity vs. upward mobilization

The inconclusive opinions within the academic community regarding the motivating factors of foreign fighters also position deradicalization efforts in a no-man's land in terms of their focus and resource allocation. Some studies emphasize that foreign fighters are being attracted to areas of conflict and Jihadist groups because of the lack of upward mobilization opportunities in their home countries and communities, and a strong sense of economic marginalization. Other studies tend to focus on the role of identity, asserting that young Muslims aspire to join Jihadi groups since this allows them to overcome sentiments of alienation and social marginalization in their home countries and to develop feelings of belonging and solidarity with a Jihadi transnational community. Thus, their inability to develop emotional attachment to the national collective in their home countries, because of the marginalization of their cultural heritage and ethnicity, is overcome by joining an alternative community (i.e., Jihadi collective).

Naturally, each of these sets of factors which drive individuals to become foreign fighters demands different sets of counter-policies. However, in both cases there is a clear necessity for long-term solutions which are actually not focusing on the individuals and their families but on their communities. More specifically, policies which aim to deal with socio-economic factors and marginalization need to address the root causes which prevent some immigrant communities from providing their young people opportunities for economic mobilization and the tools to position themselves better within the labor market. Improving educational, vocational, and social efficacy seems to be an effective long-term step. But it is also important, it seems, to identify how intra-communal services can help deal with the more economically vulnerable within immigrant communities. Studies which show that large portions of foreign fighters are from the lower economic echelons of immigrant communities hint that it is not enough to help the community at large, but also identifying mechanisms that in the short term can provide direct assistance to the low economic tiers of the community (Perliger and Milton 2016). While such solutions cannot provide immediate "medicine" to the current "symptoms," they can generate effective responses to the root causes of the threat.

Addressing foreign fighters who seem to be attracted to the Jihadi struggle as a result of their desire to become part of an alternative collective identity is even more challenging since some of the major policies which were implemented so far to tackle this problem have seemed to fail miserably.

Both the adoption of multiculturalism in places like the UK, as well as policies which emphasized homogenization of national practices in public (i.e., France), seem to have failed to instill a sense of belonging among second- and third-generation immigrants, many of whom constitute contemporary foreign fighters. The tendency of immigrant communities to cluster in specific areas, which facilitates segregation, may add to the related challenges. Lastly, the intensifying process of globalization and the emergence of transnational communities, which seem to erode some aspects of national identity and cohesiveness, definitely do not make it easier to find effective policies that can facilitate emotional integration and help marginalized communities to feel part of the national collective.

Mixed messages: the politics of deradicalization of foreign fighters

In democracies, political leaders are traditionally trying to shape counter-terrorism policies that strike a balance between ensuring the security of the nation/citizens and the preservation of democratic/liberal principles (Schmid 1992). Studies on the factors which shape counter-terrorism policies in democracies identified however that governments tend to adopt more aggressive policies when fighting terrorist groups that represent marginal communities which are not part of the mainstream culture, and have limited political capital (Perliger 2012). This trend is even more enhanced in non-democratic regimes. Hence, it is not surprising that most countries tend to distance themselves from "soft" deradicalization policies when dealing with the threat of foreign fighters. After all, most of the foreign fighters originate from such sub-cultures or marginalized communities (Perliger and Milton 2016). Moreover, it explains also why in several of the case studies which were discussed above it was clear that one of the challenges of implementing "soft" deradicalization policies was related to political counter-pressure, as well as opposition by the general public (see the cases of the UK and Tunisia).

Another issue which may contribute to public pressure against "soft" deradicalization policies is the strong sense of betrayal which proliferates in some of the societies which "export" foreign fighters. These sentiments, at least in North America and Western Europe, are further stimulated by various far-right parties and movements which promote sentiments such as that the foreign fighters' phenomenon represents the "ungratefulness" of immigrant communities, and that immigrants are not really interested in integrating and embracing loyalty to their new countries. Thus, any effective deradicalization efforts must also engage in practices which will refute such xenophobic views, and promote further interaction and understanding between immigrants and mainstream society/culture, as well as rejecting perceptions which tend to blame the communities for the acts of individuals. Such policies can in the long term reduce the backlash towards soft deradicalization programs and increase the likelihood of their effectiveness.

References

Bakke, M. Kristen. (2013). "Copying and Learning from Outsiders? Assessing Diffusion from Transnational Insurgents in the Chechen Wars." In Jeffrey T. Chekel (ed) *Transnational Dynamics of Civil Wars*. Cambridge, UK: Cambridge University Press, pp. 31–62.

Bakrania, Shivit. (2014). *Counter and De-Radicalisation with Returning Foreign Fighters*. GSDRC.

Bjørgo, Tore, and John G. Horgan. (2009). *Leaving Terrorism Behind: Individual and Collective Disengagement*. London: Routledge.

Briggs, Rachel, and Tanya Silverman. (2014). *Western Foreign Fighters: Innovations in Responding to the Threat*. Institute for Strategic Dialogue. London: Institute for Strategic Dialogue.

Bryan, Ian. (2010). "Sovereignty and the Foreign Fighter Problem." *Orbis* 54 (1): 115–129.

Cohen, Chanan, and Oren Barak. (2013). *The "Modern Sherwood Forest": Theoretical and Practical Challenges, in Nonstate Actors in Intrastate Conflicts*. Philadelphia: University of Pennsylvania Press.

Committee, Home Affairs. (2009). *Project CONTEST: The Government's Counter-Terrorism Strategy.* London: Stationery Office Limited.
Davis, L. Paul, and Kim Cragin. (2009). *Social Science for Counterterrorism: Putting the Pieces Together.* Santa Monica: RAND Corporation.
Dodwell, Brian, Brian Milton, and Don Rassler. (2016). *The Caliphate's Global Workforce: An Inside Look at the Islamic State's Foreign Fighter Paper Trail.* West Point: Combating Terrorism Center.
Fink, Naureen Chowdhury, and El-Said Hamed. (2011). *Transforming Terrorists: Examining International Efforts to Address Violent Extremism.* Washington, DC: International Peace Institute.
Gall, Carlotta. (2017). "Tunisia Fears the Return of Thousands of Young Jihadists." *New York Times,* February 25.
Githens-Mazer, Jonathan, and Robert Lambert. (2010). *Islamophobia and Anti-Muslim Hate Crime: A London Case Study.* University of Exeter, Exeter: European Muslim Research Centre.
Gregg, Heather S. (2010). "Fighting the Jihad of the Pen: Countering Revolutionary Islam's Ideology." *Terrorism and Political Violence* 22: 292–314.
Griffith-Dickson, Gwen, Andrew Dickson, and Robert Ivermee. (2014). "Counter-extremism and De-radicalisation in the UK: A Contemporary Overview." *Journal for Deradicalisation* 1: 26–37.
Gurski, Phil. (2016). *Western Foreign Fighters: The Threat to Homeland and International Security.* London: Rowman & Littlefield.
Hegghammer, Thomas. (2010). "The Rise of Muslim Foreign Fighters: Islam and the Globalization of Jihad." *International Security* 35 (3): 53–94.
Holman, Timothy. (2015). "Belgian and French Foreign Fighters in Iraq 2003–2005: A Comparative Case Study." *Studies in Conflict & Terrorism* 38 (3): 603–621.
Horgan, John, and Kurt Braddock. (2010). "Rehabilitating the Terrorists? Challenges in Assessing the Effectiveness of Deradicalisation Programs." *Terrorism and Political Violence* 22 (2): 267–291.
Koehler, Daniel. (2013). "Family Counselling as Prevention and Intervention Tool against 'Foreign Fighters'. The German 'Hayat' Program." *Journal EXIT-Deutschland* 3: 182–204.
Kohler, Daniel. (2014). "Deradicalization." In Nathan Hall, Abbee Corb, Paul Giannasi, John G. D. Grieve, and Neville Lawrence (eds) *Routledge International Handbook of Hate Crime.* New York: Routledge.
Lasse, Lindekilde, and Mark Sedgwick. (2012). *Impact of Counter-Terrorism on Communities: Denmark Background Report.* Institute for Strategic Dialogue.
Lister, Charles. (2015). *Returning Foreign Fighters: Criminalization or Reintegration?* Doha: Brookings Doha Center.
Malet, David. (2013). *Foreign Fighters: Transnational Identity in Civil Conflicts.* Oxford: Oxford University Press.
———. (2015). "Foreign Fighter Mobilization and Persistence in a Global Context." *Terrorism and Political Violence* 27 (3): 454–473.
Mustapha, Jennifer. (2013). "The Mujahideen in Bosnia: The Foreign Fighter as Cosmopolitan Citizen and/or Terrorist." *Citizenship Studies* 17 (3): 742–755.
Nilsson, Marco. (2015). "Foreign Fighters and the Radicalization of Local Jihad: Interview Evidence from Swedish Jihadists." *Studies in Conflict & Terrorism* 38 (5): 343–358.
Parlapiano, Alicia, Wilson Andrews, Haeyoun Park, and Larry Buchanan. (2015). "Finding the Links among the Paris Attackers." *The New York Times,* March 18.
Perliger, Arie. (2012). "How Democracies Respond to Terrorism: Regime Characteristics, Symbolic Power and Counterterrorism." *Security Studies* 21 (3): 490–528.
Perliger, Arie, and Daniel Milton. (2016). *From Cradle to the Grave: The Lifecycle of Foreign Fighters in Iraq and Syria.* West Point: Combating Terrorism Center.
Project Denmark. (2015). *Project Denmark: Extremism and Counter Extremism.* Institute for Strategic Dialogue.
Rabasa, Angel, Stacie L. Pettyjohn, Jeremy J. Ghez, and Christopher Boucek. (2010). *Deradicalizing Islamic Extremists.* Santa Monica: RAND Corporation.
Ramalingam, Vidhya. (2014). *On the Front Line: A Guide to Countering Far-right Extremism.* Oslo: Institute for Strategic Dialogue.
Ribetti, Marcella. (2009). "Disengagement and Beyond: A Case Study of Demobilization in Colombia." In Tore Bjørgo and John Horgan (eds) *Leaving Terrorism Behind: Individual and Collective Disengagement.* New York: Routledge, pp. 152–159.
Ryan, Johny. (2007). *Countering Militant Islamist Radicalisation on the Internet.* Dublin: Institute of European Affairs.

Schmid, P. Alex. (1992). "Terrorism and Democracy." *Terrorism and Political Violence* 4 (4): 14–25.
Schori Liang, Christina. (2015). *Cyber Jihad: Understanding and Countering Islamic State Propaganda*. Geneva: Geneva Center for Security Policy.
Smith, Tuva Julie Engebrethsen. (2015). *Islamic Radicalization in Norway: Preventive Action*. Herzlia: International Institute for Counter-Terrorism.
Stenersen, Anne. (2011). "Al Qaeda's Foot Soldiers: A Study of the Biographies of Foreign Fighters Killed in Afghanistan and Pakistan between 2002 and 2006." *Studies in Conflict & Terrorism* 34 (3): 171–198.
Stock, Jurgen. (2015). "Statement before the United Nations Security Council Ministerial Briefing on Foreign Terrorist Fighters." *Speech*, New York: U.N. headquarters, May 29.
Watanabe, Lisa. (2015). *Foreign Fighters and Their Return – Measures Taken by North African Countries*. Center for Security Studies. ETH Zurich: Zurich Center for Security Studies, ETH Zurich.
Zelin Aaron, and Prohov Jonathan. (2014) "The Foreign Policy Essay: Proactive Measures-Countering the Returnee Threat". *Lawfareblog*, May 1. www.lawfareblog.com/2014/05/the-foreignpolicy-essay-proactive-measures-countering-the-returnee-threat/.

PART II

Actors

9

PRISON-BASED DERADICALIZATION

What do we need to determine what works?

Jessica Stern and Paige Pascarelli

Criminologists have long argued that, rather than serving as a place of rehabilitation, prisons are often a space where offenders become more deeply committed to a culture of crime. Just as prison time can lead prisoners to adopt criminal values, a process known as "prisonization," it can also prompt incarcerated offenders to accept terrorist values, including the belief that violence is a legitimate way to achieve ostensibly political goals (Naderi 2014).[1] A number of governments and private organizations have developed deradicalization and disengagement programs, but there is no agreed-upon definition of success, or a common method of evaluation.[2] This chapter provides an overview of several of these programs and analogous programs for ordinary criminals, and proposes an approach to measuring their impact.

There are fewer terrorists than ordinary prisoners in most prisons globally, but terrorist prisoners' ability to influence others can be proportionally greater than that of ordinary prisoners (Silke 2014, p. 3). Prison can strengthen incarcerated terrorists' commitment to their stated cause and their determination to use violence to achieve it. Terrorists who go to prison can recruit, and spread terrorist ideologies among ordinary offenders, as was the case of Ahmad Rahimi, the "Chelsea Bomber," who even after arrest, reportedly disseminated Osama Bin Laden and Anwar al-Awlaki speeches and bomb-making instructions while awaiting trial (NBC 2017).[3] They can form new groups, plot attacks, develop new strategies, or incite others.

The extent of terrorist recruitment or radicalization in prison is currently unknown,[4] but there are some important examples. Islamic State in Iraq and Syria (ISIS) leader, Abu Bakr al-Baghdadi, was incarcerated at Camp Bucca in 2004, a US-run detention facility in Iraq. He had been relatively unknown, a minor jihadi at the time he was jailed. But it is now understood that Camp Bucca served as a kind of terrorist university for the group that would eventually be the Islamic State, even despite the existence of deradicalization efforts in these facilities (Stern and Berger 2015, pp. 33–34).[5] According to General Stone, who ran the US detention facilities in Iraq, jihadists who get out of US detention develop a kind of aura when reintegrated into their home communities, making it easier for them to recruit others, or to represent defiance against the West.[6] Baghdadi left Camp Bucca and immediately joined the ranks of the Islamic State of Iraq (ISI), later announcing the formation of the Islamic State in 2014.[7] Baghdadi is but one of many prominent terrorist recidivists.

Though this chapter is primarily concerned with those in prison on terrorism-related charges, there are also examples of ordinary offenders who radicalized in prison or shortly after they were released, and were subsequently convicted of terrorist crimes. British Richard Reid, the "shoe-bomber," and American Jose Padilla both converted to Islam while in prison for non-terror-related offenses but may have radicalized shortly after their release. There are also cases of regular criminals becoming radicalized while in prison. The following two cases mirror one another: Harry Sarfo (German) and Amedy Coulibaly (French) were both radicalized by known al-Qaeda recruiters while each was serving time in prison for armed robbery.[8] Sarfo claimed that it was in prison where he "learned the ideology of jihad," whereas Coulibaly would meet his future accomplice, Cherif Kouachi (Chrisafis 2015; Dearden 2017).[9] Figures for European ISIS fighters range from 50 to 80 percent having criminal records (Gaub and Lisiecka 2017, p. 1).[10] Among ISIS attackers in the West, at least 57 percent had a criminal background (Vidino et al. 2017, p. 17). Importantly, the University of Maryland START program has found that individuals who engaged in non-violent or violent crime before radicalizing were 1.85 times more likely to engage in violent extremism after radicalizing than extremists without criminal histories (Jensen et al. 2018, p. 1). This suggests that individuals convicted of ordinary crime could be useful recruits for terrorist organizations.[11]

With the increase of terror-related arrests and convictions around the globe, prisons could become larger breeding grounds for the jihadist movement (Basra et al. 2016, p. 4). As such, deradicalization is an important development in an overall counterterrorism strategy, as there are notable examples of terrorists who recidivated upon release. The US government reports that nearly 30 percent of released Guantanamo detainees are suspected of or confirmed to have re-engaged in terrorism (DNI n.d., p. 1). Still, deradicalization is not a panacea: several of the January 2016 Jakarta attackers had undergone Indonesian deradicalization programming, and graduates of Saudi Arabian deradicalization programs have returned to the battlefield; some of them would become senior leaders of al-Qaeda. Deradicalization will never completely prevent terrorist recidivism, but with better evaluation of the programs that do exist, there may be a greater chance of improvement and success.

The first section of this chapter lays out the problem that deradicalization programs aim to address, and provides a brief survey of scholars' critiques of existing methods of deradicalization and assessment. The second section provides an overview of several prison-based deradicalization and disengagement programs, and lists the components of these programs and the variables that are hypothesized to reduce recruitment and recidivism. The third section provides an overview of counter-recidivism programs successfully deployed for "ordinary" criminals. Unlike countering violent extremism (CVE) programs, these efforts incorporate a common method of evaluation. The final section concludes that, in order for prison-based deradicalization programs to benefit from the experience of others around the globe, an agreed-upon system of rigorous evaluation is needed.

We hypothesize that some aspects of existing programs to counter ordinary criminal recidivism and, most importantly, the standard method of evaluation that is now in use, may be applicable to decreasing terrorist recidivism. Our analysis thus far suggests that programs that are tailored to individual needs are more likely to be effective, as is the case for ordinary criminals. But in the absence of common evaluation tools, it is not yet possible to make a firm recommendation about which aspects of counter-recidivism (disengagement, deradicalization, and post-release stabilization) are most likely to be effective, nor is it possible reliably to compare programs as they have different goals and employ a variety of methodologies and metrics.

How big is the terrorist recidivist problem?

There is no single database that reports the number of terrorists incarcerated around the globe. One study found that between September 11, 2001 and 2011, there were 119,044 anti-terror arrests and 35,117 convictions across 66 countries (Mendoza 2011).[12] At the time of this writing, there were approximately 300 terrorist prisoners in US prisons, nearly 90 of whom are due to be released in the next five years (NCTC Current 2017, p. 1). Some of them "will probably reengage in terrorist activity," the National Counterterrorism Center (NCTC) warned (p. 1). However, dynamics have changed since 2001. Of the 45,000 foreign fighters from around the world who left for Syria and Iraq, some have returned to their home countries of origin, and some have already died. But others have been or will be imprisoned, either in their home country or detained in Syria or Iraq (or elsewhere). In Europe, there were 718 arrests related to jihadist terrorism in 2016 alone, a number that has sharply increased for each of the previous three years (Europol 2017, p. 7). Thus, the number of incarcerated terrorists is likely to have grown significantly since the above-mentioned tally was published.

Daniel Koehler notes that there are approximately 40–50 deradicalization (or CVE) programs in operation globally (Koehler 2017, p. 1). Some of them have been evaluated, to some extent, often by the same organization that is providing the service, creating potential conflicts of interest. There is no overall measurement of how many terrorists have undergone deradicalization and what worked for those who did. There are many qualitative overviews, such as the "Rome Memorandum on Good Practices for Rehabilitation and Reintegration of Violent Extremist Offender," which presents over 20 useful best practices for prison deradicalization, but the report does not analyze the conditions under which certain practices work better than others (Global Counterterrorism Forum 2013). Other studies have analyzed the methodology of assessments that do exist. IMPACT Europe assessed 55 evaluations of deradicalization or prevention programs, and found that only 12 percent provided quantitative and qualitative data on effectiveness. A majority of the evaluations were not empirically based, but rather "theoretical" and/or "anecdotal" (Feddes and Gallucci 2015, p. 11). Koehler warns that ill-designed and ineffective deradicalization programs can *increase* the risk of terrorism by failing to detect high-risk cases (2017, p. 1).

Understanding why terrorists disengage is essential for formulating deradicalization programming. In John Horgan's study of 29 former terrorists, he found no identifiable patterns among the reasons they offered for their decision to disengage. Many remained dedicated to the cause, even though they no longer espoused violence in support of it. Disillusionment with terrorist group members and leaders was a notable factor for why the terrorists began to question their involvement, as well as shifting personal priorities (Horgan 2009, p. 31). Horgan notes people can vacillate between violent action and inaction, while still holding radical beliefs (Bjørgo and Horgan 2009; Horgan 2008, 2010). Thus, a program that focuses solely on ideology may not be effective in bringing about behavioral changes.

Individuals get involved in terrorism for many reasons. Some individuals become terrorists because it is their best employment option. Others are attracted to the ideology the terrorist group claims to promote, while others are seeking a new identity, adventure, glamour, or fun.

Most importantly, extremist, violent-promoting ideologies do not necessarily lead to violent action, and terrorist violence is not necessarily motivated by terrorist ideology. It follows that programming must be flexible enough to respond to the constellation of reasons individuals are drawn to violent extremism, calling for multi-pronged approaches, but should not focus on ideology alone (Stern 2003, 2014).

Mary Beth Altier et al. find that, for those who *voluntarily* disengaged, push factors were more important than pull factors, such as disillusionment with the group's strategy or actions, leaders, or members, or day-to-day tasks (Altier et al. 2017, p. 320). This finding is important because many European programs are voluntary. For the involuntary control group, pull factors, such as employment and educational opportunities, positive interactions with moderates (or formers), and financial incentives, were more prevalent. Saudi Arabia's programming, for example, is largely mandatory (p. 320). Still, she argues, "pull factors may also play a role in terrorist rehabilitation and re-integration and in deterring re-engagement" (p. 332). This means that providing alternatives to the terrorist lifestyle may reduce the inclination to rejoin a terrorist group or recidivate.

Horgan, Stern, and Altier all contend that only rarely does one factor drive someone's decision to engage in or disengage from terrorism. As such, options for addressing such processes should be adaptable enough to be individualized.

Overview of country-specific deradicalization and disengagement programs

The goal of these brief summaries is to provide a general overview of several prison-related deradicalization programs. These programs were selected either because of their purported success, or because they incorporated some evaluative measures. Except for a study of a Sri Lankan program that measured success in terms of a reduction in extremist beliefs, most programs profiled view success in terms of decreased terrorist recidivism, or behavior.

Saudi Arabia

Saudi Arabia first implemented its well-funded and comprehensive counter-radicalization programs in 2004, and has continued to expand its programs into new areas, including addressing online recruitment. Though Saudi Arabia's programs incorporate ideological "re-education," they also include psychological and vocational assistance, and post-release stabilization. Individuals are constantly re-evaluated in and out of the program. Compensation is provided to family members upon the observation that many of the individuals in the program joined terrorist groups to make money. After the program ends, surveillance and control continue (Holmer and Shtuni 2017, p. 8). Though the Saudi program claimed a remarkable 1–2 percent recidivism rate in 2008, two years later Saudi Arabia admitted that as many as 10–20 percent of program graduates had returned to illicit activity[13] (Boucek 2008, p. 21; Porges 2010). Without an external evaluation of these programs, their impact on reducing recidivism cannot be confirmed.

Sri Lanka

A Sri Lankan terrorist rehabilitation program entails seven components: educational, vocational, psychological, spiritual, recreational, cultural/family, and community. The program was modeled on the Saudi and Singaporean program. The program was available to convicted Tamil Tiger (LTTE) terrorists, but those designated as high-risk (frontline leaders and members) were detained and went through the judiciary process. Only then, and upon another assessment, could individuals be offered rehabilitation (Hettiarachchi 2013, p. 109).

Rather than measuring recidivism rates, a study of the Sri Lankan program assessed changes in program participants' ideological commitment to determine "success." The study found that participants displayed decreased levels of extremist beliefs over one year after the program concluded, and that "feelings of significance" provided a buffer against extremism.[14] The study argues that the program was successful because it addressed the individual, cultural, and social reasons individuals initially got involved with terrorism by providing non-violent, pro-social routes for personal significance. However, those individuals who, upon release, retained social connections to members of the LTTE and "family and friends in diaspora" expressed higher levels of extremism. Additionally, at the time of the program's implementation, the Tamil Tigers were already defeated. As such, the appeal of Tamil ideology and/or the opportunities to recidivate may have both been decreased (Webber et al. 2017, pp. 6–7, 13–14).

United Kingdom: The Unity Initiative (TUI)

Founded by British-Pakistani cage-fighting coach, Usman Raja, TUI conducts ideologically based interventions and provides counseling to prisoners in group and individual settings (The Unity Initiative n.d.). The UK Probation Service's Central Extremism Unit now channels cases to them. Utilizing former extremists, the program employs indirect means such as cage-fighting to achieve the main goal of prompting ideological changes through a sense of belonging and community. The interventions use individualized risk assessments to better tailor their programming and measure change. TUI has been enlisted to work with at least 30 ISIS returnees (The Unity Initiative n.d.; Kirkpatrick 2017; Robertson and Cruickshank 2012).

TUI claims to have successfully reintegrated over 50 released terrorist prisoners over eight years, and none have committed a terrorist act (The Unity Initiative n.d.). Still, without external evaluation, it is impossible to confirm TUI's self-reported success at reducing recidivism.

Germany: Violence Prevention Network (VPN)

VPN is a network of programs, several being prison-related, that have been externally evaluated. In contrast to the "first-generation" deradicalization programs of Saudi Arabia, VPN is a multi-faceted network of programs throughout Germany that includes prevention and intervention services in addition to deradicalization programs that address a variety of ideologically and religiously motivated forms of extremism. The programs provide assistance with employment, housing, and counseling, and some work with juveniles, and many involve family members. VPN programs begin in prison, but once prisoners are released, programming can continue for up to 12 months. While this highly individualized and comprehensive approach may be expensive, the model is flexible enough to respond to specific contexts and the variety of underlying reasons for an individual's initial interest in terrorism (Korn et al. 2015, pp. 6, 12; Radicalisation Awareness Network 2017, p. 104; Stern 2014, p. 450; Violence Prevention Network 2014).

The programs' effectiveness is continually measured, both externally and internally. For recidivism to violence (but not necessarily terrorist violence), rates have decreased from

41.5 percent to 13.3 percent for those who took part in their programs (VPN Annual Report 2014, p. 14). But it is unclear which aspects of the programs yielded such positive results.

Germany: EXIT

EXIT helps individuals leave extreme far-right movements. Founded by a criminologist and former Neo-Nazi, participation in EXIT is voluntary. They arrange contacts, provide practical aid and individual counseling, and answer questions regarding personal safety and social problems. EXIT helps individuals with obtaining education and employment, as well as providing family counseling as needed. EXIT also offers awareness training to prison staff. As with VPN, EXIT offers a variety of services for extremists, making it flexible and adaptable, and uses the narratives of former extremists.[15] There are, however, impediments to EXIT's ability to reach prisoners, since prisoners often need to write letters to EXIT or go through a tutor or social worker to contact the program.

While it is unclear whether the program was externally evaluated, EXIT claims a very small 3 percent recidivism rate. As with VPN, it is unclear which program elements yielded positive results, when and why, and whether success rates are based on general recidivism or terrorist recidivism.

The United States

To date, the authors are unaware of any prison-based deradicalization or disengagement program existing in the United States.[16] Abdulahi Yusuf, a young Somali-American who was arrested for attempting to travel to Syria, is undergoing some form of deradicalization provided by a Minneapolis non-profit for troubled youth and adults, Heartland Democracy. The program reportedly includes counseling and courses on "civic engagement" (Temple-Raston 2017). But this initiative appears to be a one-off and administered upon the personal conviction of the judge on Yusuf's case, Judge Michael A. Davis.

However, American Jesse Morton has provided a personal account of his own experience post-incarceration for terrorist offenses. Morton was convicted in 2011 for terror-related charges, having founded the group Revolution Muslim and recruited for al-Qaeda. Morton says he deradicalized on his own and became an informant for the FBI. Later, he became the first former jihadist to step into a "public role" in the United States (Callimachi 2016). However, there was no post-release stabilization plan for Morton. Though not a recidivist to terrorist activity, he was re-arrested in early 2017 on drug and prostitution charges. The authors asked Morton what could have prevented his return to illegal activity. He told the authors, despite personally requesting psychotherapy, appropriate therapy was not provided and was difficult to obtain. Morton contends, without proper post-release stabilization, it did not matter what progress he had made in prison. Unsupported and needing mental health assistance, he returned to criminal behavior (Jesse Morton, personal communication, September 19, 2017).

Linking studies on criminal recidivism to terrorist recidivism

Criminals and terrorists both use illegal violence, though terrorists claim to be motivated by a violence-promoting ideology. Just as the reasons for and the process of joining a gang may be similar to joining a terrorist group, the recidivism process may be similar across the two populations. As such, we hypothesize that programs that have decreased ordinary criminal recidivism may be relevant to decreasing terrorist recidivism, both in terms of the program's substance and how the programs are evaluated.

Several programs have turned to rehabilitative, rather than purely punitive, approaches in order to address high recidivism rates across the West.[17] A study by Mark W. Lipsey (2009) tests seven different intervention philosophies for juveniles: surveillance, deterrence, discipline, restorative, counseling, skill-building, and coordinated (an array of services provided in a package). Lipsey found that interventions that provided "therapeutic" services, such as counseling and skills training, were more effective than strategies of control or coercion (p. 144).

The Boston Reentry Initiative (BRI) has helped transition violent adult offenders, including gang members, back into society (Braga et al. 2009). The methods tailored each intervention to the individual using mentoring, social service assistance, and vocational development. Those who went through the program were approximately 30 percent less likely to be rearrested for a violent crime (p. 11).

BRI and Lipsey's study found success in decreasing recidivism rates by equipping individuals for life after release. But importantly, by directly impacting recidivism rates, these programs and studies show what can actually make communities safer.

Research on gang disengagement

The study of gangs in the context of terrorism is a potentially fruitful avenue for study. A study by RAND and IMPACT Europe finds that nearly all gang evaluations reviewed were applicable and/or transferable to CVE (Davies et al. 2017, p. vii). These parallels may exist because, unlike analysis of general crime, group dynamics, feelings of camaraderie, group-think, and social identity all operate within gangs in similar ways as they may operate among extremists (Decker et al. 2014, p. 270). For many terrorists, the search for identity and group dynamics may be more important than grievances (Stern 2010).

Researchers have found that several key factors prompted or helped facilitate the gang member's desire to leave. For some, exposure to violence gave way to disillusionment with the lifestyle and leaders, and propelled them to re-think the directions of their lives. Seventy-three percent of respondents, however, noted that family was a main motivator for leaving (Decker et al. 2014, p. 277). Second was obtaining new employment, or acquiring new "adult responsibilities" (p. 277). Skills training and counseling were seen as the *most* effective strategies in rehabilitating individuals for life after prison. Similar to Altier et al.'s findings, providing alternatives to the criminal life was important in compelling some to leave.

The use of former gang members has also been seen as useful in gang interventions. In many gang intervention and rehabilitation programs, such as Grasp in Denver, CO; the Professional Community Intervention Training Institute in Los Angeles, CA; or BUILD in Chicago, IL, former gang members were founders and/or worked as mentors or interventionists (Leitner 2014; Build n.d.; The Professional Community Intervention Training Institute n.d.; GRASP n.d.). Irving A. Spergel, who created one of the first comprehensive and evaluated models to reduce gang violence, found that former gang members were useful as youth workers because they had respect and legitimacy among gang members, and could use that respect to garner trust as a foundation for mentoring and providing assistance with aligning themselves with "legitimate institutions" (OJJDP 2009). Overall, Spergel's model was found to be successful in reducing serious violent and property crimes, gang re-involvement, violent crime, and drug arrests for the target group, and increased involvement of gang members in educational and employment endeavors (Spergel and Grossman 1997).

Evaluating programs targeting regular criminals

Substantive elements of the programs discussed above may be directly applicable to terrorist prisoners. But elements of how these programs are evaluated may also be applicable to deradicalization efforts.

Risk assessment

Initial and standardized evaluations of the prisoners are linked to the overall effectiveness of a program. Programs that holistically evaluate the risks and needs of individual prisoners, and tailor the findings to interventions and programs, are shown to be more effective in reducing recidivism. The Risk-Needs-Responsivity (RNR) model, which is widely used in correctional settings, is based upon a psychological assessment of a criminal and the nature of a criminal's conduct. It evaluates an offender's underlying needs that led him or her to criminality ("criminogenic needs"), putting the individual at risk of reoffending (Bonta and Andrews 2007, p. 1). Utilizing the tool has been shown to reduce recidivism rates by as much as 17–35 percent in certain settings (p. 12). A separate study found that those programs that targeted 3–8 criminogenic needs, as opposed to targeting 1–2, showed a 29 percent reduction in recidivism – this is possibly because there is unlikely to be one or two causal risk factors (Gendreau and French 2006, p. 201). The incorporation of the RNR model is crucial in overall program evaluations, because it more clearly shows what mechanisms work best in which settings. Notably, there are now risk assessment models geared towards extremists specifically, such as the VERA-2, the ERG 22+, TRAP18, and RRARP. VERA-2 contains at least 30 indicators specifically related to violent extremism, divided between five areas: beliefs, attitudes, and ideology; social context and intention; history, action, and capacity; commitment and motivation; and protective/risk-mitigating indicators. There are another 30 additional indicators based on the scientific literature, divided between five domains: criminal history; personal history; radicalization; personality traits; and psychiatric characteristics. The use of the model allows for the collection of information that can provide evidence of behavioral change, a key component of program evaluations (Pressman 2016).

Program evaluation

The need for individualized programming does not preclude the possibility of developing common assessments. The Correctional Program Assessment Inventory (CPAI) and the Correctional Program Checklist (CPC) are widely used assessment tools that incorporate indicators shown to be effective in reducing recidivism, and discern how well a program adhered to the principles of effective intervention ("program integrity"). The CPC measures a program's capacity to deliver interventions, and the substance of the program's offerings (University of Cincinnati Corrections Institute n.d.). Both tools use criteria based on empirically derived principles of effective programming across eight different domains. Since the CPAI is now standardized and widely used, it allows for comparison between different programs. Programs that scored better on the CPAI assessment showed a 10–14 percent decrease in recidivism, compared to programs that scored worse and showed a 11–17 percent *increase* in recidivism (Lowenkamp et al. 2006, p. iii). Moreover, Edward J. Latessa found that, in each of his studies, the more the programs incorporated tested tools of effective intervention, the greater the reductions in recidivism (2013, p. 72). As such, a reverse process can occur: if adhering to program integrity yields such good results, it may be beneficial to design programs with the CPAI, or other standardized assessments in mind. When programs incorporate standardized evaluations – both of individuals and of the program itself – and continually measure results, it helps program-designers to continually tweak their programs, ideally improving recidivism rates over time.

Assessment and evaluation do not have to be completely "in house." Roca, a Boston-area intervention program for young people at high risk of reoffending, uses the Social Solutions' Efforts to Outcomes platform, an external software program that helps organizations gather and arrange data and measure impact (Roca n.d.; Social Solutions n.d.). In fact, Social Solutions advertises its services for "acing" the CPAI *and* the CPC assessments (Social Solutions 2017).

Conclusions

We propose that programs consider adapting counter-recidivism tools designed for ordinary criminals to terrorist offenders, with the caveat that continuous evaluation is imperative for determining success. We also propose that deradicalization programs adopt a common definition of recidivism and that they subject their programs to outside evaluation. Below is a synthesis of our findings and tentative conclusions.

1. *Programs should span time in prison and time beyond prison*: The immediate security risk posed by a terrorist inmate is temporarily mitigated by incarceration. Based on descriptive evaluations available in the literature as well as the experience in anti-gang programs, we hypothesize that deradicalization or disengagement programming should begin in prison, and should continue post-release. If programming begins in prison, there may be a decreased chance of radicalizing others within prisons, mitigating the net risk posed by incarcerated and released terrorists alike. A shortcoming of this approach is that programs that start earlier may be more expensive, and require sustained dedication.
2. *Outside resources should be utilized*: Those implementing rehabilitation post-release can benefit from the experiences of what worked in other fields. The Rome Memorandum notes that a broad range of experts, psychologists, former terrorists, and scholars should be involved. VPN and EXIT Germany are examples of this utilization of outside resources.
3. *Programs should not focus on ideology alone*: It is impossible to measure a shift in beliefs: participants may simply lie. In addition, people engage and disengage from violence while still holding radical beliefs. Therefore, it does not make sense for programs to adopt a solely ideological approach because ideological beliefs may have little bearing on an individual's behavior. However, we argue that different cultures may call for different approaches, some more ideologically oriented than others. Most of the programs that claim to be successful incorporate a variety of tools, such as both vocational training and dismantling of extremist beliefs.
4. *Promoting alternatives to involvement in terrorism*: All three of the following possible alternatives were provided in the programs that report low recidivism rates. However, what remains unclear is in which contexts these options worked.

a *Using former terrorists may be useful in prison settings*: Former gang members were useful in mentoring and assisting with other gang members' disengagement. The use of former terrorists may be equally useful. Many successful "Exit" programs in Germany and Sweden, for example, employ formers in their deradicalization approaches. But as far as has been reported, the effectiveness of using formers has not yet been compared with similar programs that do not rely on formers as service providers.

b *Incorporating family and friends*: Socially re-anchoring individuals has been proven to be useful in both juvenile and gang member rehabilitation. Similarly, this has been beneficial in several of the deradicalization programs that report high rates of success, such as VPN.

c *Vocational training and employment assistance*: Such options were found to be successful in decreasing both criminal and gang involvement, and are used in many deradicalization programs. While these options may not compel people to leave terrorist groups, they may deter recidivism.

5. *Individualized and tailored programming*: As noted, terrorists engage and disengage in terrorism for a number of reasons, meaning that there can be no one-size-fits-all approach to deradicalization. A downfall of truly individualized programming is that it could be cost-prohibitive. The Rome Memorandum notes that utilizing effective intake forms and ongoing assessments and classifications for terrorist prisoners could allow for easier implementation of individualized approaches. An example used for normal criminals includes the "risk-needs assessment," discussed above, while the VERA-2 presents an analogous model specifically for extremist prisoners. Importantly, programs for regular criminals are more successful when risk assessments are utilized. It has been argued that there is no agreed-upon way to house terrorists in prison; dispersal, concentration, isolation, and so on. But, similar to our argument that deradicalization should be individualized, we also argue that perhaps there shouldn't be an agreed-upon way to house terrorists in prison. Different social and cultural contexts, just like different individual contexts, make it difficult to determine a common set of housing practices. Terrorists vary in the severity of their extremist commitment and activity, and cultural differences can affect the success of terrorist recruiters.
6. *Addressing broad prison reform in connection with prison radicalization and deradicalization is important*: As long as prisons remain symbols of repression and marginalization, prison time can be harnessed and manipulated by terrorists. If prisons are not doing enough to address poor conditions, overcrowding, mistreatment, and so on, these negative experiences can eclipse the benefits of deradicalization and disengagement programs. Many studies note that poor conditions, poorly trained staff, and mistreatment can in fact have a "criminogenic" effect, meaning systems, places, or situations that are likely to cause or increase criminal behavior.[18] The same may hold for terrorist prisoners, who carry a powerful narrative of victimhood and martyrdom with them, for which they can leverage mistreatment.
7. *There is more to learn from general criminality*: Both in terms of program substance and evaluation, there are many future avenues for comparison. This may be particularly true for gang intervention models and evaluations, since some elements of joining, belonging to, and leaving a gang resonate with the process of radicalization and joining and leaving terrorist groups.

8. *A common approach to evaluation is urgently needed*: Without a common approach to evaluations of current deradicalization and disengagement programs, claims of success are difficult to compare, and may be only speculative. It is imperative that outside entities perform evaluations to prevent conflicts of interest, and that evaluations include controls. Moreover, it will be important for common definitions to be created and adhered to. Finally, if clear program targets, definitions, and goals (outcomes) are stated along the lines of a broadly agreed upon system of possibilities, it will be easier to discern which programs can and cannot be compared. Until then, it will be impossible to determine definitively what works, and what does not, and in which legal and social context. Notably, IMPACT Europe is developing a toolkit and database for evaluations of CVE programs in Europe, where best practices and approaches to evaluations will be organized.[19]

Notes

1 According to Clarke R. Jones, prisonization can also have the opposite effect. Variables such as the quality of the prison, the religious make-up, activities offered, and policies of isolation or segregation can either contribute to further radicalization or encourage the prisoner to disengage from violent extremism (Jones 2014).

2 Daniel Koehler notes in Chapter 2 that a main difference between disengagement and deradicalization is that deradicalization is the reduction of ideological commitment, while a physical role change and desistance from illegal behavior would be disengagement. Koehler's chapter discusses how the process is often far more complicated; disengaging from terrorist activity does not necessarily mean a reduction in ideological commitment. Koehler highlights several scholars' contention that, while disengagement may be more feasible, it is necessary to address extremist beliefs in order to reduce recidivism (2017).

3 By "ordinary," we mean those incarcerated for non-terror related offenses.

4 Mark Hamm notes that "very few" prisoners who convert to a cause actually end up turning to violence upon release (2008). Clark R. Jones, citing a study by the United States Congressional Research Service (2011, p. 23), finds that "widespread terrorist-inspired radicalization or recruiting" is *not* occurring in prisons (Jones 2014, p. 78).

5 The authors acknowledge that there are different types of prisons, jails, and detention centers which have different goals and methods of detention, or are affected by broader social or cultural contexts – all of which have different effects on individuals. For example, Abu Ghraib held combatants without charge, where the main purpose was interrogation and intelligence collection. It is unlikely that deradicalization attempts would work within such a context. In short, despite similar programming, individuals may react differently in different places (Clarke Jones, personal communication, August, 2018).

6 Interviews with General Stone published in Stern and Berger (2015).

7 Other terrorists who became more violent after time in prison include Ayman al Zawahiri and Abu Musab al Zarqawi.

8 Cherif Kouachi, Coulibaly's accomplice and close friend, had been previously imprisoned for attempting to fight with jihadists in Iraq (and was, like Coulibaly, also previously a pretty criminal) (Chrisafis 2015).

9 Harry Sarfo is now convicted for his role in a Syrian mass execution. Amedy Coulibaly was one of several terrorists who launched coordinated attacks on the offices of *Charlie Hebdo* and the Hypercacher Kosher Supermarket.

10 Of those attackers who converted to Islam, 73 percent had criminal backgrounds, compared to 53 percent of those who did not convert (Vidino, Entenmann and Marone 2017, pp. 17, 56). https://extremism.gwu.edu/sites/extremism.gwu.edu/files/FearThyNeighbor%20Radicalizationand JihadistAttacksintheWest.pdf.

11 While prison deradicalization programs are not offered to ordinary prisoners, these individuals could be indirectly affected by deradicalization programs that target terrorists in prison who may have, otherwise, recruited or influenced them.

12 AP reporters in 100 countries filed requests and conducted hundreds of interviews to obtain these numbers.

13 Two prominent al-Qaeda members, Said Ali al-Shihri and Mohammed Atiq al-Harbi of al-Qaeda, were formerly Guantanamo detainees, had been repatriated to Saudi Arabia, and enrolled in Saudi Arabian deradicalization programs. Upon release, Shihri stated that "By Allah, imprisonment only increased our persistence in our principles for which we went out, did jihad for, and were imprisoned for." Harbi reemerged as an al-Qaeda field commander (CBS 2009).

14 This study claims to be the first external and empirical study of a deradicalization program.

15 Demant et al. (2008, p. 163) found that former extremists were useful in an Exit program in Stockholm, and lend the program credibility and make the program more approachable and relatable.

16 Peter Neumann has discussed how the United States and several other Western countries have relied on "security first" approaches, ignoring rehabilitative or reformative options (2010, p. 13). Tony Parker notes that, without attention to this issue, the United States will remain in "a reactive posture" to both prisoners who may have radicalized in prison, and those who went into prison radicalized and remained so (2013, p. 3).

17 France has a reconviction rate of 59 percent over a 2-year period, the Netherlands has a reconviction rate of 48 percent over a 2-year period, and the United Kingdom has a reconviction rate of 45 percent over a 1-year period (Fazel and Wolf 2015). In the United States, for those who served time in federal prisons, 49.3 percent are rearrested, and 24.7 percent are re-incarcerated (The United States Sentencing Commission 2016, p. 1).

18 For more on how prisons can be criminogenic, see: Chen and Shapiro (2007); Drago et al. (2009); Ruderman et al. (2015); Vacca (2004).

19 Additionally, RAND has developed a toolkit to assist with evaluation of CVE programs generally, and how to utilize evaluation findings (Helmus et al. 2017).

Bibliography

Andersen, Synøve Nygaard, and Torbjørn Skardhamar. (2015). "Pick a Number: Mapping Recidivism Measures and Their Consequences." *Crime & Delinquency* 63, no. 5, pp. 613–635. http://journals.sagepub.com/doi/abs/10.1177/0011128715570629#articleCitationDownloadContainer.

BUILD. (n.d.). "BUILD Chicago: About Us." *BUILD (Broader Urban Involvement & Leadership Development).* Accessed January 20, 2018. www.buildchicago.org/about-us.

Casptack, Andreas. (2015). "Deradicalization Programs in Saudi Arabia: A Case Study." *Middle East Institute*, June 10. www.mei.edu/content/deradicalization-programs-saudi-arabia-case-study#_ftn10.

Chulov, Martin. (2014). "Isis: The Inside Story." *The Guardian*, December 11, 2014. www.theguardian.com/world/2014/dec/11/-sp-isis-the-inside-story.

Cilluffo, Frank et al. (2006). "Out of the Shadows: Getting Ahead of Prisoner Radicalization." *George Washington University: Homeland Security Policy Institute.* www.tc.pbs.org/weta/crossroads/incl/Out-of-the-Shadows.pdf.

Good Lives Model. (n.d.). "Good Lives Model: Information." *Good Lives Model.* Accessed August 18, 2017. https://goodlivesmodel.com/information.

GRASP. (n.d.). "Grasp Youth: Home." *GRASP (Gang Rescue and Support Project).* Accessed January 15, 2018. http://graspyouth.org/.

Horgan, John, and Kurt Braddock. (2010). "Rehabilitating the Terrorists?: Challenges in Assessing the Effectiveness of Deradicalisation Programs." *Terrorism and Political Violence* (March), pp. 267–291. www.start.umd.edu/start/publications/Derad.pdf.

Ismail, Noor Huda, and Susan Sim. (2016a). "From Prison to Carnage in Jakarta: A Tale of Two Terrorist Convicts, Their Mentor behind Bars, and the Fighter with ISIS (Part 1)." *Brookings*, January 22, 2016. www.brookings.edu/opinions/from-prison-to-carnage-in-jakarta-a-tale-of-two-terrorist-convicts-their-mentor-behind-bars-and-the-fighter-with-isis-part-1/.

Ismail, Noor Huda, and Susan Sim. (2016b). "Predicting Terrorist Recidivism in Indonesia's Prisons (Part 2)." *Brookings*, January 28, 2016. www.brookings.edu/opinions/predicting-terrorist-recidivism-in-indonesias-prisons/.

Leary, Kimberly. (2009). "Engaging Extremists: Diplomacy through Deradicalization." *Kennedy School Review* 9.

Liebling, Alison, Helen Arnold, and Christina Straub. (2011). "An Exploration of Staff–Prisoner Relationships at HMP Whitemoor: 12 Years on." *Revised Final Report, Ministry of Justice, National Offender Management Service. Cambridge Institute of Criminology Prisons Research Centre* (November), pp. 1–201. www.prc.crim.cam.ac.uk/publications/whitemoor-report.

Lozano, Maria. (2014). "Inventory of the Best Practices on De-radicalisation from the Different Member States of the EU." *TerRa (Terrorism and Radicalisation): European Network Based Learning and Prevention Program*, pp. 1–58. www.terranet.eu/files/nice_to_know/20140722134422CVERLTdef.pdf.

McCants, William, Jarret Brachman, and Joseph Felter. (2006). *Militant Ideology Atlas: Executive Report*. West Point, NY: Combating Terrorism Center, U.S. Military Academy. https://ctc.usma.edu/app/uploads/2012/04/Atlas-ResearchCompendium1.pdf.

Parks, Brad. (2015). "How a US Prison Camp Helped Create ISIS." *The New York Post*, May 30, 2015. https://nypost.com/2015/05/30/how-the-us-created-the-camp-where-isis-was-born/.

Pluchinsky, Dennis. (2008). "Global Jihadist Recidivism: A Red Flag." *Studies in Conflict & Terrorism* 31, no. 3, pp. 182–200. https://doi.org/10.1080/10576100701878457.

Psychology Ministry of Security and Justice; International Centre for Counter-Terrorism. *Presented at the Council for Penological Co-operation: 11th Working Group Meeting*. January 11, 2016. https://rm.coe.int/16806f5258.

Rabasa, Angel. (2010). *Deradicalizing Islamist Extremists*. Santa Monica, CA: RAND.

Renaldi, Adi. (2016). "Indonesia's Anti-Terrorism Efforts Are Falling Short." *Vice News*, November 16, 2016. www.vice.com/en_id/article/nzwqjm/indonesian-jihadis-are-slipping-through-the-cracks-of-deradizalization-programs.

Roca. (n.d.). "Our Work: Our Intervention Model: Performance-Based Management." http://rocainc.org/work/our-intervention-model/performance-based-management/.

Social Solutions. (n.d.). "Who We Serve." *Social Solutions*. Accessed January 15, 2018. www.socialsolutions.com/who-we-serve/.

The Counter Extremism Project. (2017). "Said al-Shihri." *Profile*. www.counterextremism.com/extremists/said-al-shihri.

The Professional Community Intervention Training Institute. (n.d.). "The Professional Community Intervention Institute: About Us." Accessed January 17, 2018. http://pciti.net/.

The Soufan Group. (2013). "Indonesia." *Profile* April 11, 2013. www.soufangroup.com/tsg-intelbrief-assessing-indonesias-counterterrorism-campaign/.

The Unity Initiative. (n.d.). "Services." *Profile*. Accessed July 15, 2017. www.theunityinitiative.com/services.

Tough, Paul. (2003). "The Black Supremicist." *The New York Times*, May 23, 2003. www.nytimes.com/2003/05/25/magazine/the-black-supremacist.html.

Ungerer, Carl. (2011). "Jihadists in Jail: Radicalisation and the Indonesian Prison Experience – An ASPI–RSIS Joint Report." *Australian Strategic Policy Institute/Centre of Excellence for National Security* 40 (May). www.files.ethz.ch/isn/161633/SR40_jihadists_in_jail.pdf.

University of Cincinnati Corrections Institute. (n.d.). "Services: Program Evaluation." Accessed January 23, 2018. www.uc.edu/corrections/services/program_evaluation.html.

UNODC. (2016). *Handbook on the Management of Violent Extremist Prisoners and the Prevention of Radicalization to Violence in Prisons*. New York: United Nations Office of Drugs and Crime: Criminal Justice Handbook Series. www.unodc.org/pdf/criminal_justice/Handbook_on_VEPs.pdf.

Vallance, Chris. (2013). "How One Extremist Rejected Violence." *BBC News*, July 2, 2013. www.bbc.com/news/uk-23131706.

Violence Prevention Network. (n.d.). "Violence Prevention Network: Approaches: Deradicalisation/disengagement assistance." *Profile*. www.violence-prevention-network.de/en/approach/deradicalisation.

Ward, Tony, and Shadd Maruna. (2007). *Rehabilitation*. New York: Routledge.

Wright, Lawrence. (2006). *The Looming Tower: Al-Qaeda and the Road to 9/11*. New York: Knop.

References

Altier, Mary Beth, Emma Leonard Boyle, Neil D. Shortland, and John G. Horgan. (2017). "Why They Leave: An Analysis of Terrorist Disengagement Events from Eighty-Seven Autobiographical Accounts." *Security Studies* 26, no. 2, pp. 305–332. https://doi.org/10.1080/09636412.2017.1280307.

Basra, Rajan, Peter R. Neumann, and Claudia Brunner. (2016). "Criminal Pasts, Terrorist Futures: European Jihadists and the New Crime-Terror Nexus." *Special report, The International Centre for the Study of*

Radicalisation and Political Violence. http://icsr.info/wp-content/uploads/2016/10/crime-terror-report_20171214_web.pdf.

Bjørgo, Tore, and John Horgan. (2009). *Leaving Terrorism Behind: Individual and Collective Disengagement*. New York: Routledge.

Bonta, James, and Donald A. Andrews. (2007). "Risk-Need-Responsivity Model for Offender Assessment and Rehabilitation." *Rehabilitation* 6, no. 1, pp. 1–22.

Boucek, Christopher. (2008). "Saudi Arabia's 'Soft' Counterterrorism Strategy: Prevention, Rehabilitation, and Aftercare." *Middle East Program, Carnegie Endowment for International Peace* no. 97, pp. 1–27. http://carnegieendowment.org/files/cp97_boucek_saudi_final.pdf.

Braga, Anthony A., Anne M. Piehl, and David Hureau. (2009). "Controlling Violent Offenders Released to the Community: An Evaluation of the Boston Reentry Initiative." *Journal of Research in Crime and Delinquency* 46, no. 4, pp. 411–436. https://doi.org/10.1177/0022427809341935.

Callimachi, Rukmini. (2016). "Once a Qaeda Recruiter, Now a Voice Against Jihad." *The New York Times*, August 29. www.nytimes.com/2016/08/30/us/al-qaeda-islamic-state-jihad-fbi.html?mcubz=3&_r=1.

CBS News. (2009). "Pentagon: Prisoner Releases Not Fail-Safe." *CBS*, January 26, 2009. www.cbsnews.com/news/pentagon-prisoner-releases-not-fail-safe/.

Chen, M. Keith, and Jesse M. Shapiro. (2007). "Do Harsher Prison Conditions Reduce Recidivism? A Discontinuity-based Approach." *American Law and Economics Review* 9, no. 1, pp. 1–29.

Chrisafis, Angelique. (2015). "Charlie Hebdo Attackers: Born, Raised and Radicalised in Paris." *The Guardian*, January 12. www.theguardian.com/world/2015/jan/12/-sp-charlie-hebdo-attackers-kids-france-radicalised-paris.

Davies, Matthew, Richard Warnes, and Joanna Hofman. (2017). *Exploring the Transferability and Applicability of Gang Evaluation Methodologies to Counter Violent Radicalisation*. Santa Monica, CA: RAND Corporation. www.rand.org/pubs/research_reports/RR2120.html.

Dearden, Lizzie. (2017). "Former London Postman Charged with Murdering Syrian Captives in Isis Mass Execution." *The Independent*, July 19. www.independent.co.uk/news/world/europe/harry-sarfo-isis-germany-syria-london-postman-charged-murder-mass-execution-palmyra-video-massacre-a7849831.html.

Decker, Scott, David C. Pyrooz, and Richard K. Moule, Jr. (2014). "Disengagement from Gangs as Role Transitions." *Journal of Research on Adolescence* 24, no. 2, pp. 268–283. https://doi.org/10.1111/jora.12074.

Demant, Froukje, Marieke Slootman, Frank Buijs, and Jean Tillie. (2008). "Decline and Disengagement." *An Analysis of Processes of Deradicalisation, University of Amsterdam, IMES*. https://pure.uva.nl/ws/files/1079141/64714_Demant_Slootman_2008_Decline_and_Disengagement.pdf.

DNI. (n.d.). "Summary of the Reengagement of Detainees Formerly Held at Guantanamo Bay, Cuba." Office of the Director of National Intelligence: Reports and Publications. Accessed August 1, 2017. www.dni.gov/files/documents/Newsroom/Reports%20and%20Pubs/Summary_of_the_Reengagement_of_Detainees_Formerly_Held_at_GTMO_Ma%204_2016.pdf.

Drago, Francesco, Roberto Galbiati, and Pietro Vertova. (2009). "Prison Conditions and Recidivism." *CELS 2009 4th Annual Conference on Empirical Legal Studies Paper* (August). http://dx.doi.org/10.2139/ssrn.1443093.

Europol. (2017). "TESAT: European Union Terrorism and Situation Trend Report." *European Union Agency for Law Enforcement Cooperation*. www.europol.europa.eu/tesat/2017/.

Fazel, Seena, and Achim Wolf. (2015). "A Systematic Review of Criminal Recidivism Rates Worldwide: Current Difficulties and Recommendations for Best Practice." *PLoS One* 10, no. 3. http://dx.doi.org/10.1371/journal.pone.0130390.

Feddes, Allard R., and Marcello Gallucci. (2015). "A Literature Review on Methodology Used in Evaluating Effects of Preventive and De-radicalisation Interventions." *Journal on Deradicalization*, no. 5, pp. 1–46. http://journals.sfu.ca/jd/index.php/jd/article/view/33/31.

Gaub, Florence, and Julia Lisiecka. (2017). "The Crime-Terror Nexus." *European Union Institute for Security Studies*, Brief Issue 10, pp. 1–4. www.iss.europa.eu/sites/default/files/EUISSFiles/Brief_10_Terrorism_and_crime.pdf.

Gendreau, Paul, and Sheila A. French. (2006). "Reducing Prison Misconducts: What Works!" *Criminal Justice and Behavior* 33, no. 2, pp. 185–218. https://doi-org.ezproxy.bu.edu/10.1177/0093854805284406.

Global Counterterrorism Forum. (2013). "Rome Memorandum on Good Practices for Rehabilitation and Reintegration of Violent Extremist Offenders." *Global Counterterrorism Forum*. www.thegctf.org/Portals/1/Documents/Framework%20Documents/A/GCTF-Rome-Memorandum-ENG.pdf.

Hamm, Mark S. (2008). "Prisoner Radicalization: Assessing the Threat in U.S. Correctional Institutions." National Institute of Justice, October 27. www.nij.gov/journals/261/pages/prisoner-radicalization.aspx.

Helmus, Todd, Rajeev Miriam Matthews, Sina Ramchand, David Stebbins Beaghley, Michael A. Amanda Kadlec, Aaron Kofner Brown, and Joie D. Acosta. (2017). *RAND Program Evaluation Toolkit for Countering Violent Extremism*. Santa Monica: Rand. www.rand.org/pubs/tools/TL243.html.

Hettiarachchi, Malkanth. (2013). "Sri Lanka's Rehabilitation Program: A New Frontier in Counter Terrorism and Counter Insurgency." *Prism* 4, no. 2, pp. 104–122. http://cco.ndu.edu/Portals/96/Documents/prism/prism_4-2/prism105-122_Hettiarachchi.pdf.

Holmer, Georgia, and Adrian Shtuni. (2017). "Returning Foreign Fighters and the Reintegration Imperative." *United States Institute of Peace: Special Report* 402, no. 8 (March), pp. 1–15. www.usip.org/sites/default/files/2017-03/sr402-returning-foreign-fighters-and-the-reintegration-imperative.pdf.

Horgan, John. (2008). "From Profiles to Pathways and Roots to Routes: Perspectives from Psychology on Radicalization into Terrorism." *The Annals of the American Academy of Political and Social Science* 618, no. 1, pp. 80–94. https://doi.org/10.1177/0002716208317539.

Horgan, John. (2009). *Walking Away from Terrorism: Accounts of Disengagement from Radical and Extremist Movements*. New York: Routledge.

Horgan, John. (2010). "Deradicalization or Disengagement?" *Perspectives on Terrorism* 2, no. 4, cited in Jessica Stern. 2014. "X: A Case Study of a Swedish Neo-Nazi and His Reintegration into Swedish Society." *Behavioral Sciences & The Law* 32, no. 3, pp. 440–453. https://doi.org/10.1002/bsl.2119.

Jensen, Michael, Patrick James, Gary LaFree, and Aaron Safer-Lichtenstein. (2018). "Pre-Radicalization Criminal Activity of United States Extremists." *START Research Brief* (January). www.start.umd.edu/pubs/START_PIRUS_PreRadCriminalActivityofUSExtremists_Jan2018.pdf.

Jones, Clarke R. (2014). "Are Prisons Really Schools for Terrorism? Challenging the Rhetoric on Prison Radicalization." *Punishment & Society* 16, no. 1, pp. 74–103. https://doi.org/10.1177/1462474513506482.

Kirkpatrick, David D. (2017). "A Cage Fighter with a Soft Touch for Hard-Core Jihadists." *The New York Times*, December 29, 2017. www.nytimes.com/2017/12/29/world/europe/uk-cage-fighter-jihadis-reintegrate.html.

Koehler, Daniel. (2017). "How and Why We Should Take Deradicalization Seriously." *Nature Human Behaviour* 1, pp. 1–4. https://doi.org/10.1038/s41562-017-0095.

Korn, Judy, Christine Koschmieder, Cornelia Lotthammer, and Thomas Mücke. (2015). "Brochure: Taking Responsibility – Breaking Away from Hate and Violence." *Violence Prevention Network*. www.violence-prevention-network.de/en/publications.

Latessa, Edward J. (2013). "Evaluating correctional programs." *151st International Training Course: United Nations Asia and Far East Institute for the Prevention of Crime and the Treatment of Offenders: Resource Material Series* 88, pp. 64–76. www.unafei.or.jp/english/pdf/RS_No88/No88_00All.pdf.

Leitner, Tammy. (2014). "Former Gang Member Works to Revitalize Neighborhood." *NBC Chicago*, August 13, 2014. www.nbcchicago.com/investigations/Former-Gang-Member-Works-to-Revitalize-Neighborhood-271181791.html.

Lipsey, Mark W. (2009). "The Primary Factors that Characterize Effective Interventions with Juvenile Offenders: A Meta-Analytic Overview." *Victims and Offenders* 4, no. 2 (February), pp. 124–147. https://doi.org/10.1080/15564880802612573.

Lowenkamp, Christopher T., Edward J. Latessa, and Richard Lemke. (2006). "Evaluation of Ohio's Reclaim Funded Programs, Community Corrections Facilities, and DYS Facilities: FY 2002." *University of Cincinnati Division of Criminal Justice Center for Criminal Justice Research* (February), pp. 1–32. www.uc.edu/content/dam/uc/ccjr/docs/reports/project_reports/CCF_Evaluation_Final_2006.pdf.

Mastroe, Caitlin, and Susan Szmania. (2016). "Surveying CVE Metrics in Prevention, Disengagement and DeRadicalization Programs." *Report to the Office of University Programs, Science and Technology Directorate, Department of Homeland Security*. College Park, MD: START. www.start.umd.edu/pubs/START_SurveyingCVEMetrics_March2016.pdf.

Mendoza, Martha. (2011). "Rightly or Wrongly, Thousands Convicted of Terrorism Post-9/11." *NBC News*, September 4, 2011. www.nbcnews.com/id/44389156/ns/us_news-9_11_ten_years_later/t/rightly-or-wrongly-thousands-convicted-terrorism-post-/#.WbGZIXeGO34.

Naderi, Nader. (2014). "Prisonization." *The Encyclopedia of Criminology and Criminal Justice*, pp. 1–5. https://doi.org/10.1002/9781118517383.wbeccj124.

National Counterterrorism Center. (2017). "US Homegrown Violent Extremist Recidivism Likely." *National Counterterrorism Center Current*, January 24, 2017. https://assets.documentcloud.org/documents/3873025/NCTC-Report.pdf, cited in De Luce, Dan, et al. 2017. "John Walker Lindh, Detainee #001 in the Global War On Terror, Will Go Free In Two Years. What Then?" *Foreign Policy*, June 23, 2017. http://foreignpolicy.com/2017/06/23/john-walker-lindh-detainee-001-in-the-global-war-on-terror-will-go-free-in-two-years-what-then/.

NBC News. (2017). "Chelsea Bomber Trying to Radicalize Other Inmates: Feds." December 23, 2017. www.nbcnewyork.com/news/local/Chelsea-Bomber-Tried-to-Radicalize-Other-Inmates-Feds-Ahmad-Khan-Rahimi–466121183.html.

Neumann, Peter. (2010). "Prisons and Terrorism: Radicalisation and Deradicalisation in 15 Countries." *The International Centre for the Study of Radicalisation and Political Violence*. http://icsr.info/wp-content/uploads/2012/10/1277699166PrisonsandTerrorismRadicalisationandDeradicalisationin15Countries.pdf.

Office of Juvenile Justice and Delinquency Prevention. (2009). "OJJDP Comprehensive Gang Model: Planning for Implementation." *Institute for Intergovernmental Research* (May), pp. 1–2. https://permanent.access.gpo.gov/gpo82906/Implementation-Manual.pdf

Parker, Tony C. (2013). "Establishing a Deradicalization/Disengagement Model for America's Correctional Facilities: Recommendations for Counter Prison Radicalization." *Master's Thesis: Naval Postgraduate School*. https://calhoun.nps.edu/bitstream/handle/10945/32881/13Mar_Parker_Tony.pdf?sequence=1&isAllowed=y.

Porges, Marisa L. (2010). "The Saudi Deradicalization Experiment." *Council on Foreign Relations: Expert Brief*. January 22, 2010. www.foreignaffairs.com/articles/persian-gulf/2010-05-01/getting-deradicalization-right.

Pressman, Vera. (2016). *Risk Assessment of Radicalization to Violence Applications of VERA-2 in Prisons*. The Hague, the Netherlands: Netherlands Institute of Forensic Psychiatry and Psychology.

Radicalisation Awareness Network. (2017). "Preventing Radicalisation to Terrorism and Violent Extremism: Approaches and Practices." *Radicalisation Awareness Network*, pp. 1–523. https://ec.europa.eu/home-affairs/sites/homeaffairs/files/what-we-do/networks/radicalisation_awareness_network/ran-best-practices/docs/ran_collection-approaches_and_practices_en.pdf.

Robertson, Nic, and Paul Cruickshank. (2012). "Cagefighter 'Cures' Terrorists." *CNN*, July 23, 2012. www.cnn.com/2012/07/20/world/europe/uk-caging-terror-main/index.html.

Ruderman, Michael A., Dierdra F. Wilson, and Savanna Reid. (2015). "Does Prison Crowding Predict Higher Rates of Substance Use Related Parole Violations? A Recurrent Events Multi-Level Survival Analysis." *PLoS One* 10, no. 10, e0141328. https://doi.org/10.1371/journal.pone.0141328.

Silke, Andrew. (2014). *Prison, Terrorism and Extremism: Critical Issues in Management, Radicalisation, and Reform*. New York: Routledge.

Social Solutions. (2017). "Ace Your Correctional Program Assessment Inventory." *Social Solutions*. May 31, 2017. www.socialsolutions.com/blog/ace-your-correctional-programassessment-inventory/.

Spergel, Irving A., and Susan F. Grossman. (1997). "The Little Village Project: A Community Approach to the Gang Problem." *Social Work* 42, no. 5, pp. 456–470. www.jstor.org/stable/23718333.

Stern, Jessica. (2003). *Terror in the Name of God: Why Religious Militants Kill*. New York: Ecco.

Stern, Jessica. (2010). "Mind over Martyr: How to Deradicalize Islamist Extremists." *Foreign Affairs* 89, no. 1 (January/February). www.foreignaffairs.com/articles/saudi-arabia/2009-12-21/mind-over-martyr.

Stern, Jessica. (2014). "X: A Case Study of a Swedish Neo-Nazi and His Reintegration into Swedish Society." *Behavioral Sciences & the Law* 32, no. 3, pp. 440–453. https://doi.org/10.1002/bsl.2119.

Stern, Jessica, and J.M. Berger. (2015). *ISIS: State of Terror*. New York: Ecco. https://permanent.access.gpo.gov/gpo82906/Implementation-Manual.pdf.

Temple-Raston, Dina. (2017). "He Wanted Jihad; He Got Foucault." *New York Magazine*, November 26, 2017. http://nymag.com/daily/intelligencer/2017/11/abdullahi-yusuf-isis-syria.html.

United States Sentencing Commission. (2016). "Recidivism and Federal Sentencing Policy: Recidivism of Federal Offenders: A Comprehensive Overview." *Commission Report*. www.ussc.gov/sites/default/files/pdf/research-and-publications/backgrounders/RG-recidivism-overview.pdf.

United States Congressional Research Service. (2011). *American Jihadist Terrorism: Combating a Complex Threat*, November 15, 2011. R41416. Accessed October 9, 2019. https://www.refworld.org/docid/4f1ea1862.html.

Vacca, James S. (2004). "Educated Prisoners Are Less Likely to Return to Prison." *Journal of Correctional Education* 55, no. 4 (December), pp. 297–305. www.jstor.org/stable/23292095.

Vidino, Lorenzo, Eva Entenmann, and Francisco Marone. (2017). *Fear Thy Neighbor: Radicalization and Jihadist Attacks in the West*. Milan: Institute for International Political Studies.

Violence Prevention Network. (2014). "VPN Annual Report 2014." *Annual Report*. Accessed July 1, 2017. www.violence-prevention-network.de/en/publications.

Webber, David, Marina Chernikova, Arie W. Kruglanski, Michele J. Gelfand, Malkanthi Hettiarachchi, Rohan Gunaratna, Marc-Andre Lafreniere, and Jocelyn J. Bélanger. (2017). "Deradicalizing Detained Terrorists." *Political Psychology* 39, pp. 539–556. https://doi.org/10.1111/pops.12428vpn.

10

LOCAL GOVERNMENTS' ROLE IN DISENGAGEMENT, DERADICALISATION AND REINTEGRATION INITIATIVES

Stian Lid

The growing understanding of the complex process of leaving violent extremism and reintegrating into (mainstream) society has led to an acknowledgement that multifaceted measurements and involvement of various actors are required to promote these processes (Dalgaard-Nielsen, 2016). In many countries, local governments are made accountable for countering violent extremism (CVE), including disengagement, deradicalisation and, in particular, reintegration of former extremists (Andersson Malmros & Mattsson, 2017; Gielen, 2018; Heide & Schuurman, 2018; Hemmingsen, 2015; Lid et al., 2016; Marsden, 2017).[1] Local governments can, in some cases due to their functions, be in a position to influence the individual's motivation to leave extremism, to assist the person's reintegration into mainstream society, in addition to society's willingness and support to reintegrate the person (Marsden, 2017, p. 44). In this chapter, I discuss how local governments can promote disengagement, deradicalisation and reintegration, and local governments' challenges and opportunities to stimulate these processes.

As demonstrated in other chapters in this book, there are significant differences between countries in the role local governments take in promoting exit from violent extremism and the transition of former extremists back into society. For instance, in comprehensive welfare states, such as the Benelux countries and Scandinavia, local governments are a prominent actor, but in the US, Horn of Africa and South Asia, their role is limited and the need for non-governmental actors is greater. These differences can be explained by the variations among local governments' societal functions. The main argument in this chapter is that local governments' role in promoting disengagement, deradicalisation and reintegration processes is closely linked to their primary societal functions, which means that local governments use their ordinary functions for promoting exit and reintegration. Based on Stoker's (2011) typology of local government's core societal functions, four functions of local governments in supporting exit and reintegration processes are identified: *provision of welfare services*, *control and surveillance*, *reconciliation and community tolerance*, and *coordination*. Those prominent functions and the ability to mix these functions vary considerably between local governments.

Combining the function of control with other functions is also a significant challenge. The emergence of control and surveillance as a prominent function can reduce trust among the target groups, which local governments heavily depend on to promote other functions. It follows from this that local government has an exposed position and that a broad complexity of factors influences their role and capability to succeed.

The chapter departs from the understanding that disengagement and deradicalisation should not only be understood as a process of leaving violent extremism (physically and ideologically), but it is also about re-engaging with a non-extremist environment. Here, I draw on the logic of Barrelle's (2015) Pro-Integration Model, which underlines that sustained disengagement is about the proactive and harmonious engagement the person has with wider society. Using such holistic understanding of disengagement and deradicalisation, the role of local governments is becoming most prominent. Additionally, a broader perspective of the deradicalisation process, which includes reintegration, must also take into account to some extent the criticism by Clubb and Tapley (2018, p. 2054) that the deradicalisation literature has neglected the intersection between deradicalisation and reintegration, and how contextual factors mediate the success of these two.

The ambition of this chapter is to contribute to fill the gap in research on different *actors'* involvement in countering violent extremism (Koehler, 2017), particularly on local governments' engagement. By drawing on Stoker's (2011) typology and the analysed data, I will suggest a preliminary systematising of local governments' key functions to promote disengagement, deradicalisation and reintegration. I will utilise primary data from Norway and Kenya[2] and secondary data from various countries to provide examples to illustrate the identified key functions, and major challenges and opportunities. Hence, this is not a comprehensive comparative study of all local government systems that could ensure solid theories and models of local governments' functions.

The chapter proceeds by providing a short description of the reasons why people join and then leave violent extremist groups to help grasp how local governments can influence these processes. It continues with a presentation of local governments' core functions and tasks as a basis for the main analysis of local governments' role in promoting exit and reintegration. Thereafter, some key challenges are discussed, followed by the conclusion.

Ways in and out of extremism

Understanding who the extremists are and their motivations for joining violent extremist groups, in addition to the processes of leaving the militant group and reintegrating into (mainstream) society, is important for local governments in their effort to develop efficient interventions. Disengagement, deradicalisation and reintegration are understood as complex psychological, social and physical processes that may elapse differently between individuals. The processes vary during the desistance of illegal behaviour (disengagement), reduction of the ideological commitment (deradicalisation) and reconnection to mainstream society (reintegration) (see Chapter 2). Former extremists who have disengaged, in the sense of having reduced violent participation or leaving the violent extremist group, have not necessarily rejected ideologically based violence. Ideological changes often happen after the person has left the violent milieu (Horgan, 2009). Webber et al. (Chapter 5) suggest distinguishing between methods that can directly lead to deradicalisation (that counter the ideological narrative by articulating arguments against it) and those that indirectly facilitate it (via a non-radical network or need components). Marsden (2017) argues that the reintegration process should be understood as a two-way process; society must allow, and ideally actively support, the individual's reintegration, and the individual must demonstrate a willingness to reintegrate.

Individuals involved in terrorism have undergone rather different processes of violent radicalisation. They come from a diversity of social backgrounds and relate to ideology and politics in different ways (Bjørgo, 2011; Nesser, 2015). However, disengagement is far from being a simple reversal or mirror-image of the initial process of engagement in militant extremism, although the processes of becoming engaged in militant extremist groups have some important bearing on the processes of disengagement (Bjørgo, 2011). Individuals radicalised because of personal grievances, social, economic or health problems might have other needs for support than resourceful, educated and previously well-integrated individuals who may have been attracted because of the ideology and the thrills of activism. Thus, individual variations affect the local governments' possibilities of influencing the processes of leaving extremism and reintegrating.

Individuals' motivations for leaving violent extremism and reintegrating into mainstream society are generally not due to a single factor, but several different push, pull and inhibiting factors (Altier et al., 2017; Barrelle, 2015).[3] The most commonly cited reasons for disengagement are disillusionment with the group's strategy or actions, internal conflicts, dissatisfaction with one's day-to-day tasks and burnout (Altier et al., 2017; Barrelle, 2015). There are also important inhibiting factors that might hamper the decision to leave, such as social and penal sanctions, in addition to loss of protection and feeling of nowhere to go (Bjørgo, 2009). Important pull factors are amnesty for offences, job and education opportunities and financial incentives, interaction with moderate peers and the desire to live a normal life, be married and have children (Altier et al., 2017; Barrelle, 2015; Bjørgo, 2009; Hwang, 2018; Jacobsen, 2010; Rosenau et al., 2014). These pull factors are important not only for pushing people out of extremism, but also for dissuading re-engagement and in the reintegration process into mainstream society (Altier et al., 2017). Many of these push, pull and inhibiting factors are beyond what governmental actors can influence, and studies of former extremist processes of leaving violent extremism show that many do so unassisted (Barrelle, 2015). The role of counter-terrorism and the role of states are often overemphasised (Cronin, 2009, p. 52). However, some of the identified potential push, pull and inhibiting factors might be possible for local governments to influence. As I will show in the following text, local governments can provide new opportunities or alternatives such as a job, education, housing, financial incentives, social and psychological counselling and guidance, in addition to a safe and secure local environment. These might be within the functions and mandates of local governments.

Local governments' functions, approaches and target groups

Chandler (2001) defines local governments in a Western liberal democracy as "the authorities and dependent agencies that are established by the Parliament to provide a range of specified services and represent the general interests of a specific area under the direction of a locally elected council". They "vary in terms of the number of tiers, the comparative size of local units and the functions assigned to them" (Chandler, 2013, p. 188). Moreover, from a global perspective, the levels of autonomy and democracy vary considerably. In Africa, the process towards devolving political power and economic resources from national to local levels of governance, and creating autonomous democratic local governance has halted. Local governments remain as an agent of the national government and centralised rule (Enemuo, 2000), despite attempts from aid donors to support such devolution processes (Smith, 2007). In this chapter, a broad understanding of local governments is used, including hybrid forms of local governments that are controlled by central government and centralised rule.

Although there are major variations among local governments, Stoker (2011, p. 20) has identified five core societal functions for local governments at the beginning of the 21st century: *expressing identity, economic development, welfare provision, lifestyle coordination* and *security*. Security and the discipline function can be categorised either as embedded in each of the other four roles or as a disciplinary coercive function expressed through the controlling and surveillance power of local government. The latter categorisation is the one used in this chapter, due to the importance of this function for local governments in promoting disengagement, deradicalisation and reintegration processes. Security and the discipline function can be categorised either as embedded in each of the other four roles or as a separate disciplinary coercive function. Stoker argues that security might be considered as a fifth core function, particularly if security is more broadly defined as a disciplinary/coercive function expressed through the controlling and surveillance power of local government. In disengagement, deradicalisation and reintegration processes the controlling and surveillance power of local governments seem as significant. Security will therefore be categorised as a separate fifth function of local governments.

According to Stoker (2011), there are considerable variations between local governments in terms of which functions are prominent and their ability to mix roles. Economic development is prominent in countries such as the US, China and Brazil, but welfare provision is the prominent role in European and particularly in Scandinavian countries, the Netherlands, Germany and Britain. The welfare function is also prominent in local governments in Latin America, as well as in East Asia, China and African countries. The scale of the resources available and the effectiveness of the support provided by welfare services vary enormously, but the basic idea that local government has an embedded role in welfare provision and redistribution is a prominent one. The co-ordination role in promoting the general well-being of a community and its citizens has risen to prominence in a range of local government systems in recent decades. Moreover, the modern condition is characterised by the complexity of function, scale, purpose and responsibility, and coordination or networked community governance is the solution to this complexity (Stoker, 2011, p. 23).

All five functions may be relevant for the processes of disengagement, deradicalisation and reintegration. For instance, local economic development and sustainability may be an important underlying condition to reintegrate entire extremist groups successfully, as we have seen in the reintegration of thousands of former extremists into local communities in Colombia (Carranza-Franco, 2014). However, I will argue that the most prominent functions for local governments are *welfare provision, security* and *coordination*. In addition to these three functions, there are examples of local governments' importance in *reconciliation and community tolerance* of reintegrating former extremists. I argue that these four functions are the main functions for local governments in promoting disengagement, deradicalisation and reintegration. These identified functions might either directly support persons in their exit and reintegration process (for instance, welfare services), or ensure the conditions for successful disengagement, deradicalisation and reintegration initiatives to take place (for instance, community acceptance). Local governments do not essentially carry out all these functions and there are significant variations between local governments as to which of these functions are prominent in their efforts to support people out of extremism. Hence, in states where local governments hold these functions as prominent, they would play a greater role in promoting disengagement, deradicalisation and reintegration than in countries where these functions are weak, such as in the US. In the latter countries, non-governmental institutions[4] play a greater role (see Chapter 23).

Due to local governments' various societal core functions, local governments' target groups are several. The main target group includes *persons or groups* with extremist beliefs and behaviours, such as for the security sector. The second target group includes the extremists' *family and networks*, which can be important for reaching the main target (extremists) and in reintegration processes (Altier et al., 2014; Bjørgo & Horgan, 2009; Horgan, 2009; Koehler, 2017; Ranstorp & Hyllengren, 2013). Lastly, *local society* is essential due to the importance of the acceptance and willingness of the recipient community to welcome back former extremists (Clubb & Tapley, 2018; Kaplan & Nussio, 2018; Marsden, 2017). The last two target groups differ at least from those in the security sector.

Local governments' main societal core functions are presented above. In the following, I will elaborate on local governments' four key functions in promoting successful exit and reintegration of former extremists.

Welfare provision

Local governments can, by providing different types of welfare services such as financial and social support, offer the extremist new opportunities and alternatives to continuing in violent groups or movements. Moreover, these services may also hinder any relapse back into the group or movement, or to another type of criminal activity. In many countries, such as the UK, national laws set out the duty of government actors to provide support (economic, social, health) to people in need (HM Government, 2015). In many countries local governments are the provider of several of these services, and through this duty are pledged to engage in disengagement and reintegration processes. There are variations around which types of services local governments are in charge of, and an important role for local governments is therefore to refer the person to other institutions that provide the services required, such as hospitals, mental health clinics and other governmental institutions (Anindyaa, 2019; Lid et al., 2016). For instance, most of the deportees in Indonesia have lost their identification cards, and (some) local governments assist them in submitting their application for a new identity card to the Civil Registry and Population Agency (Anindyaa, 2019, p. 233).

In Western democratic states such as the Netherlands (Schuurman & Bakker, 2016), the United Kingdom (Neumann, 2010), Ireland (Lynch, 2015), the Scandinavian countries (Lid et al., 2016; see Chapter 18) and Colombia (Carranza-Franco, 2014) municipalities arrange accommodation and, if necessary, allocate financial assistance and benefits to former extremists. Municipalities may also allocate funds for and facilitate education and vocational training to strengthen the person's professional skills and employment opportunities in the future.

In addition to provision of financial and practical services, local governments are in some countries more directly involved in the social and psychological processes of change, by providing social and psychological counselling and guidance. For instance, in Aarhus in Denmark, the municipality does one-on-one mentoring and counselling of people who are at risk, or currently hold extremist positions or previously have been involved in violent extremism (Agerschou, 2014; see Chapter 18). The municipality and police also provide family counselling to families[5] of radical youths, or youths at risk (Agerschou, 2014). Provision of welfare services emerges as a key function of local governments in countries where this function is allocated to local governments.

Another important function for local governments is control and surveillance.

Control and surveillance

Law enforcement agencies have the main responsibility for maintaining safety and security in society and for conducting risk-assessment of identified individuals, such as returned foreign fighters. However, maintaining local security is also a task for local governments, either embedded in other functions or the control can be a more prominent or separate function (Stoker, 2011).

For instance, Norwegian municipalities are not directly given the task of controlling or monitoring released returned foreign fighters, but through the provision of economic and social welfare services they have, at least indirectly, a control and surveillance function. Local governments' detection of major negative developments or rule breaking must be reported to the police and intelligence services. As such, local governments' roles consist of providing both care and surveillance (Lid et al., 2016). The challenges of this dual role will be discussed more broadly later in this chapter.

In other countries, local governments are more involved in control of the (former) extremists who live in the communities rather than in providing care. Kenya has officially created initiatives that have consolidated the role of local governments' representatives in maintaining security. A neighbourhood watch initiative, called Nyumba Kumi, was launched after the terrorist attacks against the Westgate shopping mall in Nairobi in 2013. Nyumba Kumi is the idea that 10 households constitute one security unit that solves mainly security problems and helps security personnel with information gathering. These local committees are chaired by chiefs, who are government's local representatives, appointed and paid by the government (Lid & Okwany, 2019).[6] In practice, Nyumba Kumi is not operating well in many areas of Kenya due to implementation concerns, lack of trust in the chiefs and the entire law enforcement system (Ibid). However, some of the chiefs we have interviewed claimed they receive intelligence about returnees from Al-Shabaab in Nyumba Kumi meetings. Regardless of the success of this initiative, Nyumba Kumi is an example of how maintenance of local security, and control and surveillance are considered prominent functions of local governments in some countries.

Safety and security are, as previously described, important conditions for successful disengagement, deradicalisation and reintegration, both for the recipient society and for the person who has disengaged or is considering disengaging from a violent extremist group. Feelings of insecurity might reduce the person's interest in resettling in the local community and the recipient community's willingness to reintegrate the person. Reconciliation and community acceptance are therefore also of significant importance.

Reconciliation and community acceptance

Local communities' acceptance of reintegrating former extremists is an important condition for a successful sustained disengagement and reintegration (Clubb & Tapley, 2018; Kaplan & Nussio, 2018; Marsden, 2017). The society must allow, and ideally actively support, the individual's reintegration. Local governments can be, in some cases, in a position to influence the society's willingness and support in reintegrating the person (Marsden, 2017, p. 44). Carranza-Franco (2014, p. 257) claims local governments in Colombia played a significant role in promoting reconciliation and community acceptance in the reintegration of more than 50,000 ex-combatants from paramilitary and guerrilla groups. The high number of former combatants who needed to be reintegrated created extraordinary challenges due to pressure on the municipal services and the potential growth in unemployment and poverty. For the municipal authority, it was important to achieve a balance in the care provided to victims and to perpetrators to avoid perception among the citizens of "preference towards the perpetrators".[7] To address these challenges one of the cities, Medellín, created a model for reintegration by merging two previously separate areas of action: the reintegration process of ex-combatants and social care for victims of violence. The peace and reconciliation programme carried out activities for reparation and forgiveness in addition to integration, with the aim of reducing discrimination and grievances in the recipient communities. The advantages of the local governments compared to the central government were, among others, the possibilities of understanding the local dimensions and citizens' concerns and creating local solutions, including the flexibility of the Mayoral office to provide services to people outside the targeted population (ex-combatants) (Ibid).

Local government's representatives in Nairobi claimed in interviews that local citizens view the returnees from Al-Shabaab as enemies and criminals, and there is a need for reconciliation meetings with family, the local community and local authorities to avoid discrimination and provide human security for the returnees. Some of the local government representatives interviewed argued that they are in a position to hold such reconciliation meetings, and asserted they had facilitated such meetings.

The examples above show the importance of addressing the challenges of reluctance in the recipient society, in addition to how local governments can, due to their local presence and knowledge of the dynamics of the local society, be in a position to address the challenges of unwillingness in the society. However, the capability for stimulating acceptance in the society to reintegrate former extremists depends on the local government's capacity and legitimacy, which will be discussed later. The local presence and broad network provide local governments also with an important coordination and cooperative role, as we will investigate in the next section.

Coordination and cooperation

There has been a growing acknowledgement that multifaceted measurements and involvement of various actors are required to promote disengagement, deradicalisation and reintegration into (mainstream) society. A multi-agency initiative, which uses partnership and coordination between actors with various responsibilities and tools, is a much-used strategy also to counter violent extremism, at least in Western countries such as the UK, Netherlands and Scandinavia (see Chapters 17 and 18, Gielen, 2018; Hemmingsen, 2015; Lid et al., 2016). However, the functions, legal framework, structure and organisation of the multi-agency initiatives in these countries have interesting similarities and differences that can illustrate some variations in local governments' coordination and cooperative role.

The functions of multi-agency initiatives are similar, and consist of identifying individuals at risk, assessment of the individual concerned and developing appropriate support for the individual needed (Ibid). However, the legal framework differs between countries. In the UK, the Counter-Terrorism and Security Act 2015 (the CT&S Act) sets out the duty of local authorities to ensure that a panel (Channel programme) is in place for its area, and to list the partners required to cooperate within the panel, including local police, local government and statutory partners (such as education sector, social services, children and youth services), probation services and local communities. The nature of the case decides which partners to include (HM Government/Home Office, 2015).

In Scandinavia and the Netherlands, local governments are not obliged by law to establish multi-agency initiatives. These are mainly initiated locally by municipalities and local police (Agerschou, 2014; Gielen, 2018; Lid et al., 2016). However, the national governments strongly recommend that local actors establish local multi-agency initiatives and they have set up protocols for multi-agency case management (Gielen, 2018; Hemmingsen, 2015; Lid et al., 2016). It is left to the local actors to decide which partners to include, and this depends on the case. To a large extent the same actors are invited as in the UK.

However, a main experience from the Netherlands is that the larger cities and other municipalities that have been confronted with cases of violent extremism have initiated multi-agency strategies, whereas many smaller municipalities have not established these, or initiated them later than the larger municipalities (Gielen, 2018).

The organisation and structure of the initiatives vary also between countries. Channel is chaired by the local authority (CT&S Act, 37(1)), but it is coordinated by the Channel Police Practitioner (CPP). Channel police investigators will assess whether or not the received referral falls under the responsibilities of Channel. Partners in a panel may be requested to provide information about an individual to the CPP during the information-gathering stage (HM Government/Home Office, 2015).

In the Danish Aarhus model, which has many similarities to other multi-agency initiatives in Scandinavia, the leadership is divided between local police and the municipalities. The coordination group also consists of representatives from local police (two police officers) and the municipality (several social service officers representing different social sectors). This coordination group assesses the received referral. In serious cases such as returned foreign fighters, the police undertake an individual risk assessment (Johansen, 2018).

These multi-agency initiatives have overall many similarities, but as highlighted above, there are some key differences between them that can illustrate variations in local governments' coordination and cooperative role: in particular, whether agencies are required to participate or if it is voluntary, and the relationship between local government and the police. For instance, in the Aarhus model, the municipalities' position seems stronger and more equal to the police than in Channel. Furthermore, the structure, regulations and framework of these coordination initiatives may also influence target groups and citizens' trust in local governments. Later I will discuss how this can influence local governments' opportunities to succeed in promoting exit from violent extremism and reintegration.

Above, I have tried to illustrate how the identified core functions of local government might, under specific circumstances, be valuable and useful in supporting disengagement, deradicalisation and reintegration initiatives. In countries where local governments have societal functions that are relevant for promoting disengagement, deradicalisation and reintegration, their importance can be significant. For instance, the evaluation of the resettle programmes of more than 50,000 ex-combatants from paramilitary and guerrilla groups in Colombia in the 2000s summarises the role of the municipalities as essential. The evaluation underlined that the economic and social services provided by the municipalities to the ex-combatants, and the peace and reconciliation programme carried out for reparation and forgiveness, were crucial for successful reintegration. This made it possible for the ex-combatants to settle in a specific community instead of becoming predators on it. The extraordinary effort by the municipalities was possible due to the institutional capacity, political will and successful cooperation with civil society (Carranza-Franco, 2014).

Moreover, local governments' opportunities to promote disengagement, deradicalisation and reintegration are, in addition to their societal functions, closely related to local governments' local presence. The local-based position provides them with insight into the society that is very important, for instance, to understand the dynamics in the local society and citizens' concerns. This is vital to address the challenges of reluctance in society, and the local network can be used to find, for example, jobs, vocational training, housing and so on. Local governments' use of ordinary societal functions for promoting disengagement, deradicalisation and reintegration means they can use already-existing institutions, structures, personnel and services, but as I will discuss below, the existing systems are not always sufficient, especially for minor local governments.

Challenges for local governments

Local governments' challenges to fulfil their functions depend significantly on the allocated functions and tasks, in addition to the governmental structure and economic and human resources. This is clear in developing countries such as Kenya, where local government's economic and human resources are limited, but these challenges are also evident in developing countries. At least several European countries have chosen a decentralised approach where local governments are made accountable. That strategy entails local resources, capacity, knowledge and services. Some local governments have the required resources, but for many local governments, especially for minor municipalities, strengthening their capacity, knowledge and programmes is required (Gielen, 2018; Lid et al., 2016). However, the number of cases is usually limited for most local governments, which constrains the scope of the programme and expertise that is reasonable to develop and maintain locally. That can result in varying quality of the services delivered. The challenges to maintain appropriate knowledge, resources, capacity and services locally is an argument for reducing the tasks and duty of local governments, and rather strengthening the national level or civil actors. However, as this chapter has highlighted, it is necessary to maintain a programme and competence locally to ensure at least an adequate reintegration process. The best balance between national, regional and local level has to be negotiated within each country taking into consideration its demographic and governmental structure.

In addition to these structural challenges, a major challenge for local governments is to gain trust and legitimacy among the target groups, which they depend on to fulfil tasks, in particular welfare provision and reconciliation. In the following, I will discuss three issues that can influence local governments' trust and legitimacy.

State as the enemy

Which actor implements counter-initiatives may have a significant impact on their potential credibility and effectiveness (Bjørgo, 2016; Koehler, 2017). Christensen argues in this volume (Chapter 11) that this is particularly evident in the process of leading individuals out of violent extremism, due to participants in political radical or extreme environments often acting in opposition to political issues and against specific powerholders. That often leads to categorisation of the state and its actors as part of "the enemy" and political position (Karpantschof, 2014). The public institutions' lack of distance and independence from the state might reduce the trust the institutions need (Koehler, 2017).

This challenge appears prominent also in countries with generally relatively high levels of trust and legitimacy in government and local governments. For instance, the right-wing group, the Nordic Resistance Movement (DNM), considers the Norwegian authorities to be directly linked to the team of the Zionist power channel they wish to fight. They consider the authorities, and especially the police, as a power tool to fight their movement (Gjelsvik and Bjørgo, 2018). Furthermore, some returned foreign fighters from Syria have expressed little or no trust in public authorities in the light of their experiences after they returned and their previous experiences with Norwegian police, health and welfare services. Their experience is that the services they are offered aim to monitor them and reveal them as radical and dangerous (Kristiansen & Lid, 2019). That might explain why returning foreign fighters and their families have rejected the efforts of several Norwegian municipalities to offer assistance and support. However, the police and welfare agencies in Norway report they are able to establish solid trust relationships in some cases, although this is often among those who want to exit from the extremist groups (Lid et al., 2016).

The potential challenges due to lack of independence of the state are difficult for local governments to unravel. However, local governments' legitimacy and trust are also influenced by how they balance the function of providing care and control, which they may influence to a greater extent.

Balancing care and control

Welfare service and control and surveillance are, as previously described, two of the major functions of local governments in fostering disengagement, deradicalisation and reintegration. Local governments' capability to mix care and control are essential, especially due to their impact on trust and legitimacy. I will use the experiences from Norway (Lid et al., 2016) to discuss the challenges of balancing the roles of care and control.

There is traditionally a relatively close link between care and control in Norway, due to how the function of control is embedded in the provision of services, as described earlier. The close link between care and control seems to be enhanced within CVE, including in exit and reintegration processes. Among municipalities and other welfare providers their priorities have been to strengthen their ability to identify people at risk, and handle specific cases of concern.[8] Additionally, local governments' cooperation with local police is strengthened. A few social workers in Norwegian municipalities reported they had experienced an expectation from the police to assist in police intelligence work, and some of them had collected the information the police requested. The Norwegian social workers' argument for collecting information on behalf of the police was that the municipality and the police have the same goal of a safe local community (Ibid). Relevant questions include how close the partnership between local governments and police should be, and what is the role of the actors. Could police and other criminal justice partners make use of local social workers to collect information in local areas and about families and people to whom the police have no access?

The question is whether the strengthening cooperation, and what is seen as blurry definitions of roles, responsibilities and tasks, can have unforeseen consequences. A key lesson from crime prevention policy and practice is that police involvement can undermine the integrity and effectiveness of preventative diversion (Cherney, 2016, p. 86). Close cooperation with the police and intelligence services might increase the perception of local governments as part of the control regime, and raise the target group's scepticism about the local governments. That will hamper local governments' chances of forming relations with the target group and providing services. This may be a decisive factor in why Norwegian municipalities have had comprehensive challenges in gaining contact and trust among returned foreign fighters, although the municipalities' approach to the extremists and their families is mainly care (Lid et al., 2016). If this is the reality, cooperation and multi-agency initiatives, which seem to be crucial for success in disengagement, deradicalisation and reintegration, may become major reasons for failure.

National policies' influence on local governments' legitimacy

CVE initiatives throughout the world have several similarities, but also dramatic differences (Harris-Horgan et al., 2016; Vidino & Brandon, 2012). By demonstrating some of the variations between the national CVE approaches in the UK and the Scandinavian countries, I will discuss how national policies might influence the legitimacy and trust of local governments.

The UK's Counter-Terrorism Strategy (CONTEST), including Prevent,[9] has been heavily criticised for securitisation of social and political life (see, for instance, Chapter 17).

These types of criticism have occurred to a lesser extent in Denmark than in the UK (Lindekilde, 2015, p. 224) and in Norway such criticism has been almost absent (Lid & Heierstad, 2019). There are undoubtedly various reasons for these differences, but the foundation and legal framework of the programmes emerge as essential. In the UK, as part of CONTEST a new Act (the CT&S Act) has been implemented. The CT&S Act sets out, as presented above, the duty of local authorities to cooperate with the police and the panel (Channel programme) in carrying out the functions "so far as appropriate and reasonably practicable" (Prevent duty) (HM Government/Home Office, 2015). This Prevent duty has been criticised particularly for putting inappropriate pressure on actors to report terrorism-related concerns which result in increased surveillance and securitisation (Busher et al., 2017; Saaed & Johnsen, 2016). However, the educationalists mainly understood the Prevent duty as a continuity of previous practice, such as how the government presented the duty, and they broadly support Prevent and the Prevent duty (Busher et al., 2017).

The Scandinavian countries have not implemented a specific counter-terrorism strategy and associated act. The primary strategy is to build CVE initiatives on previous crime prevention work and (mainly) use existing legislation. For instance, the Aarhus model is a further development of the long-standing multi-agency approach consisting of police, social services and school (SSP) (see Chapter 18). Moreover, in Denmark, governmental authorities have a statutory duty to safeguard children, young people and adults. These regulations oblige these partners to provide support to the people concerned, but also to report cases to the police to prevent crime (Johansen, 2018; Lindekilde, 2015).

These substantial differences in the foundation and legal framework of the CVE approach in the UK and in Scandinavia might generate varying impressions of the models. Although the British Government claims the aim of Prevent is to "safeguard people against the risk of radicalisation", impressions and criticisms of Prevent are that it leads to securitisation of society. It appears to be a programme dominated by security and control where local government agencies and other welfare providers perform as a tool to protect society. For the Scandinavian countries, the CVE model, which is deeply rooted in the welfare state, appears to be dominated by care and integration (Johansen, 2018; Lid & Heierstad, 2019). These variations may influence citizens' and target groups' perception of the national counter-terrorism strategy, the role of the agencies (including local governments) and the legitimacy of the interventions. This may explain to some extent the variations in criticism in these countries, although, some of the practice on the ground does not seem to be as different. For instance, the introduction of the Prevent duty in the UK caused a sharp increase in the number of referrals to the police. Many referrals were not related to radicalisation, but out of "inappropriate behaviour" duty (Busher et al., 2017). In Norway, which has a mostly similar model to Denmark, the number of reported cases from statutory agencies, particularly from schools, to local police due to concern about radicalisation grew rapidly after increased attention on the topic. Many of the reported cases were easily disproved by the police as radicalisation, but assessed as another type of concern (Lid et al., 2016).

To sum up, the apparently security and control-dominated British CVE programme may have reduced the legitimacy of and trust in the public actors, and led to a stronger critical perspective of the practice. However, some of the criticism of Prevent may also be applicable to the Scandinavian countries at least, but the apparently care and integration-dominated Scandinavian CVE programme may have covered some of the fundamental problems with the practice, such as surveillance and securitisation of some arenas and groups, increased number of unnecessary referrals to the police and the extent of information sharing between collaborating partners in multi-agency initiatives. From a local government perspective the influence of the national policy on their legitimacy is an aspect that is hard to address.

Conclusion

In this chapter, I have illustrated how local governments can, in some cases, be in a position to influence exit and reintegration processes, building bridges between individuals and societies, due to their local presence and their core societal functions. Control and surveillance, reconciliation and coordination are all functions that are important to ensure the conditions for successful disengagement, deradicalisation and reintegration initiatives to take place. Moreover, welfare services can offer new opportunities and alternatives to continue in the extremist environment. However, which of the functions are the prominent function(s) varies significantly between local governments. For many local governments around the world the identified functions are probably more a description of what local governments can ensure under certain conditions, rather than what many of them do.

Local governments' capability to fulfil these functions is primarily governed by their general resources, functions and mandate. The political and practical willingness to engage in cases seems crucial in addition to the target groups' and local citizens' trust in and legitimacy of the local government. Trust and legitimacy are determined by a range of elements, such as the foundation of the national and local counter-terrorism strategy, how local governments balance the roles of promoting care and control, collaboration with the police and the level of expertise and capacity, in addition to general trust in local government.

Local governments' greatest challenge is that they are part of the state, which some extremist groups perceive as an enemy. That is a challenge that cannot be modified, and this constricts the position of local governments in many cases. However, local governments have greater impact on other factors that influence trust. In this regard, it seems important to clarify the role of local governments, their area of responsibility and tasks in disengagement, deradicalisation and reintegration, in addition to transparency and clear procedures in partnership with other actors and make these procedures visible for all stakeholders and target groups (see also Koehler, 2017, p. 156). This probably may not entirely solve these challenges, but it may help to diminish the potentially undesirable consequences of combining these functions and being in close cooperation with the police.

Moreover, it seems clear local governments' opportunities to promote welfare services and reconciliation particularly are best ensured if local governments are not dragged too far into control and surveillance, but keep an appropriate distance from the actors in the security sector. If local governments' function of control and surveillance is becoming too dominating, it may be at the expense of other functions and limit the role of local governments in control and surveillance. Especially for those local governments that have the resources, mandate and structure to promote welfare services, that will seriously reduce their importance. Probably even more importantly, it will also constrict the services from which individuals in exit processes will benefit and reduce their chances of a successful disengagement, deradicalisation and reintegration process.

There has been an increasing recognition of the intelligence and security services' limitations in successfully promoting exit and reintegration processes, and the need for involvement of other public and civilian actors. The involvement of these actors must not be reduced to being the extended hands and helpers of intelligence and security services. It is probably more important that these actors strengthen their efforts to provide services that are attractive for target groups, and build bridges between individuals and society. Addressing some of the challenges described in this chapter may strengthen local governments' role in disengagement, deradicalisation and reintegration in the future.

Notes

1 In several countries, such as the Scandinavian countries, Austria, the Netherlands and the UK, the national action plans make local governments responsible and highlight the importance of their involvement. Moreover, national networks (Götsch, 2017), and global networks, such as the United Nations' Strong Cities Network (SCN) and the EU Radicalisation Awareness Network (RAN), are established to strengthen the capacity to counter violent extremism among local governments. This shows how local governments are considered to be a prominent partner.

2 The primary research is mainly a comprehensive study of Norwegian municipalities' role in countering violent extremism. The study consisted of more than 70 interviews, mostly group interviews, with representatives from the most relevant municipal agencies and political and administrative leaders in five Norwegian municipalities, in addition to cooperating partners such as local police, intelligence services and civil society organisations (Lid et al., 2016). Additionally, a smaller study was conducted in Nairobi, Kenya, in April 2018. Twelve local government representatives (members of county assembly and local chiefs) in informal settlements in Eastleigh and Majengo were interviewed about their engagement in disengagement, deradicalisation and reintegration initiatives of returnees from Al-Shabaab. The interviews were conducted as an extension of another current research project about community policing, which included citizens' relations to local government representatives.

3 Push factors are often defined as "negative social incidents and circumstances that make it uncomfortable and unappealing to remain in a particular social movement", and pull factors refer to the "positive factors attracting the person to a more rewarding alternative than continuing in the movement or group" (Bjørgo, 2016, p. 234).

4 Koehler (2017, p. 133) argues that the level of social services delivered through governmental institutions affects the need for non-governmental actors in deradicalisation processes. This need might either be broad (including vocational training, employment facilitation, financial support, etc.) or narrow (focused on ideological debate, networking, guidance or contact provision).

5 Other European countries, such as Germany, the Netherlands and France, have organised family counselling differently. It is a joint project between national government and non-governmental organisations (Koehler, 2017).

6 The chiefs are part of the executive power structure of the old public administration implemented by the colonial administration, and their main functions are gathering intelligence for the president. Although the 2010 Kenyan Constitution dissolved this old public administration, it still exists and is supported by the president. However, the local levels in the new public administration engagement in promoting exit and reintegration are assessed as limited (BRICS, 2017; Taita, 2016; see Chapter 22, this volume). At the Kenyan coast, which is the area that has received most returnees from Al-Shabaab, the county governments' involvement was considered to be reluctant, and the county governments failed to take initiatives and responsibility (BRICS, 2017, Taita, 2016). Hence, in Kenya, the local representatives from the old public administration appear to have the most prominent role in countering violent extremism, due to their function of gathering intelligence.

7 See Clubb and Tapley (2018) for a similar challenge in Nigeria.

8 Van de Weert and Eijkmann (2018) and Mattsson (2017) describe a similar development in the Netherlands and Sweden.

9 Prevent is one of four pillars (prevent, pursue, protect, prepare) in CONTEST.

References

Agerschou, T. (2014). "Preventing radicalization and discrimination in Aarhus." *Journal for Deradicalisation*, 2014/2015 (1), pp. 5–22.

Altier, M.B., Boyle, E.L., Shortland, N.D., & Horgan, J.G. (2017). "Why they leave: An analysis of terrorist disengagement events from eighty-seven autobiographical accounts." *Security Studies*, 26 (2), pp. 305–332.

Altier, M.B., Thoroughgood, C.N., & Horgan, J.G. (2014). "Turning away from terrorism. Lessons from psychology, sociology, and criminology." *Journal of Peace Research*, 51 (5), pp. 647–661.

Andersson Malmros, R. & Mattsson, C. (2017). *Från ord till handlingsplan. En rapport o kommunala handlingsplaner mot våldsbejakande extremism*. Stockholm: Svergies kommuner och Landsting.

Anindyaa, C.R. (2019). "The deradicalisation programme for Indonesian deportees: A vacuum in coordination." *Journal for Deradicalisation*, Spring 2019 (18), pp. 217–243.

Barrelle, K. (2015). "Pro-integration. Disengagement from and life after extremism." *Behavioral Sciences of Terrorism and Political Aggression*, 7 (2), pp. 129–142.
Bjørgo, T. (2009). "Process of disengagement from violent groups of the extreme right." In T. Bjørgo & J. Horgan (eds). *Leaving terrorism behind. Individual and collective disengagement*. London/New York: Routledge, pp. 30–48.
Bjørgo, T. (2011). "Dreams and disillusionment: Engagement in and disengagement from militant extremist groups." *Crime, Law and Social Change*, 55, pp. 277–285. DOI: 10.1007/s10611-011-9282-9.
Bjørgo, T. (2016). *Preventing crime: A holistic approach*. Basingtoke and New York: Palgrave Macmillan.
Bjørgo, T. & Horgan, J. (2009). "Introduction." In T. Bjørgo & J. Horgan (eds). *Leaving terrorism behind. Individual and collective disengagement*. London: Routledge, pp. 1–14.
BRICS. (2017). "Project completion report. Building resilience in civil society for preventing violent extremism in East Africa." *Building Resilience in Civil Society (BRICS) Report.*
Busher, J., Choudhury, T., Thomas, P., & Harris, G. (2017). *What the Prevent duty means for schools and colleges in England: An analysis of educationalists' experiences*. Coventry: Centre for Trust, Peace and Social Relations, Coventry University.
Carranza-Franco, F. (2014). "A sub-national approach to state-building and security: The role of municipal institutions in Colombia's DDR process." *Conflict, Security & Development*, 14 (3), pp. 245–274.
Chandler, J.A. (2001). *Local government today*. Manchester: Manchester University Press.
Chandler, J.A. (2013). *Local government in liberal democracies: An introductory survey*. London: Routledge.
Cherney, A. (2016). "Designing and implementing programmes to tackle radicalization and violent extremism: Lessons from criminology." *Dynamics of Asymmetric Conflict*, 9 (1–3), pp. 82–94. DOI: 10.1080/17467586.2016.1267865.
Clubb, G. & Tapley, M. (2018). "Conceptualising de-radicalisation and former combatant re-integration in Nigeria." *Third World Quarterly*, 39 (11), pp. 2053–2068.
Cronin, A.K. (2009). *How terrorism ends: Understanding the decline and demise of terrorist campaigns*. Princeton, NJ: Princeton University Press.
Dalgaard-Nielsen, A. (2016). "Countering violent extremism with governance networks." *Perspectives on Terrorism*, 10 (6), pp. 135–139.
Enemuo, F. (2000). "Problems and prospects of local governance." In G. Hyden, D. Olowu, & H.W.O. Okoth Ogendo (eds). *African perspectives on governance*. Eritrea: African World Press, Inc, pp. 181–204.
Gielen, A.J. (2018). "Exit programmes for female jihadists: A proposal for conducting realistic evaluation of the Dutch approach." *International Sociology*, 33 (4), pp. 454–472.
Gjelsvik, I.M. & Bjørgo, T. (2018). "Politiets virkemidler og rolle i forebygging av høyreekstremisme." I.T. Bjørgo (red), *Høyreekstremisme i Norge. Utviklingstrekk, konspirasjonsteorier og forebyggingsstrategier. PHS Forskning*, 2018, p. 4.
Götsch, K. (2017). "Austria and the threats from Islamist radicalisation and terrorist involvement: An overview of governmental and non-governmental initiatives and policies." *Journal for Deradicalisation*, Fall 2017 (12), pp. 169–191.
Harris-Horgan, S., Barelle, K., & Zammit, A. (2016). "What is countering violent extremism? Exploring CVE policy and practice in Australia." *Behavioral Sciences of Terrorism and Political Aggression*, 8 (1), pp. 6–24.
Heide, L. & Schuurman, B. (2018). "Reintegrating terrorists in the Netherlands: Evaluating the Dutch approach." *Journal for Deradicalisation*, Winter 2018/2019 (17), pp. 196–239.
Hemmingsen, A.S. (2015). "An introduction to the Danish approach to countering and preventing extremism and radicalisation." *DIIS Rapport.*
HM Government/Home Office. (2015). "Channel duty guidance. Protecting vulnerable people from being drawn into terrorism. Statutory guidance for Channel panel members and partners of local panels." *HM Government publication.*
Horgan, J. (2009). *Walking away from terrorism: Accounts of disengagement from radical and extremist movements*. London/New York: Routledge.
Hwang, J.C. (2018). *Why terrorists quit: The disengagement of Indonesian jihadist*. New York: Cornell University Press.
Jacobsen, M. (2010). *Terrorists dropouts: Learning from those who have left (Vol. 101)*. Washington: Washington Institute for Near East Policy.
Johansen, M.L. (2018). "Aarhus-indsatsen: Udveksling og relationsarbejde i den danske velfærdsstat." In A. Andersson, S. Høgestøl, & A.C. Lie (eds). *Fremmedkrigere*. Oslo: Gyldendal Akademisk, pp. 265–296.

Kaplan, O. & Nussio, E. (2018). "Community counts: The social reintegration of ex-combatants in Colombia." *Conflict Management and Peace Science*, Online November 24. DOI: 10.1177/0738894215614506.

Karpantschof, R. (2014). "Violence that matters! Radicalization and de-radicalization of leftist, urban movements – Denmark 1981–2011." *Behavioral Sciences of Terrorism and Political Aggression*, 7 (1). DOI: 10.1080/19434472.2014.977330.

Koehler, D. (2017). *Understanding deradicalization. Methods, tools and programs for countering violent extremism*. London & New York: Routledge.

Kristiansen, S.H. & Lid, S. (2019). "Mistenkt og dømt for terrortilknytning, hva nå, og hva med fremtiden? In S. Lid & G. Heierstad (eds). *Forebygging av radikalisering og voldelig ekstremisme. Norske handlemåter i møtet med terror*. Oslo: Gyldendal Akademisk, pp. 223–242.

Lid, S. & Heierstad, G. (2019). "Norske handlemåter i møtet med terror Den gjenstridige forebyggingen nå og i framtiden." In S. Lid & G. Heierstad (eds). *Forebygging av radikalisering og voldelig ekstremisme. Norske handlemåter i møtet med terror*. Oslo: Gyldendal Akademisk, pp. 15–48.

Lid, S. & Okwany, C.C.O. (2019). "Protecting citizens or an instrument for surveillance? – The development of community policing models in Kenya." *Journal of Human Security*, 7 (2).

Lid, S., Winsvold, M., Søholt, S., Hansen, S.J., Heierstad, G., & Klausen, J.E. (2016). "Forebygging av radikalisering og voldelig ekstemisme Hva er kommunenes rolle?" *NIBR-rapport* 2016:12.

Lindekilde, L. (2015). "Refocusing Danish radicalization prevention: The (problematic) logic and practice of individual 'de-radicalization' interventions." In C. Baker-Beall, C. Heath-Kelly, & L. Jarvis (eds). *Counter-radicalisation – Critical perspectives*. London/New York: Routledge, pp. 223–241.

Lynch, O. (2015). "Desistance and deradicalisation – The case of Northern Ireland." In S. Zeiger & A. Aly (eds). *Countering violent extremism: Developing an evidence-base for policy and practice*. Perth: Curtin University, pp. 111–118.

Marsden, S.V. (2017). *Reintegrating extremists. Deradicalisation and desistance*. London: Palgrave Macmillan.

Mattsson, C. (2017). "Caught between the urgent and the comprehensible. Professionals' understanding of violent extremism.' *Critical Studies on Terrorism*, 11 (1), pp. 111–129. DOI: 10.1080/17539153.2017.1337327.

Nesser, P. (2015). *Islamist terrorism in Europe, a history*. London: Hurst Publishers.

Neumann, P.R. (2010). *Prisons and terrorism: Radicalisation and de-radicalisation in 15 countries*. London: ICSR, King College.

Ranstorp, M. & Hyllengren, P. (2013). *Prevention of violent extremism in third countries. Measures to prevent individuals joining armed extremist groups in conflict zones*. Sweden: Center for Asymmetric Threat Studies, National Defense College.

Rosenau, W., Espach, R., Ortiz, R.D., & Herrera, N. (2014). "Why they join, why they fight and why they leave: Learning from Colombia's database of demobilized militants." *Terrorism and Political Violence*, 26 (2), pp. 277–285.

Saaed, T. & Johnsen, D. (2016). "Intelligence, global terrorism and higher education: Neutralising threats or alienating allies?" *British Journal of Educational Studies*, 64 (1), pp. 37–51. DOI: 10.1080/00071005.2015.1123216.

Schuurman, B. & Bakker, E. (2016). "Reintegrating jihadist extremists: Evaluating a Dutch initiative, 2013–2014." *Behavioral Sciences of Terrorism and Political Aggression*, 8 (1), pp. 66–85. DOI: 10.1080/19434472.2015.1100648.

Smith, B.C. (2017). *Good governance and development*. New York: Palgrave Macmillan.

Stoker, G. (2011). "Was local governance such a good idea? A global comparative perspective." *Public Administration*, 89 (1), pp. 15–31.

Taita Teveta University College. (2016). "Working with the National Government and Coastal Counties to counter violent extremism in the Coast Region of Kenya." *Report of a survey project done under the Brics East Africa project submitted to Development Alternatives Initiatives (DAI) Europe*.

Van de Weert, A. & Eijkman, Q.A.M. (2018). "Subjectivity in detection of radicalisation and violent extremism. A youth workers' perspective." *Behavioral Sciences of Terrorism and Political Aggression*, Published online 21 March 2018. DOI: 10.1080/19434472.2018.1457069.

Vidino, L. & Brandon, J. (2012). "Europe's experience in countering radicalization: Approaches and challenges." *Journal of Policing, Intelligence and Counter Terrorism*, 7 (2), pp. 163–179.

11

CIVIL ACTORS' ROLE IN DERADICALISATION AND DISENGAGEMENT INITIATIVES

When trust is essential

Tina Wilchen Christensen

Based on ethnographic interviews[1] with around 50 individuals who have participated in radical and/or violent right- or left-wing groups in Northern Europe (Christensen 2009, 2015, Christensen & Mørck 2017), this chapter provides insight into extremists' experiences and frameworks of understanding and interpretation. It will illustrate why participants in radical and extreme groups represent a difficult target group to reach by initiatives aimed at disengagement and deradicalisation run by state and public actors in North European welfare states and why, as the chapter argues, civil actors *per se* seem better positioned to gain legitimacy among them.

By shedding light on some of the experiences (former) participants acquire by participating in radical and/or extreme groups, the chapter demonstrates the different positions state and civil actors have in responding to individuals' particular needs when they leave extreme environments and why civil society actors can play a particular role in disengagement and deradicalisation initiatives.

The idea is to convey, as the chapter argues, that who is in charge of programmes and initiatives aimed at deradicalisation and disengagement has a significant impact on their credibility in the eyes of the target groups and with it the possibility of reaching them. The individuals' particular experiences as activists in a political and violent context with its crucial factors, moments and dynamics often result in them coming to categorise the state and its actors as part of 'the enemy' (Karpantschof 2014). Participants in political radical or extreme environments[2] act in opposition to political powerholders and issues on the national and international agenda (Christensen 2009, Christensen & Mørck 2017). Over the course of their engagement some participants develop into violent extremists as an outcome of a complex interplay of internal and external factors (Karpantschof 2014, p. 3).

Becoming an extremist is an outcome of people's engagement in a community defined by some sort of common practice and discourse. Once they have become involved their participation entails that they develop or reinforce an ideological orientation, and some gradually come to accept and/or use violence. Becoming an extremist is thus an outcome of a social and psychological development the individual goes through, which is conditioned by a specific social, historical and political context where no one can be perceived as neutral (Berntzen & Sandberg 2014, Karpantschof 2014, Porta 2009, 2013). By zooming in on the social process making an individual develop an identity as an extremist the chapter demonstrates how participation in extreme groups influences the individual's life-world (Schutz 1967). In untangling this process, the chapter provides an empirically informed understanding of the personal implication of participation in extreme groups to make participants' outlook and acquired experiences tangible and thus the conditions which need to be considered in disengagement and deradicalisation initiatives.

During the last decades initiatives and programmes aimed at combating violent extremism have emerged across Europe. State agencies such as probation services, the police and the secret services, among others, have been in charge of initiatives aimed at disengagement and deradicalisation. As the chapter demonstrates, such actors might have a high risk of having setbacks from the very beginning, because the target group's trust in them may be low or non-existent (Koehler 2017, Lid & Heierstad 2018). Acknowledging that state agencies and non-governmental organisations (NGOs) cooperate to various degrees, civil society actors seem initially better positioned to reach out and gain trust among people leaving extremist groups, which is crucial. Building a trusting relation is essential in any effort aimed at disengagement and deradicalisation, as trust is what makes people become open to input from an outside party, which is necessary for change to occur (Christensen 2015). Trust in the provider on a personal and institutional level is thus key to any successful initiatives as everything in an exit process depends on it (Christensen 2015, Christensen & Bjørgo 2018, Dalsgaard-Nielsen 2013).

The chapter identifies some of the critical differences between state, public and civil society actors and discusses the possibilities and challenges involved conditioned by the outlook people in an exit process might have and the sort of personal support they require if reintegration into mainstream society should become a genuine possibility.

Becoming a violent extremist is recognised here as an outcome of an individual's engagement in a situated learning process, implying that learning is perceived as embedded within activity, context and culture and is unintentional (Lave & Wenger 1990). For the sake of clarification 'radical' is understood here as anything that deviates from the comparable mainstream, and thus only makes sense within a wider societal context. 'Violent extremism' is when individuals approve of and/or use non-democratic and illegal means in a liberal democratic system, such as threats, harassment and violence against political opponents and others categorised as enemies in the pursuance of political goals (Schmid 2013).

Civil society actors

Civil actors are NGOs or any association that manifests the interests and will of citizens, such as religious communities, relief organisations and recreational associations. Such organisations in Northern Europe are in general perceived as actors that have a positive role to play in crime-preventive measures and venues supporting the reintegration of former extremists. Yet, handling extremists who have defected or just left a violent environment is a challenge requiring knowledge, insight and understanding, which makes some civil actors more relevant than others. The chapter acknowledges that different actors like governmental non-governmental organisations (GNGOs) also work with violent (extremist) offenders and that civil actors like religious communities and recreational associations have a huge role to play in the process of reintegrating former violent extremists. Yet, the focus will mainly be on NGOs, which have the experience required to risk assess, handle and support violent extremists, who are motivated to disengage or have just left an extremist environment. Such NGOs are often working against (violent) extremism on several levels. On the one hand they offer support to individuals motivated to leave violent extremist groups and environments, while on the other hand they spread information, training and knowledge about how to prevent violent extremism to a public audience and people working in the field.

Several civil actors with expertise within this field exist across Northern Europe; for example, the German NGO EXIT Germany and the GNGO Violence Prevention Network,[3] both of which aim at disengagement, deradicalisation and exit assistance. The Violence Prevention Network is an example of an NGO which has become a GNGO, as its approach has been implemented across Germany and is now co-funded jointly by the EU, federal governments and others. The organisation works inside and outside prisons with violent offenders from right-wing extremism, Islamism and neo-Salafism. EXIT Germany offers counselling services for individuals who have held high-ranking positions in right-wing extremist groups.[4] It has also expanded its target group as HAYAT, a sub-organisation within EXIT Germany, has been established building on its experiences. HAYAT[5] targets what is defined as Muslim supremacists. In contrast, a different sort of programme is the Danish society Breathe Prison Smart,[6] which runs meditation courses inside and outside prisons across the world and offers individual trauma treatment aimed mainly at violent offenders from gangs and/or extremist groups (Hviid 2017). The Swedish NGO EXIT approach is based on a mentorship programme supporting right-wing extremists leaving the Swedish White Power movement. It is from EXIT Sweden that the present chapter will draw its main examples, stemming from an anthropological investigation as part of a Ph.D. project I conducted based on the organisation and its approach in 2012 (Christensen 2015).

Founded in 1998, EXIT Sweden is the oldest programme of its kind in Europe and is based on cooperation between former neo-Nazis, social workers and academics (ibid). While a few of the employees have a past in extreme groups, the programmes in general share some important characteristics with other similar programmes, such as: participation is voluntary; individuals in the programmes are expected to be motivated for change; methods and approaches are informed by a detailed understanding of the social practices and culture at work in extreme groups; a detailed insight into the impact of participation in extreme groups for the individual; and the benefit of their existence being known among individuals in the target group as well as a high degree of legitimacy.

The entanglement of the state and the impossibility of staying neutral

The national strategies implemented by the municipalities, the probation service and the police and other public institutions aimed at countering violent extremist (CVE) initiatives in Northern Europe are two-fold. They are both preventive, targeting what are opaquely defined as 'people at risk of radicalisation', as well as seeking to motivate people who are or have been involved in extremist groups, or who are convicted of illegal military involvement in armed conflicts also called 'foreign fighters' or being charged with terrorism by providing support instigating an exit through exit programmes (Christensen & Bjørgo 2018, Christensen & Mørck 2017, Lid et al. 2016, National handlingsplan 2016).

In Northern Europe societal structure is based on a universal welfare state and principles of United Nations statements of human rights. The state is responsible for protecting citizens and grants their freedom of speech and promotes their economic and social wellbeing (Lid & Heierstad 2018). Citizens in Northern Europe enjoy almost unlimited freedom of expression and thus the right to express even extreme viewpoints. At the same time school teachers and front-desk personnel in public institutions in, for example, Denmark have over the last decade received training in 'preventing radicalisation' by being instructed in the risky endeavour of identifying youth 'at risk of radicalisation' and potential 'violent political offenders'.[7] Part of the training emphasises the right to freedom of expression, yet employees are encouraged to react to expressions of 'a concerning conviction' and 'a rhetoric legitimating or encouraging violent actions'.[8] Such expressions are identified as one of the signs – among others – of radicalisation, which can be interpreted as of 'concern' and are identified by the Danish National Center for Prevention of Extremism as worth paying attention to (ibid). The example indicates that, even though initiatives that aim to (risk) assess and reintegrate former extremists generally differentiate between behaviour and attitude relating to the mainly analytical difference between the terms *radicalisation/deradicalisation*, which concern changes in attitudes/ideology, and *engagement/disengagement*, which involve changes in behaviour and involvement in violent groups and activities or desisting from this (Bjørgo & Horgan 2009), in practice it can be difficult to separate the two. The difficulty in separating the two may also explain why initiatives targeting people motivated or in the process of disengaging now seek to support individuals reintegrated in democratic society (Marsden 2017).

The state's responsibility for securing citizens places high demands on the political system and impacts the legislation in relation to CVE and the state and public institutions' room for manoeuvre. Yet, the ideological orientation to the government in power and the public discourse in relation to radical and/or extreme groups and their activities also influence state and public actors' understanding of the raison d'être for such groups and the individuals' involvement in them. This will in turn have an impact on what is identified as the problem, who the target groups are and which measures are required in disengagement and deradicalisation initiatives. The coherence can be illustrated by the present political and public debate in Europe.

Over the last decade a general negative discourse about Islam, immigrants and immigration, combined with numerous terror attacks by violent Islamic groups or individuals, has resulted in a general greater political will to apply significant control, surveillance and legal sanctions (Christensen & Bjørgo 2018, Høgestøl 2018 in Lid & Heierstad 2018). But it has also tended to reduce extremism and radicalisation to issues linked to broad categories such as 'Islam' and 'Muslims' in the public perception. The result is that the daily media discourse and the initiatives merge and tend to stigmatise a minority group, with the outcome that prevention runs the risk of developing into a self-fulfilling prophecy (Gemmerli & Hemmingsen in Hemmingsen 2015). Such tendencies might also explain why, for example, several Norwegian municipalities have been rejected by returning foreign fighters and their families in their efforts to offer assistance and support (Lid et al. 2016). Individuals who have returned from Syria/Iraq and been convicted as foreign fighters have expressed little or no trust in the authorities in the light of their experiences after they returned and previous experiences with Norwegian police, health and welfare services. Their experience is that the services they are offered aim to monitor them and reveal them as radical and dangerous (Kristiansen & Lid, 2019).

The current public and political debate affects people's perception of the risk, the target groups and positions of state actors in the eyes of individuals in the target group. Such conditions also make measures aimed at, for example, reintegration of returned foreign fighters from Syria in Norwegian prisons at the same time a difficult and controversial issue (Christensen & Bjørgo 2018).

While state actors in the perception of the target groups are influenced by the ruling political ideology, discourse and state actors' activities, civil actors are in general much less so. The target group's perception of the link between the government, the state and public actors' ideological stand is crucial compared to NGOs, which is perceived as less influenced by the given political order as well as bearing the heavy burden of securing the public from terror attacks. The difference between the two has a critical impact on initially reaching the target group and the chance of building up trusting relations, which becomes apparent by zooming in on individuals' experiences when active in radical and/or violent extremist groups and especially their individual outcomes.

An identity shaped by opposition to outer enemies

Interviewing radical left-wingers as well as former extremists from violent extremist right- or left-wing groups reveals that only a few get involved because of a clear political ideology or undefined feelings of political discontent (Christensen 2009, 2015, Christensen & Mørck 2017). On the contrary, many of them joined initially because of non-ideological reasons, such as being on the lookout for community, excitement and curiosity by attending social events like concerts, parties or other types of informal meetings. These events enabled them to strike up new acquaintances and expand their social network in political environments (ibid). Even though individuals became involved because of multiple reasons, many would eventually increase their social interaction with others from the group. Thereby they would get involved in political discussions and activities as political actions are an integrated part of the social life within radical and/or violent political environments (ibid).

Many radical and/or extreme groups work for a fundamental change in society and the political system. This has an impact on the sort of perception participants develop of the surrounding society and the public and civil actors in it. Being part of a violence-prone radical or extreme group positions the participant vis-à-vis the surrounding society; in addition social life in these environments involves political discussions about local, national and international news and conflicts (Christensen 2009, 2009a). The interpretation of the different events – in radical and extremist groups – is based on an ideologically defined understanding and interpretation framework identifying the problem, friends and enemies and actions the individual ought to take to support the group's desired goal or changes in society (Christensen 2009, Polleta 2007, Snow et al. 2007). The individual's framework of interpretation and understanding of the world as well as his or her own position in it will in time be constituted by the group and the narratives and propaganda at work within it (ibid).

In qualitative interviews former right-wing and left-wing extremists from across Scandinavia described how they moved from being active in social gatherings and events to becoming increasingly involved in demonstrations or other political events and handing out leaflets arguing against the existing political and social order. Such activities often involved fights with political opponents and others categorised as legitimate targets for violence, which for some resulted in clashes with the police, detention in custody, trials and imprisonment (Christensen 2009, 2009a, 2015; Christensen & Mørck 2017).

To illustrate the sort of influence of clashes with the police and how this impacts the individual's perception of state actors, this quotation from a former left-wing radical is illustrative. The quotation described the individual's experience, when the person travelled from a neighbouring country with a radical left-wing group known to contain both radical and violent extreme individuals to participate in a demonstration in a middle-sized Swedish town and the influence such experiences can have on a person's perspective:

> I changed my mind about the use of violence while I was in a Swedish town until then I was against it. My experience was that we were stopped at the border, the bus was searched and we had no weapons. We started to walk from the buses up to the main street. Then we heard that the police ordered us to turn around. Then I remember turning around. So, in my mind, I thought they gave us an order and we turned around. Then we saw the police run, while they kept the shields in front of their chest while striking the protesters. The crowd panicked, people started running and every other fell. I remember we turned around and then there was one that had fallen, and the face was full of blood, and then the protesters started throwing what they found ... So I remember, I thought; 'Why do they beat us when we did as they said?' That was completely incomprehensible. So, I thought they used dogs and batons on defenseless people. They knew we had no weapons of any kind, and we did as they said. It changed my picture of ... I felt stepped on, violated and that it was so deeply unfair how the system has just kind of revealed itself in ways it shouldn't. I totally lost faith in the police. Then after that, I was just; 'let's use so much violence we can handle. No limits'. But that does not mean that in practice. I participated in demonstrations, I wanted a conflict to occur, but I did not commit violence. But when I entered the extreme right those constraints were gone.
>
> *(Christensen & Mørck 2017, pp. 92–93)*

The social interaction with other participants in the group, the shared narrative and the personal experience of highly intense and violent situations in general change involved individuals' perspective of how far-reaching their political struggle is, the use of violence, the legitimacy of the police and sometimes, as this person says, the 'system' itself. Clashes in demonstrations and the experience of violence directed against oneself or others can lead to a dramatic change in participants' overall perspective and their perspective on the legitimacy and use of violence and their own willingness to use it (Christensen & Mørck 2017).

Personal experiences confirm the propaganda about state actors

A civil actor with a status as an independent NGO stands a better chance of gaining a position with a higher degree of legitimacy among individuals motivated to disengage (Christensen 2015) as people's perception of state actors is shaped by personal experience combined with the framework of interpretation and understanding circulation in the radical or extreme environment (Christensen 2009, 2015, Holland et al. 2018). To give an example of the perspective to be found in extreme environments, the case of the neo-Nazi group Nordic Resistance Movement (DNM), which is represented across Scandinavia, is illustrative. They consider the authorities to be directly linked to what the group perceives as the 'Zionist power' they wish to fight, so they perceive the authorities, and especially the police, as a power tool to fight their movement (Gjelsvik & Bjørgo 2019). In contrast, the autonomous movement on the extreme left tends to perceive the state and powerholders as part of an illegitimate 'capitalistic and imperialistic' system (Karpantschof 2014). Negative perception of the state and its actors such as the police is at work for different reasons at both ends of the political spectrum.

Narrative circulation in radical and extreme environments about the police being biased and violent changes from general perceptions into an accurate rendering of the truth when it becomes a personal experience. The quotation below is from a former participant in a left-wing group which contained both radical and violent extreme individuals. It illustrates how his perception of the police changed when he was participating in a demonstration at the beginning of his involvement in the environment (Christensen 2009, 2009a, Christensen & Mørck 2017). He relates:

> 'I was in a demonstration in Germany during the first year I was part of the environment, where I saw a man being kicked in the head by a police officer while lying down. It was extremely violent, so I felt really bad about it ... where I was thinking ... fuck ... they are such pigs, the peelers. Again, here many years after, I can see that a police officer's violence has conditioned my perception of them all, not only because it confirms the tale being told ... well, I was so ready to confirm the understanding amongst my buddies and ... their anger. I really wanted to understand it, so if I saw it happen once, then ...' (interviewer): 'Yes, then it makes sense, or ... Yes, so I signed to everything they said, you could say'.
>
> *(Christensen & Mørck 2017, p. 94)*

The description illustrates how shocked he was by the event. Yet, his interpretation of the experience is also informed by the general narrative established inside the left-wing environment of which he was part at the time. What the person sees in the demonstration is informed by descriptions of the police and 'the system' as such shared by radical individuals in the environment and the episode comes to constitute his overall framework of interpretation and understanding.

Violence-ridden situations have the potential to alter individuals' ontology and reshape their world-view, thereby allowing an alternative sense of identity to emerge and of the individual's position and perception of the conflict and the actors involved (Christensen 2009, 2009a, Christensen & Mørck 2017).

Interviews with former violent right- and left-wing extremists also include descriptions of how, when arrested by the police, the individuals were very conscious of what to say and what not to say in order to avoid being charged. And if they were charged, they knew how to handle the situation to minimise the sentence when going to court.[9] Such knowledge and perceptions of institutions might prove impossible or difficult to override if the same actors were suddenly to cooperate and trust one another in a disengagement and deradicalisation process.

The above gives an insight into individuals' experiences and framework of understanding and interpretation of themselves and other actors in society when they leave extremist groups, illustrating why building a trusting relationship seems challenging and why civil actors *per se* seem better positioned to gain legitimacy among individuals in the target group – at least initially.

When everything builds on a trustful relationship

Extreme groups have in general a high turnover. Soon after joining, many people realise that it is not what they expected, while only a few stay for years (Bjørgo 2009). The longer an individual stays the more difficult it becomes for the person to reintegrate into mainstream society. As illustrated above, participation in extreme groups can have a major impact on a person's cogitation, embodied knowledge and communal life (Christensen 2015). This quotation from a former participant in an extreme right-wing group illustrates how the feelings of confusion, loss and meaninglessness when leaving an extreme group are far-reaching:

> I think it's very important to understand how much the one leaving the group has invested in it. For that's what people do not seem to understand. I did not just leave a group; I left an entire life, I left my views, I left my friends, or what I, moreover, had come to see as my family. They were the ones I could do anything with; at least, I thought so. I left a whole lifestyle! I may have developed a lifestyle that did not work in any other context than in the group, really, a way of being, a behavior, a way of supporting myself which could not work afterwards. And you have invested a number of years in it, be it two years or ten, you have still invested quite a large part of your life in it, and it remains important to understand that: it's a bit like leaving oneself. So, for someone to leave such a group is as if Svensson[10] would have to pack his bags and leave his wife, children and house to go to Tunisia to live in a tent. That's almost as likely! It's not something you just do in a jiffy, and it's not easy.
>
> *(Christensen 2015)*

As the quotation illustrates, some people are utterly lost when they leave an extreme environment. They are in a vulnerable situation where everything is at stake. Former participants in violent extreme groups in general need support in handling many different issues such as post-traumatic stress disorder, aggression, violent response patterns, difficulties in handling stress and in resolving conflicts, mistrust of other people combined with feelings of guilt and shame (Bjørgo 2009, Bjørgo & Horgan 2009, Christensen & Bjørgo 2018). They also often struggle with an ideologically coloured black-and-white mind-set, which means some individuals need support to establish a new framework of references, as the quotation indicates (Christensen 2015). Less acute demands might be their lack of employment opportunities and stigma from society at large and their need for support to further develop social skills making reintegration in mainstream society a real option (ibid).

On top of such issues that it is important to be able to act on, the motivation for disengaging and leaving might only be short-lived (Bjørgo 2009). Such issues are crucial to act on for disengagement and deradicalisation initiatives to work. This means that it might be the end of any motivation for an individual if he/she has to contact what potentially is perceived as 'the enemy' if the motivation for an exit occurs. Therefore putting the least offensive providers – from the target group's perspective – at the forefront of the initiatives is crucial. This is not to argue that state actors have no role in the process; it is just to emphasise the importance of having the right actors in the right place at the right time. The lack of trust in state actors is an issue to be taken seriously. Fortunately, this seems only to be the case initially as the individual's trust will increase in general the more he or she establishes an alternative identity and life course.

Trust, recognition of individuals in an exit process and legitimacy of the institutions behind it – in the one disengaging perspective – are only crucial initially. Whenever individuals leaving extremist groups have started the process of (re)gaining a position outside the group, the importance of such issues decreases, and other actors become relevant when the need to build new social networks, to find a job, a stable place to live or start an education becomes a core issue (Christensen 2015, Christensen & Bjørgo 2018).

Similarities and differences between state and civil actors

To identify the role of civil actors in disengagement and deradicalisation processes it is important to compare aspects of civil and state actors to expose differences and similarities between them. Research into state actors and NGOs in regard to supporting people leaving extremist groups shows that they each have a number of possibilities and constraints built into their different positions, organisational structure and economic support (Christensen 2015, Christensen & Bjørgo 2018).

First and foremost, civil actors have, as mentioned, a crucial advantage from their position as they do not carry the burden of responsibility of protecting the public from terror attacks. This means that they can also to a much larger extent avoid becoming entangled in any attempt to predefine 'people at risk of radicalisation' and identify people being 'radicalised' or 'extreme', avoiding categorisation and the potential stigmatisation of categories of people.

People in an exit process are in a vulnerable and difficult situation with potentially many (urgent) needs, and this touches upon a key element in disengagement and deradicalisation efforts, being easy to localise and to get in touch with. NGOs tend to be small in organisational structure compared to a municipality or other public and state actors, making it relatively easy for the target group and their relatives to identify how to get in touch. This might not be the case with a public institution, where it can be difficult for an outsider to identify who to get in touch with and how, running the risk of exacerbating an already urgent situation (Lid et al. 2016). Besides, a municipality and any state actor seldom have the opportunity to act at short notice, which leads to the next point – timing.

Timing is crucial, as motivation for an exit can occur once and be short-lived. Ideally there should be the opportunity to initiate action at very short notice – often within 24 hours (Christensen & Bjørgo 2018). Some NGOs are open for personal contact 24/7, which can be crucial as the problems occurring in the target group are often unexpected and severe. As a young woman who was dragged to EXIT Sweden by her father explained in an interview that:

> she had no intent of disengaging from the extreme right at the time of the meeting, but she none the less kept the number to one of the employees. One evening she was raped by a man from the groups she was part of and called the employee during the night, which initiated her disengagement.
>
> *(Christensen 2015)*

The example also goes to show that, even though the woman could have called the police, she did not. Instead she called an employee from EXIT Sweden, whom she had already met and who she knew would know the environment and whom she apparently trusted more than anybody else (ibid).

NGOs in general are flexible and can coordinate an initiative across few people, which makes responding easier (Christensen 2015, Lid et al. 2016). In contrast, state actors and municipalities often need to categorise the person first according to a much more complex system. Their action often involves an estimation of the individual's situation in relation to age, economics, job, housing and personal life situation, which can require personal issues to be sorted out before help can be provided. This can be risky as the individual's motivation for an exit might be lost in the process, and even worse if it turns out that the individual is in urgent need of protection. Some police units in Scandinavia have specific units to handle gang members who are defecting. But can they also handle people leaving extremist groups?

The police and the secret services may have much better opportunities in supporting an individual who is in need of protection over time, as in general they have more resources and can provide a cover apartment and address and, in very rare cases, even an identity. Yet, it often seems to be a prerequisite that they acknowledge the personal needs and that the individual is already somehow known within the system.

It can be beneficial for initiatives aimed at (former) violent extremists to have formers among their employees – even though it can be difficult to attract the right ones. Provided they develop the right qualifications they can be of great value for a programme because of their personal insight into issues at stake and at the same time their position as an employee also means they gain the possibility of reintegration into mainstream society (Christensen 2015). When organisations succeed in doing so, it gives credibility to the overall programme and makes it easier to support individuals in an exit process. People leaving extreme groups are often ashamed and full of regret, which can make it difficult or impossible for them to communicate with somebody who they perceive to be a complete outsider or even part of 'the enemy' (ibid). To have formers as employees counters people's fear of denunciation and their belief that, in order to understand you must have had the experience yourself, and provides role models to people in the process, as a former is a living proof that leaving is possible (ibid).

By using formers or working very closely with their cases, EXIT Sweden, EXIT Germany and others have gained a thorough knowledge of ways in and out of violent extreme groups and of what it requires of the individual to reintegrate after extremism, imprisonment or other sorts of detention (ibid). It can be hard to reach an employee with the kind of insight formers have for more established initiatives, as these individuals often get involved because they started out by receiving support themselves (ibid). Nonetheless, state and public actors do also possess a thorough knowledge of the target group, but, as argued above, they have initial difficulty in approaching or attracting them. As some positions in municipalities or the probation service, for example, require that employees have no criminal record, which can – at least for a number of years – make it impossible to be employed as a former, it might also prove difficult to attract them to such institutions.

Extremists seeking to disengage are often a small target group, which can make it easier for a small unit such as an NGO to build up and keep the specialised knowledge required over time than a bigger and more complex public system. In an economical calculation it might also be much cheaper for a state system to cooperate with an NGO with the knowledge and capacity than to develop a system of their own, which runs the risk of being unable to justify keeping employees with such qualifications if they are not in reasonable demand. Besides, it can be hard for a public system to build up the required expertise based on a target group that potentially consists of a few hundred individuals spread across a country (Christensen & Bjørgo 2018).

NGOs on the other hand can struggle to maintain the knowledge due to instability in funding, which can result in the loss of experienced staff. To lose core employees can be fatal for NGOs on different levels as it might also imply losing some legitimacy among individuals in extreme environments, because of their profound understanding of the culture and social mechanisms at work within such groups. If rumours start spreading that NGOs working in this field make mistakes leading to people being put at risk because they lack understanding of the potential threats involved, it will soon reach individuals in the target group who often monitor such organisations closely – despite their open disdain for them (Christensen 2015).

The role of other (civil) society actors and concluding remarks

Social relationships play an equally important role in an individual's reintegration as they do in the preceding radicalisation processes (Christensen 2015). Learning new social skills and behavioural norms, developing an alternative identity and a desire for social involvement in society are necessary to prevent the individual from (re)engaging with violent groups. This increases the chances of his/her (re)integration into mainstream society (Barrelle 2014, Christensen 2015). The development of relationships with others outside the group and social support, irrespective of whether this occurs in a formal setting (mentor/employee from the municipality and/or state actors or an NGO) or an informal one (friends/family), is of decisive importance for a person's further chances of regaining a non-criminal lifestyle outside the extreme group (Barrelle 2014, Christensen 2015, Christensen & Mørck 2017, Dalsgaard-Nielsen 2013). While NGOs play a vital role in an exit process, other civil society actors like religious communities and associations of different kinds are equally important from a reintegration perspective, as they offer individuals the potential to develop new interests and social networks and thus expand their social skills.

This chapter has argued that it is a disadvantage for public institutions that they do not have a distance and independence from the state, which reduces the trust necessary for reaching out to the target group. As indicated in the introduction, disengagement and deradicalisation initiatives are not a question of either public initiatives *or* civil actors, but rather a question of which institutions are best positioned to offer which kind of support at what time, in an often prolonged exit process. While NGOs seem well positioned to initially reach out to people who might consider leaving or have just left an extreme environment, other civil actors can offer new social networks and the development of social skills and interests. Public actors can support the individual's further reintegration into the labour market or the educational system and might provide a place to live. A partnership shared between several different civil state and public actors and institutions that are well informed about the importance of credibility and the task at hand seems a most promising cooperation in the practical field of disengagement and deradicalisation work.

Notes

1 The empirical materials behind the chapter are several ethnographic studies: (1) participant observation of 'the youth house movement' – Ungdomshusbevægelsen – a radical left-wing social movement consisting of both radical youths who fought for social change through democratic means and an extreme core that used violence and malicious damage to obtain political goals in Copenhagen in 2007, leading to the largest uprisings since World War II in Denmark. The study also contained 16 qualitative interviews of participants aged between 16 and 44. I participated in demonstrations and analysed much of the written materials, internet pages and films produced by the social movement and other allied political groups (Christensen 2009, 2009a); (2) an ethnographic study of former right-wing extremists leaving the scene with the help of EXIT, Fryshuset – a Swedish non-governmental organisation. The study included two months of participant observation and analysis of autobiographies of former right-wing extremists. I conducted a total of 21 interviews of 15 people, each lasting from one to three hours. The majority were interviewed once, whereas the coaches at EXIT (former right-wing extremists) have been interviewed twice. The study also included 11 interviews of former right-wing extremists who had been clients at EXIT (Christensen 2015); (3) qualitative interview-based research on people moving in and across extremist environments, biker groups and gangs, involving 42 interviews with practitioners and former extremists, of whom 16 people had participated in several extremist and/or criminal groups (Christensen & Mørck 2017).

2 Both terms are in use as extra-parliamentary environments can contain both categories of political agents – radical non-violent and violent (extreme) individuals.
3 www.violence-prevention-network.de/en/projects/deradicalisation-in-prison/59-menue-deutsch/projekte/projekte-nach-titel/projektunterseiten/941-deradicalisation-in-prison-approach-and-methods (31.12.2018).
4 www.exit-deutschland.de/english/ (23.12.2018).
5 https://hayat-deutschland.de/english/.
6 http://breathesmart.dk/ (3.1.2019).
7 Regeringen (2016). *Forbyggelse og bekæmplelse af ekstremisme og radikalisering, National handlingsplan.* www.justitsministeriet.dk/sites/default/files/media/Pressemeddelelser/pdf/2016/National-handlingsplan-Forebyggelse-og-bekaempelse-af-ekstremisme-og-radikalisering.pdf (27.3.2019).
8 Vuderingsværktøj til anvendelse ved bekyrming for radikalisering og ekstremisme, 'Analyse af Risiko & Trussel', Nationalt Center for Forebyggelse af Ekstremisme.
9 The insights come from a research project by the author and Line Lerche Mørck 'Bevægelser i og på tværs af ekstreme grupper og bande- og rockermiljøet. En kritisk undersøgelse og diskussion af "Cross-over" in 2016 ('Movements in and across extreme groups and gangs, a critical discussion of "cross-over"'). As part of the investigation I conducted 16 qualitative interviews of people who had moved across political violent extremist groups and gangs. The example is from an interview with a former right-wing extremist.
10 Svensson is a typical Swedish surname, but in this context it is used as slang to convey an image of a sort of average middle-class Swedish person, working from 9 to 5 with two children, a wife, a villa and a Volvo.

References

Barrelle, K. (2014). *Pro-Integration: Disengagement and Life after Extremism.* PhD Philosophy, Department of Politics, Monash University. http://arrow.monash.edu.au/hdl/1959.1/965357

Berntzen, L. E., & Sandberg, S. (2014). "The Collective Nature of Lone Wolf Terrorism: Anders Behring Breivik and the Anti-Islamic Social Movement." *Terrorism and Political Violence*, 26, pp. 759–779.

Bjørgo, T. (2009). "Processes of Disengagement from Violent Groups of the Extreme Right." In T. Bjørgo & J. Horgan (Eds.). *Leaving Terrorism Behind.* New York: Routledge. pp. 30–49.

Bjørgo, T., & Horgan, J. (2009). "Introduction." In T. Bjørgo & J. Horgan (Eds.). *Leaving Terrorism Behind.* New York/London: Routledge. pp. 1–15.

Christensen, T. W. (2009). "Forrest eller bakerst i demo'en – aktivist i Ungdomshusbevegelsen." *Norsk Antropologisk Tidsskrift*, 20, no. 4, pp. 236–250.

Christensen, T. W. (2009a). "Den ensrettede mangfoldighet." In R. Karpantschof & M. Lindblom (Eds.). *Kampen om Ungdomshuset, studier i et oprør, Karpantschof.* København: Frydenlund & Monsun: København. pp. 229–251.

Christensen, T. W. (2015). *A Question of Participation: Disengagement form the Extremist Right. A Case Study from Sweden.* Roskilde: Roskilde Universitet.

Christensen, T. W., & Bjørgo, T. (2018). *How to Manage Returned Foreign Fighters and Other Syria Travellers? Measures for Safeguarding and Follow-up.* Oslo: Universitet i Oslo, Senter for ekstremismeforskning: Høyreekstremisme, hatkriminalitet og politisk vold (C-REX).

Christensen, T. W., & Mørck, L. L. (2017). *Bevægelser i og på tvers av ekstreme grupper og bande- og rockermiljøet – En kritisk undersøgelse og diskussjon av "Cross-over".* Aarhus: DPU, Aarhus Universitet.

Dalsgaard-Nielsen, A. (2013). "Promoting Exit from Violent Extremism: Themes and Approaches." *Studies in Conflict & Terrorism*, 36, pp. 99–115.

Gjelsvik, I. M., & Bjørgo, T. (2019). "Med flere tanker i hodet samtidig: Politiets forebyggende arbeid mot radikalisering og voldelig ekstremisme." In Stian Lid & Geir Heierstad (Eds.). *Forebygging av radikalisering og voldelig ekstremisme. Norske handlemåter i møtet med terror.* Gyldendal Akademisk. ISBN 9788205518346. Kapittel 6, pp. 133–151.

Hemmingsen, A.-S. (2015). *The Danish Approach to Countering and Preventing Extremism and Radicalisation.* Copenhagen: DIIS Danish Institute for International Studies. http://pure.diis.dk/ws/files/470275/DIIS_Report_2015_15_2_ed.pdf

Holland, D., Price, C., & Westermeyer, W. H. (2018). "Political Becoming in Movements: Lessons from the Environmental, Tea Party, and Rastafari Movements." In C. Strauss & J. R. Friedman

(Eds.). *Political Sentiments and Social Movements: The Person in Politics and Culture*. Cham, Switzerland: Palgrave Macmillan. pp. 265–295.
Hviid, P. (2017). *Traumebehandling og resocialisering, Gennem åndedræt og meditation*. Aarhus: Turbine Akademisk.
Karpantschof, R. (2014). "Violence That Matters! Radicalization and Deradicalisation of Leftist, Urban Movements – Denmark 1981–2011." *Behavioral Sciences of Terrorism and Political Aggression*. Lokaliseret. http://doi.org/10.1080/19434472.2014.977330.
Koehler, D. (2017). *Understanding Deradicalisation. Methods, Tools and Programs for Countering Violent Extremism*. London: Routledge.
Kristiansen, S. H., & Lid, S. (2019). "Minstenkt og dømt for terrortilknytning – hva nå?" In S. Lid & G. Heierstad (Eds.). *Forebygging av radikalisering og voldelig ekstremisme*. Oslo: Gyldendal Akademisk. pp. 223–240.
Lave, J., & Wenger, E. (1990). *Situated Learning: Legitimate Peripheral Participation*. Cambridge, UK: Cambridge University Press.
Lid, S., & Heierstad, G. (2018). *Countering Violent Extremism in a Welfare State – Strengthens and Weakness of the Norwegian Approach*. Unpublished paper from the conference Nordic conference on violent extremism: Theory and Practice, University of Oslo.
Lid, S., Winsvold, M., Søholt, S., Hansen, S.J., Heierstad, G., & Klausen, J. E. (2016). "Forebygging av radikalisering og voldelig ekstemisme: hva er kommunenes rolle?" *NIBR-rapport*, 2016, p. 12.
Marsden, S. (2017). *Reintegrating Extremists: Deradicalisation and Desistance*. London: Palgrave Pivot.
Polleta, F. (2007). "It Was Like a Fever ...." In Jeff Goodwin & James Jasper (Eds.). *Social Movements: Critical Concepts in Sociology, Volume IV, Culture and Emotions*. New York: Routledge. pp. 367–376.
Porta, D. D. (2009). "Leaving Underground Organizations: A Sociological Analysis of the Italian Case." In T. Bjørgo & J. Horgan (Eds.). *Leaving Terrorism Behind*. New York: Routledge. pp. 66–88.
Porta, D. D. (2013). *Clandestine Political Violence*. Cambridge, UK: Cambridge University Press.
Regeringen. (2016). *Forbyggelse og bekæmpelse af ekstremisme og radikalisering, National handlingsplan*. Danmark file: www.justitsministeriet.dk/sites/default/files/media/Pressemeddelelser/pdf/2016/National-handlingsplan-Forebyggelse-og-bekaempelse-af-ekstremisme-og-radikalisering.pdf
Schmid, A. (2013). "Radicalisation, Deradicalisation, Counter-radicalisation: A Conceptual Discussion and Literature Review." *ICCT Research Paper* 97.
Schutz, A. (1967). *The Phenomenology of the Social World*. Evanston, IL: Northwestern University Press.
Snow, D., Burke Rochford Jr, A. E., Worden, S. K., & Benford, R. D. (2007). "Frame Alignment Processes, Micromobilization, and Movement Participation." In Jeff Goodwin & James Jasper (Eds.). *Social Movements: Critical Concepts in Sociology, Volume IV, Culture and Emotions*. New York: Routledge. pp. 193–225.
Udlændinge-, Integrations og Boligministeriet. (2016). Forebyggelse og bekæmpelse af ekstremisme og radikalisering. Rosendahls a/s: København – downloaded 11.10.2019: http://www.justitsministeriet.dk/sites/default/files/media/Pressemeddelelser/pdf/2016/National-handlingsplan-Forebyggelse-og-bekaempelse-af-ekstremisme-og-radikalisering.pdf

12
DERADICALIZATION THROUGH RELIGIOUS EDUCATION

Rached Ghannouchi

Violence is a phenomenon that is present in all societies, whether at the individual or public level, and for a variety of motivations that range from the personal and psychological to the social, political, ideological and economic. The potential for violence exists within every individual, but can either be weakened through educational, social and cultural processes that elevate individuals to higher values and standards for resolving tensions and conflicts, or strengthened by educational, social and cultural processes that further fuel conflict and violence.

While the world's leaders focus on combatting the tide of violent extremism through heightened security and military acts, it can be argued that far less attention has been paid to deradicalization or reintegration of the young people who constitute the largest and most susceptible pool for recruitment.

As illustrated by the introduction to this handbook (see Chapter 1), there are various approaches to deradicalization and disengagement, some focusing on deradicalization as preventing violent actions, some on deradicalization as changing ideas.

Following the latter view, deradicalization requires the confrontation of the misguided ideas of extremist and terrorist groups head on. In the case of violent extremist groups of a religious background, which is the focus of this chapter, these ideas must be challenged on two levels – contesting the textual basis of their interpretations of their religion and challenging their historical basis, to show that these interpretations have little precedent these interpretations are not supported by strong historical and textual evidence. If violent extremists use religion to justify their actions, religious leaders have the capacity to challenge and debunk their arguments, thus weakening their narrative. The vast majority of studies conducted on the educational background of terrorists who use religious arguments show that an extremely small percentage has received any form of formal religious instruction. The vast majority are largely ignorant of religious principles or texts. Among the most noteworthy of these studies are those conducted by Britain's Intelligence Agency MI5 in 2008 (Travis 2008) and Andrew Lebovich in 2016, which conclude that religious literacy is low among the predominantly young Muslim men who have travelled internationally to join violent extremist organizations (VEOs) such as Daesh and others. These two studies undermine the widespread notion that these terrorists are fundamentally driven by a deep-seated understanding and practice of Islam. Rather, we find that these individuals had barely engaged with the Muslim faith prior to their recruitment into VEOs, and that VEOs are able to exploit their ignorance of religious precepts to persuade them that violent acts are a religious duty. This leads us to the conclusion that a concerted effort to fill the void in religious literacy and counter extremist religious interpretations and misrepresentations of religious precepts might go a long way towards strengthening counterterrorism and deradicalization efforts. As expressed by Oliver Roy (2006), it is also "new intellectuals" – individuals with little formal education – who spearheaded the development of, for example, Al Qaeda and later the Islamic State; these ideologies are "invention" rather than tradition. Religious foundations have been stated to be important for deradicalization and disengagement work. Indeed, the relatively young term "deradicalization" began to emerge through Middle Eastern countries' attempts to use theological debates in order to convince prisoners to abandon militant extremist ideology. In one sense, moderate theologians can develop alternative narratives to those of the violent extremists.

One of the reasons behind the appeal of extremist narratives – whether xenophobic, nationalistic or religious – is how they simplify the complex. Reality is complex, as are religious texts and how people view, interpret and live by them. Extremism presents a seductively simplified version of reality and of religion that strips out all the complexity and relativity of lived experience. It is no coincidence that this narrative tends not to appeal to many social science graduates, for instance, whose education focuses on the complexity and relativity of the human experience. These simplistic narratives are thriving today, driven by the spread of social media, which itself simplifies reality by reducing it to a Facebook status or a 140-character tweet.

Counter-narrative work is growing in importance with regard to deradicalization; introducing religious and ideological narratives that counter the narratives of the violent extremism might be a tool to produce such counter-narratives. Braddock and Horgan (2016) and Kahn (2017) show that psychological research has argued that psychological transportation – "a process whereby all mental systems and capacities are focused on events in a narrative" increases the reception likelihood of a narrative, and that perceived relationships between consumers of narratives and the characters contained in the narrative encourage trust, and such characters might indeed be religious. The source of the narrative has to be trusted, and religious institutions, such as Al-Zaytouna, might contribute to trust, as it has a more than millennium-long tradition in interpreting Islam. Braddock and Morrison (2018) highlight the importance of who is seen as being behind the counter-narrative, as crucial for the acceptance of the narrative. The counter-narrative has to come from a source that has some form of credibility in the eyes of the violent extremist, in order to be more efficient. If the radical narrative is claiming to be religious, religious leaders, in some form, or denomination can have access to forms of such trust.

The irony is perhaps that scholars such as Braddock and Morrison (2018) highlight the importance of the Internet in such quests, a medium many religious leaders still have to develop skills in using.

Religious counter-narratives also must be simplified if they are to reach the target audience. This means efforts must be made to simplify complex concepts and convey them in accessible ways through popular channels. This is a task that requires multiple actors – religious institutions and scholars, intellectuals, social scientists and psychologists, educators as well as community leaders. There is no shortage of research or scholarly writings relating to questions of religion, but these must be actively and effectively disseminated through a concerted and comprehensive campaign that uses multiple channels of communication and education to engage young people. We must reform our public education systems in a manner that reflects a diversity of opinions and approaches, and our curricula must integrate both a greater and more profound appreciation of history and civilization with an openness to all the best the world has to offer. We must equip our religious leaders and psychological experts to meet the changing demands of our youth who feel alienated and excluded in many ways, by organizing lectures and teach-ins where they can make direct contact with young people and speak to their concerns and anxieties. We must also develop multi-media productions, through television, radio and print, that synthesize and incorporate the values of citizenship and democratic practice without seeming condescending or presumptuous.

This chapter will present my own thoughts on these issues, the thoughts of as a practitioner and Islamic thinker rather than an outright academic expert on deradicalization and disengagement.

A religious approach to deradicalization and disengagement

A religious approach does have some advantages, including speaking to violent extremist individuals from a platform that some of them might see creating common ground, and addressing extremist brainwashing that might have taken place inside a radical organization.

In that vein, it is important to keep in mind that the religious sphere of interpretation is a broad space comprising widely varying views, interpretations, schools and sects. In fact, the deeper and more detailed an individual's religious education, the more developed is that person's understanding that very few matters in religion – or life – are black and white. There are widely varying views and shades of grey in interpreting any issue, a matter that has been respected by religious scholars throughout Islamic history.

The first element of such a deradicalization approach must be to work with religious leaders and educators who enjoy widespread recognition, credibility and respect among young people. A key element of this process is to build trust, which requires credibility. Just as there are charismatic preachers responsible for terrorist recruitment, we must work with the many more inspiring and compelling religious figures around the world who are trusted by their local communities, who understand the concerns and anxieties of young people and who can speak in their language. This is a long-term, grassroots effort that requires time and patience, neither of which is in large supply in the fast-moving world of politics, but which are nevertheless vital in effectively addressing this phenomenon. Such trust will allow interventions amongst radicalized individuals as well; the radicalized will share a foundation that can be an opening for deradicalization work.

A second part of the solution is to integrate respected historic religious institutions. Mainstream institutions such as Al-Zaytouna in Tunis and Al-Azhar in Egypt and imam training institutes throughout the world need to be strengthened in order to play an effective role in producing mainstream religious leaders who have a deep knowledge of religious texts and thought, and an appreciation of how the concepts of freedom, individual rights and pluralism have been developed through centuries of Islamic reformist thought. Again, the solution would continue to create trust; institutions with experience and credibility might use this to create openings in the radicalized; challenge extremist narratives and engage with those who have been exposed to them.

Key concepts from the Qur'an: breaking the radical narrative

In this section, I will put forward the basis for a religious counter-discourse to the arguments used by violent extremism groups that claim to base their actions on Islam. Such groups adopt a very selective interpretation of *jihad* to justify the use of violence, whereas the term in Arabic and in Islamic jurisprudence denotes "struggle" or exertion, and ranges from personal spiritual self-purification through to the use of force in very specific circumstances subject to clear conditions. These groups justify their use of *jihad* on one of two broad grounds – either as a means of forcing non-Muslims to become Muslims (i.e. through individual conversion) or as a means of destroying all so-called non-Islamic structures and systems so that Islamic law becomes universal and societies are placed under their version of Islamic governance. They interpret some verses of the Qur'an so as to justify this position, arguing that *jihad* is an offensive weapon inherently designed to confront disbelief, or *kufr*.[1]

By doing so, these groups violate nearly every single accepted norm of textual and historical interpretation and venture far beyond anything that resembles classical, traditional or mainstream Islam.

There is a clear, compelling and textually sound response to this argument that has long constituted the mainstream opinion in Islam held by the majority of scholars. If we look at all the verses of the Qur'an holistically, it becomes clear that the holy text emphasizes the idea that God created mankind with a distinguishing feature from other forms of creation – freedom of choice. The Qur'an makes clear that, had God so wished, He could have created all of mankind in the same mould, with the same beliefs, culture, language and so on. God says in the Qur'an, "Had God willed, He would have made you one nation [united in religion], but [He intended] to test you in what He has given you; so race to [all that is] good" (Verse 5:48), and in another verse:

> Had your Lord so willed, He would surely have made mankind one community. But they will not cease to differ among themselves except for those on whom your Lord has mercy. And it is for this [exercise of freedom of choice] that He has created them.
>
> *(Verses 11:118–119)*

The Qur'an stresses that God chose diversity to be a fundamental characteristic of the human race, manifested in multiple racial, ethnic and religious groups, and endowed humans with the freedom to choose their values and belief systems. Thus, Islam recognizes and affirms that pluralism and diversity were intended to be universal and natural laws of the human species that cannot be subverted or obliterated by any individual or group. Any attempt to do so would, from the Qur'anic perspective, go against the very nature of creation. Hence, God says in the Qur'an, "There shall be no compulsion in religion" (Verse 2:256). To seek to dominate people's hearts and dictate their beliefs directly and categorically violates this basic commandment of all Muslims. Indeed, this is the case of most world religions. We can give some examples from Islam.

Readings of Islamic history

These interpretations must also be confronted using Islamic history. As a matter of historical fact, the *Khilafah*, Caliphate or Islamic state recognized diversity, both externally and internally. Externally, it recognized non-Muslim states and carried out regular diplomatic and trade relations with them. Successive caliphates sent ambassadors to non-Muslim lands and in turn received ambassadors from them. If Islam had required that Muslims impose Islamic governance everywhere and viewed all forms of non-Muslim governance as illegitimate, such relations certainly could not have existed.

Internally, another constant feature of Islamic history that belies the extremist narrative is the fact of pluralism. Muslim-majority societies across the world have for centuries contained non-Muslim minorities. Indeed, Islamic rule has recognized religious, intellectual and even legal pluralism throughout its history. Religious minorities could conduct their personal affairs according to their own religious law and had their own religious institutions and courts. Within Sunni Islam, each of the main four schools of thought had its own religious scholars, muftis and courts. In fact, the history of Islamic governance is full of examples of the coexistence of diverse religious communities and their laws and practices being respected and protected by the main political authorities. This model of multiple legal structures and codes coexisting in the same state may seem unfathomable today in light of the modern nation-state with its centralized legal system, but it went a long way to protecting religious pluralism for centuries. In Tunisia, for example, while the Ottoman-era ruling dynasty largely adhered to the Hanafi school of jurisprudence, there were Hanafi and Maliki courts as well as Jewish courts for the sizeable Jewish community in the country.

This practice goes back to the first Muslim society established by the Prophet Muhammad, which was in its essence a pluralistic society. The society of Medina was composed of Muslims of different ethnic and tribal origins as well as non-Muslims. In the founding document of the Medinan system, the *Sahifa* – its constitution – we find that the first Muslim society ever established recognized non-Muslims as equal and integral parts of the *ummah*, or community. The *Sahifa* stated, "Jews are one community (*ummah*) with the believers". While Jews in Medina were part of this community, Muslims from outside Medina were not. Thus, if a Jewish member of Medinan society was attacked by an outsider from another state, the *Sahifa* obliged members of the community to protect him or her, while the same rights and obligations did not extend to Muslims outside Medina. This shows that, from the Islamic perspective, the political community is based on territory and not religious belonging. This is the basis for what we today call "citizenship", and what I believe ought to be developed as the basis for equal rights and democracy in the Arab and Muslim worlds.

Many elements of Islamic history – in particular, the diversity of Muslim societies throughout history – are erased by the extremist narrative. Thus, an important strategy within deradicalization efforts is to challenge the religious arguments deployed within extremist narratives by showing that they have little basis in Islamic texts or in Islamic history. A methodological dismantling of these arguments is essential in order to persuade those attracted to it that they have, in fact, been led astray by charlatans posing as religious authorities who are presenting a misleading religious narrative.

It is essential to put these facts before individuals who hold extremist views and to push them to question the narrative they have embraced by asking critical questions – Why is it that Muslim societies have always been plural? Why did the Prophet Muhammad include Jews and other non-Muslims as members of the first Muslim society and guarantee their protection if pluralism is not accepted in Islam? Why is it that the oldest churches and synagogues in the world are, to this day, in Muslim countries? If Islam did not respect and protect pluralism and ensure the continued survival of these minorities and their places of worship, groups such as ISIS would not have found minorities to persecute nor churches and temples to destroy in the first place.

The central role of religious institutions

Religious institutions doubtless have an important role to play in challenging extremist religious discourse. In fact, throughout Islamic history, when social or political conditions gave rise to the emergence of extremist interpretation, groups, religious institutions and scholars played a key role in rebutting the arguments of these groups and protecting mainstream religious thought against the attacks of extremist factions.

However, religious institutions in the Arab world today are no longer able to fulfil that function as effectively as they once did, due to many factors. In many Arab countries, religious institutions have seen their independence constrained by authoritarian regimes, which have sought to either marginalize these institutions or exploit them for their own interests. In Tunisia, for example, decades of authoritarian policies aimed at weakening and controlling religious institutions mean that they have lost their capacity to produce credible religious leaders and a religious discourse that is able to relate to the developments and needs of modern life. The resultant religious vacuum that has been created has been filled, frequently, by self-appointed religious figures with little religious training or by religious discourse on satellite television channels based overseas and social media promoting extreme interpretations of Islam.

Challenging and undermining extremist narratives requires filling the religious vacuum that is being exploited by extremist voices to promote their interpretations. This calls for strengthening mainstream religious institutions and improving training and support to religious leaders.

Imams, through their weekly sermons at Friday prayer services and other religious services throughout the week, are the most prominent conduit of religious thought and understanding in local communities throughout the Arab and Muslim worlds. Indeed, it is to their local imams that many observant Muslims primarily look for guidance and direction in religious matters. In Tunisia, for example, each of the 5,300 mosques in the country receives on average 1,500 persons in Friday prayer services, the largest weekly congregation, making it an optimal platform for promoting a compelling and tolerant religious vision and combatting extremist ideologies among a broad and religiously observant audience. In such a context, in a population of roughly 11 million people, the impact of imam training would be far reaching.

It is therefore imperative that comprehensive training initiatives for imams constitute a pillar of any deradicalization effort. At present, this critical group are largely undertrained, underpaid and overlooked as critical vectors for delivering counter-narratives. Imams in Tunisia, for example, are paid the equivalent of roughly $100 per month and receive little training. The vast majority do not have any higher education. Many young people complain that their sermons are repetitive and uninspiring, which is not surprising since they tend to avoid touching on important social topics that concern young people. Without adequately trained imams, and when young people find nowhere to turn to for compelling and inspiring religious teaching within formal state institutions, they become susceptible to fringe voices that speak directly to their concerns and fears. Equipping imams and religious scholars with a simple yet compelling religious discourse based on the concept of citizenship and training that promote the values of freedom and pluralism by drawing on Islamic history and texts would directly challenge extremist narratives.

Conclusion

Some may question the role of religion in countering violent extremism, preferring models of hard-line secularism that believe the key to peace and social harmony is to erase religion from the public sphere. However, this approach has been shown to yield further extremism and fuel conflict and polarization. The answer to deradicalization is therefore not less religion, but to collectively rethink and reform our understanding of religion and strengthen the efforts and voices of religious scholars and leaders who are best able to counter violent extremist discourse that misuses religious terms in order to promote the narrow interests and thirst for power of a tiny minority at the expense of the vast majority of peaceful Muslims.

What I have outlined above is in no way a small endeavour, and is only one part of an overarching set of measures and reforms needed to address the rise of violent extremism. The phenomenon of violent extremism in any society indicates the presence of a deep crisis on some level – whether economic, social, political, intellectual or moral. The crises facing the world, and in particular the Arab world, as evidenced by the explosion of social unrest in 2011, require immediate, medium-term and long-term considered solutions that seek to address the roots of these crises, rather than attacking only the symptoms. This chapter is an attempt to elaborate one solution, among many, to address this crisis on a religious and intellectual level.

Note

1 According to the consensus (*ijma'*) of Islamic scholars throughout history, armed *jihad* is permitted only in defence against direct attack, and is considered the weakest form of *jihad* from an Islamic perspective. In its broadest and most widely used sense, *jihad* is a deeply spiritual, often internal struggle to improve oneself and thereby reaffirm one's commitment to goodness and God consciousness.

References

Braddock, Kurt & John Horgan (2016) "Towards a Guide for Constructing and Disseminating Counter-narratives to Reduce Support for Terrorism", *Studies in Conflict & Terrorism* 39(5), 381–404

Braddock, Kurt & John F. Morrison (2018) "Cultivating Trust and Perceptions of Source Credibility in Online Counternarratives Intended to Reduce Support for Terrorism", *Studies in Conflict & Terrorism*, online. doi: 10.1080/1057610X.2018.1452728

Kahn, Humera (2017) "Countering Violent Extremism and the Role of Meta Narratives", *Sicureza e Science Sociali* 5(2), 159–178

Lebovich, Andrew (2016) "How 'Religious' Are ISIS Fighters? The Relationship between Religious Literacy and Religious Motivation", *Brookings Rethinking Politicall Islam Series*, April 2016.

Roy, Oliver (2006) *Globalized Islam: The Search for a New Ummah*, New York: Columbia University Press.

Travis, Allan (2008) "MI5 Report Challenges Views on Terrorism in Britain", *Guardian*, August 20, www.theguardian.com/uk/2008/aug/20/uksecurity.terrorism

13

UNITED NATIONS AND COUNTER-TERRORISM

Strategy, structure and prevention of violent extremism conducive to terrorism: a practitioner's view

Hans-Jakob Schindler

Over the last nearly two decades, Member States mandated the United Nations system to respond to the threat posed by global terrorism. This sparked a wide range of structural and conceptional developments, driven both by the United Nations General Assembly and the Security Council. The global threat posed by al-Qaida and more recently by the Islamic State in Iraq and the Levant (ISIL) enabled a global coalition of Member States to be built, which on other issues hold diverging, in some cases opposing, positions. By focusing mainly on this specific terror threat the new structure could avoid the political difficulties of the negotiations concerning a general definition of the term terrorism, which have been deadlocked for several decades, with little hope of progress.

While significant parts of the response from this structure of the United Nations focus on security and preventative measures, a fairly recent addition to the work of the United Nations system focuses on the issue of deradicalization, in particular with a focus on returning or relocating foreign terrorist fighters. In this context, the United Nations uses the terminology "rehabilitation" and "reintegration", rather than "deradicalization". The United Nations does not set global standards for what rehabilitation, reintegration or deradicalization entails and consequently also does not offer definitions for these terms. This is a recognition that these processes are culturally specific and can only be defined within a specific social context. Therefore, it is the responsibility of Member States to define the specifics of these processes. However, the United Nations does deliver capacity support for deradicalization efforts of Member States, such as for example the sharing of best practices and experiences across regions, and advises Member States on the compatibility of respective measures with human rights and international law. This support is part of a broader structure of various counter-terrorism and prevention of extremism strategies and mandates of the United Nations and cannot be fully understood in isolation. Therefore, it is important to address both the conceptual as well as the institutional structures currently in place.

After a short summary of the historical development of the United Nations counter-terrorism and preventative structures, this chapter will first focus on the two basic normative documents guiding the counter-terrorism work of the United Nations system, the United Nations Global Counter-Terrorism Strategy (GCTS) and the Plan of Action to Prevent Violent Extremism (PVE Plan), outlining their major provisions and the effect these documents have on the operational work of the United Nations.

These documents have two central functions. They present a normative framework in which Member States should develop their counter-terrorism and prevention of violent extremism strategies and they guide the United Nations system by outlining priority areas for its work. These documents primarily address Member States as the principal actors. The United Nations system is only mandated to support Member States in their operational efforts but is not assigned a role as an independent actor or standard setter. This also relates to efforts to deradicalize, rehabilitate and reintegrate foreign terrorist fighters. One important role of the United Nations system in this regard is to ensure that the conceptual and normative frameworks outlined in the GCTS as well as the PVE Plan are an integral part of the efforts of Member States.

The third part of this chapter will outline the various institutional counter-terrorism structures of the United Nations, aimed at providing analysis and needs assessment, capacity building as well as coordination and coherence. These various actors within the United Nations system have the responsibility to assist the General Assembly and the Security Council in the continuing development of the conceptual and normative framework, including the framework for rehabilitation and reintegration measures. In addition, they support Member States in the implementation of the various measures outlined in the GCTS, the PVE Plan and the various Security Council resolutions.

Finally, the chapter will conclude with a discussion on potential ways the United Nations counter-terrorism structure could further evolve to more effectively and efficiently support the international community. This includes a more systematic engagement with regional and sub-regional organizations to ensure that all politically significant decision-making levels are addressed, a more systematic and structured engagement with civil society in order to ensure that the substate level is adequately included in counter-terrorism and prevention of radicalization efforts and finally a structured engagement with private sector stakeholders to ensure that relevant expertise and knowledge developed in this sector feed into the work of the United Nations system.

Historical development of the United Nations counter-terrorism structure

Since 1999 the counter-terrorism efforts of the United Nations in significant aspects have developed in response to the rise of al-Qaida and since 2014 have been modified in response to the emergence of the ISIL. Following the bombings of the embassies of the United States of America in Nairobi, Kenya and Dar es Salaam, Tanzania on 7 August 1998 the United Nations Security Council passed resolution 1267 (1999), establishing a global sanctions regime, focusing on the leaders of al-Qaida as well as the Taliban, and the 1267 Sanctions Committee of the Security Council entrusted with the management of the regime. This entails decisions concerning the sanctioning of individuals and entities, the delisting of individuals and entities that are no longer relevant as well as the management of all information that is included in the sanctions list. In 2011, the Security Council decided to remove the Taliban from the counter-terrorism sanctions list (resolution 1989 (2011)) and to create a new Taliban-centred sanctions regime (resolution 1988 (2011)). In 2015 the Security Council, with resolution 2253 (2015), expanded the listing criteria of the Al-Qaida sanctions regime to also include individuals and entities supporting ISIL.

In addition to the global sanctions' architecture, the Security Council developed a general global counter-terrorism structure. Following the terror attacks of 11 September 2001, the Council passed resolution 1373 (2001). The resolution, passed under Chapter 7 of the United Nations Charter, is legally binding for Member States, and asked Member States to adapt their national legal systems to counter the threat of global terrorism, including to counter-terrorism financing. The resolution also mandated the newly formed Counter Terrorism Committee of the Security Council to oversee the implementation of its provisions.

In the same year, the Security Council also passed resolution 1540 (2004). The resolution affirms that the proliferation of nuclear, chemical and biological weapons and their means of delivery constitutes a threat to international peace and security. It decides that Member States must refrain from providing support to non-State actors that attempt to develop, acquire, manufacture, possess, transport, transfer or use nuclear, chemical or biological weapons and their means of delivery (resolution 1540 (2004), para. 1). The Security Council also established the 1540 Committee mandated to oversee the implementation of the provisions of the resolution. To augment these Security Council structures, the Secretary General established the Counter Terrorism Implementation Task Force (CTITF) in 2005 (A/60/825, para. 3) after wide-ranging consultations with Member States. This demonstrated that, while the Secretary General does not have an independent decision-making role, his office can act as an important driver of innovation if it is possible to build sufficient political will among Member States. CTITF was endorsed by the General Assembly in 2006 when the Assembly adopted the United Nations Global Counter-Terrorism Strategy (60/288, para. 5). CTITF is tasked to ensure overall coordination and coherence in the counter-terrorism efforts of the United Nations system. Within this framework the United Nations Counter-Terrorism Centre (UNCCT) was established in 2011 and endorsed by the General Assembly in resolution 66/10.

In order to address the continuing spread of violent extremism and recognizing that such radical tendencies form the basis for global terrorism, the Secretary General presented the PVE Plan to the General Assembly on 15 January 2015 (A/70/674). This innovation was received with a mixed reaction by Member States, some of which saw this as a potential intrusion into their domestic affairs while others criticized the plan's provisions as too general to be effective. Consequently, it took nearly two years to build political acceptance for the PVE Plan. Finally, in 2017 the General Assembly through resolution 71/291 established the United Nations Office of Counter Terrorism (UNOCT), headed by Under-Secretary General for Counter-Terrorism Vladimir Ivanovich Voronkov. The role of this new office is to strengthen coordination and coherence between the different elements of the United Nations counter-terrorism entities and to provide strategic leadership on the issue for the organization as a whole. To achieve these aims CTITF and UNCCT have been incorporated into UNOCT. The establishment of this office was a reflection that the growth of the mandated counter-terrorism and prevention work for various entities of the United Nations system had led to a loss in efficiency and the risk of duplication. To further enhance coordination between the various CTITF entities, the Secretary General and the heads of the various CTITF entities signed the United Nations Global Counter-Terrorism Coordination Compact in 2018 (Annex III to A/72/840).

Basic normative documents: United Nations Global Counter-Terrorism Strategy and Plan of Action to Prevent Violent Extremism

Since 1999 the United Nations Security Council has passed a significant number of resolutions to adapt its global sanctions regime and the global counter-terrorism structure. A useful compendium of the relevant Security Council resolutions can be found in Annex I of the 2018 report of the Secretary General on the Activities of the United Nations system in implementing the GCTS (A/72/840). As far as the wider United Nations system is concerned, the operational work in this area is guided by the GCTS and the PVE Plan of the Secretary General.

The adoption of the GCTS by the consensus of the General Assembly in 2006 was hailed as a major achievement, since this was the first time the full membership of the United Nations agreed on a common framework to fight terrorism globally since the issue was raised with the League of Nations in 1934 (The Stanley Foundation, 2007 p. 1). As one expert framed it, "the synchronization of international objectives in the global strategy has created an opening for better technical and political multilateral coordination" (Millar, 2010). Despite this positive reception, some Member States and academic specialists immediately pointed to the lack of a commonly agreed definition of terrorism as one of the enduring weaknesses of the strategy (The Stanley Foundation, 2007, p. 22). This debate continues to date. For example, during the meeting in which the General Assembly adopted the resolution containing the sixth biennial review of the GCTS, the representative of Brazil highlighted that the absence of a universally agreed-upon definition of terrorism was detrimental to the shared goal of eliminating it and stressed the need to overcome the stalemate preventing the adoption of the comprehensive convention on international terrorism (United Nations Meeting Coverage GA/12035, 26 June 2018).

The GCTS falls into two major parts. In the short resolution text Member States commit to implement it (60/288, para 3 (d)), to encourage non-governmental organizations and civil society to contribute to its implementation (60/288, para. 3 (e)) and to review the GCTS every two years (60/288, para. 3 (b)).

The Annex of the resolution consists of a Plan of Action in which the details of the GCTS are outlined. Member States commit themselves to becoming party to all legal instruments against terrorism, for example international counter-terrorism conventions, and to implement those as well as all relevant General Assembly and Security Council resolutions. The strategy outlines specific measures grouped into four pillars: measures to address the conditions conducive to terrorism; measures to prevent and combat terrorism; measures to build States' capacity to prevent and combat terrorism and to strengthen the role of the United Nations system; and measures to ensure respect for human rights and the rule of law as the fundamental basis of the global and domestic fight against terrorism.

The responsibility to implement the GCTS rests primarily with the Member States (72/284, para. 5). However, in addition to Member States, the General Assembly calls on the United Nations and other appropriate international, regional and subregional organizations to implement its provisions (72/284, para. 2). While not a legally binding document, the GCTS does carry political weight since it is backed by all Member States of the United Nations. The biennial review of the GCTS by the General Assembly aims to adapt the specific measures to the changing nature of the global threat of terrorism, making it into an evolving document. Currently, the review process involves several steps. In its review resolution, the General Assembly requests the Secretary General to submit two reports, one in the year after the review and one during the year of the next review. In the first report, the

Secretary General submits recommendations on how the implementation of the measures outlined in the GCTS can be assessed and progress can be measured (72/284, para. 83). In the second report, submitted several months prior to the next review, the Secretary General is to report on the progress made in implementing the GCTS and to make suggestions on how the United Nations system can implement it in the future (72/284, para. 84). Therefore, the review process is a continuous discussion between the United Nations system and Member States rather than a singular biennial event. This ensures that the GCTS reflects the consensual political will of all Member States and that this consensus is able to evolve organically as the threat emanating from global terrorism changes. The review process also regularly triggers close engagements by academic and political experts with Member States and the United Nations system, influencing the ongoing debate. For example, the Global Center on Cooperative Security regularly publishes a series of reports in advance of the review negotiations (Cockayne, Millar, Cortright, & Romaniuk, 2012; Cockayne, Millar, & Ipe, 2010; Chowdhury Fink, Romaniuk, Millar, & Ipe, 2014; Millar, 2018; Millar & Chowdhury Fink, 2016).

As far as content is concerned, the current version of the GCTS is a wide-ranging document. Rather than explicitly outlining new measures for the individual pillars, the document covers a range of issues related to the four broad topics of the GCTS. In its latest review (72/284) the General Assembly encourages Member States and the United Nations to take a broad approach to counter-terrorism and to involve non-governmental organizations, civil society, women and youth in their efforts. The resolution also addresses a range of security-related issues such as biometric information exchange to counter the threat posed by foreign terrorist fighters or the importance of countering the threat of the misuse of the internet and other media by terrorists (72/284, paras. 34–35, 41). The issue of deradicalization is addressed only in the context of returning foreign terrorist fighters. Member States are in general terms called upon to enhance efforts to implement respective programmes (72/284, para. 37) and to develop rehabilitation and reintegration strategies (72/284, para. 39). The document does not specify what such programmes should look like and avoids defining this issue further. This limits the role of the United Nations system only to supporting Member States in their efforts rather than giving the various United Nations entities an independent role.

However, in order to counter the risk that counter-terrorism measures are misused to unduly limit fundamental rights, the General Assembly uses the reviews of the GCTS to continue to emphasize the centrality of the protection and respect for the rule of law, international law, the Charter of the United Nations, international humanitarian law and refugee law, human rights and fundamental freedoms (72/284, para. 10) while countering terrorism. This provides a general framework for the activities of Member States and allows the United Nations system to advise Member States on which strategies fall within these boundaries.

In addition to the negotiations concerning the GCTS, the issue of deradicalization and reintegration of foreign terrorist fighters has been part of the ongoing discussion between Member States and the United Nations system for a number of years. Already in 2015, the ISIL, Al-Qaida and Taliban Monitoring Team, in its special report on foreign terrorist fighters, highlighted the importance of a deliberate "returnee policy" for Member States, including deradicalization strategies (Monitoring Team, 2015, para. 58). The Security Council addressed the issue of returning foreign terrorist fighters in a separate section of resolution 2396 (2017), in which the Council urges Member States to implement appropriate reintegration and rehabilitation strategies (S/RES/2396 (2017), paras. 29–41). Finally, the recent Trends Report of the Counter-Terrorism Executive Directorate (CTED) emphasized that

Member States "have continued to investigate the appropriateness and effectiveness of rehabilitation and reintegration programmes for incarcerated FTFs [foreign terrorist fighters]" (CTED, 2018b, p. 14).

The GCTS also elaborates on the issue of preventing violent extremism leading to terrorism (72/284, para. 16). The GCTS connects this issue to the PVE Plan of the Secretary General (A/70/674). The current review document recommends Member States to consider the implementation of relevant recommendations of the PVE Plan as applicable to their national contexts (A/72/284, para. 18), leaving political space for Member States to adapt the provisions of the PVE Plan to their specific political, economic and cultural conditions. Recognizing that violent extremism is the underlying social basis for global terrorism, in 2015 the Secretary General presented his comprehensive PVE Plan to the General Assembly (A/70/674). The Secretary General argued for an "interdisciplinary 'All-of-society' and 'All-of-government' approach to address the drivers of violent extremism" (A/70/675).

The PVE Plan envisions itself to be an integral part of the GCTS and argues that addressing violent extremism entails reinvigorating measures covered under the GCTS pillars concerning eliminating conditions conducive to terrorism and the respect for human rights and the rule of law (A/70/674, para. 7). The PVE Plan explains that the term "violent extremism" covers a wider category of manifestations than "terrorism" (A70/674, para. 4). However, the PVE Plan does not offer a more precise description of the term and makes clear that definitions of "terrorism" and "violent extremism" are the prerogative of Member States. However, the PVE Plan emphasizes that such definitions must be consistent with the obligations of Member States under international law, in particular international human rights law (A70/674, para. 5).

The PVE Plan emphasizes that there is no authoritative statistical data on the pathways towards individual radicalization but that research demonstrates that one can distinguish between "push factors", the conditions conducive to violent extremism and "pull factors", individual motivations (A/70/674, para. 23). This conceptualization is similar to the one presented by Koehler in Chapter 2 of this book. Since the PVE Plan aims to provide a general framework, which can be adapted to various regional situations around the globe and adapted to guide political decision making, the analysis of the causes of radicalization remains broad.

As far as "push factors" are concerned, the PVE Plan lists lack of socioeconomic opportunities, marginalization and discrimination, poor governance, violations of human rights and the rule of law, prolonged and unresolved conflicts and radicalization in prisons (A/70/674, paras. 25–31). The "pull factors" include both individual backgrounds and motivations, collective grievances and victimization, the distortion and misuse of beliefs, political ideologies, as well as ethnic and cultural differences and social networks (A/70/674, paras. 33–37).

In order to counter these factors, the PVE Plan recommends that Member States develop their own national action plans to prevent violent extremism (A/70/674, para. 44) and calls for greater regional and subregional cooperation (A/70/674, para. 45). It recommends that these national action plans should be developed in a multidisciplinary manner aiming to both counter and prevent violent extremism. The PVE Plan also connects these national plans to national development policies connected with the Sustainable Development Goals (General Assembly resolution 70/1) agreed to by Member States (A/70/674, para. 44 (e)).

The issues of disengagement and rehabilitation of violent extremists are addressed under the second priority area, strengthening good governance, human rights and the rule of law (Counter Terrorism Implementation Task Force (2018) Summary Plan of Action to Prevent

Violent Extremism, p. 4). As in the GCTS, the PVE Plan does not specify or define how disengagement should be achieved but only calls on Member States to develop respective programmes (A/70/674, para. 50(g)). This leaves the responsibility for such programmes solely with the Member States and mandates the United Nations system only in a supporting role.

The PVE Plan also outlines the support the United Nations will give Member States in countering violent extremism. The PVE Plan explains that the United Nations system is already addressing the underlying drivers and triggers of violent extremism through its work (A/70/674, para. 57). However, the Secretary General pledges that the United Nations entities will redouble their efforts to adapt existing programmes so that they target the drivers of violent extremism more precisely (A/70/674, para. 58). The Plan then outlines 12 practical measures the United Nations system will take (A/70/674, para. 57), including capacity-building support for Member States (A/70/674, para. 57). In essence, the PVE Plan suggests mainstreaming prevention of violent extremism into all areas of work of the United Nations system. As a practical step, the Secretary General regularly convenes a "high-level action group on the prevention of violent extremism, which consists of the heads of 22 United Nations departments, agencies, funds and programmes" (A/72/840, para. 54).

Some Member States and experts highlighted the importance of the PVE Plan's role to focus on preventative approaches and strategies as part of the wider counter-terrorism work of the United Nations (Millar, 2016). Millar and Chowdhury Fink argue that "there will be no way to balance a militarized, law enforcement-centric response to terrorism without institutionalizing a preventative approach" (Millar & Chowdhury Fink, 2016, p. 4). Others highlighted that the PVE Plan presents a "reaffirmation of the centrality of human rights in any policies, strategies or actions by Member States and indeed by the UN itself" (Megally, 2017).

However, the PVE Plan was also met with mixed reactions among Member States. In a resolution, the General Assembly only took note of it (70/254, para. 1) and to consider it further as part of the biennial review of the strategy in 2016 (70/254, para. 2), a rather weak initial endorsement. Recognizing that the concept of "violent extremism" is very broad, the General Assembly has also begun using the more specific terminology "violent extremism as and when conducive to terrorism" (see, for example, 70/291, para. 40). The PVE Plan also elicited criticism from academics and specialists. One common argument among critics of the PVE Plan is that the lack of a clear definition of the term "violent extremism" is a serious gap since the phenomenon is supposed to include wider manifestations than "terrorism". Atwood argues that, consequently, "the term obscures more than it illuminates by potentially lumping tougher diverse forms of protest, insurrection and radicalism" (Atwood, 2016). Modirzadeh (2016) outlines further that the lack of definition, in combination with the very general terms in which the drivers of extremism are analysed, clashes with the fairly prescriptive recommendations contained within the PVE Plan. In her analysis this risks the misuse of the concept by subsuming legitimate interests under the banner of suppressing "violent extremism". Furthermore, Modirzadeh is concerned that the mainstreaming of the concept into humanitarian work would result in the risk of integrating humanitarian efforts in the security field.

However, the prescriptive terms used within the PVE Plan are fairly broad and consequently leave sufficient room to avoid these potential pitfalls while translating the provisions of the PVE Plan into the work of the United Nations system. In addition, while assessing the impact of the PVE Plan, it is useful to consider its

> normative impact rather than its practical effects. The Plan [...] may at least nudge the international community towards a fuller understanding of the threat of terrorism, and perhaps compel a more holistic approach by some of the more receptive member states.
> *(Ucko, 2018, p. 270)*

Rather than giving specific instructions to Member States on how to implement the PVE Plan, the document presents a broad framework that can be tailored to the various specific circumstances and challenges Member States in different regions of the globe face. The United Nations mandate to support Member States in their efforts in turn allows the various United Nations stakeholders to support Member States in their understanding of this framework and to ensure that national counter-terrorism measures are tailored accordingly and are broader than only the development of repressive instruments, including efforts to develop disengagement and rehabilitation programmes for violent extremists.

The operationalization of the GCTS and the PVE Plan within the United Nations system is the task of the various counter-terrorism structures of the organization. Analysing the current status of these structures is crucial in order to assess the capability and capacity of the United Nations system to support the efforts of the international community.

United Nations counter-terrorism structure

As outlined above, the current counter-terrorism structure within the United Nations systems spans both the Security Council as well as the General Assembly. The current structure is broadly oriented on three overarching goals (71/858, para. 10): analysis/needs assessment, capacity building, coordination/maintenance of coherence.

Analysis and needs assessment

The analysis of the threat and the gaps in the capacities of Member States and needs assessment is mainly accomplished by the three bodies under the purview of the Security Council: the ISIL, Al-Qaida and Taliban Monitoring Team, CTED and the 1540 Expert Group.

ISIL, Al-Qaida and Taliban Monitoring Team

A useful summary of the counter-terrorism mandate of the ISIL, Al-Qaida and Taliban Monitoring Team can be found on the website of the ISIL and Al-Qaida Sanctions Committee and in Annex I of Security Council resolution 2368 (2017). The team has three main tasks.

Firstly, it analyses the global threat emanating from ISIL, Al-Qaida and their affiliated individuals and entities. This global threat analysis feeds into the discussions of the ISIL and Al-Qaida Sanctions Committee as well as the regular reports of the Secretary General concerning the threat posed by ISIL and foreign terrorist fighters and the United Nations efforts in support of Member States (Security Council resolution 2368 (2017), para. 101).

Secondly, it supports the Sanctions Committee and the Ombudsperson in listing, delisting and decisions concerning amendments to the sanctions list as well as the various annual and triannual reviews of the sanctions list. Finally, in cooperation with Member States, international organizations and private sector stakeholders, the team develops recommendations to the Sanctions Committee on how the operational implementation of the three sanctions measures (asset freeze, travel ban and arms embargo) can be more effectively implemented by Member States in order to ensure that these measures reflect the evolving nature of the threat emanating from ISIL, Al-Qaida and their affiliated individuals and entities. These recommendations are regularly accepted by the Sanctions Committee and subsequently implemented as legally binding provisions of Security Council resolutions. Therefore, the Team is also involved in creating new capacity needs by Member States.

Counter-Terrorism Executive Directorate

The current mandate of CTED is outlined in Security Council resolution 2395 (2017). CTED's mandate is to assess and analyse capacity and implementation gaps of Member States, in particular with regard to Security Council resolutions 1373 (2001), 1624 (2005) and 2178 (2014) (resolution 2395 (2017), para. 14). Therefore, CTED plays a central role as the "monitor, facilitator and promoter of the implementation by Member States of the relevant Security Council resolutions" (A/71/858, para. 17). It assesses counter-terrorism capacities and identifies gaps, new trends and challenges. In order to compile these assessments, CTED conducts country visits, which regularly include experts from relevant international, regional and subregional organizations (CTED Factsheet, 2018).

CTED reports its findings to the Counter Terrorism Committee and makes recommendations on how gaps and implementation challenges can be mitigated. Through this work, CTED is also involved in the process supporting Member States in the implementation of the various provisions of the GCTS and is mandated to cooperate closely with UNOCT (resolution 2395 (2017), para. 14). Finally, CTED maintains a Global Research Network, which enables it to analyse emerging threats, trends and developments (resolution 2395 (2017), para. 15). The quickly expanding mandate of CTED during the past several years raised concerns with some experts that the mission would slowly be overburdened and that CTED should refocus its efforts on its core business of gap analysis (Millar, 2017). Some even called for a wider reform of the United Nations counter-terrorism structure, which would practically subsume CTED under the newly created UNOCT (Rosand, 2017; Baage & Stoffer, 2017). However, with resolution 2395 (2017), the Security Council opted against such a wide-ranging and fundamental reform but highlighted the importance of close and regular cooperation and coordination between CTED and UNOCT (resolution 2395 (2017), para. 18–20).

1540 Expert Group

The 1540 Expert Group has a mandate focused on supporting Member States in the implementation of Security Council resolution 1540 (2004), which asks Member States to refrain from providing support to non-State actors that attempt to develop, acquire, manufacture, possess, transport, transfer or use nuclear, chemical or biological weapons and their means of delivery (resolution 1540 (2004), para. 1). The 1540 Committee and the 1540 Expert Group also monitor the implementation of the resolution and play a clearinghouse role to facilitate assistance to Member States (A/71/858, para. 18).

Capacity building

The United Nations system is currently undertaking a significant amount of capacity-building projects in the framework of the GCTS (Annex II of A/72/840 offers an overview of these projects). Capacity building is operationalized by the various entities of the CTITF and oriented along the four pillars of the GCTS (A/72/840, para. 42). The UNCCT, the Terrorism Prevention Branch (TPB) of UNODC and the United Nations Interregional Crime and

Justice Research Institute (UNICRI) are considered to be the main United Nations counter-terrorism bodies for capacity-building support (A/71/858, para. 21). The counter-terrorism-related capacity-building efforts of other United Nations entities, such as for example the United Nations Development Programme (UNDP), are also coordinated by CTITF.

The Under-Secretary General for Counter-Terrorism serves as the executive director of UNCCT (A/71/858, para. 62). UNCCT currently follows a five-year programme of work launched in 2016 (The Beam, 2016, p. 13). This programme ensures that the activities do not overlap with the activities of other CTITF entities but leverage experience through joint efforts (A/71/858, para. 23). UNODC-TPB

> promotes the ratification of the international conventions and protocols relating to terrorism and supports Member States in their implementation. It provides legal assistance for the review and drafting of national counter-terrorism legislation and builds the capacity of criminal justice systems to effectively respond to terrorism.
>
> *(A/71/858, para. 25)*

UNICRI assists intergovernmental, governmental and non-governmental organizations in formulating and implementing improved policies of crime prevention and control, including counter-terrorism and preventing violent extremism. This is achieved through research, training, field activities and information collection and dissemination (A/71/858, para. 26). For example, since 2015 UNICRI, in cooperation with the European Union, has been implementing a capacity-building project in the Sahel-Maghreb region which aims to promote deradicalization activities (UNICRI, 2015, p. 1).

The role of the United Nations system in supporting Member States' capacity-building efforts allocates the responsibility of the conceptual definition of what deradicalization, rehabilitation and reintegration entail and when they are achieved, solely to Member States. Consequently, this includes the risk that standards can vary significantly between Member States. Due to its supporting mandate, the United Nations cannot officially develop its own internal definitions or benchmarks for these terms. However, the United Nations system does play a significant role in helping Member States to design respective measures in accordance with human rights and international law and therefore is able to outline principle standards for such measures. For example, UNCCT, in cooperation with the CTITF Working Group on Protecting Human Rights while Countering Terrorism, has developed five Basic Human Rights Reference Guides for Member States that include practical tools outlining how to protect human rights while countering terrorism. In addition to addressing issues such as stopping and searching of persons, security infrastructure, detention and the right to a fair trial and due process, these guides address the issue of the compatibility of counter-terrorism legislation with international human rights law (CTITF, 2014).

Coordination and coherence

Since 2017, the area of coordination and coherence has seen significant reforms. Chiefly among these was the establishment of UNOCT (General Assembly resolution 71/291). UNOCT provides leadership and overall coordination and coherence for all capacity-building support efforts of the United Nations system with regard to counter-terrorism (71/291, para. 1 and A/71/858, para. 64). The establishment of this new office by the General Assembly was aimed at reducing administrative inefficiencies, duplication of work and competition between the various United Nations entities in the area of counter-terrorism capacity building.

The establishment of UNOCT concluded a debate among Member States and experts that took nearly half a decade on how the United Nations counter-terrorism structure could be more efficiently organized. Some experts had consistently argued the case for a high-ranking coordination office since 2012 (Cockayne, Millar, Cortright, & Romaniuk, 2012; Millar & Chowdhury Fink, 2016; Stoffer, 2013). In order to ensure that UNOCT has the institutional means to fulfil its leadership and coordination mandate, CTITF and UNCCT were integrated into the office.

CTITF has the operational responsibility to coordinate the relevant activities of the currently 33 member entities and five entities that are observers of CTITF and to ensure that coherence among the various activities is maintained (A/71/858, para. 12 and Figure II). The Under-Secretary General for Counter-Terrorism is the Chief of CTITF and, therefore, ultimately responsible for system-wide coordination of counter-terrorism activities within the United Nations (A/71/858, para. 62). CTITF is organized into 12 thematic working groups (A/71/858, para. 15), covering a wide range of issues including among others the prevention of violent extremism. Currently, there is no working group solely dedicated to deradicalization issues. In order to further enhance the coordination between capacity-building efforts across the United Nations system, the Secretary General in 2018 signed the United Nations Global Counter-Terrorism Coordination Compact with the heads of the CTITF entities (Annex III to A/72/840). The signatories of the non-binding compact (Annex III, para. 10 (e) of A/72/840) commit themselves to a range of concrete coordination, collaboration and information exchange standards (Annex III para. 11 of A/72/840). Furthermore, in a separate report, requested by paragraph 18 of Security Council resolution 2395 (2017), UNOCT and CTED laid out a number of concrete recommendations on how both institutions can increase their cooperation and coordination (Annex of S/2018/435 and Annex IV of A/72/840). Both documents clearly demonstrate the "efforts made in improving coordination and cooperation between the UNOCT and CTED and with other CTITF entities" (Millar, 2018, p. 15).

The mandate of UNCCT is to promote international counter-terrorism cooperation and support Member States in the implementation of the Global Counter-Terrorism Strategy, in particular through capacity-building support, by providing relevant legal and technical expertise, including for deradicalization efforts for Member States. UNCCT also provides fora in which Member State officials can exchange experiences and best practices and strengthen their bilateral and multilateral cooperation. Furthermore, UNCCT, as part of UNOCT, currently conducts in-depth research to enhance the understanding of the foreign terrorist fighters' phenomenon among Member States and the United Nations system. A first study concerning foreign terrorist fighters in Syria was published in 2017 (UNOCT, 2017).

In addition to these internal reforms and initiatives, the Secretary General, following a suggestion by UNOCT, convened in June 2018 the first ever gathering of the heads of counter-terrorism agencies of Member States in a High-Level Conference on Counter-Terrorism. After discussions with Member States and lobbying efforts (ICAN, 2018), the event also included representatives of civil society organizations and regional organizations. Although the conference did not produce a negotiated outcome document, it led to the establishment of a new unit within UNOCT to ensure that the views of civil society feed into the office's work and the establishment of a Global Network of Counter-Terrorism Coordinators to better share expertise and best practices (Secretary General Closing Remarks, 2018).

Conclusion and outlook

The United Nations system with its international reach and global legitimacy is ideally placed to counter global threats. The threat of terrorism posed by al-Qaida and ISIL to all Member States, helped to build and maintain a broad consensus among all Member States of the United Nations that this system should play a role in counter-terrorism efforts. However, at the same time, Member States have avoided giving the United Nations system an independent role. The various mandates given to the United Nations system on the issue of counter-terrorism and preventative measures as well as rehabilitation and reintegration of foreign terrorist fighters are aimed to support Member States' efforts. In this regard, the various United Nations stakeholders are not mandated to be independent actors, giving prescriptive advice to Member States, but to generate and deliver knowledge and expertise, provide fora for Member States to cooperate multilaterally and to convene Member State officials and experts from specialized agencies and international organizations. Consequently, the priority areas of the work of the various United Nations stakeholders are adjusted according to the evolving global terror threat, the changing challenges that Member States face, their capacity needs as well as donor priorities. This ensures that the actions of the United Nations system are based on the widest possible political consensus among Member States, something that would not be easy to achieve if the United Nations system acted independently.

Building political consensus among Member States concerning key terminology such as "terrorism", "extremism" or "deradicalization" remains a challenge and, therefore, conceptual developments will remain evolutionary and only oriented on the operational needs as well as challenges faced by Member States. Nevertheless, during the past two decades the General Assembly and the Security Council have made major and significant contributions through the development of the various Security Council resolutions as well as the GCTS and the PVE Plan as basic normative documents that provide a flexible and evolving framework for Member States countering the challenge of global terrorism. The complex system of normative documents and institutional structures of the counter-terrorism architecture of the United Nations has evolved organically over nearly two decades, at each point responding to the changing threat of global terrorism, violent extremism and demands by Member States.

The development of the operative mandates of a significant number of stakeholders within the United Nations system risks operative duplication, inefficiency and administrative competition. Consequently, in order to ensure the effective and efficient functioning to implement the aims of the GCTS and the PVE Plan, strong coordination among all the actors of the United Nations system continues to be needed. With the creation of UNOCT in 2017 and its strong coordination mandate this challenge was addressed. However, a new opportunity was also created to continue further internal reforms. These reforms should aim to involve a wider range of stakeholders, above and below the level of Member States, in the implementation of counter-terrorism, preventative and deradicalization efforts of the United Nations. Chief among these are regional and subregional organizations, civil society and non-governmental organizations and private sector stakeholders.

Regional and subregional organizations have built their own counter-terrorism and preventative structures over the last few years and a stronger engagement by the United Nations system with these structures would ensure that capacity-building efforts are addressed also at the level between Member States and the global structure. For example, in Southeast Asia, the Southeast Asia Regional Center for Counter-Terrorism (SEARCCT) has developed into an influential regional platform for research and project work, while in

East Africa, the Intergovernmental Authority on Development's (IGAD's) Security Sector Program (SSP) does important work on counter-terrorism issues and IGAD's Center of Excellence in Preventing and Countering Violent Extremism (ICEPCVE) works on conceptual and operational issues. The United Nations system has already engaged with these and other organizations; for example, there is a long-standing cooperation with the European Union Agency for Law Enforcement Cooperation, EUROPOL. However, these engagements have been driven more by individual project demands rather than conducted in a systematic fashion. Creating such specific mechanisms for these engagements would enable the United Nations system to tap into a wealth of knowledge and capacities, aiding in more effective project design and delivery processes. The Financial Action Task Force (FATF) global structure with its FATF-style regional bodies (FSRBs) could be a potential blueprint for such a network. The announcement of the Secretary General in June 2018 that the United Nations is establishing a network of counter-terrorism coordinators could be an appropriate forum to achieve this.

Secondly, civil society and non-governmental organizations are important stakeholders in counter-terrorism, preventative as well as deradicalization efforts due to their local knowledge and close connection to various communities. Some organizations also have a global reach, such as for example the International Civil Society Action Network (ICAN) or the Counter Extremism Project (CEP), which co-hosted the Global Youth Summit Against Violent Extremism, a side event to the General Assembly Plenary meeting in 2015. It is therefore crucial to involve these actors in a more systematic way. Despite the fact that civil society is named as an important stakeholder in several counter-terrorism-related United Nations documents, institutional engagement with such stakeholders in the field of counter-terrorism remains largely ad hoc and unsystematic. One example of a more structured engagement is the Global Research Network (GRN) of CTED. The establishment of a new unit within UNOCT to engage with civil society and non-governmental organizations is a first important step in this direction.

Finally, private sector stakeholders can bring important information, experience and innovations to the counter-terrorism and preventative work of the United Nations. Often it is the private sector that is the operational implementor of counter-terrorism measures, such as international sanctions, air travel security mechanisms or financial transfer regulations. For several years, some counter-terrorism actors within the United Nations system have engaged the private sector intensively. For example, in 2016, the ISIL, Al-Qaida and Taliban Monitoring Team published a report focusing on the challenges private sector stakeholders face in implementing Security Council sanctions measures (S/216/213). In 2017, CTED and ICT4Peace launched the Global Internet Forum to Counter Terrorism (The Beam, 2017, p. 9). Here too, non-governmental organizations can provide already existing private sector networks and open doors for the United Nations system. For example, CEP has built up a significant private sector network and developed eGLYPH, software capable of detecting and removing extremist images, videos and audio messages that have been pre-determined to violate the terms of service of internet and social media companies (CEP, 2016). Further structured engagement of the United Nations system, under the leadership of UNOCT, with private sector stakeholders in a wide range of industries, such as the travel, financial and logistics sectors, could result in the development of more effective measures as it would connect the operational implementors with the designers of counter-terrorism, preventative and deradicalization measures.

References

General Assembly

A/RES/60/288. *The United Nations Global Counter-Terrorism Strategy*. 20 September 2006. Retrieved from: www.un.org/en/ga/search/view_doc.asp?symbol=A/RES/60/288
A/RES/66/10. *United Nations Counter-Terrorism Centre*. 7 December 2011. Retrieved from: www.un.org/en/ga/search/view_doc.asp?symbol=%20A/RES/66/10
A/RES/70/254. *Secretary-General's Plan of Action to Prevent Violent Extremism*. 10 March 2016. Retrieved from: www.un.org/en/ga/search/view_doc.asp?symbol=A/RES/70/254
A/RES/70/291. *The United Nations Global Counter-Terrorism Strategy Review*. 19 July 2016. Retrieved from: www.un.org/ga/search/view_doc.asp?symbol=A/RES/70/291
A/RES/71/291. *Strengthening the Capability of the United Nations System to Assist Member States in Implementing the United Nations Global Counter-Terrorism Strategy*. 19 June 2017. Retrieved from: www.un.org/en/ga/search/view_doc.asp?symbol=A/RES/71/291
A/RES/72/284. *The United Nations Global Counter-Terrorism Strategy Review*. 2 July 2018. Retrieved from: www.un.org/en/ga/search/view_doc.asp?symbol=A/RES/72/284

Security Council

S/RES/1267. (1999). *Resolution 1267 (1999). Adopted by the Security Council at Its 4051st Meeting on 15 October 1999*. Retrieved from: www.un.org/ga/search/view_doc.asp?symbol=S/RES/1267%281999%29
S/RES/1373. (2001). *Resolution 1373 (2001). Adopted by the Security Council at Its 4385th Meeting, on 28 September 2001*. Retrieved from: www.un.org/en/ga/search/view_doc.asp?symbol=S/RES/1373%20%282001%29
S/RES/1540. (2004). *Resolution 1540 (2004), Adopted by the Security Council at Its 4956th Meeting, on 28 April 2004*. Retrieved from: www.un.org/en/ga/search/view_doc.asp?symbol=S/RES/1540(2004)
S/RES/1624. (2005). *Resolution 1624 (2005). Adopted by the Security Council at Its 5261st Meeting, on 14 September 2005*. Retrieved from: www.un.org/en/ga/search/view_doc.asp?symbol=S/RES/1624%20%282005%29
S/RES/1988. (2011). *Resolution 1988 (2011). Adopted by the Security Council at Its 6557th Meeting, on 17 June 2011*. Retrieved from: www.un.org/ga/search/view_doc.asp?symbol=S/RES/1988%20%282011%29
S/RES/1989. (2011). *Resolution 1989 (2011). Adopted by the Security Council at Its 6557th Meeting, on 17 June 2011*. Retrieved from: www.un.org/ga/search/view_doc.asp?symbol=S/RES/1989%20%282011%29
S/RES/2178. (2014). *Resolution 2178 (2014). Adopted by the Security Council in Its 7272nd Meeting on, 24 September 2014*. Retrieved from: www.un.org/en/ga/search/view_doc.asp?symbol=S/RES/2178%20%282014%29
S/RES/2253. (2015). *Resolution 2253 (2015). Adopted by the Security Council at Its 7587th Meeting, on 17 December 2015*. Retrieved from: www.un.org/en/ga/search/view_doc.asp?symbol=S/RES/2253%282015%29
S/RES/2368. (2017). *Resolution 2368 (2017). Reissued for Technical Reasons on 27 July 2017. Adopted by the Security Council at Its 8007th Meeting, on 20 July 2017*. Retrieved from: www.un.org/en/ga/search/view_doc.asp?symbol=S/RES/2368%282017%29
S/RES/2395. (2017). *Resolution 2395 (2017). Adopted by the Security Council at Its 8146th Meeting, on 21 December 2017*. Retrieved from: www.un.org/en/ga/search/view_doc.asp?symbol=S/RES/2395%20(2017)&referer=www.un.org/en/documents/index.html&Lang=E
S/RES/2396. (2017). *Resolution 2396 (2017). Adopted by the Security Council at Its 8148th Meeting, on 21 December 2017*. Retrieved from: www.un.org/en/ga/search/view_doc.asp?symbol=S/RES/2396%20(2017)&referer=www.un.org/en/documents/index.html&Lang=E
S/2018/435. *Letter Dated 8 May 2018 from the Chair of the Security Council Committee Established Pursuant to Resolution 1373 (2001) Concerning Counter-Terrorism Addressed to the President of the Security Council, 8 May 2018*. Retrieved from: www.un.org/en/ga/search/view_doc.asp?symbol=S/2018/435&referer=/english/&Lang=E

General Secretary

A/60/825. *Uniting against Terrorism: Recommendations for a Global Counter-Terrorism Strategy. Report of the Secretary-General, 27 April 2006.* Retrieved from: www.un.org/ga/search/viewm_doc.asp?symbol=A/60/825

A/70/674. *Plan of Action to Prevent Violent Extremism. Report of the Secretary-General, 24 December 2015.* Retrieved from: www.un.org/ga/search/view_doc.asp?symbol=A/70/674

A/71/858. *Capability of the United Nations System to Assist Member States in Implementing the United Nations Global Counter-Terrorism* Strategy. *Report of the Secretary-General, 3 April 2017.* Retrieved from: www.un.org/ga/search/view_doc.asp?symbol=A/71/858

A/72/840. *Activities of the United Nations System in Implementing the United Nations Global Counter-Terrorism Strategy. Report of the Secretary-General, 20 April 2018.* Retrieved from: www.un.org/en/ga/search/view_doc.asp?symbol=A/72/840

Secretary General. (2018). *UN Secretary-General's Closing Remarks at High-Level Conference on Counter-Terrorism (As Delivered).* Retrieved from: www.un.org/sg/en/content/sg/statement/2018-06-29/secretary-generals-closing-remarks-high-level-conference-counter

Other sources

Atwood, R. (2016). "The great debate. the dangers lurking in the U.N.'s new plan to prevent violent extremism". *Reuters* unknown. Retrieved from: http://blogs.reuters.com/great-debate/2016/02/07/why-is-the-wolf-so-big-and-bad/

Baage, H.O. & Stoffer, H. (2017). *Strengthening the United Nations' Strategic Approach to Countering Terrorism.* The Hague: International Center for Counterterrorism. Retrieved from: https://icct.nl/publication/strengthening-the-united-nations-strategic-approach-to-countering-terrorism/

Chowdhury Fink, N., Romaniuk, P., Millar, A., & Ipe, J. (2014). *Blue Sky II. Progress and Opportunities in Implementing the UN Global Counter-Terrorism Strategy.* New York: Global Center on Cooperative Security. Retrieved from: www.globalcenter.org/wp-content/uploads/2014/04/Blue-Sky-II-Low-Res.pdf

Cockayne, J., Millar, A., Cortright, D., & Romaniuk, P. (2012). *Reshaping United Nations Counterterrorism Efforts. Blue Sky Thinking for Global Counterterrorism Cooperation 10 Years after 9/11.* New York: Center on Global Counterterrorism Cooperation. Retrieved from: http://globalcenter.org/wp-content/uploads/2012/07/Reshaping_UNCTEfforts_Blue-Sky-Thinking.pdf

Cockayne, J., Millar, A., & Ipe, J. (2010). *An Opportunity for Renewal. Revitalizing the United Nations Counterterrorism Program. An Independent Strategic Assessment.* New York: Center on Global Counter-terrorism Cooperation. Retrieved from: http://globalcenter.org/wp-content/uploads/2012/07/Opportunity_for_Renewal_Final.pdf

Counter Extremism Project (CEP). (2016). *"Counter Extremism Project Unveils Technology to Combat Online Extremism. New Algorithm Will Quickly and Accurately Identify Extremist Content on Internet and Social Media Platforms, Including Images, Videos, and Audio Clips" Counter Extremism Project Public Statement.* Retrieved from: www.counterextremism.com/press/counter-extremism-project-unveils-technology-combat-online-extremism

Counter-Terrorism Executive Directorate. (2018a). "United Nations Security Council Executive Directorate (CTED) factsheet". Counter-Terrorism Executive Directorate. Retrieved from: content/uploads/2018/07/ctc_cted_fact_sheet_25_june_2018_designed.pdf

Counter-Terrorism Executive Directorate. (2018b). "The challenge returning and relocating foreign terrorist fighters: research perspectives". *CTED Trends Report March 2018.* Retrieved from: www.un.org/sc/ctc/wp-content/uploads/2018/04/CTED-Trends-Report-March-2018.pdf

Counter-Terrorism Implementation Task Force. (2018). "Plan of action to prevent violent extremism". *Counter-Terrorism Implementation Task Force* homepage. Retrieved from: www.un.org/counterterrorism/ctitf/sites/www.un.org.counterterrorism.ctitf/files/plan_action.pdf

Counter-Terrorism Implementation Task Force. CTITF Working Group on Protecting Human Rights while Countering Terrorism. (2014). *Basic Human Rights Reference Guide: Conformity of National Counter-Terrorism Legislation with International Human Rights Law.* New York: United Nations. Retrieved from: un.iborn.net/counterterrorism/ctitf/sites/www.un.org.counterterrorism.ctitf/files/CounterTerrorismLegislation.pdf

International Civil Society Action Network (ICAN). (2018). *Civil Society Engagement with the UN Office of Counter-Terrorism. Letter to Under-Secretary General for Counter-Terrorism.* Washington: ICAN. Retrieved from: www.icanpeacework.org/wp-content/uploads/2018/01/Civil-Society-Engagement-with-the-UN-Office-of-Counter-Terrorism.pdf

ISIL, Al-Qaida and Taliban Monitoring Team. (2015). "Analysis and recommendations with regard to the global threat from foreign terrorist fighters". *Report S/2015/358.* Retrieved from: www.un.org/en/ga/search/view_doc.asp?symbol=S/2015/358

Megally, H. (2017). *Preventing Violent Extremism by Protecting Rights and Addressing Root Causes.* New York: NYU Center on International Cooperation. Retrieved from: https://cic.nyu.edu/news_commentary/preventing-violent-extremism-protecting-rights-and-addressing-root-causes

Millar, A. (2010). *Multilateral Counterterrorism: Harmonizing Political Direction and Technical Expertise. The Stanley Foundation Policy Analysis Brief December.* Retrieved from: www.stanleyfoundation.org/publications/pab/MillarPAB1210.pdf

Millar, A. (2016). "Is UN equipped to deliver new plan on preventing extremism?". *The Global Observatory Blogg January* 28. Retrieved from: https://theglobalobservatory.org/2016/01/is-un-equipped-to-prevent-extremism/

Millar, A. (2017). *Mission Critical or Mission Creep? Issues to Consider for the Future of the UN Counter-Terrorism Committee and Its Executive Directorate.* Washington: Global Center on Cooperative Security. Retrieved from: www.globalcenter.org/wp-content/uploads/2017/10/CTED-Mandate-Renewal_Policy-Brief-1.pdf

Millar, A. (2018). *Blue Sky IV: Clouds Dispersing? An Independent Analysis of UN Counterterrorism Efforts in Advance of the Sixth Review of the UN Global Counter-Terrorism Strategy in 2018.* Washington: Global Center on Cooperative Security. Retrieved from: www.globalcenter.org/wp-content/uploads/2018/05/GC_2018-May_Blue-Sky.pdf

Millar, A. & Chowdhury Fink, N. (2016). *Blue Sky III. Taking UN Counterterrorism Efforts in the Next Decade from Plans to Action.* Washington: Global Center on Cooperative Security. Retrieved from: www.globalcenter.org/wp-content/uploads/2016/09/Blue-Sky-III_low- res.pdf

Modirzadeh, N. (2016). "If it's broke, don't make it worse: a critique of the U.N. secretary-general's plan of action to prevent violent extremism". *Lawfare blogg.* 23 January Retrieved from: www.lawfareblog.com/if-its-broke-dont-make-it-worse-critique-un-secretary-generals-plan-action-prevent-violent-extremism

Rosand, E. (2017). "UN counterterrorism reform: now it's the security council's turn". *The Global Observatory Blogg.* 15 September. Retrieved from: https://theglobalobservatory.org/2017/09/terrorism-countering-violent-extremism-guterres/

Stoffer, H. (2013). *The Need for a United Nations Global Counter-Terrorism Coordinator.* The Hague: International Center for Counterterrorism. Retrieved from: www.icct.nl/download/file/Stoffer-The-Need-For-A-UN-Global-Counter-Terrorism-Coordinator-August-2013.pdf

The Beam Newsletter of the CTITF and UNCCT. (2016). "The UNCCT 5-year programme kicks-off in 2016". *The Beam Newsletter of the CTITF and UNCCT Vol. 11, June 2016.* Retrieved from: www.un.org/counterterrorism/ctitf/sites/www.un.org.counterterrorism.ctitf/files/beam/BEAM%2011_June_2016.pdf

The Beam Newsletter of the CTITF and UNCCT. (2017). "CTED and ICT4Peace host U.S. launch of global internet forum to counter terrorism in San Francisco". *The Beam Newsletter of the CTITF and UNCCT Vol. 13 January–July 2017.* Retrieved from: www.un.org/counterterrorism/ctitf/sites/www.un.org.counterterrorism.ctitf/files/beam/BEAM%2013_FINAL.pdf

The Stanley Foundation. (2007). "Implementation of the UN global counterterrorism strategy. 42nd conference on the United Nations of the next decade, June 2007". *42nd Conference on the United Nations of the Next Decade.* Retrieved from: www.stanleyfoundation.org/publications/report/UNND807.pdf

Ucko, D.H. (2018). "Preventing violent extremism through the United Nations: the rise and fall of a good idea". *International Affairs,* 94:2, pp. 251–270. Retrieved from: www.chathamhouse.org/sites/default/files/images/ia/INTA94_2_02_Ucko.pdf

United Nations General Assemblage. (2018). "GA/12035 general assembly unanimously adopts resolution calling for strong coordinated action by member states to tackle terrorism, violent extremism worldwide. Speakers welcome new references in annual text to foreign fighters, financing". *UN Meetings Coverage 26 June 2018.* Retrieved from: www.un.org/press/en/2018/ga12035.doc.htm

United Nations Interregional Crime and Justice Research Institute. (2015). "Countering radicalisation and violent extremism in the Sahel-Maghreb region". Project homepage. Retrieved from: www.unicri.it/news/article/2015-09-10_Countering_Radicalisation_and_Violent

United Nations Office of Counter-Terrorism. (2017). "Enhancing the understanding of the foreign terrorist fighters phenomenon in Syria." *Special Report* June. Retrieved from: www.un.org/en/counter terrorism/assets/img/Report_Final_20170727.pdf

14
PREVENTING RADICALISATION AND ENHANCING DISENGAGEMENT IN THE EUROPEAN UNION

Sarah Léonard, Christian Kaunert, and Ikrom Yakubov

Europe has seen significant and varied terrorist activities in the twentieth and twenty-first centuries, ranging from the Provisional Irish Republican Army through the German Red Army Faction to al Qaeda- and Daesh-inspired individuals and groups. These episodes have provided European states with a wealth of experience in combating terrorism (Chalk, 1996). Although there has been continued concern over separatist groups in some states and growing unease about the activities of far-right groups in others, jihadist terrorism has been the primary focus of counter-terrorism efforts in many Western states since the terrorist attacks on 11 September 2001. Moreover, since 2013, against the backdrop of the Syrian civil war, the issues of radicalisation and foreign terrorist fighters (FTFs) have become focal points in counter-terrorism debates in Europe and on the EU's policy agenda.

Actually, the EU had already begun to reflect on how to address radicalisation a few years before. As early as November 2005, following the terrorist attacks in Madrid and London, it had published a 'European Union Strategy for Combating Radicalisation and Recruitment to Terrorism' (Council of the European Union, 2005b). Preventing radicalisation was also an important dimension of the EU Counter-Terrorism Strategy, which was adopted around the same time (Council of the European Union, 2005a). The EU Strategy for Combating Radicalisation and Recruitment to Terrorism was subsequently revised in 2008 and 2014, which demonstrates the continued salience of this issue on the EU's policy agenda.

This chapter examines the EU's efforts to tackle radicalisation. The specific formulation of its title (i.e. 'preventing radicalisation and enhancing disengagement') reflects the EU's emphasis on *preventing* radicalisation. Most of the radicalisation-related measures adopted by the EU belong to the 'Prevent' dimension of its Counter-Terrorism Strategy, whilst 'disengagement' has become more prevalent in recent years, in contrast to 'deradicalisation', which is rarely used in EU official documents. The chapter begins by locating the EU's efforts to address radicalisation in the wider context of its counter-terrorism policy. It briefly presents the evolution of EU counter-terrorism cooperation in both its policy and institutional dimensions for the benefit of readers who may not be familiar with the EU's role in counter-terrorism. The following section reflects on the controversial concept of 'radicalisation' and how it has been used by the EU. The chapter then delves into the EU's activities aiming to prevent or counter radicalisation. In that respect, it begins by examining the EU's strategic thinking towards addressing radicalisation, before examining the main policy measures that it has adopted. The chapter concludes by offering some reflections on assessing the effectiveness of the EU's measures aiming to address radicalisation.

EU counter-terrorism cooperation

It is only relatively recently that EU Member States began to cooperate in combating terrorism. Some observers may point out that some degree of European counter-terrorism cooperation could be observed as early as the 1970s within the so-called 'Trevi Group' (Kaunert and Léonard, 2019: 264). However, these early efforts, which took place on an intergovernmental basis, yielded only modest results. This pattern continued to repeat itself even after counter-terrorism became a formal competence of the EU with the entry into force of the Treaty of Maastricht in 1993 (Argomaniz, 2011; Bossong, 2013; Reinares, 2000). This considerably changed in the aftermath of the terrorist attacks on 11 September 2001 (European Council, 2001a). Although those took place in the United States, they had a profound impact on the development of EU counter-terrorism cooperation (see notably Argomaniz, 2009; Baker-Beall, 2016; Bures, 2011; Kaunert, 2005, 2010a; O'Neill, 2012; Zimmermann, 2006). This was because they were interpreted by European governments as signalling that Islamist terrorism was a global problem and that fundamentalist terrorists could strike again, not only in the United States, but in Europe as well (Kaunert and Léonard, 2019: 265). As a result, EU Member States decided to develop their cooperation on counter-terrorism on the basis of the so-called 'Anti-terrorism Roadmap' (European Council, 2001b), which was adopted very shortly after 9/11.

Over the years, although the Member States have remained the principal policy actors in the fight against terrorism, an EU counter-terrorism policy has gradually taken shape. Its development has been underpinned by the EU Counter-Terrorism Strategy, which was adopted in 2005 (Council of the European Union, 2005a). This has four pillars, namely 'prevent', 'protect', 'pursue' and 'respond' (Council of the European Union, 2005b). 'Prevent' concerns all the measures aiming to ensure that individuals are not drawn into terrorism; 'protect' refers to improving the security of critical infrastructure, transport and borders; 'pursue' mainly concerns the investigation of terrorist activities; and 'respond' relates to dealing with the consequences of terrorist attacks.

In addition, the EU Counter-Terrorism Strategy has been complemented by other programmatic documents that have built on the above-mentioned Anti-terrorism Roadmap, including the EU Plan of Action on Combating Terrorism (Council of the European Union, 2004) and the Revised Strategy on Terrorist Financing (Council of the European Union, 2008a). Against this backdrop, various EU counter-terrorism measures have been adopted, such as rules to prevent money laundering and terrorist financing (Léonard and Kaunert, 2012), a directive to harmonise the use of passenger name record (PNR) data in the EU for the prevention, detection, investigation and prosecution of terrorist offences and serious crime (Directive (EU) 2016/681), as well as the measures to prevent and counter radicalisation that are at the heart of this chapter.

As observed by various scholars, the development of the EU counter-terrorism policy has not been linear, but has rather been characterised by periods of inertia followed by accelerations, usually in the aftermath of significant terrorist attacks (Argomaniz, 2009; Bossong,

2013). In addition, the implementation by Member States of measures adopted at the EU level has often lagged behind (Argomaniz, 2010; Monar, 2005). This has frequently led scholars to question the effectiveness of the EU counter-terrorism policy (Bossong, 2008, 2013; Bures, 2006, 2011; Coolsaet, 2010; De Londras and Doody, 2015). Nevertheless, the fact that any significant terrorist attack in Europe nowadays tends to lead to questions about possible EU failings and calls for reinforced cooperation amongst Member States testifies to the recognition of the EU as an established policy actor in counter-terrorism (Kaunert and Léonard, 2019).

Before considering the EU's activities concerning radicalisation in greater detail, a few words on the institutional arrangements currently in place in that policy area are in order. From an institutional point of view, it is important to note that there is a wide range of actors involved in the development of the EU's counter-terrorism policy, including the measures relating to radicalisation. At the EU level, the European Commission makes legislative proposals, which are then negotiated and adopted by the Council, in which each Member State is represented, and the European Parliament. The Commission is also responsible for managing a range of EU funds supporting activities aiming at countering and preventing radicalisation. Within the Juncker Commission (2014–2019), terrorism was dealt with by the Directorate-General for Migration and Home Affairs (DG Home). In addition, from 2016 onwards, in the context of the development of the Security Union, the Commissioner for the Security Union supported the Commissioner for Migration, Home Affairs and Citizenship. The European Council – which gathers the Heads of State or Government of the Member States, the President of the European Council and the President of the European Commission – also plays a significant role by defining the EU's political priorities. It usually does so by issuing 'Conclusions' during European Council meetings.

Various EU agencies are also active in counter-terrorism, including radicalisation-related activities. The most important is arguably Europol, the EU's law enforcement agency (Kaunert, 2010b). It releases various annual reports, including the EU Terrorism Situation and Trend (TE-SAT) reports. Those present an overview of terrorism within the EU in a given year, including a significant amount of information concerning radicalisation. Since January 2016, Europol has also hosted the European Counter Terrorism Centre (ECTC) (European Commission, 2015), which presents itself as 'a central hub in the EU in the fight against terrorism'. All of its priorities concern radicalisation to some extent, including 'providing operational support upon a request from an EU Member State for investigations', 'tackling foreign fighters', 'sharing intelligence and expertise on terrorism financing (through the Terrorist Finance Tracking Programme and the Financial Intelligence Unit)', 'online terrorist propaganda and extremism (through the EU Internet Referral Unit)', and 'international cooperation among counter terrorism authorities' (Europol, 2019). Eurojust, the EU's Judicial Cooperation Unit, is another European agency dealing with terrorism, notably through its publication of the 'Terrorism Convictions Monitor' (TCM) three times per year. This report provides an overview of concluded court proceedings, amendments to relevant legislation at European and national levels, as well as a selection of upcoming and ongoing trials across the EU.

To add to the institutional complexity, the EU also has a Counter-Terrorism Coordinator (CTC), who is appointed by the High Representative of the Union for Foreign Affairs and Security Policy (previously, the High Representative for Common Foreign and Security Policy). This post was created in the aftermath of the 2004 terrorist attacks in Madrid, but its scope has never been clearly defined (MacKenzie, Bures, Kaunert and Léonard, 2013). Broadly speaking, the office of the CTC mainly aims to promote the EU's role in fighting terrorism, both internally (i.e. cooperation amongst Member States) and externally (i.e. cooperation between the EU and third countries). The CTC notably does so by monitoring the implementation of the EU's counter-terrorism measures, making policy recommendations and suggesting priority areas for EU action in regular reports, including in relation to preventing and countering radicalisation. Finally, as the EU has increasingly cooperated with third countries in order to address the terrorist threat, terrorism has also been on the agenda of the European External Action Service (EEAS), which is the EU's diplomatic service headed by the High Representative of the Union for Foreign Affairs and Security Policy. For example, the EU holds Counter-Terrorism Political Dialogue meetings with various countries, which notably address the issue of radicalisation.

The EU and the concept of 'radicalisation'

Although there had long been a scholarly interest in matters relating to 'radicalisation', it is only in the aftermath of 9/11 that this concept gained popularity amongst policy-makers and researchers alike. As observed by Sedgwick (2010: 480),

> [b]efore 2001, 'radicali[s]ation' was rarely referred to in the press, although the term was occasionally used in academia (...). The greatest increase in frequency of use of 'radicalisation' in the press was between 2005 and 2007, timing that strongly suggests that the term's current popularity derives from the emergence of 'home-grown' terrorism in Western Europe, notably the London bombings in July 2005.

However, as is so often the case with concepts, there is no single, universally accepted definition of 'radicalisation'. Coolsaet (2019: 29) describes 'radicalisation' as a multi-layered concept with a 'twisted history', whilst Sedgwick (2010: 479) notes that 'the term is understood and used in a variety of different ways, which in itself produces confusion'. Scholars generally agree on the basic understanding that 'radicali[s]ation can be defined as the process whereby people become extremists', although there are differences amongst the various conceptualisations of the specific factors and dynamics at play in this process (Neumann, 2013: 874). However, there is no agreement over the definition of 'extremism' and, more particularly, whether this refers to political ideas or methods. Thus, as summarised by Neumann and Kleinmann (2013: 362),

> like terrorism, radicali[s]ation remains a contentious concept, and there continues to be no consensus definition, with some scholars rejecting the concept altogether, others using it exclusively to describe processes that culminate in the use of violence, and yet others including both violent and nonviolent forms of extremism.

Unsurprisingly, this means that the related concept of 'deradicalisation' also lacks clarity, despite its frequent use. According to Horgan and Altier (2012: 86), '[b]roadly speaking, de-radicali[s]ation includes any effort to change or re-direct views that are supportive of – and thereby, the assumption goes, conducive to – violent action'. They also observe that, to make matters even more confusing, a lot of programmes and initiatives aiming to tackle radicalisation actually do not contain any mention of 'deradicalisation' in their formal description (Horgan and Altier, 2012: 86).

When it comes to the EU, the idea of 'radicalisation' initially did not occupy a prominent place in its conceptualisation of terrorism and in its counter-terrorism policy. The understanding of terrorism that underpinned the first phase of the development of the EU counter-terrorism policy following 9/11 was that it was largely an external security threat. The European Security Strategy, which was adopted in 2003, depicted terrorism as a consequence of 'regional conflicts' and 'state failure'. It also argued that '[t]he most recent wave of terrorism is global in its scope and is linked to violent religious extremism' (European Council, 2003). The document also identified the causes of terrorism as comprising 'the pressures of modernisation, cultural, social and political crises, and the alienation of young people living in foreign societies'. It is not entirely clear what was meant by 'foreign societies', although it seems to refer to societies outside the EU, as it was noted in the next sentence that '[this] phenomenon is also part of our own society'. Nevertheless, the European Security Strategy mainly presented terrorism as a threat external to the EU.

A turning point came with the Madrid terrorist attacks in March 2004, in which 193 people died and nearly 2,000 were injured. Those came to be widely seen as a case of 'homegrown terrorism', which led to a new emphasis in the EU's official discourse on addressing radicalisation. Actually, as pointed out by Reinares (2009: 16), 'a closer look at the individuals involved in the network behind the attack reveals a more complicated picture'. Although most of the members of the network became radicalised while in Spain, none of them had been born in Spain (or in Europe, for that matter) or held the citizenship of one of the EU Member States. Moreover, several group members had strong links to international terrorist groups, such as al Qaeda and the Moroccan Islamic Combatant Group (GICM) (Reinares 2009: 17).

Nevertheless, in the 'Declaration on Combating Terrorism' issued on 25 March 2004, the European Council emphasised the importance of 'combating the threat posed by terrorism and *dealing with its root causes*' (European Council, 2004: 1; emphasis added). This marked a departure from the previous emphasis on the external origin of terrorism. Nevertheless, although this was the first time that it was mentioned in an EU official document made public, the idea of understanding and tackling the root causes of terrorism had already entered national security debates in some of the EU Member States, especially following 9/11. In particular, in Belgium and in the Netherlands, security and intelligence officials had begun to notice a growing number of individuals acquiring 'radical' or 'fundamentalist' Islamic beliefs and, in some cases, being recruited by foreign 'Islamist fighters' (Coolsaet, 2019: 30–31). In the run-up to the Iraq War, they had become increasingly concerned that the so-called 'War on Terror', rather than increasing the security of Western states by defeating terrorism abroad, might actually be fuelling resentment and bottom-up radicalisation processes in some communities in Europe (Coolsaet, 2019: 32).

A document entitled 'European Union Objectives to Combat Terrorism (Revised Plan of Action)' was appended to the March 2004 Declaration on Combating Terrorism. It identified seven key objectives, the sixth of which was '[t]o address the factors which contribute to support for, and recruitment into, terrorism' (European Council, 2004: 16). An important aspect of this process, the document further argued, was to '[c]ontinue to investigate the links between extreme religious or political beliefs, as well as socio-economic and other factors, and support for terrorism, building on work already undertaken in this area, and identify appropriate response measures' (European Council, 2004: 16). Thus, in that way, addressing the causes of radicalisation – although the specific term 'radicalisation' had not been used yet – became an important part of the EU counter-terrorism policy from March 2004 onwards.

With regard to the issue of the precise meaning of 'radicalisation' in the EU, it is noteworthy that the EU's first strategic document on radicalisation – the 2005 EU Strategy for Combating Radicalisation and Recruitment to Terrorism – did not explicitly define 'radicalisation'. In the document, it appears to be understood as the process through which 'people are drawn into terrorism' (Council of the European Union, 2005b: 2). The document on which the Strategy built, namely the 2005 Communication of the European Commission on Terrorist Recruitment, was more precise in that respect. It started by defining 'violent radicalisation' as 'the phenomenon of people embracing opinions, views and ideas which could lead to acts of terrorism as defined in Article 1 of the Framework Decision on Combating Terrorism' (Commission of the European Communities, 2005: 2). It can also be noted that 'deradicalisation' is rarely used in EU documents. Those far more frequently mention 'preventing radicalisation', as well as 'countering radicalisation', which is in line with the fact that most radicalisation-related measures in the EU are part of the 'prevent' pillar of its Counter-Terrorism Strategy (see also Martins and Ziegler, 2018). The concept of 'disengagement' also appears in EU official documents. Following the adoption of Council Conclusions in 2012 (Council of the European Union, 2012), the 2014 Revised EU Strategy for Combating Radicalisation and Recruitment to Terrorism defined 'disengagement' as a process 'through which a radicalised individual can come to renounce violence, leave a group or movement, or even reject a worldview supporting or promoting an extremist ideology linked to terrorism' (Council of the European Union, 2014: 11).

The next two sections elaborate upon the EU's efforts at preventing and countering radicalisation, considering first their strategic aspects, before turning to the policy measures that have been adopted over the years.

Preventing and countering radicalisation in the EU: strategic aspects

As previously mentioned, the first key EU document on radicalisation was the EU Strategy for Combating Radicalisation and Recruitment to Terrorism, which was published in November 2005. This drew on work that had been carried out since the adoption of the Declaration on Combating Terrorism in March 2004. In particular, two EU working groups (Council Working Group on Terrorism – International Aspects (COTER) and the Terrorism Working Group (TWG)) had produced a confidential document on the 'Underlying factors in the recruitment to terrorism' in May 2004. It concluded that:

> [in the] context of sometimes real grievances [in Europe], a lack of any real opportunities to effect change or vent frustration and a consequent sense of anger and helplessness, the unambiguous messages of extremist propaganda can become very attractive, particularly to the youth population.
>
> *(Coolsaet, 2019: 34)*

Moreover, in September 2005, the European Commission had published a Communication on radicalisation. Bearing the title 'Terrorist recruitment: addressing the factors contributing to violent radicalisation', it identified a series of 'core areas of immediate focus', namely 'broadcast media, the internet, education, youth engagement, employment, social exclusion and integration issues, equal opportunities and non-discrimination and inter-cultural dialogue' (Commission of the European Communities, 2005: 3). It also highlighted the importance of supporting the sharing of knowledge and further research into radicalisation in order to inform policymaking. The idea of developing an external dimension to these activities in collaboration with third countries and regional partners was also included, although it appeared to be viewed more as an idea for the future than an immediate concern.

The Commission's Communication was followed by the adoption of the EU Strategy for Combating Radicalisation and Recruitment to Terrorism in November 2005. It identified three priorities for the EU, namely: (1) '[disrupting] the activities of the networks and individuals who draw people into terrorism; (2) [ensuring] that voices of mainstream opinion prevail over those of extremism; and (3) [promoting] yet more vigorously security, justice, democracy and opportunity for all' (Council of the European Union, 2005b: 3). In addition, the Strategy emphasised the importance of respecting fundamental rights whilst countering radicalisation. It is also noteworthy that the 2005 Strategy focused on al Qaeda and the terrorists inspired by al Qaeda and made various references to the Muslim communities (see Martins and Ziegler, 2018). This was markedly different to the 2008 Revised Strategy, which adopted a broader approach and highlighted 'Europe's desire to combat all forms of terrorism, whoever the perpetrators may be' (Council of the European Union, 2008b: 2). Nevertheless, the three main priorities for the EU remained the same in that document. Thus, the 2008 version of the Strategy did not fundamentally differ from the 2005 version.

In contrast, the 2014 Revised Strategy was significantly different from its predecessors. It notably built on the Communication on Preventing Radicalisation to Terrorism and Violent Extremism, which the European Commission published in January 2014 and which drew itself notably upon the work of the Radicalisation Awareness Network (RAN) (see below). The revision of the Strategy was prompted to a large extent by significant changes in the EU's environment. Amongst those was the rise in the number of European foreign fighters travelling to Syria. It was feared that they could use the experience acquired in the conflict zones in the Middle East and carry out terrorist attacks in Europe in the short term, as well as '[acting] as catalysts for terrorism' in the longer term (European Commission, 2014: 2). Other changes identified included 'the roles of public communications, the Internet and Social Media', particularly how 'the Internet and social media present a new potential for mobilisation and communication' (Council of the European Union, 2013: 3–4). In its Communication, the Commission identified ten types of 'actions that Member States and the EU could take to prevent and counter radicalisation more effectively' (European Commission, 2014: 12). Those were largely echoed in the 2014 Revised Strategy. This document emphasised that 'the means and patterns of radicalisation and terrorism are constantly evolving', which makes it necessary for the EU 'to consistently revisit [its] priorities and ensure that [its] security approach can address emerging forms of threats' (Council of the European Union, 2014: 4). As a result, ten priorities were identified: (1) '[promoting] security, justice, and equal opportunities for all'; (2) '[ensuring] that voices of mainstream opinion prevail over those of extremism'; (3) '[enhancing] government communications'; (4) '[supporting] messages countering terrorism'; (5) '[countering] online radicalisation and recruitment to terrorism'; (6) '[training], [building] capacity and [engaging] first line practitioners across relevant sectors'; (7) '[supporting] individuals and civil society to build resilience'; (8) '[supporting] disengagement initiatives'; (9) '[supporting] further research into the trends and challenges of radicalisation and recruitment to terrorism'; and (10) '[aligning] internal and external counter-radicalisation work' (Council of the European Union, 2014: 5). One may object that ten is too large a number of priorities. However, this can be explained by the nature of the role of the EU in this policy area, which is mainly to support the efforts of the Member States. Those remain the main policy actors when it comes to addressing radicalisation. Since then, although further documents relating to radicalisation have been released by the EU institutions, such as a Communication of the European Commission (2016) on Supporting the Prevention of Radicalisation Leading to Violent Extremism, the EU Strategy for Combating Radicalisation and Recruitment to Terrorism has not been further revised.

Nevertheless, some discussions have been held within the Council to that effect. In 2017, it was noted that a 'revision of the guidelines should duly reflect the changed threat picture and recent policy developments', including 'the growing challenge of European returning foreign terrorist fighters, including women and children, from Syria and Iraq' (Council of the European Union, 2017: 3).

Preventing and countering radicalisation in the EU: policy measures

In line with the priorities identified in its key programmatic documents, the EU has adopted a wide range of measures aiming at addressing radicalisation over the years. As previously mentioned, it is important to emphasise that the Member States remain the main actors in this policy area, whilst the EU mainly seeks to support their efforts and to facilitate their cooperation. An important exception in that respect is Directive (EU) 2017/541 on Combating Terrorism, which *obliges* Member States to criminalise various terrorism-related acts, including recruiting for terrorism, providing or receiving terrorist training, as well as public incitement to commit terrorist offences or advocating terrorism, including online.

This section focuses on three key aspects of the EU's activities relating to radicalisation, namely sharing knowledge and experience within the EU RAN, countering online radicalisation and recruitment to terrorism, as well as supporting research on radicalisation.

Sharing knowledge and experience relating to radicalisation: the EU RAN

One of the EU's main achievements in preventing and countering radicalisation has been the establishment of the RAN. This network finds its origins in the decision of the European Commission in 2006 to establish the Expert Group on Violent Radicalisation, which, as suggested by its name, was a group of experts providing policy advice to the Commission on fighting violent radicalisation. This group was succeeded by the European Network of Experts on Radicalisation (also referred to as the 'European Network of Experts on Violent Radicalisation') from 2009 and then the RAN from 2011 onwards.

RAN is an EU-wide umbrella network (or 'network of networks'), which brings together local actors and practitioners involved in preventing and countering radicalisation, such as teachers, youth workers, social workers, healthcare professionals, prison officers, non-governmental organisations, local authorities, researchers and law enforcement officers. As of 2019, the activities of RAN are organised around nine thematic working groups, as follows: Communication and Narratives (RAN C&N); Education (RAN EDU); EXIT (in the sense of moving away from violence) (RAN EXIT); Youth, Families and Communities (RAN YF&C); Local Authorities (RAN LOCAL); Prison and Probation (RAN P&P); Police and Law Enforcement (RAN POL); Remembrance of Victims of Terrorism (RAN RVT); and Health and Social Care (RAN H&SC). Within each working group, participants exchange their knowledge, experience and practices relevant to the specific dimension of radicalisation. As a result, a large number of guidelines, handbooks, recommendations and reports on best practices have been produced over the years, such as a manual on 'Responses to Returnees' aiming to support Member States in addressing the challenges posed by returning FTFs, which was presented in June 2017 (European Commission, 2017c: 8). There are ongoing debates as to the inclusion of more categories of practitioners in future (European Commission, 2017a: 15). All working-group leaders also sit on the Steering Committee of RAN, which is chaired by the European Commission.

Also represented on the Steering Committee is the RAN Centre of Excellence (CoE), which the European Commission has presented as 'the main policy tool in countering and preventing radicalisation' (European Commission, 2017a: 15). It has developed state-of-the-art knowledge about radicalisation and has supported both the European Commission and the Member States in their efforts to counter and prevent radicalisation. Nevertheless, it has its limitations, as it is a virtual entity that provides its services under a five-year procurement contract (2014–2019) (European Commission, 2017a: 17).

Countering online radicalisation and recruitment to terrorism

Modern communications technologies can be used for terrorism purposes. The Internet may be employed for spreading radicalising propaganda, which can then be easily accessed by individuals in their own homes (European Commission, 2014: 8). For example, the European Commission (2018a: 1) noted that 'in January 2018 alone, almost 700 new pieces of official Da'esh propaganda were disseminated online'. The acknowledgement of this major problem has led the EU to take several initiatives aiming to address online radicalisation.

One of the key actions for tackling online terrorist content has been the establishment of the EU Internet Forum in 2015, which gathers participants, notably online platforms, on a voluntary basis. It has two main objectives, namely decreasing the accessibility of online terrorist content and supporting civil society in increasing the volume of effective, alternative narratives online. The EU Internet Referral Unit at Europol has played a key role with regard to the first objective by flagging terrorist content for removal to the Internet companies (European Commission, 2017c: 8). The second objective has been supported since December 2016 by the Civil Society Empowerment Programme (CSEP), which has a budget of EUR 10 million. The European Strategic Communications Network (ESCN), which gathers representatives of the EU Member States and is funded by the European Commission, has also contributed to this second objective through the sharing of knowledge and good practices concerning the use of strategic communications in countering and preventing violent extremism. The ESCN emerged from the Syria Strategic Communications Advisory Team (SSCAT), which had been set up in January 2015 with the aim of discouraging EU citizens from travelling to Syria or other conflict zones in order to participate in terrorist activities (Council of the European Union, 2016: 32).

Another noteworthy development has been the 'Code of conduct on countering illegal hate speech online', which was launched by the European Commission in May 2016. Facebook, Microsoft, Twitter and YouTube were the four platforms that initially signed up to the code of conduct, before being joined by others, including Instagram, Google+, Snapchat and Dailymotion (European Commission, 2018a: 2). The code of conduct has set out several public commitments aiming to help users notify illegal hate speech on these platforms, as well as improving the support to civil society and the coordination with national authorities.

Moreover, in July 2017, the members of the EU Internet Forum adopted an Action Plan to combat terrorist content online. As explained by the European Commission (2017b: 9),

> [this] includes measures to step up the automated detection of illegal terrorist content online, share related technology and tools with smaller companies, achieve the full implementation and use of the 'database of hashes' [which aims to prevent terrorist material removed from one platform being re-uploaded on to another], and empower civil society on alternative narratives.

In addition, in March 2018, the European Commission (2018b) made several recommendations to Member States and companies in order to address online radicalisation more effectively. Having considered that progress had not been swift and sufficient enough, the European Commission (2018a) tabled a proposal for new rules in September 2018. Those aim at ensuring that online terrorist content is swiftly removed (i.e. within an hour from the time of notification by the national authorities).

Supporting research on radicalisation

The EU institutions, the European Commission in particular, have regularly expressed the belief that research plays a crucial role in preventing and countering radicalisation. The research evidence generated by various projects helps Member States develop new practices and programmes and fine-tune existing ones. Several research projects on radicalisation were supported by the Seventh Framework Programme for European Research and Technological Development (FP7). These projects mainly aimed to better understand the dynamics at play in radicalisation processes and to establish methodologies to assess the effectiveness of the measures taken to address radicalisation (European Commission, 2016: 4). The recent terrorist attacks in Europe have led the European Commission to conclude that there are 'new trends in the process of radicalisation which need to be further investigated' (European Commission, 2016: 4). Research topics on radicalisation have therefore been included in the Horizon 2020 Programme. Priorities for the future, according to the European Commission (2016: 4), include further bridging the gap between researchers and practitioners in the field of radicalisation, as well as harnessing the power of big data for better understanding the communication practices of violent radicalisation. Research on radicalisation is not only funded by these research budgets, but is also supported by security funds, such as the Internal Security Fund – Police, which supports the efforts of Member States in tackling terrorism, including countering radicalisation and supporting civil society in disseminating alternative narratives. It is noteworthy that there has recently been more emphasis on better exploiting the findings of research projects that have already been completed. As underlined by the Expert Group 'Steering Board for Union Actions on Preventing and Countering Radicalisation' that advises the European Commission,

> [w]hile we need to deepen discussions on a closer interaction between researchers and policy-makers within the context of the different actions (e.g. undertaken by the RAN or ESCN), it is equally important to increase the accessibility of what is already available, both on EU and national level.
>
> *(Expert Group 'Steering Board for Union Actions on Preventing and Countering Radicalisation', n.d: 3)*

Conclusion

This chapter has shown that the EU has assumed an increasingly important role in preventing and countering radicalisation. After a first phase in the development of its counter-terrorism policy shaped by a view of terrorism as a largely external security threat, heightened concerns about homegrown terrorism have led the EU to give more importance to the issue of radicalisation, in particular understanding the dynamics at play in radicalisation processes and identifying the most effective measures to prevent and counter radicalisation. Since 2005, preventing radicalisation has been an important dimension of the 'prevent' pillar of the EU Counter-Terrorism Strategy. In addition, in the same year, the EU adopted a dedicated Strategy for Combating

Radicalisation and Recruitment to Terrorism, which has been regularly updated since then. Given that each Member State remains responsible for national security, the EU mainly aims to support the efforts of Member States and to facilitate cooperation amongst them. As a result, various EU initiatives aiming to prevent and counter radicalisation have been developed. Amongst the aspects of radicalisation that have received particular attention in the EU, one can mention sharing knowledge and expertise through initiatives such as setting up the RAN, addressing online radicalisation and supporting research into radicalisation. The EU's activities in this area are set to further grow in future, as the report of the High-Level Commission Expert Group on Radicalisation has identified a series of priority areas where, in its view, 'further action at EU level could offer significant benefit' (European Commission, 2018c: 5; see also High-Level Commission Expert Group on Radicalisation, 2017).

Against the backdrop of this flurry of activities, a crucial question has been that of the effectiveness of these measures. A study for the European Parliament (2017: 63) published in 2017 emphasised that:

> [n]o mechanisms or reporting obligations are in place to monitor follow-up and implementation of the policy objectives that are formulated in the Strategy documents. In that sense it is impossible to measure the formal effectiveness in this policy field, let alone the material effectiveness.

Difficulties are compounded by the fact that this is a very wide and fragmented policy area, given that, with the exceptions previously noted, the EU has mainly sought to encourage the initiatives of Member States, rather than legislating in order to oblige them to take specific measures. In 2018, the European Court of Auditors (2018: 4) conducted a performance audit of the Commission's policy on the prevention of radicalisation and concluded that 'the Commission addressed the needs of Member States, but there were some shortfalls in coordination and evaluation'. It notably noted that '[t]he Commission has not sufficiently developed its framework for assessing whether its support is effective and offers value for money' and that there was a tendency to focus on the amount of activities, rather than their effectiveness (European Court of Auditors, 2018: 5).

One can therefore conclude that the EU's role in preventing and countering radicalisation has undoubtedly grown to a very significant extent in recent years. Nevertheless, the question of the effectiveness of all its activities will remain largely unanswered until reporting and evaluation tools are more systematically used.

References

Argomaniz, J. (2009) "When the EU is the 'Norm-taker': The Passenger Name Records Agreement and the EU's Internalization of US Border Security Norms", *Journal of European Integration*, 31(1): pp. 119–136.

Argomaniz, J. (2010) "Before and After Lisbon: Legal Implementation as the 'Achilles Heel' in EU Counter-terrorism?", *European Security*, 19(2): pp. 297–316.

Argomaniz, J. (2011) *The EU and Counter-terrorism: Politics, Polity and Policies after 9/11*, London: Routledge.

Baker-Beall, C. (2016) *The European Union's Fight Against Terrorism: Discourse, Policies, Identity*, Manchester: Manchester University Press.

Bossong, R. (2008) "The Action Plan on Combating Terrorism: A Flawed Instrument of EU Security Governance", *Journal of Common Market Studies*, 46(1): pp. 27–48.

Bossong, R. (2013) *The Evolution of EU Counter-Terrorism: European Security Policy after 9/11*, London: Routledge.

Bures, O. (2006) "EU Counterterrorism: A Paper Tiger?", *Terrorism and Political Violence*, 18(1): pp. 57–78.

Bures, O. (2011) *EU Counterterrorism Policy: A Paper Tiger?*, Farnham: Ashgate.

Chalk, P. (1996) *West European Terrorism and Counter-terrorism: The Evolving Dynamic*, Basingstoke: Macmillan.

Commission of the European Communities. (2005) "Communication from the Commission to the European Parliament and the Council Concerning Terrorist Recruitment: Addressing the Factors Contributing to Violent Radicalisation", COM(2005) 313, 21 September 2005. Brussels: Commission of the European Communities.

Coolsaet, R. (2010) "EU Counterterrorism Strategy: Value Added or Chimera?", *International Affairs*, 86(4): pp. 857–873.

Coolsaet, R. (2019) "Radicalization: The Origins and Limits of a Contested Concept", in Fadil, N., de Koning, M. and Ragazzi, F. (eds) *Radicalization in Belgium and the Netherlands: Critical Perspectives on Violence and Security*. London: I.B. Tauris, pp. 29–51.

Council of the European Union. (2004) "EU Plan of Action on Combating Terrorism", *10586/04*, 15 June 2004. Brussels: Council of the European Union.

Council of the European Union. (2005a) "The European Union Counter-Terrorism Strategy", *14469/4/05, REV 4*, 30 November 2005. Brussels: Council of the European Union.

Council of the European Union. (2005b) "The European Union Strategy for Combating Radicalisation and Recruitment to Terrorism", *14781/1/05*, 24 November 2005. Brussels: Council of the European Union.

Council of the European Union. (2008a) "Revised Strategy on Terrorist Financing", *11778/1/08, REV 1*, 17 July 2008. Brussels: Council of the European Union.

Council of the European Union. (2008b) "Revised EU Strategy for Combating Radicalisation and Recruitment to Terrorism", *15175/08*, 14 November 2008. Brussels: Council of the European Union.

Council of the European Union. (2012) *Council Conclusions on De-radicalisation and Disengagement from Terrorist Activities, 3162nd Justice and Home Affairs Council meeting, Luxembourg, 26 and 27 April 2012*, Brussels: Council of the European Union.

Council of the European Union. (2013) "Draft Council Conclusions Calling for an Update of the EU Strategy for Combating Radicalisation and Recruitment to Terrorism", *9447/13*, 15 May 2013. Brussels: Council of the European Union.

Council of the European Union. (2014) "Revised EU Strategy for Combating Radicalisation and Recruitment to Terrorism", *9956/14*, 19 May 2014. Brussels: Council of the European Union.

Council of the European Union. (2016) "Implementation of the Counter-terrorism Agenda Set by the European Council", *13627/16, ADD1*, 04 November 2016. Brussels: Council of the European Union.

Council of the European Union. (2017) "Review of the Guidelines for the EU Strategy for Combating Radicalisation and Recruitment to Terrorism", *6700/17*, 09 March 2017. Brussels: Council of the European Union.

De Londras, F. and Doody, J. (eds) (2015) *The Impact, Legitimacy and Effectiveness of EU Counter-Terrorism*, London: Routledge.

European Commission. (2014) "Communication from the Commission to the European Parliament, the Council, the European Economic and Social Committee and the Committee of the Regions: Preventing Radicalisation to Terrorism and Violent Extremism: Strengthening the EU's Response", *COM(2013) 941*, 15 January 2014. Brussels: European Commission.

European Commission. (2015) "Communication from the Commission to the European Parliament, the Council, the European Economic and Social Committee and the Committee of the Regions – The European Agenda on Security", *COM(2015) 185*, 28 April 2015. Strasbourg: European Commission.

European Commission. (2016) "Communication from the Commission to the European Parliament, the Council, the European Economic and Social Committee and the Committee of the Regions – Supporting the Prevention of Radicalisation Leading to Violent Extremism", *COM(2016) 379*, 14 June 2016. Brussels: European Commission.

European Commission. (2017a) "Commission Staff Working Document: Comprehensive Assessment of EU Security Policy Accompanying the Document 'Communication from the Commission to the European Parliament, the European Council and the Council – Ninth Progress Report Towards an Effective and Genuine Security Union'", *SWD(2017) 278, PART 2/2*, 26 July 2017. Brussels: European Commission.

European Commission. (2017b) "Communication from the Commission to the European Parliament, the European Council and the Council: Ninth Progress Report Towards an Effective and Genuine Security Union", *COM(2017) 407*, 26 July 2017. Brussels: European Commission.

European Commission. (2017c) "Communication from the Commission to the European Parliament, the European Council and the Council: Tenth Progress Report Towards an Effective and Genuine Security Union", *COM(2017) 466*, 07 September 2017. Brussels: European Commission.

European Commission. (2018a) "State of the Union 2018: Commission Proposes New Rules to Get Terrorist Content Off the Web", *IP/18/5561*, 12 September 2018. Brussels: European Commission.

European Commission. (2018b) "A Europe That Protects: Commission Reinforces EU Response to Illegal Content Online", *IP/18/1169*, 01 March 2018. Brussels: European Commission.

European Commission. (2018c) *High-Level Commission Expert Group on Radicalisation (HLCEG-R): Final Report*, 18 May 2018. Luxembourg: Publications Office of the European Union.

European Council. (2001a) "Conclusions and Plan of Action of the Extraordinary European Council meeting on 21 September 2001", *SN 140/01*. Brussels: European Council.

European Council. (2001b) "Anti-terrorism Roadmap", *SN 4019/01*, 26 September 2001. Brussels: European Council.

European Council. (2003) *European Security Strategy: A Secure Europe in a Better World*, Vol. 12, Brussels: European Council.

European Council. (2004) *Declaration on Combating Terrorism*, 25 March 2004. Brussels: General Secretariat of the Council.

European Court of Auditors. (2018) *Special Report – Tackling Radicalisation that Leads to Terrorism: The Commission Addressed the Needs of Member States, but with Some Shortfalls in Coordination and Evaluation*, Luxembourg: European Court of Auditors.

European Parliament. (2017) "The European Union's Policies on Counter-Terrorism: Relevance, Coherence and Effectiveness", Study for the LIBE Committee, Directorate-General for Internal Policies, Policy Department C: Citizens' Rights and Constitutional Affairs. Brussels: European Parliament.

Europol. (2019) *European Counter Terrorism Centre – ECTC*, The Hague: Europol. Available at www.europol.europa.eu/about-europol/european-counter-terrorism-centre-ectc (last accessed on 11 June 2019).

Expert Group 'Steering Board for Union Actions on Preventing and Countering Radicalisation'. (n.d.) *Strategic Orientations on a Coordinated EU Approach to Prevention of Radicalisation for 2019*, Brussels: Expert Group 'Steering Board for Union Actions on Preventing and Countering Radicalisation'.

High-Level Commission Expert Group on Radicalisation. (2017) *Interim Report (Preliminary Findings and Recommendations*, Brussels: High-Level Commission Expert Group on Radicalisation.

Horgan, J. and Altier, M.B. (2012) "The Future of Terrorist De-Radicalization Programs", *Georgetown Journal of International Affairs*, 13(2): pp. 83–90.

Kaunert, C. (2005) "The Area of Freedom, Security and Justice: The Construction of a 'European Public Order'", *European Security*, 14(4): pp. 459–483.

Kaunert, C. (2010a) *European Internal Security: Towards Supranational Governance in the Area of Freedom, Security and Justice?* Manchester: Manchester University Press.

Kaunert, C. (2010b) "Europol and EU Counterterrorism: International Security Actorness in the External Dimension", *Studies in Conflict and Terrorism*, 33(7): pp. 652–671.

Kaunert, C. and Léonard, S. (2019) "The Collective Securitisation of Terrorism in the European Union", *West European Politics*, 42(2): pp. 261–277.

Léonard, S. and Kaunert, C. (2012) "'Between a Rock and a Hard Place?': The European Union's Financial Sanctions against Suspected Terrorists, Multilateralism and Human Rights", *Cooperation and Conflict*, 47(4): pp. 473–494.

MacKenzie, A., Bures, O., Kaunert, C. and Léonard, S. (2013) "The European Union Counter-Terrorism Coordinator and the External Dimension of the European Union Counter-terrorism Policy", *Perspectives on European Politics and Society*, 14(3): pp. 325–338.

Martins, B.O. and Ziegler, M. (2018) "Counter-Radicalization as Counter-Terrorism: The European Union Case", in Steiner, K. and Önnerfors, A. (eds) *Expressions of Radicalization: Global Politics, Processes and Practices*. Basingstoke: Palgrave, pp. 321–352.

Monar, J. (2005) "Justice and Home Affairs", *Journal of Common Market Studies*, 43(s1): pp. 131–146.

Neumann, P. and Kleinmann, S. (2013) "How Rigorous Is Radicalization Research?", *Democracy and Security*, 9(4): pp. 360–382.

Neumann, P.R. (2013) "The Trouble with Radicalization", *International Affairs*, 89(4): pp. 873–893.

O'Neill, M. (2012) *The Evolving EU Counter-Terrorism Legal Framework*, London: Routledge.

Reinares, F. (ed) (2000) *European Democracies against Terrorism: Government Policies and Intergovernmental Cooperation*, Aldershot: Ashgate.

Reinares, F. (2009) "Jihadist Radicalization and the 2004 Madrid Bombing Network", *CTC Sentinel*, 2(11): pp. 16–19.

Sedgwick, M. (2010) "The Concept of Radicalization as a Source of Confusion", *Terrorism and Political Violence*, 22(4): pp. 479–494.

Zimmermann, D. (2006) "The European Union and Post-9/11 Counterterrorism: A Reappraisal", *Studies in Conflict and Terrorism*, 29(1): pp. 123–145.

15

AFRICAN UNION INITIATIVES TO COUNTER TERRORISM AND DEVELOP DERADICALISATION STRATEGIES

Anneli Botha

Violent extremism leading to acts of terrorism is not new to Africa, requiring the focus of countermeasures to change throughout the years. Initially, the focus has been on actively addressing the direct threat, calling for political, legislative and physical measures, in line with United Nations (UN) directions. Since the introduction of the UN Global Counter-Terrorism Strategy – based on four pillars, namely measures to address the conditions conducive to terrorism; measures to prevent and combat terrorism; measures to build states' capacity to prevent and combat terrorism and to strengthen the role of the UN system in this regard; and measures to ensure respect for human rights for all and the rule of law as the fundamental basis of the fight against terrorism – countries on the continent again followed the lead by introducing measures and strategies to (in addition to the direct threat) address the conditions conducive to radicalisation and terrorism (the manifestation of violent extremism). However, instead of the African Union (AU) introducing similar steps as when it introduced the Organization of African Unity (OAU) Convention on the Prevention and Combating of Terrorism and subsequent Protocol and Plan of Action, countries most directly affected by terrorism and its aftermath took the lead in developing regional strategies through Regional Economic Communities (RECs). Starting initially with counter-terrorism strategies, RECs more recently introduced strategies to counter and prevent radicalisation. For example, the Economic Community of West African States (ECOWAS)[1] and Intergovernmental Authority on Development (IGAD)[2] took the lead, introducing specific strategies against terrorism and radicalisation into violent extremist organisations. These strategies – in addition to measures to address the immediate threat of terrorism – also made provision to curb the growing threat of radicalisation by introducing initiatives to address the underlying reasons for radicalisation. From a pure counter-terrorism perspective, deradicalisation is however still very new to the agenda of many countries, especially those not directly affected.

When deradicalisation efforts in Europe are being compared to that of Africa, the initial assumption is that the continent is light-years behind. However, it is easy to forget that Africa is the size of the United States, Eastern and Western Europe, China and India combined and similar to the diverse nature of these areas are the different regions on the African continent. Furthermore, the manifestation of radicalisation in acts of terrorism in Africa is completely different to the experiences in Europe. Although both Europe and Africa are being confronted with foreign fighters, the manifestation of the associated threat is different: Europe is confronted with radicalisation and recruitment of its nationals into Islamic State in Syria and Iraq, to be used to commit acts of terrorism at home and/or participate in the then conflict in Syria and Iraq. As a result, returning foreign fighters are considered to be one of the most prominent security challenges to countries in Western Europe and Scandinavia. Africa, on the other hand, has been the recipient of foreign fighters to especially Somalia and Libya, but its nationals have also been recruited to Afghanistan and later Iraq and Syria. That being said, the manifestation and level of recruitment of foreign fighters in southern Africa cannot even be compared to the situation in northern Africa. Preventing and countering terrorism – as well as radicalisation – through a one-size-fits-all approach will not be effective as long as the respective counter-strategies are not developed after understanding the local threat and associated challenges and acknowledging the different nature of the threat in Africa in the form of insurgencies versus radicalisation into terrorist organisations in Europe.

One can identify three hotspots in Africa: Eastern Africa, with Somalia as the epicentre; Western Africa, with Nigeria as the centre of gravity; and Northern Africa (Algeria, Libya and Egypt spreading to Mali, Niger and Mauritania). Unlike in Europe, radicalisation in Eastern, Western and North Africa manifested first in insurgencies, driven by domestic circumstances and local frustration. Not being able to bring these conflicts under control the initial national crisis became increasingly transnational. As a result, the reasons for and manifestation of radicalisation and associated terrorism under al-Shabaab are different in Somalia (predominantly an insurgency where control of territory is important) and Kenya (where al-Shabaab manifests itself as a purely terrorist organisation). Practically, the counter and deradicalisation strategies also need to be different to speak to the realities in each of these countries, despite being in the same region. Therefore, although direction from the AU may add some guidance to countries not experiencing the same level of radicalisation to initiate preventative measures, initiatives taken by RECs addressing similar challenges and realities will be far more effective.

The following chapter will start with providing a brief introduction to AU initiatives to prevent and counter terrorism and institutions within the AU to take the lead in developing relevant strategies. As an example of where the AU took the lead in developing a dedicated strategy, reference will be made to the AU strategy for the Sahel region. In the absence of a specific AU deradicalisation strategy for the continent the AU, as part of its conflict and mitigation strategies, instead focused on disarmament, demobilisation and reintegration (DDR) efforts. In contrast to the driving factors of radicalisation in Europe, where ideology play a more prominent role, radicalisation into violent extremist movements is caused by an array of factors that also include governance, ethnic and religious marginalisation, need for revenge and financial incentives. As a result, peacekeeping and DDR are often more relevant to address the broader manifestation of violent extremism in Africa.

Historical overview of African initiatives to prevent and combat terrorism

Efforts to improve African regional cooperation in countering terrorism predate the 9/11 attacks and even the 1998 bombings of the United States' embassies in Kenya and Tanzania. As early as July 1992, the OAU Heads of State and Government meeting in Dakar adopted

Resolution 213. The objective of this resolution was to strengthen cooperation and coordination between the African states, to enhance the effectiveness of its initiatives against the first real manifestations of extremism. According to the Resolution, Member States committed themselves

> not to allow any movement using religion, ethnic or other social or cultural differences to indulge in hostile activities against Member States as well as to refrain from lending any support to any group that could disrupt the stability and the territorial integrity of Member States by violent means, and to strengthen cooperation and coordination among the African countries in order to circumvent the phenomenon of extremism and terrorism.
>
> *(Organization of African Unity, 1992, p. 1)*

The Member States furthermore agreed not to allow any movement using religion, ethnic or other social or cultural differences to incite and justify hostile activities against the Member States.

In June 1994, during its session in Tunis, the Assembly of Heads of State and Government adopted a "Declaration on the Code of Conduct for Inter-African Relations". In that Declaration, the Summit rejected fanaticism and extremism, whatever their nature, origin and form, particularly those based on religion as unacceptable and detrimental to the promotion of peace and security on the continent. The Summit unreservedly condemned the terrorist acts, methods and practices and expressed its determination to strengthen cooperation between Member States (African Heads of State and Government, 1994, pp. 9–10).

Although the rest of the world refers to 9/11 as the watershed in the emergence of major international terrorism, African countries were abruptly awakened to the dangers of transnational terrorism when terrorists bombed the US embassies in Dar-es-Salaam and Nairobi in 1998. The vehicle-borne improvised explosive devices (VBIEDs) caused a large number of casualties among residents as well as US officials. In reaction to these attacks, African countries in July 1999 adopted the OAU Convention on the Prevention and Combating of Terrorism (Algiers Convention) during the 35th Ordinary Session of the Assembly of Heads of State and Government. The Convention called on the Member States not to justify terrorism under any circumstances, origin, causes and objectives. Article I included a lengthy definition of a terrorist act. However, the OAU Convention also stipulated that "armed struggle against colonialism, occupation, aggression and domination by foreign forces shall not be considered as terrorist acts" (Organization of African Unity, 1999, p. 208). This provision reflects the African historical context in which liberation movements were labelled terrorist organisations. During this period, the focus of African leaders has been on developing the capacity to implement practical counter-terrorism measures, such as enhanced border control and surveillance, information-sharing and financial controls. Following the introduction of the OAU Convention, most notably defining a terrorist act, countries domesticated the Convention through counter-terrorism legislation. The example set by the AU further facilitated cooperation between countries – especially amongst those directly confronted by terrorism.

As a sign of greater awareness by the AU Member States to the terrorist threat posed to the stability and security of Member States, the Constitutive Act of the African Union listed among its principles the rejection of acts of terrorism (Article 4 (o)) (African Union, 2000,

p. 7). In addition, the Solemn Declaration on the Conference on Security, Stability, Development and Cooperation in Africa (CSSDCA) was adopted by the Lome Summit in July 2000. Further reference was made to condemn terrorism and for countries on the continent to cooperate.

To build momentum towards ratification, the AU convened an "Inter-Governmental High-Level Meeting" during September 2002 in Algiers where the Action Plan to implement the Convention was designed (African Union, 2002b). Largely at the insistence of Algeria (also the host of the meeting), the meeting also recommended that the AU started work on an implementation and monitoring mechanism (to be reflected in a Protocol). Furthermore, the AU proposed the establishment of the African Centre for the Study and Research of Terrorism (ACSRT), that will be referred to below, to be based in Algeria.

The Convention was the first concrete regional step to address and deal with the devastating impact of terrorism on the African continent. It was however only after 9/11 – on 6 December 2002 – that the Convention came into force. Illustrating the impact of 9/11, only six countries ratified the convention before those attacks, while 28 ratified the convention soon after 9/11. Furthermore, in the aftermath of 9/11, African countries felt that the Algiers Convention was not sufficient to develop a comprehensive counter-terrorism strategy and suggested an additional Protocol and Plan of Action. Furthermore, the Peace and Security Council (PSC) was formed to work towards a stable and conflict-free Africa, to be discussed below.

The Constitutive Act of the African Union provides a sound basis for the prevention and combating of terrorism. Article 4(o) calls for "respect for the sanctity of human life, condemnation and rejection of impunity and political assassination, acts of terrorism and subversive activities" (African Union, 2000, p. 7). The Preamble also underscores the need to promote peace, security and stability as a prerequisite for the implementation of Africa's development agenda.

The emergence of a new peace and security architecture on the continent, particularly the PSC in the AU, introduced a new chapter in addressing increasing threats the continent faces (to be discussed below).

Protocol to the OAU Convention on the Prevention and Combating of Terrorism

The primary focus of the Protocol was to enhance the effective implementation of the Convention (African Union, 2002a). The Protocol also acknowledged new developments in the threat of terrorism, such as the growing interest of terrorists in weapons of mass destruction as well as the use of sophisticated and electronic technology to plan, organise and commit terrorist activities.

In addition to the above-mentioned role of the AU in developing a regional counter-terrorism strategy, the AU has also facilitated technical assistance delivery to its Member States. Despite a Convention, Protocol and a Plan of Action, AU Member States requested the Commission of the AU to draw up a roadmap indicating timelines and priorities in the implementation of the Plan of Action (African Union, 2004, p. 4). This illustrates a real problem, namely a lack of capacity among Member States and the AU's inability to provide the necessary guidelines and resolve to implement existing UN and AU instruments.

Plan of Action of the African Union High-Level Inter-Governmental Meeting on the Prevention and Combating of Terrorism in Africa

The primary aim of the Plan of Action as presented in its Preamble is:

> to give concrete expression to commitments and obligations (presented in the Algiers Convention and UN Resolution 1373 adopted in the immediate aftermath of 9/11), to enhance and promote African countries' access to appropriate counter-terrorism resources through a range of measures establishing a counter-terrorism cooperation framework in Africa.
>
> *(African Union, 2002b, p. 1)*

The Plan of Action sets out a series of measures and actions it requires Member States to comply with, including the structuring of two inter-related structures that would enable better cooperation between the Member States on security-related issues:

- the PSC; and
- the ACSRT that was established under the authority of the PSC.

Peace and Security Council

The PSC succeeded the OAU Central Organ of the Mechanism for Conflict Prevention, Management and Resolution. The Central Organ was the OAU's operational body mandated to the prevention, management and resolution of conflicts on the continent. Under Article 7 of the Protocol, the PSC's key powers, according to the AU website, include: To anticipate and prevent disputes and conflicts, as well as policies, which may lead to genocide and crimes against humanity. Undertake peace-making, peace-building and peace-support missions and recommend intervention in a Member State in respect of grave circumstances, namely war crimes, genocide and crimes against humanity and institute sanctions where necessary. Implement the AU's common defence policy, ensure implementation of key conventions and instruments to combat international terrorism; promote coordination between regional mechanisms and the AU regarding peace, security and stability in Africa (Africa Union, 2002c, p. 9).

In line with measures to address the conditions conducive to terrorism, the PSC calls for the promotion of democratic practices, good governance, the rule of law, protection of human rights and fundamental freedoms, respect for the sanctity of human life and international humanitarian law. Furthermore, the PSC promotes and encourages the implementation of conventions and treaties on arms control and disarmament; examines and takes action in situations where the national independence and sovereignty of a Member State are threatened by acts of aggression, including by mercenaries; and supports and facilitates humanitarian action in situations of armed conflict or major natural disasters.

The PSC is therefore primarily responsible and tasked to prevent and combat terrorism in Africa. Under Article 3(d) the PSC is tasked with coordinating and harmonising continental efforts in the prevention and combating of terrorism in all its aspects, as well as the implementation of other relevant international instruments (African Union, 2002b, p. 3). Furthermore, under Article 7(i) the PSC gives the Organ the power to "ensure the implementation of the OAU Convention on the Prevention and Combating of Terrorism and other relevant international, continental and regional conventions and instruments and harmonize and coordinate efforts at the regional and continental levels to combat international terrorism" (African Union, 2002b, p. 9).

Paragraph 16 of the Plan of Action and Article 4 of the Protocol further provide for a detailed role of the PSC, including, among others, the following (African Union, 2002b, p. 9). Firstly, prepare, publicise and regularly review a list of persons, groups and entities involved in terrorist acts (related to UN Security Council Resolution 1267). Secondly, establish mechanisms to facilitate the exchange of information among State Parties on the patterns and trends in terrorist acts, the activities of terrorist groups and on successful practices in combating terrorism (UN Security Council Resolution 1373). Thirdly, request all Member States on an annual basis to report on the steps taken to prevent and combat terrorism and, where appropriate, on the implementation of the Algiers Convention (Counter-Terrorism Committee established under UN Security Council Resolution 1373 and UN Resolution 1624). Lastly, monitor, evaluate and make recommendations on the implementation of the Convention and the Plan of Action.

Under Article 10(e) of the Plan of Action, Member States undertake to "promote policies aimed at addressing the causes of terrorism, in particular, poverty, deprivation and marginalisation".

In addition to coordinating initiatives on the continent to address the threat of terrorism (listed as number 6 under Article 7 – see above), the PSC undertakes peace-making, peace-building and peace-support missions (listed as number 2) and promotes coordination between regional mechanisms and the AU regarding peace, security and stability in Africa (listed as number 7). The PSC is, therefore, the best placed to propose initiatives and strategies on deradicalisation. As will be discussed below, the PSC under its mandate to undertake peacekeeping and peace-building initiatives, especially DDR, plays an increasingly relevant role in deradicalisation through reintegration as part of DDR.

African Centre for the Study and Research on Terrorism

The Centre was launched during the Second High-Level Inter-Governmental Meeting on the Prevention and Combating of Terrorism in Africa held in Algiers, Algeria on 13–14 October 2004. The Centre was established under paragraphs 19–21 of the AU Plan of Action on the Prevention and Combating of Terrorism, based in Algiers and serves as a structure of the Commission of the AU and the PSC. The Centre performs, among others, the following functions (ACSRT, n.d., pp. 3–4): assists Member States of the AU in developing strategies for the prevention and combating of terrorism; establishes operating procedures for information gathering, processing and dissemination; and provides technical and expert advice on the implementation of the AU counter-terrorism instruments. The Centre also updates and strengthens policies and programmes of the Union relating to counter-terrorism; and develops and maintains a database on a range of issues relating to the prevention and combating of terrorism, particularly on terrorist groups and their activities in Africa. This database, as well as other analyses, will be accessible by all Member States. The Centre further promotes the coordination and standardisation of efforts aimed at enhancing the capacity of Member States to prevent and combat terrorism; and initiates and disseminates research studies and policy analyses periodically, through an *African Journal for the*

Prevention and Combating of Terrorism. It also develops training programmes with the assistance of individual countries and organisations.

Since its inception, ACSRT through Memoranda of Understanding (MoU) with RECs, the Committee of Intelligence and Security Services of Africa (CISSA) and national security institutions established relationships to enhance the effectiveness of counter-terrorism efforts (Peace and Security Council, 2012, p. 6).

In its report, the Chairperson of the Commission on Terrorism and Violent Extremism in Africa stipulated that:

> Countering radicalization and extremism lies at the heart of the efforts to address the conditions that are conducive to the spread of terrorism. It is a long-term process that requires the development of sound national policies and programs based on a thorough understanding of the radicalization threat. Terrorist acts cannot be justified under any circumstances. However, the fact that some segments of society may have sympathy for extremist and terrorist groups warrants a closer look at domestic grievances, ideological tendencies and trust gap between Government and population. Hence the need for Member States to adopt counter-radicalization and de-radicalization policies and programs that encompass engaging and working with civil society, including community leaders and religious authorities, formal and informal educational institutes. Furthermore, addressing socio-economic problems to reduce vulnerability to extremist ideology, legislation reform, prison rehabilitation programs and building national capacities, to ensure effective implementation and sustainability of related measures.
>
> *(Peace and Security Council, 2012, p. 11)*

In April 2012, the ACSRT organised a seminar to examine and evaluate national experiences, establish broad guidelines of analysis for radical discourse and design a common methodology for the African states for developing and implementing counter-radicalisation and deradicalisation programmes, as well as effective legal and administrative measures. The seminar was attended by 40 government officials, members of the religious organisations and representatives from civil society (Peace and Security Council, 2012, p. 6).

African Union strategy for the Sahel region

Although the AU assists and work with RECs in developing regional strategies through the PSC and ACSRT, the AU took the lead (with the UN) in developing an AU strategy for the Sahel. Dealing with the instability in Chad, Mali, Mauritania and Niger, resulting from trafficking and terrorism through groups – such as al-Qaeda in the Islamic Maghreb (AQIM), the Movement for Unity and Jihad in West Africa (MUJAO) and Ansar Dine – the AU associated with the UN proposed a strategy for the Sahel region. This strategy consists of elements of preventative and counter (including deradicalisation) initiatives.

This strategy is centred on three main pillars: (1) governance; (2) security; and (3) development under the AU Mission for Mali and the Sahel (MISAHEL) that will be responsible for the effective implementation of this strategy. Following the Libyan crisis of 2011, the AU and UN conducted a fact-finding mission to the region. Based on the "United Nations Integrated Strategy for the Sahel" the PSC of the AU endorsed the conclusions of this joint AU–UN experts meeting at a ministerial-level meeting in Bamako on 20 March 2012. Additionally, the March 2012 military coup in Mali and intensification of the crisis in the north of Mali (emergence of armed terrorist groups) called for action against the causes of recurring insecurity in the region (Peace and Security Council, 2014, p. 2).

The strategy under governance as the first priority identifies that

> the lack of respect for principles of good governance and the rule of law and the manipulation of constitutional provisions relating to power alternation play an important role in the occurrence of political crises in the Sahel region and on the continent as a whole.
>
> *(Peace and Security Council, 2014, p. 7)*

To ensure the implementation of the strategy, it calls for the "close monitoring of political developments in the countries of the region and undertake good offices and structural conflict prevention initiatives" (Peace and Security Council, 2014, p. 7). It further recommends:

> support civil society organisations, including women's associations, parliamentarians, political parties and the media professionals in the region with a view to enabling them to play their role for the effective implementation of these instruments in their respective fields of action.
>
> *(Peace and Security Council, 2014, p. 7)*

Under paragraph 22, it promotes "a culture of respect for human rights and curb injustices, inequalities and the perceptions of marginalisation". Specifically recognising the main nomadic populations in the Sahel region, namely the Tuareg (Algeria, Burkina Faso, Libya, Mali and Niger), the Toubus (Chad, Libya and Niger) and, to a lesser degree, the Fulani or Peuls and the role perceptions of marginalisation play in radicalisation and conflict. The AU through this strategy encourages dialogue and development within these communities, but also encourages "the promotion of languages and cultural symbols of the nomadic populations, within a framework of national harmony, in order to enhance their integration into the national community" (Peace and Security Council, 2014, p. 9).

Directly associated with deradicalisation, the "AU proposes to continue its engagement in the dialogue and reconciliation processes, both in Mali and at the regional level". To ensure its success, the strategy is committed to "mobilize funds to support the field actions of institutions in charge of the dialogue and reconciliation processes in Mali, particularly in relation to the development of programs of activities and the conduct of [its] hearings". Recognising the role religious and traditional leaders play in the promotion of peace and national cohesion, it specifically recalled the

> African Charter for the Cultural Renaissance stressed that elders and traditional leaders are important cultural actors. Their role and importance deserve an official recognition through their integration in the modern mechanisms of conflict resolution and the systems of intercultural dialogue.
>
> *(Peace and Security Council, 2014, p. 11)*

To ensure the implementation of this approach, the strategy calls for the following four steps (Peace and Security Council, 2014, p. 11). Firstly, facilitate regular exchanges between and with religious and traditional leaders around values of tolerance and strategies to better convey these messages through the media to the young people and in places of worship. Secondly, strengthen the position of religious and traditional leaders to enable them to better play their role as actors of peace, and preaches common values and messages of tolerance and harmonious cohabitation. Thirdly, support civil society organisations and youth associations working in the field of the promotion of religious tolerance and sensitisation of young people on the consequences of intolerance and religious extremism. Lastly, promote inter-faith dialogue using the existing cultural mechanisms in the Sahel region to avoid the stigma and violence against other beliefs.

Under the framework, this strategy provided for individual countries to develop tailored initiatives.

Dealing with radicalisation as part of broader AU conflict mitigation strategies

Recognising the different realities on the African continent, "traditional" deradicalisation programmes are being developed and implemented in countries directly affected by radicalisation on a national level. However, the AU focuses predominantly on bringing stability to areas affected by conflict. From this perspective initiatives from the AU on "deradicalisation" took the format of DDR processes in the aftermath of insurgencies. Acting as a bridge between immediate security and longer-term recovery priorities, DDR is the first step in peace-building. While the AU is actively developing and guiding policy on the continent on DDR best practices, the ACSRT facilitated discussion groups on radicalisation in the past. Whether DDR can be associated with deradicalisation is up for debate when approached from a Western perspective. However, within the African context, organisations associated with conflicts over the continent and responsible for the worst acts of terrorism were executed by insurgencies. Insurgencies represent the following prominent characteristics: the primary focus of an insurgency is to overthrow the existing government or to obtain a share in government by forcing the existing government to the negotiation table. Secondly, the objective is to gain control over territory by enhancing access to resources, a tax base and recruitment opportunities (Hammes, 2006, p. 24).

In response, the UN in partnership with the AU directly receives ex-combatants through its DDR programmes in Somalia, the AU/UN Hybrid operation in Darfur (UNAMID) as well as the Economic Community of Central African States (ECCAS) mission in the Central African Republic and the AU counter-LRA (Lord's Resistance Army) mission. The AU (through the UN) enhanced its DDR capacity-building and support infrastructure as an answer to this growing operational need. It is especially in Somalia through the AU mission (AMISOM) that al-Shabaab members are being reintegrated through its DDR project that supports the decision to consider the connection between deradicalisation and DDR. In contrast to the arrest of individuals implicated in acts of terrorism in Europe or who were individually radicalised into violent extremism, al-Shabaab and Boko Haram, to name a few, are closely associated with insurgencies, bringing them into the DDR framework. Similarly, only a minority of the individuals who had been part of these organisations were actually radicalised; instead, most joined out of necessity. For example, living in areas controlled by organisations such as al-Shabaab and Boko Haram contributed to the impression that, by not joining, young males especially might be suspected of supporting government forces. Secondly, joining the organisations as a form of employment calls rather for classical DDR-related initiatives to equip the person for better employment opportunities instead of deradicalisation efforts addressing the ideology of the organisation.

Implementing DDR-type of programmes instead of traditional deradicalisation programmes found in Europe was reinforced especially in Somalia, where linkages between poverty and radicalisation/recruitment were established when 12% of former al-Shabaab members interviewed in 2017 as part of a United Nations Development Programme (UNDP) study into radicalisation indicated that they had joined al-Shabaab for the employment opportunities it presented after religious/nationalism motivations. Ten per cent of the same sample referred to losing their employment as a catalyst in joining al-Shabaab. Lastly, the majority of al-Shabaab respondents identified employment as the most prominent need.[3] Although defending Somalia against "foreign occupation" in the form of AMISOM played a prominent role in the radicalisation process, economic reasons justifying joining al-Shabaab cannot be ignored. Indicating a lack of ideological commitment to the "cause" of al-Shabaab, deradicalisation and reintegration strategies (currently implemented through the United Nations Assistance Mission in Somalia (UNSOM) with the assistance of other partner institutions) need to address these employment challenges through vocational training and the creation of employment opportunities.

Disarmament, demobilisation and reintegration

Based on the unique manifestation of the threat through well-defined organisations such as al-Shabaab and Boko Haram, whose aim it was to capture territory in Somalia and Nigeria, these organisations in those two countries became a hybrid between an insurgency and a terrorist organisation. In addition to the structuring and overall aim of these organisations – associated with an insurgency – increasing attacks directed at the local population placed the said organisations increasingly in the realm of terrorism. In considering the magnitude of resources required to deal with the threat effectively, the Nigerian government deployed its military, followed by establishing the Multinational Joint Task Force (MNJTF) with troop-contributing countries from Benin, Cameroon, Chad, Niger and Nigeria to find a solution to Boko Haram. Faced with state failure in Somalia, the AU through its mission in Somalia (AMISOM) with military support from Ethiopia, Kenya, Uganda, Burundi and Sierra Leone instituted a peacekeeping mission in Somalia to bring an end to al-Shabaab. Within peace-keeping circles DDR has been well known since March 1990, when the UN Security Council expanded the mandate of the peacekeeping operation known as ONUCA (UN Observer Group in Central America) to demobilise anti-government elements in Nicaragua (United Nations, 2010, p. 3).

Recognising the changing environment in which peacekeeping operations in recent years have been being conducted, the UN introduced "Second Generation Disarmament, Demobilization and Reintegration (DDR) Practices in Peace Operations: A Contribution to the New Horizon Discussion on Challenges and Opportunities for UN Peacekeeping". According to this report, whereas "traditional DDR focuses mainly on combatants that are present within military structures, the focus of Second Generation programs shifts away from military structures towards the larger communities that are affected by armed violence" (United Nations, 2010, p. 3).

In February 2012 the AU Commission, through the Peace and Security Department (PSD), initiated the Disarmament, Demobilization and Reintegration Capacity Program (DDRCP) by holding a Consultation Seminar on DDR with the RECs and Regional Mechanisms for Conflict Prevention, Management and Resolution (RMs). This was conducted within the framework of the 2004 Common African Defence and Security Policy (CADSP), the 2006 Post-Conflict Reconstruction and Development (PCRD) and the 2010

African Peace and Security Architecture (APSA) Roadmap. Each of the AU Member States is a member of at least one of the eight RECs and two RMs:

1. ECOWAS
2. Common Market of East and Southern Africa (COMESA)
3. ECCAS
4. Southern Africa Development Community (SADC)
5. Arab Maghreb Union (UMA)
6. Economic Community of Sahel-Saharan States (CEN-SAD)
7. East African Community (EAC)
8. IGAD.

The two RMs refer to the Eastern African Standby Brigade Coordination Mechanism (EASBRIGCOM) and North Africa Regional Capability (NARC). Although the AU PCRD Policy Framework of 2006 provides guidance on roles and responsibilities of AU and RECs as well as on mechanisms to be established for the effective implementation of PCRD measures at Member State level, there is still a lack of clear definitions of roles and responsibilities of the AU and the RECs (African Union Commission, 2015, p. 41).

The purpose of the DDRCP is to strengthen capacities within the AU, its Member States and regional partners, namely the RECs and RMs, to support national and regional DDR initiatives on the continent. The Defence and Security Division (DSD) is the office within the PSD responsible for developing policy on emerging issues the CADSP is confronted with (African Union Commission, 2012, p. 7).

Following an integrated process, the DSD works in partnership with the other sections in the Commission, including the Peace Support Operation Division (PSOD) and the African Standby Force. The World Bank Transitional Demobilization and Reintegration Program (TDRP), the UN Office at the AU (UNOAU) and the UN Department of Peacekeeping Operations (UN DPKO) financially support the AU's DDR capacity-building initiatives.

Following requests made by the Member States, the AU supports national DDR programmes. These include assistance to the Republic of South Sudan, the Central African Republic and Somalia.

Phases in the DDR process

Although the focus is on reintegration, disarmament consists of the collection, control and disposal of small arms, ammunition, explosives and light and heavy weapons from combatants, as well as in many cases from the civilian population. Secondly, demobilisation is the formal discharging of active combatants. According to the UN, "reinsertion" serves as a step between demobilisation and reintegration. During this step, assistance is being provided to former combatants by supplying the basic needs of former combatants and their families that can include "transitional safety allowances, food, clothes, shelter, medical services, short-term education, training, employment and tools" (United Nations, 2010, p. 23). Lastly, reintegration is considered the most difficult stage in the DDR process during which former combatants are prepared to be integrated back into their communities. During this process, former combatants are retrained to secure employment, as explained above.

Through demobilising former combatants, equipping them with the necessary skills to provide for themselves and their families and reintegrating them back into society, these initiatives create a platform for long-term stability. In addition to creating employment opportunities for former combatants, the DDR framework equally emphasises the need for economic, political and social reforms. Consequently, these initiatives include strengthening of governance, the rule of law, gender and youth vulnerability – all elements in the prevention and countering of a violent extremism agenda. That said, DDR does not necessarily focus on the ideological factors influencing radicalisation that deradicalisation programmes would concentrate on. It is, however, important to note that the DDR process in Somalia incorporated religious education as part of the programme.

Facilitating reintegration under DDR, vocational training is being provided in the following basic skills (African Union, 2007, p. 3): functional literacy; hygiene, nutrition, sanitation, and disease prevention, including HIV/AIDS prevention; and family life skills, including parental care and domestic skills. Especially applicable in deradicalisation is the following training recipients receive: namely creative thinking and analysis of information skills; and human relations and interpersonal skills to enable more constructive interaction with others from different ethnic backgrounds. This is further supported by communication and language skills – if necessary learning a second language – in multilingual societies; human rights and good governance practices; politics, culture and history; and lessons on national unity and reconciliation.

Guiding the delivery of vocational training in a post-conflict situation, these projects address skill acquisition, particularly in areas related to infrastructure development, basic socioeconomic activities and local community needs. More specifically, the AU recommends the following types of programme (African Union, 2007, p. 5):

- agriculture, for example, crop and animal production, agro-food processing, irrigation, etc.
- building and construction services, including masonry, carpentry, painting and decorating, interior design, electrical installation, plumbing, etc.
- water and sanitation systems maintenance
- welding and fabrication, including the manufacture of simple agricultural implements and tools
- electrical and electronic equipment repair
- vehicle repair and maintenance
- handicrafts and traditional crafts, for example, carvings, weavings, basketry, leatherwork, etc.
- basic ICT skills, including word processing, data management, internet, etc.
- tourism-related skills, for example, hotel management, tour guides, cooks, waiters, etc.
- business entrepreneurial skills and attitudes, including time management, marketing, basic accounting, microbusiness management, joint ventures.

To ensure the success of the said programmes, those benefiting need to be employed as a measure to prevent these individuals from returning to the conflict. Associated with deradicalisation programmes, the AU recommended psychological trauma counselling, post-training support including follow-up, mentoring of graduates and the initiation of monitoring and evaluation mechanisms with appropriate indicators (African Union, 2007, p. 5).

Although the focus of the reintegration process is the former combatant, the long-term success of the programme is to secure the support of the communities these individuals will be reintegrated into. Without community acceptance, the possibility of returning to the organisation increases substantially.

One of the most challenging parts of the reintegration process is to differentiate between commanders and combatants. In contrast to deradicalisation, under reintegration, the prosecution of those who committed crimes might be a requirement. Therefore, the classification system to differentiate between high-risk and low-risk individuals is critical in both the deradicalisation and reintegration framework. Furthermore, identification and differentiation between the different reasons and levels of radicalisation are required to implement different reintegration procedures and deradicalisation programmes. Intelligence is therefore critical in differentiating between low- and high-risk and between commanders and combatants to facilitate different reintegration programmes.

A similar process will also be applicable in the deradicalisation process. Within the DDR framework, the UN in its "Second Generation Disarmament, Demobilization and Reintegration (DDR) Practices in Peace Operations" guidelines refers to specific commander incentive programmes (CIPs), to ensure that middle- and high-ranking commanders do not spoil the peace as these individuals may have the means, status and connections to engage in illicit activities, particularly arms and drug trade. Part of this strategy may be to place commanders in positions of authority, including political or administrative positions, or to head reintegration programmes without promoting a culture of impunity. However, identifying "suitable and trustworthy commanders who would be eligible to assume political or administrative authority requires extra training, monitoring and mentoring mechanisms" (United Nations, 2010, pp. 25–26).

Conclusion

The primary role of the AU, as with any regional organisation, is inter alia to provide guidance and coordinate efforts to address a common challenge. Terrorism and all the associated themes, including preventing and addressing this threat, regarding counter-terrorism, preventing radicalisation into violent extremist organisations, countering violent extremism and deradicalisation call for coordinated guidance. Although the AU initially provided a counter-terrorism framework, the threat of terrorism and what is required to prevent it changed dramatically over time. Recognising the different manifestations of the threat of terrorism and radicalisation on the continent, the implementation of these counter and preventative measures occurs more effectively in a regional (driven by RECs) and national setting. In other words, although the threats associated with radicalisation and terrorism changed, its manifestation is confined to specific countries and neighbouring countries; for example, al-Shabaab in Somalia as the epicentre that spread to Kenya, Uganda, Tanzania, Djibouti and to a lesser extent Ethiopia. In another example, Boko Haram in Nigeria expanded to Cameroon, Niger and Mali. Lastly, AQIM with its historical origins in Algeria spread to Mauritania, Mali and Burkina Faso as the most severely affected. It is also for this reason that RECs are particularly active in developing and implementing strategies to address the different manifestations and counter changing trends associated with terrorism. Recognising the different manifestations of radicalisation associated with recruitment to national and/or transnational operations and the different local dynamics, it is to be expected that the type, strategies and role players involved in preventing and countering radicalisation followed by deradicalisation initiatives will take different forms across the continent.

In considering the magnitude of especially al-Shabaab and Boko Haram and the nature of their operations as insurgencies resorting to acts of terrorism as part of its broader strategy, the AU instituted peacekeeping operations in Somalia (AMISOM) and the MNJTF to deal with Boko Haram. Within military circles, DDR has been a well-known concept and integral part of any peacekeeping operation since 1990. It therefore came as no surprise that AMISOM, supported by the UN, introduced rehabilitation centres in Somalia to facilitate the reintegration of former al-Shabaab members. Furthermore, the fact that the entire continent doesn't have to address the same type and level of radicalisation and terrorism means that the urgency for a continental framework and its focus differ. In contrast to the OAU Convention on the Prevention and Combating of Terrorism that called for efforts to facilitate cooperation through, for example, the introduction of specialised counter-terrorism legislation, to leap to the development of a continental prevention and countering of violent extremism and deradicalisation strategy might be remote and even practically unrealistic. Instead, the AU Commission seems to be more inclined to develop countering violent extremism strategies as part of the DDR framework and as part of regional initiatives driven by RECs. Working on the technical level (peacekeeping), instead of the political (required in introducing a continental framework), means that initiatives could be tailored to the specific needs and realities of the affected areas. The implementation of these strategies and measures can also be monitored and revised when necessary.

Should the AU decide to develop a continental prevention and countering of violent extremism strategy that makes provision for deradicalisation, the PSC and ACSRT will be the two institutions to take the lead in developing and implementing these initiatives. In particular, the ACSRT that is tasked with providing technical assistance and expert advice on counter-terrorism instruments, as well as the updating and strengthening of policies and programmes relating to counter-terrorism, would be best placed to take the lead. However, considering the realities described above, it is to be expected that the ACSRT will continue to provide technical support to RECs for the immediate future and for the latter to develop regional and guide national strategies. That being said, the ultimate test will not be how many meetings and strategies are being developed, but rather how many and to the extent these strategies will be implemented.

Notes

1 ECOWAS developed the Counterterrorism Strategy and Implementation Plan in 2013.

2 Initiatives started focusing on counter-terrorism with the IGAD Capacity Building Programme Against Terrorism (ICPAT) in 2006, to be followed in 2011 by the IGAD Security Sector Programme to restructure the IGAD Capacity-Building Programme Against Terrorism. More recently IGAD launched the Regional Strategy for Preventing and Countering Violent Extremism in the Horn and Eastern Africa Region in 2018.

3 Specific data on the Somalia sample was not published separately, but included in "Journey to Extremism in Africa: Drivers, Incentives and the Tipping Point for Recruitment", published in 2017. Available at http://journey-to-extremism.undp.org/content/downloads/UNDP-JourneyToExtremism-report-2017-english.pdf.

References

African Centre for the Study and Research on Terrorism (ACSRT) (n.d.) "African Centre for the Study and Research on Terrorism (ACSRT)", *Brief about the Centre*. http://caert.org.dz/About%20us.pdf

African Heads of State and Government meeting in Tunis (1994) "Declaration on a Code of Conduct for Inter-African Relations, Assembly of Heads of State and Government", *Adopted by the African Heads of State and Government meeting in Tunis, Thirtieth*, Ordinary Session, Tunis, Tunisia, 13–15 June 1994. http://hrlibrary.umn.edu/africa/INTAFN.htm

African Union (2000) "Constitutive Act of the African Union", *Adopted by the Thirty-sixth Ordinary Session of the Assembly of Heads of State and Government 11 July, 2000* – Lome, Togo. www1.uneca.org/Portals/ngm/Documents/Conventions%20and%20Resolutions/constitution.pdf

African Union (2002a) "Protocol to the OAU Convention on the Prevention and Combating of Terrorism", Algiers, Algeria, 11–14 September.

African Union (2002b) "Plan of Action of the African Union High-Level Inter-Governmental Meeting on the Prevention and Combating of Terrorism in Africa, Mtg/HLIG/Conv.Terror/Plan (I)", *Mtg/HLIG/Conv.Terror/Plan (I)*, 11–14 September.

African Union (2002c) "Protocol Relating to the Establishment of the Peace and Security Council of the African Union", *Adopted by the 1st Ordinary Session of the Assembly of the African Union*. Durban, 9 July. www.peaceau.org/uploads/psc-protocol-en.pdf

African Union (2004) "Draft Declaration of the Second High-Level Inter-Governmental Meeting on the Prevention and Combating of Terrorism in Africa", Algiers, Algeria, 13–14 October.

African Union (2007) *Framework for Post-Conflict Reconstruction and Technical and Vocational Education and Training (TVET)*, Addis Ababa: Department of Human Resource Science and Technology, Division of Human Resource and Youth.

African Union Commission (2012) "African Union Disarmament, Demobilization and Reintegration Capacity Program (AU DDRCP), Project Document and Funding Proposal", *Project Document and Funding Proposal*, October.

African Union Commission (2015) *African Peace and Security Architecture APSA Roadmap 2016–2020*, Addis Ababa: African Union Commission, Peace and Security Department.

Conference on Security, Stability, Development and Cooperation in Africa (CSSDCA) (2000) "CSSDCA Solemn Declaration", *AHG/Decl.4 (XXXVI)*. www.peaceau.org/uploads/ahg-decl-4-xxxvi-e.pdf

Hammes, T. X. (2006) "Countering Evolved Insurgent Networks". *Military Review* Vol. 86, No. 4: 150.

Organization of African Unity (1992) "Resolution on the Strengthening of Cooperation and Coordination among African States", *AHG/Res. 213 (XXVIII)*.

Organization of African Unity (1999) *OAU Convention on the Prevention and Combating of Terrorism*, Algiers, Algeria. www.peaceau.org/uploads/oau-convention-on-the-prevention-and-combating-of-terrorism.pdf

Peace and Security Council (2012) "Report of the Chairperson of the Commission on Terrorism and Violent Extremism in Africa", *Report of the Chairperson of the Commission on Terrorism and Violent Extremism in Africa*, 13 November.

Peace and Security Council (2014) "The African Union Strategy for the Sahel Region", *Adopted at peace and security council 449th meeting 11 August 2014*, Addis Ababa, Ethiopia.

United Nations (2010) *Second Generation Disarmament, Demobilization and Reintegration (DDR) Practices in Peace Operations: A Contribution to the New Horizon Discussion on Challenges and Opportunities for UN Peacekeeping*, New York: Department of Peacekeeping Operations, United Nations.

PART III

Regional case studies

16

DERADICALISATION AND DISENGAGEMENT IN THE BENELUX

A variety of local approaches

Amy-Jane Gielen

Belgium has the highest number of foreign fighters per capita in Western Europe (Colaert, 2017; Van Ostaeyen en Van Vlierden, 2018). It is closely followed by The Netherlands, which produced over 300 foreign fighters. With the so-called Caliphate defeated, many foreign fighters have surrendered or have already returned home. Belgium has over 130 returnees (Segers, 2019) and The Netherlands 60 (AIVD, 2019). The question of what to do with these foreign fighters has sparked heated political and societal debate varying from sentencing (to death) in Iraq and Syria to prosecuting them in The Netherlands and Belgium and offering exit progammes. Such programmes are often a combination of interventions aimed at changing extremist beliefs (deradicalisation) or dissuading from violent extremist action (disengagement) (Horgan & Braddock, 2010). These programmes have become of particular importance in Belgium and The Netherlands as these countries are not only confronted with the terrorist threat of returnees, some of whom were responsible for (foiled) terrorist attacks, but are also dealing with an increase in home-grown violent extremism due to the fact that the Caliphate has been defeated and because extremist right-wing organisations are on the rise again (NCTV, 2019; Segers, 2019).

Exit programmes have become common across the world in the fight against violent extremism. However, the approaches used in different geographical locations differ substantially. While, for instance, disengagement and deradicalisation attempts in South East Asia and the Middle East revolve around theology and ideology, in Germany, Norway and Sweden, exit interventions focus less or not at all on ideology (Dalgaard-Nielsen, 2013). In Mali, Niger and Chad, one study found that radio programmes were an effective part of a strategy to counter violent extremism (Aldrich, 2014). Yet, the strategy does not necessarily transfer to digitalised countries (Gielen, 2017a). Thus programmes for deradicalisation and disengagement are very much country-dependent. However, both Belgium and The Netherlands have not only organised their countering violent extremism (hereafter: CVE) policies on a national and in the case of Belgium on a federal level, but have also made municipalities responsible for CVE policy.

Belgium is a federal state, composed of communities and regions. Belgium has three communities: the Flemish community, the French community and the German-speaking community. The country is further divided into 10 provinces and 589 municipal councils (Belgium.be, 2019). The Netherlands is not a federal state, but consists of 390 municipalities. Most municipalities that are confronted with violent extremism (e.g. due to travel of foreign fighters) have their own local CVE programmes. As a consequence, deradicalisation and disengagement not only vary by country, but also very much locally in both countries. This contextuality, in combination with the high number of foreign fighters from the Benelux, warrants a separate chapter on deradicalisation and disengagement programmes in the Benelux. The Benelux consists not only of Belgium and The Netherlands, but also of Luxembourg. However, Luxembourg has nowhere near the amount of foreign fighters and the threat level Belgium and The Netherlands have. In the words of the High Commission for National Protection (HCPN): "While 'tak[ing] the threat seriously and act[ing] accordingly by implementing the necessary policies and measures'," the situation is "less acute than in other EU countries" (quoted from Van Ginkel & Entenmann, 2016: 46).[1] As a consequence Luxembourg will not be further discussed in this chapter.

This chapter will start off by briefly discussing the broader national, (federal) and local policy frameworks, of which deradicalisation and disengagement programmes are part, also known as CVE. It will focus on how deradicalisation and disengagement are organised on a local level, highlighting the multi-agency and tailor-made approach. It will then go on to discuss the effectiveness of these efforts. It will do so by drawing on both our empirical research in municipalities as well as desk research of previous studies that have been conducted. The chapter concludes with several reflections on the Benelux exit approach and how the effectiveness of these programmes can be further improved.

The Belgian CVE context

As part of its counter-terrorism (CT) effort since the attacks in Madrid in March 2004 and in London on July 2005, the Belgian federal government launched the action plan Radicalisation (Stratégie fédérale belge contre la radicalisation violente), also known as "Plan R", in 2005. In 2013 it became apparent that dozens of Belgian citizens had travelled to Syria to initially fight against the regime of Bashar al-Assad. Since then, Belgium has been heading the list in Western Europe of the highest number of foreign fighters per capita (Colaert, 2017). Plan R was updated in 2015 and still forms the cornerstone of the Belgian CT policy with the adoption of an increasing number of CVE measures, instruments, laws and/or institutions at federal, regional and local level (Wittendorp et al., 2017). An overview of the Belgian local, regional and federal initiatives has been provided by Gielen (2018d) and is summarised below:

- In April 2015, the Flemish Government approved the *Action plan for the prevention of violent radicalisation processes* (*Actieplan ter preventie van radicaliseringsprocessen*) that can lead to extremism and terrorism. This was updated in 2017 to an *Action plan for the prevention of violent radicalisation and polarisation* (*Actieplan ter preventie van gewelddadige radicalisering en polarisering*) (Colaert, 2017).
- In the Brussels-Capital Region *Brussels–Prevention and Security* (BPS) was set up in 2015 to play a central role in coordinating the various regional prevention and security chain operators. The BPS drafted the *Global Security and Prevention Plan* (GSPP) in 2017, which also includes the topic of polarisation and radicalisation.

- A similar initiative was undertaken by Wallonie-Bruxelles which launched their *Initiatives de prévention du radicalisme et du bien-vivre ensemble* (*Initiatives to prevent radicalisation and well-being together*) in 2015 and set up a new service called CAPREV (Centre for the Assistance of People concerned by any Radicalism or Extremism leading to Violence) in December 2016.
- Confronted with the foreign fighter phenomenon, the municipalities of Vilvoorde, Brussels, Mechelen, Antwerp and Liège were the first to respond and appointed "deradicalisation officials" in 2013 who were responsible for setting up a local approach to prevent and counter violent extremism (Renard & Coolsaet, 2018). These cities are also known as the "pilot cities". In the following years many municipalities (e.g. Aalst, Charleroi, Ghent, Maaseik, Menen, Namur, Oostende, Verviers and Zele) – often supported by the regional government – followed their example and developed CVE policies.

In Belgium the mayor has to take the initiative to set up a Local Integral Security Cell (LIVC) to ensure that preventative and social services can share information together with the Local Task Force (LTF). The LTF is a multi-agency platform between the federal police, security services and the local public prosecution office. Within the LTF information is shared and radicalised individuals are monitored. The mayor forms a bridge between the security and the social domain and makes it possible to undertake legal and administrative measures or interventions aimed at deradicalisation and disengagement (Van Broeckhoven & Gielen, 2015). In Belgium, efforts to deradicalise and disengage are thus very much a local responsibility. The regions support the local level with finances and expertise (exchange), but do not carry out interventions aimed at deradicalisation and disengagement (Figure 16.1).

The Dutch CVE context

The Netherlands was first confronted with homegrown jihadism in 2004 when Mohammed B. assassinated the film maker Theo van Gogh. Mohammed B. turned out to be part of an extremist network of mostly Dutch-born young Muslims who were planning attacks as early as 2002 (Vidino, 2007). The network was also known as the Hofstad group. In the aftermath of the assassination and the arrest of members of the Hofstad group, the first "counter-polarisation and radicalisation" programmes were developed on both a national (Ministerie BZK, 2007) as well as a local level. The City of Amsterdam, for example, developed an action plan called "Wij Amsterdammers", and Amsterdam boroughs followed suit (Gielen,

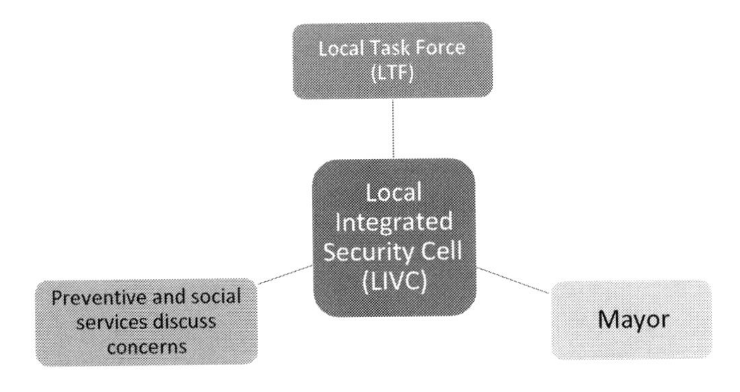

Figure 16.1 Belgium's multi-agency approach.
Source: Van Broeckhoven & Gielen, 2015.

2008; Uitermark & Gielen, 2010). The essence of these plans is that they attempted to address the root causes and drivers of radicalisation and violent extremism and enhance protective factors against violent extremism. Lousberg et al. (2009) provide an overview of the types of intervention that were part of the Dutch national and local programmes. The interventions aim to prevent both Islamic radicalisation and right-wing radicalisation. Lousberg et al. (ibid) structured 213 interventions used by practitioners, of which 106 were targeted at right-wing individuals and 174 at Muslims. The clustering led to an overview of 15 clusters of interventions in the preventive, curative and repressive stage. In the curative stage, mentoring and deradicalisation are offered to (potential) radicalised individuals.

The Dutch national and local CVE programmes came to an end in 2012, because violent extremism was not considered a serious threat any more by security services (Ministerie Veiligheid en Justitie, 2012, NCTV; 2012). One year later the conflict in Syria led to Dutch citizens travelling to join terrorist organisations such as Islamic State in Iraq and Syria (ISIS). It was at that time, in March 2013, that the threat level had to be raised (NCTV, 2013) and a new national CVE action plan (Ministerie van Veiligheid & Justitie et al., 2014) was developed.

As in 2007, the local approach became the cornerstone of Dutch CVE policies in which municipalities are responsible for setting up local CVE programmes. These CVE programmes are most often a combination of preventive approaches (e.g. training for practitioners, community engagement) as well as individual case management ("persoonsgerichte aanpak") for radicalised individuals (Gielen, 2015b). The individual case management takes place within a multi-agency setting in which municipalities are in the lead and reports of (potential) radicalised individuals are assessed and discussed. These signals can come from practitioners, members of the public and communities, the Police, the Public Prosecution Office, the General Intelligence and Security Service (AIVD) or the Office of the National Coordinator for Security and Counter-terrorism (NCTV). The signals are either directly passed to the responsible policy officer of the municipality or are given to the mayor of the municipality. The signals are discussed within a multi-agency setting consisting of the municipality, the Police, the Public Prosecution Office, the Child Protection Service, the Probation Service, the Mental Health Service and the NCTV. Together they make a risk assessment of each (potentially) radicalised individual and decide on the best course of action. This can consist of (a combination of) legal, administrative and/or softer measures. Measures can include ideological/psychological counselling; family support; practical support with housing and a job; no contact with the former extremist network to prevent further grooming; social media ban to prevent further grooming and involving Child Protection Services to enforce necessary change in (troubled) family systems (Gielen, 2015b; Gielen, 2018a; NCTV, 2014). The individual case management within a multi-agency setting is visually presented in Figure 16.2.

It is thus within this multi-agency setting that exit programmes are offered. Exit programmes refer to "all efforts undertaken by or under the responsibility of a municipality aimed" *at* deradicalisation (changing extremist beliefs), disengagement (dissuading from violent extremist action), reintegration and rehabilitation (quoted from Gielen, 2018a: 456 based on Horgan & Braddock, 2010; Veldhuis, 2012). Exit programmes can be undertaken at different stages: to prevent imprisonment, during imprisonment or after imprisonment (Gielen, 2018a: 457). Based on the CVE prevention classification model (Gielen, 2017a), Dutch exit programmes fall in the secondary and tertiary category of CVE. Secondary prevention is aimed at preventing further radicalisation, tertiary prevention programmes are offered once someone has already engaged in acts of violent extremism, for example foreign fighters. Unlike secondary prevention, tertiary prevention is offered after criminal prosecution and possible imprisonment. So Dutch municipalities

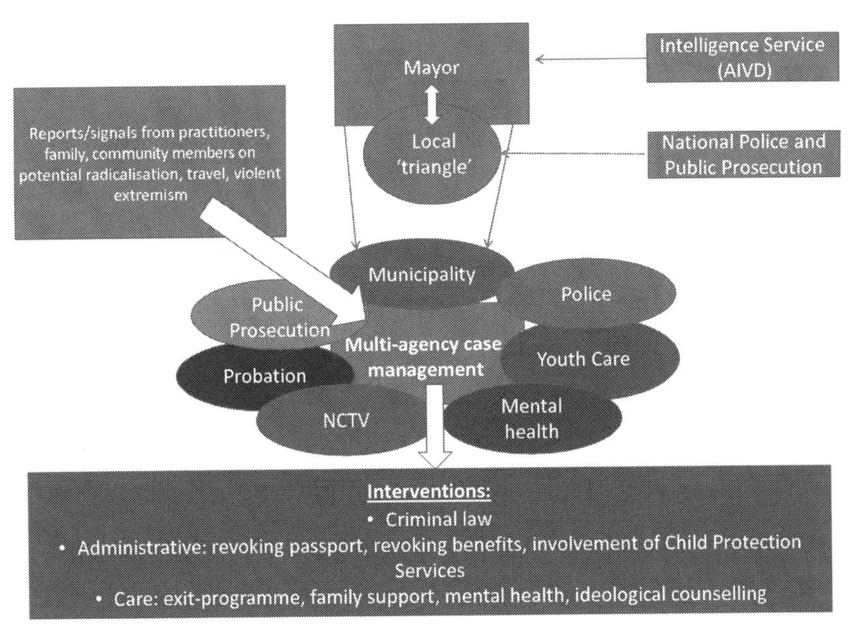

Figure 16.2 Dutch multi-agency approach. NCTV, Office of the National Coordinator for Security and Counter-terrorism.

Source: Gielen, 2015b.

are responsible for deradicalisation and disengagement (Gielen, 2018a: 457). However, they can also make use of national facilities that have been set up and/or funded by the NCTV: the TER team and Forsa. The TER (Terrorism, Extremism and Radicalisation) team is a reintegration programme of the Dutch Probation Service (Reclassering Nederland, RN) for convicted violent extremists and Forsa is a national voluntary exit outreach facility for radicalised individuals. The nature of these programmes will be addressed shortly, but for now it is important to know that municipalities can request the help of both the TER team and Forsa for the deradicalisation and disengagement of radicalised individuals in their municipalities. Some municipalities call upon their help, others do not, while some combine the TER or Forsa with their own local tailor-made exit programme. The above-mentioned factors make deradicalisation and disengagement in The Netherlands very complex, contextual and specific.

Effectiveness of the Dutch and Belgium exit approach

The Dutch AIVD as well as the NCTV report that most returnees remain active in the jihadist network upon return, because they are welcomed by the jihadist network with open arms and sucked back into the network (NCTV, 2016a). The AIVD (2016a) has also stated that single interventions, such as only revoking a passport, are ineffective, as individuals are likely to attempt to travel to ISIS territory a second and third time with either fake or alternative identification. So, the question is, are effective deradicalisation and disengagement at all possible and how should they be done?

There is very little empirical evidence on exit programmes in general, let alone in the Benelux. Based on the limited scientific evidence, the few empirical studies that have been conducted and practice-based experiences, such as for example collected by the EU

Radicalisation Awareness Network (RAN), some important lessons can be drawn. These lessons have been drawn up by Gielen (2017a, 2018a) and are reiterated in this section. El-Said (2012) reviewed several exit programmes around the globe and concluded that exit programmes must be tailor-made and take into account the contextual factors of each country, including culture, traditions, history and laws. The RAN, set up by the European Commission with at the time more than 2,000 practitioners working in CVE, has collected approaches and inspiring practices in CVE. Its collection of approaches and practices (Radicalisation Awareness Network, 2017), too, underlines that exit programmes should be tailor-made. It furthermore advises that exit programmes take a long-term approach and consist of multiple interventions aimed at the individual level via mentoring, psychological counselling, theological guidance and practical interventions such as provision of schooling and housing, as well as interventions aimed at the family level, such as family support. Furthermore, the *RAN Collection* underlines that exit programmes require a multi-agency approach, properly trained staff knowledgeable on the issue of violent extremism and specific competences in terms of, for example, relationship formation and communication skills.

Demant et al. (2008) similarly stressed the importance of an integral approach to deradicalisation and disengagement. In their opinion, exit programmes for jihadists focus too much on normative factors, concentrating on theological and ideological issues, and as a consequence overlook affective factors such as the family and peer network (ibid: 181). Demant et al. (ibid) argue that European exit programmes would benefit from a more comprehensive focus, dealing with all exit factors – normative, affective and practical – without favouring one factor over the others. This argument is also made in more recent studies on exit programmes (Koehler, 2016; Weggemans & De Graaf, 2017).

In sum, the success of an exit programme is dependent on the extent to which the exit programme is integral and holistic and addresses ideological, social and practical issues. The next sections will discuss the extent to which this is the case in the Benelux by discussing several evaluations (or the lack of them) in The Netherlands and Belgium.

Evaluations of the Dutch Probation Service

In 2012, the NCTV and the Dutch Probation Service developed a plan to improve the reintegration of extremist offenders in The Netherlands. The aim was to: (1) improve reintegration efforts of violent extremist prisoners whilst still in detention; (2) provide better aftercare upon their release; and (3) create a central and coordinated approach for dealing with violent extremists in the future (Schuurman & Bakker, 2016; Van der Heide & Schuurman, 2018).

This has led to the TER team being set up. The team has a legal mandate to work with people either suspected or convicted of offences related to violent extremism. The TER team becomes involved during a probationary sentence awaiting trial or after the sentence for violent extremism (related acts) is nearly finished and the individual is coming up for parole. The TER team conducts the same tasks as their "regular" probation colleagues: (1) making an assessment and reporting on the risk of recidivism; and (2) suggesting interventions to minimise recidivism and supervising individuals accordingly (ibid). To carry out these tasks, the TER team makes use of risk assessment tools (e.g. "RISc" and VERA-2R), protocols and guidelines on how to work with prisoners and probationers, as well as oversight measures such as electronic (GPS) monitoring systems (ibid).

The TER team differs from a regular Probation Service approach in the following aspects. First of all, the (suspected) violent extremist is supervised by two staff members in order to increase accuracy in conducting the risk assessment. Moreover, the team has meetings twice a week to exchange knowledge, share experiences and discuss best ways forward with a particular individual (ibid). Furthermore, members of the TER team, which now consists of 15 team members, have been extensively trained on violent extremism, ideology and conversation techniques (Reclassering Nederland, 2019).

Schuurman and Bakker (2016) conducted a process evaluation of the Dutch Probation Service and their TER team. They provide a process evaluation of the team concerned with the reintegration of formerly imprisoned violent extremists. Although this study cannot provide any hard conclusions on the effectiveness of the Probation Service in terms of deradicalisation and disengagement, the evaluation is particularly helpful in illustrating crucial contextual factors that influence the effectiveness of an exit programme. Relevant contextual conditions include managerial support for probation staff and good cooperation with other stakeholders such as municipalities. The process evaluation also highlighted a difference of opinion between the NCTV and the Probation Service about the theory of change and aim of the programme. The Probation Service mainly focused on behavioural aspects instead of also applying cognitive interventions. This also had implications for the ultimate goal of the programme, as the behavioural interventions can only achieve disengagement and not deradicalisation. The latter aim is a strong desire of the NCTV (ibid).

Van der Heide and Schuurman (2018) evaluated that same TER team two years later, but this time much more extensively with a theoretical evaluation, process evaluation and a qualified impact assessment of the reintegrate programme of the TER. This time they followed the programme for a 27-month period in which they interviewed 72 staff members, clients and stakeholders and the TER team responsible for 189 individuals. Whilst the evaluation results seem promising in the sense that the programme seems to consist of sound theory of change and terrorist-related recidivism is exceptionally low in comparison to regular Dutch recidivism figures, Van der Heide and Schuurman present the results with caution and disclaimers which underline the complexity of deradicalisation and disengagement and challenges related to their evaluation. First of all, no form of longitudinal structured risk assessment is applied, nor are recidivism rates collected after the oversight period by the Probation Service has ended. In the absence of these metrics, it means "effectiveness" is very much based on the (subjective) professional judgement by the TER team (ibid). As most individuals receive guidance from the TER team whilst they are awaiting their trial, one must always take into consideration that individuals have a vested interest in presenting a best (and disengaged) version of themselves (ibid).

The importance of context is reflected in the process evaluation, which highlights contextual factors that contribute to specific outcomes. Workload-induced stress, financial constraints and working with municipalities that were either less experienced with the issue of violent extremism or municipalities that followed their own specific course with a very different approach to deradicalisation and disengagement from the rest of the country (e.g. Amsterdam) were considered as limiting the effectiveness of the TER team. Working together in pairs to supervise individuals and having a psychologist for staff members to talk to were considered important contextual factors in the deradicalisation and disengagement efforts of the TER team (ibid).

Evaluation of the Dutch local exit approaches

Most municipalities have not evaluated their CVE programme let alone their deradicalisation and disengagement initiatives. To stimulate evaluation the NCTV has now developed an evaluation toolkit for municipalities (ESS, 2019). Gielen (2018c) has conducted an evaluation of the exit programme of one of the biggest cities in The Netherlands based on 19 case files. The municipality in question has set up a team of mentors/intervention providers who can be deployed in cases of violent extremism or (possible) radicalisation. This team consists of several professionals who have different kinds of backgrounds and who already work for or within the municipality (e.g. social services, youth care, employment office). They have received extensive training on violent extremism, jihadism and conversation techniques about goals in life and religion. They are capable of making assessments in cases of violent extremism and mentoring and providing interventions for (potential) violent extremists. The team is diverse in terms of gender, culture and religious background which means there is always someone available who fits the needs and background of the case at hand. The municipal intervention providers are made available one day a week from their regular work and are able to work on a case for a longer period of time. They have contact with the cases on a weekly basis and work on the basis of outreach in the sense that they (can) make home visits, and so on. The intervention providers receive individual coaching and participate in monthly intervision (a form of peer-to-peer learning) and also receive ongoing training (ibid).

Gielen concluded that a proper evaluation was not possible because the municipality in question did not make risk assessments of their cases, nor did they log their interventions.

Table 16.1 Evidence and practice-based model for the design of exit programmes.

- Exit requires a long-term and holistic approach that takes into account the push and pull factors, combining multiple interventions that activate different mechanisms. For example, such a programme might entail mentoring, practical support, family support, physical and psychological assessment and counselling and theological and ideological guidance
- The sequence of interventions in the exit programme is important and must be tailored to the needs of the individual. Practical interventions can help participants gain sufficient trust to move forward with other interventions. Creating a safe and stable family environment can be an important precondition to mentoring and learning self-reflection
- Creating an alternative social network is essential to compensate for loss of friends or brother- and sisterhood
- The success of an exit programme does not seem to be dependent on the size or experience of a municipality. Rather, it seems determined more by the extent to which the exit programme is integral and holistic and addresses normative, affective and practical issues
- The success of an exit programme is also dependent on the intervention provider. The ability to establish a trust-based relationship with the individual and the family and operate in a multi-agency setting is imperative. These elements are also acknowledged in the empirical small-scale pilot study ($n = 5$) of a deradicalisation programme conducted by Hallich and Doosje (2017). These authors emphasised that a successful exit depends not only on "best practices" but also on "best people". Establishing trust-based relationships between the intervention provider, the individual and the individual's family and being able to provide support in a multi-agency setting are crucial elements for exit programme success
- While a soft approach seems more promising, legal and administrative instruments can be helpful in creating the right conditions for exit. Specific conditions are: no contact with the former extremist network to prevent further grooming, a social media ban to prevent further grooming and involvement of Child Protection Services to enforce necessary changes in troubled home situations

Source: Evidence and practice-based model for the design of exit programmes.

A proper before-and-after measurement therefore was not possible (ibid). It seems that lack of documentation and structural risk assessment is representative for the situation in other municipalities too. Gielen has proposed how to conduct such evaluations of the Dutch municipal approaches in the future (Gielen, 2018a).

Evaluation of national exit facility Forsa

As part of the Integral Action Plan Jihadism (Ministerie van Veiligheid en Justitie et al., 2014) a national exit facility was set up in The Netherlands in October 2015. The facility is aimed at individuals with violent extremist attitudes who are or were involved in violent extremist networks. The exit facility was initially only aimed at people involved in jihadist networks but is now also aimed at right-wing extremists. Forsa works on an outreach basis, which enables them to work nationwide. They offer:

- critical reflection
- trauma counselling
- empowerment in dealing with the (former) extremist network
- stimulating societal participation
- help to improve family and social relations
- increasing resilience
- dealing with religious and existential questions (AEF, 2018).

In an evaluation (AEF, 2018), researchers concluded the following on the basis of case file analysis:

- 90% of clients who received a tailor-made exit programme no longer posed a risk in terms of violent extremist behaviour. In the remaining 10% it was hard to establish an effect.
- None of the clients travelled to a conflict zone after receiving an exit programme.
- No concerns have been raised by municipalities that individuals who have been helped have formed a (new) concern.
- No individuals have reapplied to the exit programme.

These results are the short-term outcomes on the basis of case file analyses. Only a longitudinal analysis in which the individuals are extensively monitored will be able to provide indications of the impact of Forsa.

Evaluation of the Belgium (exit) approach

Gielen (2018d) has drafted a road map for CVE evaluation in Belgium. As part of this road map she made an inventory of the attempts that were and are being undertaken to monitor and evaluate the Belgian CVE approach (including deradicalisation and disengagement) on a federal, regional and local level. She concludes that monitoring and evaluation are not systematic parts of Belgium CVE policy. However there have been several initiatives from a policy, civil society and academic level to conduct evaluation in the Belgian context. This section provides an overview of the CVE evaluation initiatives that have been undertaken by policy and academic actors and is based on the above-mentioned road map which was commissioned by the Open Society Foundation (ibid).

After the terrorist attacks on the Brussels underground and at Brussels airport in 2016 a Parliamentary Commission evaluated the Belgian CT approach and identified a number of shortcomings, one of them being the imbalance between prevention and repression (Renard & Coolsaet, 2018). The Federal Plan to counter terrorism and radicalisation, "Plan R", is continually evaluated but the results are not made public (Wittendorp et al., 2017). On a regional level, the Flemish Peace Institute has been commissioned by the Flemish Parliament to evaluate the local approaches in nine cities and municipalities (Flemish Parliament, 2018). This evaluation revolves around two questions: are the local measures in line with scientific knowledge and needs on the ground, and how are they implemented? This evaluation is a result of the Flemish Parliament placing the issue on the agenda by inviting academics to Parliament in 2017 and the Flemish Peace Institute editing a book *'De-radicalisation': Scientific Insights for Policy* (Colaert, 2017).

On a local level, the policy officers of most of the pilot cities (Antwerp, Vilvoorde, Mechelen, Brussels and Liege) state that evaluation has not been an integral part of their CVE programme. The cities were initially so overwhelmed by the flux of foreign fighters that they focused on controlling the situation and developing a CVE policy. Nevertheless, most cities have a form of monitoring via their LIVCs in which they discuss the up-to-date statistics (how many are radicalised, how many have travelled, how many have returned?) and discuss what interventions have been implemented for each. Two cities have CVE programmes that are embedded in a broader organisation/department and that have to comply with the monitoring and evaluation framework of that organisation/department. Consequently, one of the cities has to comply with a quarterly process evaluation in which they have to provide an update on what kinds of intervention have been organised. The other city's programme includes (impact) evaluation in the sense that effect measurements are undertaken before, during and after the intervention (Gielen, 2018d).

On an academic level the universities of Louvain (UCL), Brussels (VUB) and the National Institute of Criminalistics and Criminology (NICC) are collaborating in a research project called AFFECT. The objective of AFFECT is to assess the effectiveness of Belgian deradicalisation and CT policies and programmes and their impact on social cohesion and liberties. It aims to offer a comprehensive evaluation of the effectiveness of these policies in order to identify good practices, but also loopholes, gaps and duplication of effort.

Professor van San from the Erasmus University of Rotterdam recently published a report (Van San, 2018) in which she is very critical of the Flemish CVE policy. The report states that most policies and interventions are not aimed at preventing and countering violent extremism, but are focused on the detection of the phenomenon, which can have counterproductive effects such as first-line practitioners becoming the extended arm of security services. She questions the added value of CVE programmes as there is little to no scientific evidence that they are effective. Her critical analysis only highlights the need for more evaluation. The latter point has also been made by Belgian youth workers who are very critical of the report and do believe in the importance of Belgian CVE programmes (Struys, 2018).

Conclusion

This chapter has provided an overview of the broader national, (federal) and local CVE frameworks of which deradicalisation and disengagement programmes are part in The Netherlands and Belgium. It has illustrated that a local and multi-agency approach forms the cornerstone of both the Belgian and Dutch exit programmes. It has also shown that, due to the administrative complexity and the variety of tailor-made exit programmes, it is very difficult to assess the effectiveness of these programmes. There is no "one-size-fits-all" programme; rather deradicalisation and disengagement in the Benelux consist of a variety of local approaches. Thorough evaluation of deradicalisation and disengagement initiatives remains scarce in both countries, although The Netherlands has a slightly better track record than Belgium. That is due to the fact that these countries were overwhelmed by the foreign fighter phenomenon. All the attention went towards containing the problem instead of reflection and evaluation. The evaluations illustrate a variety of evaluation methods, e.g. interviews, case file analysis, document analysis, and so on. It is not possible to make statements about the effectiveness of the Dutch and Belgian deradicalisation and disengagement programmes.

The evaluations that have been conducted do however all highlight the importance of contextual factors that need to be taken into account, such as the importance of a multi-agency approach, funding and properly trained staff who can establish a trust-based relationship with individuals. More evaluations and specifically longitudinal evaluations in which (de)radicalised individuals are monitored for a longer period are crucial to gain more insight into effectiveness. This requires that municipalities invest much more in conducting thorough risk assessments before and after and log all the interventions they have provided to individuals with the aim of deradicalisation and disengagement.

Note

1 Luxembourg does have a CVE programme in place which is mostly executed by the Respect, the centre against radicalisation, founded mid-2017. Their annual report provides an overview of the activities: https://www.respect.lu/documents/Jahresbericht-2017-respect.lu-Centre-contre-la-radicalisation.pdf

References

AEF (2018). *Evaluatie Forsa en Familiesteunpunt*. The Hague: Andersson Elders Felix, 30 November 2018. Accessed via: https://www.nctv.nl/documenten/rapporten/2019/03/11/evaluatie-forsa-en-familiesteunpunt

AIVD (2016a). *Life with ISIS: The Myth Unravelled*. The Hague: AIVD. https://english.aivd.nl/publications/publications/2016/01/15/publication-life-with-isis-the-myth-unvravelled

AIVD (2019). "Uitreizigers en terugkeerders", *Hoeveel Nederlanders zijn uitgereisd naar een jihadistisch strijdgebied?* AIVD: 1 May 2019. www.aivd.nl/onderwerpen/terrorisme/dreiging/uitreizigers-en-terugkeerders

Aldrich, Daniel P. (2014). "First Steps Towards Hearts and Minds? USAID's Countering Violent Extremism Policies in Africa", *Terrorism and Political Violence*, Vol. 26 (3), pp. 523–546.

Belgium.be (2019). *De gemeenten*. Accessed via: https://www.belgium.be/nl/over_belgie/overheid/gemeenten

Colaert, Lore (2017). *'De-radicalisation'. Scientific Insights for Policy*. Brussels: Flemish Peace Institute.

Dalgaard-Nielsen, Anja (2013). "Promoting Exit from Violent Extremism: Themes and Approaches", *Studies in Conflict and Terrorism*, Vol. 36 (2), pp. 99–115.

Demant, Froukje, Marieke Slootman, Frank Buijs & Jean Tillie (2008). *Decline and Disengagement. An Analysis of Processes of Deradicalisation*. Amsterdam: IMES.

El-Said, Hamed (2012). *De-radicalising Islamists: Programmes and Their Impact in Muslim Majority States*. London: ICSR.

ESS (2019). *Toolkit Evidence Based Werken ter Preventie van Radicalisering*. Den Haag: Expertise-unit Sociale Stabiliteit, Ministerie van Sociale Zaken en Werkgelegenheid, 26 August 2019. Accessed via: Expertise-unit Sociale Stabiliteit, Ministerie van Sociale Zaken en Werkgelegenheid: https://www.socialestabiliteit.nl/si-toolkit

Flemish Parliament (2018). *Evaluatie van Vlaamse antiradicaliseringsbeleid*. 15 February 2018. Accessed via: https://vlaamsparlement.tv/evaluatie-van-het-vlaamse-antiradicaliseringsbeleid/

Gielen, Amy-Jane (2008). *Radicalisering en Identiteit. Radicaal rechtse en moslimjongeren vergeleken*. Amsterdam: Aksant.

Gielen, Amy-Jane (2015b). *Rol gemeenten in integrale aanpak radicalisering*. Den Haag: VNG, 2 June 2015. https://vng.nl/files/vng/publicaties/2015/20150528-gemeenten_en_radicalisering.pdf

Gielen, Amy-Jane (2017a). "Countering Violent Extremism. A Realist Approach for Assessing What Works, for Whom, in What Circumstances and How?", *Terrorism & Political Violence*, pp. 1147–1169. DOI: 10.1080/09546553.2017.1313736

Gielen, Amy-Jane (2018a). "Exit Programmes for Female Jihadists: A Proposal for Conducting a Realistic Evaluation of the Dutch Approach", *International Sociology*, pp. 454–472.

Gielen, Amy-Jane (2018c). *GER. Een methodiek- en procesbeschrijving*. Rotterdam: A.G. Advies, 18 September 2018.

Gielen, Amy-Jane (2018d). *Executive Summary. A Road Map for Monitoring and Evaluation of PVE policies in Belgium*. Brussels: Open Society Foundations.

Hallich, Benaissa & Bertjan Doosje (2017). *"DIAMANT-plus": een methodiek voor de- radicalisering en vergroting van weerbaarheid tegen extremistische invloeden*. Amsterdam: Universiteit van Amsterdam.

Horgan, John & Kurt Braddock (2010). "Rehabilitating the Terrorists?: Challenges in Assessing the Effectiveness of Deradicalisation Programs", *Terrorism and Political Violence*, Vol. 22 (2), pp. 267–291.

Koehler, Daniel (2016). *Understanding Deradicalization*. London: Routledge.

Lousberg, Maaike, Dianne van Hemert & Saar Langelaan (2009). *Ingrijpen bij radicalisering. De mogelijkheden van de eerstelijnswerker*. Soesterberg: TNO Veiligheid en.

Ministerie BZK (2007). *Actieplan polarisatie en radicalisering 2007–2011*. Den Haag: Ministerie van Binnenlandse Zaken en Koninkrijksrelaties.

Ministerie Veiligheid en Justitie (2012). *Nr. 213 Brief van de minister van Veiligheid en Justitie*. Den Haag: ministerie van Veiligheid en Justitie, 22 June 2012. Accessed via: https://zoek.officielebekendmakingen.nl/kst-29754-213.html

Ministerie van Veiligheid en Justitie; Nationaal Coördinator Terrorismebestrijding en Veiligheid and Ministerie van Sociale Zaken en Werkgelegenheid (2014). *Actieprogramma Integrale Aanpak Jihadisme*. Den Haag: Ministerie van Veiligheid en Justitie; Nationaal Coördinator Terrorismebestrijding en Veiligheid and Ministerie van Sociale Zaken en Werkgelegenheid, 29 August 2014. https://www.rijksoverheid.nl/documenten/rapporten/2014/08/30/actieprogramma-integrale-aanpak-jihadisme

NCTV (2012). *Samenvatting Dreigingsbeeld Terrorisme Nederland 28*. Den Haag: NCTV, 26 March 2012. Accessed via: https://www.nctv.nl/documenten/kamerstukken/2012/03/26/samenvatting-dreigingsbeeld-terrorisme-nederland-28

NCTV (2013). Samenvatting Dreigingsbeeld Terrorisme Nederland 32. Den Haag: NCTV, 13 March 2013. Accessed via: https://www.nctv.nl/documenten/kamerstukken/2013/03/13/samenvatting-dtn-32

NCTV (2016). *Samenvatting 'De jihad beëindigd? 24 teruggekeerde Syriëgangers in beeld'*. Den Haag: NCTV. www.nctv.nl/binaries/samenvatting-jihad-beeindigd-def_tcm31-32539.pdf

NCTV (2019). *Samenvatting dreigingsbeeld terrorisme Nederland 50*. Den Haag: NCTV, 24 June 2019. Accessed via: https://www.nctv.nl/documenten/publicaties/2019/6/24/samenvatting-dreigingsbeeld-terrorisme-nederland-50

Radicalisation Awareness Network (2017). *RAN Collection. Approaches and Best Practices* (4th edition). Brussels: RAN. https://ec.europa.eu/home-affairs/sites/homeaffairs/files/what-we do/networks/radicalisation_awareness_network/ran-best-practices/docs/ran_collection-approaches_and_practices_en.pdf

Reclassering Nederland (2019). *Aanpak Radicalisering*. Accessed via: https://www.reclassering.nl/samenwerken-met-de-reclassering/gemeenten/aanpak-radicalisering

Renard, Thomas & Rik Coolsaet (eds.) (2018). "Returnees: Who Are They, Why Are They (Not) Coming Back and How Should We Deal With Them? Assessing Policies on Returning Foreign Terrorist Fighters in Belgium, Germany and the Netherlands", *Egmont Paper* 101.

Schuurman, Bart & Edwin Bakker (2016). "Reintegrating Jihadist Extremists: Evaluating a Dutch Initiative, 2013–2014", *Behavioral Sciences of Terrorism and Political Aggression*, Vol. 8 (1), pp. 66–85.

Segers, Frank (2019). "Paul Van Tigchelt: 'Terugkerende IS-moeders geval per geval bekijken'", VRT homepage. 7 January. www.vrt.be/vrtnws/nl/2019/01/07/paul-van-tigchelt-terugkerende-is-moeders-geval-per-geval-beki/

Struys, Bruno (2018). "HulCVErleners betwisten vernietigend rapport: 'Wij geloven wél in deradicalisering'", *DeMorgen*, 13 December. www.demorgen.be/binnenland/hulCVErleners-betwisten-vernietigend-rapport-wij-geloven-wel-in-deradicalisering-bc343151/?referer=www.google.nl/url?sa=t&rct=j&q=&esrc=s&source=web&cd=1&ved=2ahUKEwiN85Kx44HgAhUBblAKHbgjCCkQFjAAegQIAhAB&url=https%253A%252F%252Fwww.demorgen.be%252Fbinnenland%252FhulCVErleners-betwisten-vernietigend-rapport-wij-geloven-wel-in-deradicalisering-bc343151%252F&usg=AOvVaw1F-Oqj_xKU8fRDWvEwnKza

Uitermark, Justus en Amy-Jane Gielen (2010). "Islam in the Spotlights. The Mediatisation of Politics in an Amsterdam Neighbourhood", *Urban Studies*, Vol. 47 (6), pp. 1325–1342.

Van Broeckhoven, Kato & Amy-Jane Gielen (2015). *Handvaten voor een lokale aanpak radicalisering*. Brussels: VVSG. www.vvsg.be/knowledgeitem_attachments/Handvaten-Lokale-Aanpak-Radicalisering-met-bijlagen.pdf

Van der Heide, Liesbeth & Bart Schuurman (2018). "Reintegrating Terrorists in the Netherlands: Evaluating the Dutch Approach", *Journal for Deradicalization*, 17 Winter 2018/2019, pp. 196–236.

Van Ginkel, Bibi & Eva Entenmann (2016). *The Foreign Fighters Phenomenon in the European Union*. The Hague: ICCT. www.nctv.nl/binaries/icct-report-foreign-fighters-phenomenon-full-version-including-annexes_tcm31-30169.pdf

Van Ostaeyen, Pieter & Guy Van Vlierden (2018). "Citizenship and Ancestry of Belgian Foreign Fighters", *ICCT Policy Brief*, May 2018. https://icct.nl/wp-content/uploads/2018/06/ICCT-Van-Ostaeyen-Van-Vlierden-Belgian-Foreign-Fighters-June2018.pdf

Van San, Marion (2018). *De onvoorspelbare terrorist: het 'magisch denken' over preventie van radicalisering en de mogelijkheden tot deradicalisering*. Brussels: Itinera. www.itinerainstitute.org/wp-content/uploads/2018/12/Rapport-radicalisering.pdf

Veldhuis, Tinka (2012). *Designing Rehabilitation and Reintegration Programmes for Violent Extremist Offenders: A Realist Approach*. The Hague: ICCT.

Vidino, Lorenzo (2007). "The Hofstad Group: The New Face of Terrorist Networks in Europe", *Studies in Conflict and Terrorism*, Vol. 30 (7), pp. 579–592.

Weggemans, Daan & Beatrice de Graaf (2017). *Reintegrating Jihadist Extremist Detainees – Helping Extremist Offenders Back into Society*. London: Routledge.

Wittendorp, Stef, Roel de Bont, Jeanine de Roy van Zuijdewijn en Edwin Bakker (2017). *Beleidsdomein aanpak jihadisme. Een vergelijking tussen Nederland, België, Denemarken, Duitsland, Frankrijk, het VK en de VS*. Leiden: Universiteit Leiden. www.universiteitleiden.nl/binaries/content/assets/governance-and-global-affairs/isga/rapport_beleidsdomein-aanpak-jihadisme_1.pdf

17

DESISTANCE AND DISENGAGEMENT PROGRAMME IN THE UK PREVENT STRATEGY

A public health analysis

Mohammed Samir Elshimi

Introduction

The purpose of this chapter is to examine the introduction of the Desistance and Disengagement Programme (DDP) in the Prevent strand of the UK's Counter-Terrorism Strategy (CONTEST). Little is known about DDP in the public domain and no academic investigation has been conducted to understand how it works and the impact it is having. This chapter therefore attempts to answer the following questions: Why has a counter-terrorism (CT) programme such as DDP been incorporated into a preventing and countering violent extremism (P/CVE) strategy such as Prevent? What does the emergence of DDP in the Prevent strand tell us about how Prevent is evolving?

A revised version of CONTEST was released in June 2018. CONTEST has undergone three iterations (2006, 2011, 2018) and comprises four pillars: Prevent, Pursue, Protect and Prepare. Prevent aims to 'safeguard and support vulnerable people to stop them from becoming terrorists or supporting terrorism' (HO 2018: 31) and is now in its fourth iteration (2006, 2009, 2011, 2018). The new element to Prevent 2018 was the integration of DDP under its purview (HO 2018: 40). DDP targets individuals already engaged in terrorism, who are required to disengage from terrorism and re-integrate back into society. DDP targets a wider category of persons than those convicted of terrorism, such as individuals who have not been convicted in court due to a lack of evidence but who are subject to court-approved restrictions, such as the Terrorism Prevention and Investigation Measures (TPIMS), and those who have returned from conflict zones in Syria or Iraq and are subject to Temporary Exclusion Orders (TEOs) (HO 2018: 40).

CONTEST 2018 states that DDP work complements the Pursue strand, which aims to stop terrorist attacks happening in the UK and overseas (HO 2018: 29). This move towards working across the four 'P' strands is framed as both natural and necessary considering the shift in threats facing the UK. The cross-fertilisation between Prevent and Pursue is also presented as an opportunity to make the Home Office's capabilities and resources increasingly interconnected, especially with respect to 'managing the risks from terrorist travellers and prisoners, and to multi-agency work' (Ibid).

However, preventive CT and DDP have conflicting logics. Prevent seeks to work with communities and individuals in the 'pre-criminal space' to prevent them from crossing over to terrorism or supporting terrorism. Although the term 'pre-criminal space' is not recognised in criminology and social science (Goldberg, Jadhav & Younis 2017; Heath-Kelly & Strausz 2018: 10), it nevertheless aptly encapsulates the tension inherent in a strategy eager to eschew criminalising individuals and communities on the one hand, while balancing this with the perceived need to provide corrective support on the other hand. In contrast to Prevent's pre-criminal work, programmes such as DDP operate in the post-criminal space and target individuals with a previous involvement in terrorism. These programmes are designed to ensure that individuals who previously contributed to terrorism do not return to such activities and are therefore reactive, not preventive. Since June 2018, then, Prevent – a pre-emptive strategy designed to reduce the risk of people turning to terrorism – is now also concerned with people already engaged with terrorism.

And yet at this point little is known about DDP and what the blurring between P/CVE (Prevent) and CT (Pursue) means in practice. No research has hitherto examined the integration of DDP into Prevent. The lack of research on DDP is significant given that keeping the public safe is a priority for policymakers, and that de-radicalising Islamic State returnees and prisoners (sentenced under the Terrorism Act 2000 and its successors, and known as TACT offenders) is a pressing political and security issue that attracts a lot of media and public attention. In addition, the programme is currently undergoing a transition between piloting phase and having to expand rapidly (HO 2018: 40); it has to deal with scores of TACT offenders who are coming to the end of their sentences and who will re-join society; it also has to contend with the presence of various offenders with different forms of licensing arrangements and the wider issue of rehabilitating fighters, women and children linked to the Islamic State. A failure, then, to understand DDP and how it fits into Prevent can potentially lead to ill-informed policy decisions.

This chapter makes three arguments. The first is that the literature has not fully explored the implications of having a post-criminal CT programme integrated into the UK Prevent strategy. The second is that it is more intelligible to understand the incorporation of DDP into Prevent through the conceptual framework of the Public Health Model (PHM). The use of the PHM has recently gained prominence in the literature on P/CVE (Aly, Balbi & Jacques 2015; Bhui & Jones 2017; Challgren et al. 2016; Sumpter 2017; Weine, Eisenman, Kinsler, Glik & Polutnik 2017) but has not yet been applied to the analysis of Prevent in the UK. Seen therefore through the PHM framework, the inclusion of interventions that evince a rehabilitative logic within Prevent 2018 must be understood as an attempt to address different levels of risk. The incorporation of DDP under Prevent also indicates that the Prevent delivery model is being restructured in the image of the PHM.

The third argument is that, rather than being something entirely new, the advent of DDP in Prevent 2018 represents rather a culmination of longer historical trends, in which responses to terrorism have become increasingly medicalised. The medicalisation of terrorism has expanded the medical gaze to include an ever-growing category of persons within the purview of CT, as well as individualising, pathologising and de-politicising Prevent's responses to terrorism.

This chapter is divided into the following sections. The next section examines what is known about DDP in the literature and identifies the pre-existing limitations of trying to analyse DDP through the existing literature on Prevent. The second section introduces the PHM and how the literature has treated the role of public health approaches in relation to P/CVE. In the third section Prevent is situated in a historical context in order to highlight its evolution and how it has reconfigured its activities, over the years, in the paradigmatic image of the PHM. The section after applies the PHM framework to Prevent and attempts to demonstrate that Prevent fits well into the PHM. Lastly, the implications of viewing Prevent through the PHM is analysed through the concept of 'medicalisation' and explores what this means for current Prevent practices.

DDP, de-radicalisation and Prevent

Little is known about DDP in the public domain, except for what is conveyed in Prevent. A freedom of information request by the *Guardian* newspaper to the Home Office revealed that 116 people were subject to the DDP between October 2016 and September 2018 (Grierson 2019). Due to the sensitive nature of DDP work and the fact that the programme has not fully matured yet, details of individuals and organisations selected to deliver interventions are not known. In addition, data on how DDP operates in practice, how it interacts with the rest of Prevent work and an understanding of the impact it is having is not available.

Prevent 2018 does not define several key terms associated with DDP, such as 'desistance', 'disengagement', 're-integration' and 'rehabilitation'. Although these terms are often employed interchangeably, they nonetheless connote subtle conceptual and operational differences, which in practice impact the approach taken by rehabilitation programmes. Many European governments employ the terms 'de-radicalisation' and 'disengagement' to refer to the process of moving away from terrorism, whereas the terms 're-integration' and 'rehabilitation' refer to the aims of such interventions (RAN 2017: 43). In the literature, 're-integration', which is often synonymous with 'rehabilitation', is understood as a safe transition to the community, by which individuals proceed to live a law-abiding life following their release and acquire attitudes and behaviours that generally lead to productive functioning in society (Veldhuis 2012: 2). The use of these terms to distinguish between the process and objective of programmes echoes Prevent's use of the terms, where the objective of DDP is 'rehabilitation', with 'desistance' and 'disengagement' denoting the process itself (HO 2018: 40).

It is significant that Prevent frames its terrorist rehabilitation programme as 'desistance and disengagement' and not 'de-radicalisation', not least because DDP measures include mentoring, psychological support and theological and ideological advice, all of which are components of a typical de-radicalisation intervention (HO 2018: 40). Prevent, notably, alludes to 'de-radicalisation mentors' once, but not to de-radicalisation programmes/interventions (HO 2018: 50). De-radicalisation is commonly conceptualised as a social and psychological process that results in attitudinal change, effectively reducing an individual's commitment to the belief that personal involvement in violence is necessary and justified (Schuurman & Bakker 2016: 3). Key to understanding the concept of de-radicalisation is the notion of a cognitive shift and the use of counter-ideology and theological deconstruction in inducing a fundamental change in behaviour.

However, Prevent's reticence to employ the term 'de-radicalisation' can be attributed to the conceptual and practical challenges inherent in the concept. De-radicalisation is criticised for its emphasis on belief change, because it represents a reductive conceptualisation of the process and posits an intervention objective that diverts resources away from more realistic policy aims. Conceptually, it also excludes the dynamic interplay between various non-ideational factors involved in the process of leaving terrorism behind (Bjorgo & Horgan 2009; Ferguson 2016; Horgan 2008). Research, for example, emphasises that ideational and ideological factors play little or no role in persuading individuals to enter or leave such groups and movements (Bjorgo 2009: 36–40).

The term de-radicalisation is also seen as problematic in liberal democratic societies because of the implicit implication that the state is interested in regulating the beliefs and views of its citizens (Elshimi 2017: 60–61). De-radicalisation, then, is not merely about reducing the risk of terrorism and ideological transformation but is also about normative change; participants' pre-intervention worldview is not only construed as being risky, but it is also assumed to be wrong. De-radicalisation therefore suggests that intervention participants should adopt a preferred ideational worldview.

Historically, in the UK, the meaning and practice of de-radicalisation have evolved over the last 12 years. Between 2006 and 2010, de-radicalisation was used as a broad catch-all term to encompass different-but-related methods and techniques aimed at reducing society's risk from terrorism, such as 'countering violent extremism' and 'preventing violent extremism' (Elshimi 2017). In other words, the UK Prevent strategy was synonymous with the term 'de-radicalisation'. De-radicalisation was subsequently employed as a concept to describe the police-administered and multi-agency referral mechanism, the Channel programme, between 2011 and 2015 (Home Office 2011: 65) – an association that was only severed after the Prevent Duty became statutory law in 2015 and when Channel re-framed itself as a safeguarding programme. It is for these, and the above reasons, that policymakers prefer to brand Prevent's post-criminal rehabilitation work as 'desistance and disengagement programmes' rather than 'de-radicalisation', even though de-radicalisation work appears to be taking place in DDP.

Equally important, it is not clear how 'desistance' is distinguished from 'disengagement' in Prevent 2018. It is notable that 'desistance' from terrorism does not appear to be used anywhere else in the world except the UK, and actually has a longer track record in offenders' programmes in the UK than 'disengagement' (Dean 2016; Marsden 2017; McNeil 2005). Christopher Dean, who designed an offender's programme called the 'Healthy Identity Intervention' (HII), claims that the programme was not referred to as de-radicalisation or disengagement because of concerns surrounding the terms' applicability to other offending behavioural programmes in prison (Dean 2016: 27, footnote 21). The primary goal of HII is to facilitate desistance, which may require changes to personal identity, thinking, behaviour and relationships (Dean 2016: 27, footnote 21). Desistance, simply, denotes the process by which individuals cease criminal activity or offending (Altier, Thoroughgood & Horgan 2014: 17).

According to Dean's conception, then, desistance may be commensurate with the goals of de-radicalisation and disengagement but not reduced to either. Disengagement is not considered necessary for desistance to occur, especially temporary or even lifelong desistance, which may require identity change (Dean 2016: 27, footnote 21). In the literature, disengagement is the process whereby an individual undergoes a change in role or function that is usually associated with a reduction of violent participation. It may not necessarily involve leaving the movement but is most frequently associated with significant temporary or permanent role change. Additionally, while disengagement may stem from role change, that role change may be influenced by psychological factors such as disillusionment, burnout or the failure to reach the expectations that influenced initial involvement (Horgan 2009a: 152). In relation to Prevent, 'desistance' seems to refer to the cessation of terrorist activity, while the ideological dimension of terrorism is confusingly subsumed by the term 'disengagement', and not the usual term 'de-radicalisation'.

Significantly, research has not been conducted on DDP. Most of the scholarship treats de-radicalisation, disengagement, desistance, re-integration and rehabilitation programmes through the lens of CT *and not* how they operate in a preventive pre-criminal strategy like Prevent. This body of work primarily examines these programmes in prisons with the view of reducing the risk of terrorism (Silke 2013). Attention has primarily focused on descriptive case studies of programmes in different countries (Ashour 2009; Bjorgo & Horgan 2009a; El-Said 2012; Horgan 2009b; Horgan et al. 2010; Khalil et al. 2019; Sukabdi 2015); the process of leaving terrorism behind (Alonso 2011; Ashour 2009; Altier, Boyle, Shortland & Horgan 2017; Bjorgo & Horgan 2009; Clubb 2017; Ferguson 2016; Hwang 2017; Reinares 2011); the efficacy of programmes (Cherney 2018; Koehler 2017; Schuurman & Bakker 2016; Veldhuis 2016; Webber et al. 2017); the re-integration of extremist offenders back into society (Barrelle 2015; Marsden 2017; Weggemans & De Graaf 2017); the modelling of de-radicalisation pathways (Altier et al. 2014; Barrelle 2015; Harris, Gringart & Drake 2017); and conceptual and terminological issues (Horgan 2008; Schmid 2013).

Meanwhile, the literature on Prevent has addressed the development of the strategy in the pre-criminal, and not in the post-criminal space. Prevent has been critiqued for enabling the performance of state sovereignty (Heath-Kelly 2013); creating a spatial pre-criminal geography of detection (Heath-Kelly 2017b); creating suspect communities (Pantazis & Pemberton 2009); delegating the responsibility of surveillance to self-policed communities (Ragazzi 2016); securitising health (Heath-Kelly 2017a), education (Durodie 2016; McGovern 2017; O'Donnell 2015) and citizenship (Jarvis & Lister 2015); using counter-insurgency to manage British Muslim populations (Sabir 2017); undermining community cohesion policies (Thomas 2015); depoliticising and delegitimising dissent (Kundnani 2009); straining community–police relations (Innes, Roberts, Innes, Lowe & Lakhani 2011), re-configuring domestic multiculturalism (Brighton 2007); and suppressing and asserting new forms of identity (Elshimi 2017; Martin 2014).

There has been limited treatment of the concept and practice of de-radicalisation in the pre-criminal space in the wider P/CVE literature. The most relevant contributions have come from works that employ a Foucauldian analysis, in which P/CVE is viewed through the prism of governmentality. Lindekilde (2012, 2015) and Elshimi's works (2015, 2017), for example, argue that de-radicalisation practices in P/CVE aim at regulating the ideational boundaries of the nation-state and the conduct of citizens in European societies. While these works engage critically with the concept and practice of de-radicalisation, they do so in relation to P/CVE and not specially with respect to how de-radicalisation in the post-criminal space operates in the context of P/CVE.

While both academic communities have significantly contributed to the scholarly understanding of rehabilitation programmes in the post-criminal space on the one hand, and Prevent in the pre-criminal space on the other hand, the knowledge of behavioural change programmes, which are designed to mitigate the risk of terrorism in the P/CVE and CT fields, has nevertheless developed along mutually exclusive lines. Research has thus not yet investigated what the adoption of DDP within Prevent entails and what the implication of this move in British CT means.

The Public Health Model

One promising avenue that allows us to understand the adoption of DDP within the Prevent paradigm can be found in the burgeoning prominence of the PHM in the classification of P/CVE (Aly et al. 2015; Bhui & Jones 2017; Challgren et al. 2016; Sumpter 2017; Weine et al. 2017). Public health approaches have been applied to violence prevention in general (Mitton, 2019) and to behaviours such as suicide, drug taking, crime and now, also, to radicalisation and terrorism. According to the World Health Organization public health refers to:

> all organized measures (whether public or private) to prevent disease, promote health, and prolong life among the population as a whole. Its activities aim to provide conditions in which people can be healthy and focus on entire populations, not on individual patients or diseases. Thus, public health is concerned with the total system and not only the eradication of a particular disease.
>
> *(World Health Organization 2016: 9)*

The PHM refers to the study of 'the distribution and determinants of health-related states or events and the application of this study to the control of diseases and other health problems' (WHO). It relies on a three-pronged approach of identification, interruption and behavioural change (Riemann 2019: 147). The PHM tries to collate data on contagious areas, communities, spaces and individuals in order to map and localise populations at 'risk' and 'vulnerable' to disease. It classifies the population into three levels that correspond to varying degrees of risk: the 'primary level' refers to the pre-risk stage among the generation population; the 'secondary level' refers to individuals and communities at risk of radicalisation; and the 'tertiary level' comprises individuals and groups who actually have the 'disease'.

The PHM is appealing for some academics and practitioners working in P/CVE because it offers a coherent, structured and multi-pronged approach to identifying and responding to different types of risk among populations. For Bhui and Jones (2017), public health approaches improve the understanding of radicalisation pathways because they seek to understand the social and psychological conditions and promote interest in protective factors. For Hardcastle et al. (2019), public health approaches afford other ways of addressing the problem of terrorism beyond the conventional criminal justice approach to CT. Weine et al. (2017: 210) identify a gap in social services for those at-risk for terrorism who have not yet committed a crime. The pre-criminal space of the P/CVE field becomes their public health focus. The PHM is therefore seen as a way of limiting the use of law enforcement in P/CVE and reducing the stigma associated with it. The PHM also encourages commitment to improving the monitoring and evaluation of programmes, leveraging existing public health resources, as well as promoting multi-sectorial cooperation (Mitton 2019: 136).

Other scholars have critiqued the deployment of the PHM to address terrorism and other forms of violence (Aggarwal 2018; Heath-Kelly 2017b; Riemann 2019). Neil Aggarwal (2018) argues that the American Government is using public health systems to extend the net of surveillance to a wider population (Aggarwal 2018: 4). According to Aggarwal, public health screening assumes that clinical procedures can detect risk factors for an illness whose early detection leads to effective interventions (Aggarwal 2018: 2). He also claims that there is a danger of health professionals becoming co-opted into the American Government's security agenda and that the health system risks serving governments by sequestering populations that are deemed undesirable at the expense of promoting the health interests of individuals. Aggarwal's analysis does not evaluate the effectiveness of the PHM and is based on a critical analysis of a few public documents, but it does draw our attention to the challenges that arise from the deployment of the PHM in P/CVE.

Only a couple of scholars have drawn parallels between public health approaches and the delivery of UK Prevent (Goldberg et al. 2017; Heath-Kelly 2017b). Heath-Kelly (2017b) argues that Prevent under the Labour Government (2006–2010) borrowed from historical models of public health to imagine radicalisation risk as an epidemiological concern in areas showing a 2% or higher demography of Muslims (p. 298). She lays out the public health 'geography' characterising UK Prevent and how it was constituted around notions of proximity and contagion. According to Heath-Kelly, tertiary level interventions were considered preventive rather than punitive because the judicial response to crime aimed at the reduction of recidivism through the separation of offenders from the population (imprisonment), rehabilitation programmes and treatment programmes for addiction (p. 303).

While Heath-Kelly draws our attention to the geographical and epistemological shifts in the deployment of the UK Prevent strategy between 2007 and 2017, she nevertheless wrote her article at a time when there were no tertiary level interventions in the UK. This explains why her reference to tertiary level interventions was vague, describing it in a generic way, without pinning her analysis to a specific example (p. 306). Heath-Kelly also presents tertiary level interventions in the UK as eliding with secondary level interventions, encapsulated in Channel's rehabilitative work (p. 304). Importantly, however, she argues that early iterations of Prevent were premised on public health approaches, as well as the pre-profiling of suspect communities. For Heath-Kelly, Prevent 2011 marked the move away from the deductive logic of public health approaches and towards the adoption of modern surveillance techniques based on inductive big data logic. While she presents a compelling case, this article argues instead that it is not until the introduction of DDP in Prevent in 2018 that Prevent can be said to have fully restructured itself in the image of the PHM. In other words, Prevent has been gradually evolving in the direction of the PHM and has not moved away from it.

Hardcastle et al.'s study (2019) examines the challenges facing Prevent and highlights the criticism it has received, the lack of an evidence-base underpinning its interventions and the lack of rigorous evaluations (p. 58). For these authors, the real strength of the public health approach is its ability to address individual and community level risk and protective factors by adopting early interventions and utilising multi-disciplinary and multi-agency approaches (p. 62). They argue that public health approaches could address the multiple risk factors that contribute to terrorism – poverty, inequality, isolation, abusive childhoods, difficulties with identity and mental ill health. They also claim that Prevent has failed to adopt a personal life course history approach, which would enable Prevent practitioners to identify when and how an individual becomes vulnerable to terrorism (p. 61).

Hardcastle et al.'s analysis exaggerates the extent to which Prevent specifically, and P/CVE more generally, has developed according to a criminal justice framework, while understating the increasing prominence of public health approaches in Prevent. Prevent, for example, already uses the language of vulnerability and risk; targets community resilience; acknowledges the multiple factors of radicalisation; has due regard for mental health issues; targets different forms of terrorism; and uses multi-agency approaches to identify individuals in need of support. This article does not advocate that Prevent adopts public health approaches, but argues, instead, that the PHM represents a useful conceptual framework for understanding the emergence of DDP in Prevent, while also underscoring the shift of the Prevent delivery model towards the PHM.

Prevent: a strategy in evolution

To appreciate the subtle conceptual, spatial and operation shifts taking place in the delivery of Prevent, it is useful to situate Prevent in a historical context. CONTEST was developed according to principles found in risk management frameworks (Omand 2010). The architect of CONTEST, Sir David Omand, highlighted the importance of using risk management principles to reduce the security threat:

> the aim has to be to take sensible steps to reduce the risk to the public at home and to our interests overseas, on the principle known in risk management as ALARP, to a level as low as is reasonably practicable.
>
> *(Omand 2010: 93)*

The influence of risk management on the Prevent strategy is reflected in its aim, which does not seek to eliminate terrorism or bring it to an end, but to 'reduce the risk' of terrorism (HO 2018: 8). The term 'prevent', which describes preventive counter-terrorism, is a misnomer, given that UK Prevent has been driven by a pre-emptive logic. Pre-emption is different from prevention. Pre-emption can be understood as a forceful intervention aiming to neutralise an imminent threat from materialising (Massumi 2007). The notion is encapsulated in military doctrines that propose that threats should be neutralised as soon as possible by seeking to strike first so that the enemy cannot attack. Crucially, pre-emptive logic in the sphere of politics is shaped more by the realm of imagination and the imperative of averting the worst-case scenario from happening (Massumi 2005). While pre-emption is less concerned with facts and empirical data, preventive logic is rooted in the principle that policy objectives are based on data and facts (Massumi 2007).

In the political sphere governed by a pre-emptive logic, risk becomes based on the social construction of what the culture determines to be a threat (Githens-Mazer 2012). In 2006, the imperative for Prevent arose in response to blowback from the Iraq War and the threat of terrorism emanating from second- and third-generation British Muslims. This threat became articulated in the concept of 'radicalisation', which consequently justified mass-scale interventions in segments of the population through Prevent (Elshimi 2017). Prevent was thus concerned with re-engineering Muslim communities in order to govern ungoverned spaces in the country (Martin 2014), colonise an unknown future and, as a result, bring a new future into existence (Massumi 2005: 6), one in which radicalisation is drastically reduced to an acceptable level. It is in this sense that Prevent could be said to be governed more by a pre-emptive logic than a preventive one.

Prevent also exhibits a pre-emptive logic due to the challenges of identifying positive cases of terrorist profiles. The absence of a terrorist profile makes it difficult to predict which high-risk individuals will turn to terrorism in the pre-criminal space. As a result, the first two iterations of Prevent (2006–2010) attempted to map the spatial configuration of British Muslim communities in order to locate the perceived threat of radicalisation (Heath-Kelly 2017b). Funding was distributed according to the population size of Muslim communities in a locality (HO 2006, 2009; HC 2010: 50): areas with populations over 5% Muslims in the first iteration (2006) and over 2% in the second (2009). At the time, the Department for Communities and Local Government (DCLG) was responsible for delivering Prevent through the distribution of funds to local organisations and charities across the country.

During these years, Prevent was comprised almost entirely of primary level interventions. Channel, a secondary level intervention, was still a pilot project and had not been rolled out nationally yet. Tertiary level intervention was not a feature of the strategic vision of Prevent. Based on fragmented literature, we know that as early as 2007 the National Offender Management Service (NOMS) endeavoured to develop interventions targeting the drivers of radicalisation in prisons (HO 2011: 88; Spalek, Lambert & El-Awa 2008: 45–46). In 2011, under the Coalition Government, Prevent officially rolled out the Channel programme, marking the emergence of secondary level interventions (HO 2011: 65). Channel, which is a platform in which information is shared among experts from different disciplines, embodies the multi-agency approaches promoted by public health approaches. Multi-agency approaches involve representatives from a plurality of municipal agencies and local organisations – education, health, social welfare, youth, police and corrections – meeting on a regular basis for the identification, development and delivery of interventions to benefit individuals referred to the unit. Rather than focusing on the stigmatising issue of violent extremism, Channel in 2011 was framed as a programme designed to provide 'support to vulnerable people' (HO 2011: 65).

Prevent 2011 was organised around three 'Is': ideas, individuals and institutions (HO 2011). 'Ideas' referred to the objective of countering Islamist ideology; 'individuals' denoted that the strategy focused on supporting vulnerable individuals 'at risk' of radicalisation, while 'institutions' referred to the way that state institutions were tasked with the responsibility of identifying individuals at risk of radicalisation. The responsibility for delivering was also taken away from DCLG and given to the Office for Security and Counter-Terrorism (OSCT) at the Home Office, indicating the growing centralisation of Prevent operations and the relegation of local approaches and the disentanglement of community cohesion policy from Prevent (Elshimi 2017: 146). With the development of secondary level interventions and the centralisation of Prevent there was thus an evolution in its scope, language and delivery mechanism.

With Prevent 2011, however, we see the first indications that tertiary level prison interventions were being developed. Prevent 2011 stated that 'progress has been slower' due to the lack of 'proven methodology' and the lack of templates to develop interventions from (HO 2011: 89), although national implementation was planned for 2012. One of the goals of Prevent 2011 was 'significantly scaling up' de-radicalisation interventions in prisons. By 2012, there were two intervention programmes in prisons for extremist offenders – the Healthy Identity Intervention and Al Furqan (Dean 2016; PSJ 2012: 31). But beyond descriptive and fragmented references to prison de-radicalisation, Prevent did not officially have a prison de-radicalisation programme. It was not until 2018, then, that we see the advent of tertiary level interventions in the form of DDP.

The passing of the Counter-Terrorism and Security Bill of February 2015 that enshrined the Prevent Duty in statutory law was a critical watershed moment in the development of Prevent. The Act made it a legal requirement for specified authorities to have due regard to the need to prevent people from being drawn into terrorism. Firstly, it led to a huge spike of referrals to Channel after 2015. In the year 2017/18, for example, a total of 7,318 individuals were subject to a referral (HO 2018b), whereas between 2007 and 2010 only 1,120 individuals were referred to Channel (HO 2011: 59). Secondly, it led to Prevent being reframed as a 'safeguarding' strategy in Prevent 2018 (HO 2018: 31). Safeguarding is a measure used by local authorities to intervene in vulnerable people's lives (children, young people and vulnerable adults) to protect them from physical, sexual or criminal abuse (DHSC 2018). In Prevent, safeguarding is framed as a form of protection against terrorism, in which radicalisation is compared to a form of grooming, whereby an abuser exerts control over a victim. Potential terrorists are now seen as individuals who are vulnerable to ideological indoctrination on the one hand and a potential danger to the public on the other hand.

While the adoption of DDP in 2018 indicated the turning point in which Prevent reconfigures itself in the paradigmatic image of the PHM, there have been several other developments historically with the delivery of Prevent that underscore the adoption of public health approaches. Although the PHM is often invoked to promote more universal and upstream approaches in policy, many of its other core aspects, such as multi-disciplinary and multi-agency work, identifying the multifaceted nature involved in behaviour change, improving the protective factors and reducing the risk factors at the individual level, now characterise the work taking place in Prevent.

Classifying Prevent through the Public Health Model

Prevent 2018 has three objectives, illustrated in the following model:

1. Tackle the causes of radicalisation and respond to the ideological challenge of terrorism.
2. Safeguard and support those most at risk of radicalisation through early intervention, identifying them and offering support.
3. Enable those who have already engaged in terrorism to disengage and rehabilitate.

Instead of the Prevent delivery model depicted in Figure 17.1, it is more fruitful to situate the inherent paradox of having DDP localised in a Prevent strategy through the lens of a PHM framework. Figure 17.2 is an adapted version of the PHM and reveals in more detail how the PHM frames the P/CVE field.

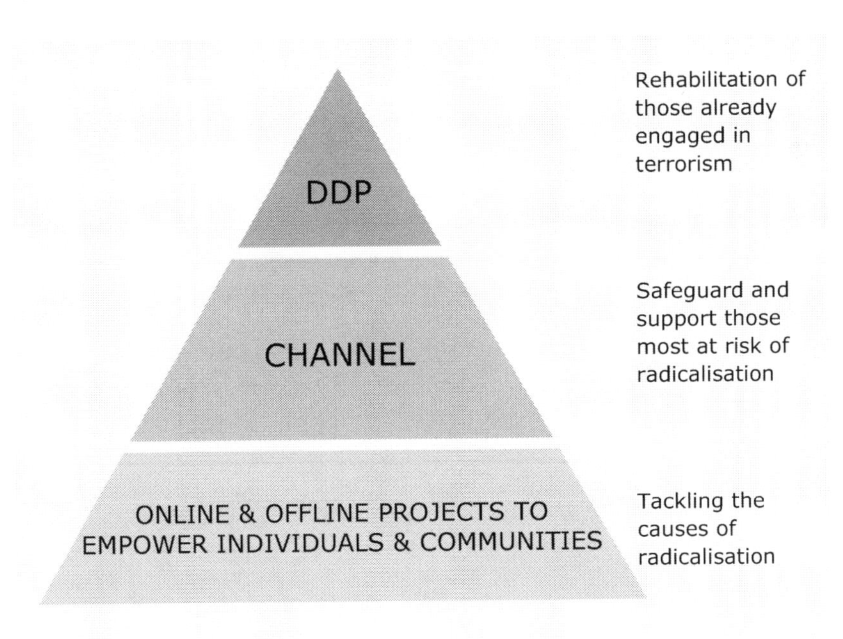

Figure 17.1 Prevent Delivery Model. DDP, Desistance and Disengagement Programme.
Source: Adapted from CONTEST 2018, p. 32.

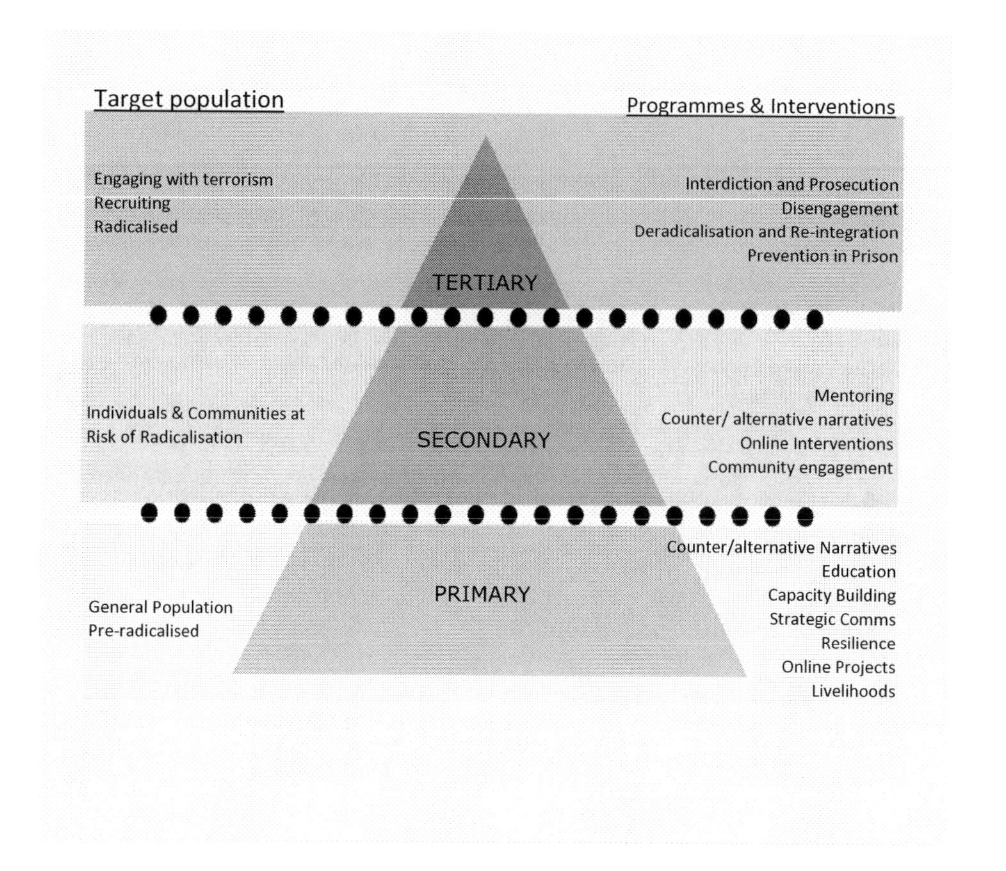

Figure 17.2 Public Health Model (PHM).
Source: Adapted from Challgren et al. 2016, p. 17.

The PHM not only represents the Prevent delivery model more accurately but also reflects the evolution of the Prevent strategy. The difference is that, while the Prevent strategy does not see itself in the PHM mould – there are no references, for example, to it in CONTEST – it has nonetheless inadvertently reconfigured its delivery model in the paradigmatic image of the PHM.

Following the emergence of DDP in 2018, Prevent is now organised according to three levels. The primary level describes broad-based, mass prevention programmes that target the general population. Interventions at this level aim to address the causes of radicalisation. Activities at this level focus on awareness raising, delegitimising terrorism and equipping individuals and communities with the skills to mitigate the threat of radicalisation. These include strategic communication and counter-narratives, community-based interventions, educational initiatives, social activities, skills development and capacity building. The communication aspect of primary interventions includes removing extremist content online by the Internet Referral Unit (HO 2018: 35), as well as various types of products produced by the Research, Information and Communications Unit (RICU) at the Home Office. The goal at the primary level is articulated in terms of building individual and communal 'resilience' against radicalisation (Edwards 2016; HO 2018: 33).

Secondary level interventions refer to tailor-made activities that target 'at-risk' populations/individuals. The aim is to prevent the progression of radicalisation and reduce the potential for future radicalisation. At this level, activities include mentoring, psycho-social support and counter-messaging (both offline and online). In the UK, secondary level interventions refer to the Channel programme, a voluntary initiative delivered through a multi-agency approach. Channel has Prevent coordinators working across local authorities and some of the police forces. Channel performs the role of a referral mechanism and 'conduit' between local authorities, various sectors of the state and intervention providers. A multi-agency panel meets regularly to review referrals, conduct a risk assessment and make decisions about each case, including whether to assign the individual to an intervention provider. Often, 'support' here means that the individual is assigned a mentor (Elshimi 2017; Thornton & Bouhana 2017).

The tertiary level describes tailor-made activities targeting radicalised individuals, those engaging with terrorism who have not been convicted, as well as those convicted of a terrorism offence. The aim is to stop and prevent various type of offenders from supporting and re-engaging with terrorism, as well as supporting their re-integration back to normal life. DDP has been running in pilot through 2017 and 2018 and plans to expand in 2019. In contrast to Prevent's Channel programme, participation in DDP is mandatory. Interventions include counter-theology/counter-ideology which involves theological refutation of ideas, undertaken either by a mentor or an imam; mentoring, which involves providing pastoral support and guidance to participants, as well as counter-ideology; psychological support through assessment, counselling and therapy; and, where possible, supporting their 'universal needs for identity, self-esteem, meaning and purpose' (HO 2018: 40).

Prevent: medicalising counter-terrorism

Medicalisation refers to 'a process by which nonmedical problems become defined and treated as medical problems, usually in terms of illness and disorders' (Conrad 2007: 4). Medicalisation compares terrorism to a disease. With the inclusion of DDP at the tertiary level, the medical gaze has extended not only to those who have the disease of violent extremism to various degrees, and hence must be cured, but also to a new category of unknown threat embodied by men, women and children linked to the Islamic State, as well as those who have not been convicted in court, but who are subject to licensing conditions. This extension of the medical gaze is also evidenced by the growing preoccupation at the tertiary level with the re-integration of ex-offenders into society, and concerns about potential recidivism in the future. Combining the target populations of primary, secondary and tertiary level interventions reveals the vast scope of surveillance of human life that is subjected to the medical gaze, regulation and behavioural correction under the Prevent infrastructure. This is represented in the adaptation of the 'career terrorist' model set out by Horgan and Taylor (2015: 179), shown below.

I. 'pre-radicalised' individuals
II. vulnerable individuals
III. extremism (non-violent advocates of extreme change)
IV. radicalisation (involvement with terrorism)
V. violent radicalisation (engagement with terrorism)
VI. desistance and disengagement
VII. de-radicalisation
VIII. reintegration and rehabilitation
IX. recidivism (?).

Another example of the medicalisation of Prevent is seen in the way it now defines itself as a 'safeguarding and support' strategy. Although the Prevent Duty of 2015 introduced the notion of safeguarding, it was not until 2018 that Prevent defined its remit in terms of protection against terrorism, as well as support for terrorism. This conception of Prevent as a strategy that provides protection to vulnerable people is new and softens the implication of this subtle change. By transforming itself into a safeguarding strategy, Prevent has legitimised the power to monitor and regulate the various spaces and institutions of the state, as well as intervene against signs of potential radicalisation at a population scale level. The UK remains the only nation in the world to deliver CT within its education and healthcare and social care sectors as safeguarding (Heath-Kelly & Strausz 2018: 10).

With this re-framing of Prevent into a safeguarding strategy, the spatial differentiation between the outside–inside dichotomy required for paradigmatic systems of classification in the biopolitical management of human life was reconfigured (Heath-Kelly 2017a). This is exemplified by the fact that the threat is no longer external (international terrorism) or internal (home-grown terrorism) but ubiquitous – everyone in the 'pre-radicalised' phase (Silber & Bhatt 2007: 22) is vulnerable to catching the disease. It is no longer just Muslims, therefore, who are under scrutiny for signs of radicalisation but it is also now the general population that is being observed and examined for latent radical tendencies. Given that the safeguarding threshold is ambiguous and appears to be low in the pre-criminal space, every member of society is a potential subject of safeguarding intervention.

Medicalisation is further illustrated with the de-politicisation of CONTEST's conception of the radicalisation process. Treating terrorism as the symptom of a psychiatric disorder de-politicises it. The political dimension of terrorism is one of the very components that defines it. This de-politicisation can be seen in the mainstreaming of Channel referrals, the rendering of political violence into a problem of 'safeguarding' and with the diminishing prominence of 'ideology' from the grammar of Prevent, e.g. 'ideology' is mentioned 13 times in CONTEST 2018, which pales in comparison to 2011, where ideology is mentioned 103 times (HO 2011). By de-emphasising the ideological and political motivations of terrorism, Prevent is moving away from the very boundaries that distinguish terrorism from other forms of violence, such as pathological and criminal violence.

Through medicalisation, terrorism also becomes reduced to individual pathology, divorced from the social ecological factors that allow radicalised settings to emerge in the first place. While Prevent acknowledges the diverse factors involved in radicalisation to violent extremism, it nevertheless has a static view of 'vulnerability'. This is evident with how Prevent conceptualises the 'pre-radicalised' person as a 'vulnerable' person (HO 2018: 37). According to this framing, the general and personal vulnerabilities that a person has become conflated with vulnerability to radicalisation. Here, a distinction must be made: individuals vulnerable to 'radicalisation' may include 'vulnerable individuals', but it remains to be demonstrated that 'vulnerable individuals' are necessarily 'vulnerable to radicalisation' (Corner, Bouhana & Gill 2018: 3). The profile of the violent radical is left vague so that anyone can potentially pick up the disease of radicalisation.

Research suggests that vulnerability to terrorism is situational and not innate within individuals (Corner et al. 2018: 4). Some individuals have a greater propensity to recruitment to terrorism due to personal temperaments, biographies, looser moral control and other idiosyncratic factors. However, vulnerability to recruitment is more dependent on exposure to radicalised settings and social processes (Bouhana & Wikstrom 2011). Viewed in this way, vulnerability to recruitment is something that becomes expressed in response to a specific situation. It matters substantially whether an individual becomes exposed to a radicalised setting, interacts with recruiters and socialises in places of recruitment. In other words, the turn to political violence cannot be explained by reference to individual vulnerability alone.

Consequently, 95% of Channel referrals do not receive safeguarding support (HO 2018b). In 2017/18, for example, a total of 7,318 individuals were subject to a referral but only 394 individuals received Channel support following a Channel panel (HO 2018b: 4). There is a substantial discrepancy between the numbers being referred and actual participation in interventions. Equally significant is the fact that 40% of referrals are being re-directed to other services prior to Channel discussion taking place (HO 2018b: 4). This suggests that during a period in which public services in the UK were slashed by central government due to austerity for the best part of a decade, people with actual personal and social issues in need of support were being channelled into the British CT infrastructure (Heath-Kelly & Strausz 2018: 54). The deployment of care structures in the service of CT has diverted attention and resources away from addressing the social structures that can produce real vulnerabilities and alienation in the first place. It underscores the way that the medicalisation of CT has eviscerated the boundaries between public health and CT issues.

Conclusion

This chapter has made three arguments. Firstly, research has not yet examined the significance of incorporating a tertiary level programme such as DDP in a Prevent strategy that operates in the pre-criminal space. Specifically, this chapter has tried to understand what the introduction of DDP tells us about how UK Prevent is evolving. Secondly, as the existing research on tertiary level programmes is written primarily from a CT perspective, and the literature on Prevent from a P/CVE perspective, the chapter has attempted to bridge this aporia by utilising the PHM. The PHM allows us to conceptualise Prevent in terms of a three-level intervention system, structured around different risk levels. Seen therefore through the lens of the PHM, post-criminal tertiary level intervention such as DDP complements primary and secondary interventions in the pre-criminal space. Viewing DDP through the PHM re-frames our conceptual understanding of the boundaries between CT and P/CVE, between Pursue and Prevent, and renders the cross-fertilisation between both domains more intelligible.

Lastly, this chapter has also explored the implication of viewing Prevent through a PHM. A major consequence of adopting a public health approach is the medicalisation of terrorism: the PHM treats terrorism as a disease and takes the population into view, rather than confining the problem to specific domains or groups, and fails to treat terrorism as a social, cultural and political phenomenon. While this approach has advantages for the government in terms of organising a structured response to the threat of terrorism, it nevertheless has the effect of depoliticising terrorism and, in the process, removes the agency and culpability of individuals, not to mention pathologising pathways to terrorism; it also divorces such processes from the social ecological conditions that generate recruitment to terrorism. The medicalisation of the Prevent paradigm has hauled more activities and people under the purview of CT.

This chapter has therefore argued that the emergence of DDP in Prevent 2018 signified the advent of tertiary level interventions and represented the culmination of a historical process in which Prevent has increasingly, over the years, appropriated the language and practice of public health solutions. Given the protean and rapidly shifting security threats facing the UK, academic, political and media scrutiny of DDP will only continue to grow.

References

Aggarwal, N.K. (2018). 'Questioning the current public health approach to countering violent extremism', *Global Public Health*, 14:2, pp. 309–317.

Alonso, R. (2011). 'Why do terrorists stop? Analyzing why ETA members abandon or continue with terrorism', *Studies in Conflict & Terrorism*, 34, pp. 696–716.

Altier, M.B., Boyle, E.L., Shortland, N.D., & Horgan, J.G. (2017). 'Why they leave: An analysis of terrorist disengagement events from eighty-seven autobiographical accounts', *Security Studies*, 26:2, pp. 305–332.

Altier, M.B., Thoroughgood, C.N., & Horgan, J.G. (2014). 'Turning away from terrorism: Lessons from psychology, sociology and criminology', *Journal of Peace Research*, 51, pp. 647–666.

Aly, A., Balbi, A., & Jacques, C. (2015). 'Rethinking countering violent extremism: Implementing the role of civil society', *Journal of Policing, Intelligence and Counter Terrorism*, 10:1, pp. 3–13.

Ashour, O. (2009). *The De-radicalisation of Jihadists: Transforming Armed Islamist Movements*. London; New York: Routledge.

Barrelle, K. (2015). 'Pro-integration: Disengagement from and life after extremism', *Behavioral Sciences of Terrorism and Political Aggression*, 7:2, pp. 129–142.

Bhui, K., & Jones, E. (2017). 'The challenge of radicalisation: A public health approach to understanding and intervention', *Psychoanalytic Psychotherapy*, 31:4, pp. 401–410.

Bjorgo, T. (2009). 'Processes of disengagement from violent groups of the extreme right'. In T. Bjorgo & J. Horgan (eds), *Leaving Terrorism Behind: Individual and Collective Disengagement*. London: Routledge, pp. 30–48.

Bjorgo, T., & Horgan, J. (2009). *Leaving Terrorism Behind: Individual and Collective Disengagement*. London: Routledge.

Bouhana, N., & Wikstrom, P.H. (2011). Al-Qaeda-influenced radicalisation: A rapid evidence assessment guided by Situational Action Theory, Home Office, https://assets.publishing.service.gov.uk/government/uploads/system/uploads/attachment_data/file/116724/occ97.pdf.

Brighton, S. (2007). 'British Muslims, multiculturalism and UK Foreign policy: "Integration" and "Cohesion" in and beyond the state', *International Affairs*, 83:1, pp. 1–17.

Challgren, J., Kenyon, T., Kervick, L., Scudder, S., Walters, M., & Whitehead, K. (2016). *Countering Violent Extremism: Applying the Public Health Model*. Washington: Georgetown University.

Cherney, A. (2018). 'Evaluating interventions to disengage extremist offenders: A study of the proactive integrated support model (PRISM)', *Behavioral Sciences of Terrorism and Political Aggression*, pp. 1–21.

Clubb, G. (2017). *Social Movement De-Radicalisation and the Decline of Terrorism: The Morphogenesis of the Irish Republican Movement*. London: Routledge.

Conrad, P. (2007). *The Medicalisation of Society: On the Transformation of Human Conditions into Treatable Disorders*. Baltimore: The John Hopkins University Press.

Corner, E., Bouhana, N., & Gill, P. (2018). 'The multifinality of vulnerability indicators in lone-actor terrorism', *Psychology, Crime & Law*, pp. 1–22.

Dean, C. (2016). 'Countering violent extremism in prisons: Principles for effective interventions and programmes', *Global Center on Cooperative Security*, pp. 18–27.

DHSC. (2018). 'Department of Health & Social Care', *Care Act 2014*, www.gov.uk/government/publications/care-act-statutory-guidance/care-and-support-statutory-guidance

Durodie, B. (2016). 'Securitising education to "prevent" terrorism or losing direction?', *British Journal of Educational Studies*, 64:1, pp. 21–35.

Edwards, P. (2016). 'Closure through resilience: The case of Prevent', *Studies in Conflict and Terrorism*, 39:4, pp. 292–307.

El-Said, H. (2012). *De-Radicalising Islamist Programmes and Their Impact in Muslim Majority Societies*. London and New York: Routledge.

Elshimi, M. (2015). 'De-radicalisation interventions as technologies of the self: A Foucauldian analysis', *Critical Studies on Terrorism*, 8:1, pp. 110–129.

Elshimi, M. (2016). 'Prevent 2011 and counter-radicalisation: What is de-radicalisation?' In Baker-Beall, C., Heath-Kelly, C., & Jarvis, L. (eds), *Counter-Radicalisation: Critical Perspectives*. London and New York: Routledge, pp. 258–276.

Elshimi, M. (2017). *De-Radicalisation in the UK Prevent Strategy: Security, Identity and Religion*. London and New York: Routledge.

Ferguson, N. (2016). 'Disengaging from Terrorism: A Northern Irish experience', *The Journal for Deradicalisation*, 6, pp. 1–23.

Githens-Mazer, J. (2012). 'The rhetoric and reality: Radicalization and political discourse', *International Political Science Review*, 33:5, pp. 556–567.

Goldberg, D., Jadhav, S., & Younis, T. (2017). 'Prevent: What is pre-criminal space?', *BJPsych Bulletin*, 41:4: 208–211.

Grierson, J. (2019). 'Extremists Living in UK under secretive counter-terror programme'. *The Guardian*, www.theguardian.com/uk-news/2019/apr/05/extremists-living-in-uk-under-secretive-counter-terror-programme

Hardcastle, K., Bellis, M., Middleton, J., Harrison, D., Flecknoe, D., & Hopkins, J. (2019). 'Preventing violent extremism in the UK: Public health solutions', Public Health Wales, Faculty of Public Health, www.fph.org.uk/media/2475/preventing-violent-extremism-in-the-uk_public-health-solutions-web.pdf

Harris, K.J., Gringart, E., & Drake, D. (2017). 'Leaving ideological groups behind: A model of disengagement', *Behavioural Sciences of Terrorism and Political Aggression*, 10:2, pp. 91–109.

Heath-Kelly, C. (2013). 'Counter-terrorism and the counterfactual: Producing the "radicalisation" discourse and the UK prevent strategy', *The British Journal of Politics and International Relations*, 15:3, pp. 394–415.

Heath-Kelly, C. (2017a). 'Algorithmic autoimmunity in the NHS: Radicalisation and the clinic', *Security Dialogue*, 48:1, pp. 29–45.

Heath-Kelly, C. (2017b). 'The geography of pre-criminal space: Epidemiological imaginations of radicalisation risk in the UK Prevent Strategy, 2007–2017', *Critical Studies on Terrorism*, 10:2, pp. 297–319.

Heath-Kelly, C., & Strausz, E. (2018). 'Counter-terrorism in the NHS: Evaluating prevent duty safeguarding in the NHS', *The Welcome Trust*.

(HC) House of Commons, Communities and Local Government Committee. (2010). Preventing Violent Extremism, Sixth Report of Session 2009–2010, www.publications.parliament.uk/pa/cm200910/cmselect/cmcomloc/65/65.pdf

(HO) Home Office. (2006). CONTEST, the United Kingdom's Strategy for Countering Terrorism.

(HO) Home Office. (2011). CONTEST, the United Kingdom's Strategy for Countering Terrorism.

(HO) Home Office. (2018). CONTEST, the United Kingdom's Strategy for Countering Terrorism.

(HO) Home Office. (2018b). Individuals referred to and supported through the prevent programme. April 2017–March 2018. London: Crown Copyright.

(HO) Prevent Strategy. (2009). 'CONTEST, the United Kingdom's strategy for countering terrorism'.

Horgan, J. (2008). 'Deradicalization or disengagement? A process in need of clarity and a counterterrorism initiative in need of evaluation', *Perspectives on Terrorism*, 2:4, pp. 3–8.

Horgan, J. (2009a). *Walking Away from Terrorism: Accounts of Disengagement from Radical Extremist Movements*. London: Routledge.

Horgan, J. (2009b). 'Assessing the effectiveness of current de-radicalization initiatives and identifyingimplications for the development of US-based initiatives in multiple settings', National Consortium for the Study of Terrorism and Responses to Terrorism, www.start.umd.edu/start/research/investigators/project.asp?id=56

Horgan, J., & Braddock, K. (2010). 'Rehabilitating the terrorists? Challenges in assessing the effectiveness of de-radicalization programs', *Terrorism and Political Violence*, 22:2, pp. 267–291.

Horgan, J., & Taylor, M. (2015). 'Disengagement, de-radicalization and the arc of terrorism: Future directions for research'. In Coolsaet, R. (ed), *Jihadi Terrorism and the Radicalisation Challenge: European and American Experiences*. 2nd ed. London: Routledge.

Hwang, J. (2017). 'The disengagement of Indonesian jihadists: Understanding the pathways', *Terrorism and Political Violence*, 29:2, pp. 277–295.

Innes, M., Roberts, C., Innes, H., Lowe, T., & Lakhani, S. (2011). *Assessing the Effects of Prevent Policing. A Report to the Association of Chief Police Officers*. Cardiff: Universities' Police Science Institute, Cardiff University.

Jarvis, L., & Lister, M. (2015). *Anti-Terrorism, Citizenship and Security*. Manchester: Manchester University Press.

Khalil, J., Brown, R., Chant, C., Olowo, P., & Wood, N. (2019). *Deradicalisation and Disengagement in Somalia Evidence from a Rehabilitation Programme for Former Members of Al-Shabaab*, RUSI Whitehall Report 4-18, January 2019.

Koehler, D. (2017). *Understanding Deradicalisation: Methods, Tools and Programmes for Countering Violent Extremism*. London: Routledge.

Kundnani, A. (2009). *Spooked! How Not to Prevent Violent Extremism*, Institute of Race Relations, October 2009.

Lindekilde, L. (2012). 'Neo-liberal governing of "radicals": Danish radicalization prevention policies and potential iatrogenic effects', *International Journal of Conflict and Violence*, 6:1, pp. 109–125.

Lindekilde, L. (2015). 'Refocusing Danish counter-radicalisation efforts: An analysis of the (problematic) logic and practice of individual de-radicalisation interventions'. In Baker-Beall, C., Heath-Kelly, C., & Jarvis, L. (eds), *Counter-Radicalisation: Critical Perspectives*. London: Routledge.

Marks, L., Hunter, D., & Alderslade, R. (2011). *Strengthen Public Health Capacity and Services in Europe*. Durham: World Health Organization and Durham University.

Marsden, S. (2017). *Reintegrating Extremists: Deradicalisation and Desistance*. Basingstoke: Palgrave Macmillan.

Martin, T. (2014). 'Governing an unknowable future: The politics of Britain's "Prevent" policy', *Critical Studies on Terrorism*, 7:1, pp. 62–78.

Massumi, B. (2005). 'The future birth of the affective fact', *Conference Proceedings: Genealogies of Biopolitics*, http://browse.reticular.info/text/collected/massumi.pdf

Massumi, B. (2007). 'Potential politics and the primacy of preemption', *Theory & Event*, 10:2.

McGovern, M. (2017). 'The university, "Prevent" and cultures of compliance', *Prometheus*, 34:1, pp. 49–62.

McNeil, F. (2005). 'A desistance paradigm for offender management', *Criminology and Criminal Justice*, 6:1, pp. 39–62.

Mitton, K. (2019). 'Public health and violence', *Critical Public Health*, 29:2, pp. 135–137.

O'Donnell, A. (2015). 'Securitisation, counterterrorism and the silencing of dissent: The educational implications of "Prevent"', *British Journal of Educational Studies*, 64:1, pp. 53–76.

Omand, D. (2010). *Securing the State*. London: C Hurst & Co Publishers Ltd.

(PSJ) Prison Service Journal. (2012). 'Combating extremism and terrorism', September, No. 203, www.crimeandjustice.org.uk/sites/crimeandjustice.org.uk/files/PSJ%20September%202012%20No.%20203.pdf

Pantazis, C., & Pemberton, S. (2009). 'From the "old" to the "new" suspect community: Examining the impacts of recent UK counter-terrorist legislation', *British Journal of Criminology*, 49:5, pp. 646–666.

Radicalisation Awareness Network (RAN). (2017). 'Responses to returnees: Foreign terrorist fighters and their families', https://ec.europa.eu/homeaffairs/sites/homeaffairs/files/ran_br_a4_m10_en.pdf

Ragazzi, F. (2016). 'Suspect community or suspect category? The impact of counterterrorism as "policed multiculturalism"', *Journal of Ethnic and Migration Studies*, 42:5, pp. 724–741.

Reinares, F. (2011). 'Exit from terrorism: A qualitative empirical study on disengagement and deradicalization among members of ETA', *Terrorism and Political Violence*, 23, pp. 780–803.

Riemann, M. (2019). 'Problematizing the medicalization of violence: A critical discourse analysis of the "Cure Violence" initiative', *Critical Public Health*, 5, pp. 146–155.

Sabir, R. (2017). 'Blurred lines and false dichotomies: Integrating counterinsurgency into the UK's domestic "war on terror"', *Critical Social Policy*, 37:2, pp. 202–224.

Schmid, A.P. (2013). *Radicalisation, Deradicalisation, Counter-radicalisation: A Conceptual Discussion and Literature Review*. Hague: International Centre for Counter-Terrorism.

Schuurman, B., & Bakker, E. (2016). 'Reintegrating jihadist extremists: Evaluating a Dutch initiative, 2013–2014', *Behavioral Sciences of Terrorism and Political Aggression*, 8, pp. 66–85.

Silber, M., & Bhatt, A. (2007). 'Radicalization in the west: The homegrown threat', The NYPD Jihadist Report.

Silke, A. (2013). *Prisons, Terrorism and Extremism: Critical Issues in Management, Radicalisation and Reform*. London: Routledge.

Spalek, B., Lambert, R., & El-Awa, S. (2008). 'Preventing violent extremism in prison: Key policy and practice issues', *Prison Service Journal*, 180, pp. 45–54.

Sukabdi, Z.A. (2015). 'Terrorism in Indonesia: A review on rehabilitation and deradicalization', *Journal of Terrorism Research*, 6, pp. 36–56.

Sumpter, C. (2017). 'Countering violent extremism in Indonesia: Priorities, practice and the role of civil society', *Journal for Deradicalisation*, Nr. 11, pp. 112–147.

Thomas, P. (2015). 'Britain's Prevent programme: An end in sight?' In Jarvis, L., & Lister, M. (eds), *Critical Perspectives on Counter-Terrorism* London: Routledge, pp. 169–186.

Thornton, A., & Bouhana, N. (2017). 'Preventing radicalization in the UK: Expanding the knowledge-base on the Channel programme', *Policing: A Journal of Policy and Practice*, pp. 1–14.

Veldhuis, T. (2012). 'Designing rehabilitation and reintegration programmes for violent extremist offenders: A realist approach', ICCT Research Paper.
Veldhuis, T. (2016). *Prisoner Radicalization and Terrorism Detention Policy: Institutionalized Fear or Evidence-based Policy Making?* London/New York: Routledge.
Webber, D., Chernikova, M., Kruglanski, A.W., Gelfand, M.J., Hettiarachchi, M., Gunaratna, R., Lafreniere, M.A., & Belanger, J.J. (2017). 'Deradicalizing detained terrorists', *Political Psychology*, 39:3, pp. 539–556.
Weggemans, D., & De Graaf, B. (2017). 'Reintegrating Jihadist extremist detainees: Helping extremist offenders back into society', Contemporary Terrorism Studies. (WHO) World Health Organization, www.who.int/topics/epidemiology/en/
Weine, S., Eisenman, D., Kinsler, J., Glik, D., & Polutnik, C. (2017). 'Addressing violent extremism as public health policy and practice', *Behavioral Sciences of Terrorism and Political Aggression*, 9:3, pp. 208–221.
World Health Organization (WHO). (2016). Public health, trade foreign policy, diplomacy and health. World Health Organization. Retrieved from http://www.who.int/trade/glossary/story076/en/

18

PROMOTING DISENGAGEMENT FROM VIOLENT EXTREMISM IN SCANDINAVIA

What, who, how?

Anja Dalgaard-Nielsen and Jakob Ilum

The purpose of this chapter is to provide an overview of the central principles, actors, and instruments of efforts to promote disengagement from violent extremism in Denmark, Norway, and Sweden and to identify strengths and weaknesses that might inform and inspire the efforts of a broader set of countries. As elaborated below, Scandinavian efforts, and thus this chapter, focus on disengagement from violent extremist groups and networks, not deradicalization, e.g., revising and moderating extremist ideas. The inclination to target behavior rather than beliefs and ideology is evident across time and from efforts to promote exit from different forms of violent extremism in Denmark, Norway, and Sweden. This aligns with general liberal democratic values – as long as you do not break the law you should be free to think what you like. But it also reflects the strong Scandinavian institutional tradition for social crime prevention work embodied in networks and collaboration structures like the Danish SSP, the Norwegian SLT, and the Swedish SSPF.[1] In light of the preexistence of these mechanisms and the opportunity to leverage economic, social, and general educational services to incentivize pro-social and law-abiding behavior, it is hardly surprising that the Scandinavian countries leaned towards disengagement rather than trying to establish ideological and religious counseling and reeducation services to attempt to deradicalize violent extremists.

The chapter argues that the Scandinavian tradition of institutionalized, cross-governmental efforts to prevent crime, the welfare state, and the emerging willingness of the municipal level to engage with violent extremism, even if this has traditionally been handled by central government security agencies, represent major strengths. But Scandinavian efforts to promote disengagement also face challenges. They include different views of national policy-makers and local actors in collaboration with "gray-zone" actors, e.g., former extremists and individuals or organizations that condemn violence, but still represent conservative, sometimes illiberal, religious and social values. Local level actors tend to take a pragmatic view, stressing the importance of these groups as bridge builders that permit them to reach into otherwise closed extremist groups and subcultures. National level politicians, particularly in Denmark, tend to emphasize the importance of displaying allegiance to a set of core Western, democratic values before collaboration can take place – rejecting violence is not enough.

Another challenge is the lack of agreement on the appropriate balance between efforts to sanction and efforts to rehabilitate violent extremists. This issue has come to the fore as individuals who joined or attempted to join militant Islamist groups in Syria or Iraq return to Scandinavia. Local level actors attempt to reach out to and facilitate the reintegration of returnees. The national level appears more prone to focus on sanctions, not least in Denmark, where major political parties compete to be "tough on crime" and where recent court cases have led to harsh sentences.

The diverging priorities combined with the absence of clear and consensual measures of success of disengagement programs represent a vulnerability, which proponents of disengagement efforts would arguably do well to address. They raise the specter of a backlash against disengagement efforts in case of a high-profile case of recidivism. The absence of clear and explicit definitions of exit or disengagement in the major national policy strategies pertaining to violent extremism underscores the point.

Below, we first provide a brief overview of violent extremism in Scandinavia since the 1990s. We proceed to address, in turn, the what, who, and how of efforts to promote disengagement in Denmark, Norway, and Sweden. What are the core principles? Who are the major actors? What are the ways and means of disengagement efforts? In the last two sections, we discuss strengths and weaknesses of the Scandinavian efforts and argue the need for national dialog about success criteria. The chapter is based on official government documents and policies, threat assessments, evaluation reports, and academic research on deradicalization, exit, and disengagement. Supplementary interviews were carried out with national and local level government officials and civil society actors in Denmark, Norway, and Sweden.[2]

Violent extremism in Scandinavia: a brief overview

This section provides a brief overview of violent extremism in the Scandinavian countries from the 1990s till 2017 including violent right-wing and left-wing extremism and militant Islamism. The focus is on movements, groups, and individuals who reject democracy, favoring violent means in pursuit of political, ideological, or religious aims.

Right-wing extremism in Scandinavia in the late 1980s and 1990s was characterized by a move from loosely organized or spontaneous violence targeting immigrants towards more organized and ideologically motivated groups and networks (Ravndal, 2017, 773). The emergence of right-wing extremism in this period can be seen as a reaction to perceived lenient government immigration policies as well as to the more general structural challenges posed by increasing globalization, e.g. migration of labor, outsourcing of jobs, and so on (Ignazi, 2003). However, many of the groups, especially in Sweden, emanated from older political groups adhering to traditional national socialist political agendas, with racism and anti-semitism cutting to the core of their ideology. Amongst the emerging groups and networks this core ideology was supplemented with an increasingly activist agenda morphing into youth cultures and subcultures, especially white-power music and football hooliganism (Fangen, 1998, 203; Lööw, 2000). Today the common ground for right-wing extremism in Scandinavia is a deeply rooted anti-semitism as well as opposition to immigrants and refugees – in particular a strong opposition to a perceived "Islamization" of European and Scandinavian societies. The ideological underpinnings of right-wing extremism in Scandinavia today are characterized by a patchwork of sometimes conflicting streams of thought, political ideology, religious references, and Nordic mythology detached from their original context.

The most extreme act of violence carried out against this background is the terrorist attack committed by Norwegian right-wing extremist Anders Behring Breivik, who on July 22, 2011 killed 77 people and injured more than 300 in subsequent bomb and handgun attacks on the office of the Prime Minister in Oslo and the participants at a Workers Youth League camp at the island of Utøya. Despite recurring attacks on immigration centers and despite ideologically being fueled by anti-semitism and strong Islamophobic viewpoints, much of the violence committed by right-wing extremists in Scandinavia is aimed at immediate left-wing political opponents, especially left-wing political activists, themselves seeing their right-wing opponents as prime targets for violent actions (SFI, 2014, 67).

A systematic and activist opposition to all sorts of perceived "right-winging" cuts to the core of the identity of the extremist left-wing, defining itself as anarchist, anti-fascist, anti-imperialist, and anti-capitalist (Ibid, 41). This has resulted in violent attacks on individuals from right-wing groups and organized violent clashes with right-wing demonstrations as well as violent street and city riots, such as at the EU summit in Gothenburg in 2001 and on several occasions in Copenhagen in the 1990s and 2000s, oftentimes leading to violent clashes with police being seen as the repressive tool of a potentially fascist state (Ibid 42).

Although individuals in the political extremist milieus in Scandinavia have the capacity to commit acts of violence, the Security and Intelligence Services of Sweden, Norway, and Denmark assess it to be less likely that a terrorist threat currently emanates from here (CTA, 2017; NCT, 2017; PST, 2017). Violent left- and right-wing extremism in Scandinavia today therefore often ends up in a reciprocal relationship in which activity and violence on the one side trigger an adverse response from the other side. In this sense the two mutually constitute each other by engaging in a conflict fundamentally on how Muslim minorities in Scandinavia should be treated (Ibid, 40; Ravndal, 2017, 784).

Throughout the 1990s relatively little attention (from Scandinavian media, academia, and government alike) was given to militant Islamism. The relatively few cases that came to public knowledge were associated with some individuals with contacts to militant Islamist groups in their countries of origin – the Middle East, North Africa, and South Asia. This obviously changed with September 11, 2001. As in other European countries throughout the 2000s, the Scandinavian countries saw an increasing number of young individuals – many of them descendants of immigrants from Muslim-majority countries – attracted to an Islamist and in some instances militant Islamist ideology. Especially in Denmark a series of terrorism-related court cases in the mid-2000s reflected the much-debated phenomenon of homegrown extremism brought to the forefront with the July 7 and 22, 2005 attacks in London.

For the Scandinavian countries and Denmark in particular the 2005 printing of a series of cartoons intended to depict the Prophet Mohammed marked a watershed. On December 30, 2005 the Danish newspaper *Jyllands-Posten* published an editorial on free speech and self-censorship, "The Face of Muhammad," illustrated by 12 cartoons, most of which depicted the Prophet Mohammed. The events following the printing of the cartoons arguably prompted the greatest foreign policy and security crisis Denmark had seen since the Second World War.

The printing and the political aftermath – an unequivocal defense of the cartoonist's freedom of expression on the part of the Danish Government – prompted strong reactions across a number of countries and were seized by militant Islamist movements, including al-Qaida, depicting a presumed global war against Islam. Not only were the cartoons seized upon by international militant Islamist media outlets, they also came to play a significant role in the radicalization to violence of individuals in Sweden, Norway, and Denmark (PST, 2016).

In January 2010 the Danish cartoonist Kurt Westergaard was attacked in his home by a 28-year-old Somali man living in Denmark. In Norway three men were arrested in July 2010 and charged with attempting to attack *Jyllands-Posten* and Kurt Westergaard. Two of them were later convicted on the charges. And in late December 2010 four men traveled from Sweden to Denmark in order to launch an attack on *Jyllands-Posten*. All of them were arrested and later convicted on charges of planning a terrorist attack. Prior to this, on December 11, 2010, Sweden and Scandinavia saw the region's first militant Islamist suicide attack, when two bombs went off in the midst of Christmas shopping around Drottninggatan in central Stockholm – an attack in which only the attacker died. In an email statement made just before the attack, the perpetrator declared that the attack was in response to Swedish military presence in Afghanistan and the cartoon drawn by Swedish artist Lars Vilks depicting the Prophet Mohammed as a dog.

Lars Vilks has been the target of several violent attacks and assassination plots, most recently in February 2015, when two shootings took place in Copenhagen at an event attended by Lars Vilks and at the Jewish Synagogue. Two people were killed. Apparently the street gang-affiliated perpetrator was inspired by ISIS.

In sum, the cartoons and the controversies surrounding them still seem to play a central role in the radicalization of militant Islamists in the Scandinavian countries and beyond.

Since the beginning of 2012 the authorities in the Scandinavian countries have expressed increasing concern about the number of individuals traveling from Scandinavia to join the fighting in Syria and Iraq. In parallel with what is seen in other European countries, the fight against the Assad regime in Syria has been the single most important recruiting ground for the various Islamist groups in Scandinavia. More than 500 individuals are estimated to have left Sweden, Norway, and Denmark to join Islamist groups – especially ISIS in Syria – since 2012 (CTA, 2017; PST, 2016; SÄPO, 2017).

In April 2017 Drottninggatan was again the scene of a terrorist attack when a hijacked truck was rammed into a crowd, resulting in five deaths. In the course of the trial the perpetrator explained his motivation had been to punish Sweden for its participation in the fight against ISIS. As of 2018 the flow of fighters appears to have almost stopped, due to difficulties in entering Syria, the harsh conditions on the ground, and the dismantling of the proclaimed Islamic Caliphate. However the threat from militant Islamist terrorism prevails and together with right wing solo terrorists like Breivik, it is regarded as the most serious terrorist threat to Scandinavian societies by intelligence services in Sweden, Norway, and Denmark alike. Returnees from the battlefield constitute a particular concern due to the skills and networks they may have acquired during their stay abroad. Additional concern is being raised in relation to the women who left Scandinavia for the "Caliphate," some bringing their children and some giving birth abroad. While some of these women, provided they return, might pose direct threats to their home countries, concern is also centering on their children and how they have been influenced and impacted by their stay in the Islamic State's "Caliphate."

Efforts to promote disengagement: what, who, how?

This section outlines and explains the central principles (what), major actors (who), and activities (how) of efforts to promote disengagement in Denmark, Norway, and Sweden.

Today, disengagement efforts are nested within broader national action plans and policies to prevent violent extremism early on. The specific measures of the action plans differ from country to country, but they all emphasize the need to collaborate across different government sectors and across national and local levels. Typically, national level actors provide funding, knowledge, and best-practice tools. Local actors are supposed to leverage existing collaboration structures (SSP, SLT, SSPF) to engage individuals or groups believed to be at risk of radicalizing (Government Communication, 2014; National Coordinator to safeguard democracy against violent extremism, 2016; Norwegian Ministry of Justice, 2014; Danish Ministry of Immigration, Integration and Housing, 2016).

Efforts to prompt individuals to leave violent extremist groups and networks are longstanding in Scandinavia. In Norway and Sweden they date back to before the national action plans to the 1990s when the focus was on right-wing extremism. Disengagement efforts targeting militant Islamism are more recent, with Denmark being the first country to develop exit interventions specifically targeting this type of extremism in the late 2000s. Respondents from all three Scandinavian countries point out that, initially, efforts to promote exit from violent extremism met with skepticism – the notion that it is possible to leave violent extremist groups and that one should actually "help these kinds of people" (R1, R3, R4) appeared alien to many. Today, the social and political acceptance of exit, disengagement, and rehabilitation efforts appears firm, at least in so far as the major policy documents pertaining to violent extremism, the national action plans, include such measures (Government Communication, 2014, 35–39; National Coordinator to safeguard democracy against violent extremism, 2016, 5; Norwegian Ministry of Justice, 2014, 21; Danish Ministry of Immigration, Integration and Housing, 2016, 6).

While the plans carefully define violent extremism and radicalization, the terms "deradicalization" and "disengagement" are not used. But a focus on voluntariness and behavioral change is evident from the general wording. The Norwegian action plan calls for establishing "exit schemes for persons who *want* to withdraw" (emphasis added) (Norwegian Ministry of Justice, 2014, 21) and the Swedish strategy underlines that, whereas municipalities, non-governmental organizations (NGOs), friends, and family may support an individual who wishes to leave violent extremism, the driving force and the motivation need to be present in that individual him- or herself (National Coordinator to safeguard democracy against violent extremism, 2016, 16). Along the same lines the Danish action plan speaks of "targeted exit programs and rehabilitation efforts in cases where there is a *will* to change" (emphasis added) (Danish Ministry of Immigration, Integration and Housing, 2016, 3).

In line with the official government texts, the respondents also lean on a behavioral definition, but point out that attitudinal change may follow track if someone physically disengages. In the words of a Norwegian municipal government official: "In our experience, disengagement is the first step. If over time, via mentoring etc. we can also make them deradicalize, that's a bonus" (R2). A Danish police officer, along similar lines, points out: "We do not aim at changing the mindset of the individual, however this is what often happens. When we focus upon the basic elements of life, i.e. work, education, family and social networks, the mindset will typically change" (R4). The notion that you can engineer a deradicalization process by means of external intervention is rejected. In the words of a Swedish respondent working at the national level: "I do not believe in deradicalization [programs]. You cannot initiate it externally. And how do you judge sincerity?" (R3).

In sum, the Scandinavian approach contrasts with more ideologically focused deradicalization programs in South East Asia and the Middle East that explicitly aim to "re-educate" violent extremists (Barrett and Bokhari, 2009, 175; Dalgaard-Nielsen, 2013, 100; Gunaratna, 2011, 65). As argued above, this might be seen as an expression of general liberal values such as freedom of thought, but also of a strong, institutional tradition of preventing crime via economic, social, and general educational initiatives.

Turning to the major actors of Scandinavian disengagement efforts, the three countries again resemble each other. While violent extremism is conceived as partly a law enforcement problem and thus the responsibility of the police, it is also conceived as a social problem that needs to be tackled at multiple levels of government by a broad coalition of actors, including civil society actors (Danish Ministry of Immigration, Integration and Housing, 2016, 12; National Coordinator to safeguard democracy against violent extremism, 2016, 2; Norwegian Ministry of Justice, 2014, 1). Municipalities and the range of social and economic measures they dispose of play a central role next to the security services, the police, probation services, mental health services, educational institutions, and a handful of NGOs (Lid et al., 2016, 27–29).

NGOs are widely believed to have an easier time reaching individuals with limited trust in government authorities – they are in a position to offer counseling and social support, but may also funnel disengagers towards the municipal services, e.g., housing, education, jobs, needed to build a life outside extremist groups (R1, R2). The Swedish NGO "Fryshuset" is one of the most well established. It has helped individuals leave right-wing extremist groups since 1998. Individuals need to volunteer for the program and they receive social support and guidance from former right-wing extremists and professional social workers. Partners or families are often involved and Fryshuset collaborates with the municipalities in providing the disengager with practical help and support (www.fryshuset.se).

NGOs seem to play a stronger part in exit and disengagement efforts in Sweden than in Norway and Denmark. In the Danish case this may be a reflection of the less pragmatic attitude of Danish national level policy-makers vis-à-vis collaboration with "gray-zone" actors.

Some respondents point out that, with the plethora of actors, roles and responsibilities are not always clear (R2, R4). However, and in line with conclusions from academic research, they also emphasize the complexity and case-to-case variation of the phenomena of extremism and disengagement. Supporting disengagement therefore takes a broad coalition of actors, who between them dispose of a variety of tools, permitting them to customize interventions to different individual cases (Bjørgo and Carlsson, 2005, 47–50; Dalgaard-Nielsen, 2017; Horgan, 2009, 140).

A distinctive feature of the Scandinavian approach is the crucial part played by municipal authorities and local collaborative structures aimed at crime prevention. In Denmark, schools, social authorities, and police work together to prevent youth delinquency in the so-called SSP collaboration.[3] Norway has a comparable set-up in the so-called SLT model. Sweden has local level coordinators of the efforts against violent extremism as well as the so-called SSPF collaboration[4] and, in some municipalities, local crime prevention councils (National Council for Crime Prevention, 2005, 1; Norwegian Ministry of Justice, 2014, 13; Danish Ministry of Immigration, Integration and Housing, 2016, 12).

Whereas other countries have established separate, publicly funded organizations to handle violent extremism and exit, in Scandinavia, existing actors and collaborative structures have largely been willing and able to absorb the task (Lid et al., 2016, 21–22) (Table 18.1). An example is what has become known as the Aarhus model. The local authorities in the city of Aarhus, Denmark, have created a multiagency collaboration aiming at preventing extremism amongst youth and rehabilitating extremists into society. Based upon the existing legal framework for sharing information to prevent crime, the model essentially brings together relevant authorities and civil society actors with the aim of including the at-risk individual in mainstream cultural, social, and societal life.

The advantage to building on existing structures is that, in principle, this ensures strong geographical coverage and close integration between social work, "normal" crime

Table 18.1 Major central, local, and non-governmental actors in the Scandinavian countries' efforts to promote disengagement from violent extremism.

	Central government	*Regions, municipalities, and police districts*	*Non-governmental organizations*
Denmark	National Center for the Prevention of Extremism PET (Security and Intelligence Service) NFC (National Crime Prevention Centre) Prison and Probation Service	SSP, PSP, and KSP (fora for coordination of crime prevention measures) and info houses bridging relevant actors in the disengagement efforts	
Norway	Ministry of Justice and Public Security Probation Service PST (Security Service)	SLT (forum for coordination of crime prevention measures)	
Sweden	National coordinator for protecting democracy against violent extremism (from 2018 replaced by Center for Preventing Violent Extremism) SÄPO (Security Police)	SSPF, municipal coordinators (not yet in all municipalities)	Fryshuset Another Side of Sweden Save the Children

prevention, and efforts against violent extremism. A downside, as elaborated below, is the risk of undermining trust between social workers and citizens if social workers come to be perceived as the prolonged arm of law enforcement and security services.

The laws that regulate the ability of social authorities and the police to exchange information as well as the institutional traditions and sharing habits differ somewhat from country to country, resulting in differences when it comes to how much is actually shared. Denmark has the most permissive laws for exchanging information between government agencies for the purpose of crime prevention. But, as pointed out by a local level respondent, the extensive amount of sharing is a double-edged sword as it runs the risk of compromising the trust that is crucial to effective social work and the credibility of local efforts (R4). The same concern appears to apply in Sweden and Norway, yet respondents simultaneously express reservations about whether flows of information between central and local authorities and from law enforcement to social authorities are sufficient (R2, R3; Lid et al., 2016, 31).

The activities – the how of disengagement – are manifold in the Scandinavian countries. But they tend to cluster into: (1) mentoring and social-psychological support; and (2) practical support with housing, jobs, and education. The primary target group is individual disengagers. Families and friends are a secondary target group, reflecting a realization that they are crucial actors when it comes to providing emotional and social support to a disengager (Norwegian Ministry of Justice, 2014, 21 and 23).

As regards mentoring, respondents, in line with established research, point out that openness, willingness to listen, and a non-judgmental attitude are essential, not least in the early phase of a disengagement process (Arnstberg and Hållén, 2000, 38; Rabasa, Petty, Ghez and Boucek, 2010, 9). Mentoring, in a Scandinavian context, is not about providing alternative ideologies or telling individuals what is right or wrong. It works more subtly, aiming to facilitate the mentee's own reflection and realization that things are not as black and white as suggested by extremist ideology (R1, Ministry of Refugee, Immigration and Refugee Affairs, 2010, 26). In the words of a local level respondent from Denmark: "Although we may personally dislike the extremist mindset and ideas of an individual this is not our focus, instead we try to introduce more perspectives to life" (R4).

Disengagers may also receive practical and economic support. The relative affluence of Scandinavia and the welfare-state tradition appear to play important roles. Lack of economic opportunities may aid violent extremist recruitment and complicate disengagement, even for individuals who are ideologically disillusioned (Rabasa, Petty, Ghez and Boucek, 2010, 35). Still, some respondents call for more flexibility and creativity on the part of municipal authorities when it comes to the forms of help offered. From a democratic accountability point of view, it might be advantageous to observe standard procedures, bureaucratic areas of responsibility, and costs. But successful disengagement often requires willingness to adapt measures to individual, even idiosyncratic, cases. A Swedish respondent relates that not all municipalities are willing to fund, for example, the removal of tattoos: "I had these guys who had been competing. Who could get more swastika tattoos? I believe the guy who led had 17. Now, if you want to disengage and start a new life, it could be good to have them removed" (R1).

To sum up, the what, who, and how of disengagement vary somewhat across the Scandinavian countries. However, a focus on behavioral disengagement, a broad involvement of actors from central and local government as well as civil society, and intervention efforts that tend to cluster into mentoring and practical support characterize all three countries.

Dilemmas and differing perspectives: central and local perspectives

How firm is the political and popular legitimacy of the efforts and the consensus across from central and local level actors about means and ends? This section identifies some fault lines between key stakeholders as well as dilemmas inherent to the Scandinavian approach to disengagement.

A major strength of the Scandinavian efforts is the willingness of municipal actors to take responsibility. Despite initial skepticism, a national consensus appears to have emerged in all three countries that efforts to prevent and counter violent extremism are not just the responsibility of central government, the police, and security service, but should involve a broader set of actors (Lid et al., 2016, 21; Winsvold, 2017, 7). The municipal level has largely, in the assessment of our respondents, stepped up and accepted responsibility, even if the naturalness and ease of collaboration differ across the region (R1, R2, R3, R4, R5). Particularly in Sweden, the pressure placed on municipalities from national level actors to adopt local action plans has been criticized, amongst others on the grounds that the process was hurried and resulted in local action plans that were rarely based on local needs and threat assessments (Malmros and Mattsson, 2017, 5).

The engagement of local level government is nevertheless a major organizational and political achievement that positions the Scandinavian countries well to tackle a complex and diverse phenomenon like violent extremism. This type of coalition facilitates the mobilization of a variety of resources and permits a tailored approach to individual cases. It also ensures that local government actors, who are closer to the everyday life of citizens and most likely to be plugged into local atmospherics, are committed to the effort to prevent violent extremism.

In Denmark, larger municipalities and police districts have emerged as crucial driving forces in the further development of programs and intervention methods, also inspiring other actors. The Aarhus model has for instance gained widespread attention and served as inspiration both nationally and internationally (R2, R4).

Whilst acknowledging local achievements, a Danish central government respondent points to the need for strengthening the strategic support for local level efforts, including developing common national definitions, tools, and success criteria (R5). Additionally the established "infohouse structure" seems to be in need of incorporating further local authorities to deal with the substantial increase in cases and the plethora of social challenges to address.

While local level respondents tend to agree with the need for such support, they point to a different and more thorny aspect of local–national level cooperation and coordination: across Denmark, Norway, and Sweden, respondents call for more sensitivity on the part of national policy-makers when it comes to local consequences and complications of, for example, tightening legislation or talking tough. One example brought up is national legislation that criminalizes foreign fighting in, for example, Syria and Iraq. The ability of municipal workers to reach returnees is hardly underpinned by the prospect of potential prosecution. In the words of a Swedish respondent: "All I'm saying is, we should think through the consequences of legislation for social workers. I'm not for or against, but how should practitioners work with this?" (R1).

The issue points to a broader dilemma: local level actors, due to their closer interaction with citizens, play a crucial role preventing, but also detecting, violent extremism. Yet, citizens' trust in social workers, health professionals, and educators could suffer if they are perceived as collaborating too closely with the police and security service, undercutting their ability to fulfill their primary roles as caregivers and educators (R2, R4; Lid et al., 2016, 31). The same goes for civil society actors, for example, religious communities (Winsvold, Mjelde and Loga, 2017, 68). There are no easy solutions here. A mutual commitment to dialog across levels of governance to raise awareness of the trade-offs between hard and soft measures together with a commitment to seek to balance the needs seems to be the best way to proceed.

The perspectives and priorities of national policy-makers and local practitioners also seem to diverge somewhat on the question of whether to collaborate with "gray-zone" actors – e.g., former extremists and individuals or organizations that might represent conservative or even illiberal values, but who reject violence. Such collaboration can be highly controversial politically, which might explain why there is limited government-sanctioned NGO involvement in disengagement efforts in Denmark and Norway – civil society actors must clear a high bar.

While setting the bar high might reduce political risks, it arguably increases the risk that local level actors lose touch with specific subcultures and must forgo the possibility of exerting vicarious influence on individuals in such subcultures. Several respondents highlight the need for bridge builders and go-betweens to enable them to reach vulnerable individuals and be in touch with population segments that distrust the authorities. A Norwegian local level respondent explains:

> Our principle is that if they do not break any laws, we should be in touch with them … We have an understanding with the mosques that they don't maintain a low threshold for expelling individuals, but instead remain in touch with us and the police. That way, at least these individuals are in some kind of a community (R2).

Conceivably, local actors who do not have access to classified intelligence reports might find it difficult to judge who to work with and who not to work with. Nevertheless, local level respondents are vocal that national policy-makers should not attempt to micromanage local networks as that would reduce much-needed local flexibility to find workable and customized solutions to local problems. They converge on the notion that central government should provide tools and legal advice, but leave it to the municipalities to decide how to deal with individual cases and in collaboration with whom.

To sum up, underneath the emerging national consensus on the need for broad coalitions to tackle violent extremism, including via programs and efforts aimed at promoting disengagement, there are still fault lines and dilemmas with no easy solution.

Success criteria and legitimacy

How successful have Scandinavian efforts been and how is success conceived of in the Scandinavian context? The short answer to both questions is that it remains unclear.

The difficulties of formulating appropriate success criteria and measuring the impact of disengagement and deradicalization efforts are broadly recognized (Horgan and Braddock, 2010, 266; Lindekilde, 2012, 342; Rabasa, Petty, Ghez and Boucek, 2010, xvi; Spalek and Davies, 2012, 363). Frequently, several factors are in play when individuals disengage from violent extremism. How do you isolate the effect of the external intervention? Moreover, oftentimes a disengagement process is gradual and entails some going back and forth. How long should someone have stayed clear of extremist groups to be considered disengaged? Should "formers" be monitored by the authorities? And how much recidivism is acceptable? Considering general recidivism rates for violent criminal offenders in Scandinavia (ranging from 18 to 34 percent), a zero recidivism success criterion for disengagement programs would not be fair or realistic. Yet the public and political tolerance for recidivism might be very low, considering the potential seriousness of crimes related to violent extremism and the emotions activated by terrorist violence (Direktoratet for Kriminalforsorgen, 2016, 17; Nordic Prison and Probation Services, 2010, 32).

The longer-standing Scandinavian programs targeting right-wing extremism have been evaluated and generally found successful. Disengagers state that the help they received from the programs was crucial. As underlined in the evaluation of the Norwegian "Prosjekt Exit" of the late 1990s, however, it is difficult to isolate the effect of the program, given its core philosophy of working with the natural, preexisting factors that push or pull towards disengagement, e.g., disillusionment with the extremist group or leadership, longing for a normal life, stress, or burn-out (National Council for Crime Prevention, 2001, 8; Voksne for barn, Undated, 51).

Most of the initiatives of current national action plans and strategies have not yet undergone systematic and independent evaluation. Respondents report anecdotal evidence of success, but also difficulties, in particular when it comes to reaching into extremist Islamist subcultures (R2, R3; Lid et al., 2016, 27). Frequently, individuals in these subcultures lack trust in government authorities and are disinclined to accept help. In the words of a Norwegian respondent: "These guys will not trust us. You start on minus twenty and work your way up" (R2). And yet, the respondent continues: "We should keep on trying, because motivation [to accept help] may eventually emerge over time" (R2). The inclination to keep at it appears well founded. A Danish respondent indicates that it is possible to overcome trust deficits by establishing a track record of constructive engagement and practical assistance: "The program has increasingly gained such a level of credibility amongst relatives, parents and sometimes extremists themselves that they come to us acknowledging there is help to be found" (R4).

But what would happen if an individual who went through a disengagement program became involved in a high-profile terrorism case? Would a blame game and a backlash ensue? In the words of one respondent: "Yes, probably. But what would be the alternative to having exit programs? We have to conceive of this in terms of risk. What is the risk of having these programs and what is the risk of not having them?" (R3). Even if the inclusion of exit and disengagement efforts in national action plans across from Scandinavia seems to indicate a high level of political legitimacy and even if respondents point to growing acceptance since the 1990s, it is premature to consider this an irreversible development.

It appears advisable for proponents of disengagement to seek a dialog between the relevant stakeholders and with the broader public about realistic and acceptable success criteria in a Scandinavian context. It will probably remain difficult to isolate the impact and quantify the success rate of disengagement efforts. However, researchers have suggested a variety of possible success indicators, which might serve as a point of departure for debate. They include: disengagement from operational activity; disengagement from violent extremist groups, networks, and subcultures; collaboration with authorities, e.g., testifying in court or providing intelligence; meeting victims or intended victims; publicly denouncing violent extremism; and becoming active in efforts to prevent violent extremism (Bjørgo and Horgan, 2009, 250; Horgan and Braddock, 2010, 281; Rabasa, Petty, Ghez and Boucek, 2010, 35; Spalek and Davies, 2012, 363).

Absent common ground in terms of success criteria, it is difficult to envision an informed debate about how to balance diverging local and national perspectives and priorities discussed above. Arguably, the long-term legitimacy of disengagement efforts as well as the ability to navigate the inherent dilemmas of such efforts hinge on achieving a level of national agreement on realistic success criteria.

Conclusion

This chapter has provided an overview of efforts to promote disengagement from violent extremism in Denmark, Norway, and Sweden.

The chapter shows how an emphasis on voluntariness and behavioral rather than attitudinal definitions of disengagement dominates. It also points to an emerging willingness of central government, municipal authorities, and civil society actors to take responsibility and engage with the tasks of promoting disengagement, even if the degree and closeness of collaboration vary across the region and even if the pressure placed on municipal actors from central actors has been problematized in the Swedish case.

The chapter highlights three major strengths of the Scandinavian efforts: the tradition of institutionalized, cross-governmental efforts to prevent crime, which has offered an established platform and collaboration mechanism for tackling violent extremism; the willingness of the municipal level to accept co-responsibility for disengagement efforts despite the fact that violent extremism has traditionally been handled by central government security agencies; and the ability to offer practical and economic support to disengagers via the Scandinavian welfare state.

Unclear success criteria for disengagement efforts combined with divergence between government authorities at local and national level regarding whether to collaborate with "gray-zone" actors and how to balance sanctions and rehabilitation efforts represent the greatest political and institutional challenges to current efforts. A backlash against disengagement programs is not inconceivable if, for example, an individual who had received aid via a disengagement program later became involved in a high-profile incidence of extremist violence. Other countries, absent the welfare-state tradition and the presence of a legal and institutional platform for collaborating across government actors in crime prevention, could not easily copy Scandinavian solutions. Yet, the Scandinavian case could still offer inspiration for others. First, deep knowledge of the political and theological foundations of various forms of extremism might help when trying to promote disengagement. But focusing simply on the practical and social needs of the disengager seems to go a long way. Second, working in a coalition that spans several levels of government is a huge advantage. But a durable coalition will need some mechanism for addressing and negotiating the right balance between divergent needs and priorities. Finally, even if measuring the success of disengagement efforts is no easy task, it appears prudent to address the question explicitly in political and public debates as well as in the policy documents and strategies that guide national efforts.

Notes

1 SSP stands for Schools, Social Services, Police. SLT stands for "Samordning af Lokale rus og kriminalitetsforebyggende Tiltag" (in English: Coordination of local efforts to prevent crime and substance abuse). SSPF stands for Schools, Social Services, Police and "Fritid," which is the Swedish term for after-school and leisure activities.

2 Five supplementary interviews were carried out with national and local level government officials and civil society actors in Denmark, Norway, and Sweden. Respondents were selected based on seniority and experience from working at the policy level or from working hands on with violent extremists. Interviews were semi-structured and with a particular focus on questions of collaboration across central and local government and civil society. All respondents were promised anonymity. Interviews were conducted during spring and summer 2017, each lasting between one and two hours.

Respondent	Country	Sector	National/local
R1	Sweden	NGO	National level
R2	Norway	Government	Local level
R3	Sweden	Government	National level
R4	Denmark	Government	Local level
R5	Denmark	Government	National level.

3 Similar collaboration structures are established with the psychiatric services (PSP) and the Prison and Probation Service (KSP).

4 The F in Sweden's SSPF stands for "fritid," which translates roughly to leisure and after-school activities. See also note 1 above.

References

Arnstberg, Karl-Olov and Jonas Hållén. (2000). *Smaka kanga. Vägen tillbaka. Intervjuer med avhoppade nynazister.* Stockholm: För Exit, Fryshuset.

Barrett, Richard and Laila Bokhari. (2009). "Deradicalization and rehabilitation programmes targeting religious terrorists and extremists in the Muslim world. An overview." In Tore Bjørgo and John Horgan (eds) *Leaving Terrorism Behind. Individual and Collective Disengagement*, London: Routledge, pp. 170–180.

Bjørgo, Tore and Yngve Carlsson. (2005). "Early Intervention with Violent and Racist Youth Groups." *NUPI Paper 677.*

CTA. (2017). Assessment of the terror threat to Denmark 2017." *CTA assessment*, February 7. www.pet.dk/English/Center%20for%20Terror%20Analysis/~/media/VTD%202017/VTD2017ENpdf.ashx

Dalgaard-Nielsen, Anja. (2013). "Promoting Exit from Violent Extremism: Themes and Approaches." *Studies in Conflict and Terrorism*, 36: 2, pp. 99–115.

Dalgaard-Nielsen, Anja. (2017). "Patterns of Disengagement from Violent Extremism: A Stocktaking of Current Knowledge and Implications for Counterterrorism". In Andreas Önnerfors and Kristian Steiner (eds) *Expressions of Radicalization: Global Politics, Processes and Practices*, London: Palgrave, pp. 273–293.

Danish Ministry of Immigration, Integration and Housing. (2016). *Preventing and Countering Extremism and Radicalisation*, Copenhagen: Danish Ministry of Immigration, Integration and Housing.

Direktoratet for Kriminalforsorgen. (2016). *Kriminalforsorgens recidivstatistik 2015*, Copenhagen: Direktoratet for Kriminalforsorgen.

Fangen, Katrine. (1998). "Living Out Our Ethnic Instincts: Ideological Beliefs Among Right-Wing Activists in Norway." In Jeffrey Kaplan and Tore Bjørgo (eds) *Nation and Race*, Boston: Northeastern University Press, pp. 202–230.

Government Communication. (2014). *Actions to Make Society More Resilient to Violent Extremism*, Stockholm: The Government.

Gunaratna, Rohan. (2011). "Terrorist Rehabilitation: A Global Imperative." *Journal of Policing, Intelligence and Counter Terrorism*, 6: 1, pp. 65–82.

Horgan, John. (2009). *Walking Away from Terrorism: Accounts of Disengagement from Radical and Extremist Groups*. London: Routledge.

Horgan, John and Kurt Braddock. (2010). "Rehabilitating the Terrorists? Challenges in Assessing the Effectinveness of Deradicalisation Programs." *Terrorism and Political Violence*, 22, pp. 267–291.

Ignazi, Piero. (2003). *Extreme Right Parties in Western Europe*. Oxford: Oxford University Press.

Jyllands-Posten. Muhammeds ansigt. 30.09.2005 https://jyllands-posten.dk/indland/ECE4769352/Muhammeds-ansigt/ (accessed October 10, 2019).

Lid, Stian, Marte Winsvold, Susanne Søholt, Stig J. Hansen, Geir Heierstad and Jan E. Klausen (2016). "Forebygging av radikalisering og voldelig ekstremisme – Hva er kommunernes rolle?" *NIBR-rapport* 12.

Lindekilde, Lasse. (2012). "Assessing the Effectiveness of Counter-Radicalisation Policies in North-Western Europe." *Critical Studies on Terrorism*, 5: 3, pp. 335–344.

Lööw, Helene. (2000). *Nazismen i Sverige 1980-1997: Den rasistiska undergroundrörelsen: Musiken, myterna, riterna*. Stockholm: Ordfront.

Malmros Robin Andersson and Christer Mattsson. (2017). *Från ord til handlingsplan. En rapport om kommunala handlingsplaner mot våldsbejakende extremism*. Stockholm: Sveriges Kommuner och Landsting.

Ministry of Refugee, Immigration and Refugee Affairs. (2010). *The Challenge of Extremism. Examples of Deradicalisation and Disengagement Programmes in the EU*, Copenhagen: Ministry of Refugee, Immigration and Refugee Affairs.

National Coordinator to safeguard democracy against violent extremism. (2016). *Nationell strategi mot väldsbejakande extremism*. Stockholm: Nationelle samordnaren mot väldsbejakande extremism.

National Council for Crime Prevention. (2001). "Exit för avhoppare. En uppföljning och utvärdering av verksamheten åren 1998-2001." *BRÅ-rapport* 8.

National Council for Crime Prevention. (2005). *On the Right Track. A Survey of Sweden's Local Crime Prevention Councils*. Stockholm: National Council for Crime Prevention.

NCT. (2017). *Bedömning av terrorhotet mot Sverige 2017*, Stockholm: NTC. www.sakerhetspolisen.se/download/18.1beef5fc14cb83963e73383/1484663040490/NCT_Helarsbedomning_2017.pdf

Norwegian Ministry of Justice. (2014). *Action Plan Against Radicalization and Violent Extremism*. Oslo: Norwegian Ministry of Justice.

Nordic Prison and Probation Services. (2010). *Retur. Nordisk recidiv*. Oslo: Kriminalomsorgen i Danmark, Finland, Island, Norge, Sverige.

PST. (2016). *What Background Do Individuals Who Frequent Extreme Islamist Environments in Norway Have Prior to Their Radicalization?*, Oslo: PST. www.pst.no/media/82364/Radikaliseringsprosjektet_rapport_ugrad_eng_12-09-16.pdf

PST. (2017). *National Threat Assessment 2017*. Oslo: PST. www.pst.no/media/82645/pst_trusselvurd-2017_eng_web.pdf

Rabasa, Angel, Stacie L. Petty, Jeremy J. Ghez and Christopher Boucek. (2010). *Deradicalizing Islamist Extremists*. Santa Monica: RAND.

Ravndal, Jacob Aasland. (2017). "Right-Wing Terrorism and Militancy in the Nordic Countries: A Comparative Case Study." *Terrorism and Political Violence*, 30: 5, pp. 772–792. doi: 10.1080/09546553.2018.1445888

SÄPO. (2017). *Färre reser från Sverige till terroristorganisationer*. Stockholm: SÄPO. www.sakerhetspolisen.se/ovrigt/pressrum/aktuellt/aktuellt/2017-06-27-farre-reser-fran-sverige-till-terroristorganisationer.html

SFI. (2014). *Anti-democratic and Extremist Environments in Denmark*. Copenhagen: The Danish National Centre for Social Research.

Spalek, Basia and Lynn Davies. (2012). "Mentoring in Relation to Violent Extermism: A Study of Role, Purpose, and Outcomes." *Studies in Conflict and Terrorism*, 35, pp. 354–368.

Voksne for barn. (Undated). *Prosjekt exit. Sluttrapport*. Oslo: Voksne for barn. www.vfb.no/filestore/Publikasjoner/Informasjons-_og_vervemateriell_om_VFB_og_tiltak/EXIT-Sluttrapport_95-99.pdf (accessed June 14, 2017).

Winsvold, Marte, Hilmar L. Mjelde and Jill Loga. (2017). *Trossamfunn som arena for forebygging av radikalisering og voldelig ekstremisme*. Bergen and Oslo: Senter for forskning på sivilsamfunn & frivillig sektor.

19

DERADICALISATION

China's panacea for conflict resolution in Xinjiang

Bhavna Singh

As a strategic response to the terrorist threat faced by countries the world over, many states have introduced governmental counter-terrorism policies or what may be called attempts aimed at deradicalisation and prevent strategies. These are intended to assist the public agencies and departments in understanding their role in dealing with terrorism as well as to assist investigations by local authorities and firefighters in dealing with radicalised combatants (Lowe, 2018: 58). For instance, the UK's CONTEST policy is based on four "p"s – prepare, protect, prevent and pursue – which echoes closely the EU counter-terrorism strategy, which is also based on four strands of disengagement and exit strategies, and the Canadian Government's counter-terrorism strategy, which has four strands to it. The US policy listed in the National Strategy for Counter-terrorism also discusses the measures and procedures that have been strengthened in order to "improve" US capabilities in countering terrorism, especially by preventing it from occurring (Ibid: 59). China is no exception; it too grapples with the threat of radicalisation at various levels in different parts of its territories. Keeping this in mind, it has initiated several measures as a prevent strategy in view of increased radicalisation, both religious and ethnic, in Xinjiang over the last two decades. Heeding the clarion call given by many scholars who had warned of the likely "Palestinisation" of conflict in Xinjiang if alternative strategies are not adopted for conflict resolution, China has brought in prevent strategies to curtail the menace of severe political and social instability, often instigated by troublesome forces, organisations and mechanisms from abroad. This also bears from the fact that China's approach of using development as an antidote to ethnic tensions in Xinjiang has failed miserably, forcing it to adopt prevent strategies against terrorist elements.

With China now focusing on the Belt and Road initiative, touted as its foremost foreign policy apparatus for the present century, curbing extremist instances in Xinjiang has become even more important to maintain stability in its frontier regions. Keeping this in view, President Xi Jinping has urged the security forces to erect a "Great Wall of Steel/Iron" around the violence-hit western region of Xinjiang. These attempts are deemed even more important to change China's image which has often attracted criticism for its restrictive policies and widespread harassment of religious groups, and understandably so, as it faces the challenge of grappling with 55 minority nationalities (56 including the Han majority), some of which occupy large territorial swathes of its polity. The Uyghurs in fact do not even constitute the largest Muslim population; it is the Hui community with its 10.5-million-strong population that has emerged as the second largest ethnic minority in China. They exhibit a lot of cultural affinity to the Hans and are virtually indistinguishable from them. They have close trade linkages across the country and do not pose a severe challenge to the central administration. It is the Turkic Muslims in Xinjiang who are considered "bad Muslims" and hence have been at the receiving end from the state for resisting the central authority. A recent study by the Pew Research Centre placed China at a high position of number two just behind Egypt amongst countries with a high degree of religious restrictions using data from 2015 (Williams, 2017). Rising inequality from state-orchestrated migration as well as natural migration has been at the heart of separatist movements in the form of Han–Uyghur clashes in Xinjiang. Given this rise in radical tendencies it would be prudent to examine why the state's policies have been rendered counter-productive to the goal of integrating Xinjiang's minorities in its larger nation-building exercise and whether deradicalisation as a strategy can show the way forward.

Though there is no major consensus on how to define the terms "radicalisation" and its counterpart "deradicalisation", for the purpose of this paper Dalgaard-Nielsen's definition of radicalisation, that is, as Koehler points out in this volume, a "growing readiness to pursue and support far-reaching changes in society that conflict with, or pose a direct threat to the existing order" will be used. This would subsume the trend that radicalisation occurs due to networks, group dynamics and peer pressure and a constructed reality as propounded by Kepel (2004). Whether or not the use of violence is actually a key aspect of radicalisation remains contested, as Koehler points out, since even non-violent radicalisation can occur. This may be understood as the "social and psychological process of incrementally experienced commitment to extremist political or Islamist ideology", as explained by Horgan and Braddock (2010: 152). Both violent and non-violent radicalisation has been witnessed in the case of Xinjiang. Deradicalisation is understood in terms of deliberately focusing on an ideology or the psychological aspects of an existing violent phenomenon to wean away the radicalised groups and minimise the risk of re-radicalisation. This occurs through a process of voluntary or involuntary attempts to turn from a position of perceived deviance or conflict with the surrounding environment towards moderation and equilibrium, deriving from a societal negotiation, also explained by Koehler earlier in this volume. It is often used in combination with attempts at disengagement of the deviant groups from their parent movements.

Ethnic radicalisation in Xinjiang

China's endeavours to assimilate Xinjiang as an autonomous region have been marked by an oscillating hard and soft policy over the last few decades. The region, which has abundant oil resources like the Tahe oilfield and Dushanzi refinery and boasts of the largest natural gas-producing capabilities in China, has emerged as a key strategic location facilitating oil and gas trade, making it even more indispensable to China. While Muslim Uyghurs had traditionally been the predominant majority in the province prior to mass migrations of Hans into the region, the current demography exhibits equal proportions of Turkic-speaking Uyghurs and Mandarin-speaking Hans. This alteration in the demographic component is a major source of instability and disgruntlement for the locals as well as the central government.

Historically, the ethnic minorities in Xinjiang have enjoyed widespread cultural autonomy as the Qing rulers did not bother interfering with their religious practices or even bureaucratic practices. However, after the establishment of Xinjiang as an autonomous region under the People's Republic of China (PRC), the state has constantly sought to keep a firm rein on both political and religious aspects. The Communist Party's Anti-Rightist Policy of 1957, which opposed "local nationalism" and the Cultural Revolution of 1966–76 under which the minorities witnessed most of their religious texts and institutions being destroyed, left many scars on the psyche of the Muslim minorities.

The unwieldiness of their aspiration for a separate state of "East Turkestan" sought by the Uyghurs, led by fragmented ideologies, continues to be a major source of dissatisfaction amongst the local communities, especially since the other ethnic groups – Kazaks, Kyrgyz, Uzbek and Tajik – who had been vying for independence realised their goals and formed their own independent nations (Central Asian Republics) as a result of the disintegration of the Soviet Union in the 1990s. This explains the surge in dissent in Xinjiang post-1990. In fact a combination of ethnicity and religion has made the region more vulnerable to the movement of religious and political ideologies, groups and weapons (Davis, 2008). The state's response to the outbreaks of unrest in Xinjiang in the 1990s, especially bombings in Beijing in 1997, has been mostly ham-fisted as the state maintains a heavy hand on the administrative and traditional customs in the region. While the "Strike hard campaign" had been announced as one of the foremost measures in 1996 in an attempt to curb separatism, a "war on terror" has been declared more recently to curb the "three evils" of religious extremism, separatism and terrorism in the wake of the 9/11 attacks and the larger augmentation of the "Global war on terror".[1]

More significantly, there has been a parallel rise in violence in Xinjiang as the PRC has sought to assert its rise on the international stage, perhaps both as a cause and effect. In 2006, Wang Jinxiang, deputy director of the National Development and Reform Commission, had assured the National Committee of the Chinese People's Political Consultative Conference (CPPCC) that the national strategy to develop the country's western region under the Western Development Campaign had made great progress.[2] But on the ground, the radical groups utilised the opportunities provided by economic modernisation and the soft policies of the state to further their agenda, often abetted by their Muslim Brotherhood abroad and local support from Muslim clerics and influential businessmen. Ever since, violent outbreaks have been occurring sporadically as the groups that claim responsibility frequently merge and collapse depending on the unofficial support they derive from extremist elements and governments, for instance, from Turkey and other states in their neighbourhood.

This was even more evident in the extremist instances that flared up around the Beijing Olympics and subsequent to the event, since it was seen as an opportunity by the minorities in China to bring the issue of human rights violations to the forefront of international politics. An aircraft attack in March and multiple killings in August 2008 had put the Chinese authorities on high alert. The state has ever since maintained a strict vigil on minorities in Xinjiang as well as Tibet. The scale of radicalisation and the rise in violence in Xinjiang till 2005 had been mapped by Bovingdon and Garner (2010), who identified 158 political violent events and organised protests from 1949 to 2005, of which 142 had a clear ethnic component. China claims that there has been a rise in Islamist-inspired terrorism and inter-ethnic violence especially after 2009; the year 2013 alone witnessed at least five major incidents in Kashgar, Turpan and Khotan (Clarke, 2017). The Uyghurs have, however, failed to emerge as a unitary force harbouring a single agenda which has been a major drawback for their struggle – while some aspire for a separate state, others wish for cultural autonomy while some others are in fact integrating into the Chinese system (Ibid). The central government has tried to wean away many of these radical elements by making efforts to co-opt the local elite, especially the Uyghurs who have spearheaded the struggle for an independent state of East Turkestan. At the same time, it has begun to identify Muslim institutions and practices that are a source of instability.[3]

The rise in violence in Xinjiang can be attributed to several socio-economic and political factors: a ban on religious activities which the state considers illegal and human rights issues, which have surfaced as a major reason for discontent amongst the local population and differences in perception on balancing indigenous cultural developments. There is a constant struggle for resources and opportunities between Uyghurs and Hans due to ethnic-based discrimination policies of the government as most of the decision-making authoritative jobs fall under the purview of Hans, leaving the middle-rung and lower-category jobs for the other ethnic minorities. The human resource development also suffers as a result of the biased education policies which lay more stress on Mandarin education in comparison to ethnic language-based education – leading to widely differing career prospects for them (Dillon, 2004: 21) and difference of availability of health amenities, which fuels a discourse of deprivation amongst the Uyghurs (Schuster, 2009: 423).

The state has termed the religious revival as an ethno-nationalist and splittist threat (*fenlie zhuyizhe*), thereby targeting the theoretical and ritualistic manifestations of religion. For instance, it has restricted the celebration of regional holidays, study of religious texts and free expression of religious preferences through personal appearances, including the way they prefer to dress to the naming of their children, which has drawn a backlash from the Uyghur community. An example of the state's heavy-handed approach to discourage Uyghur women from wearing traditional headscarves or veils was the "Project Beauty campaign" (Leibold and Grose, 2015). In December 2014, some county-level authorities in Xinjiang began disseminating a brochure that identified 75 forms of "religious extremism" for local officials to be aware of, as reported in the *Global Times*. In March 2017, the Xinjiang legislature Standing Committee passed a law to curb religious extremism which bans wearing veils or "abnormal beards" without specifying the term. It deems it illegal to refuse to watch state television and listen to state radio, or prevent children from receiving national education – activities deemed "manifestations" of extremism (Gan, 2017).

China has closed down several mosques and increased control over the Islamic clergy through the China Islamic Organisation. Anyone deemed in contravention of the rules is punishable or liable for detention in China's notorious and discredited Re-education Through Labour (RTL) programme. Of late it has even banned dozens of baby names with religious meanings that are widely used by Muslims elsewhere in the world under the "Naming Rules for Ethnic Minorities", such as Islam, Quran, Mecca, Jihad, Imam, Saddam, Hajj and Medina, stating that any babies registered under such names would be barred from the "hukou" household registration system that gives access to health care and education. Night markets have been closed and the process of assimilation has been pushed hard, including cash incentives for mixed marriages between Han and Uyghurs.

These measures have naturally given rise to resentment amongst the local population which views these attempts by the government as a challenge to their personal and religious freedom. The government, however, refuses to take note of the social disruption that its policies are causing and attributes the religious disorientations to the "dramatic social transformation" that is taking place in China today (Annual Report on China's Religions 2010 by the Chinese Academy of Social Sciences (CASS)) and the confusion amongst the ethnic groups resulting from China's soft and hard policies. The soft policies include positive discrimination in terms of concessions from the one-child policy and reservation of government jobs for locals (Article 17, 18, 22), priority to ethnic minorities in enterprises and institutions (Article 23), fiscal transfer, poverty reduction and arranging for assistance from developed provinces in the East, which the government had earlier doled out on various occasions (instituted through the Law of Regional Ethnic Autonomy in 1984 and amended in 2001). Interestingly, it has been observed that the chances of violence in Xinjiang have increased with gross domestic product (GDP) per capita increases as the frequency of protests over ethno-nationalist issues increased with urbanisation because economic development fostered the very conditions for local minorities to form ethnic networks (Cao, Duan, Liu and Wei, 2018). In this sense, economic integration through trade has not led to assimilation of Uyghurs as in the case of the Hui minority.

These soft measures have failed to address the sentiments of relative deprivation as higher population density has exacerbated resource scarcity and worsened inter-group competition, leading to further radicalisation amongst the Uyghurs. The government is now hard pressed to come up with alternative strategies to deradicalise. Though the cavalcade of measures brought forth during the earlier part of 2017 may seem prudent to the government since it wants to maintain a complete grip over the minority regions given its Belt and Road summit initiative, it may be hard for the government to justify its approach to the indigenous people.

The process – modes and agents of radicalisation

The militant movement in Xinjiang led by the East Turkestan Islamic movement (ETIM)/ Tu-Dong forces and later by the Tukistan Islamic Party (TIP) has reorganised along religious lines after the demise of the Eastern Turkestan People's Party. Drawing inspiration from the victory of the Afghan Mujahideen over the Red Army, most Uyghurs have sought to mobilise local support through various slogans like "Down with socialism", "Take Barin, establish East Turkestan" and so on (Castets, 2003: 38). Militant Uyghur groups often exploit Xinjiang's porous border with Kazakhstan, Tajikistan, Kyrgyzstan and Afghanistan to establish training camps and move explosives and small arms into China (Wolfe, 2004).[4] Many young students and entrepreneurs who travel to the neighbouring regions for study and business become easy targets of recruitment by "terrorist and splittist" organisations operating abroad.

The Chinese Government has alleged that since 1997 the ETIM has been leading pious Muslims astray by offering board, lodging and scholarships as bait through its offices in different Asian countries. Besides physical training they receive basic skill drills such as assembling and disassembling different weapons and shooting. More and more Uyghurs are being radicalised and trained overseas by groups such as al-Qaeda, Islamic State and most probably more localised Southeast Asian groups (Sainsbury, 2017). However, the evidence provided by the Chinese Government and the international agencies, in the form of documentaries and video clippings that argue these acts of violence in Xinjiang are infiltrated as part of a larger terrorist network, is very often fabricated and by no means involves entire movements or their leaders; some of these acts are no more than ordinary crimes.[5] Wang Lequan, secretary of Xinjiang's Chinese Communist Party (CCP) committee in 1998 highlighted the preliminary nature of these attacks – "Since early 1996, a series of criminal activities involving violent attacks have taken place in Xinjiang" carried out by "a handful of criminals".

The term terrorism has been increasingly used only after 2001 in the context of the global wave of the fight against terrorism and that too with unclear definitions and purposes in the present context. In its Document No.7 issued in 2000, the CCP had briefly identified the principal danger to Xinjiang's stability as the "separatist force and illegal religious activities" without defining these terms in a precise manner. There is an attempt to manipulate the discourse on terrorism by Beijing by exploiting the remoteness of Xinjiang and its cultural distance and restricted information. This exaggeration of the narrative on the crimes of Eastern Turkestan Terrorist Power (*Dongtu kongbu shili zuixing jishi*) further radicalises the Uyghur youth.

Meanwhile, other organisations which have been critical of the cause of a separate Turkestan but which do not have terrorist links are also often dubbed as extremist by the Chinese Government, especially the World Uyghur Congress and the East Turkestan Government-in-exile. Earlier in 2014, US National Security Advisor Susan Rice alleged that Chinese Uyghurs from Xinjiang had been sighted in Iraq and Syria fighting among the ranks of the Islamic State in Iraq and Syria (ISIS) insurgency. In the same year China also took action by seizing passports to prevent its citizens from travelling to Syria and Iraq as many Chinese citizens had been reported to have worked in tandem with the Islamic State of Iraq and the Levant (ISIL) in the Middle East. In November, ISIL claimed to have executed Chinese citizen Fan Jinghui, prompting strong condemnation from President Xi Jinping. Two weeks later, ISIL posted a song online in Mandarin calling for Chinese Muslims to take up arms against their country.

Palpably, there is an increasing trend amongst Uyghurs to relate their nationalism more in terms of an ideological religious nationalism instead of ethnic religious nationalism which also targets co-ethnics viewed as collaborators with the state (Country Reports on Terrorism, 2015). The state has tried to wean away some of these radicalised groups by stating that "religious extremism under the banner of Islam runs counter to Islamic doctrines and it is not Islam and that these ethnic groups should not turn a blind eye to the diverse and splendid cultures of Xinjiang" (White paper, 2019).

State responses to Uyghur radicalisation

The Chinese state has responded deftly to the radicalisation movement in the province, firstly by ensuring international support and secondly by churning out indigenous initiatives. To begin with, the inclusion of ETIM in the terrorist list by the UN Security Council has provided China the needed international support to wage a war against terrorism and at the same time led to a loss of sympathy for the independence movement of the Uyghurs. Simultaneously, China has been relentlessly trying to establish evidence on the funding of these terrorist organisations by various local and international financing mechanisms (China Daily, 2002). The state has also tried to a keep a firm control over the polity through the Xinjiang Production and Construction Corps (XPCC) which, being the main organ of the state in the defence realm, is also one of the main reasons for intensification of Uyghur–Chinese conflict. In addition the state has tried to suppress all dissent by imprisoning prominent intellectuals, as illustrated by the case of Ilham Tohti.

The pressing need to check radicalisation was brought to the fore by Chinese dissident Wang Lixiong in his 2007 book, *My West China: Your East Turkestan*, where he cautions on the likely "Palestinisation" of conflict in Xinjiang in which "the full mobilization of a people and the full extent of its hatred would be directed against the state" (Lixiong, 2014). From 2014 onwards, the state's reaction has been largely framed under an attempt to strengthen security and counter-terrorism measures by increasing Xinjiang's internal security budget. President Xi Jinping now heads a specially formed committee on China's new National Security Council to deal with security and counter-terror strategies in Xinjiang. At the same time the state has declared a "people's war" to exterminate the "savage and evil" separatists who are directed by foreign extremists to incite violence at home. It has accelerated counter-terrorism and deradicalisation initiatives through three specific local regulations, including "the *Regulations of Xinjiang Uyghur Autonomous*

Region on Religious Affairs", "the *Measures of Xinjiang Uyghur Autonomous Region on Implementing the Counter-terrorism Law of the People's Republic of China*" and "the *Regulations of Xinjiang Uyghur Autonomous Region on De-radicalization*". Under these legal measures

> since 2014, the state has destroyed 1,588 violent gangs, arrested 12,995 terrorists, seized 2,052 explosive devices, punished 30,645 people for 4,858 illegal religious activities and confiscated 345,229 copies of illegal religious materials.
>
> *(White Paper on The Fight Against Terrorism and Extremism and Human Rights Protection in Xinjiang, 2019)*

Besides co-opting the elite the authorities have tried to elicit assistance of ordinary Uyghurs through the offer of financial rewards for tip-offs to police regarding suspicious individuals and activities. In 2014, China made a forceful attempt to link violence in Xinjiang to the radical Islamic threat and the rise of ISIS and also used soft-power techniques to target radicalisation through anti-extremism campaigns. For instance, in a commemoration speech at China's National People's Congress in March 2014 in the honour of the victims of a knife attack in Kunming train station in which 33 were killed and 144 injured, the deputy chair of the China Dancer's Association, Dilnar Abdulla, complained that "religious extremists" in the Muslim region of Xinjiang were "campaigning for the commoners not to sing and dance".

Several such campaigns have been introduced with the intent of inculcating an alternative set of behaviours in addition to criminalising Islamic behaviours. The most prominent part of these campaigns is the organisation of song and dance events by the cultural bureau for displays of loyalty to the party and nation and singing of revolutionary songs. The emphasis on public demonstrations of happiness is another recurring theme in the reports of these campaigns. Some of these programmes have drawn displeasure from the media in international Islamic countries and organisations; for instance, it was the reports of the Imams publicly dancing to the Chinese internet hit song "*Little Apple*" that aroused the ire of the Turkish media in 2015. Nonetheless, the state has equipped the mosques and imams with modern infrastructure with access to medical services, LED screens, computers, drinking water and electricity facilities and automatic dispensers of shoe coverings to better satisfy their reasonable religious demands (White Paper, 2019).

However, despite these local measures the biggest challenge for China in countering terrorism and extremism emerges from the lack of clear definitions on its understanding of the terms "terrorism and extremism". *Country Reports on Terrorism*, published by the US Government (Bureau of Counter terrorism and Countering Violent Terrorism, 2015) lament that the lack of transparency and information provided by China about violent incidents that the government characterised as terrorist incidents greatly complicates the effort to verify details and its tendency to prevent foreign journalists and international observers from independently verifying media accounts leads to improper reporting (White Paper, 2019). This is also the primary reason why counter-terrorism cooperation between China and the US has remained limited. Yet China remains committed to implementing the resolution of the General Assembly of the United Nations concerning the United Nations Global Counter-Terrorism Strategy (60/288) through a people-centred approach.[6] So far the two countries have initiated several technical workshops on countering the spread of improvised explosive devices (IEDs) and increased consultations aimed at stemming the transnational flow of foreign terrorist fighters, countering terrorist funding networks, increasing information sharing on terrorist threats and sharing evidentiary best practices.

A more successful regional attempt to curb extremist influence and radicalisation of Uyghur youth has emerged under the Shanghai Cooperation Organisation (SCO) framework with the Central Asian countries.[7] For its part, China has also been a member of the Financial Action Task Force (FATF), as well as the Asia/Pacific Group on Money Laundering and the Eurasian Group on Combating Money Laundering and Terrorist Financing, both of which are FATF-style regional bodies. China and the US have met at least once a year (for the last four years) to engage in a technical discussion related to anti-money laundering (AML) and countering the financing of terrorism (CFT) under the AML/CFT Working Group within the Strategic and Economic Dialogue (S&ED).

In May 2015 the Chinese state media reported that it had dismantled 181 "terror groups" in Xinjiang. In December 2015, the National People's Congress Standing Committee approved the country's first comprehensive counter-terrorism law to "provide legal support for counter-terrorism activities as well as collaboration with the international community".[8] In addition to the provisions under the Constitution of the PRC, China's anti-terrorism law system is currently composed of:

1. the Criminal Law of the PRC
2. the Criminal Procedure Law of the PRC
3. the National Security Law of the PRC
4. the Counter Terrorism Law of the PRC
5. the Regulations on Religious Affairs and Opinions issued by the Supreme People's Court, the Supreme People's Procuratorate, the Ministry of Public Security and the Ministry of Justice.

These responses have helped to curtail the threat of Islamic radicalisation to some extent but not yet effectively.

Deradicalisation as a strategic tool

The necessity to deradicalise is imminent if the state wants to avert the growth of separatism as a challenge to long-term political stability in Xinjiang. The Chinese state is coming to terms with the fact that military, enforcement and intelligence measures alone will not be sufficient to combat religious extremism. Hence there is an emerging consensus amongst Chinese scholars and policy makers that if rigorous deradicalisation (*qu jiduanhua*) measures are brought into practice, it can reduce the risk of violent extremism (Congressional-executive, Commission on China, Annual report 2016). It also has to be curbed for the reasons that it lends support to the active independence movement in Tibet and influences nascent ethnic unrest in Inner Mongolia (George, 1998, No. 73).

Though there has been a reversal of policy approach since the 2009 Urumqi riots in terms of adopting a stringent apparatus, as reflected in the change of guard at the top levels and the two Work Forums in 2010 and 2014, the current government under Xi Jinping is more open to accept alternatives for the resolution of Xinjiang conflict. Under the larger parapet, Xi Jinping called on Xinjiang residents to identify themselves, regardless of their ethnicity, with China, the Chinese nation, its culture and socialism with Chinese characteristics.[9] Endorsing the deradicalisation approach, Zhang Chunxian, then top leader of Xinjiang, used the term "deradicalisation" for the first time in January 2012. In a study on the approach to deradicalisation, Angel Rabasa, a senior political scientist with RAND Corporation, had explained that "getting militants to refrain from violence is only part of the process; ideally the goal is to get the individual to change his belief system, reject the extremist ideology and embrace a moderate worldview". The Chinese Government has made efforts in this direction by obtaining intelligence on extremist organisations and by discrediting the extremist ideology and bringing about a shift in belief from extremist ideas to mainstream values.

In May 2013, the strategy of deradicalisation materialised in a policy document entitled "Several Guiding Opinions on Further Suppressing Illegal Religious Activities and Combating the Infiltration of Religious Extremism in Accordance with Law", issued by Xinjiang's CCP Committee. The policy document, often referred to as the "No. 11 Document", elaborated and defined the borders between ethnic customs, normal religious practices and extremist manifestations. In 2014, the No. 11 Document was supplemented by a "No. 28 Document" that referred to another policy guideline entitled "Several Opinions on Further Strengthening and Improving the Work with Regard to Islam" (Zhou, 2017). By and large the deradicalisation approach has been high on its agenda since the Second Work Forum in 2014 and has been pursued in different forms by multiple CCP and government organs and civil society groups.

To project its approach towards deradicalisation in Xinjiang, China has postulated several approaches under the "five keys", "four prongs", "three contingents", "two hands" and "one rule" strategy. The "five keys" approach in its documents highlights five methods respectively to solve five different categories of problems, that is, ideological, cultural, customary, religious and legal keys – ideological problems should be solved by means of ideology, cultural problems should be solved through the means of culture, folk customs should be treated with an attitude of respect, religious problems should be solved in accordance with religious rules and violent terrorism should be combated in line with the rule of law and by means of iron-fisted actions (Lina, 2015).

The "four prongs" approach articulated by Zhang Chunxian at the Xinjiang Stability Work Conference on 8 January 2016 refers to a combination of methods based on "squeezing by correct faith", "counteracting by culture", "controlling by law" and "popularizing science" (Tong and Yunyan, 2016).[10] Under its "three contingents" strategy the Chinese Government has identified its 1.28 million cadres, 0.4 million teachers and 28,000 religious figures as an integral part of a human resource pool which can help in maintaining stability and security in the region. Meanwhile, the two hands refer to "one firm hand" which cracks down on terrorists and the other firm hand which educates and guides Uyghur people and the "one rule" refers to the policy of ruling Xinjiang according to law. The emphasis on the rule of law suggests the adaptability of Xinjiang authorities to change their previous deradicalisation practices, which are perhaps not firmly based on the law (Zhou, 2016).

Besides these approaches the government has tried to legalise its standpoint on counter-terrorism through laws such as the Counter-Terrorism Law (CTL), passed on 27 December 2015, which for the first time introduces China's specific provisions on terrorist deradicalisation; Article 29 is a general stipulation on social and custodial deradicalisation while Article 30 addresses post-imprisonment deradicalisation. In addition to the National Law, it adopted the Xinjiang Uyghur Autonomous Region's Implementing Rules on the "Counter-Terrorism Law of the PRC" (Xinjiang IRCTL) – the regional law comprising 61 articles in 10 chapters featuring important provisions to supplement the national law. These laws yet again showcase a hard and soft approach of the Chinese Government to the issue of radicalisation. While the state finds it difficult to prevent radicalisation since most of it is foreign-sourced, the current approach of the state is to deradicalise imprisoned radicals, released radicals and radicals who have not been in prison. Accordingly the state has devised custodial programmes, post-imprisonment programmes and social programmes.

In an effort to upend the traditional role of prisons as hotbeds of radicalisation, the Chinese Government has made provisions of the prisons, detention centres and community correctional facilities to supervise, educate and correct criminals imprisoned on terrorism and extremism charges. The Prison Administration, a governmental agency administered by the Department of Justice in Xinjiang, has gained hands-on experiences that they are sharing with the prisons based all over country, labelling them as "Xinjiang experiences". These experiences include boosting the capabilities of prison officials for deradicalisation, familiarising themselves with local customs, traditions and culture as well as being integrated into the *Fang Hui Ju* project,[11] providing religious counselling to dispel extremist ideology by inviting reliable Islamic scholars and religious leaders to give counselling to radicalised detainees, garnering external support from other governmental agencies, for instance joint mechanisms involving partner institutions for policy interpretation legal aid and occupational help and civil society organisations, as well as utilising deradicalised prisoners to speak out against extremism (Zhou, 2017).

The implementation of these projects, though difficult, has yielded some results. Claiming its deradicalisation efforts to be successful, China has reduced sentences for some of its prisoners who have shown signs of improvement. In August 2014, two inmates, Maimaituofuti Maimaitirouzi and Guli'aman Abudula, were sent to their home prefecture Hetian, having been assigned the responsibility to use their own experiences to expose the harm caused by extremism and demonstrate the benefits of change (Zhou, 2017). More recently, China reduced sentences of 11 people in February 2016 jailed for threatening state security after declaring the success of its deradicalisation programmes. However, such claims have been discredited by Uyghur expatriates who dismiss it as Chinese political propaganda. More interestingly, the commutation of sentences occurs largely after self-criticism by the prisoners who express deep regret for having hurt their families and causing damage to their nation. This reflects the hangover of historical approaches in the Chinese psyche which still remains stuck in the self-critical approaches of its past leaders.

The reintegration of these released prisoners remains another issue of concern for the Chinese authorities. It is essential to ensure that, after the painstaking deradicalisation process, these individuals find employment and become socially integrated so as to avoid reversion to extremism. For this purpose the Chinese authorities have devised the "Placement and education" strategy which helps to generate employment for individuals redeemed from radicalisation. One such instrument was the "Beauty Project" launched in 2011, a five-year special programme with a budget of 80 million Chinese Yuan to develop industries for women's fashion, cosmetics and accessories and promote the employment rate for Uyghur women. In pursuing this strategy the government aims to create employment for 100,000 labourers in southern Xinjiang between 2018 and 2020, and a total of 1.4008 million urban jobs. It intends to popularise the already-running nine-year compulsory education rule so that minorities can benefit most from it as well as improve the social security system.

Overall the implementation of the deradicalisation strategy has been carefully planned and implemented to convey constant and coherent messages against the threat of three evils in Xinjiang and has deployed multifaceted programmes to underscore the role of community engagement to prevent and control further radicalisation. It has helped to curtail the menace of terrorism reflected in the retrieval of tourism in 2018. Recently, the CCP has created a new bureau to improve intelligence and policy coordination in Xinjiang under the Central

United Front Work department and provide advice and policy proposals to China's top leaders. This reflects Beijing's growing concern about stability in the region (Mai, 2017) and also its inability to reconcile its historical approach of treating these regions as frontier areas when seeking to constrict them within the sovereignty approach. The fact that Xinjiang is positioned geographically between neighbouring states with Islamic influence and a central polity on the other hand which demands lesser focus on religion is somewhat gloomy. Therefore, deradicalisation through cultural and innovative means seems to be the only option available for China. Lack of an integrative policy that could strike a balance between the needs of the local people and its own nationalist agenda has the potential to destabilise the entire Chinese state. Deradicalisation as a strategy to uplift the Uyghurs has the potential to resolve the ethnic issue whereby violence as a means of expression could become unnecessary. However, the costs of this transformation need to be taken into consideration. Meanwhile, not being able to track the exact source of terrorist expansion remains the most prominent detriment to deradicalisation efforts. The disenfranchisement amongst the Uyghurs resulting from state policies also cannot be disregarded. While deradicalisation has the potential to benefit some strata amongst the radicals who are able to return and assimilate with the mainstream, the state increasingly comes under the microscope for its resemblances to a police-state or an authoritarian regime.

Notes

1 Shan Wei and Weng Cuifen, China's New Policy in Xinjiang and Its Challenges, Online URl: www.eai.nus.edu.sg/publications/files/Vol2No3_ShanWei&WengCuifen.pdf
2 Uyghur Muslim Ethnic Separatism in Xinjiang, China, Elizabeth Van Wie Davis, Asia-Pacific Center for Security Studies, January 2008, Online URL: https://apcss.org/college/publications/uyghur-muslim-ethnic-separatism-in-xinjiang-china/. He said that a total of one trillion Yuan (US$125 B) has been spent building infrastructure in western China with an annual average regional economic growth rate of 10.6 per cent for six years in a row.
3 However, sometimes it was found that Chinese respondents overestimated the proportion of the Muslim population in China. On average, the respondents thought that around nine out of every 100 people in China were Muslims, when the actual share of the Muslim population was around 2 per cent in China.
4 The Chinese Government has sought to curtail the terrorist incidences through its increased economic and strategic cooperation with the Central Asian countries under the SCO grouping as it threatens their stability as well.
5 The government estimated that, from 1992 to 2001, Eastern Turkestan Forces initiated at least 200 violent terrorist attacks in which 162 people of different nationalities died and more than 440 were wounded.
6 China has also joined most international counter-terrorism conventions; for instance, International Convention for the Suppression of Terrorist Bombings, International Convention for the Suppression of the Financing of Terrorism, International Convention for the Suppression of Acts of Nuclear Terrorism and the International Convention against the Taking of Hostages.
7 Under the SCO framework, China and other neighbouring countries have signed the following documents: the Shanghai convention on Combating Terrorism, Separatism and Extremism, Cooperation Between SCO Member States on Combating Terrorism, Separatism and Extremism, SCO Convention on Combating Terrorism, and another one on Extremism, SCO Cooperation Programme on Fighting Terrorism, Separatism and Extremism for 2019–2021 and SCO Plan of Action for Cooperation with the Islamic Republic of Afghanistan on Fighting Terrorism, Drug Trafficking and Organised Crimes.
8 The law broadened China's definition of terrorism and the scope of its counter-terrorism measures, and made provisions to establish a counter-terrorism intelligence centre to better coordinate terrorism response and information sharing across different Chinese government agencies. The law also required foreign firms to provide technical and decryption assistance to Chinese authorities as part of terrorism-

related investigations. The legislation stipulated measures on tightening internet security management, inspection of dangerous materials, prevention of terrorism financing and border controls.

9 He also proposed five basic principles for governing Xinjiang: protecting legal religious activities; stopping illegal ones; deterring religious extremism; guarding against its infiltration; and cracking down on crimes related to extremism. The fifth principle involves the clear authorisation to conduct harsh crackdowns on religious extremism.

10 "Squeezing by correct faith" means using correct faith to clarify the people's understanding of Islam, awaken their minds and squeeze out extremism; "counteracting by culture" means seeking effective and practical solutions to counteracting extremism and guiding people to secularisation and modernisation; "controlling by law" means making the best of the rule of law not only in regulating social behaviour and countering religious extremism but also in guiding social expectations and building social consensus; "popularizing science" means spreading the knowledge about and promoting the use of science and technology in order to guide the people to uphold science, remove ignorance and deny extremism.

11 It is a special project/mass line campaign started by the government of Xinjiang under the leadership of Zhang Chunxian in March 2014 aimed at investigating the conditions of the people, serving the interests of the people and winning the hearts and minds of the people. At present the trainees at the centres are those who were incited, coerced or induced but were not serious enough to constitute a crime or those who did not cause actual harm.

References

Annual Report on China's Religions. (2010), Social Science Press, The Chinese Academy of Social Science.

Bovingdon, Garner, (2010), *The Uyghurs, Strangers in Their Own Land*, New York: Columbia University Press.

Cao, Xun, Duan, Haiyan, Liu, Chuyu, Piazza, James A., and Wei, Yingjie, (2018), 'Digging the Ethnic Violence in China' Database: The Effects of Inter-Ethnic Inequality and Natural Resources Exploitation in Xinjiang," *The China Review* 18, no. 1 (May 2018): 121–154.

Castets, Remi, (2003), "The Uyghur in Xinjiang: The Malaise Grows," *China Perspective* 49: 34–48. September-October, 2003.

China Daily. (2002), "East Turkistan terrorists exposed," *China Daily*, Online URL: www.chinadaily.com.cn/en/doc/2002-01/21/content_103075.htm.

China's State Council Information Office. (2019), "White paper on '*The Fight against Terrorism and Extremism and Human Rights Protection in Xinjiang*," The State Council Information Office of the People's Republic of China.

Clarke, Michael, (2017), "China and the Uyghurs: 'The Palestinization' of Xinjiang," Online URL: http://mepc.org/china-and-uyghurs-palestinization-xinjiang

Country Reports on Terrorism, (2015), United States Department of State Publication Bureau of Counter Terrorism and Countering Violent Extremism. Released. 2 June, 2016, Online URL: https://2009-2017.state.gov/documents/organisation/258249.pdf.

Congressional-Executive Commission on China, (2016), 2016 Annual report, Online URL: https://www.cecc.gov/publications/annual reports/2016-annual-report.

Davis, Elizabeth and Wie, Van, (2008), "Uyghur Muslim Ethnic Separatism in Xinjiang, China," January 2008, Online URL: http://apcss.org/college/publications/uyghur-muslim-ethnic-separatism-in-xinjiang-china/.

Dillon, Michael, (2004), *Xinjiang-China's Muslim Far Northwest*, London: Routledge Curzon, p. 21.

Gan Nectar, (2017), "Ban on Beards and Veils – China's Xinjiang Passes Law to Curb 'Religious Extremism', *South China Mornng Post*, 30 March 2017.

George, Paul, (1998), "Islamic Unrest in the Xinjiang Uyghur Autonomous Region, Commentary, Canadian Security Intelligence Service," Spring 1998, No. 73. Online URL: www.oss.net/dynamaster/file_archive/040319/023539ebdbd64ed648eb562d65081223/OSS1999-P2-27.pdf

John Horgan and Braddock, Kurt, (2010), "Rehabilitating the Terrorists?: Challenges in Assessing the Effectiveness of De-radicalization Programs," *Terrorism and Political Violence*, 22: 267–291.

Leibold, James and Grose, Timothy, (2015), "Why China Is Banning Islamic Veils and Why It Won't Work," China File, 4 February , 2015, Online URL: www.chinafile.com/reporting-opinion/view point/why-china-banning

Lina, Wen, (2015), "'Wu Ba Yaoshi' Kai 'Xinsuo' Ju Minxin ['Five Keys' Open 'the Lock of the Heart' and Win the Heart of the People]," Tianshan Wang [Tianshan Net], 2 October 2015.

Lixiong, Wang, (2014), "Excerpts from 'My West China, Your East Turkestan' — My View on the Kunming Incident," Online URL: http://chinachange.org/2014/03/03/excerpts-from-my-west-china-your-east

Lowe, David, (2018), *Terrorism: Law and Policy*, London: Routledge.

Mai, Jun, (2017), "Why the Communist Party Has Created a New Bureau for Xinjiang, *South China Morning Post,* 5 May 2017.

Sainsbury, Michael, (2017), "Suppression in Xinjiang and the Fast Tracking of Radicalization", 17 March 2017, La Croix International.

Schuster, Brenda L., (2009), "Gaps in the Silk Road: An Analysis of the Population Health Disparities in the Xinjiang Uyghur Autonomous Region of China," *The China Quarterly* 198 (June 2009): 433–441.

Shichor, Yitzhak, (2006), "Fact and Fiction: A Chinese Documentary on Eastern Turkestan Terrorism," *China and Eurasia Forum Quarterly* 4, no. 2 (2006): 89–108.

Sound Islam China "Islamic Extremism, Song and Dance, and Sonic Territoriality", 8 May 2017, Online URL: www.soundislamchina.org/?p=1646

Tong, Yao and Yunyan, Sui, (2016), "Ganyu Dandang, Zonghe Fali, Quebao 'Sange Jianjue' [Guarantee 'Three Promises' Through Accountable and Comprehensive Efforts]," *Xinjiang Ribao* [Xinjiang Daily], 9 January 2016, Online URL: http://news.ts.cn/content/2016-01/09/content_11951821.htm (accessed 26 March , 2017).

Williams, Thomas D., (2017), Pew Study: Egypt, China, Iran Most Restrictive of Religion, 11 April 2017, Online URL: www.breitbart.com/national-security/2017/04/11/pew-study-egypt-china-iran-most-restrictive-of-religion/

Wolfe, Adam, (2004), "China Takes the Lead in Strategic Central Asia," *Asia Times*, 17 September , 2004.

World News Online (2016) "Declaring De-radicalisation Success, China Reduces 11 Sentences," 3 February 2016, World News Online, URL: www.reuters.com/article/us-china-xinjiang-idUSKCN0VC0C4

Zhou, Zunyou, (2016), "Rehabilitating Terrorists: The Chinese Approach," *Counter Terrorist Trends and Analysis* 8, no. 4 (April 2016): 13.

Zhou, Zunyou, (2017), "Chinese Strategy for De-radicalisation, Terrorism and Political Violence," 9 June 2017, Online URL: www.tandfonline.com/doi/full/10.1080/09546553.2017.1330199

20

DERADICALIZATION AND DISENGAGEMENT

Context, actors, strategies and approaches in South Asia

Bahadar Nawab

Deradicalization and disengagement (DD) of radicalized individuals and organizations is a worldwide concern. Since radicalized locals have national, regional and global repercussions, their DD is a hot topic at the United Nations (UN) and regional forums and for concerned governments. The issue is more complex and multifaceted in South Asia, as the causes and motivation for radicalization are woven in religious and ethnic intolerance, nationalist and separatist movements and socio-economic disparities. DD on the other hand still lacks strong theoretical underpinning and sustainable institutional approaches.

This chapter highlights the DD processes in the South Asian countries, i.e. Bangladesh, India, Nepal, Pakistan and Sri Lanka. All the selected countries experienced conflicts of a different nature and are still prone to them due to many unsettled disputes and prevailing active root causes of radicalization, militancy and conflict. For a better understanding of DD, a detailed account of country-wise radicalization status is presented. The diverse causes of radicalization are also highlighted.

Deradicalization is a course which leads individuals to discard extremist perceptions about the world, renounce violence for bringing about social change and adopt more acceptable political pluralism (Bertram, 2016; Rabasa et al., 2010; Rana, 2011; Horgan, 2009). Deradicalization programmes became attractive and catchy to describe creative, unique and varied initiatives. Broadly speaking, deradicalization includes any effort to change or re-direct views that are supportive of violent action (Horgan and Altier, 2012, p. 86). It is a process of changing the attitudes of the militants towards the use of violence for the attainment of their ideological or political goals (Ashour, 2009). Defence and security experts were realizing the limited scope of intelligence and security approaches for counter-radicalization and terrorism and felt the need for "de-radicalization which involves the process of changing an individual's belief system, rejecting the extremist ideology, and embracing mainstream values" (Bajpai and Kaushik, 2017, p. 2).

Worldwide more than 40 DD programmes are in process (El Said, 2015; M.M. Khan, 2015). These programmes focus on the rehabilitation and reintegration of extremists into society rather than punishing them or marginalizing them from their respective communities. There are, however, some definitional issues with deradicalization. Counter-radicalization and anti-radicalization are proactive measures used to reduce the risk of radicalized society (Bajpai and Kaushik, 2017) but often ignore radicalized individuals and detainees, while deradicalization involves reactive measures trying to reverse radicalized individuals and groups (Bertram, 2016).

Causes of radicalization in South Asia

In South Asia socio-economic disparities, uneven power and resource distribution, ethnic and religious divisions, ideological contradictions, foreign interference and conflicts and different movements are still providing fertile ground for radicalization and militancy (see, for example, Basit et al., 2019; ICSR, 2010; Moeed, 2014). Further, the Jihadist philosophy in Afghanistan, Pakistan and Bangladesh, separatist movements in India and Sri Lanka and poverty and exclusion in Nepal are major factors in extremism and radicalization (D'Souza, 2017; ICSR, 2010; Kaushik, 2015; Moeed, 2014). Development is the dream in South Asia but most countries failed to trickle down the benefit of the available growth and prosperity to the common people, resulting in frustration and radicalization. Here we briefly explain the major reasons for extremism and radicalization in South Asian countries.

In Pakistan, the Afghan conflict, i.e. the Russian invasion, fighting among Mujahideen groups and US and NATO attacks, created passion and lust for Jihad among the youth of Pakistan. The madrassas and religious leaders were fanatically promoting the spirit of Jihad among the youth (Taha, 2012). In 1989, the USSR left Afghanistan but the repercussions of the Afghan war and Jihad still prevail in Pakistan in the form of crimes, drugs and arms smuggling and proliferation, extremism and radicalization in society (ibid). The decades-long unrest on the western border, fighting and conflict with India and internal political, economic and social instability left a substantial population of Pakistan unstable and extremist. Poverty, high population growth and unemployment also contributed to anarchy in Pakistani society. Weak institutions and a slow justice system and the emergence of militancy both as an ideology and as a kind of business for youth resulted in radicalization and terrorism. As a result, Pakistan today is plagued with ethnic, sectarian and economic instability. Bad governance, rifts among provinces, economic disparity, illiteracy and unemployment all contribute to radicalization, particularly among the youth (M.M. Khan, 2015).

Starting in early 1996 Maoists in Nepal used economic deprivation, inequality and discrimination against minorities as a tool for violent conflict in Nepal which continued over a decade between 1996 and 2006 (Arino, 2008). Maoists were frustrated with the monarchical regime and wanted to seize power and establish a Maoist republic (ibid). Maoists mobilized marginalized community members, women and lower-cast Hindus (Arino, 2008; Ansorg and Strasheim, 2019; Kantha, 2011) and started a violent conflict called "The People's War". Initially the conflict started in the Rolpa and Rukum districts in Western Nepal and gradually spread into 75 districts and Maoists seriously challenged state authority and legitimacy. This changed the social structure of society and the overall political landscape of the country (Thapa, 2017). The disgruntled youth played a vital role in the escalation of the armed conflict (Subedi, 2015, 2014) as they were radicalized the most (Thapa, 2017).

The Maoists used three strategies to advance their narrative: firstly, they radicalized the Nepalese by arguing for hard-line revolutionary changes in the then political system in order to achieve economic equality; secondly, they further divided people using ethnic strife (Thapa, 2017). The Maoist narrative proved very effective and attractive to women since they were marginalized and had fewer socio-economic and upward mobility opportunities from the state (Ram and Oliva, 2005). The Maoist army comprised a large number of female combatants (Arino, 2008) due to their policies of volunteers and aggressive recruitment drives (Manchanda, 2004).

India is facing violent extremism in different forms. The separatists and Jihadists in Kashmir, Maoist (also called Naxalite) separatists in the centre and Islamic State in Iraq and Syria (ISIS)/Islamic State of Iraq and the Levant (ISIL) presence in the southern part of India are active (Narain, 2016; Telford, 2001). There is rising religious and ethnic-based Hindu extremism and frequent cases of insurgency and violence across the country. These movements are triggered by freedom struggle, socio-economic exclusion of minorities and untouchable and caste systems.

According to Banerjee (2017), the causes for the radicalization and violent extremism in India include provision of poor education curriculum, religious extremism, cultural influence and involvement of the state itself in its promotion. He also provides suggestions for drastic changes in schooling, systematic changes in eradication of violence from society, alternate livelihood facility, sports and outdoor activities for physical exuberance. Communication technology and social media played an important role in connecting youth with extremists and militant networks in India (Penn, 2016). As a result extremism and radicalization are flourishing and terrorist activities are growing in the country (Narain, 2016). The inadequacy of moderate religious guidance, poverty, human rights abuses, anti-Western sentiment, lack of personal meaning and radical Islamic fundamentalists are also causes of violent extremism.

In Sri Lanka, the root cause of historical conflict and recent tension is separatist movement on ethnic affiliation, tension among majority Buddhist and minority Hindu, Christian and Muslims and power grabbing among major ethnic groups. As a result, since the 1980s, Sri Lanka has been confronted with the dilemma of two armed militancies (Manoharan, 2006). In the north, Tamils created the Liberation Tigers of Tamil Eelam (LTTE) on ethnic lines and took up arms against the state for separation and an independent state. In the south, the government encountered the People's Liberation Front or Janatha Vimukthi Peramuna (JVP), with most Sinhala fighters grabbing maximum power (Manoharan, 2006). This shattered the social harmony and unity of the country. In May 2009 the government eliminated the LTTE (Jabbar and Sajeetha, 2014) and the demand for a separate state ended after 30 years (Keerawella, 2013). The Sinhalese and Tamil conflict is almost over but ethnic strife between Sinhalese and Muslims has the potential for new conflict. In recent years, Sri Lanka has also been confronting religious extremism. The radical Buddhists are inculcating an anti-Muslim narrative (Jabbar and Sajeetha, 2014). The Sinhala-Buddhist nationalist group Bodu Bala Sena (BBS) is becoming deep-rooted in the local communities with a hard-line political-religious extremism narrative (Zylva, 2017). The BBS cause is also supported by some political parties and young Buddhist monks with an agenda of upsetting Muslims (Jabbar and Sajeetha, 2014; Zylva, 2017). The recent ISIS attack on churches in Sri Lanka shows hidden tension among ethnic and religious communities in that country.

In Bangladesh, strong religious extremist groups are a nursery for radicalization and extremism. For example, Al-Qaeda (AQ) and Islamic State (IS)-affiliated groups such as Harkat-ul-Jihad al-Islami (HUJI-B), Hizb-ut-Tahrir (HT), Shahadat-e-Al Hikma and Ansarullah Bangladesh Team (ABT) are the main fundamentalist Islamic groups blamed for terrorist activities.

The polarization in politics and institutional repression of religious parties has led to the growth of extremism and radicalization in Bangladesh (Macdonald, 2016). Weak institutions and justice system, uneven economic growth and governance issues provide space for extremist narratives (Khan, 2017). Social media and cyber crimes targeting youth are considered to be the potential causes of radicalization in Bangladesh (Munir, 2017). The spread of online radicalization of terrorist ideology has increased tenfold in Bangladesh since 2016 (Basit et al., 2019). A transnational crime nexus is becoming rooted in Bangladesh due to around one million Rohingya refugees and their involvement in drug, human and arms trafficking on the Bangladesh–Myanmar border (ibid). Targeting and victimization of the religious parties might cause a new brand of radicalized youth (Macdonald, 2016).

Deradicalization and disengagement approaches in South Asia

Pakistan

After the completion of the army's counter-terrorism offensive against militants in the Federally Administered Tribal Areas (FATA) and Swat, Pakistan started its first deradicalization programme in 2009. Most of the militants arrested during the army assaults were juveniles who were indoctrinated and trained as suicide bombers.[1] With time the government has learnt that violent and radical Islamic extremism cannot be defeated by the use of force. They understand that dialogues and rehabilitation and deradicalization of militants might help curb violent ideology and deviant interpretations of Islam.[2] For this purpose an institutionalized effort has also been started by the state of Pakistan with the help of civil society organizations to deradicalize the extremists in society (Qazi, 2013).

At present there are six main deradicalization programmes running throughout the country, including the Sabaoon, Mishal, Sparley, Rastoon, Pythom and Heila rehabilitation centres, mostly run by government and civil society organizations (S.A. Khan, 2015; Basit, 2015). The main purpose of the centres is to impart formal education to the detainee militants. The curriculum includes formal education, moderate religious education, skill training, advice and therapy. More specifically, rehabilitation training includes psychological counselling, religious education and their proper interpretation, information education and vocational training and reintegration back into society (Basit, 2015). In addition detainees are given an opportunity to discuss social issues (Qazi, 2013). To achieve speedy and good results, militants are first separated into groups, based on their level of indoctrination and age, and then training is provided accordingly (S.A. Khan, 2015). Most of these centres were initiated in 2009, with a good success rate: more than 2,500 Taliban fighters have been rehabilitated in different rehabilitation centres in Swat (Basit, 2015; Rana, 2011). In Punjab more than 1,000 Jihadists went through DD training to make them part of mainstream society (Basit, 2015). In the absence of independent evaluation, however, these statistics cannot be corroborated. Three of the rehabilitation centres working in Punjab are now closed due to lack of funding (ibid).

Most of the rehabilitation centres are run by civil society organizations but under the overall supervision of the army. These include deradicalization projects that incorporate interfaith dialogues and establishing madrassas to counter the existing religious schools that promote violence (S.A. Khan, 2015). Project Mishal, which is run by the Pakistan army in Swat, focuses its efforts on adult detainees; Project Sparley extends the initiative to the families of detainees. Limited assistance in finding jobs is also provided by the Pakistani authorities. The ultimate aim is to reintegrate former terrorists and radicalized individuals back into mainstream civil society. Other programmes operate across the country, especially in Punjab, but are poorly resourced (Burke, 2013). A few are run by the police and have seen success when the police have been able to keep up surveillance after prisoners have been released. However, it is important to note that Pakistan's efforts to date have essentially concentrated on low-risk militants – foot soldiers or low-level facilitators. Very little, if any, effort has been made, unlike in Indonesia, at rehabilitating high-risk or high-ranking militants (Abuza, 2003). Disengaging militants and the general population without violating sacred beliefs is critical (ibid).

In addition, in Pakistan governments have framed and passed numerous anti-terrorism laws and have banned many militant groups in different stages (Ahmed, 2014) after the brutal Army Public School (APS) attack on 16 December 2014 in Peshawar which unified the Pakistani nation and institutions. Hence, the National Action Plan (NAP) was announced by the government of Pakistan (Farwa, 2016). The National Counter Terrorism Authority (NACTA) was established through an act of Parliament in 2013. According to this act the NACTA is mandated and empowered to prepare, plan and provide guidelines for DD. It is also empowered to evolve and review mechanisms for their implementation (NACTA, 2018).

The government of Pakistan developed NAP for counter-terrorism and DD. As of today NAP measures are predominantly counter-radicalization, reactionary, administrative and legal to stop radicalization and terrorism. Little focus is given to rehabilitation and DD. The NAP provides a broad framework of action in diverse areas but specific mechanisms and its implementation in each sector are still not set out. There are apex committees represented both at federal level and in the four provinces to serve as a forum for civil–military coordination and to monitor progress in NAP implementation. Despite these initiatives, the status of NAP implementation in the federal and provincial governments of Pakistan needs further clarity and proper implementation (PILDAT, 2016). There still seems to be some gaps that cause delay in the full implementation of NAP. New efforts are underway in the current government for full implementation of NAP as this is demanded of all political parties and international communities.

In 2014, the National Internal Security Policy (NISP) was formulated. In this policy, the Ministry of the Interior pledged to ensure the internal security and interests of Pakistan. The policy constitutes the Comprehensive Response Plan (CRP), also called the soft plan, as well as the Composite Deterrent Plan (CDP), known as the hard plan. The government of Pakistan is aggressively pursuing the hard plan through ongoing Radd-al-Fasad operation of the security forces; however, few interventions are in place in the proposed soft plan which should focus more on DD. Dialogue with all parts of society is the main theme of CRP. Development of infrastructure, rehabilitating victims of terrorism, process of reconciliation, legal reforms, developing national narratives and the larger process of reintegration are the main focus of this plan. The NACTA coordinates with all relevant agencies for impartial reconstruction, rehabilitation, reintegration, reconciliation and creating national narratives to counter violence and extremism and DD.

Similarly, the main purpose of CDP is to ensure the internal security of Pakistan through a shift from reactive policy to proactive policy. However, efforts are needed to bridge gaps in coordination with the intelligence agencies to develop proactive systems for the elimination of extremism and implementation of DD approaches (Government of Pakistan, 2014). NACTA, through federal and provincial stakeholders, also developed policy interventions in six key governance areas: (1) rule of law and service delivery; (2) citizen engagement; (3) media engagement; (4) integrated education reform; (5) reformation, rehabilitation, reintegration and renunciation; and (6) promotion of culture (NACTA, 2018).

Quite recently, the government of Pakistan also built a national counter-narrative "Pigham-e-Pakistan" for handling radicalization, extremism, sectarianism, terrorism and militancy as an ideological response to non-traditional threats (Government of Pakistan, 2018). In Pigham-e-Pakistan, key relevant stakeholders from across society were engaged for the promotion of peace, tolerance and values of democracy that could lead to freedom ownership and hence DD. In this process, religious and academic scholars sat together and first drafted the ideology of Pakistan and the major progress and achievements of the country since independence. Afterwards, issues and challenges being faced by the country, such as fighting and militancy against government and public and misinterpretation and misuse of Jihad, were elaborated. At the end of the Pigham-e-Pakistan, a joint declaration negated the narrative of militants, the punishment of Fasad Fil Ardh (corruption on earth) and promotion of peace with reference to the Quran and the saying of Prophet Peace Be Upon Him (PBUH). In this initiative, the broader segment of religion, academic circle and government collectively condemned terrorism and opened up avenues for DD.

Nepalese efforts

In Nepal the seven political parties signed an agreement with Maoists in 2006. The parties agreed on the 12-point agenda for future cooperation and restoration of peace (NIPS, 2013). Building on this agreement a Comprehensive Peace Agreement (CPA) was signed by the Maoists and the major political players of Nepal (Tandukar et al., 2016). This resulted in the end of a decade-long violent conflict in which over 13,000 people lost their lives and over 200,000 were internally displaced (Arino, 2008). Subsequently an interim government was created with the representation of Maoists (Valente, 2013).

The peace agreement included political and military reform, disarmament, demobilization and reintegration of the Maoist combatants (Ansorg and Strasheim, 2019; Kantha, 2011). Under the DD programme, within a week of the peace agreement, Maoist combatants moved into different camps which were set up under a UN mission. All weapons were stored (United Nations, 2007). Afterward DD became part of the wider demobilization agenda, focusing on changing the potential of violence rather than opinions (Dahal, 2012). During DD, more than 15,000 ex-combatants opted for a "retirement package" that included a cash payment (Bogati, 2015). A total of 1,400 ex-combatants joined the National Army (Subedi, 2015). Under the peace agreement the Maoist militant group was converted into a political party, even won an election and came to power and thus this is one of the successful reintegration processes in South Asia (Ishiyama and Anna, 2011). In order to gain societal legitimacy the political actors pledged to establish a high-level Truth and Reconciliation Commission to reach truth and identify those who had committed human rights violations and crimes against humanity during the process of violent conflict (MOPR, 2011), as well as the Ministry of Peace and Reconstruction in March 2007, which was demanded by civil society during the peace process (Thapa, 2007). This ministry has a mandate to lead the peace process negotiations and agreements. The ministry established the national level commission supported by the local committee to identify conflict-affected communities and displaced populations, meet their grievances and develop social harmony in the reconciliation and reconstruction process (Tandukar et al., 2016). In this sense Nepal focused on allowing the voices of former combatants to be heard, and in so doing remove the potential for violence. The government of Nepal also introduced the "Enforced Disappearances Enquiry Commission and Truth and Reconciliation Commission Act #2071" in May, 2014. The aim was to investigate and explore the facts related to human rights violations at a mass level during the armed conflict (Nepal Gazette, 2014).

In 2015 Nepal introduced a National Youth Policy (NYP). The objective was to streamline the youth population and ensure their basic needs and aptitude building (Thapa, 2017). Unfortunately, this youth policy was not as successful because the earlier youth who became part of the Maoist movement and were recruited as combatants were ignored. Therefore, the repercussions of an almost decade-long armed conflict are very negative, particularly for the youth of Nepal. The increased level of aggression and violence in the youth is an adverse result (ibid).

As a considerable number of ex-Maoist fighters have been disengaged but have not reintegrated into society completely, there is a chance that these ex-combatants may reorganize and promote violence if not completely reintegrated into society (Subedi, 2014). Currently, the newly organized federation in Nepal has a great responsibility to make the peace process sustainable through developing and promoting tolerance and harmony in politics. If the federation of Nepal fails to fulfil its responsibilities then it is possible that the society may become violent, radicalized and extremist. Therefore, terrorism may emerge which will swamp the whole of Nepal (Thapa, 2017).

India

To handle the Islamic radicals, intelligence and security capabilities have been built up as pre-emptive measures (Bajpai and Kaushik, 2017). In 2010 the central government started a surrender-cum-rehabilitation approach for Naxalites (Indian Maoists). Under this a 0.15 million initial and 2,000 monthly Indian Rupees (IRS) stipend would be given to those who surrender for three years along with vocational training (ibid). This amount was increased to 2.5 million and 3,000 IRS for senior members in 2013. As a result of this policy around 4,000 radicalized left-wing extremists surrendered. For long-term proactive measures the government also focused on security, development, ensuring rights and entitlements of local communities and management of public perception to counter home-grown left-wing extremists. Some developments of infrastructure, sports and vocational training were undertaken and still continued but their volume, relevance and impact are considered as inadequate.

Similarly, in Maharashtra state, in order to include youth and the minority community, the state introduced activities such as National Cadet Corps and Bharat Scout Guides in minority schools. Some reforms were introduced in education, sports, urban planning, law and order, skill development, women and children, social justice and health for mainstreaming the youth and minority population (Vyas, 2016). Other initiatives include teaching the text of all religions and Urdu in selected minority schools, provision of subsidized textbooks, promoting democratic values and developing minority urban clusters (ibid). The Maharashtra state government had engaged and trained religious, academic and community leaders for deradicalization (Rasheed, 2016). As in the Maharashtra and Telangana states, it worked with Muslim community members and clerics.[3] The state authorities and Muslim clerics/leaders provide counselling which stops youths from engaging in violent activities.

To counter radicalization, mass media and social networks have great potential in India. Yet, instead of winning the hearts and minds of militants, India often uses more common counterinsurgency (COIN) approaches involving violence and enemy-centric approaches of suffocating insurgency through saturation of forces (Mukherjee, 2010; Lalwani, 2011). Torture, disappearance, encounter killing and mass graves are counter-militancy approaches that are commonly used in India (Lalwani, 2011).

Sri Lanka

In countering radicalization, the government of Sri Lanka legislated and used several counter-terrorism mechanisms (Manoharan, 2006). The government is now working on Sustainable

Development Goals (SDGs) to address the grievances of socio-economically excluded classes. The national anthem in Tamil as well as Sinhala is also promulgated (Arnmarker, 2017) to please separatists. Further legislative efforts include: (1) the Public Security Ordinance (PSO) and its promulgation; and (2) the Prevention of Terrorism Act (PTA) 1979. These laws were seen as discriminatory and against human rights; thus the UN Human Rights Committee Council and EU pushed Sri Lanka to replace the PTA with a new counter-terrorism act (PLFCT, 2017). As part of the drafting process, the government held many consultations with civil society and international actors, who were critical about the early drafts of the counter-terrorism act and aimed to make it conform with international standards (Government of Sri Lanka, 2016). More recently, the country adopted the Policy and Legal Framework of Counter-Terrorism (PLFCT) of Sri Lanka on 25 April 2017 (PLFCT, 2017).

Counter-terrorism policies in Sri Lanka mostly revolved around the elimination of LTTE, while an external threat was seen in 2016. Law enforcement forces continued to act under the PTA, promulgated in 1982 to counter terrorism, check, arrest and detain people (Government of Sri Lanka, 2016). It is still the LTTE that is the main focus for DD efforts (Hettiarchchi, 2015; Kruglanski et al., 2014). In Sri Lanka, the focus was on the rank and file of the militants of LTTE but not on their leadership as such, who were presented before the courts. Under the PTA government ensured one-year rehabilitation for captured LTTE ex-combatants. Earlier, around 12,000 ex-combatants were rehabilitated. There were also DDR-focused groups targeting both ex-army soldiers and Tamil fighters from the De-Mining group DASH (Delvon Association for Social Harmony) (ibid). Prison deradicalization efforts were also common.

In another approach towards deradicalization, disengagement and reintegration (DDR) programmes, the Sri Lankan government invited successfully disengaged key figures from the LTTE, as well as former LTTE members turned businessmen, to use them as role models in the media (Hettiarachchi, 2015). The DD programmes of Sri Lanka were and still are successful because the government addresses those weak areas that motivated the LTTE community to become radicalized and militants. Another reason for the success could be that the LTTE were already defeated and they have few options and hope to remain militants (ibid). The main actor carrying out DD in Sri Lanka remains the state, using tools targeting LTTE; it remains to be seen if this is efficient in the new wave of religious violence facing the country.

Bangladesh

The government of Bangladesh initially focused on mitigative measures in 2005 by stopping radicalization instigated by Jama'atul Mujahideen of Bangladesh (JMB) and Harajat-ul-Jihad-al-Islami (HuJI). Here the government used tools of incarceration, intelligence and intellectual intervention (IPI, 2010). The government of Bangladesh initiated hybrid programmes of counter-radicalization and a series of DD programmes (Fink and El-Said, 2011; Harrigan, 2011). For example, already radicalized and vulnerable groups were targeted in a series of village/madarsa/mosque level seminars, workshops and training by engaging Imams, village leaders and civil society organizations. Anti-militant commercials were prepared and aired to stop radicalization. In 2017, the elite force of Bangladesh published a book on "Misinterpretation of Verses by Militants and the Right Interpretation of the Qur'an and Hadith" as a move towards disengagement and reintegration (Hasan, 2017). The Bangladesh Islamic Foundation worked with the imams of the mosques to make DD part of their Friday sermon (Anik and Rabbi, 2018; Rahman, 2016). The Ministry of Education launched a programme for teacher and student awareness in academic institutions through seminars and workshops.

The hybrid counter-radicalization and DD approach of Bangladesh remains quite successful (Harrigan, 2011). However, most of these programmes were short-term and, due to a lack of proper coordination among the relevant government agencies, some of these initiatives have already been stopped (Anik and Rabbi, 2018).

In addition, in order to take a resolute stance on extremism and terrorism, the government of Bangladesh established 17 member committees to tackle these challenges and mobilize public interest to eradicate these issues. As a result, the government banned five extremist groups in the following six years. Bangladesh has also formulated laws and policies, including the Anti-Terrorism Act 2009 and 2013, Money Laundering Prevention Act 2012 and Mutual Legal Assistance Act 2012 (CRI, 2015). Bangladesh also works with civil society organizations and religious leaders to raise awareness. Muslim clerics are engaged in madrassa education reforms to create awareness of extremism and terrorism and highlight the true picture of Islam (Basit et al., 2019). The government also organised community engagement programmes and inter-faith dialogues at different levels. The relevant government agencies are working with academic institutions in research on better understanding how to prevent radicalization and disengage radicalized individuals and organizations (ibid). However, very few concrete efforts are in progress for DD in Bangladesh. The legal and other interventions are mostly a reaction to counter terrorism. There is a need for more efforts to rehabilitate already radicalized youth and disengage militants.

Who does the deradicalization in South Asia? Common patterns

The main actors, i.e. militants, radicalized individuals and groups in South Asia, have different motivations, interests and goals. The initial motivations of individuals and groups who took arms against their state and people are for independence (for example, cases of Kashmiri and Maoists in India, LTTE in Sri Lanka), land, rights, control over resources (Maoists in Nepal) or undue occupation (again, Kashmiri in India). In the case of Pakistan, Tahreq-e-Taliban Pakistan (TTP) took up arms against government when they supported NATO allies in Afghanistan. In Bangladesh the Jihadists aim for Khilafat, i.e. Islamic State. The militants develop their narratives in the form of a freedom struggle, Jihad, fighting for rights, or fighting the illegal rulers. However, as time goes by, the fighting has been converted into business and attraction for the unemployed, illiterate and the poorest youth. This can be seen in the form of TTP (Ashour, 2009), Maoists in Nepal (Subedi, 2014; Ram and Oliva, 2005), LTTE in Sri Lanka (Hettiarachchi, 2015; Keerawella, 2013; Webber et al., 2018) and scores of Jihadist, separatist and freedom fighters in India (Lalwani, 2011; Mukherjee, 2010) and religious militants in Bangladesh (Khan, 2017). In South Asia, terrorism is a billion-dollar industry with different interest groups that make their ends meet. Such a complex nature of actors within militants would definitely need diverse DD strategies and approaches to bring them into mainstream society.

For DD, the government remains the most important actor in the region. Police and other relevant government institutions provide other required support, including information sharing on local dynamics and grassroots networking, or agents controlled by the army. The police, local administration, local politicians, civil society organizations and community are major actors. However, ironically most of these actors, except the army, have a limited say over the limited DD centres, for example, in Pakistan (Basit, 2015), Bangladesh (Khan, 2017) and India (Lalwani, 2011; Mukherjee, 2010). It is in general the armed forces that decide who should be referred to the centres, which DD and rehabilitation approach should be adopted, what should be the content of the rehabilitation process and what kind of resources a person should use. These centres can take care of limited groups of radicalized individuals who are already engaged in militancy and terrorism. A close coordination among the relevant actors could make DD a successful and continuous model for mainstreaming radicalized individuals and groups in South Asia. A regional forum will provide opportunities to learn from the member countries' experiences of how to make South Asia peaceful and progressive.

In the context of the South Asian countries little attention has been placed on DD. Some of the successful DD programmes in Sri Lanka, Pakistan and Nepal were short-term and limited. Most of the DD initiatives were good with some impact but still not really in line with the main causes of radicalization and militancy. Organized efforts are still lacking in addressing the root cause of radicalization such as poverty reduction, illiteracy, inclusion of the marginalized segment of society, and so on. Also how to deradicalize youth and others is not prioritized. Very little input is taken from local administration, local politicians, police, civil society and the local community who live with the issue of extremism and militancy and need to be engaged in the process of DD. They have local cultural and traditional knowledge of the root causes and psyche of youth and radicalized individuals and groups.

Overall in South Asia, fighting terrorism and terrorists is a commonly used approach. Fighting militants (mostly natives) is a long and tiring journey and has a huge cost in terms of financial and human losses. For example, in India, Nepal and Sri Lanka the waves of militancy and freedom struggle before 9/11 were all subdued by use of hard components, i.e. military forces. Sri Lanka was at war with LTTE for three decades before defeating them by military means. After a decade of fighting and human suffering, Nepal reconciled with the Maoists. India is still struggling with freedom fighters, separatists and radicalized militants. All these countries used the hard option (fighting) to eliminate militants. In post-9/11 South Asia, religious radicalization took place in Pakistan and Bangladesh and a hard-core military approach was used. The real fighting and wars in South Asia have somehow subsided but their ramifications are still continuing in the form of extremism, radicalization and sporadic militancy. The root causes triggering radicalization and taking arms are still in effect. Instead of addressing the root causes, the respective governments in the region are more inclined to use force to eliminate the militants. The danger with this approach is that you kill one and five new terrorists are produced, and a handsome amount of others are radicalized. Despite some success stories in Sri Lanka, Nepal and Pakistan, the South Asian countries, however, still have to develop target-oriented effective DD programmes for radicalized individuals and groups.

In a counter-radicalization approach in South Asia, militants who survive or put down their arms are arrested. In such cases different options prevail in handling those arrested militants. In Pakistan, the government established military courts for two years (2015–16) which were extended for two more years until 2018. The trial of militants took place in these courts. In Bangladesh, India, Nepal and Sri Lanka arrested militants are generally detained and put in isolation centres for investigation. The whereabouts of such militants are not known to the public and, most of the time, rights-based organization would declare them missing. The numbers of enforced disappearances and missing persons are claimed to be in the thousands in India, Pakistan, Nepal and Sri Lanka, while in Bangladesh this number is reported to be in the hundreds. The security agencies would usually categorize radicalized individuals and militants into hard and soft categories. The hard-core militants remain in jail for an indefinite time while the soft militants (freshly radicalized, mostly youth) are sent to a small number of rehabilitation centres. Yet individuals going to these centres are the exception. As of today, normally militants spend time in jail without passing through any DD process and when they are released from jail, instead of normal citizens, they remain frustrated and prone to further radicalization (Bajpai and Kaushik, 2017).

Conclusion

South Asia is hit hard by conflicts and terrorism. Socio-economic disparities, uneven power and resource distribution, marginalization and exclusion, separatist movements and Jihadist movements against Western policies and invasion are common reasons for radicalization, insurgency and terrorism. The root cause for this menace may vary from country to country and region to region; however, the DD policies, strategies and approaches, though successful in Sri Lanka, Pakistan and Nepal, are short-term and need to be strengthened.

Extremism and radicalization are still on the rise in South Asian countries. Unfortunately, none of the South Asian countries has ever made a serious effort to understand the causes of radicalization and address them. No evidence-based policies and strategies are ever drafted and implemented for DD. The DDR programmes of Sri Lanka and Nepal can be considered quite successful but need to be adapted in Pakistan, India and Bangladesh. There is a need for research on concrete, and also non-military, soft approaches and strategies and how to engage the local population in developing evidence-based DD approaches, strategies and action against militancy.

There is also a need for grassroots level DD institutions where the selection, rehabilitation and mainstreaming of radicalized youth and militants are carried out by local institutions with the support of local people. The respective governments in South Asia need to carefully address the root causes of radicalization and bridge the economic, social, institutional and religious gaps in society.

Notes

1 Burke, J. (2013). "Fighting Terrorism: Do 'De-radicalisation' Camps Really Work?" *Guardian*, June 9, 2013, available at: www.theguardian.com/world/2013/jun/09/terrorism-do-deradicalisation camps-work
2 Hesterman, J. L. (2010, May 4). "Catch and Release Jihadist Recidivism." Retrieved Dec 1, 2013, from policeone.com www.policeone.com/terrorism/articles/3295091-Catch-andrelease-Jihadist-recidivism/
3 The government plans several strategies to counter ISIS threat to India; see www.dnaindia.com/india/report-government-plans-several-strategies-to-counter-sis-threat-to-india-2110252 (visited May 2019).

References

Abuza, Z. (2003). *Militant Islam in Southeast Asia: Crucible of Terror*. Boulder, CO: Lynne Rienner Publishers.

Ahmed, N. (2014). "Pakistan's Counter-Terrorism Strategy and Its Implications for Domestic, Regional and International Security." *Hal Special Report*.

Anik, S. S. B., and Rabbi, A. R. (2018). "No Coordination in Bangladesh Government Deradicalization Programs." *Dhaka Tribune* (n.d.), available at: www.dhakatribune.com/bangladesh/mili tancy/2018/11/29/experts-no-coordination-in-bangladesh-govt-de-radicalization-programs (visited June 2019).

Ansorg, N., and Strasheim, J. (2019). "Veto Players in Post-Conflict DDR Programs: Evidence From Nepal and the DRC." *Journal of Intervention and State Building*, 13(1), pp. 112–130. https://doi.org/10.1080/17502977.2018.1501981

Arnmarker, L. (2017). Reconciliation in Post-war Sri Lanka: A Study on Reconciliation Possibilities after a Victor's Peace. MS thesis, Department of Political Sciences, Lund University, Sweden.

Arino, M. V. (2008). "Nepal: A Gender View of the Armed Conflict and the Peace Process." *Quaderns De Construcció De Pau*, 4, pp. 1–16.

Ashour, O. (2009). *The De-Radicalization of Jihadists: Transforming Armed Islamist Movements*. London; New York: Routledge.

Bajpai, G. S., and Kaushik, A. (2017). "Thwarting Radicalization in India: Lacunae in Policy Initiatives." *Journal of Sociology and Criminology*, 5(1), pp. 1–12.

Banerjee, D. (2017). *Countering Youth Radicalization in South Asia. Countering Youth Radicalization and Violent Extremism in South Asia*. Kathmandu: Consortium of South Asian Think Tanks.

Basit, A. (2015). "Countering Violent Extremism: Evaluating Pakistan's Counter-Radicalization and de-Radicalization Initiatives." *IPRI Journal*, 15, pp. 44–68.

Basit, A., Bashar, I., Siyech, M. S., Mahmood, S., and Unasingham., A. (2019). "South Asia – Afghanistan, Bangladesh, India, Pakistan, Sri Lanka." *Counter Terrorist Trends and Analysis, Annual Threat Assessment*, 11(1), pp. 33–64.

Bertram, L. (2016). "How Could a Terrorist Be De-radicalized?" *Journal for Deradicatization*, 5, pp. 120–149.

Bogati, S. (2015). *Assessing Inclusivity in the Post-War Army Integration Process in Nepal*. Berlin: Bergh of Foundation, available at: http://ips-project.org/wp-content/uploads/2015/11/IPSPaper11-Assessing-Inclusivity-in-the-Post-War-Army-Integration-Process-in-Nepal_English.pdf

Burke, J. (2013). "Fighting Terrorism: Do 'De-radicalization' Camps Really Work?" *Guardian*, June 9, 2013.

CRI. (2015). *Bangladesh: Combating Terrorism Ensuring Peace*. Dhaka: Centre for Research and Information.

D'Souza, S. M. (2017). "Countering Insurgencies, Terrorism and Violent Extremism in South Asia." *Small Wars & Insurgencies*, 28(1), pp. 1–11.

Dahal, P. (2012). "Army Takes Charge of PLA Fighters, Weapons." *Kathmandu Post*, April 11. Kathmandu, Nepal: Nepal National Newspaper.

El-Said, H. (2015). *New Approaches to Countering Terrorism: Designing and Evaluating Counter Radicalization and Deradicalization Programs*. Hampshire, United Kingdom: Palgrave Macmillan.

Farwa, U. (2016). "National Action Plan: The Need for a National Narrative, Young ISSI Professional." *ISSI Homepage*, available at: www.issi.org.pk/national-action-plan-the-need-for-a-national-narrative/

Fink, N. C., and El-Said, H. (2011). *Transforming Terrorists: Examining International Efforts to Address Violent Extremism*. Washington: International Peace Institute, available at: www.ciaonet.org/attachments/18073/uploads

Government of Pakistan. (2014). *National Internal Security Policy*. Islamabad: Ministry of Interior.

Government of Pakistan. (2018). *Pigham-e-Pakistan*. Islamabad: Islamic Research Institute Press.

Government of Sri Lanka. (2016). *Country Reports on Terrorism*. Colombo: Bureau of Counterterrorism and Countering Violent Extremism.

Hettiarachchi, M. (2015). "Sri Lanka's Rehabilitation Programme: The Humanitarian Mission." In R. Gunaratna and M. Bin Ali (Eds.), *Terrorist Rehabilitation: A New Frontier in Counter-Terrorism*. London, United Kingdom: Imperial College Press, pp. 103–131.

Horgan, J. (2009). "Individual Disengagement: A Psychological Analysis." In T. Bjorgo and J. Horgan (Eds.), *Leaving Terrorism Behind: Individual and Collective Disengagement*, 1st ed. London; New York: Routledge, pp. 17–29.

Horgan, J., and Altier, M. B. (2012). "The Future of Terrorist De-Radicalization Programs." *Georgetown Journal of International Affairs*, 13, p. 2.

ICSR. (2010). "Prisons and Terrorism Radicalisation and De-radicalisation in 15 Countries." *A Policy Report Published by the International Centre for the Study of Radicalisation and Political Violence (ICSR)*, Kings College London, South Asia, Geneva, Switzerland.

International Peace Institute (IPI). (2010). *A New Approach? De Radicalization Programs and Counter Terrorism*. Oslo: Norwegian Ministry of Foreign Affairs.

Ishiyama, J., and Anna, B. (2011). "Swords into Plowshares: The Organizational Transformation of Rebel Groups into Political Parties." *Communist and Post-Communist Studies*, 44(4), pp. 369–379. doi: 10.1016/j.postcomstud.2011.10.004.

Jabbar, M. A., and Sajeetha, T. F. (2014). "Conflict Transformation in Post War Sri Lanka." *Paper Presented at the Conference: 4th International Symposium 2014 At: South Eastern University of Sri Lanka.*

Kantha, P. K. (2011). "Maoist-Madhesi Dynamics and Nepal's Peace Process." In M. Lawoti and A. K. Pahari (Eds.), *The Maoist Insurgency in Nepal: Revolution in the Twenty-First Century*. New York: Routledge, pp. 156–172.

Kaushik, R. (2015). *Frontiers, Insurgencies and Counter-Insurgencies in South Asia*. New Delhi: Routledge.

Keerawella, G. (2013). "Post-War Sri Lanka: Is Peace a Hostage of the Military Victory? Dilemmas of Reconciliation, Ethnic Cohesion and Peace-Building." *International Centre for Ethnic Studies Report*, Colombo.

Khan, M. M.. (2015). "Countering Violent Extremism in Pakistan: An Appraisal of Pakistan's CVE Initiatives." *Strategic Studies*, 35 (4), available at: www.researchgate.net/publication/305109189

Khan, S. A. (2015). "Deradicalization Programming in Pakistan." *United States Institute of Peace, Peace Brief Report.*

Khan, S. E. (2017). "Bangladesh: The Changing Dynamics of Violent Extremism and the Response of the State." *Small Wars & Insurgencies*, 28(1), pp. 191–217.

Kruglanski, A. W., Gelfand, M. J., Belanger, J. J., Sheveland, A., Hetiarachchi, M., and Gunaratna, R. (2014). "The Psychology of Radicalization and Deradicalization: How Significance Quest Impacts Violent Extremism." *Political Psychology*, 35(S1), pp. 69–93.

Lalwani, S. (2011). "India's Approach to Counterinsurgency and the Naxalite Problem." *Combating Terrorism Centre Report*, 4(10). Available at: https://ctc.usma.edu/indias-approach-to-counterinsurgency-and-the-naxalite-problem

Macdonald, G. (2016). "Preventing Violent Extremism through Inclusive Politics in Bangladesh." *Peace Brief*, 200.

Manchanda, R. (2004). *Maoist Insurgency in Nepal: Radicalizing Gendered Narratives*. Kathmandu: South Asia Forum for Human Rights.

Manoharan, N. (2006). "Counterterrorism Legislation in Sri Lanka: Evaluating Efficacy." *Policy Studies*, 28, pp. 1–76. Washington, DC: East West Center.

Moeed, Y. (2014). *Insurgency and Counterinsurgency in South Asia: Through a Peace Building Lens*. Washington, DC: United Institute of Peace.

MOPR. (2011). "Government of Nepal Ministry of Peace and Reconstruction Singhadurbar, Kathmandu 1st February 2011." *National Action Plan On Implementation of the United Nations Security Council Resolution* 1325 & 1820 [2011/12 – 2016/17].

Mukherjee, A. (2010). "India's Experiences with Insurgency and Counterinsurgency." In S. Ganguly, A. Scobell, and J.C. Liow (Eds.), *Handbook of Asian Security Studies*. London: Routledge, pp. 139–157.

Munir, S. (2017). *Radicalization without Borders: Understanding the Threat of Youth Radicalization in Cyberspace. Countering Youth Radicalization and Violent Extremism in South Asia*. Kathmandu: COSATT.

NACTA. (2018). "National Counter Extremism Policy Guidelines." Homepage, available at: www.nacta.gov.pk.

Narain, A. (2016). *Revamping India's Counter-Terrorism Approach*. Singapore: Nanyang Technological University.

Nepal Gazette. (2014). "The Enforced Disappearances Enquiry, Truth and Reconciliation Commission Act, 2071 (2014)." *Nepal Gazette* 2071/01/28.

NIPS. (2013). "Nepal's Peace Process: A Brief Overview." *Nepal Institute for Policy Studies (NIPS) brief.*

Penn, M. J. (2016). "Views from Around the Globe: Countering Violent Extremism." *A CSIS Commission on Countering Violent Extremism Survey.*

PILDAT. (2016). "Monitor Implementation of National Action Plan to Counter Terrorism in Punjab Volume 1."

PLFCT. (2017). *Policy and Legal Framework Counter Relating to the Proposed Terrorism Act of Sri Lanka*. Colombo: PLFCT.

Qazi, S. H. (2013). "A War without Bombs: Civil Society Initiatives against Radicalization in Pakistan," *Policy Brief* no. 60, available at: www.ispu.org/pdfs/ISPU_Brief_CounterDeradicalization_2_14.pdf

Rabasa, A., Pettyjohn, S. L., Ghez, J. J., and Boucek, C. (2010). *Deradicalizing Islamic Extremists*. Santa Monica, CA: Rand Corporation.

Rahman, M. A. (2016). "The Forms and Ecologies of Islamist Militancy and Terrorism in Bangladesh." *Journal of Deradicalization*, 7, pp. 68–106.

Ram, S., and Oliva, F. (2005). *The Maoist Insurgency in Nepal: A Comprehensive Annotated Bibliography*. Geneva-Kathmandu: Graduate Institute of International Studies.

Rana, A. (2011). "Swat De-radicalization Model: Prospects for Rehabilitating Militants." *Special Report PIPS*, 4(2).

Rasheed, A. (2016). "Countering the Threat of Radicalization: Theories, Programmes and Challenges." *Journal of Defence Studies*, 10(2), pp. 39–76.

Subedi, D. B. (2014). "Ex-combatants, Security and Post-conflict Violence: Unpacking the Experience from Nepal." *Millenial Asia*, March.

Subedi, D. B. (2015). "Security Dimension of Post-Conflict Recovery: Nepal's Experience in Disarmament and Demobilisation of People's Liberation Army Fighters." *International Journal of Politics Culture, and Society*, 28(2), pp. 143–159.

Taha, S. M. (2012). "History Culture and Cross-Border Migration: Impact of Afghan Refugees on Socio-Economic Environment of Peshawar." *International Journal of Independent Research and Studies*, 1(4), pp. 174–185.

Tandukar, A., Upreti, B. R., Paudel, S. B., Gopikesh Acharya, G., and Daniel Harris, D. (2016). "The Effectiveness of Local Peace Committees in Nepal: A Study from Bardiya district." *Nepal Center for Contemporary Research Technical Report*, 40.

Telford, H. (2001). "Counter-insurgency in India: Observations from Punjab and Kashmir." *Journal of Conflict Studies*, 21(1), pp. 1–29.

Thapa, M. (2007). "Nepal: Ministry of Peace and Reconstruction – A Foundation for Peace." Unknown available at: www.researchgate.net/publication/232253114

Thapa, R. R. (2017). "An Overview of Youth Movements and Youth Radicalization in Nepal: Countering Youth Radicalization and Violent Extremism in South Asia." *Kas paper*.

United Nations. (2007). "Report of the Secretary-General on the Request of Nepal for United Nations Assistance in Support of Its Peace Process." *S/2007/235*.

Valente, C. (2013). *Education and Civil Conflict in Nepal*. Washington, DC: The World Bank Development Economics Vice Presidency Partnerships, Capacity Building Unit.

Vyas, S. 2016. "IS Threat: Maharashtra Rolls Out Deradicalization Plan." *The Hindu*, (n.d.) (downloaded in June 2019).

Webber, D., Chernikova, M., Kruglanski, A. W., Gelfand, M. J., Hettiarachchi, M., Gunaratna, R., Lafreniere, M. A., Jocelyn, J., and Belanger, J. J. (2018). "Deradicalizing Detained Terrorists." *Political Psychology*, 39(3), pp. 539–556.

Zylva, A. D. (2017). *International Engagement in Countering Youth Radicalization: Sri Lanka's Untapped Opportunities, Countering Youth Radicalization and Violent Extremism in South Asia*. Colombo: COSATT (Consortium of South Asian Think Tanks).

21

THE POLITICS OF DERADICALIZATION IN ISRAEL/PALESTINE

Lihi Ben Shitrit

This chapter uses the Israel/Palestine case to make a broader claim about deradicalization efforts in non-democratic contexts. Therefore, before delving into the case, important clarifications with regard to premises, assumptions, and concept definitions are in order. First, by non-democratic contexts I mean situations in which the targets for deradicalization come from communities that do not enjoy equal civil and political rights. Such rights include the right to vote and to be elected, freedom of expression and association, alongside other rights specified in the UN's International Covenant on Civil and Political Rights (ICCPR). These communities could be occupied by a foreign power or disenfranchised by their own government due to their ethnic, racial, religious, gender, political, or other affiliation. Non-democratic contexts of course most clearly also include authoritarian regimes, where the entire citizenry is denied civil and political rights. The premise of this chapter is that, in such non-democratic situations, the state-centered security approach to deradicalization is both ineffective and normatively questionable.

The efforts of states in non-democratic contexts to deradicalize members of disenfranchised communities are ineffective for several reasons. First, if we take this volume's definition of categorizing an ideology as radical not based on its substance, but rather on its relational approach to competing or alternative ideologies – i.e., a radical ideology is one that is intolerant of differences and alternatives and seeks hegemony and dominance rather than democratic co-existence with competing worldviews – then in non-democratic situations both state and non-state actors fall under the radical category. A state-centered security approach to deradicalization, where the state targets members of disenfranchised groups using its repressive-security apparatuses: (1) is not likely to be viewed as legitimate by the larger communities to which radical dissidents belong as these communities do not have access to other, democratic, means for grievance expression such as voting, being elected, lobbying, demonstrating, organizing, and so forth; and (2) will assist the state in fortifying its own radical ideology (of non-democratic intolerance of different political visions), by suppressing political opponents. Second, in non-democratic situations, both non-state actors and state actors engage in political violence. By political violence I mean the use of violent means toward political ends. Non-state actors might employ methods such as attacks on military, security, and civilian targets. State actors in non-democratic situations would employ methods such as extrajudicial killings, disproportionate use of force against protestors, torture, and arrests without charges or trial. State-centered deradicalization by the security apparatuses aims to curb the political violence of non-state actors, but does nothing to curb the political violence of the state.

Next, the state-centric security approach is questionable normatively in these cases. Of course, it is questionable only from a standpoint that upholds a commitment to democracy with equal civil and political rights. However, I assume that at least most scholars engaged with research, writing, and even practice of deradicalization initiatives share this normative commitment. The normative challenge entailed in the state-centric security paradigm in non-democratic contexts is that lines between deradicalization efforts and political suppression efforts by the state are extremely blurry. In non-democratic situations, states arrest and imprison large numbers of political dissidents, both ones that use violence and ones that do not. In the absence of due process, transparency, equality before the law, and general equal civil and political rights, the targets for deradicalization held at state prisons and detention camps often include both actual criminals and political dissidents. Scholars or practitioners advising or collaborating with the state's deradicalization efforts could be complicit in a state's efforts to silence, suppress, and reduce or eradicate political opposition to the regime by disenfranchised groups. In this capacity, the scholar and practitioner lend support to one radical ideology and actor (the non-democratic state aiming to establish a monopoly by silencing alternatives) in the suppression of another, competing radical actor (if the target indeed advocates a radical worldview) and non-radical actor (in cases where the target is a political dissident advocating democratic inclusion and equal civil and political rights).

Yet, the contention of this chapter is not that deradicalization initiatives are impossible in non-democratic situations and that scholars and practitioners should simply disengage from them. In this chapter, I also offer an example from Israel/Palestine of an alternative approach that can replace the state-security paradigm. This alternative focuses on civil society and adopts a political-transformative approach. It addresses the problem that both the state and non-state actors employ political violence and uphold radical ideologies. It does so by recruiting and targeting for joint deradicalization efforts people who have taken part in different forms of political violence both on behalf of non-state organizations *and* people who have used violence on behalf of the state. Furthermore, beyond simply aiming at a change in individual behavior and ideology, the objective of this work is to transform the political situation from one that perpetuates various forms of political violence to one that strives to resist and overcome the underlying structural roots of such violence. This transformation entails political efforts to change the status quo from a non-democratic to a democratic one, where all individuals and communities enjoy equal civil and political rights.

The case of Israel/Palestine

There are significant challenges to employing the concept of "deradicalization" in the context of Israel/Palestine. In particular, the politicized use of the terms "radicalization" and "deradicalization" by agents of the state, security services, the popular media, and even within academic research requires vigilant scrutiny. Given the fact that the Israeli state, as well as the Palestinian Authority government in the West Bank and the Hamas government in the Gaza Strip, suffer from severe democratic deficits, their use of the term "radicalization" to label dissidents who dispute the status quo must be critically evaluated. As Daniel Koehler helpfully outlines in this book, violent radical ideologies

> constantly erase and negate alternative or competing definitions of the ideology's core values and concepts and try to establish a monopoly in this regard. At the same time, the propaganda and group dynamics constantly increase the urgency and importance of the core problems stated through the movement and ideology.
> *(Chapter 2)*

But what of cases where the states or governments purporting to target radicalism themselves promote and propagate violent radical ideologies, as well as the use of violence against those who disagree with the state's or government's agenda? If deradicalization is understood as a "process of turning from a position of perceived deviance or conflict with the surrounding environment" or the degree of an individual's or group's accordance with "the legal, ideological or moral view of the surrounding majority (or mainstream) environment" (Chapter 2), what paradigms can we use to evaluate these processes when the mainstream environment itself is non-democratic and intolerant?[1] In these situations, how do we draw a distinction between government efforts to deradicalize radicals and government efforts to eliminate dissent and opposition?

The focus of much of the research and policy work in Israel/Palestine, as it is elsewhere, is on the radicalization and deradicalization of non-state actors (for example, see: Della Porta and LaFree, 2012; Horgan, 2009; Horgan and Braddock, 2010, p. 279). In turn, the designation of a group as radical, and in extreme cases as "terrorist," often borrows from lists or designations determined by states' security apparatuses. Yet these representatives of the state, including in government, the police, military, and intelligence and security services, are rarely themselves defined as "radicalized," even when they hold extreme intolerant ideologies and employ licit and illicit violence. While this immunity of state actors from the category of radicalization and from being potential targets for deradicalization is problematic even in democratic contexts, it is even more tenuous in non-democratic settings, such as repressive regimes and instances of military occupation, as in Israel/Palestine. What I propose in this chapter is that legitimate (from a democratic standpoint respectful of the principle of equal civil rights) and effective deradicalization efforts in non-democratic situations such as this one must target *both* violent non-state actors, often designated as "terrorists," *and* state actors and bodies who also use violence and hold intolerant ideologies.

This approach is particularly apt to the evaluation of deradicalization initiatives in Israel/Palestine. While some studies place Israel in the company of democratic states in Western Europe and the US, which have grappled with what has been termed home-grown "Islamic radicalism" (Ganor, 2011; Ganor and Falk, 2013), a much more accurate frame would place Israel in the context of studies of radicalization under repressive regimes (for example, Davenport et al., 2012; Larzillière, 2012). Another apt comparison is of foreign military occupation or the imprisonment of non-citizens in military prisons, as in the case of Guantanamo (for example, Olesen, 2011). Israel itself within its pre-1967 borders, which do not include the West Bank and Gaza, is indeed a democracy. However, a majority of those whom Israel designates and imprisons as radicals or terrorists (called "security prisoners") are not citizens entitled to equal civil rights, but rather residents of the occupied Palestinian territories that are under Israel's military control.[2] Because the territories it occupies are adjacent to its own territory, political violence[3] against security services and Israeli civilians has been compared to home-grown radicalism in Western democracies. However, while home-grown radicalism in these countries originates in communities of citizens, in the Israeli context non-state actors using political violence are almost exclusively composed of residents who, because they are Palestinians and not Israeli or Jewish, do not enjoy civil rights. As an occupied population, they cannot vote or be elected to the Israeli parliament, serve in its police or military, and do not enjoy full civil liberties such as freedom of movement, association, assembly, expression, and so on. The non-violent avenues available for this population to express grievances are much more limited in comparison to those available to citizens in a democratic country (for example, protest, lobbying, organizing political parties, pressuring elected officials). The category for comparison, therefore, should be non-democratic contexts such as occupation (for example, Kashmir, Tibet, Iraq, and Afghanistan under US occupation) or non-democratic or semi-democratic regimes (for example, Egypt, Jordan, Russia, and Turkey).

In addition, the state has designated as terrorist or illegal organizations a spectrum of Palestinian organizations with a plethora of ideological commitments – from the nationalist Fatah whose stated aim is the establishment of an independent Palestinian state alongside Israel, to Hamas and the Islamic Jihad that officially call for immediate or gradual reclamation of all of the lands of the historic mandatory Palestine (an aim which entails the cessation of the existence of Israel) and the establishment of a religious Islamic state. However, Israeli governments themselves, since at least 1977, have included political parties that advocate similar ideologies from the Jewish-Israeli side. Some of them today, like the Jewish Home party, advocate for the primacy of the ethno-nationalist religious Jewish identity of Israel over and at the expense of its democratic character (an aim which entails the prevention of Palestinian statehood by extending Israeli sovereignty to the occupied territories and making permanent the legal apartheid that exists there). Others hope to establish an illiberal religious Jewish state (for example, the ultra-Orthodox parties within the government).[4] Moreover, even from the narrower prism of radical violence or the use of political violence the Israeli government and military have engaged in repression and retaliation acts that have led to the deaths of thousands of Palestinian civilians, and the country's security services have employed an array of violent tactics, including the use of torture and persistent violations of human rights.[5] Compounding matters, the Fatah-controlled Palestinian Authority on the one hand, and the Hamas government in Gaza on the other hand, likewise cannot be considered fully democratic, and their security apparatuses also participate in repression of Palestinian dissenters under the guise of countering radicalism and terrorism.[6]

In non-democratic contexts such as the Israel/Palestine case (whether it be classified in the category of repressive regimes or military occupations) where the targets for intended deradicalization lack full civil rights, two divergent approaches have been employed. One focuses on security services and prison administration – the representatives of the state – as the agents to potentially implement deradicalization initiatives. The second approach is vested in civil society and operates under a political-transformative paradigm rather than a purely state-centered security paradigm. In what follows I briefly outline these two approaches and argue that in the current political climate in Israel/Palestine, the first is highly ineffective and normatively questionable, from a democratic perspective of respect for equal civil rights, while the latter possesses tremendous potential, and merits the investment of much greater resources and funding than are currently available to it.

"Security prisoners" and the state-security approach

The Israeli Prisons Service (IPS) currently holds a large number of what it terms Palestinian "security prisoners." The term officially refers to

> a prisoner who was convicted and is serving a sentence for an offence, or who is detained for suspicion of committing an offence, which by its nature or circumstances is defined as a distinctly security offence, or that the motivation for its perpetration stems from nationalistic reasons.
>
> *(Ronen, 2019b, p. 2, translated from Hebrew)*

The designation of a detainee as a "security prisoner" is not based on legislation but is rather the purview of the IPS as part of its administrative authority (Ronen, 2019b, p. 2). What acts are classified as a security offense are extremely broad. These range all the way from planning or committing violent attacks on military or civilian targets, to participating in an unauthorized gathering or unruly demonstration, spraying graffiti, posting of poems or social media statuses considered to be inciting, and simply being political members in organizations which Israel designates as unlawful or illegal. The criterion of "nationalist" motives casts even non-violent acts as security offenses, if they are motivated by Palestinian demands for self-determination. Moreover, and perhaps most problematic, while inside Israel there are proper procedures for declaring an organization illegal, in the occupied territories the situation is different. There, an area commander can declare any association an illegal association, and furthermore, a person can be convicted of being involved in an illegal association even if that association was not declared as illegal, and finally, an organization and association can be declared illegal even if it has not actually taken any action that poses a threat to security. Finally, Palestinians, including minors, are tried for all offenses (criminal and security) in military courts, while Israeli citizens living in the same territories are tried in civilian courts (see IDF, 2016; IPS, 2018; ACRI, n.d.; B'tselem, 2018).

The number of such prisoners spiked significantly during the first Palestinian intifada (uprising) in 1987–1993 and averaged 4,000. Following the Oslo Peace Accords between Israel and the Palestinian Liberation Organization (PLO) in 1993, many prisoners were released and by the year 2000 their numbers dropped to about 800. The onset of the second intifada in 2000 again saw rising arrests, reaching a peak of about 10,000 security prisoners in 2007. As of May 2017, there were 6,189 such prisoners (Figure 21.1) and these constitute about 30% of the entire prison population in the country. Facilities established by the military to hold the prisoners were transferred to the IPS by 2006, and the IPS is currently the authority in charge of this population. Because of their designation as a security threat these prisoners are held separately from regular prisoners and their conditions, rights, and privileges are different from those of the general prisoner population. It should be noted

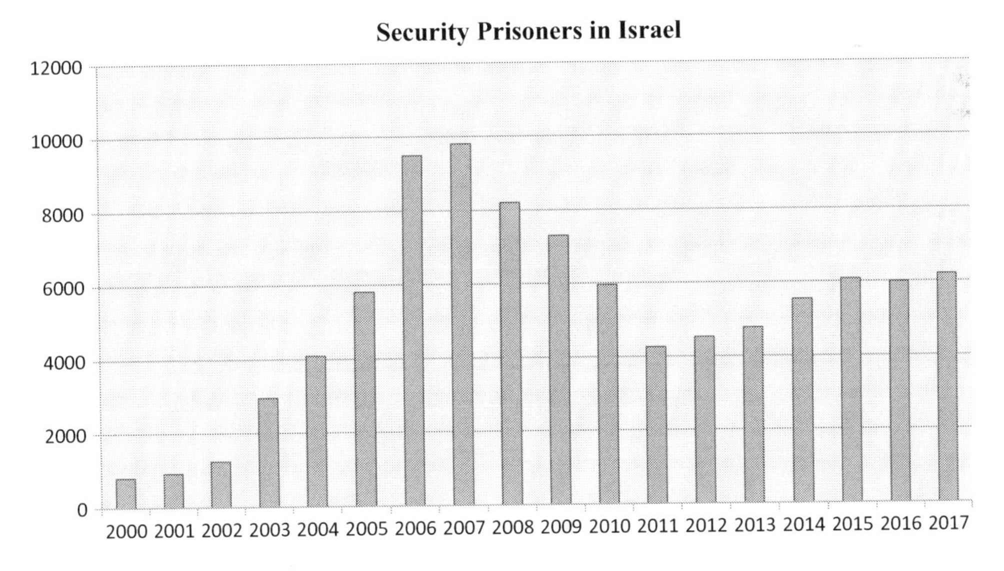

Figure 21.1 Security prisoners in Israel.

Source: Data combined from B'tselem, 2018; Ganor and Falk, 2013; Hamoked, 2019[7]

that the incarceration of Palestinian prisoners from the West Bank and Gaza inside Israel proper constitutes a violation of the fourth Geneva Convention, which prohibits the transfer of detainees and prisoners out of an occupied territory (Hamoked, 2019).

The administration of these prisoners by the IPS presents opportunities for deradicalization initiatives within a framework of a larger political process of settlement and peace building between the Israeli government and the different Palestinian organizations. However, in the absence of interest in a political settlement, extant and future efforts at the prison level implemented by state agents and with security, rather than political-transformative, objectives, are bound to be ineffective.

When arrested, security prisoners are sent to wards in accordance with their organizational affiliations (for example, Fatah, Hamas, Islamic Jihad, Popular Front for the Liberation of Palestine, etc.). They hold bi-yearly elections to select a spokesperson to represent each organization in dealings with the prison administration. In general, the leadership of the different factions enjoys some autonomy in running the daily life of its members within the prison. This structure has also allowed them to coordinate collective action such as strikes or hunger strikes to extract concessions from prison authorities on living conditions, treatment, and privileges. In addition, the Palestinian Authority transfers funds to the personal accounts of dominant prisoners, which are used collectively to buy products in the prison's commissary and for other purposes (according to a report by the Israeli Knesset, between 2000 and 2006 prisoners received 17 million NIS in this way (Ronen, 2019b). The evolution of this system of affiliation and representation stems from two sources. The first is the prisoners' self-identification as "political prisoners," rather than as terrorists, as they are defined by the IPS. They hold Israel accountable to articles 70 and 102 of the third Geneva Convention, which grant prisoners of war the right to elect their own representatives (Baker, 2016). The second is Israel's tacit acknowledgment of this state of affairs and of the effectiveness of such mechanisms to maintain order among the security prisoner population. In addition, maintaining separate factions also helps to entrench the internal Palestinian split, especially between Fatah and Hamas (although the prisons have been one arena where occasionally the two factions in the past have effectively negotiated intra-Palestinian détentes (Noy, 2017)).

This level of organization and the collective action coordination and negotiation skills prisoners develop could serve an Israeli government keen on reaching a political solution to the conflict. The high status and nationalist credentials of prisoners make them credible representatives in the eyes of the Palestinian population and potential partners for an effective Israeli–Palestinian agreement. However, especially since 2009 the Israeli government has relied on a coalition of parties and Members of Knesset (Israeli Parliament) who object to the notion of a Palestinian state and hope to contain and manage the conflict while expanding settlements and Israel's hold on the occupied territories, rather than make any political concessions to the Palestinians. In this context, Israel's strategy toward security prisoners has seen a combination of: (1) using prisoners as bargaining chips with Palestinian factions by occasionally hardening their conditions and depriving them of privileges such as family visits or access to higher education, for example; and (2) an individualist approach of carrot-and-stick tactics to influence individual prisoners' cost–benefit calculations with regard to what Israel defines as "radical" behavior (Baker, 2016; Ganor and Falk, 2013).

In their study of deradicalization efforts in Israeli prisons, Ganor and Falk outline this individualist approach. They explain:

> Prison authorities have a variety of rewards and sanctions at their disposal, all of which can be used to convince inmates to participate in the deradicalization process,

> or which may influence their individual cost–benefit calculations. In return for cooperating with and participating in meetings, deradicalization lessons, indoctrination sessions, non-religious/non-ideological work, or academic, vocational or professional education, a prisoner may be rewarded with family visits, telephone calls, canteen purchases (goods and food), preferred cooking facilities and accommodations, and leisure activities. A prisoner who fails to cooperate with or participate in such activities may be penalized in these same areas.
>
> *(Ganor and Falk, 2013, p. 125)*

There are several problems with this method that render it largely ineffective. In her excellent study of security prisoners in Israel, Abeer Bake, a human rights lawyer who has represented some of these prisoners in court, outlines the major logistical and political flaws of the individualist approach (Baker, 2016). First, since security prisoners are designated by the prison administration to an organizational affiliation, they encounter a Catch-22 dilemma when presented with the opportunity to take the individual cost–benefits approach outlined by Ganor and Falk above. In order to be considered for certain benefits, such as participation in rehabilitation programs or early release eligibility, security prisoners have to demonstrate that they have renounced all affiliation with their organization. However, since the prisoners' life is administered by these organizations, with the consent and support of the prison administration, proving non-affiliation requires active defiance by individual prisoners of their elected prison leadership. For instance, if the leadership declares a hunger strike, a prisoner must request and actively engage in consuming food in front of his peers to demonstrate an active breaking of the strike. If he does not eat, in solidarity with his peers, the act is taken as an affirmation of membership, and denies him eligibility to privileges available to regular criminal prisoners.

The problems with this are that: first, as explained here, logistically the prison administration makes it close to impossible for prisoners not to be affiliated, as it assigns them collective affiliation. Second, it is clear that renunciation of the organization serves the political interest of Israel and is detrimental to the political and collective bargaining power of Palestinians. The aim of conditioning privileges on the severing of affiliation with the prisoner's organization is clearly to weaken the collective action capacity of the organization within the prison, and also outside of it, rather than a concern for the use of violence by the prisoner. Finally, as Baker explains, only few Palestinian prisoners in fact pursue the individual track. This is not only because of the logistical difficulty, but also because they do not see themselves as criminals in need of rehabilitation programs (which is a condition for early release) but rather as patriotic nationalists resisting a military occupation. Moreover, even for those who take the individual track, most requests for early release are usually denied by military courts (Baker, 2016).

Even Ganor and Falk, who subscribe to the state-centric security paradigm, admit that it has proved ineffective. Measured by "rate of return to terrorism," in their words, they state that Israel's

> deradicalisation efforts have not been effective in preventing released terrorists from returning to lethal terrorism. In fact, of the 6,912 convicted Palestinian terrorists released as part of the confidence-building measures that attended the Oslo Peace Process between 1993 and 1999, 854 of them had been rearrested for acts of terrorism by August 2003. Moreover, since 2000, 180 Israelis have been killed and hundreds injured by terrorists released from Israeli jails.
>
> *(Ganor and Falk, 2013, pp.127–128)*

This approach, beyond its logistical and structural flaws, also maintains a tenuous double standard. It sees non-state actors' "radical" ideology, affiliation, and violence as a target for deradicalization, while ignoring or even condoning the same type of ideology and violence by the state or state actors.[8]

The questionable nature of the security approach in a non-democratic setting is as apparent when examined in the intra-Palestinian context too. In a fascinating research, Björn Brenner has looked at a deradicalization initiative undertaken by Hamas, the Palestinian Islamic Resistance Movement, in Gaza starting in 2009 (Brenner, 2017). Hamas, which itself is considered a terrorist organization by Israel, violently took over the Gaza Strip in 2007 in a fight with Fatah, and has formed an unelected repressive government in the Strip. Increasingly, Hamas has been challenged by Salafi-Jihadis, many of them former Hamas members who felt that the organization was not radical enough both in terms of religious doctrine and resistance to Israel. The Hamas government's first step in countering this trend included sweeping purges of Hamas's own membership focusing mainly on its military wing, the Qassam Brigades. This was followed by heavy restrictions of Salafi-affiliated mosques, including shutdowns of some mosques or replacing their imams with Hamas sympathizers. In tandem, Hamas conducted massive arrests and began the construction of five new detention centers to house around 1,200 security detainees, among them many Salafis.

In prison, Hamas sought to implement a deradicalization approach centered on Islamic re-education by religious teachers and scholars. As Brenner outlines:

> The religious scholars engaged with the detainees through lectures, one-on-one sessions, and group seminars. The sessions began with the scholars listening to the experiences and views of the detainees. They then moved on to a traditional form of religious dialogue, with the goal of re-educating the subjects to accept Hamas's interpretation of Islam. The second part of the program was political and involved lectures and group sessions with Hamas leaders from the movement's political echelon … The third and final part of the program sought to engage the Salafi jihadists after their release from detention. Upon release, they had to sign pledges not to violate truces agreed between Hamas and Israel or to engage in any activities that compromised Gaza's internal security. The former prisoners received regular home visits by security officers who continued to monitor them.
>
> *(Brenner, 2017, pp. 30–31)*

This initiative yielded few results, according to Brenner, exactly due to the non-democratic nature of the regime implementing it. Arrested Salafi individuals were not only those who participated in violent activities, but also those who simply had ideological and political disagreements with Hamas. Deradicalization programs for Salafis were not voluntary but rather mandatory. Moreover, repressive detention and interrogation methods used in Hamas's prisons included and continue to include the use of torture and violations of human rights, as well as periodic executions of political rivals. The US State Department's Bureau of Democracy, Human Rights, and Labor stated in its latest human rights report that in 2016:

> Human rights abuses under Hamas included security forces killing, torturing, arbitrarily detaining, and harassing opponents, including Fatah members and other Palestinians with impunity … Human rights organizations reported authorities held prisoners in poor conditions in detention facilities in the Gaza Strip, and Hamas publicly and unlawfully executed persons without trial or after proceedings that did

> not meet "fair trial" standards. Hamas also infringed on privacy rights. Hamas restricted the freedoms of speech, press, assembly, association, religion, and movement of Gaza Strip residents.
>
> *(US Department of State, 2016, p. 70)*

It is not surprising, then, that Salafi radicals interviewed in Brenner's research stated that the religious re-education felt like ideological indoctrination and not a form of equal, meaningful, and transformative dialogue. Like the Israeli prisons case, this example is a stark illustration of the limited effectiveness and normative dubiousness, in terms of respect for basic democratic civil rights, of attempts at deradicalization undertaken by non-democratic authorities.

The same also applies to the security practices of the Fatah-controlled Palestinian Authority in the West Bank. Here too, as numerous Palestinian and international human rights organizations consistently document, violations of human rights of prisoners in Palestinian prisons is rampant, and security pretexts are often used to arrest political dissidents and critics of the political status quo.[9] The US government has contributed an average of $100 million annually since the mid-1900s to the Palestinian Authority's security sector. In recent years, this aid has been used to "train, reform, advise, house, and provide non-lethal equipment for PA [Palestinian Authority] civil security forces in the West Bank loyal to President Abbas." The stated aim of this support has been "countering militants from organizations such as Hamas and Palestine Islamic Jihad-Shaqaqi Faction, and establishing the rule of law for an expected Palestinian state" (Zanotti, 2016, p. 8). Yet, as the US State Department itself acknowledges, human rights violations under the Palestinian Authority in the West Bank routinely include "abuse and mistreatment of detainees, overcrowded detention facilities, prolonged detention, and infringements on privacy rights" alongside restrictions on freedom of speech, press, and assembly and limits on freedom of association and movement (US Department of State, 2016, p. 70).

Israel, the Palestinian Authority, and Hamas's security apparatuses are unlikely to produce meaningful deradicalization results in their prisons. As this section reviewed, these state or proto-state actors are themselves engaged in the use of illegitimate violence inside and outside prisons and use incarceration as a measure to curb political opposition to the status quo. For Israel, membership in organizations that resist the Israeli occupation is labeled radicalism and terrorism. For Fatah and Hamas, political opponents, even those who simply criticize these respective organizations but do not engage in violence, are routinely arrested and mistreated in detention centers. Furthermore, these three governments themselves uphold unpalatable intolerant ideologies. The Israeli government continues to invest in a system of occupation, civilian settlements, and repression of the occupied population in contravention of international law and out of a belief in Jewish supremacy in rights to the land. The Palestinian Authority and its affiliated media and social media herald as "martyrs" Palestinians who die while executing attacks against Israeli civilians and security personnel (US Department of State, 2016). Hamas's rhetoric is explicit in its incitement against Israel and Jews and often resorts to anti-Semitism and incitement to violence in its media operations and public speeches by its cadres (US Department of State, 2016).

As under other repressive regimes, deradicalization efforts in prisons of such state actors are not likely to be seen as legitimate by their targets and their communities, and should not be lumped in the same category as prison-based deradicalization efforts in democratic contexts. In democratic contexts, citizens have formal non-violent avenues to express their grievances, engage in politics, and have their interests heard and represented by elected officials. In non-democratic contexts lacking freedom of expression, association, and basic civil rights such as the right to participate in free and fair elections, "deradicalization" is often a way to silence opposition or regime critiques. This is not lost on prisoners, who see themselves as political prisoners rather than radical deviants (Baker and Matar, 2011; Della Porta and LaFree, 2012). In the next section, I outline an alternative strategy employed by civil society groups, which I argue has a much greater transformative potential and more sound moral legitimacy from a democratic standpoint that upholds the principle of equal civil rights.

Civil society and the political-transformative approach

The political-transformative approach addresses the problem of state vs. non-state violence by recruiting and targeting people who have taken part in different forms of political violence on behalf of both the state and of non-state organizations. Furthermore, beyond simply aiming at a change in individual behavior and ideology, the objective of this work is to transform the political situation from one that perpetuates various forms of political violence to one that strives to resist and overcome the underlying structural roots of such violence.

To illustrate this strategy, I will use the example of the Israeli–Palestinian organization Combatants for Peace (CfP). CfP was established in 2006 by former Palestinian combatants, many of whom spent time in Israeli prisons, and former Israeli soldiers, including some currently serving on reserve duties, who served in the Israeli military (the Israel Defense Force – IDF). It is run jointly by a steering committee currently consisting of 15 Palestinians and 18 Israelis. The individuals who originally established the organization found their individual paths toward a commitment to non-violence but decided to take action for the benefit of their wider societies, which are the victims of the violence of the ongoing conflict. By outlining the organization's mission and work in what follows, I highlight the fundamental difference in the logics of the political-transformative approach and the state-centric security approach explained in the previous section.

Definitions

In introducing themselves, the members of CfP define themselves in the following words:

> We are a group of Palestinians and Israelis who have taken an active part in the cycle of violence in our region: Israeli soldiers serving in the IDF and Palestinians as combatants fighting to free their country, Palestine, from the Israeli occupation.[10]

The language here is clearly vastly different from the language of the security approach. If the IPS and academics subscribing to the security paradigm use words such as "radicals" and "terrorists" to describe Palestinians who have taken part in political violence, CfP talks about Palestinian "combatants" involved in resistance to a military occupation. Furthermore, both Israeli soldiers and Palestinian combatants are acknowledged as having taken an "active part in the cycle of violence." The purpose here is not necessarily to equate the two sides or the political rationale for each side's engagement in violence, but simply to recognize that in so far as violence is rejected as a political tool, both sides have been implicated in using this illegitimate tool. The use of the word combatant is not meant to justify or legitimize the members' participation in violent action, but rather to recognize their self-perception as having been motivated by a desire to act in defense of their national collectives.

Politics

The security paradigm completely obfuscates the question of politics by designating its targets as radicalized terrorists in need of rehabilitation, similarly to criminals who have broken the law. Its objective is therefore to rehabilitate the "terrorist" so that s/he relinquishes violent action and eventually also disassociates from organizations designated as terrorist. Presenting itself as apolitical, the security paradigm is quintessentially political in that it works to maintain a political status quo that favors a monopoly by the state and its agents over the use of political violence. The political-transformative approach recognizes that, while for some the choice to engage in political violence may stem from personal anti-social or syncretic motivations, for the majority on both sides the motivation and self-understanding are largely political. Without working to change the structural political reality that is the root cause of political violence, an approach that addresses only its symptoms remains inherently limited.

CfP, therefore, describes its mission statement as striving to create

> a model for humanistic values of freedom, democracy, security and dignity for all. We envision Combatants for Peace as a strong, significant, influential bi-national community – a community that exemplifies viable cooperation: co-resistance to the occupation and violence, which forms the basis for future co-existence. Through joint nonviolence in the present, we lay the foundations for a nonviolent future.[11]

A commitment to non-violent action is here embedded in a larger political vision that includes freedom, democracy and security for both sides. Moreover, rather than simply pacifying people who have previously engaged in violence in a way that benefits the status quo, the organization includes co-resistance to military occupation as a stated objective and recruits Israelis to this cause as well. There is, then, a transformation in which both people formerly involved in the security apparatuses of the state and people who have in the past been imprisoned and branded as "radicals" or "terrorists" commit to a joint effort toward a political goal. This approach rejects their former use of violence while still affirming the legitimacy of their original political motivations.

Community

Finally, in contrast to the security approach that seeks to pacify the individual by separating him/her from a perceived "radical" collective or environment, the civil society approach focuses on individuals as always embedded within communities. CfP's goals thus emphasize community work. They include, in their words:

> 1) Building an ever-expanding Palestinian–Israeli joint activist *community* based upon CfP's bi-national regional groups that embody our vision and serve as a model for both societies and their future; 2) Motivating broad and effective bi-national, nonviolent activity promoting freedom and security for both peoples in their homeland; 3) Changing attitudes on a wide scale, both within the Israeli and Palestinian *public*, as well as with governmental decision makers (stress added).[12]

The organization's activities reflect this community-centered approach. There are six regional bi-national groups that bring Israelis and Palestinians in their areas for joint activities (Nablus–Tel Aviv, Qalailya–Tel Aviv, Bethlehem–Jerusalem, el-Quds/Jericho–Jerusalem, Ramallah–Jerusalem, North and Hebron–Beer Sheva). The focus of activities is determined by the regional group itself according to local priorities. These include social and recreational activities such as bi-national tours and meetings, as well as more explicitly activist work such as helping villagers re-build after army demolitions, advocating against land expropriation, and non-violent protests on local issues. The organization also runs a theater group and a women's group, and former combatants visit with schools and communities to share their stories about transition from violence to non-violent activism.

The most far-reaching action by the group is the Joint Israeli–Palestinian Memorial Day, run jointly with other peace organizations, which has been held annually for the past 11 years. The Memorial Day brings people from both sides to remember together the victims of the conflict who have lost their lives in the violence it perpetuates. In 2016 there were 2,500 attendees, and by 2017 the number had grown to 4,000. Hostility toward the event still exists in both societies. In 2017 the Israeli army prevented Palestinian families attending the event, and right-wing Jewish protestors attacked participants. Nevertheless, the high attendance is noteworthy, and the wide media coverage of the event has raised awareness of it in both communities.

Other civil society initiatives abound in Israel/Palestine, although CfP is unique in that it was established and is managed by former combatants on both sides. Fascinating examples of non-governmental efforts include the Bereaved Families Circle, a group of Israeli and Palestinian families who have lost loved ones in the conflict and who meet with students and other groups on both sides to share their stories and advocate an end to the occupation and to violence. The Circle has organized the joint Memorial Day ceremony with CfP in order to highlight the human costs of the violent status quo. Another example, from the Israeli side, is the Adam Institute for Democracy and Peace (n.d.), which runs educational programs throughout the country that focus on pluralism, tolerance, respect for human rights, democratic practices, and peaceful conflict resolution. Participants in the Institute's programs over the years number in the thousands and include children and youth – from kindergarten to high school – educators, journalists, women's rights activists, and civil society leaders.[13] There are many other civil society initiatives on the Israeli side. Many of them coordinate through the Peace NGOs Forum, which is a platform aimed at networking and coordinating their efforts to get Israelis to recognize the need for a peaceful resolution of the Israeli/Palestinian conflict through an end to the occupation.[14]

On the Palestinian side, given the asymmetric nature of the situation where Palestinians lack the same resources and freedoms available to Israelis, there also exist some civil society initiatives that promote non-violent approaches to the occupation. The Holy Land Trust, for example, established in 1998 and based in Bethlehem, works "through a commitment to the principles of nonviolence … to strengthen and empower the peoples of the Holy Land to engage in spiritual, pragmatic and strategic paths that will end all forms of oppression."[15] The Wasatia (moderation) project, started in 2007 by Prof. Mohammed S. Dajani Daoudi (formerly of Al-Quds University in Jerusalem) is another such initiative. The goals of his work, as he articulates them, are to simultaneously promote religious moderation and to end the occupation through non-violent means, seeing these two as interconnected. The most high-profile project in the initiative was an educational trip for Palestinian university students to Auschwitz and other death-camp sites in Poland in 2014. The goal was to learn about the Holocaust and become familiar and more empathetic with the Jewish historical narrative. Even though this work has been limited and did not generate much support in Palestine, it is noteworthy to quote here the ambitious mission statement of Wasatia (n.d.):

(a) To bring a deeper and more rational understanding of Islam to Moslems as well as to non-Moslems. (b) To clarify the distortions to which Islam has been subjected at home and in the West. (c) To educate Palestinians on taboo topics such as the Holocaust taking a new humanistic approach. (d) To seek answers for the deep religious, political, social, and economic crises inflicting the Palestinian society. (e) To strive and work for ending the Israeli military occupation through negotiations and peaceful means. (f) To spread and promote Islamic tolerant concepts, values and principles within the Palestinian community. (g) To encourage the practice of moderation among Palestinians in order to mitigate religious radicalism and bigotry and reduce political extremism. (h) To bring a message of peace, moderation, justice, coexistence, tolerance, and reconciliation to Palestinian community through vocal civic leaders. (i) To teach creative and critical thinking and open-mindedness. (j) To empower the potential for leadership in their society. The goal of dialogue and education is to deconstruct mythologies and distortions and misinterpretations and to promote knowledge and empathy for the other. Wasatia addresses all aspects of life: the way we eat, the way we dress, the way we spend money. Moderation is a value shared with the various thinkers and philosophers as well as all faiths and therefore could become a fruitful foundation for dialogue to achieve peace and reconciliation.[16]

Wasatia now works in cooperation with a German university to offer MA and PhD courses in peace and non-violence research. Another example is Middle East Nonviolence and Democracy (MEND), which was founded in 1998 and has engaged in projects such as:

Active Nonviolence Network in 9 centers throughout Palestine, including the Gaza Strip; Preparing alternate curriculum which aims to promote acceptance of the "Other"; Distribution of Bumper Stickers which question the outcome of violence; Radio Soap Opera program which promotes the value of nonviolence; Training for children and teachers in over 35 schools including the Jerusalem, Ramallah, Jericho, and Bethlehem areas; Video Conferencing Debates on Nonviolence between activists in the West Bank and Gaza Strip.[17]

Despite their lofty aims, there are several major challenges that plague these civil society political-transformative efforts. First, in terms of resources, civil society organizations of this nature are at an incredible disadvantage in comparison to the funding available to the state security apparatuses (both Israeli and the Palestinian Authority), and to non-state armed groups (such as Hamas). While a group like CfP relies on small and often non-sustainable donations from foundations, Western governments, and communities (CfP's total budget, for example, was around 900,000 NIS in 2014 and 2015),[18] state and non-state military actors enjoy budgets of hundreds of millions of dollars. Funding for civil society organizations is often project-based, entailing short life-cycles for projects, little sustained support for long-term operational costs, the need to compete with other organizations for funding, and of course the need to adjust to the objectives and agendas of donors at the expense of autonomy and grassroots independence. Second, due to limited resources, not enough funding is available for systematic evaluation of such groups' impact and the creation of strategic planning for scaling their work. This is an area where academics might assist practitioners. While civil society practitioners often lack the funding for scientific evaluation of outcomes, academics might volunteer their time and social scientific skills to collaborate in such an endeavor. Even though most organizations cannot afford to pay for these services, academics might benefit otherwise through access to data, generating publications, and contributing to the accumulation of a rigorous body of knowledge (see Chapter 2).

Finally, because of their bi-national joint activities, such organizations are often branded as "collaborators" and "traitors" by hawkish groups in their respective societies, and even by representatives of the state. For example, a different organization called "Breaking the Silence," consisting of IDF soldiers who have served in the occupied territories and who strive to raise awareness of the toll of the occupation on the moral and mental wellbeing of soldiers, has been a target of government attacks. Ministers and politicians have taken steps to bar the group from giving lectures in high schools, military bases, and community centers, and some have even tried to outlaw the group (Alon, 2016; Lem, 2016). On the Palestinian side, those who work jointly with Israelis are increasingly accused of "normalizing" the occupation and denounced as unpatriotic. A stark illustration of this is the fate of Prof. Mohammed S. Dajani Daoudi, founder of the Wasatia project. He had to resign from his university position and leave for several years to the US due to death threats and denunciations from students and colleagues who accused him of collaboration with Israel and normalization of the occupation following his trip to Auschwitz (Alexander, 2016).

Conclusion

Israel/Palestine presents a unique case for the implementation of "deradicalization" projects. Israel is often viewed in the literature on security and terrorism as a democratic country facing similar War on Terror challenges as Western democracies, but its situation is far more complex. Because the territories it occupies are adjacent to its own territory, political violence against security services and Israeli civilians has been compared to home-grown radicalism in Western democracies. However, while home-grown radicalism in these countries originates in communities of citizens, in the Israeli context non-state actors using political violence are almost exclusively composed of residents who, because they are Palestinians and not Israeli or Jewish, do not enjoy civil rights. As an occupied population, they cannot vote or be elected to the Israeli parliament, serve in its police or military, and do not enjoy full civil liberties such as freedom of movement, association, assembly, expression, and so on. The non-violent avenues available for this population to express grievances are much more limited in comparison to those available to citizens in a democratic country (for example, protest, lobbying, organizing political parties, pressuring elected officials). The category for comparison, therefore, should be non-democratic contexts such as occupation (for example, Kashmir, Tibet, Iraq, and Afghanistan under US occupation) or non-democratic or semi-democratic regimes (for example, Egypt, Jordan, Russia, and Turkey). Similarly, the Palestinian Authority on the one hand and the Hamas-controlled Gaza Strip on the other, are both semi- or proto-states in the sense that they have a government (although under severe restrictions of autonomy by the Israeli occupation) that also displays repressive authoritarian tendencies toward the Palestinian civilian population under their control.

In other non-democratic or semi-democratic cases there indeed have been some successful episodes of deradicalization of non-state actors resulting from various state policies of repression and cooptation, as part of a state-centered security paradigm. There have also been many failures (Loyle, Lindekilde, Nets-Zehngut, Diehl and Steinmann, 2012). Yet in the absence of a true transition to democracy, examples touted as successes have often simply entailed the restoration of the state actor's monopoly over the use of political violence, rather than a move away from political violence. In this respect, the security approaches to deradicalization employed by Israel, the

Palestinian Authority, and Hamas outlined in this chapter are not very different from these other experiences. However, the civil society political-transformative paradigm as it is taking shape in Israel/Palestine, and which of course draws on examples such as anti-apartheid activism in South Africa or the civil rights movement in the US among others, can perhaps serve as a model for other contexts of military occupation or repressive regimes. The uniqueness of this approach is that it recognizes that political violence is perpetrated by *both* state and non-state actors, and that deradicalization efforts must target both non-state individuals *as well as* representatives of the state who participate in such violence. Furthermore, this approach aims at the political, systematic root causes that give rise to political violence and to its legitimation and justification on both sides. Instead of the piecemeal targeting of individuals for "rehabilitation," the paradigm endows individuals and communities with recognition for the legitimacy of their grievances. It encourages the option of working together with those who are considered "enemies" to address these grievances non-violently. Significant challenges remain in the way of this approach in non-democratic contexts, especially in the absence of willingness by major state and non-state official parties to a conflict to move toward democracy. Even so, both moral-normative and practical considerations, as discussed in this chapter, still make the political-transformative path a more preferred and effective course of action.

Notes

1 By intolerant, I mean Koehler's definition in this book regarding radical ideologies being ones that "constantly erase and negate alternative or competing definitions of the ideology's core values and concepts and try to establish a monopoly in this regard. At the same time, the propaganda and group dynamics constantly increase the urgency and importance of the core problems stated through the movement and ideology (Chapter 2).

2 The Gaza Strip has not been internally under Israeli occupation since 2005, but Israel controls its airspace, sea, and all entry points (except for the Rafah crossing that is controlled by the Egyptian military). As part of its ongoing siege Israel heavily restricts the movement of people and goods in and out of the Strip. In October 2018 there were 310 Gazans among the over 5,000 Palestinian security prisoners held in Israeli prisons (B'tselem, 2019).

3 By political violence I mean the use of violence toward political ends. Political violence can be perpetrated by individuals, non-state actors, and states.

4 Between 1964 and 2018, Israel declared as illegal 404 organizations, out of which only two were right-wing Jewish organizations (or 0.4% of the total); the rest were all Palestinian or Muslim organizations. See Terrorists Organization in accordance with the Defense Regulations (Emergency) 1945 and the Prohibition on Terrorist Financing Law 5765–2004 and Declarations on Terrorist Organizations in accordance with the Prevention of Terrorism Ordinance No 33 5708–1948 and the Counter Terrorism Law 2016. Available here: www.mod.gov.il/Defence-and-Security/Fighting_terrorism/Pages/default.aspx (Accessed Nov. 30, 2018).

5 See for example: Public Committee Against Torture in Israel (2016) *2016 report,* Tel Aviv: Public Committee Against Torture in Israel http://stoptorture.org.il/wp-content/uploads/2016/06/INT_CAT_NGO_ISR_23475_E-Last.pdf; Human Rights Watch pages on Israel/Palestine at www.hrw.org/middle-east/n-africa/israel/palestine (Accessed May 13, 2017).

6 ibid.

7 The vast majority of security prisoners are Palestinians from the West Bank and Gaza, but the data also include a few Palestinian citizens of Israel and Israeli Jews.

8 For example, a Palestinian organization calling for Palestinian sovereignty over all of the territories of Israel and Palestine from the river to the sea could be declared an illegal organization and its participants can be prosecuted as committing a security offence. A Jewish-Israeli organization calling for Israeli sovereignty over the whole same territory, and the denial of Palestinian right to self-determination would not be considered an illegal organization, and in some cases (like the Jewish Home party) would even be invited to join the government. A Hamas capturing of an Israeli soldier would be considered a radical act of violence, while an Israel Defense Forces capturing and

holding of thousands of Palestinians, and hundreds imprisoned without charges or a trial (through administrative arrest) is not considered a radical act of political violence.

9 See, for example, Amnesty and Alhaq www.amnesty.org/en/countries/middle-east-and-north-africa/palestine-state-of/report-palestine-state-of/; www.alhaq.org/advocacy/topics/palestinian-violations.

10 CFP (n.d. a, b) "Homepage" *CFP* Homepage n.d. http://cfpeace.org/about-us/.

11 CFP (n.d. c) "Our Vision" *CFP* Homepage n.d. http://cfpeace.org/about-us/our-vision/.

12 ibid.

13 Adam Institute (n.d.) "Homepage" *Adam Institute* n.d. www.adaminstitute.org.il/language/en/whats-new/.

14 פורום ארגוני השלום Peace NGO's Forum (n.d.) "Homepage" *פורום ארגוני השלום Peace NGO's Forum* n.d. www.facebook.com/%D7%A4%D7%95%D7%A8%D7%95%D7%9D-%D7%90%D7%A8%D7%92%D7%95%D7%A0%D7%99-%D7%94%D7%A9%D7%9C%D7%95%D7%9D-Peace-NGOs-Forum-304163972991820/ (Accessed April 18, 2018).

15 Holyland trust (n.d.) "About Us" *Holyland trust Homepage* n.d. https://holylandtrust.org/about-us/home (Accessed April 18, 2018).

16 Wasatia (n.d.) "Our Goals" *Wasatia Homepage* n.d. www.wasatia.info/goals.html (Accessed April 18, 2018).

17 Middle East Nonviolence and Democracy (n.d.) "Homepage" *Middle East Nonviolence and Democracy* n.d. www.mendonline.org (Accessed April 18, 2018).

18 CfP Financial Reports are available here: www.guidestar.org.il/organization/513797902/documents (Accessed May 30, 2019).

References

ACRI (n.d.) "One Rule, Two Legal Systems. Association for Civil Rights in Israel." *Blog entry*. https://law.acri.org.il//pdf/2laws-presentation.pdf.

Adam Institute (n.d.) "Homepage." *Adam Institute*. www.adaminstitute.org.il/language/en/whats-new/

Alexander, N. (2016). "The Palestinian Professor Who Took Students on Auschwitz Trip and Paid a Heavy Price." *Haaretz*. www.haaretz.com/israelnews/.premium.MAGAZINE-the-palestinian-who-leads-tours-through-auschwitz-1.5435444.

Alon, Gideon (2016). "MK Mualem-Refaeli: Outlaw Breaking the Silence." *Israel Hayom Report*, 14 January. www.israelhayom.co.il/article/347629.

B'tselem (2018). "Report on Palestinian Minors in the Israeli Military Courts System." *Organisational Homepage*. www.btselem.org/sites/default/files/publications/201803_minors_in_jeopardy_heb.pdf.

B'tselem (2019). "Data on Palestinian Detainees and Prisoners in Israel." *Organisational Homepage*, 22 May 2019. www.btselem.org/hebrew/statistics/detainees_and_prisoners.

Baker, A. (2016). "Palestinian Prisoners Between the Community and the Individual: An Insider's View." *Ma'asei Mishpat*, *8*, 95–112. In Hebrew.

Baker, A., & Matar, A. (Eds.). (2011). *Threat: Palestinian Political Prisoners in Israel*. London: Pluto Press.

Brenner, B. (2017). "The Deradicalization of Islamists by Islamists: Hamas's Kid Glove Approach to Salafi Jihadists in the Gaza Strip, 2010–2015." *Strategic Assessment*, *20*(1), 23–34.

CfP (n.d.a) "Homepage." *CFP Homepage*. http://cfpeace.org/about-us/.

CfP (n.d.b) "Our Vision." *CFP Homepage*. http://cfpeace.org/about-us/.

CfP (n.d.c) "Financial Reports." *CfP*. www.guidestar.org.il/organization/513797902/documents.

Davenport, C., & Loyle, C. (2012). "The States Must Be Crazy: Dissent and the Puzzle of Repressive Persistence." *International Journal of Conflict and Violence (IJCV)*, *6*(1), 75–95.

Della Porta, D., & LaFree, G. (2012). "Guest Editorial: Processes of Radicalization and De-Radicalization." *International Journal of Conflict and Violence (IJCV)*, *6*(1), 4–10.

Ganor, B. (2011). "An Intifada in Europe? A Comparative Analysis of Radicalization Processes Among Palestinians in the West Bank and Gaza Versus Muslim Immigrants in Europe." *Studies in Conflict & Terrorism*, *34*(8), 587–599.

Ganor, B., & Falk, O. (2013). "Deradicalisation in Israel's Prison System." *Studies in Conflict & Terrorism*, *36*(2), 116–131.

Hamoked (2019). "Security Prisoners in Israel." *Center for the Defense of the Individual*. www.hamoked.org.il/Prisoners.aspx.

Holyland trust (n.d.) "About Us." *Holyland Trust Homepage.* https://holylandtrust.org/about-us/home (Accessed April 18, 2018).
Horgan, J., & Braddock, K. (2010). "Rehabilitating the terrorists?: Challenges in Assessing the Effectiveness of Deradicalisation Programs." *Terrorism and Political Violence, 22*(2), 267–291.
Horgan, J. G. (2009). *Walking Away from Terrorism: Accounts of Disengagement from Radical and Extremist Movements.* London: Routledge.
IDF (2016). "Military Prosecution Instruction, Judea and Samaria." *IDF Military Instruction.* www.idf.il/media/42943/הנחיה-מס-602.pdf.
IPS (2018). *Designation of Security Prisoners, Israeli Prisons Services.* Tel Aviv: IPS. www.gov.il/BlobFolder/policy/040500/he/04.05.00%20תהליך%20הגדרת%20אסיר.pdf.
Larzillière, P. (2012). "Political commitment under an authoritarian regime: Professional associations and the Islamist movement as alternative arenas in Jordan." *International Journal of Conflict and Violence, 6* (1), 11–25.
Lem, A. (2016). "Bennet is promoting a law to outlaw breaking the silence." *Arutz 20.* www.20il.co.il/חוק-חדש-יאסור-על-גופים-שפועלים-נגד-צה%D7%B4ל/
Loyle, C., Lindekilde, I. E. L., Nets-Zehngut, R., Diehl, I. C., & Steinmann, J. P. (2012). "Focus: radicalization and deradicalization." *IJCV, 6*(1), 2.
Middle East Nonviolence and Democracy (n.d.) "Homepage." *Middle East Nonviolence and Democracy.* www.mendonline.org (Accessed April 18, 2018).
Noy, Orly (2017). "If this Hunger Strike Succeeds, It Could Mean Revolution." *972Mag.com.* https://972mag.com/if-this-hunger-strike-succeeds-it-could-mean-revolution/127273/.
Olesen, T. (2011). "Transnational Injustice Symbols and Communities: The Case of al-Qaeda and the Guantanamo Bay Detention Camp." *Current Sociology, 59*(6), 717–734.
Public Committee Against Torture in Israel (2016). *2016 Report.* Tel Aviv: Public Committee Against Torture in Israel. http://stoptorture.org.il/wp-content/uploads/2016/06/INT_CAT_NGO_ISR_23475_E-Last.pdf.
Ronen, Y. (2019b). "Security Prisoners in Israeli Prisons." *Report by the Knesset Research and Information Center.* www.knesset.gov.il/mmm/data/pdf/m03332.pdf (Accessed May 10, 2017).
US Department of State (2016). "Israel and the Occupied Territories." *Country Reports on Human Rights Practices for 2016 United States Department of State Bureau of Democracy, Human Rights and Labor.*
Wasatia (n.d.) "Our Goals." *Wasatia Homepage.* www.wasatia.info/goals.html (Accessed April 18, 2018).
Zanotti, J. (2016). *U.S. Foreign Aid to the Palestinians.* Washington: Congressional Research Service. https://fas.org/sgp/crs/mideast/RS22967.pdf
רום ארגוני השלום Peace NGO's Forum (n.d.) "Homepage." *פורום ארגוני השלום Peace NGO's Forum.*

22

DISENGAGEMENT AND PREVENTING/COUNTERING VIOLENT EXTREMISM IN THE HORN OF AFRICA

An analysis of contemporary approaches and discussion of the role disengagement can play in preventing/countering violent extremism

Martine Zeuthen

The Horn of Africa (predominantly Mogadishu and South Central Somalia) has suffered from a series of brutal attacks since the establishment of Al-Shabaab in 2006. The Al-Qaeda-aligned group view having a regional aspect to their fight as a necessary part of their strategy (Maruf & Joseph, 2018). This was seen most recently by the 2019 attack on the Dusit Hotel in Nairobi. The regional nature of their violence is used by them to legitimise their claim to be an "international" terrorist organisation and helps attract financing and new recruits. Consequently, over the past years, the wider region and in particular Somalia and Kenya have been subjected to numerous initiatives to prevent violent extremism as well as to disengage fighters who have been members of Al-Shabaab.

Looking at primary, secondary and tertiary prevention the chapter shall describe and discuss the initiatives currently focusing on preventing/countering violent extremism (P/CVE) and disengagement. It shall become apparent that there is a lack of understanding of the multifaceted processes of both joining and leaving violent extremist organisations and that there is a lack of cross-programme integration and knowledge sharing between disengagement and P/CVE work. It will be argued that a more integrated knowledge-sharing approach could be of significant benefit to the greater field of terrorism prevention. P/CVE is understood to be an emerging field of practice that includes a range of non-coercive and preventative measures (Khalil & Zeuthen, 2016). Formal disengagement from a terrorist or violent organisation can be seen to form part of P/CVE but due to its focus on individuals who were previously directly or indirectly involved in the production of violence, for the purpose of this analysis it is considered as a distinct area of intervention. Programmatic terminology such as initiatives, interventions and programmes shall be used interchangeably when describing P/CVE and disengagement. Furthermore, there is also a lack of conceptual clarity regarding the differences between disengagement and deradicalisation. This chapter uses the term disengagement deliberately as it is measurable and has an emphasis on behaviour rather than belief. To explain the difference between disengagement and deradicalisation Horgan (2008) stated that:

> While "deradicalization" has become the latest buzzword in counterterrorism, it is critical that we distinguish it from disengagement and stress that not only are they different, but that just because one leaves terrorism behind, it rarely implies (or event necessitates) that one becomes "deradicalized".

Horgan has extensively studied how, when and why people leave terrorist organisations. He describes how it is a process and how it can be individual or collective, that there is both a psychological and a physical dimension to it and finally that it can be both voluntary and involuntary. Highlighting that this is not a simple straightforward process, he explains that

> of course the disengaged terrorist may not necessarily be repentant or "de-radicalized" at all. Often there can be physical disengagement from terrorist activity, but no concomitant change or reduction in ideological support or indeed, the social and psychological control that the particular ideology exerts on the individual.
>
> *(Horgan, 2008, p. 5)*

Horgan goes on to explain in his research that deradicalisation is understood as: "a softening of views, an acceptance that the individual's pursuit of his objectives using terrorism were illegitimate, immoral and justifiable" (Horgan, 2008). When practitioners and policy makers describe programmes in the region, references are often arbitrarily made to deradicalisation and/or disengagement without clearly clarifying what is meant specifically. When this lack of clarity is transferred to programming it causes a lack of clarity of the objective and intended impact of a programme, namely if the focus is on change of behaviour, change of beliefs or both. Leaving the academic discussions behind and looking at the programmes focusing on former fighters in the region, it is evident that there is often an element of both disengagement and deradicalisation approaches built into the programmes. Most programmes have gone through limited evaluation and assessment, therefore the specific analysis of what the programmes are actually achieving as opposed to what they are seeking to achieve are mostly not available.

Methodology and limitations

The chapter focuses on Kenya and Somalia as they face the greatest threats and have advanced the furthest in their response. The analysis of P/CVE and disengagement also draws on publicly available information, policy documents, regional academic literature, reports and information shared during regional terrorism prevention conferences. The few studies referenced in this chapter of direct interviews with disengaged or former fighters mostly focus on the background of the individuals, their journey into the groups, their experiences while being in the groups, the process of leaving the group as well as their route to re-integration. Some studies include interviews with families and some with a control group for comparison. It is important to note some possible concerns around the quality of the data; however, filling gaps in knowledge, these studies have contributed and will significantly contribute to bringing the thinking forward regarding the understanding of violent extremism in the Horn of Africa.

Terrorism-related research, disengagement and P/CVE programmes only share information to a very limited extent, partly for security concerns and partly to protect organisational interests in a highly competitive and possibly saturated field. Therefore, it is possible that other initiatives exist that only those involved in are aware of and are therefore not reviewed here. In some parts of the chapter specific names of programmes or details have been deliberately omitted out of consideration for the sensitivity of this work for implementers and managers in particular.

One major challenge of a review of this kind is the limited articulation of the logic of the programmes and therefore their focus. For example, in Kenya a number of traditional developments, humanitarian and peacebuilding actors have started doing work under the P/CVE banner. However, the objectives of such programmes are only tangentially relevant to certain aspects of terrorism prevention; for example, reducing unemployment for youth, inter-faith dialogue between youth of different faiths or female empowerment projects. All are designed on the assumption that the respective area of work will contribute to enhancing resilience to violent extremism or preventing recruitment, where resilience is often not clearly defined. Many programmes describe that they work with "vulnerable" youth without specifying the nature of the vulnerability. On this particular debate Corner, Bouhana and Gill (2018) discuss the concern over the lack of clarity of the terms:

> Prevent guidance not only mentions vulnerability in terms of people who are "vulnerable" due to personal and/or social circumstances but also a "vulnerability to radicalisation". This distinction is important. "People vulnerable to radicalisation" may include "vulnerable people", but it remains to be demonstrated that "vulnerable people" are of necessity "vulnerable to radicalisation".

If the programme is not specific on being focused on individuals "vulnerable to radicalisation" or "vulnerable to recruitment" it remains uncertain how the intervention is intended to prevent or counter violent extremism specifically. Only by looking at a programme in detail is it clear whether it is a programme that: (1) seeks to contribute to terrorism prevention by addressing structural motivators tangentially linked to violent extremism; (2) has a specific P/CVE focus on reducing recruitment and sympathy for violence before individuals engage in violence; or (3) seeks to directly disengage individuals already actively involved with the organisation. Moreover, programmes differ in their approaches in terms of their intention to address violent behaviours separately from attitudes that legitimise and support the use of violence (Khalil, 2014).

P/CVE initiatives in the region are generally designed based on the following identified key factors: (1) how the risk is defined (in particular if the initiative is close to the front line or further afield); (2) what the objective is; and (3) who is the implementing actor. However, one key factor which is often overlooked in P/CVE discussions is the motivations and drivers for an individual to join a violent extremist organisation and in particular the role of proximity to armed conflict in recruitment. While motivations and drivers to join violent extremist groups are complex and diverse, it should be noted that there are a higher number of recruits in areas of close proximity to the front lines of Al-Shabaab territory. Al-Shabaab is utilising clan conflicts and clan grievances in their recruitment approach in close proximity to their territories. Proximity to conflict can also increase the likelihood of forced recruitment. As such the proximity of the specific effort to the ongoing armed conflict is an additional crucial factor to consider when designing prevention as well as disengagement initiatives.

Adapting P/CVE policies and approaches

Individuals actively engaged in violent extremist organisations have taken and continue to take many lives across East Africa and cause significant human, economic, political and infrastructural harm in the region. The focus of this chapter is predominantly on Al-Shabaab, although affiliated groups and other violent extremist organisations continue to evolve as well as their recruitment strategies, financing needs, weapon and fighter-based needs and the communities' response to violent extremist organisations. The response offered by governments and organisations therefore must continue to adapt to the changing approaches and strategies in order to ensure continued effectiveness. As an example, the increased involuntary recruitment from parts of Kenya as well as a larger focus of recruitment of women is such a change in approach that has been observed in recent years, which implementing actors and governments must adapt to with high flexibility (Badurdeen, 2018; Zeuthen & Sahgal, 2018). Implementing organisations may not have information in real time as government actors do and therefore, to ensure interventions being as effective as possible it is important that governments share information that will help enhance the effectiveness of the interventions.

There are different P/CVE and disengagement approaches in Kenya and Somalia. In Kenya there are many terrorism prevention efforts done at the community level, with the government as well as disengagement work done in prisons and with former fighters. In South Central Somalia the focus is primarily on disengagement alongside an emerging field of terrorism prevention which is inextricably linked to broader stabilisation efforts. In that sense the labelling of interventions as P/CVE efforts becomes significantly more challenging the closer they are to the armed conflict, as most development efforts in one sense or the other in South Central Somalia are seeking to have a positive impact in relation to the ongoing conflict being youth employment, gender empowerment, political dialogue and so on. That said, if the aim is not articulated specifically in relation to P/CVE, such as prevention of recruitment or support to communities receiving returning fighters, they cannot be defined as P/CVE programmes. Thereby, there are a range of ongoing activities within "stabilisation" which may also be playing a critical role in P/CVE but which are not incorporated into the broader P/CVE context and therefore are not readily available to learn from and analyse.

Governments in the region – led by Somalia and Kenya, as well as some local counties in Kenya – have developed publicly available national and county-based strategies. Through consultations with multiple government and non-government actors they have defined the strategic focus of efforts of P/CVE. The Kenyan National Strategy to Counter Violent Extremism (NSCVE) is based on pillars outlining the key areas of focus in terrorism prevention work, such as media, education, religious narratives and so on, involving a diverse set of actors and emphasising that terrorism prevention can only be done by involving multiple actors such as media houses, journalists, teachers, religious leaders, civil society leaders, political leaders and government officials in a coordinated effort. Based on the experiences of rolling out the strategy over the past years, the National Counter Terrorism Centre (NCTC) is currently undertaking a review of the strategy which is leading to an updated version due to be published during 2019.

At county level, several counties have followed up and developed county level strategies with collaboration between local government structures, security officials representing the County Commissioner, representatives from the national government as well as non-state actors from civil society. The county action plans are based on analysis of the specific context in the county and the plans reflect the national framework for specific efforts in that particular county. The strategy for Somalia was developed earlier and must be seen as part of an overall strategic framework where the National Rehabilitation Programme Strategy is an equally important document in their approach to prevent terrorism and disengage former fighters (a list of publicly available plans can be found in the reference list).

Categorising prevention approaches

To better understand P/CVE and disengagement programmes this chapter builds on a framework presented in a study by a group of researchers from Georgetown University Centre for Security Studies by the National Security Critical Issues Task Force in 2016. The framework suggests categorising prevention according to primary, secondary and tertiary approaches (Chalgren et al., 2016, p. 2). According to this study primary prevention is a broad approach directed towards society as a whole. Activities include education, health, social and cultural programmes. Secondary prevention focuses on individuals and groups identified as "at risk" for violent extremism. Activities include group-based interventions and counter-messaging. Finally, tertiary prevention is for radicalised individuals and groups who are actively planning attacks or recruiting for a violent extremist cause. Activities here include disengagement, deradicalisation, isolation and re-direction (Chalgren et al., 2016).

Primary prevention approaches

Primary prevention approaches focus on addressing drivers described as "structural motivators" (Khalil & Zeuthen, 2016) and comprise the majority of interventions in East Africa in terms of volume and financial support from donors. These are programmes focusing on the general population, such as job creation, vocational training, youth empowerment, education, governance and so on. They are large in monetary terms compared to smaller bespoke P/CVE and disengagement projects with budgets often in the region of 3–10 million Euro. They commonly have a large reach in terms of beneficiaries and are typically implemented by traditional development actors, national and international non-governmental organisations (NGOs) and civil society organisations. They primarily focus on violent extremism before violence happens and mostly work at the community level through civil society organisations.

The beneficiaries of such programmes are identified based on a geographical analysis of marginalised areas, assuming a causal link between perceived (or real) marginalisation and susceptibility of recruitment to Al-Shabaab. These programmes do not clearly state what their specific objectives are in relation to violent extremism as it is assumed providing opportunities for youth in so-called marginalised areas will reduce the appeal of recruitment, assuming violent extremist groups offer an alternative to the marginalisation in terms of job opportunities and financial compensation. The lack of specific clarity is often intentional because the subject is generally viewed as highly sensitive or carrying too high a risk of stigmatising the communities they work in (Khalil & Zeuthen, 2014).

In Somalia, operational considerations around access and where it is physically possible to work are also typically key criteria considered in the selection of the communities. Similar considerations around access and safety are made in the North-East, the North Coast (Lamu and Tana River) as well as other harder-to-access areas in Kenya. It is important to note that these considerations are rarely made explicit in programme documents or external articulation of the programmes. As such considerations of operational security will weigh in above assessments of strategic concerns around areas of specific vulnerability to recruitment and radicalisation. Members of targeted and so-called marginalised communities are often included in the design of programmatic intervention, based on the assumption that they have useful insights into how to tackle the challenges their communities face and that they understand the problem. For example, studies of violent extremism often become studies of local communities' perceptions of violent extremism, which of course is valid to understand perceptions but there is no guarantee that a community member has specific knowledge of violent extremism, just because he or she comes from a community where there have been cases of recruitment (Young et al., BRICS 2018). As such, this community consultation method is borrowing lessons from community-driven development and community-led peacebuilding (Bennett & D'Onofrio, 2015; Holmer, 2013), but is not always explicit about the limitations and problems of such approaches. Communities are not interest-free and individuals active in their community seeking to improve their conditions will have a position, based on their political views and interests. This must be taken into account when basing assessments and analysis uncritically on community perspectives to inform programmes.

Secondary prevention approaches

Secondary prevention approaches have the individual in focus and seek to address primarily individual incentives going beyond individual financial incentives and other structural drivers. That said, most programmes within secondary prevention will need to take structural motivators into account, as they are dominant in many of the communities in Kenya and Somalia where recruitment and radicalisation are taking place. Also, the enabling factors and enhancing resilience against the appeal of enablers and recruiters is important in secondary prevention initiatives focusing on reducing the risk of recruitment and radicalisation.

Only a few examples can be found in Kenya that attempt to address the ideological and individual incentives a person may face and then, subsequently, try to debunk these narratives. Such interventions require deep, technical knowledge and are labor-intensive to implement, which could possibly be said for all of the most effective measures to curb violent activity. Moreover, these types of secondary prevention initiatives are more vulnerable to risks such as stigmatisation of the person who seeks to debunk the narrative (often being religious leaders), risk of being perceived as pro-government campaigns and when effective a potential negative response by the violent extremist groups. The best examples of secondary prevention are strategic communication initiatives as well as mentorship programmes such as STRIVE II,[1] which focus on individual support and advice. Both Kenya and Somalia have seen various counter-narrative campaigns in recent years which sought to counter the extremist narrative through communication (Avis, 2016; Media Council of Kenya, 2014; Menkhaus, 2014; Williams, 2018).

Mentorship programmes often seek to provide guidance to young people identified through carefully considered risk analysis of who may be at risk of recruitment or radicalisation. Such programmes include, to a varying extent, approaches to establish alternative peer networks for at-risk individuals, as well as softer skills in trying to challenge violent extremist narratives that include intolerance that legitimises violence towards people considered to be of different or of a "wrong" faith. Understanding the legitimisation of violence within some interpretations of Salafi Jihadism is an important aspect of such campaigns (Maher, 2016). While this type of programme can face finding the "needle in a haystack" problem, they do seek to individually identify and closely work with those who may be at risk of recruitment, achieving a narrower but deeper intervention. Secondary prevention interventions are tailored to individuals at risk of recruitment and radicalisation and, as such, criteria for vulnerability measures must be developed. This has led to significant debates in the literature recently and interventions seeking to identify who is at risk of radicalisation and recruitment must carefully consider and seek to mitigate the risk associated with "at-risk" categorisation (Corner, Bouhana & Gill, 2018; Khalil & Zeuthen, 2016; Sarma, 2017).

Tertiary prevention approaches

Tertiary prevention approaches, of key interest in this chapter, are those that take place through formal disengagement programmes and in prisons after an individual has been directly involved with violent extremist organisations and has left or wishes to leave. Recent studies of disengagement in Somalia point out that the disengagement process can take many forms and individuals who are seeking to disengage can follow different routes. One is disengagement back into communities without a formal process. This process often takes place in areas where there is limited access and knowledge of available disengagement opportunities and also for individuals who perceive limited risk associated with informal re-integration into the communities. This informal disengagement does not directly involve any organised intervention or external deradicalisation or rehabilitation efforts but is likely to be the highest proportion in terms of numbers of defectors. While the studies have a very small sample of women, this informal route appeared to be the most common for female defectors.

Other defectors follow the formal process of disengaging by going through government officials and following a screening asserting the level of risk the individual poses. Individuals who are found to pose a high risk will not be found suitable for rehabilitation and will be incarcerated. There are a number of disengagement centres run by the Federal Government of Somalia in close collaboration with different international actors. The overall process is managed according to the National Rehabilitation Programme as the official governing framework. The process post-screening going to a disengagement centre is, according to the established policy, voluntary and individuals can choose the specific centre which suits them best. According to recent studies, considerations around clan, socio-economic opportunities and risk are a part of the decision-making process when former fighters choose a centre. The activities in the centres vary but common to all of them is that they focus on rehabilitation activities including livelihoods skills, educational opportunities and physical wellbeing. There is a varying degree of attention paid to the ideological aspects or "deradicalisation". Re-integration to the community is also of primary concern in most centres, though they have different approaches to this process (Felbab-Brown, 2018; Khalil & Zeuthen, 2016).

Upon receiving a defector, the centre staff seek to assess the individual in terms of socio-economic background, clan and prior perception of the government. This is done through entry interviews, which also include capturing data on their physical journey to the centre as well as their experiences prior to arriving at the centre. This provides an indication of their intention and interests in being at the centre, which will inform how the individual is likely to perform, what level and type of support are required and how risk needs to be managed. Finally, the screening interview also supports the development of plans for when the defector has completed the programme at the centre.

Discussions around very high-level defectors such as Robow who surrendered to the Somali National Army in 2017 have been a subject of significant debate and controversy. When senior commanders are accepted back into society and political life with no punishment, it has been accused of sending a message of impunity (Felbab-Brown, 2018). A year after his surrender, Robow announced his candidature for presidency in Somalia's South West State. The Federal Government was against his candidature and subsequently during the campaign he was arrested.[2] The management of the process has been discussed by analysts as a factor that could potentially discourage others from defecting. Evidently the management of such high-level defectors is highly political and a clear policy is required to enable clear, transparent political action and to send a consistent message to other potential high-level defectors.

In Kenya disengagement is also a key priority for managing risk regarding citizens returning from having fought with Al-Shabaab. The Kenyan disengagement programme was rolled out after the government initiated an amnesty in 2015, which included a process of accepting returning fighters who voluntarily came forward. The government has announced that a formal policy and framework are under development and will be shared in the near future. The end goal of disengagement is a risk mitigation process leading to re-insertion and rehabilitation back into the communities, therefore information to the communities about the risk associated with re-integration of these individuals is crucial. The UN researcher Felbab-Brown who recently did a study on re-integration in Somalia outlines that:

> Perceptions towards individuals associated with Al-Shabaab vary enormously, ranging from acceptance to extreme ostracization. Views are often based on whether a community, clan or family's experience with Al-Shabaab has predominantly been marked by brutality or the delivery of justice and protection services … Many local communities indicate they are afraid of ex-Al-Shabaab members returning to their areas.
>
> *(Felbab-Brown, 2018, p. 8)*

In Kenya the front line is further away and families will rarely, except for in the north of Lamu and parts of Mandera, Wajir and Garissa, have been directly affected by the presence of Al-Shabaab but perceptions and fear associated with the group as well as the government's response cannot be neglected. Further clarity around amnesty rules and processes will contribute to communities feeling safer in supporting rehabilitation and re-integration of returning fighters who have completed disengagement programmes.

Just as with disengagement centres in Somalia, running programmes for returnees in Kenya requires strong collaboration and trust between government agencies and implementing actors such as NGOs, religious groups and other community-based service providers like social workers. Implementing actors have a role to play that most likely could not be undertaken by the government. Likewise, non-state implementing actors need support from the government in order to undertake screening of participants when designing their interventions, as well as general support in handling individuals who are not suitable for re-integration. As such, working together within an agreed framework is essential to maximise the possibility of success.

This process is iterative and both security actors and community-based actors must continue to share information should initial assessments prove to have been wrong or indeed if an individual changes as a part of the process and the risk level changes.

Rehabilitation of offenders of terrorism in prisons is another key aspect of disengagement undertaken in the region. Working with individuals in this way is a unique opportunity but also poses a unique challenge as they may wish to further radicalise and recruit other inmates. This brings a focus to the physical arrangements in the prison, something which has been documented as a challenge in other recruitment cases globally (Jones, 2014; Silke & Veldhuis, 2017). Purposeful isolation of such offenders is one option but there may be others which work to prevent further prison-based radicalisation (Jones & Morales, 2012). In Somalia, as with the rest of the world, some of the lessons learned appear to be centred on defining a rehabilitation programme that suits the individual's needs, as well as increasing attempts to reduce the risk of negatively influencing others while in prison. Similar initiatives are ongoing in the region, and in Kenya in particular, the prison service in collaboration with the NCTC are continuing to improve the provision of opportunities for offenders such as better visiting conditions, better education options, religious guidance and recreational activities, as well as continuing to do research and study what works (Sahgal & Zeuthen, 2019).

Sharing of experiences and lessons is vital for a continued improvement of longer-term disengagement and re-integration processes for the benefit of regional stability as a whole. While contexts differ, authorities and actors involved in rehabilitation can learn from each other's experience and inspire ideas for innovative solutions feasible in the given context. Learning from each other across the region would significantly benefit all actors – security, political as well as community-based actors – engaging on this topic. The steadily growing body of research and evidence on these topics and initiatives is essential to enhancing learning around how to do screening, how to design interventions, how to manage risk, how to engage with religious actors and so on, which will help to contribute to programmatic improvements.

By establishing a framework for P/CVE, noting the importance of understanding drivers for individuals to join violent extremist groups, critical insight from disengagement activities would similarly serve to enhance the development of P/CVE activities. This has been seen recently in the information garnered from recent rare accounts of current disengagement programmes. These publications are highly commendable, allowing for implementers and governments to draw lessons from other initiatives when designing new initiatives or adjusting existing efforts.

One essential aspect of the conversation around disengagement is the role of ideology and defining the relationship between deradicalisation and disengagement approaches. For interventions in the region these terms remain widely interpreted in the different interventions and suffer from unclear articulation of the approaches regarding ideology specifically. In particular, disengagement efforts would benefit from clearly articulated and measurable indicators highlighting the different areas that the disengagement process is intending to have an impact on for the individual as well as when the risks are considered to have reduced to an extent that would justify re-integration into the community. Some of the lessons evolving from Somalia-based disengagement centres are focusing on why people enlisted in Al-Shabaab, why and how they disengage and also how they experience re-integration post-exit from the centres (Khalil et al., 2019; Taarnby, 2018) could potentially be relevant for interventions in Kenya, and potentially Tanzania, and vice versa.

Conclusion

When seeking to provide an overview of P/CVE and disengagement programmes addressing violent extremism, both before violence occurs as well as after, this chapter highlighted some of the limitations and concerns regarding lack of conceptual clarity in many interventions. The chapter has argued that there is a need for greater collaboration and utilisation of state and non-state actors' different skills and approaches in order to have a holistic and integrated approach. It is evident that religious leaders, civil society and social workers can play unique roles that security actors cannot and vice versa. There is a need when fighting and preventing terrorism in the Horn of Africa for all expertise to come together and acknowledge each other's role in addressing this complex phenomenon.

The chapter has highlighted some specific recommendations and suggestions in relation to each type of approach (primary, secondary and tertiary). At a broader level, the main recommendation from this chapter is the need for further integration of three levels of prevention including disengagement approaches within a comprehensive integrated framework. Primary, secondary and tertiary prevention need more robust evaluations and assessments to better understand the intended impact versus the actual outcome. For disengagement programmes specifically this will further clarify when and if "deradicalisation" happens and if it is a feasible objective of disengagement initiatives. A lot can be learned from the past years of work on terrorism prevention and disengagement in Kenya and Somalia at the community level, in disengagement centres as well as in prisons, but very limited information is publicly available or otherwise shared. More importantly, a lack of evidence sharing reduces the opportunities to share experiences and learnings between programmes and initiatives in order for them to become more effective in defining and achieving core objectives in the prevention of violent extremism.

The analysis of disengagement programmes in the region showed that a disengagement process is unique to each individual and highly multifaceted, which highlights the need for very specific programmatic approaches and clear articulation of the objectives. This could also highlight the need for a higher degree of interventions tailored specifically to the individual involved to enhance effectiveness. Finally, re-integration after risks have been reduced through disengagement programmes requires clear communication and assurances to gain support from families and the wider community.

Notes

1 Strengthening Resilience to Violent Extremism (STRIVE) II is implemented by the Royal United Services Institute (RUSI) funded by the EU and the author of this paper is working as the team leader.

2 Mohamed Olad Hassan (2018). "Former Al-Shabab No. 2 Arrested in Somalia". *VoA*, 13 December www.voanews.com/a/former-al-shabab-no-2-arrested-in-somalia-/4698968.html.

References

W. Avis (2016). "The Role of Online/Social Media in Countering Violent Extremism in East Africa". *Helpdesk Report*, June 2016.

F. Badurdeen (2018). "Women and Recruitment in the Al-Shabaab Network: Stories of Women Being Recruited by Women Recruiters in the Coastal Region of Kenya". *The Africa Review*, 45(1), pp. 19–48.

S. Bennett & A. D'Onofrio (2015). "Community-Driven Development in Conflict-Affected Contexts: Revisiting Concepts, Functions and Fundamentals". *Stability: International Journal of Security and Development*, 4(1), p. Art.19.

Jonathan Challgren, Ted Kenyon, Lauren Kervick, Sally Scudder, Micah Walters & Kate Whitehead (2016). "Countering Violent Extremism – Applying the Public Health Model". *A Special Report Prepared by the NATIONAL SECURITY CRITICAL ISSUES TASK FORCE (NSCITF)*, October 2016.
E. N. Corner & P. G. Bouhana (2018). "The Multifinality of Vulnerability Indicators in Lone Actor Terrorism". *Psychology, Crime & Law*, 25(2). DOI: 10.1080/1068316X.2018.1503664
V. Felbab-Brown (2018). "The Limits of Punishment: Transitional Justice and Violent Extremism: Somalia Case Study". *Institute for Integrated Transitions and United Nations University Case Study*, May.
G. Holmer (2013). "Countering Violent Extremism: A Peace Building Perspective". *USIP Special Report*, September 2013.
J. Horgan (2008). "Deradicalization or Disengagement? – A Process in Need of Clarity and a Counterterrorism Initiative in Need of Evaluation". *Perspectives on Terrorism*, 2(4), pp. 3–8.
C. Jones (2014). "Are Prisons Really Schools for Terrorism? Challenging the Rhetoric on Prison Radicalization". *Punishment and Society*, 16(1), pp. 74–103.
C. Jones & R. Morales (2012). "Integration versus Segregation: A Preliminary Examination of Philippine Correctional Facilities for Deradicalisation". *Studies in Conflict & Terrorism*, 35(3), pp. 211–228.
J. Khalil (2014). "Radical Beliefs and Violent Actions Are Not Synonymous: How to Place the Key Disjuncture Between Attitudes and Behaviors at the Heart of Our Research into Political Violence". *Studies in Conflict & Terrorism*, 37(2), pp. 198–211.
J. Khalil, R. Brown, C. Chant, P. Olowo & N. Wood (2019). "Deradicalisation and Disengagement in Somalia – Evidence from a Rehabilitation Programme for Former Members of Al-Shabaab". RUSI, Whitehall Report 4–18.
J. Khalil & M. Zeuthen (2014). "A Case Study of Counter Violent Extremism (CVE) Programming: Lessons from OTI's Kenya Transition Initiative". *Stability: International Journal of Security & Development*, 3(1): 31, pp. 1–12. DOI: http://dx.doi.org/10.5334/sta.ee
J. Khalil & M. Zeuthen (2016). *Countering Violent Extremism and Risk Reduction. A Guide to Programme Design and Evaluation*. London: Royal United Services Institute.
S. Maher (2016). *Salafi-Jihadism – The History of an Idea*. London: Hurst and Company.
H. Maruf & D. Joseph (2018). *Inside Al-Shabaab – The Secret History of Al-Qaeda's Most Powerful Ally*. Indiana: Indiana University Press.
Media Council of Kenya (2014). *Deconstructing Terror: Assessing Media's Role in Religious Intolerance and Radicalisation*. Nairobi: Media Council of Kenya.
K. Menkhaus (2014). "Al-Shabaab and Social Media: A Double-Edged Sword". *The Brown Journal of World Affairs*, XX(11), pp. 309–327.
G. Sahgal, & M. Zeuthen. (2019). "The Nexus between Crime and Violent Extremism in Kenya: A Case Study of Two Maximum Security Prisons". CreateSpace.
K. Sarma (2017). *Risk Assessment and the Prevention of Radicalization from Nonviolence into Terrorism*. Galway: National University of Ireland.
A. Silke & T. Veldhuis (2017). "Countering Violent Extremism in Prisons: A Review of Key Recent Literature and Research Gaps". *Perspectives on Terrorism*, 11(5), pp. 2–11.
M. Taarnby (2018). "Serendi – Inside Somali's Terrorist Rehabilation Project". London: RUSI.
P. Williams (2018). "Strategic Communications for Peace Operations: The African Union's Information War Against al-Shabaab". *Stability: International Journal of Security and Development*, 7(1), pp. 3–17.
E. Young et al. (2018). "Preventing Violent Extremism: Understanding At-risk Communities". BRICS report by Wasafiri Consulting, December 2018.
M. Zeuthen & G. Sahgal (2018). "Gender and Violent Extremism". RUSI Occasional Paper, September 2018.

Policy documents

Draft Document on the Establishment of the IGAD Centre of Excellence for Preventing and Countering Violent Extremism (ICEPCVE). March 2017.

Kenya's National Strategy to Counter Violent Extremism (2016).

Draft and final County Action Plans:

- Isiolo County Action Plan, Isiolo Peace Link & Isiolo County Government, 2018
- Kilifi County Action Plan, H. Shauri & Kilifi County Government, 2017

- Kwale Action Plan, Huria & Kwale County Government, 2017
- Lamu County Action Plan, H. Shauri & Lamu County Government, 2017
- Mandera County Action Plan (draft), Mandera County Government & Mandera County Commissioners Office
- Mombasa County Action Plan, Haki Africa, Mombasa County Government & Mombasa County Commissioners Office, 2017
- Tana River County Action Plan (draft), KEKOSCE & Tana River County

Somalia National Strategy and Action Plan for Preventing and Countering Violent Extremism, Federal Republic of Somalia, 2016.

23
TURNING THE PAGE ON EXTREMISM
Deradicalization in the North American context

Mubin Shaikh, Hicham Tiflati, Phil Gurski, and Amarnath Amarasingam

ISIS-related attacks in North America, overwhelmingly committed by born citizens of the respective countries, have shown the urgency and necessity to directly deal with these individuals in order to temper their overall views, and move away from violent extremism. Particularly in the American context, this has become more important since the December 2015 attack of San Bernardino where a couple, husband and wife, attacked and killed 14 people and wounded 20. The June 2016 Orlando night club attack that led to the death of 50 individuals and the injury of the same number was explicitly claimed by an ISIS supporter. In October 2017, another attack took place on a Manhattan pedestrian walkway, where a man used a rented U-Haul truck to kill eight, and wound 11.

According to figures released by George Washington University's "Program on Extremism," there have already been 196 persons charged with offenses related to ISIS, with 146 having pleaded guilty (George Washington University, 2019). Prior to the emergence of ISIS there, of course, have been similar cases and arrests related to extremism in the name of Islam. In 2001, shortly after the war in Afghanistan against the Taliban and Al Qaeda, John Walker Lindh, dubbed "the American Taliban," was captured and imprisoned by the United States for his involvement with the terrorist group. Moreover, approximately 40 Americans and 20 Canadians, overwhelmingly of Somali origin, had gone to join the Al Qaeda affiliate, Al Shabab, in Somalia. This included the first American suicide bomber, Shirwa Ahmed, from Minneapolis. A number of factors were given for this: bicultural identity integration and rejecting Western identity, heightened interest in Islam, and the lure of "jihadi culture" (King & Mohamed 2011). In the American context, however, the United States remains a primary target for these extremist and terrorist groups, not just for operations but also for recruiting potential future perpetrators.

There is a prevalent assumption in the popular media, as well as among some terrorism scholars, that Canada is largely immune from terrorist attacks and has experienced the problem of radicalization at a much lower scale than Europe and the United States (Tomlinson

2014; Canadian Press 2017). There is some truth to this, comparatively speaking, but there is also a heavy dose of wishful thinking involved. In 2006, for instance, 18 young people in Canada were arrested for planning and preparing for a series of attacks, including one on Canada's Parliament Hill (Teotonia 2010; Speckhard & Mubin 2014). Canadians have also been among foreign fighter mobilizations in the past, whether it be Bosnia, Chechnya, or Somalia. More recently, our own research shows that close to 100 young men and women have left Canada to join a variety of militant and terrorist groups active in Syria and Iraq (Amarasingam 2015; Gurski 2016).

Several Canadians have also been involved in plots and attacks locally and abroad that have caused a significant number of civilian casualties. In October 2014, Michael Zehaf-Bibeau fatally shot Corporal Nathan Cirillo and then entered the parliament buildings in Ottawa before being shot dead. Two days earlier, Martin Couture-Rouleau rammed his car into two Canadian Forces members, killing one. Salman Ashrafi, a young man from Calgary, blew himself up in Iraq in November 2013, killing and injuring over 40. Tamim Ahmed Chowdhury, who lived for a time in both Windsor and Calgary, somehow found his way into the leadership of ISIS in Bangladesh and masterminded the Holey Artisan Bakery attack in July 2016, which saw 22 people hacked to death (Amarasingam 2016).

Canadian law enforcement and policy makers have wrestled with how to handle this situation for some time, but there has been renewed urgency and increased funding particularly since 2011 with the launch of the Kanishka Project, a five-year $10-million initiative designed to not only address gaps in the understanding of terrorism in Canada but also establish a better[1] knowledge-sharing relationship between academics, law enforcement, and policy makers. As the Kanishka Project came to an end, Ottawa established the Canada Centre for Community Engagement and Prevention of Violence[2] (CCCEPV), which is focused on providing funding at the local level to organizations working on the issue of radicalization and prevention. While still in its infancy, this broader federal program seeks to aid local community groups to intervene to prevent radicalization to violence, rehabilitate imprisoned terrorists and returning foreign fighters, and provide alternatives to a variety of violent ideologies. It is important to note for both the American and Canadian context; governmental agencies are not direct service providers of deradicalization interventions or disengagement from violent extremism.

Radicalization, deradicalization, and disengagement

Much attention has been given to the role of radicalization in violent extremism and terrorism. In a way, understanding mechanisms of radicalization, which is usually seen as a pre-extremism stage, is relevant to understanding the origins and processes of violent extremism and, therefore, key for preventing and countering it. With this in mind, what states and actors are trying to prevent and counter is a radicalization that is problematic. Problematic radicalization means a noticeable change in the individual's or the group's beliefs and behaviors in ways that justify illegal violence against the state's institutions or members of an out-group. However, it is difficult to tackle radicalization outside the realms of violence and illegality. In politically vibrant societies, opponents and their views can be defined as radicals or even extremists.

As terrorism is a political activity (Cottee & Hayward 2011, 966), so is radicalization. It is a contested term that means different things to different people. Rather than providing a general theoretical frame of the phenomenon, it is essential to separately theorize radicalization of thought (which usually falls within the boundaries of the law and legality), and behavioral radicalization, which promotes violence, be it political or religious (Tiflati 2016).

Using a slightly different terminology, McCauley and Moskalenko (2008, 213) state that "Radicalization of opinion is a phenomenon of mass psychology, whereas radicalization of action is a phenomenon of individual and small-group psychology." However, while the focus is usually on the violent part of radicalization, its social aspect should not be ignored. For instance, involvement in many radical groups can be more of a matter of "joining" than being recruited and lured by an agent (Cronin 2006, 34).

There is no single profile or cause behind radicalization. Looking at the "profiles" of radicals, Bjørgo (2011, 279) stated that radicalization is not, and cannot be, linked to one specific status, be it ideological or non-ideological, political or apolitical, socially adapted or marginalized. In fact, radicals come from all sorts of backgrounds. While a few may fantasize about adventures, heroism, and militancy (Bjørgo 2011, 283), others might be drawn by feelings of victimization and a sense of injustice. Profiling seems to be very limited in terms of identifying "potential terrorists." Individuals who really constitute a threat may go unnoticed because "they do not fit the stereotype" (Bjørgo 2011, 278). Cottee and Hayward (2011), for instance, identify three main motives for engaging in violent radicalization, which are excitement, meaning, and glory. Furthermore, McCauley and Moskalenko (2008) distinguish between individual, group, and mass radicalization. The first is usually linked to victimization, political grievances, and affiliation with radical groups; the second refers to radicalization within like-minded groups competing for support or for political power; and the third happens in relation to a "hated" out-group. While responding to non-state terrorism from threatening non-state groups, states can also become radicalized when facing interstate conflicts or homegrown terrorism.

Socialization into radicalization is a complex process during which individuals become radicalized for multiple reasons (i.e., political, religious, social, cultural, personal, ideological). Many feel that the real challenge at this point is how to prevent and/or reverse radicalization. Just as radicalization is a complex non-linear process, so is the process of deradicalization and disengagement from violent extremism. That said, there are many narratives and initiatives of deradicalization. According to Daniel Koehler (2017), there are three different counter-terrorism methods: prevention, repression, and intervention, and these methods operate in three dimensions "macrosocial/national; mesosocial/regional/local; and microsocial/individual." As we cannot address them all in one go, we will examine a few that we think are more relevant to this volume.

According to Koehler (2017, 20), debates surrounding deradicalization have resulted in the birth of two main schools of thought; whereas the first sees success in abstaining from violence, the second insists that rejecting the ideology of violence is also crucial to "long-term disengagement." Additionally, ideology, be it religious or political, cannot – and does not – flourish in a vacuum; it always has a context and a frame (i.e., political, religious, social, cultural, etc.). Violent radicals, religiously or politically inspired, engage in an "identity project of personal self-affirmation" (Cottee & Hayward 2011, 976). Therefore, disengagement from terrorism is not a sign of deradicalization (Horgan 2009). Furthermore, deradicalization programs need to be tailored to the would-be deradicalized or disengaged (Bjørgo 2011, 279). When tackling questions of deradicalization, it is important to distinguish radical groups from radical individuals. Unlike radical groups which cannot flourish without having a popular base, most individuals can easily get radicalized without such support or sympathy (Cronin 2006, 27).

Moreover, deradicalization can be seen as a moral disengagement or an ideological disenchantment from violent extremism-justifying ideologies. According to Kruglanski et al. (2014, 77), these ideologies have three main components: grievance because of an injustice, a presumed perpetrator for such grievance, and a (moral) obligation to fight and remove this injustice. Whereas disengagement might infer giving up the radical behavior, deradicalization infers fully disregarding the radical ideology. Likewise, understanding the target audience and the target ideology is crucial to producing the right counter-narrative. For example, if the aim is to counter a religious radicalization, a theological discourse should be employed. While some experts insist that "evilizing" terrorists is the right strategy to deal with and prevent their threat, others (such as Dawson 2017, 4) suggest that humanizing them might help us understand how normal and balanced individuals make the transition from law-abiding citizens to violent extremists.

Even though everyday discourse links terrorism to non-state actors that represent a challenge or a threat to the state (McCauley & Moskalenko 2008, 416), states are also perpetrators of terrorism. There is also a focus on Islamist extremism "at the expense of right-wing, nationalist, neoliberal, and/or state violence" (Finn & Momani 2017). Although the emphasis of CVE is usually on Muslim perpetrators, incidents committed by lone-wolf terrorists such as Alexandre Bissonnette (the Quebec mosque attacker who killed six Muslims and injured many others) show that the danger of national security arises from multiple forms of violent ideologies. In what follows, we briefly examine the definitional and theoretical issues around the question of deradicalization before examining some not-for-profit prevention and deradicalization initiatives in Canada and the United States.

Deradicalization programs in Canada and the United States

Due to the small number of individuals in the North American Muslim community engaging in terrorism, there are very few actual deradicalization programs. In fact, the discourse related to the topic is significantly underdeveloped in the North American context, especially the United States. "Countering violent extremism," popularly referred to as "CVE," has been introduced into the American context very recently and is "best understood as a series of fits and starts" (Hughes 2017). Beginning in 2011, it has since gone through a number of attempts at seeking to create a mechanism whereby the issues related to the identification and intervention of extremist individuals and groups can be discussed maturely. This, however, seems obfuscated by the fact that CVE in the United States has undergone significant criticism and repudiation by various Muslim communities as well as non-Muslim ones, both having shared as well as divergent views about the theoretical program.

One of the primary arguments made by Muslim organizations critical of CVE is that such community-wide change cannot occur as a top-down, government-driven approach (CAIR 2015). Furthermore, they argue that such programs which identify only one minority group (Muslims) and ignore others (far-right radicalization) are marginalizing the community and reinforcing systemic discrimination. While their respective view of CVE may be flawed in relation to understanding the theories underpinning the subject there was also the mistaken view that the CVE program of 2011 only focused on one group. Unfortunately, recent changes under the Trump administration to refocus CVE solely on the so-called Islamist threat and largely ignore the far right has further eroded the trust that Muslim organizations were developing in these initiatives (Pasha-Robonson 2017).

While the policy prescriptions around who is identified, how they are identified, and what works is still being debated, organizations critical of the government-driven CVE model have begun developing their own in-house capacity at the community level (Haus-lohner 2016). It will remain to be seen how effective and legitimate such programs are, and whether they will alienate members of their community. It will also be important to watch how these ideas develop in light of increasingly violent attacks by the far right and other white supremacist groups in Canada and the United States, as well as increasing Islamophobia serving to focus the community on the threat against them from the outside, as opposed to from within.

Based on our research in North America, it is clear that a basic distinction needs to be made between prevention programs and initiatives dedicated to targeted interventions. The former is what many Muslim organizations are already doing in terms of castigating unlawful violence in the name of Islam, promoting pro-social values, and the teaching of traditional Islamic values. As research has shown, individuals who have a solid religious identity are in fact better "inoculated" against violent ideas than those who lack it (Tiflati 2016). The latter category has much fewer examples in the North American context. While some organizations are contacted by friends and families of individuals with the hope that some kind of "intervention" will take place, these programs are scattered and do not operate according to any established set of practices. Nevertheless, there are indeed a select few organizations working in this space. Below, we briefly examine their work.

Deradicalization initiatives in Canada

One of the earliest-established organizations that continue to work in this space is the Anjuman-E-Islahul Muslimin (AIM), founded and administered by Mohammad Shahied Shaikh. Based in Toronto (full disclosure: Mr. Shaikh is also the father of the lead author) the primary demographic of Masjid El Noor is South Asians from India and Pakistan. The center also caters to African and Arab worshippers as well as converts from diverse backgrounds. It also administers an Islamic school for children, as well as public lessons on Islam. Alongside devotional services, some members of the organization participate in professional social service projects. They are professionals in their respective fields and have varying knowledge of psychosocial counseling. On the prevention side, the organization acts as other Canadian Muslim organizations with the madrasa-style Islamic school for children and provides a standard version of Islam that rejects violent extremism. Masjid El Noor has also proactively engaged with young people on issues of youth violence in general and also participates in local interfaith events and meetings with government and grassroots community organizations.

At an initial judicial hearing, the lawyer for the defendant can submit to the court that this counseling will be undertaken and a report will be issued by the organization for consideration by the presiding judge. Often, the accused is put on probation and released to the care of the organization. In cases where an individual is remanded into custody and a bail hearing is required, participation in the counseling can result in relaxed or removed probation conditions. It is worthwhile noting that most clients' cases in this regard are not extremism- or violent extremism-related but rather deal with general issues of violence including weapons charges. The organization understands that the context of gang-related violence is intimately connected as an at-risk factor in joining other violent extremist groups.

Interviews with the clients of this program were conducted anonymously in full protection of their privacy. Unstructured, open-ended questions were asked in order to understand the person's personal history, the issues being counseled for and what they thought of the program, and why they thought it would work for them to begin with. A thematic arrangement of the testimonies yields two primary pillars as to what works: the use of trusted intermediaries and consultation with subject matter experts. Trusted intermediaries include community members who are known to care for their community and constituents. They may also be subject matter experts and professionals such as lawyers and teachers who earned the community's trust. Besides their professional profiles, trusted intermediaries have qualities such as a non-judgmental approach, patience, compassion, kindness, and the desire to help. This secures buy-in from the client and, in doing so, makes receiving instruction a process in which the client is personally invested.

Since this is psychosocial counseling, the content that is used in counseling violent offenders is drawn from both religious and non-religious sources. According to the service providers, religious ideology can either be the main driver or a mere passenger, with other psychosocial factors as the driver. A knowledge of basic Islamic scripture is required, as well as issues of mental health, considered against a personal background, including socioeconomic and education status. This allows the service provider to tailor the counseling to the individual, to appeal to sacred values in correcting what is defined as deviant behavior, and to frame their reintegration in the larger context of Canadian society at large.

The second organization that loosely works in the deradicalization space in Canada is known as Paradise4Ever. Founded by Mohammed Robert Heft in 2005 and funded by donations from the public, it deals primarily with new converts (Babin 2015). It is a well-known organization in Toronto and around the country, which attempts to ease the conversion process for new Muslims. Since a number of the new Muslims with whom Heft deals come from troubled backgrounds and carry with them personal experiences that put them at risk for violent extremism, Heft has found himself having to address the issue in some way. New converts often come with stories of childhood physical and sexual abuse, criminality, and imprisonment, as well as issues related to identity conflicts and a sense of meaning and belonging.

Heft's counseling program is built on three pillars: (1) theological detox; (2) social services; and (3) community responsibility. Theological detox refers to correcting and calibrating certain theological arguments which permit outright, or otherwise encourage sympathy for, violent action in the name of Islam. The social service pillar deals with vocational and educational training for individuals. The third pillar refers to the inclusion of the individual into a larger network of peers who are supportive and reflect the sacred values held in esteem by the young person being counseled. Unlike most other Canadian Muslim organizations, Heft has a unique competency in extremism intervention due to his own firsthand experiences as well as dealing with high-profile extremism cases in Canada. Based on our research with some of the individuals Heft has worked with, it is clear that personal rapport, integrity, and authenticity are the core components of why these young people find him approachable (CBC News 2014). Heft also may make available to the client other new Muslims and individuals in order to provide the client with a larger circle of positive role models, which sometimes entails camping trips where stable social settings are introduced to the client in an environment of brotherhood and belonging.

The third organization that operates in the deradicalization space in Toronto is Imam Ramzy Ajem and Shaykh Abdul Aziz Suraqah's Risalah Foundation. Both of these religious leaders are experts trained in classical Islamic law and provide counseling services as well as chaplaincy services for the community at large. They also administer teachings on Islam which range from matters of jurisprudence to personal matters of spirituality. The Risalah caters to first- and second-generation Muslims from various ethnic backgrounds. Both Ajem and Suraqah participated in the deradicalization counseling for two convicted and incarcerated violent extremists arrested in the 2006 Toronto terror plot. The two individuals were found guilty of planning to drive explosive-laden vehicles as part of a criminal extremist conspiracy. The two had shown a willingness to reform their views after having had time to rethink what choices in their lives brought them to where they found themselves. The deradicalization counseling in this context was heavily influenced by traditional Islamic teachings which reframe the epistemological framework from which individuals take their knowledge, what is defined as authority in Islamic law, and why such acts are illegal in Islam to begin with. The two individuals seemed to have benefited from the intervention by admitting responsibility for the actions, repenting from the faith perspective and resolving to be engaged in CVE once released from prison.

The counseling style employed by Ajem and Suraqah is personal and up close. Once again, considering that the instructors are both trusted intermediaries as well as subject matter experts, and due to the personable nature of the instructors, individuals who work with them seem to respond positively to their approach. Furthermore, the counseling is unstructured and ad hoc and recognizes that a case-by-case basis approach to deradicalization is best. The instructors have some basic familiarity in the theories of radicalization as well as the concept of deradicalization and augment their approach by consulting professionals involved in countering radicalization.

Outside of Ontario, there are two other important initiatives in the deradicalization space, one in Calgary, Alberta, and the other in Montreal, Quebec. In Calgary, the program is led by Imam Navaid Aziz, formerly out of the 8th and 8th Musallah, a prayer space that became notorious after several individuals from there left Canada to travel to Syria and Iraq (Roberts 2016; White 2017). Aziz became the imam at this location after the center was already known in the media as a "radicalization hotspot" and was asked to identify and deal with the issues faced by young people at this location.

It is important to note that Aziz is also on contract with the Calgary police service as a chaplain where young people requiring theological intervention can be referred to by the police services. Calgary's police service has been one of those Canadian police agencies to receive funding to deal with extremism (Graveland 2017). It has implemented its REDIRECT program, which links at-risk youth with a police officer and a social worker who attempt to steer them away from dangerous ideologies. REDIRECT gets its referrals from the schools and the community where people come forward and say they're worried about the youth and then engage with that family to make sure they're getting the help that they need.

Imam Aziz uses an approach where he attempts to restructure the cognitive framework in which young Muslims interpret the environment around them. It draws on historical examples of the early Muslim community as well as an introduction to Islamic legal concepts which repudiate extremist thinking and violent behavior. Furthermore, he frames his program to the youth as an opportunity to build future leaders in Canada, avoiding any mention of phrases such as CVE or buzz words like deradicalization. The reason for this is to de-securitize the approach and place it in a public, social setting removed of pejorative labels. This, according to the imam, allows community members at large, parents in particular, and at-risk youth to be able to come forward and partake in such services without fear of judgment and outside the scrutiny of security services.

While the imam does engage at-risk youth on a one-on-one basis, he deals typically with small groups (of up to 15). One strategy is to engage in a participatory approach where group activities and group projects are conducted and youth are given leadership roles within the circle. Interviews conducted with three of his clients made clear that the main reason why the program was positively received by these individuals was due to the personable nature of the imam, as well as a sense of empowerment from studying Islam in a more relaxed and friendly environment without fear of being judged or labeled (Daigle 2015).

The Centre for the Prevention of Radicalization Leading to Violence (CPRLV) in Montreal, unlike many of the initiatives thus far discussed, operates with the support of the

Quebec government. It is a not-for-profit organization aimed at preventing violent radicalization and providing support to individuals affected. It also provides support to individuals who are radicalized or undergoing radicalization, family or friends of such individuals, teachers, professionals, or field workers. The CPRLV is a provincially mandated organization whose work also includes the prevention of hate crimes and incidents as well as the provision of support and counseling for victims of such acts.

Interviews by the lead author were conducted with five staff members of CPRLV, as well as five young Muslims implicated in ISIS-related activity (either directly by having thought of joining ISIS overseas or family members who had done the same). Individuals who were detained but not arrested were sent to the CPRLV for assessment and intervention. The CPRLV uses a psychosocial counseling approach which does not deal with religion at all but rather, to develop a rapport between client and counselor. It utilizes creative art and group activity to achieve this. Where clients may require specialist attention with religious issues, they will direct them to Muslim experts who can speak to the issues related to Islam.

The Canadian Practitioners Network for the Prevention of Violent Extremist (CPN-PREV), established in 2016, is a research and practitioners-centered network funded by the Canadian Public Safety Center: Community Resilience Fund (CRF). The network struggles to develop Canadian leadership and excellence in countering violent radicalization and extremism. CPN-PREV supports other initiatives and collaborates with intervention teams, through sustained knowledge mobilization practitioners, policy makers, researchers, and various communities.

CPN-PREV examines the level and nature of collaboration amongst Canadian initiatives, and strengthens collaborations to build expertise in areas of urgent and high need. It also generates evidence-based practices and expands to fit the needs of Canadian practitioners. Finally, CPN-PREV, in collaboration with RAPS (www.sherpa-recherche.com/fr/sherpa/equipes-recherche/raps/), develops, adapts, and expands diverse training modules, toolkits, and other programs and activities to multiple sectors (e.g., health, social services, education, community) that work on radicalization.

Sensing some of the limitations that government agencies could have with direct deradicalization, some have moved towards a multi-agency approach, akin to the U.K.'s "Channel programme" (Home Office 2017). Recently, this same initiative has been rebranded into Canada by the FOCUS Tables of Toronto. In an initiative led by the City of Toronto, the United Way, and the Toronto Police Service, the aim is to reduce crime and victimization and to improve community resiliency and well-being. The model attempts to bring together the "most appropriate community agencies at a weekly situation table model to provide a targeted, wrap around approach to the most vulnerable individuals, families and places that are experiencing heightened levels of risk in a specific geographic location" (FOCUS Toronto 2018). A multi-agency team meets once a week to "identify individuals, groups and places that are at a high risk of anti-social and/or criminal behavior as either perpetrators or victims" (FOCUS Toronto 2018). FOCUS Toronto uses the skills and resources of diverse community partners to respond quickly to situations of elevated risk, with the hope that individuals can be reached and helped before they move into violence.

Deradicalization in the United States

According to researchers and policy practitioners, CVE initiatives in the United States "can best be understood as a series of fits and starts" (Hughes 2017). The 2011 domestic CVE strategy sought to better engage with local communities, build local expertise on issues of countering extremism, and to counter extremist messaging, all with a broader push away from federal programs in favor of "local governments and partners" (Hughes 2017). While there are indeed dozens of local initiatives at work in the United States, both formal and informal, we focus on a select few below.

First, the World Organization for Resource Development and Education (WORDE), led by Hediah Mirahmadi, is a non-profit, educational organization which promotes tolerance and pluralism and counters extremism. Their specialists come from various disciplines, academic as well as spiritual. Some have held government positions. WORDE uses one-on-one counseling as well as group sessions when referred to by community members as well as law enforcement. Like other Muslim organizations engaged in this space, they appeal to a hierarchical Islamic tradition (Sufi Islam) and a counseling style that is non-judgmental and in which a long-term approach is taken where religious training is augmented with vocational and educational support. While originally called the "Montgomery County Model," it has since been renamed BRAVE (Building Resilience Against Violent Extremism) and transitioned into the University of Maryland, Baltimore's Center for Health and Homeland Security to institutionalize the program.[3]

Another notable organization active in the United States is Muflehun, via the executive director, Humera Khan; this is a Muslim grassroots organization that provides a wide variety of services to ethnic Muslim communities. Referrals originate with the community, including family and friends; online engagement handled by the executive director employs genuine and sympathetic approaches, which lead to building personal rapports with clients. The counseling style is non-judgmental but does not lean heavily on Islamic epistemology. Rather, it is utilitarian in that it encourages individuals to think for themselves in a critical manner (Volsky & Fleischer 2015).

The personal counseling component is primarily implemented by a Sudanese-American and Islamic scholar, Imam Mohamed Magid, who employs a community-level social service approach informed by pro-social Islamic values. One of the ways in which young individuals come to his knowledge is by community members and their children as well as government agencies. Imam Magid is, at times, used as a referral by the Federal Bureau of Investigation (FBI). In the case of Ali Shukri Amin, the FBI sought to have the imam have Amin take part in one of the mosque's week-long camps, a spring retreat where teens play sports, hike trails, paddle canoes, and attend lectures on Islam (Abutaleb & Kristina 2016). It did not bear fruit and Amin was arrested, and eventually sentenced to 10 years in prison.

Another initiative working on this problem is the Muslim Public Affairs Council's Safe Spaces program. Safe Spaces was designed to be a practical resource that uses a pluralistic approach to building resilience and healthy communities, and one which aims to reduce harm among young people as well as adults. The Safe Spaces program was predicated on the Prevention Intervention Model of Public Health, which attempts to deal with problems before they occur, and also addresses issues when community members need care. It focuses on trying to resolve difficult issues affecting the community with interventions seeking to address "troubled individuals, potentially harmful behaviors, and violence through education, outreach, assessment, treatment and referral" (Muslim Public Affairs Council 2016). The intervention component of Safe Spaces includes a basic risk assessment to properly categorize a situation that has been brought to the attention of the Community Response Team. The intervention team is trained on properly assessing situations, and distinctly identifying the differences between an individual who is making a threat and an individual who is posing a threat. At the most concerning end of the spectrum is "extreme risk." This is when the Community Response Team should report a case to law enforcement because the chance for a potential act of violence or suicide is eminent, as the individual has clearly made a threat with specific indicators. Next is "high-risk," which suggests a referral and a follow-up to a mental health provider, social services worker, or a theological guide. The Safe Spaces strategy looks to be an alternative to law enforcement-run CVE strategies.[4]

Finally, we have the promising case of the "Terrorism Disengagement and Deradicalization" program in *Minnesota News* source:[5] a program developed in conjunction with the German Institute for Radicalisation and Deradicalisation Studies (GIRDS) and the U.S. Probation Office, District of Minnesota. The program came from the request of the Federal Judge overseeing an ISIS prosecution of four young Somali men.[6] It is the first of its kind to formally institutionalize such a program, one which pools together the expertise of trusted intermediaries and subject matter experts, based on the attempt to employ a standard related to violent extremism recidivism as well as its repudiation (Horgan & Braddock 2010; Koehler 2017). Daniel Koehler of GIRDS in fact testified as an expert that the defendants scored highly in relation to his metric, and that they warranted continuous and ongoing probationary support once eventually released.[7]

All said, this is only the start. There are already individuals in U.S. prisons for whom such programs could be very helpful. The U.S. Government has been aware of this issue for some time,[8] but has not moved beyond the standard surveillance and undercover operation heavy approach and instead, planning for the eventual release of such individuals. By linking such programs directly to the Judges and Probation Offices to whom the task of prosecution and post-incarceration will ultimately fall, it begins to establish the off-ramp from the outset. Moreover, in working with community and family influences, it is more likely to support a reduction in violent extremism recidivism because of the long-term, ongoing, and intimate approach. Of course, programs of this type should be done parallel to intelligence-related operations and, if anything, can be used to inform each other to support a holistic approach to disengagement and deradicalization overall.

Conclusion: the trouble with deradicalization

The first consideration with deradicalization in the North American context is the difference in the way the two countries of America and Canada operate while handling this issue. At the state level, both countries are largely aligned through long-standing security, political, and economic treaties but there are marked cultural differences when it comes to the way these three issues are viewed by the public at large. The United States is engaged in major wars in the Middle East and Canada has supported all operations, including the 2003 Iraq War in which it did not join militarily as a country. This has resulted in politicization of radicalization and terrorism in both countries, ostensibly linked to the real fact that Muslim extremists are engaged as the enemy in these wars, the consequences of which have visited us all here at home.

Another marked difference is the legal system and its approaches to dealing with crime. The United States has a prison–industrial complex that is not the case in Canada. While judges are elected in the United States, they are appointed in Canada. The United States has two parallel and sovereign judicial systems. The U.S. federal justice system applies federal law, while the state systems are sovereign over the interpretation of state law. Canada has a unified system where all courts are parts of the same scheme. Systemic discrimination in the United States is greater than in Canada. These parts, taken together, especially the more liberal judicial philosophy in Canada, usually mean there will be no "counseling programs" that will mitigate or influence sentencing, which is usually set in decades when it comes to terrorism offenses. Individuals in Canada, even if sentenced to 20 years for terrorism offenses, may get out sooner and, even then, without any specific deradicalization programs made available to them while incarcerated. For all the research projects related to this topic, there is yet to be a specifically designed deradicalization program implemented and, at the moment, this remains a venture at its beginning stages.

An optimistic note related to Canada is that Muslim organizations generally have a positive relationship with government at large and are socially and politically active. Numerous professionals staff these organizations and have made clear their objections to any state-driven program that would focus only on the extremism of one group, and neglect others. Canada has been careful to frame countering extremism of any and all such groups and there are numerous non-governmental organizations and faith communities that network with each other, in order to make this a larger social issue and not just one related to terrorism.

On the practical front, the greatest challenge to deradicalization lies with what security services and law enforcement should do. These agencies are responsible for determining whom to investigate in order to stop potential attacks. Having been told that someone has been deradicalized and no longer poses a threat is not a sufficient reason to end or not start a case. Security intelligence and police organizations cannot afford to make decisions on priorities based on alleged deradicalization for fear that they are wrong. The public do not forgive errors by their protectors and do not want to hear that an act was carried out by an individual deemed to no longer be of interest. As no one can offer guarantees that treatment/care has worked, security services cannot use such criteria to determine workload and attention.

Here is also another point to consider: the separation of roles of responsibilities by government agencies and community organizations. Intelligence and/or police agencies will not cease surveillance of an individual just because s/he is seeking counseling. To err on the side of caution, they cannot risk the individual using such programs as a cover. In one Canadian case, an individual was under watch by the police, and was going to an imam, only to suddenly end up attacking two Canadian Forces members, killing one of them with his vehicle (MacCharles & Allan 2014). On the other hand, if an imam is thought to be feeding information to the authorities, parents and community members will not come forward with their children for counseling or anything else. Government-driven top-down programs will just not work in these settings and intelligence and police agencies have limited interest and ability to try to administer them where they focus on this one area of crime.

Perhaps we have the wrong focus when we elect to see deradicalization as a goal in light of the difficulties in determining whether success has been achieved. A related, but sometimes confused, term is disengagement. Those who have effectively disengaged have not necessarily deradicalized but have chosen to no longer act on their underlying ideology. Disengagement is overtly visible because it is based on observable behavior: one's social circle, online browsing and postings. This is significantly different than deradicalization where underlying psychology, which is inherently less visible, is more difficult to measure.

Even with disengagement there are problems. Just as an allegedly deradicalized individual can "reradicalize" under the right (or wrong) circumstances, someone who has disengaged can "reengage" in terrorism under the right (or wrong) circumstances. If the underlying ideology is indeed present, such might facilitate a return to violent extremism. At best, disengagement is all we can hope for since it is the only phenomenon that is readily observable. This is not to suggest that deradicalization programs should not be supported or administered as it is likely that there are benefits, planned or otherwise.

Still, we are far from a world where we can take deradicalization claims as guarantees of non-threats and the authors agree that, as a natural process, there are many individuals who we can say have been deradicalized as they are now deeply involved with countering violence, be they ex-Islamists, gang members, neo-Nazis, and others. However, it is the deradicalization process manufactured in think tanks and universities, with limited research especially related to long-term implementation, which gives us reason to be cautious with programs claiming to have successfully changed the mind of an extremist in a short period of time.

Notes

1 For more details on Kanishka Project see: www.publicsafety.gc.ca/cnt/ntnl-scrt/cntr-trrrsm/r-nd-flght-182/knshk/index-en.aspx
2 For more details on Canada Centre for Community Engagement and Prevention of Violence (CCCEPV), visit: www.publicsafety.gc.ca/cnt/bt/cccepv-en.aspx
3 For more details see: www.mdchhs.com/wp-content/uploads/2016/12/BRAVE-program-overview.pdf
4 Special thanks to Mustafa Allahrakha and Alejandro Beutel for their contribution to the Safe Spaces section.
5 Ivy Kaplan (2019) "An Inside Look at the First US Domestic Deradicalization Program." *The Defence Post*. February 12. https://thedefensepost.com/2019/02/12/us-minnesota-deradicalization-program-inside-look/
6 See Stephen Montemayor and Mila Koumpilova (2016) "Terror Suspects Will Test Deradicalization Program." *Star Tribune*. March 2. www.startribune.com/judge-orders-de-radicalization-study-for-4-terror-defendants/370806141/
7 See Doualy Xaykaothao (2016) "Deradicalization Expert Finishes Testimony in ISIS Case." *MPR News*. September 21. www.mprnews.org/story/2016/09/21/deradicalization-expert-finishes-testimony-minnesota-isis-case
8 For reference see https://docs.house.gov/meetings/HM/HM05/20151028/104102/HHRG-114-HM05-Wstate-BjeloperaJ-20151028.pdf

References

Abutaleb, Y., & Kristina C. (2016). "A Teen's Turn to Radicalism and the US Safety Net that Failed." *Reuters*. June 6. www.reuters.com/article/us-usa-extremists-teen-special-report-idUSKCN0YS1PH

Amarasingam, A. (2015). "Canadian Foreign Fighters in Syria: An Overview." *Jihadology.net*. March 4. http://jihadology.net/2015/03/04/the-clear-banner-canadian-foreign-fighters-in-syria-an-overview/

Amarasingam, A. (2016). "Searching for the Shadowy Canadian Leader of ISIS in Bangladesh." *Jihadology.net*. August 2. http://jihadology.net/2016/08/02/guest-post-searching-for-the-shadowy-canadian-leader-of-isis-in-bangladesh/

Babin, T. (2015). "Positive Relationships Key to Defusing Extremism, Says Former Radical." *The Calgary Herald*. October 2. https://calgaryherald.com/news/national/video-positive-relationships-key-to-defusing-extremism-says-former-radical

Bjørgo, T. (2011). "Dreams and Disillusionment: Engagement in and Disengagement from Militant Extremist Groups." *Crime, Law and Social Change*, 55, 4, pp. 277–285.

Canadian Press. (2017). "Canada Is Not Immune to Reach of Terrorist Networks, Experts Say." *Maclean's*. October 7. www.macleans.ca/news/canada/canadian-involvement-in-new-york-terror-plot-shows-growing-reach-of-isis/

CBC News. (2014). "Muslim Deradicalisation Councilor." *CBC News*. August 23. www.cbc.ca/news/canada/muslim-deradicalisation-councillor-1.2745004

Cottee, S., & Hayward, K. (2011). "Terrorist (E)motives: The Existential Attractions of Terrorism." *Studies in Conflict & Terrorism*, 34, 12, pp. 963–986.

Council on American-Islamic Relations. (2015). "Brief on Countering Violent Extremism (CVE)." *Council on American-Islamic Relations webpage*. August 20, 2015. www.cair.com/government-affairs/13063-brief-on-countering-violent-extremism-cve.html

Cronin, A. K. (2006). "How al-Qaida Ends: The Decline and Demise of Terrorist Groups." *International Security*, 31, 1, pp. 7–48.

Daigle, C. (2015). "Navaid Aziz: Empowering Youth and Countering Extremism." *Muslim Link*, March 19. https://muslimlink.ca/in-focus/navaid-aziz-interview

Dawson, L. (2017). *Sketch of a social ecology model for explaining homegrown terrorist radicalisation.* The Hague: International Center for Terrorism and Counter-Terrorism Studies.

Finn, M., & Momani, B. (2017). "Building Foundations for the Comparative Study of State and Non-State Terrorism." *Critical Studies on Terrorism*, 24, pp. 1–25.

FOCUS Toronto. (2018). "Focus Toronto Situation Tables. City of Toronto." *Focus Homepage.* www.toronto.ca/community-people/public-safety-alerts/community-safety-programs/focus-toronto/

George Washington University (2019). GW Extremism tracker. Terrorism in the United States. October 2019. https://extremism.gwu.edu/sites/g/files/zaxdzs2191/f/Oct19%20Tracker.pdf

Graveland, B. (2017). "Calgary Pilot Project to Prevent Youth Radicalization Gets Full Federal Funding." *The Canadian Press.* December 18. https://calgaryherald.com/news/local-news/calgary-pilot-project-to-prevent-youth-radicalization-gets-full-federal-funding

Gurski, P. (2016). *Western foreign fighters: The threat to homeland and international security.* Lanham, MD: Rowman & Littlefield Publishers.

Hauslohner, A. (2016). "How a Muslim Advocacy Group in Florida Is Doing What the Government Has so Far Failed to Do." *Washington Post.* July 4, 2016. www.washingtonpost.com/national/from-muslim-groups-to-federal-agencies-efforts-aimed-at-countering-violent-extremism-take-hold/2016/07/03/7af82c44-3f9f-11e6-84e8-1580c7db5275_story.html?utm_term=.60b4e7e57557

Home Office. (2017). "The Channel Programme. Government of the United Kingdom." *Home Page.* www.gov.uk/government/case-studies/the-channel-programme

Horgan, J. (2009). "Deradicalization or Disengagement? A Process in Need of Clarity and a Counterterrorism Initiative in Need of Evaluation." *Revista De Psicología Social*, 24, 2, pp. 291–298.

Horgan, J., & Braddock, K. (2010). "Rehabilitating the Terrorists?: Challenges in Assessing the Effectiveness of Deradicalisation Programs." *Terrorism and Political Violence*, 22, 2, pp. 267–291.

Hughes, S. (2017). "Combatting Homegrown Terrorism." *Testimony before the U.S. House of Representatives Oversight and Government Reform.* https://extremism.gwu.edu/sites/extremism.gwu.edu/files/HughesCombattingHomegronTerrorism727.pdf

Kaplan, Ivy (2019). "An Inside Look at the First US Domestic Deradicalization Program." *The Defence Post.* February 12. https://thedefensepost.com/2019/02/12/us-minnesota-deradicalization-program-inside-look/

King, M., & Mohamed, A. (2011). *Youth radicalization: Somali identity and support for Al-Shabaab in the U.K., the U.S., and Canada.* Ottawa, ON, CA: Canadian Friends of Somalia.

Koehler, D. (2017). *Understanding deradicalization: Methods, tools and programs for countering violent extremism.* New York: Routledge.

Kruglanski, A. W., Gelfand, M. J., Bélanger, J. J., Sheveland, A., Hetiarachchi, M., & Gunaratna, R. (2014). "The Psychology of Radicalization and Deradicalization: How Significance Quest Impacts Violent Extremism." *Political Psychology*, 35, 2, pp. 69–93.

MacCharles, T., & Allan W. (2014). "Quebec Attacker Gave No Hint of Deadly Plan, Say RCMP, Family, Friends." *The Toronto Star.* October 21. www.thestar.com/news/canada/2014/10/21/attack_on_soldiers_linked_to_terrorist_ideology.html

McCauley, C., & Moskalenko, S. (2008). "Mechanisms of Political Radicalization: Pathways toward Terrorism." *Terrorism and Political Violence*, 20, 3, pp. 415–433.

Montemayor, S., & Koumpilova, M. (2016). "Terror Suspects Will Test Deradicalization Program." *Star Tribune.* March 2. www.startribune.com/judge-orders-de-radicalization-study-for-4-terror-defendants/370806141/

Muslim Public Affairs Council. (2016). "Safe Spaces: An Updated Toolkit for Empowering Communities and Addressing Ideological Violence." MPAC report. Available at: https://www.mpac.org/safespaces/files/MPAC-Safe-Spaces.pdf

Pasha-Robonson, L. (2017). "Charlottesville: Donald Trump Quietly Slashed Funds to Groups Fighting White Supremacy Months Ago." *The Independent.* August 15. www.independent.co.uk/news/world/americas/us-politics/charlottesville-latest-donald-trump-slashed-funds-groups-fighting-white-supremacy-rally-riot-a7894271.html

Roberts, N. (2016). "Peace Be Upon You: Meet The Calgary Imam Who Saves Muslim Men from Radicalization." *The Walrus.* December 14. https://thewalrus.ca/peace-be-upon-you/

Speckhard, A., & Mubin S. (2014). *Undercover jihadi: Inside the Toronto 18*. McLean, VA: Advances Press.
Teotonia, I. (2010). "Toronto 18." *The Toronto Star*. n.d. Accessed July 15, 2017. www3.thestar.com/static/toronto18/
Tiflati, T. (2016). "Western Islamic Schools as Institutions for Preventing Behavioral Radicalization: The Case of Quebec." *Journal for Deradicalization*, 6, pp. 180–205.
Tomlinson, L. (2014). "Canada Lost Its Innocence Long Ago and Tried to Cover It Up." *Huffington Post*. October 27. www.huffingtonpost.ca/dr-lisa-tomlinson/canada-violence_b_6050702.html
Volsky, I., & Fleischer, V. (2015). "How this Clever Imam Has Kept Americans From Joining the Islamic State." *ThinkProgress*. June 4. https://thinkprogress.org/how-this-clever-imam-has-kept-americans-from-joining-the-islamic-state-f95b08c1b71/
White, R. (2017). "Mosque with Reputation Tied to Radicalization to Relocate, Imam Embraces Fresh Start." *CTV News*. March 30. http://calgary.ctvnews.ca/mosque-with-reputation-tied-to-radicalization-to-relocate-imam-embraces-fresh-start-1.3347809
Xaykaothao, D. (2016). "Deradicalization Expert Finishes Testimony in ISIS Case." *MPR News*. September 21. www.mprnews.org/story/2016/09/21/deradicalization-expert-finishes-testimony-minnesota-isis-case

24

DERADICALIZATION AND DISENGAGEMENT IN LATIN AMERICA

Irina A. Chindea

In Latin America, the deradicalization process is framed in the context of disarmament, demobilization, and reintegration (or DDR) initiatives adopted at the end of left-wing insurgencies and civil wars that plagued the region in the second half of the 20th century. During this time, left-wing ideology and right-wing counter-responses to the actions of Marxist guerrillas drove internal violence, with Islamic fundamentalism making few inroads in Latin America, even after 9/11. Hence, the post-9/11 deradicalization processes at work in Middle Eastern and Western European countries battling Islamic extremism never took shape in the region, which explains the slightly "off" tone of this chapter when compared to the other ones in the handbook.

Although the lines between deradicalization and DDR are in general difficult to draw (Cockayne and O'Neil 2015), in the case of Latin America deradicalization has been – in an indirect fashion – an integral part of the peace processes. It has often taken the shape of individual psychological and physical disengagement from violence, and preceded the demobilization and reintegration activities of ex-combatants. Consequently, for the purpose of this chapter, building on Koehler's discussion on disengagement in Chapter 2, I define ideological disengagement as the militant's abandonment of ideology, and I use it as a proxy concept for deradicalization in the Latin American context. Due to personal and environmental factors as well as intra-group dynamics, ideology may become over time less attractive to the militant and shape less and less his/her worldview and behavior. Ideological disengagement can be psychological and physical. When psychological disengagement occurs, the militant stops valuing and identifying with the ideological principles of the group. When physical disengagement occurs, the militant refuses to carry out violence in the name of the ideology, and ultimately leaves the organization. Psychological and physical disengagement can occur independently as well as in tandem.

As the cases presented in this chapter illustrate, many countries in Latin America had no deradicalization programs in place during and at the end of their respective internal conflicts. For this reason, individual and collective demobilization at the end of the conflict did not come as a result of successful government initiatives. Individual demobilization was mainly a product of individual disengagement of militants who had become disillusioned with the armed group or switched priorities from aspiring to make a contribution to the success of "the revolution" to desiring and pursuing a family life. The absence of government deradicalization programs was especially felt in Central American countries such as Nicaragua, El Salvador, and Guatemala, which – until the 1990s – had been mired in decades-long civil wars. In the absence of official deradicalization programs, their governments relied on propaganda to discourage local support for the guerrillas and prevent new members from joining the conflict.

For combatants demobilizing collectively (or as a group) – irrespective of ideological orientation – the decision to disarm and demobilize was the outcome of a rational assessment at group level that the costs of continuing to fight were too high while the prospects of winning were too slim. For the combatants demobilizing in the early and mid-1990s, the end of the Cold War, the termination of Soviet sponsorship, and the ideological demise of Marxism-Leninism were all factors contributing to this assessment.

Left-wing vs. right-wing disengagement

For left-wing militants, individual disengagement came as the result of guerrilla members growing disillusioned with the organization as a whole and abandoning the ideological goals for more pragmatic or personal considerations. For the groups that demobilized collectively, some of the leaders entered politics to further the group's political goals in a legitimate way, as was the case for M-19 guerrillas in Colombia in 1990.

However, the demobilization of right-wing paramilitaries remains a contentious point until today, especially in Colombia where some former combatants continue to engage in violent extremism. For several decades, the violent activities of Colombian paramilitaries were part of a state-sanctioned culture of deliberate violence against the left-wing armed groups, which often went hand in hand with drug violence. As the trade in cocaine grew extremely lucrative in the 1990s, the Colombian paramilitaries became increasingly involved in drug trafficking, with their violent activities being not entirely driven by genuine political principles, but also by desire for personal enrichment. Similar dynamics of violence are currently occurring in the drug cultivation and trafficking areas formerly under the control of Fuerzas Armadas Revolucionarias de Colombia (Revolutionary Armed Forces of Colombia: FARC), control, which the ex-paramilitaries took over when FARC started to demobilize in early 2017. The dominating financial motivation for right-wing violence means that deradicalization programs designed to target those who engage in politically or religiously motivated extremism are less likely to be successful in this case.

Also, in Latin America most post-conflict transitional justice mechanisms have been predominantly designed to bring and maintain peace and stability after decades of internal conflict. As combatants were less likely to disarm and demobilize unless granted some form of amnesty, transitional justice processes focused less on bringing to justice the perpetrators of violence. Hence, former guerrilla and paramilitary members have not only been included in peace negotiations, but some of them also entered the political process at local and national level. While on the one hand this approach brought to an end most of the insurgencies and civil wars in the region, on the other hand, it had the undesired effect of de facto legitimizing violence, with criminal violence replacing ideologically motivated attacks.

Chapter roadmap

The next sections of this chapter cover the ideological disengagement (as a conceptual proxy for deradicalization in the Latin American context), and DDR into society of the major Colombian left-wing guerrilla groups (i.e., M-19, the FARC, and the National Liberation

Army (ELN)), and of the right-wing paramilitary organization (the Autodefensas Unidas de Colombia (AUC) or the United Self-Defense Forces of Colombia). An analysis of the circumstances leading to the ideological disengagement of members of the Peruvian Maoist insurgency "Sendero Luminoso" (also known in English as the "Shining Path"), and of the disengagement and DDR into society of former civil war combatants in Nicaragua, El Salvador, and Guatemala follows. As this is a handbook on deradicalization and disengagement, the cases discussed in the following sections try to keep focus on ideological disengagement, with the extent of emphasis placed on DDR varying from case to case. The last section concludes the chapter.

The M-19 demobilization and reintegration process

In Colombia, the first successful guerrilla reintegration process took place in 1990, under President Virgilio Barco (1986–1990). Five guerrilla groups demobilized at the time, with M-19 (also known in English as the April 19th Movement) being the most prominent among them. The small size of the organizations, the relatively high level of education of the members, and the political acumen of their leaders contributed – among other factors discussed below – to the success of the demobilization (Porch and Rasmussen 2008), with deliberate government-led deradicalization initiatives playing little to no role in this case.

M-19 had emerged in 1974 as a Marxist-Leninist insurgent organization (Mapping Militants Project: https://cisac.fsi.stanford.edu/mappingmilitants/content/mapping-militants) in response to the alleged electoral fraud that had occurred during the 1970 elections. Inspired by the Cuban Revolution (Colombia: The 19th of April Movement), M-19 aimed to change what its members "believed to be a corrupt Colombian electoral system" (Mapping Militants Project) and to advance an inclusive and representative democratic structure. Although leaning strongly towards the left of the political spectrum, the group's core goals focused on extending democratic representation and curbing government corruption.

The insurgent organizations that demobilized in 1990 did so collectively, but some guerrilla members also demobilized individually (Guáqueta 2007). Although the FARC and the ELN – the two other major guerrilla groups in Colombia – continued the fight against the government, the demobilization and reintegration process of M-19 into society was successful. Moreover, among the three major leftist guerrilla organizations, M-19 was the least ideological one. Given the group's political agenda and focus on promoting democratic inclusion and representation, the demobilization process was the outcome of the group's understanding of and adaptation to the political and social circumstances in the country at the time, with two major factors contributing to the success of the peace process:

1. The conflict between M-19 and the government was perceived as a legitimate manifestation of the group's social grievances, garnering the public's support.
2. As opposed to the other guerrilla groups, M-19 was interested in becoming a player in the democratic process (Porch and Rasmussen 2008). One of M-19's preconditions to lay down arms was to obtain the government's commitment to engage in constitutional reform. In this way, M-19's political negotiations with the government during the peace process resulted in the group being perceived as a viable "political actor" committed to peace and to advancing democratic values (Guáqueta 2007). The 791 demobilized M-19 combatants became part of the "Alianza Democrática M-19" (AD M-19 or "Democratic Alliance M-19") political party, gaining at the ballot box the second largest representation in Colombia's National Constituent Assembly. They

> made a strong contribution to redrafting in 1991 Colombia's Constitution, introducing democratic reforms and provisions aimed to safeguard human rights (Guáqueta 2007). The political actions of AD M-19 after the conclusion of the peace process demonstrated their commitment to the promotion of an open and inclusive democratic process, which surpassed the group's Marxist ideological inclinations. Also, the end of the Cold War facilitated the group's legitimate abandonment of Marxist ideological principles, which its members had previously embraced.

It is worth mentioning that M-19 had made the decision to demobilize without being defeated on the battlefield (Porch and Rasmussen 2008), for as long as the government guaranteed two main basic outcomes: a legal pardon and physical protection for the demobilized M-19 members (Guáqueta 2007). The legal pardon together with the societal support of the peace process facilitated M-19's reintegration and their acceptance as legitimate political actors (Guáqueta 2007).

The FARC demobilization and reintegration process

The most recent demobilization and reintegration process in Colombia was initiated (and is currently stalling) in the context of the peace process with the FARC. The FARC was established in 1964 as a peasant insurgency that embraced Marxist-Leninist principles, aimed to defend the rights of rural poor, and opposed the privatization of natural resources (Herrera and Porch 2008). To further its cause, the FARC carried out terrorist attacks and engaged in kidnappings and extortion (Sullivan and Beittel 2016). After a confrontation that has lasted almost half a century, in 2012 the FARC and the Colombian government opened a new round of peace talks, which followed previous reconciliation initiatives in the 1980s and 1990s that did not result in a successful peace agreement.

One of the most important leftist guerrilla organizations in Latin America during the Cold War, the FARC was considered to represent a "pure Marxist" organization. However, with the end of the Cold War and the loss of Soviet support, the guerrilla movement moderated its Marxist discourse. In the second half of the 1990s – with the demise of the Cali and Medellín Cartels – the FARC became one of the top players in the drug trade in Colombia. In this context, scholars and experts questioned – for good reason – the ideological discourse of the organization, arguing that the FARC morphed into a criminal group, which has since maintained a political agenda as a mere façade for drug trafficking.

The end of the Cold War indeed reduced the appeal of Marxist ideology among FARC members, and – similar to M-19 – their ideological disengagement was not an outcome of government-initiated programs. In the post-Cold War environment, ideological disengagement – followed subsequently by individual demobilization – was often the result of individual disillusionment with life in the guerrilla movement and due to the gap between the ideological principles FARC leadership was trying to sell to the rank and file, and the actual self-interested actions in which the leaders engaged. Furthermore, in the post-Cold War environment, fewer recruits joined the FARC out of ideological conviction, with research by Saab and Taylor (2009) showing ideology ranking fourth among the main reasons why individuals joined the guerrilla movement. Many new recruits joined FARC without embracing ideological fervor and engaged in violence out of financial necessity rather than political conviction. However, the reasons why they joined the guerrilla group had an impact on their subsequent decision to abandon violence and demobilize.

According to the findings of research conducted by Rosenau et al. (2014), prior to 2012 most FARC members demobilized individually. Since 2002, over 21,000 guerrilla members belonging to FARC and ELN demobilized independently and voluntarily surrendered themselves to Colombian security forces. After 2012, they demobilized collectively. To be granted the status of "demobilized illegal combatant" – which translated into access to limited financial benefits and counseling – the guerrilla members had to agree to an interview in which they presented evidence of their membership in the organization, their activities in the armed group, and the reasons why they decided to leave the organization (Rosenau et al. 2014). FARC's forcible recruitment of combatants "through threats, violence, and intimidation" (Rosenau et al. 2014) represented one of the main reasons driving individual FARC members to desert the guerrilla movement. Besides coercion and forcible recruitment, Rosenau et al. have identified discontent with family life, family or personal ties to guerrilla members, the desire for a better life, and the desire to escape recruitment in rival armed groups such as the ELN or the AUC, as additional reasons why individuals joined the FARC (Rosenau et al. 2014). Rosenau and colleagues' findings are in line with previous research on the topic, which had identified the following four most widespread reasons for joining the FARC: forced recruitment (20%), the attraction of weapons and wearing a uniform (20%), false promises to receive a salary and good treatment (16%), and political convictions (12%) (Saab and Taylor 2009). Last but not least, the weakening of the FARC and the drop in membership after 2002 are also associated with "Plan Colombia" and the counter-narcotics (and, indirectly, counter-insurgency) measures that it entailed (Rochlin 2011; Shifter 2012) as well as with President Uribe's "scorched-earth military campaign against the Marxist FARC guerrillas" (Salazar 2018).

In the case of female recruits into the FARC, Natalia Herrera and Douglas Porch identify romantic or affective ties, the desire to emulate glamorous guerrillera (or female combatant) figures, and unhappy home situations in which the young women were physically and verbally abused, as the main reasons for joining the guerrilla group. Similar to their male counter-parts, few of the women recruited into the FARC cited ideology as the main reason for joining. However, most of the women Herrera and Porch interviewed confessed their adherence to the left-wing ideological principles to which they were exposed post-recruitment (Herrera and Porch 2008). Not only women, but all FARC recruits underwent a rigorous indoctrination process after joining the guerrilla group, with many embracing Marxist-Leninist principles by the end of their training period. Nonetheless, the discrepancy between the principles with which recruits were indoctrinated and the obvious practices of leadership disillusioned many rank-and-file recruits, who ultimately abandoned their adherence to the organization's ideological principles. Furthermore, individual needs and desires drove the recruits away from the guerrilla group, and individual demobilization was not the product of successful deradicalization programs, but a natural process of "growing out" of the organization (or ideological disengagement) as a result of intra-group dynamics (Koehler 2016) as the examples below illustrate.

Alongside identifying the motivations and circumstances under which individuals joined the FARC, Rosenau et al. also identified the main reasons why recruits left the armed group. According to their research findings, the poor treatment of lower-level combatants by their superiors, hunger and extreme fatigue, ideological disenchantment, and "perceived deviation from the revolutionary principles that had first attracted" them to the movement motivated some of the members to desert the guerrilla organization (Rosenau et al. 2014). Moreover, the desire of some guerrillas to pursue their personal lives and rebuild family connections – the FARC does not allow for family visits (Herrera and Porch 2008) – made them determined to leave behind the revolutionary goals of the group (Rosenau et al. 2014). Furthermore, the differences in the enforcement of policies prohibiting romantic relationships among members – strictly enforced for rank-and-file members but relaxed for the leadership – deepened resentment within the organization.

The personal motives are especially present in the case of the guerrilleras who demobilize from the FARC. The group's policy to ban pregnancies and force female combatants to have abortions once they become pregnant ultimately led some guerrilleras to prioritize the creation of stable family relations over revolutionary life and to, ultimately, leave the organization (Herrera and Porch 2008). For many of the women Herrera and Porch interviewed, "pregnancy, and especially the birth of a child, changed their attitude to the organization" (Herrera and Porch 2008). For other women, the discrepancy between FARC's rhetoric regarding gender equality and the actual practice that failed to accommodate female ambition, punishing it instead, represented another factor driving some guerrilleras away from the organization. However, the lack of viable alternatives outside the guerrilla organization and the difficulties of reintegrating into society as a former woman guerrilla combatant meant that women deserted the group at lower rates than their presence in the organization (Herrera and Porch 2008). Overall, the women's continued membership in the guerrilla group was not representative of their ideological inclinations or their adherence to violent extremism.

After February 2002, when one of several attempted peace processes with the government broke down, both male and female guerrillas faced the same dilemma when considering whether to desert or not: "where to go?" Given FARC's propensity to recruit from the local communities, the individuals who left the guerrilla group could not go home to areas controlled by the insurgency without risking recapture or receiving the death sentence for desertion. The members' low level of education and lack of marketable skills also made it difficult for many to survive in urban environments, which would have provided them with anonymity and some degree of protection from the insurgency (Herrera and Porch 2008). In this light, the demobilization process resulting from the November 2016 peace accord signed between the FARC and the Colombian government (Angelo 2017) was the combined outcome of gradual ideological erosion across several decades of conflict and of the lack of viable prospects for guerrilla victory. Under the 2016 accord, the demobilized FARC leaders are not to face prison time, but they are to give up their wealth – most of which comes from illicit drug trafficking – and to pay reparations to victims of their violence and abuse.

Some of the challenges associated with the implementation of the current peace process, and the disarmament and reintegration of FARC combatants, are the result of the FARC being treated as a political actor, while many of its fronts have been heavily involved over the years in the cocaine trade. Hence, the government's political incentives are not likely to compensate for the members' financial losses once they renounce drug trafficking (Norman 2017), and the peace process is unlikely to put an automatic end to narco-violence.

Furthermore, while FARC leadership benefited directly from the drug trade, the rank and file did not have access to narco-trafficking proceeds and did not receive a salary in exchange for their participation in the organization (Norman 2017). This division between leadership and rank and file is likely to create further impediments to the implementation of the disarmament and reintegration plan. Under the agreement signed with the government, each demobilized rank-and-file guerrilla is supposed to receive from the government $6,100 over a two-year period. Delays in payment or cut-backs in funding, added to broken promises for education and employment opportunities that have yet to materialize, are likely to push former combatants to resume violence and re-engage in illicit activities (Norman 2017). Furthermore, Norman's research concludes that, in the aftermath of the peace agreement, violence will continue, and it will not be ideologically motivated but driven by the quest for illicit profits (Norman 2017). These conclusions are unfortunately vindicated by the assassination since 2016 of hundreds of activists and human rights leaders who challenged the presence of paramilitaries in the coca cultivation territories that FARC vacated. In this light, government-led efforts towards combating violent extremism should take into account the lack of ideological motivation of perpetrators, and tailor the initiatives to combat criminal violence.

The Colombian paramilitaries demobilization process

The right-wing paramilitaries in Colombia formed in the early 1980s to counter the kidnapping and extortion activities of left-wing insurgent groups, such as M-19, FARC, and ELN. The right-wing paramilitaries were mainly supported by large estate landowners, ranchers, and traders, who – due to their wealth – were the principal targets of guerrillas' kidnapping and extortion activities, and could not rely on the government for protection (Guáqueta 2007). In December 2002, President Álvaro Uribe initiated negotiations with the leaders of the AUC – the main right-wing paramilitary organization in the country. The negotiations aimed to reach an agreement for a collective voluntary demobilization process (Nussio and Howe 2016). The AUC had been formed in 1997 by bringing under its umbrella the various regional paramilitary groups that had operated individually throughout Colombia since the 1980s (Guáqueta 2007). After its formation, the AUC carried out kidnappings and political assassinations, and was heavily involved in the drug trade (Ahram 2016). For Uribe, reaching an agreement with the paramilitaries was a necessary precondition for the initiation of the peace agreement with the FARC and the ELN, the two leftist insurgent groups still fighting against the government. FARC or ELN members feared that if they had demobilized and disarmed before the paramilitaries had, they would have faced certain death at the hands of the right-wing organizations (Porch and Rasmussen 2008).

The partly political, partly criminal motives driving the paramilitary groups had an impact on the success of the demobilization process. Violence in the country did not come to an end with the demobilization of the AUC. "Massacres, selective killings, extortion, robbery, and threats in support of 'social cleansing'" (Nussio and Howe 2016) continued and were carried out by newly formed organizations, which also had a partly political, partly criminal motivation. They are known as "BaCrims" – the short form for "Bandas Criminales" (or criminal bands/gangs).

Although the paramilitaries were supposed to be ideologically inclined towards the right side of the political spectrum and in direct opposition to the left-wing organizations, most individuals who had joined the "paras" did so for "the promise of money and of a better life" (Rosenau et al. 2014) or to revenge the death of a family member or friend at the hands of the leftist militant groups. Gradually, the little ideological motivation the paramilitaries had disappeared, and by the time the AUC started to demobilize, its members engaged in violence mostly to support criminal activities or purely for the sake of violence.

During the demobilization process, the Colombian government remained largely aware that many individuals had been recruited in the right-wing paramilitary groups by being promised a good wage. Hence, in addition to pull factors such as granting "amnesty from criminal investigation, prosecution and conviction to AUC fighters who voluntarily participated in demobilization" (Angelo 2017), the government added to the demobilization package social benefits such as health insurance, economic incentives, and vocational training.

However, individuals guilty of massacres and massive human rights violations were excluded from amnesty and were not covered by the provisions of Law 782 of 2002, which governed the demobilization process. The government had to make a special effort to incentivize those excluded from the benefits of Law 782 to demobilize (Angelo 2017). The emphasis the Colombian government placed on financial inducements as pull factors for demobilization was an indirect admission that profit – next to revenge – was one of the key drivers for right-wing violence, with little genuine ideological motivation being present.

Part of the formal government-led deradicalization initiative, President Uribe relied on the "Program of Reincorporation to the Civil Life" that had been in place and designed to coordinate the demobilization of the guerrillas in the 1990s. The program focused on the provision of healthcare, education, vocational training, and employment opportunities for former combatants, who demobilized either individually or collectively. Vocational training was intended to offer a viable alternative for individuals to make a living in the legal economy, and to prevent recidivism of demobilized fighters into crime and violence.

To support the reintegration of former combatants into society, the system the Colombian government set in place was supposed to monitor and assess their reintegration and their performance in the program. However, according to a 2005 Human Rights Watch Report, the monitoring system was not devised to reveal whether the demobilized paramilitary members continued to be involved in criminal activities or if they have de facto remained part of paramilitary structure (HRW 2005). In spite of these legal provisions, many demobilized combatants had a hard time finding employment in their communities. The former fighters had psychological problems that made their reintegration into society difficult, with employers refraining from hiring them due to their lack of formal training and skills, and for fear of delinquency or disciplinary problems (Angelo 2017). Also, as the AUC demobilized collectively, little individual deliberation was involved, rendering – according to Ribetti cited in Chowdhury Fink and Hearne (2008) – the AUC demobilization process less effective: most ex-paramilitaries who returned to join armed groups went through a collective – not individual – disengagement process. During the demobilization process, some 1,800 individuals refused to surrender their weapons and opted out of the mandatory registration process. They maintained control of the drug cultivation and trafficking areas of their former leaders, and reorganized themselves into BaCrims (Angelo 2017). These offspring organizations – often referred to also as neo-paramilitaries – are criminally inclined (Nussio and Howe 2016) rather than politically motivated. Some Colombian officials refer to a "reparamilitarization" of Colombia (Porch and Rasmussen 2008) taking place with the emergence of these new entities.

Furthermore, former combatants were disproportionately exposed to the risk of being killed in the aftermath of demobilization. From 2003 until 2010, 1,966 individuals who demobilized collectively died after their demobilization; among them, 1,385 former paramilitary members had been killed, with most of the killings being conducted by professional killers (Nussio 2011). The former combatants' involvement in criminal activities, outstanding disputes among the fighters, revenge killings conducted against those who assisted in the judicial process against their leaders, and the lack of law enforcement capacity to protect the demobilized fighters from those who held a grudge against them – be they previous enemies, victims, comrades, or leaders (Nussio 2011) – are the main reasons why former combatants are more likely to be assassinated post-demobilization, especially in areas of the country with a strong paramilitary presence (Nussio and Howe 2016). Moreover, the newly formed BaCrims also aim to recruit demobilized paramilitaries using a mix of economic incentives and threats to their lives or those of family members. When they resist the threats and decline reincorporation, the former combatants are very likely to be killed. In the context of the imminent threats demobilized paramilitaries face, they relocate to other areas of the country, engage in self-defense, or band together as a group to protect each other (Nussio 2011). Lack of security does not push former paramilitary members to band only with each other, but they often join others who experience a similar environment, such as former guerrillas, drug traffickers, or soldiers (Porch and Rasmussen 2008). All these responses to the threats they face to their security prevent the former AUC combatants continuing the process of reintegration into society, and make it more likely that they re-engage in violence (Nussio 2011). Also, the incentives Álvaro Uribe's government provided to AUC leadership, but not to mid-rank commanders, structured the demobilization process in such a way that mid-level commanders acted as "spoilers" (Nussio and Howe 2016).

The incorporation of the demobilized paramilitaries into the political process faced strong societal opposition, which had an impact on the government's efforts to resettle and reskill the ex-combatants, pushing some of them into joining the BaCrims. The opposition was due to the paramilitaries' involvement in drug trafficking, their record of human rights violations and perpetration of brutal massacres, and their perceived high level of influence over the economic and political environment (Guáqueta 2007). The paramilitaries and the government security forces were known to have previously collaborated at local level in certain areas of the country.

The paramilitary forces had been linked to intimidation of voters and political opponents on behalf of landed, business, and political elites, as well as the assassination of labor union leaders and left-wing and human rights activists. In the "parapolitics" scandal, over 1,000 officials with political ties to President Uribe had been investigated for their links and involvement with the AUC (Angelo 2017). In this way, the demobilization and reintegration process of the AUC had been complicated not only by the paramilitaries' deep involvement in the drug trade, but also by their close ties (see infiltration of) different government security agencies such as the military, police, and the intelligence services (Porch and Rasmussen 2008).

As these examples illustrate, the paramilitary groups enjoyed little ideological legitimacy among the population, with gruesome violence conducted for profit or revenge being their key signature. Upon their demobilization, there had been little to nothing left of their initial right-wing ideological inclination, with most of the violence being conducted in support of criminal activities or for self-defense. As BaCrims' and former paramilitaries' extreme violence is not rooted in a radical ideology, but is mostly financially or security driven, government programs aimed to counter their extreme acts of violence need to be tailored accordingly and to take into account the existing differences in motivation of the perpetrators.

The ongoing ELN peace process

The Colombian armed group Ejército de Liberación Nacional (ELN or the National Liberation Army) was created in 1964. Similar to the formation of the other leftist guerrilla groups – the FARC and the Ejército Popular de Liberación (EPL or Popular Liberation Army) – ELN's creation was a reaction to the closing of the political arena to other political actors except for the Liberal and Conservative Parties, which alternated in power after 1957 under the banner of the "National Front."

The ELN has proved to be the Colombian armed group the most difficult to demobilize, and one of the few armed groups in Latin America continuing to confront the government. Members of the organization have a strong identity, mainly built around an ideology combining "Roman Catholic morality with a strict belief in Marxist materialism," which makes it difficult for the government to bring them to the negotiations table. According to Gruber and Pospisil: "This moral component is consequently present throughout their documents and exemplified by their emphasis on living with dignity. Martyrdom for a just cause thereby becomes a messianic feature" (Gruber and Pospisil 2015).

The strong ideological identity that ELN has created for its members allowed the organization to weather well the ideological demise of Marxism-Leninism at the end of the Cold War. This identity has made the group extremely resilient throughout the past 50 years of conflict with the government. During this time, the group has demonstrated a high level of adaptability in the face of adversity without losing sight of its main ideological goals (Gruber and Pospisil 2015). Up to this moment, the guerrilla organization and the government have been unable to simultaneously sanction a collective demobilization process. Only individual desertions from the ELN have taken place, with individuals deciding to leave the organization, disarm, and reintegrate into society. Most desertions so far have been motivated by ill treatment by ELN commanders (Rosenau et al. 2014), with individual ideological disengagement being the product of intra-group dynamics and disillusionment with the cause.

However, soon after the FARC entered the peace negotiations with the Colombian government in November 2012, the ELN leadership expressed their interest in the peace process. They were rebuffed by the administration of President Santos, who demanded the release of all kidnap victims as a precondition to the talks. Between 2014 and 2018, the ELN leadership and the Colombian government have been engaged several times in "exploratory peace talks" (Sullivan and Beittel 2016), which have either been delayed or put on hold due to the continued ELN attacks against oil pipelines, civilians, or security personnel. Starting with May 2018, the peace talks between the ELN and the Colombian government have resumed in Havana, Cuba. The strong ideological hold the ELN has over its members makes the implementation of a deradicalization program tailored to the specific mix of Catholicism and Marxism-Leninism a prerequisite for a successful peace process and DDR program.

The path to defeating the Peruvian Sendero Luminoso

Sendero Luminoso – also known in English as the "Shining Path" – is a Maoist insurgency that emerged in Ayacucho, Huamanga (Friedman 2018), and has been active in Peru since 1980. Although the group has been significantly weakened over the past few years, it has remained active, committing some 13 terrorist acts in 2015, and has approximately 250–300 members (Sullivan and Beittel 2016). Similar to other leftist guerrilla movements in Latin America, Sendero Luminoso was born in the context of the land redistribution tensions which have plagued the countries in the region since their independence from Spain in the 19th century. However, as opposed to the other examples discussed in this chapter (Colombia, Nicaragua, El Salvador, Guatemala) in which the left-wing guerrillas were motivated by the lack of agrarian reform, Sendero Luminoso came in to fill the power vacuum left by a poorly designed and implemented reform. The failure of the agrarian reform made it easier for the insurgency to successfully recruit members among the indigenous communities and the university students who were unable to find employment after graduation (Kay 2001).

Among the most cited reasons why many individuals joined Sendero Luminoso are the "systematic regional and ethnic marginalization, government corruption, and extreme poverty and underdevelopment" (Friedman 2018). Alongside ideology, individual motivations to join the movement included romantic ties to some of the fighters, the desire to take revenge against the government for the human rights abuses perpetrated by the military, or the desire to "belong" resulting from low self-esteem or a tough family situation. However, irrespective of their commitment to ideology, once the personal motivations had worn off, many members – especially women recruits – started to lose their allegiance to the group and demobilized. Understanding these dynamics and to make defections harder, the new recruits were immersed in comprehensive indoctrination sessions, and Sendero forced them to commit acts of violence that would make it impossible for recruits to return to their original communities (Friedman 2018). Irrespective of its efforts, the disillusionment that many members and supporters experienced as a result of the group's "dogmatism, (ideological) rigidity and use of violence" led to individual ideological disengagement and subsequent demobilization, weakening Sendero Luminoso and leading to its near defeat (Kay 2001). According to Kay, an additional key contributing factor to Sendero's demise was its inability to provide security in the communities that supported its ideological mission and to protect the population from the human rights abuses of the government's security forces (Kay 2001) carried out in the context of an "iron fist" counter-insurgency approach. Lastly, the change in the government's tactics to less militarized ones (Friedman 2018) and the capture of Sendero's leader shifted the balance in favor of the state.

In 2001 the Peruvian government set up a Truth and Reconciliation Commission (Comisión de la Verdad y Reconciliación, broadly known as CVR). As the CVR did not offer amnesty to those who came forward and publicly testified, few militants had any tangible incentive to do so, with both Sendero Luminoso and the military avoiding taking part in any public hearings of the Commission (Friedman 2018). Furthermore, the Peruvian society at large was more focused on the missing persons and on granting support to the victims of violence rather than on the reintegration of the ex-combatants. The former fighters were often stigmatized and had to hide their past. Also, as in the other cases of post-conflict reintegration in Central and South America discussed in this chapter, women had a tougher time than men reintegrating into society, marriage rarely being an option for most of them. As a result, they were often left to fend for themselves on the margins of society (Friedman 2018).

Similar to the Colombian left-wing organizations discussed above, ideological disengagement occurred not as a result of well-established and implemented government programs, but as individual members had become disillusioned with the organization or its leadership, and abandoned the ideological cause for more pragmatic ones, including self-preservation and focus on family life.

Post-civil war ideological disengagement in Central America

In Nicaragua, El Salvador, and Guatemala, the members of the left- and right-wing organizations fighting in the civil wars had a strong degree of ideological motivation. In the Central American context, the disarmament phase of the DDR process did not concern only the guerrillas or right-wing paramilitaries as in Colombia, but government soldiers also had to surrender their weapons in El Salvador and Nicaragua (North 1998). In this light, the term ex-combatants covers both "former government soldiers as well as former members of armed opposition groups" (Spencer 1997). Across all three countries, at the end of the civil war lack of adequate funding, political will, and security stood in the way of proper implementation of demobilization and reintegration programs (Spencer 1997).

Ideology was at the heart of the civil wars in Nicaragua, El Salvador, and Guatemala, with clear divisions drawn between right-wing and left-wing supporters. Furthermore, with the United States and the USSR providing foreign aid along ideological lines, the right–left divide only grew deeper during the conflict. These decades-long internal wars exhausted the population and the resources of the state. With the end of the Cold War and the demise of the Soviet Union, the civil wars in Central America also started to unwind, and ideological considerations were subdued to pragmatic considerations: putting an end to the violence and concluding a viable peace agreement. The extreme violence that Nicaragua, El Salvador, and Guatemala experienced took place in the context of society-wide civil wars that reached far larger proportions than the left-wing and paramilitary violence in Colombia and Peru. When the peace agreements in Nicaragua, El Salvador, and Guatemala were concluded, DDR-related considerations prevailed and the ideological deradicalization of former combatants remained an afterthought. All sides suffered from the lack of state resources available to support the demobilization and reintegration process. The violence that followed the peace agreements was not ideological in nature, but represented a "learned response" and the only tool ex-combatants on both sides had available to confront a failed reintegration process.

Nicaragua

In Nicaragua, at the end of the civil war in 1990, the government of Violeta Chamorro funded the creation of "Contra-controlled" development zones aimed to facilitate the reintegration of the Contras (or right-wing combatants) into the civilian population. The creation of such zones provided the Contras with an incentive to demobilize, but many of the areas ended up lacking water and electricity due to lack of funding and for being located in rural areas where landmines were present (Cupples 2004). The funding for DDR programs fell short of the promises made during the peace process, driving some ex-Contra groups to rearm, form the "re-contras," and demand land, credit, housing, and amnesty (Rogers 2001).

Most of the government soldiers who fought on behalf of the Sandinista government were let go from the army with little support, which pushed many into a life of crime (Spear 1999). Furthermore, the attacks they suffered at the hands of the re-contras, translated into the re-armament and re-organization of ex-soldiers into groups called "recompas," aimed at defending themselves and their communities. Some of the former guerrillas and soldiers joined forces to voice their common demands for housing, credit, and amnesty, and they were called "revueltos." The Nicaraguan government re-engaged in negotiations with all sides – the "re-contras," "re-compas," and "revueltos" – and aimed to disarm them. However, with a weak economy and few financial resources available, the government achieved very little on this front (Rogers 2001).

El Salvador

In El Salvador, the civil war ended in 1992 with the Chapultepec Peace Accords that promised demobilization payments, land redistribution, and education to help ex-combatants reintegrate into society (Spear 1999). The Farabundo Martí National Liberation Front (FMLN) refused to disarm and demobilize in advance of negotiations and they demanded a full political agreement before disarming. Indeed, disarmament ended up being the last agenda item discussed with the government (Muggah, 2013). After signing the final peace agreement on January 15, 1992, the guerrillas were granted amnesty, and the main FMLN leaders returned home to El Salvador by the end of January (Munck 1993). In line with the provisions of the peace agreement, on February 1, 1992 the cease-fire came into effect, and by October 31, 1992 the full demobilization of the FMLN was to be completed as well as their transition to a legal political party. Part of the demobilization process, the FMLN forces were expected to assemble in UN-supervised "concentration zones" also called "secure areas" where they were to turn in their weapons, prior to returning to civilian life (Munck 1993). Although there were delays in implementing the agreed schedule, the guerrillas stuck to their side of the bargain. The most serious resistance to the implementation of the peace accords came from the Salvadorian Army, which refused to purge the high-level officers who had committed atrocities during the civil war (Munck 1993).

After the demobilization phase, the next step was to reinsert the former guerrillas into society. To achieve this outcome, the government sponsored programs that included "land transfers, farm loans, technical assistance and housing, as well as services for the war-wounded" (Segovia 2009). Although women accounted for approximately 30% of the guerrilla forces, the reinsertion programs did not take into account their specific needs as heads of household, with women facing discrimination in terms of access to land and credit. As a result of these practices, the reinsertion of women into productive life registered the least success (Segovia 2009). Overall, as Segovia argues, in El Salvador, demobilization and disarmament took place without being followed by the successful reintegration of ex-combatants into civilian life (Segovia 2009). The main obstacles in the successful implementation of the reinsertion programs have been limited funds (El Salvador is one of the poorest countries in Central America), delays in land redistribution, and the lack of employable skills of many ex-combatants who had fought in the civil war over the past 12 years (Spencer 1997).

Guatemala

In Guatemala, DDR had been at the forefront of the peace negotiations between the Guatemalan Government and the Guatemalan National Revolutionary Unity (URNG) to bring to an end the 36-year civil war, which had been "one of the bloodiest and longest internal armed conflicts of the Latin American continent" (Viaene 2011). The peace process lasted over a decade and focused on government and society demilitarization and on strengthening civilian power. As a result of the 1996 peace process, ex-combatants – both soldiers and guerrillas – were granted amnesty for the violent acts they committed during the civil war. However, this step – although needed to bring the war to an end – created resentment among the general population as it meant that most of the atrocities committed during more than three decades of conflict went unpunished (Spencer 1997). Furthermore, one of the outcomes of the failed demobilization efforts was the rise in organized crime and youth gang-related violence in the country.

Reintegrating female fighters

In all three cases – Nicaragua, El Salvador, and Guatemala – it is worth mentioning the experience of former female fighters who had to reintegrate into society at the end of the civil war. While fighting with the guerrillas during the civil wars, the women felt valued and respected for their skills, and they experienced a high degree of equality. However, at the end of the conflict when they demobilized, the women reintegrated "back into poverty and traditional gender relations" (Hauge 2008). In Guatemala, the worsening in post-demobilization condition was especially acute for women who demobilized individually (Hauge 2008).

As the examples above illustrate, the DDR efforts that followed the peace accords ending the Nicaraguan, Salvadorian, and Guatemalan civil wars did not include any official or government-sponsored deradicalization initiative. With the ideological demise of the Soviet Union in the early 1990s, the parties to the conflict were left animated by land redistribution and other pragmatic concerns as well as the desire to bring to an end decades-long internal conflicts. Ideology and ideological divides played little to no role in the violence that followed the peace agreements, violence that was the direct result of a poorly financed and implemented DDR process.

Conclusion

This chapter has presented an overview of the deradicalization or ideological disengagement and DDR activities of the left- and right-wing combatants fighting in insurgencies in Colombia and Peru, and in the civil wars in Nicaragua, Salvador, and Guatemala. In most of these cases, and in particular for the left-wing organizations, the initial ideological inclination of the group eroded over time, especially after the end of the Cold War. The disillusionment with life in the organization and the intra-group dynamics, together with the low prospects for victory, led to the individual psychological and physical disengagement of many group members, who ended up ultimately abandoning both the ideological cause and the organization. The individual ideological disengagement and demobilization were often precursors for collective demobilization at the end of government-led peace processes. In the cases where violence followed the demobilization process, the episodes were not born out of ideological conviction, but were either financially motivated, resulting from the lack of resources available for the reintegration of ex-combatants, or driven by self-preservation, with former combatants having to fend off attacks from former rivals or comrades.

In the case of the right-wing Colombian paramilitaries, some combatants refused to demobilize. Some of those who have demobilized continued to engage in violence to protect their access to drug-trafficking profits or to protect themselves from the violence other armed groups (e.g., BaCrims) conducted against them. Ideology played little role in post-demobilization violence, especially for the right-wing organizations, which have been since their inception less ideologically driven than guerrillas.

Regarding the DDR process, while the demobilization and reintegration of Colombian M-19 guerrillas in 1990 were a success, the jury is still out regarding the outcome of the peace process with the FARC. The negotiations with the ELN – the most ideologically motivated of all Colombian guerrillas – are still in the early stages. While some experts and Colombian government officials talk about the "re-paramilitarization" of the country, with the BaCrims often being referred to as "neo-paramilitary" groups, the balance tilts more in favor of a successful demobilization of the AUC rather than of a resounding failure, with the topic remaining rather controversial. Last but not least, the lack of adequate funding and the tough economic situation in Nicaragua, El Salvador, and Guatemala had a direct impact on the success of demobilization and reintegration of ex-combatants at the end of the civil wars.

References

Ahram, A. I. (2016). "Pro-Government Militias and the Repertoires of Illicit State Violence." *Studies in Conflict & Terrorism* 39(3), pp. 207–226.

Angelo, P. (2017). "The Colombian Peace Process: Trial and Error." *Survival* 59(1), pp. 135–148.

Cupples, J. (2004). "Counter-Revolutionary Women: Gender and Reconciliation in Post-War Nicaragua." *Gender and Development* 12(3), pp. 8–18.

James Cockayne and Shiobhan O'Neil. (2015). "UN DDR in an Era of Violent Extremism: Is It Fit for Purpose?" United Nations University.

Friedman, R. (2018). "Implementing Transformative Justice: Survivors and Ex-combatants at the Comisión de la Verdad y Reconciliación in Peru." *Ethnic and Racial Studies* 41(4), pp. 701–720.

Gruber, B. and J. Pospisil. (2015). "'Ser Eleno': Insurgent Identity Formation in the ELN." *Small Wars & Insurgencies* 26(2), pp. 226–247.

Guáqueta, A. (2007). "The Way Back in: Reintegrating Illegal Armed Groups in Colombia then and Now." *Conflict, Security & Development* 7(3), pp. 417–456.

Hauge, W. (2008). "Group Identity—A Neglected Asset: Determinants of Social and Political Participation among Female Ex-fighters in Guatemala." *Conflict, Security & Development* 8(3), pp. 295–316.

Herrera, N. and D. Porch. (2008). "'Like Going to a Fiesta' – The Role of Female Fighters in Colombia's FARC-EP." *Small Wars & Insurgencies* 19(4), pp. 609–634.

HRW. (2005). "Smoke and Mirrors – Colombia's Demobilization of Paramilitary Groups." *Human Rights Watch* 17(3 B). https://www.hrw.org/sites/default/files/reports/colombia0805.pdf

Kay, C. (2001). "Reflections on Rural Violence in Latin America." *Third World Quarterly* 22(5), pp. 741–775.

Koehler, D. (2016). *Understanding deradicalization. Methods, tools and programs for countering violent extremism.* Oxon/New York: Routledge.

Muggah, R. (2013). "Negotiating Disarmament and Demobilisation; a Descriptive Review of the Evidence." *Colombia Internacional* 77, pp. 19–41. http://www.scielo.org.co/scielo.php?script=sci_art text&pid=S0121-56122013000100002

Munck, G. L. (1993). "Beyond Electoralism in El Salvador: Conflict Resolution through Negotiated Compromise." *Third World Quarterly* 14(1), pp. 75–93.

Naureen Chowdhury Fink and Ellie B. Hearne. (October 2008). *Beyond Terrorism: Deradicalization and Disengagement from Radical Extemism.* International Peace Institute.

Norman, S. V. (2017). "Narcotization as Security Dilemma: The FARC and Drug Trade in Colombia." *Studies in Conflict & Terrorism* 41(8), pp. 638–659.

North, L. L. (1998). "Reflections on Democratization and Demilitarization in Central America." *Studies in Political Economy* 55(1), pp. 155–171.

Nussio, E. (2011). "How Ex-combatants Talk about Personal Security. Narratives of Former Paramilitaries in Colombia." *Conflict, Security & Development* 11(5), pp. 579–606.

Nussio, E. and K. Howe. (2016). "When Protection Collapses: Post-Demobilization Trajectories of Violence." *Terrorism and Political Violence* 28(5), pp. 848–867.

Porch, D. and M. J. Rasmussen. (2008). "Demobilization of Paramilitaries in Colombia: Transformation or Transition?" *Studies in Conflict & Terrorism* 31(6), pp. 520–540.

Rochlin, J. I. M. (2011). "Plan Colombia and the Revolution in Military Affairs: The Demise of the FARC." *Review of International Studies* 37(2), pp. 715–740.

Rogers, T. (2001). "Silent War in Nicaragua: The New Politics of Violence." *NACLA Report on the Americas* 34(4), pp. 11–15.

Rosenau, William, Ralph Espach, Román D. Ortiz and Natalia Herrera. (2014). "Why They Join, Why They Fight, and Why They Leave: Learning From Colombia's Database of Demobilized Militants." *Terrorism and Political Violence*, 26(2), pp. 277–285, DOI: 10.1080/09546553.2012.700658

Saab, B. Y. and A. W. Taylor. (2009). "Criminality and Armed Groups: A Comparative Study of FARC and Paramilitary Groups in Colombia." *Studies in Conflict & Terrorism* 32(6), pp. 455–475.

Salazar, M. (2018). "Once Again, the Right Wing Wins in Colombia, Amid Divisions on the Left." *The Nation*, 20 June.

Segovia, A. (2009). "Transitional Justice and DDR: The Case of El Salvador." Research Unit *International Center for Transitional Justice. Special report June.*

Shifter, M. (2012). "Plan Colombia: A Retrospective." *Americas Quarterly* (Summer 2012).

Spear, J. (1999). "The Disarmament and Demobilisation of Warring Factions in the Aftermath of Civil Wars: Key Implementation Issues." *Civil Wars* 2(2), pp. 1–22.

Spencer, D. (1997). "Demobilization and Reintegration in Central America." *Bonn International Center for Conversion Paper* 8, pp. 1–77.

Sullivan, M. and J. Beittel. (2016). "Latin America: Terrorism Issues." *CRS Report* December.

Unknown. (2017). "Colombia: What Comes Next?" *Strategic Comments* 23(1), pp. vii–viii.

Viaene, L. (2011). "Dealing with the Legacy of Gross Human Rights Violations in Guatemala: Grasping the Mismatch between Macro Level Policies and Micro Level Processes." *The International Journal of Human Rights* 15(7), pp. 1160–1181.

25
CONCLUSION

Stig Jarle Hansen and Stian Lid

This handbook's global scope demonstrates clearly that the idea of assisting people out of an extremist milieu and/or violent extreme behaviour through disengagement and deradicalisation initiatives has more or less become a manifested strategy worldwide. The phenomenon has to be studied in the light of the broader strategy of countering violent extremism (CVE), which emphasises softer measures within both preventive and reactive strategies, and the growing acknowledgement of the limited effect and high economic cost of repressive strategies. Disengagement and deradicalisation initiatives have the potential to reduce human, social and economic costs by leading to a permanent end of violent behaviour and ideology.

Although the appearance of disengagement and deradicalisation strategies is worldwide, we see important distinctions between present practices. Programmes for disengagement and deradicalisation are to a large degree country-dependent, but there are also variations within individual countries; this volume clearly shows that variations exist between both global and state levels, as well as between local and state levels.

One of the variations is between those countries that have a multifaceted approach with a range of "soft" interventions and those countries that remain in an approach dominated by repression and prosecution. Especially for those countries with a multifaceted approach, a range of actors are invited to contribute with their expertise and interventions, such as social and health institutions, local governments, non-governmental organisations and civil societies. That has led to a wide scope of disengagement and deradicalisation interventions. The interventions illustrated in many chapters in this volume can be categorised as: (1) practical support; (2) social support; (3) psychological and health treatment/counselling; and (4) ideological counselling. Practical support consists of, among other things, finding a job, vocational training and education, economic support, housing, and so on. Social support can involve both strategies to utilise the primary social networks to re-anchor the former extremist in non-radical networks such as family and friends, but also to develop the activist's social skills. Moreover, psychological counselling and health treatment are common strategies in many programmes. Finally, ideological counselling is an effort to inoculate and turn the activist against the appeal of ideologies of terrorist groups. The latter is what Webber et al. (Chapter 5) categorise as the method that can *directly* lead to deradicalisation through countering the ideological narrative, but the other interventions can *indirectly* facilitate deradicalisation in addition to disengagement by influencing underlying psychological mechanisms. They argue that to feel significant in their own and in others' eyes, which can be affected by new social networks and strengthened personal skills, will decrease the appeal of terrorist ideology.

The chapters demonstrate variations between countries and programmes in which interventions are prominent. An important distinction is the variations in ideology counselling. As demonstrated in this volume, as in other publications, ideology counselling is not a prominent strategy in Scandinavia, but it is more prominent in the Middle East and South East Asia, where the initiatives revolve to a great extent around ideology and theology. For another group of countries, such as the UK, Canada, Belgium and the Netherlands, ideological/religious counselling is offered "upon demand" and remains seen as an important disengagement/deradicalisation tool. The differences between most of the countries seem to a large extent not to be whether religious counselling is part of the potential interventions, but to what extent the programmes focus on ideological/theological re-education.

What has become evident in this book is the importance of a more holistic approach that not only focuses on the processes of leaving violent extremism, but also includes reintegration processes in a non-extremist environment. A successful and permanent disengagement is about the engagement the person has with wider society. Chapters show the significance of increasing the social skills, new social network, and so on, of the former extremist to strengthen the possibilities for resettling in mainstream society, and at the same time the importance of local conditions for reintegration. The local security situation as well as the local society's general willingness to reintegrate a former extremist are decisive for the reintegration into a law-abiding life.

As shown above, there are various strategies to promote disengagement and deradicalisation, and many of the contributors in this volume stress that combining the various strategies in multifaceted interventions tailored to individual needs is more likely to produce successful outcomes. The initiatives are also context-specific and depend on the available institutions and legal, cultural and social factors. Thus, programmes cannot be directly transferred to another country with a different cultural, social and political context, but they need to be carefully adapted to the local situation.

As highlighted by Arie Perliger in Chapter 8, the socio-political climate is important for the type of intervention accepted. Some countries have for instance experienced challenges with implementing "soft" deradicalisation policies due to political pressure against such strategies, as well as public opposition. This has been prominent for foreign fighters, who often represent marginal communities that are not part of mainstream culture, and have limited political capital, in addition to the strong sense of betrayal that proliferates in some of the societies that "export" foreign fighters. This book shows a range of relevant approaches and interventions, but at the same time, it demonstrates the importance of local context and the contextual limitation and possibilities.

Who is doing what, and why?

This book clarifies how a variety of actors, from international organisations (such as the United Nations), regional organisations (such as the African Union (AU) and European Union (EU)), state governments, civil society and religious networks implement and/or support disengagement and deradicalisation initiatives. Two other categories are also discussed in this volume: the family and the private business sector. At the micro level, the individual who tries to disengage or deradicalise a friend or an acquaintance also makes up part of the types of actors involved in deradicalisation.[1]

The chapters in this book show clearly the great variations from country to country of which actors are important, and the comparative drawbacks and advantages of different categories of actors, are discussed. For instance, in the United States, municipalities have been of limited importance, while law enforcement agencies are key. However, in Scandinavia, as illustrated in the chapters of Anja Dalgaard-Nielsen and Jakob Ilum, as well as Stian Lid, municipalities are the most significant actors; in Kenya the central state seems to delegate most responsibility, while local governance structures take some responsibility. In some scenarios, multi-national organisations become very important, such as the United Nations in Somalia (see Stig Jarle Hansen and Martine Zeuthen's contributions to this book). However, the deradicalisation field is dynamic and Amy Jane Gielen, for example, demonstrates that the picture is altering in the Benelux with the state "coming in the back way" as non-governmental organisations turn into government-organised non-governmental organisations, and government funding plays a bigger part.

Some of the contributors here stress important points with regard to both the advantages and possibilities and the liabilities of various actors. Tina Wilchen Christensen argues that civil society actors are in a better position to gain legitimacy among extremists and in building trusting relations due to their potential distance and independence from the state, considered by some segments of the population as an enemy. In totalitarian scenarios, Lihi Ben Shitrit considers civil society actors as very important alternatives to misuse of disengagement and deradicalisation initiatives in totalitarian states. These authors underline that civil society actors in some cases can enjoy more trust than state institutions amongst parts of the population. However, Mubin Shaikh, Hicham Tiflati, Phil Gurski and Amarnath Amarasingam also show how distrust between the government and parts of civil society might create problems, although they argue that in one of their cases, Canada, there is great trust in civil society.

Although state actors can have setbacks due to restricted trust among target groups, they may have other advantages depending on the available resources, structures and functions. Particularly in welfare states, state actors can provide a range of social, health and economic support. In many countries, these actors are also obliged to deliver these services, and they can use already existing institutions, structures, personnel and services, which means that at least some functions or services are available, but also sustainable over time. Yet, this can also lead to misuse: Mohammed Elshimi demonstrates how healthcare has gained a role in deradicalisation and disengagement programmes, but also how this is abused by government institutions, channelling psychologically ill individuals though channels intended for disengagement in order to save funds.

Finally, there may also be contradictions between national and local levels. Gielen illuminates how more local municipality-led or regional programmes could lead to more fragmentation. On the other hand, Dalgaard-Nielsen and Ilum argue that local programmes may have greater pragmatism and flexibility, while national programmes to a larger extent can be influenced by ideological rigour and politics.

The efficiency of the actor does not always determine which actors are emphasised and supported at a national level, but it is highly influenced by political, cultural and legal elements unique to a given country. As illustrated above, in Scandinavia municipalities are a major actor in providing welfare services, and indeed crime prevention. Hence, in one sense, it was expected that municipalities got a major role in promoting deradicalisation and disengagement. As illustrated by Bahadar Nawab, in Pakistan the army is the backbone of the state, providing the strongest and dominant institution; thus, similarly, it is to be expected that the army takes a lead in disengagement and deradicalisation work. In totalitarian states, civil society is curtailed; thus it should be expected that civil society plays a less active role. However, we also see patterns that go beyond both rational choices of actors based on their efficiency and political traditions favouring some institutions. Arie Perliger shows that patronage and personal networks could influence who gains deradicalisation and disengagement tasks.

The book also illustrates a knowledge gap in how the interaction between various actors plays out. We lack research on the interaction between the global level actors in deradicalisation and disengagement, the regional level actors and the local actors; here there are possibilities for synergic effects. Schindler highlights how the United Nations pushed for changes in national legal systems and made country assessments, recommendations, surveys and analytical products available throughout the United Nations system, and aided the implementation of various provisions. In some cases, such as in Somalia, they were directly involved with implementation on the ground. Similarly, Kaunert, Léonard and Yakubov elucidate the importance of the EU coordination mechanisms, including the Radicalisation Awareness Network (RAN), and also how the EU had an important influence on legal standardisation targeting jihadi propaganda, also because online actors were dependent on access to EU countries.

The lack of studies of interaction between the state and the regional/global level shows one of the major challenges that disengagement and deradicalisation face: lack of research. Yet this book, by bringing together many leading theoreticians and practitioners, also provides some solutions to several of these challenges. The book also clarifies several challenges that often seem to have been forgotten.

Challenges facing disengagement and deradicalisation

Some of the challenges facing the field of deradicalisation and disengagement are well known and have been discussed in many of the books and articles studying deradicalisation and disengagement in the past. A thoroughly discussed and analysed point, both in this volume and in past articles, is the problem of the measurement of success. *Firstly*, deradicalisation and disengagement programmes often have selection mechanisms focusing on what is seen as individuals with potential for deradicalisation; they may thus have selective positive recruitment, that is, recruit participants who would deradicalise or disengage themselves. Thus successes allegedly created by deradicalisation/disengagement programmes could be the result of other processes unrelated to the formal programmes. Amy-Jane Gielen in this volume rightly argues that risk assessment should be an integral part of any evaluation of a deradicalisation/disengagement programme, and many of the chapters in this book illustrate that different personalities amongst the participants in programmes also mean that different strategies are needed, and that success rates differ. *Secondly*, as illustrated by the Saudi Arabian and Yemeni cases, a correct measurement of success needs to observe the individual over time, as relapse might take time, and disengagement might lead to disengagement from ideologically induced violence, but not crime.

Thirdly, many programmes are evaluated based on their internal success criteria, which in some cases also include criteria of lesser importance, such as including meeting frequencies and procedures. We will in some cases have self-referential measurements, where the organisation in question defines the benchmarks on which it is to be measured, and fulfils them.

Fourthly, the families and outside networks are often left alone when the success rate is supposed to be measured, excluding an important source of information.

Fifthly, the conceptual discussion around disengagement and deradicalisation also influences how success is defined: is it to be non-violent behaviour, or should it be ideological change?

As suggested by Jessica Stern and Paige Pascarelli in this volume, a common approach to evaluation is urgently needed. Unfortunately, it is also a fact that another point highlighted by various contributors to this book – the need for individually tailored programmes – seemingly makes standardised approaches harder. Here there is a dilemma for future studies.

This book does however suggest that some lessons from criminology can be adapted. Hansen and Gielen, for example, both suggest that methods for measuring delinquency, including lifespan studies, are examples to be referred to, and Hansen highlights that discussions over measurements within delinquency studies hold much value for individuals who want to evaluate deradicalisation/disengagement programmes, although many factors intervening in forming behaviour over a lifespan cannot be controlled for.

Another challenge seen in this book is the limited access researchers have to information and the dependency on the willingness to share information by those in charge of the programmes. which in some cases restrict basic knowledge of the practice and the possibilities of learning from each other what are and what are not promising strategies.

Issues of coordination are also pressing. Coordination and definition of responsibility of the involved actors become important to achieve success. Multi-agency initiatives are developed in many countries to address these challenges. Yet, as illustrated by Lid in the chapter on local government, expanded cooperation might create some unforeseen consequences, especially if involving law enforcement and military state institutions. Close cooperation between local government and law enforcement and military state institutions can potentially increase scepticism among target groups of various deradicalisation and disengagement efforts towards local governments. That can hamper social service provision to these groups. This highlights some dilemmas. For example, should social and health institutions assist the police and intelligence services to collect information locally? Moreover, how to create trusting relations between the social/health workers and the former extremist in a field where surveillance and security are prominent becomes an important question. The increased number of actors creates a great need to clarify roles, area of responsibility and tasks, in addition to transparency and clear procedures in partnership.

There are also examples in this book of problems that have been overlooked, such as the agency of the radical organisation from which individuals are to be disengaged/deradicalised. In many cases, if you act against an organisation (to encourage defections), the organisation will act against you. Of course, the radical organisation will vary in capacity and strength from case to case. Nonetheless, countermeasures from radical organisations have often been underestimated, as illustrated by the examples drawn from Camp Bucca in the chapter by Stern and Pascarelli, but also in David Webber, Marina Chernikova, Erica Molinario and Arie W. Kruglanski's contribution, as well as Hansen's two chapters. The toolbox available to organisations that want to thwart the effects of disengagement/deradicalisation programmes also remains understudied. Yet the editors of this book hope that the lessons of the re-education programmes of World War II and of Camp Bucca in Iraq, that radical organisations might create an organisational hierarchy inside prison camps and target individuals seen as vulnerable to deradicalisation and disengagement, do not need to be re-learned. Nevertheless, as Lihi Ben Shitrit suggests, designating prisoners as a part of an organisation will influence their self-identification, and enhance the organisation one wants to curtail. Perhaps the Spanish strategy for handling ETA – separating members of the organisation in different prisons – is a way forward, yet a lack of resources will also constrain such measures.

Another ignored topic is the lack of thinking around gender in disengagement and deradicalisation programmes, as well as the use of gender stereotypes. Eggert argues that the specific needs of women and men wanting to leave violent extremist organisations are overlooked, and more consideration on these issues is needed.

Perhaps the greatest question is that raised by Irina A. Chindea: what happens when the organisation from which individuals are to be deradicalised suddenly emerges as a partner in potential peace processes? This is perhaps best illustrated by the overtures between the Taliban and the United States at the time of writing. In the past the Taliban was seen as an organisation to be deradicalised and disengaged from, yet the same organisation is seemingly being offered the right to influence the curriculum in Afghan schools. In such processes transitional justice suffers; transitional justice process is focused less on bringing to justice the perpetrators of violence. Hence, former guerrilla and paramilitary members have not only been included in peace negotiations, but some of them also entered the political process at local and national level. The paradoxes of such transitions have not yet been thoroughly discussed within deradicalisation and disengagement programmes.

These challenges do not mean that disengagement/deradicalisation initiatives are doomed to failure. The evidence for positive effects is simply too wide to dispute. Yet, we have to ensure that the dilemmas are discussed, and that the lessons from the various efforts do not have to be re-learned. We have to be careful that the decline of the Islamic State and the reduction of mass migration of foreign fighters (and the increasing decline of returning fighters from the Islamic State who need to be reintegrated and deradicalised) or indeed, the potential weakness of the right-wing scene, and renewed focus on great power rivalry, will be mistaken for signs of us not needing deradicalisation/disengagement. Even if radicalism declines, it may come back: Gielen's example in her chapter should be kept in mind (Chapter 16):

> The Dutch national and local CVE programmes came to an end in 2012, because violent extremism was not considered a serious threat any more by security services … One year later the conflict in Syria led to Dutch citizens travelling to join terrorist organisations such as Islamic State in Iraq and Syria (ISIS). It was at that time, in March 2013, that the threat level had to be raised … and a new national CVE action plan … was developed.

This book hopes to provide an overview of the field, which could aid the transfer of knowledge to future deradicalisation and disengagement programmes, perhaps targeting radical groups that have not yet emerged, while also keeping a critical approach containing warnings of potential misuse.

Note

1 For example, one of the neo-Nazis interviewed by one of the editors highlighted how she had participated in a formal exit programme, without any effect, but was then deradicalised by colleagues approaching her at the bar where she worked (Lid, Winsvold, Søholt, Hansen, Heierstad & Klausen 2016).

Reference

Lid, Stian, Winsvold, Marte, Søholt, Susanne, Hansen, Stig Jarle, Heierstad, Geir & Klausen, Jan Erling (2016), 'Forebygging av radikalisering og voldelig ekstremisme – Hva er kommunenes rolle?', *Nibr Raport* 2016:12.

INDEX

Made in the USA
Columbia, SC
08 June 2024